**FOURTH EDITION**

# TEACHING CHILDREN AND ADOLESCENTS WITH SPECIAL NEEDS

JUDY L. OLSON
JENNIFER C. PLATT
*Both of University of Central Florida*

PEARSON

Merrill
Prentice Hall

Upper Saddle River, New Jersey
Columbus, Ohio

**Library of Congress Cataloging-in-Publication Data**

Olson, Judy L.

    Teaching children and adolescents with special needs / Judy Olson and Jennifer Platt.
—4th ed.

      p.    cm.

    ISBN 0-13-038501-8

    Includes bibliographical references and indexes.

    Contents: Students with special needs—Beginning-of-the-year planning and organization
—Informal assessment—The instructional cycle—Instructional materials—Strategy
instruction—Content instruction—Social skills and peer-mediated instruction—Study
skills instruction—Communication and collaborative consultation—Technology for
teaching and learning—Transition from school to community living.

    1. Special education. 2. Teaching. 3. Classroom management. I. Platt, Jennifer C. II. Title.

LC3969.O47 2004
371.9—dc22

2003008694

**Vice President and Executive Publisher:** Jeffery W. Johnston
**Acquisitions Editor:** Allyson P. Sharp
**Editorial Assistants:** Penny Burleson and Kathleen S. Burk
**Production Editor:** Linda Hillis Bayma
**Production Coordination:** Cindy Miller, Carlisle Publishers Services
**Design Coordinator:** Diane C. Lorenzo
**Photo Coordinator:** Sandy Schaefer
**Cover Designer:** Jeff Vanik
**Cover image:** Corbis
**Production Manager:** Laura Messerly
**Director of Marketing:** Ann Castel Davis
**Marketing Manager:** Amy June
**Marketing Coordinator:** Tyra Poole

This book was set in New Baskerville by Carlisle Communications, Ltd. It was printed and bound by
R.R. Donnelley & Sons Company. The cover was printed by The Lehigh Press, Inc.

**Photo Credits:** pp. 2, 98, 252 by Tom Watson/Merrill; pp. 20, 198, 324 by Anthony Magnacca/Merrill; pp.
56, 132, 286, 356 by Scott Cunningham/Merrill; p. 158 by Todd Yarrington/Merrill; p. 205 by Donna
Janeczko; p. 222 by Anne Vega/Merrill.

Pearson Education Ltd.
Pearson Education Singapore Pte. Ltd.
Pearson Education Canada, Ltd.
Pearson Education—Japan

Pearson Education Australia Pty. Limited
Pearson Education North Asia Ltd.
Pearson Educación de Mexico, S.A. de C.V.
Pearson Education Malaysia Pte. Ltd.

10 9 8 7 6 5 4 3 2
ISBN: 0-13-038501-8

*To Larry R. Olson,*
*To the memory of Virginia F. Cox,*
*and*
*To our students, who inspired the writing of this text:*
*those we have worked with in the past, those we are*
*currently teaching, and those still to come.*

# PREFACE

This fourth edition is based on a personal philosophy that has evolved from the literature in special and general education and from our professional experiences. Research on teacher effectiveness in both special and general education provides many exemplary teaching practices that we include in this text. Our professional experiences include teaching both elementary and secondary students in general and special education settings, supervising interns, teaching and mentoring pre-service and in-service teachers, and participating as learners in our own professional development activities involving effective teaching practices.

The basic philosophy that keeps us actively involved in the profession after more than 30 years is that, as teachers, we can "make a difference" in the lives of our students. When the pre-service and in-service teachers we work with express concern about not affecting the lives of each of their students to the degree they wish, we remind them of the following story of a young boy walking along the beach. To paraphrase:

> That morning the tide had brought in thousands of starfish and scattered them on the hot, dry, sandy beach. A young boy was walking along the beach, tossing starfish back into the cool, blue water. As he was doing this, a man approached him. The man looked at what the young boy was doing and said, "Why are you doing that? Don't you see it's impossible? Look at the thousands of starfish. You can't possibly make a difference." The young boy slowly looked up at the man, picked up another starfish, and threw it back into the water, saying, "It makes a difference to this one."*

We hope you continue to find ideas and suggestions in this fourth edition to make a difference in your students' lives. You have the power to make a difference, for you have chosen to teach.

## FEATURES OF THE TEXT

We continue to use an informal, personal tone of writing. Additionally, we structure and organize the text to include recommendations of teacher effectiveness research, including the following effective teaching practices:

► **Advance Organizers and Post Organizers.** We begin each chapter with an advance organizer by providing an outline that highlights the key topics within the chapter. We close each chapter with discussion questions that challenge you to reflect on your professional practice and to think critically about the chapter content.

► **Reviewing/Checking for Understanding/ Monitoring Progress.** Throughout the chapters, we include several checkpoints so that you can monitor your progress as you read. These checkpoints take the form of "Important Points" sections found in the text of each chapter.

► **Active Involvement.** We provide opportunities for you to become actively involved by placing activities in each of the chapters. They are interspersed throughout each chapter to give you ample practice. Remember the Chinese proverb: "I hear and I forget, I see and I remember, I do and I understand."

*Excerpt from "The Star Thrower" in *The Unexpected Universe,* copyright © 1969 by Loren Eiseley and renewed 1997 by John A. Eichman, III, reprinted by permission of Harcourt, Inc.

▶ **Visual Aids.** We include tables, figures, diagrams, photographs, and illustrations throughout the text. We hope you use them to clarify concepts and to increase your interest.

## NOTEWORTHY CHANGES

As a result of feedback from reviewers, colleagues, and our students, along with input from users of the third edition, we have made important changes in this edition. As our field is constantly evolving, we have updated information in all of the chapters, described new legislation and national education policies, and reorganized the chapters in the text to provide additional clarity. We have included much new information such as Internet addresses; ample examples that apply to inclusive settings; new ideas for communication and collaboration among general and special education professionals, paraprofessionals, and families; ways to actively involve and include students; more examples of how students construct their own knowledge by interacting with others; and additional suggestions for movement and transition from teacher-directed to student-directed classroom activities.

Based on our philosophy that special educators must become more adept at modifying materials, adapting instruction, and communicating with general educators as our students move into inclusive classes, we have expanded the information in Chapter 5, "Instructional Materials," and Chapter 10, "Communication and Collaborative Consultation."

Based on a literature review of effective practices for teaching students with mild disabilities, we have included information on functional behavior assessment, scaffolding instruction, adapting lesson plans, and unit planning. We have also included new research on curriculum-based measurement. We believe that the fourth edition is a text that contains practical, research-based teaching strategies; relates to everyday occurrences in the schools; and describes motivating, experience-based activities. We hope that, like the boy and the starfish, our ideas and suggestions make a difference to you and your students.

## ACKNOWLEDGMENTS

We wish to acknowledge the contributions of everyone who assisted us in the completion of this text. Our thanks to Colleen Klein and Dan Ezell, who wrote Chapter 11, and to Sara Pankaskie, who wrote Chapter 12. We also wish to thank Anya Andrews for her help in researching and editing the new edition and to Sharon Dryden for her technical assistance. To Allyson Sharp, Penny Burleson, and all the Merrill/Prentice Hall staff, we express our gratitude for making our dream a reality.

Thanks to our reviewers for their critical analysis, valuable input, and suggestions: Maryann Dudzinski, Valparaiso University; Cynthia M. Okolo, University of Delaware; Patricia R. Renick, Wright State University; and Roberta Strosnider, Hood College.

A special thank-you goes to Larry Olson, whose patience with and support of a part-time wife during this process are deeply appreciated. Gratitude and appreciation are given to Chris Platt for his support and concern during the completion of the text and to Susan Wiehn for sharing her vast knowledge of children and adolescent literature.

Without the input of our students at the University of Central Florida and the support and encouragement of our families and friends, we would not have had an opportunity to make a difference in the lives of students with special needs. We are deeply grateful for these many contributions.

# DISCOVER THE COMPANION WEBSITE ACCOMPANYING THIS BOOK

## The Prentice Hall Companion Website: A Virtual Learning Environment

Technology is a constantly growing and changing aspect of our field that is creating a need for content and resources. To address this emerging need, Prentice Hall has developed an online learning environment for students and professors alike—Companion Websites—to support our textbooks.

In creating a Companion Website, our goal is to build on and enhance what the textbook already offers. For this reason, the content for each user-friendly Website is organized by topic and provides the professor and student with a variety of meaningful resources. Common features of a Companion Website include:

## For the Professor—

Every Companion Website integrates **Syllabus Manager**™, an online syllabus creation and management utility.

- ▶ **Syllabus Manager**™ provides you, the instructor, with an easy, step-by-step process to create and revise syllabi, with direct links into the Companion Website and other online content without having to learn HTML.
- ▶ Students may log on to your syllabus during any study session. All they need to know is the Web address for the Companion Website and the password you've assigned to your syllabus.
- ▶ After you have created a syllabus using **Syllabus Manager**™, students may enter the syllabus for their course section from any point in the Companion Website.

- ▶ Clicking on a date, the student is shown the list of activities for the assignment. The activities for each assignment are linked directly to actual content, saving time for students.
- ▶ Adding assignments consists of clicking on the desired due date, then filling in the details of the assignment—name of the assignment, instructions, and whether it is a one-time or repeating assignment.
- ▶ In addition, links to other activities can be created easily. If the activity is online, a URL can be entered in the space provided, and it will be linked automatically in the final syllabus.
- ▶ Your completed syllabus is hosted on our servers, allowing convenient updates from any computer on the Internet. Changes you make to your syllabus are immediately available to your students at their next logon.

## For the Student—

- ▶ **Overview and General Information**—General information about the topic and how it will be covered in the Website.
- ▶ **Web Links**—A variety of Websites related to topic areas.
- ▶ **Content Methods and Strategies**—Resources that help to put theories into practice in the special education classroom.
- ▶ **Reflective Questions and Case-Based Activities**—Put concepts into action, participate in activities, examine strategies, and more.
- ▶ **National and State Laws**—An online guide to how federal and state laws affect your special education classroom.

▶ **Behavior Management**—An online guide to help you manage behaviors in the special education classroom.

▶ **Message Board**—Virtual bulletin board to post and respond to questions and comments from a national audience.

To take advantage of these and other resources, please visit the *Teaching Children and Adolescents with Special Needs*, Fourth Edition, Companion Website at

**www.prenhall.com/olson**

# EDUCATOR LEARNING CENTER:
# AN INVALUABLE ONLINE RESOURCE

Merrill Education and the Association for Supervision and Curriculum Development (ASCD) invite you to take advantage of a new online resource, one that provides access to the top research and proven strategies associated with ASCD and Merrill—the Educator Learning Center. At **www.EducatorLearningCenter.com** you will find resources that will enhance your students' understanding of course topics and of current educational issues, in addition to being invaluable for further research.

## HOW THE EDUCATOR LEARNING CENTER WILL HELP YOUR STUDENTS BECOME BETTER TEACHERS

With the combined resources of Merrill Education and ASCD, you and your students will find a wealth of tools and materials to better prepare them for the classroom.

## Research

- More than 600 articles from the ASCD journal *Educational Leadership* discuss everyday issues faced by practicing teachers.
- A direct link on the site to Research Navigator™ gives students access to many of the leading education journals, as well as extensive content detailing the research process.
- Excerpts from Merrill Education texts give your students insights on important topics of instructional methods, diverse populations, assessment, classroom management, technology, and refining classroom practice.

## Classroom Practice

- Hundreds of lesson plans and teaching strategies are categorized by content area and age range.
- Case studies and classroom video footage provide virtual field experience for student reflection.
- Computer simulations and other electronic tools keep your students abreast of today's classrooms and current technologies.

## LOOK INTO THE VALUE OF EDUCATOR LEARNING CENTER YOURSELF

Preview the value of this educational environment by visiting **www.EducatorLearningCenter.com** and clicking on "Demo." For a free 4-month subscription to the Educator Learning Center in conjunction with this text, simply contact your Merrill/Prentice Hall sales representative.

# BRIEF CONTENTS

# CONTENTS

## 12
## Transition From School to Community Living  356
*Sara C. Pankaskie*

# PART 1

# FOUNDATIONS FOR INSTRUCTION

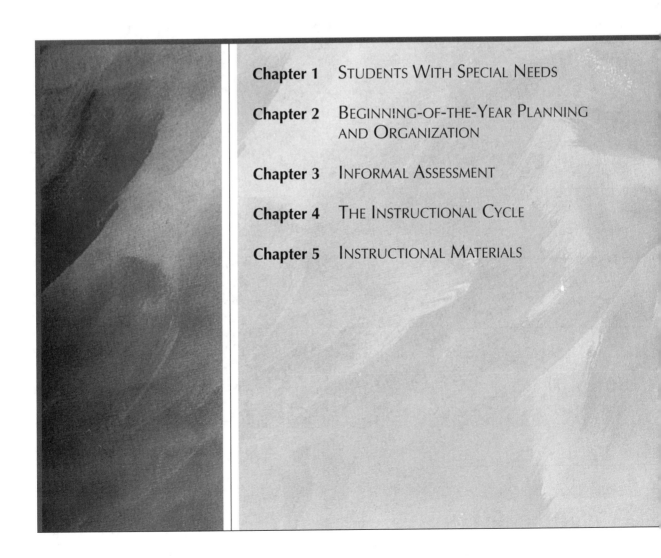

# CHAPTER 1

# STUDENTS WITH SPECIAL NEEDS

## KEY TOPICS

The field of special education will continue to grow and change in the 21st century, supported by federal legislation, such as the Individuals with Disabilities Education Act (IDEA), which has impacted students with disabilities and reframed the roles of general and special education teachers, administrators, other professionals, and families. Furthermore, as schools are restructured to meet the mandate of the No Child Left Behind Act (2001), designed to reform federal education policy, special educators are studying the impact of this legislation on students with disabilities.

In this chapter, we begin by focusing on the diverse needs and characteristics of children and adolescents with learning and behavior problems. Being knowledgeable about student characteristics means that you know your students' academic levels, can identify the skills they bring with them to the learning situation, and understand their cultural backgrounds. Children and adolescents with special needs often exhibit problems with academic and social skills that make it difficult for them to meet the demands of school, home, and community.

For optimum learning to occur, you must use effective teaching strategies based on sound research. Therefore, we provide an instructional framework based on proven educational practice, which you can use in planning, implementing, and evaluating instruction. You must also be aware of the service delivery options that are available to students with special needs, the federal government's education reform strategies, and the current emphasis on inclusion of students with disabilities in general education settings. We conclude the chapter with the Council for Exceptional Children Standards for

Professional Practice and ask you to make a commitment to students with exceptionalities, their families, and the teaching profession.

## STUDENT CHARACTERISTICS

Students with special needs often have problems in academic areas, social interactions, motivation, and transition to adult roles. In many school districts, such students are referred to as having learning disabilities (specific learning disabilities), mental disabilities (mental handicaps, mental retardation, educable mental handicaps), or emotional disabilities (emotional disturbance, behavior disorders). Often, lumped into the group of students with mild disabilities, these students have many similarities and often spend much of their school day in inclusive settings. In 1998–1999, 47.4% of students with learning disabilities, 13.8% of students with mental retardation, and 25.5% of students with emotional disturbance spent 80% or more of their time in a regular education classroom (U.S. Department of Education, 2000).

Characteristics that students with special needs or mild disabilities may display include:

*Inadequate academic achievement.* Often, such students are two or more years behind their grade-level peers in reading, mathematics, spelling, written expression, and/or oral language skills.

*Inappropriate school behaviors.* Many times, they are physically or verbally aggressive. They are frequently easily frustrated or unable to cope with the demands of the school environment. Other signs of inappropriate school behavior include noncompliance with teacher directions and instructions and lack of teacher-pleasing behaviors, such as being prepared for class, maintaining eye contact, and raising hands.

*Poor attending behaviors.* Students with special needs often have trouble following teacher directions and instructions. They seem to have difficulty attending to the relevant information in a message and are frequently unable to concentrate on an assignment or task.

*Poor memory.* Being unable to remember information from one week to the next or from one day to the next is another characteristic common to many students with special needs. These students frequently have problems remembering spelling words, basic math facts, and two or more directions.

*Poor metacognitive abilities.* Often, students do not have the necessary organizational and learning strategies to become self-regulated learners. They do not monitor their understanding of new information or develop effective strategies to complete a task.

*Poor self-concept.* For many students with special needs, school is not a comfortable, rewarding place. Instead, it is a place where they often fail to meet the standards for success.

*Inadequate social skills.* Such students often cannot maintain satisfactory interpersonal relationships, are less socially accepted by peers, and demonstrate impaired communication (pragmatic language) skills. The lack of social skills precludes adequate adjustment not only to the demands of the school environment, but also to the postschool environment. Students with special needs are frequently less accepted and less successful in the world of work due to lack of social skills.

## CULTURAL DIVERSITY

Within the population of students with special needs are students who are not members of the Anglo-American culture. These students are from Native American, Asian, Hispanic (Latino), African American, or other cultures.

The school culture frequently reflects Anglo-American values (Turnbull & Turnbull, 1986). These values include a belief in competition, individual autonomy and independence, an achievement orientation, a future orientation, timeliness, and an informal classroom atmosphere (Briganti, 1989; Grossman, 1990; Turnbull & Turnbull,

1986). Many of your students from other cultures will have adopted the same values, depending on proximity, age, birthplace, and time (Leung, 1989). Immigrants who live in ethnic centers in metropolitan areas have less opportunity to socialize with other ethnic groups, so they tend to retain their ethnic identity longer. Young people usually adapt more readily than older people, and those born in this country usually adapt more readily than do those born in another country. Succeeding generations are less steeped in ethnic traditions than the first generation.

Conversely, some of your students may find that their culture is at odds with the school culture. Some cultures may value cooperation instead of competition (Grossman, 1994; Johnson, 1987), dependent instead of independent behaviors (Rivera & Rogers-Adkinson, 1997), relationships instead of timeliness (Zirpoli & Melloy, 1993), development of the whole child, not just achievement (Wilson, 1989), immediate short-term goals instead of long-term goals (Rivera & Rogers-Adkinson, 1997), and a more formal as opposed to informal classroom atmosphere (Grossman, 1994).

Some strategies that consider these different cultural values include:

1. Allowing students to help and assist each other at times, instead of requiring students to complete work independently all the time.
2. Using cooperative learning groups and peer tutoring.
3. Giving students alternative choices (e.g., do you wish to work at the writing center or math center, instead of asking what center do you want to go to now).
4. Encouraging students to meet important deadlines by reminders of due dates.
5. Remembering to include both affective and academic objectives on the Individualized Education Program (IEP).
6. Teaching students to reach daily goals before asking them to monitor monthly goals.

You should become familiar with the cultural values of the community and invite community members to share their expertise and cultural knowledge. You should always be respectful of all cultures and try to bring in materials and perspectives from various cultures. For example, when co-teaching a unit on western expansion in the United States, Ms. Wright brought in materials that considered the Native Americans' viewpoint in addition to that of the White settlers' viewpoint.

## ENGLISH-LANGUAGE LEARNERS

In addition to the cultural differences in your classroom, you may have students who are not native English speakers. The term *English-language learners* (ELLs) refers both to students who are not proficient in English and to students who use adequate conversational English but struggle with the language of the academic curriculum (Gersten & Baker, 2000). Schools attempt to meet the needs of these students by offering immersion programs, English as a second language (ESL) programs, or bilingual programs (Gollnick & Chinn, 2002). In the structured immersion model, the teacher teaches content information through adaptations in the English language with the goal that students acquire proficiency in English while at the same time achieve in content areas. An ESL program is based on a special curriculum that typically focuses on learning the English language as opposed to content and is usually taught during specific times. Every bilingual education program has an ESL component (National Clearinghouse for English Language Acquisition [NCELA], 2002). Bilingual programs use two languages (the native language and English) for teaching and learning. Usually, the native language is used to teach concepts and knowledge, and English is used to reinforce the information (Baca & Cervantes, 1998).

There is much controversy concerning the most effective programs for teaching English-language learners. In 1998, California passed a law that ended bilingual education and required all ELLs to be educated for one year in a structured English immersion program before being placed in the general education classroom (Gollnick & Chinn, 2002). Other states, such as Colorado, rejected legislation to end bilingual programs.

To meet the needs of ELLs, Gersten and Baker (2000), along with other researchers, recommend a shift of focus from arguing over which programs should be selected to identifying the best methods for teaching these students. In a review of 24 intervention studies (research-based and descriptive) and interviews with professional educators and researchers, they identified the following "critical components" for instruction:

1. Reinforce auditory information with visual aids, such as graphic organizers and word banks.
2. Build the background knowledge of students. Going over the new vocabulary in a reading assignment and discussing what the class knows about a topic before it is presented are ways to build group knowledge.
3. Implement peer tutoring and cooperative learning.

Throughout the rest of the text, we identify other effective strategies for teaching students from different cultures and English-language learners with disabilities.

 **IMPORTANT POINTS**

1. Students with special needs often display one or more of the following characteristics: inadequate academic achievement, inappropriate school behaviors, poor attending behaviors, poor memory, poor metacognitive skills, poor self-concept, and inadequate social skills.
2. The school culture focuses on the values of the Anglo-American culture, even though students come from a variety of cultures.
3. The Anglo-American values, often at odds with those of other cultures, include an

emphasis on competition, individual autonomy and independence, timeliness, achievement orientation, future orientation, and an informal classroom atmosphere.

4. Acculturation into the school culture depends on proximity, age, birthplace, and time (Leung, 1989).
5. The term *English-language learners* (ELLs) refers both to students who are not proficient in English and to students who use adequate conversational English but struggle with the language of the academic curriculum (Gersten & Baker, 2000).
6. Currently, schools attempt to meet the needs of these students by offering immersion programs, ESL programs, or bilingual programs (Gollnick & Chinn, 2002).
7. In immersion programs, students are taught content using English language modifications; in ESL programs, the goal is to teach students English; in bilingual programs, content is taught using the native language and reinforced with English.

---

 **ACTIVITY 1.1**

Share with a colleague some of your cultural values and then compare them to the values of the school culture.

(Answers for this and other activities are found in the Instructor's Manual.)

## EFFECTIVE TEACHING STRATEGIES

In a meta-analysis of over 1,000 research studies, Forness, Kavale, Blum, and Lloyd (1997) identified effective, possibly effective, and ineffective special education interventions. The ineffective strategies included special class placement, perceptual training, the Feingold diet, modality-based instruction, and social skills training. They identified psycholinguistic training, peer tutoring, computer-assisted instruction, stimulant drugs, reduced class size, and psychotropic drugs as possibly effective. Effective strategies included early intervention, formative evaluation, cognitive-behavior modification, direct instruction, behavior modification, reading comprehension instruction, and mnemonic training. Effective teaching strategies in special education are currently based on two paradigms of the learning process. According to Heshusius (1989), a paradigm represents "the beliefs by which we ultimately think and act" (p. 403). One view is the *reductionist paradigm* (also referred to as scientific, modern empiricism, or Newtonian mechanistic), and the other is the *constructivist paradigm* (also referred to as holistic or social constructivism). In the reductionist paradigm, learners are viewed as learning in a logical, sequential, and externally arranged way (Heshusius, 1989). In the constructivist paradigm, learners are viewed as actively constructing their knowledge through interaction with the physical and social environments (Reid, Kurkjian, & Carruthers, 1994).

Both paradigms influence instructional interactions and generate heated debate in the special education field. For our discussion, we concentrate on a comparison of the two paradigms in regard to their views of the role of the teacher, the role of the student, and their influence on instructional and assessment practices.

## Reductionist Paradigm

The reductionist paradigm views the teacher's role as one of providing opportunities for systematic explicit instruction, practice, feedback, and active student involvement in learning (Kimball & Heron, 1988). Effective teachers structure the school day by providing ample instructional time and high task management. They introduce and orient, model and demonstrate, check for understanding, maintain a brisk pace and a high success rate, and monitor seatwork and progress (Englert, Tarrant, & Mariage, 1992). The teacher is in charge of instruction, and knowledge is transmitted from teacher to student. The students frequently are not involved in decision making and often engage in rote learning. Through the use of task analysis, the curriculum is separated into components with scope and sequence checklists. Sequential and hierarchical instructional objectives form the basis for curriculum-based measurement and precision teaching assessments as students' weaknesses are identified (Poplin, 1988).

## Constructivist Paradigm

In the constructivist paradigm, the teacher's role is more like that of a facilitator as students assume responsibility for their own learning. The effective teacher embeds implicit instruction in meaningful contexts, promotes classroom dialogues, demonstrates responsive instruction, links students' prior knowledge with new knowledge, and establishes classroom learning communities (Englert, Tarrant, & Mariage, 1992). Students often lead discussions, select their own objectives, and learn from other students. They construct their own knowledge through active involvement and integration into their schema. Assessment includes authentic, real-life processes, and errors provide insights not into students' weaknesses but into how students think. Subject areas are taught in authentic contexts (Englert, Tarrant, & Mariage, 1992) and integrated as a whole (Iano, 1989).

## Sample Lessons Based on Paradigms

An examination of sample lessons may assist in understanding the effects of the two paradigms on instruction. We begin with a sample lesson from a reductionist viewpoint. Then we present the same lesson based on the constructivist principles, adapted from a lesson presented by Englert, Tarrant, and Mirage (1992). Both lessons are centered around opening morning activities, a beginning routine in many primary inclusive classrooms.

### Reductionist-Based Lesson

TEACHER: It's time for our morning message. Today is Tuesday. What is today, everyone (hand signal to cue unison response)?

STUDENTS: Tuesday.

TEACHER: Correct. Today is Tuesday. (Teacher writes the sentence on the board.) Let's read our first sentence together. Everyone (signal).

STUDENTS: Today is Tuesday.

TEACHER: Good reading, everyone. Jim, what is happening today?

JIM: We are going on a field trip.

TEACHER: Yes, we are. Where are we going?

SAMANTHA: To the fire station.

TEACHER: Let's say that in a complete sentence, Samantha.

SAMANTHA: We are going to the fire station.

TEACHER: Now that's a complete sentence. (Teacher writes: We are going on a field trip to the fire station.) Everyone, let's read that sentence together (hand signal).

STUDENTS: We are going on a field trip to the fire station.

TEACHER: Good reading, everyone. So where are we going, Sherry?

SHERRY: We are going to the fire station.

TEACHER: Correct. When are we going to the fire station, Kenisha?

### Constructivist-Based Lesson

TEACHER: Anything special to write about today in our morning message?

JOSH: We are going to the fire station today.

MEGAN: A field trip.

TEACHER: Let's see. (Teacher writes: We are going to the fire station today, a field trip.) Oh! That doesn't sound right. What do you think?

KENISHA: Something's wrong with field trip.

SEBBIE: Maybe it needs a period.

TEACHER: Let's see. (Teacher adds a period before field trip and a capital A.) I added a period so now I need a capital. Let me read it, A field trip. What do you think?

STUDENTS: No.

TEACHER: Maybe, I can say for. (Teacher writes: We are going to the fire station today for a field trip. Teacher reads sentence.) What do you think?

STUDENTS: Yes.

TEACHER: What do you want to say about the field trip?

MEGAN: We leave at 11:00.

ROY: I want to say 11:00 o'clock.

STUDENTS: (Some say Yes, and some say No.)

TEACHER: Let's vote on adding o'clock. Thumbs up for Yes. Thumbs down for No.

 **ACTIVITY 1.2**

Compare and contrast the different lesson samples based on the two paradigms.

## Combining Paradigms for Effective Instructional Practice

Many experts feel that the selection of an effective instructional practice in special education depends on the task and the individual. Research indicates explicit instruction grounded in the reductionist paradigm is more effective in teaching basic decoding skills, and implicit instruction grounded in the constructivist paradigm is effective when the focus is on comprehension process or higher-level skills (Stanovich, 1994). Howell, Fox, and Morehead (1993) suggest that students who have poor prior knowledge and encounter initial failure on the task may need explicit instruction, whereas students who have good prior knowledge and early success may need implicit instruction.

Harris and Graham (1994), proponents of the constructivist paradigm, argue that extensive, structured, and explicit instruction does not need to "equate with decontextualized learning of meaningless skills, passive learning, or the teaching of gradually accruing basic skills as a prerequisite to higher-order thinking and learning" (p. 238). Instead, they urge that teachers must be responsive to individual needs, styles, and differences. We agree with Harris and Graham; therefore, in this text, we incorporate practices based on both paradigms. For example, we discuss assessments such as precision teaching (reductionist-based), the use of portfolios (constructivist-based), strategies such as direct instruction (reductionist-based), and reciprocal teaching (constructivist-based).

We include practices from both paradigms in our instructional framework of planning, presentation, independent practice, and evaluation (see Figure 1.1). In this general framework, the teacher, the students, or the combined efforts of the teacher and students may lead to the planning of the lesson.

Using a dialogue, the teacher may at first present the lesson and then turn over the lesson presentation to the students; or in classroom communities, the students may learn from one another. In the feedback and evaluation process, the involvement of both the teacher and students is essential. Students may self-evaluate or self-monitor and/or teachers may evaluate and monitor. We discuss the instructional framework in detail in Chapter 4.

**IMPORTANT POINTS**

1. In a meta-analysis of over 1,000 research studies, Forness, Kavale, Blum, and Lloyd (1997) identified early intervention, formative evaluation, cognitive-behavior modification, direct instruction, behavior modification, reading comprehension instruction, and mnemonic training as effective strategies.

2. Effective teaching strategies in special education currently are based on either the reductionist or the constructivist paradigms of the learning process.

**Figure 1.1** Instructional Framework

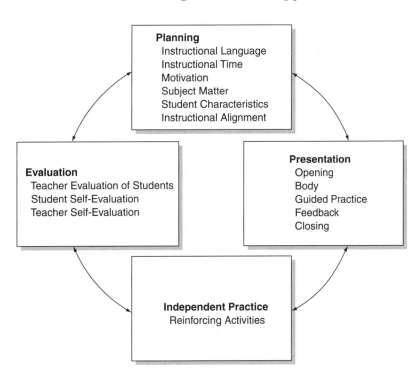

3. The reductionist paradigm views the teacher as the primary information and decision maker, the student as actively participating in the learning of isolated skills without much input, assessment as leading to sequential and hierarchical instructional objectives, and instruction as fast paced and teacher directed.

4. The constructivist paradigm views the teacher as a facilitator and one of the decision makers; the students as major decision makers as they learn from each other; assessment as occurring in authentic, real-life procedures; and instruction as purposeful and matched to students' interests and experiences.

5. Many special educators feel that both paradigms include practices that are effective for students with special needs, depending on the content and student characteristics.

6. The instructional framework of planning, presentation, independent practice, and evaluation allows for the incorporation of practices based on both paradigms.

▼ ACTIVITY 1.3

Reflect on the different practices suggested by the two paradigms. Discuss with a partner when you feel the different practices may be effective.

## CONTINUUM OF SERVICES

Students with disabilities may be found in a variety of placements and may require a variety of services (Heward, 2000). These placements and services are typically arranged on a continuum and offer a range of service options to meet the diverse needs of students. The Individuals with Disabilities Education Act Amendments of 1997, PL 105-17, which amended and reauthorized the Individuals with Disabilities

Education Act (IDEA), ensures that a continuum of placement alternatives is available for students (Yell & Shriner, 1997). Figure 1.2 illustrates a continuum of services, in which a full range of program alternatives is arranged from the most to the least restrictive. When considering educational options for students, it is important to remember that special education services should be flexible and responsive to students' needs, provide access to a variety of services, and offer the support needed for students to achieve their potential (Smith, 1998).

According to the Individuals with Disabilities Education Act (IDEA), schools must place students with disabilities in the least restrictive environment, or LRE. This means that, to the extent appropriate, students with disabilities should be educated with students without disabilities. IDEA further stipulates that placing students in special classes, separate schooling, or other removal of students with disabilities from the general education environment occurs only when the nature or severity of the disability is such that education in general education classes with the use of supplementary aids and services cannot be achieved satisfactorily. In his research, Marston (1996) calls for close attention to the least restrictive environment and the shared commitment of general and special educators along with a variety of learning opportunities across settings—in other words, the continuum of services.

As you examine Figure 1.2, notice that the model is wide at the bottom and gradually becomes narrower to reflect the number of students served at the different levels. The least restrictive setting is at the bottom and the most restrictive setting is at the top. A greater percentage of students are served in the less restrictive settings (e.g., mild/moderate needs) than in the more restrictive settings (e.g., more intensive needs). Students are moved up in levels only as necessary, and they

**Figure 1.2**   Continuum of Educational Placements and Services for Students With Disabilities

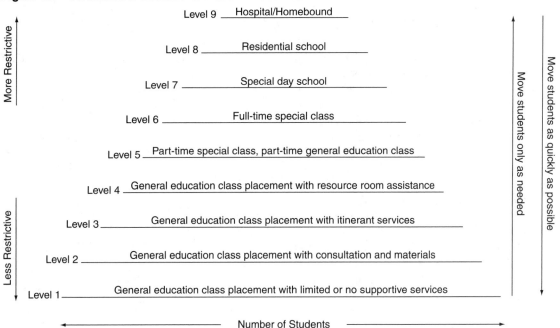

are moved down to more integrated settings as soon as possible.

Students with the types of learning and behavior problems we address in this text may be served in general education classrooms with or without supportive services or in part-time classes referred to as resource, pull-out, or part-time programs (Levels 1, 2, 3, 4, and 5). In the rest of this text, we do not refer to Levels 6 through 9. Instead, we concentrate on reporting research, providing examples, and making suggestions for the students with special needs who are being served in the first five levels. They represent the greatest percentage of the population of students with disabilities.

## INCLUSION

In 1986, Madeline Will, Assistant Secretary of Education, proposed that we place fewer students with disabilities in pull-out programs and

instead educate them in general education settings. She advocated a shared responsibility and commitment between general and special education and the use of effective special education techniques beyond the special class setting. Called the Regular Education Initiative (REI), it represented a call for alignment of programs to achieve better academic outcomes than had been demonstrated by the more traditional, pull-out programs (Zigmond et al., 1995). This initiative led to one of the major reform issues currently facing the field of education, that of inclusion. The premise of inclusion is that students with special needs benefit academically and socially by being served alongside normally achieving students as opposed to being separated from them (Banjera & Dailey, 1995).

Inclusion of students with disabilities in general education classrooms has continued to gain momentum over the last several years

(U.S. Department of Education, 2000). Proponents of the inclusion movement advocate that the majority of students with disabilities should be included in general education classrooms. Although critics of inclusion agree with some of the basic assumptions of the inclusion movement, such as the need for improvements in assessment and instruction and the need for collaboration among special and general education, they disagree with other assumptions, such as the belief that the majority of (if not all) students with disabilities can best be taught in the general education classroom. The Individuals with Disabilities Education Act (IDEA) supports the continuum of services and the belief that placement options are needed. Many proponents of inclusion believe that students with disabilities have a right to be educated with their same-age peers in general educational settings (Walther-Thomas, Korinek, McLaughlin, & Williams, 2000).

The topic remains a controversial one, making it important to define exactly what is meant by inclusion (Burnette, 1996). Some professionals support full inclusion (placing all students with disabilities in general education classrooms), whereas others favor inclusive schools that welcome students with disabilities, but at the same time, realize that general education placement may not be the best educational option (Burnette, 1996). Still others describe "responsible" inclusion, a school-based education model that is student centered and bases educational placement and service provisions on the needs of each student (Vaughn & Schumm, 1995). Most models advocating full inclusion include the following:

1. All students attend the school to which they would go if they had no disability.
2. A natural proportion (i.e., representative of the school district at large) of students with disabilities occurs at any school site.

3. A zero-rejection policy exists, so that no student is excluded on the basis of type or extent of disability.
4. Placements are age and grade appropriate, with no self-contained special education classes operative at the school site.
5. Cooperative learning and peer instruction methods receive significant use in general instruction at the school site.
6. Special education supports are provided within the context of the general education class and in other integrated environments (Sailor, 1991, p. 10).

Originally adopted at the annual conference of the Council for Exceptional Children (CEC) in 1993, the CEC Policy on Inclusive Schools and Community Settings calls for a continuum of services but supports inclusion as a meaningful goal (see Figure 1.3). Implications for schools include obtaining the support and technical assistance necessary to serve an increasingly diverse student population in inclusive settings, and facilitating collaboration among families, educators, businesses, and agencies to prepare students for membership in inclusive communities (Platt & Olson, 1997).

The Working Forum on Inclusive Schools (1994), a consortium of 10 national education associations, identified 12 characteristics of inclusive schools:

1. A sense of community (e.g., all students belong and can learn in the mainstream of the school and community).
2. Leadership (e.g., principals should involve faculty in planning and decision making).
3. High standards (e.g., all students are given the opportunity to achieve high educational standards and outcomes).
4. Collaboration and cooperation (e.g., there is an emphasis on collaborative arrangements and support networks among students and staff).

**Figure 1.3** CEC Policy on Inclusive Schools and Community Settings

The Council for Exceptional Children (CEC) believes all children, youth, and young adults with disabilities are entitled to a free and appropriate education and/or services that lead to an adult life characterized by satisfying relations with others, independent living, productive engagement in the community, and participation in society at large.

To achieve such outcomes, there must exist for all children, youth, and young adults a rich variety of early intervention, educational, and vocational program options and experiences.

Access to these programs and experiences should be based on individual educational need and desired outcomes.

Furthermore, students and their families or guardians, as members of the planning team, may recommend the placement, curriculum option, and the exit document to be pursued.

CEC believes that a continuum of services must be available for all children, youth, and young adults.

CEC also believes that the concept of inclusion is a meaningful goal to be pursued in our schools and communities.

In addition, CEC believes children, youth, and young adults with disabilities should be served whenever possible in general education classrooms in inclusive neighborhood schools and community settings.

Such settings should be strengthened and supported by an infusion of specially trained personnel and other appropriate supportive practices according to the individual needs of the child.

NOTE: From "CEC Policy Manual," 1997, Chapter 3, Special Education in the Schools, Section Three, Professional Policies, Part 1, p. 4. Reston, VA: The Council for Exceptional Children. Reprinted by permission.

5. Changing roles and responsibilities (e.g., roles of school professionals change, and everyone becomes an active participant in the learning process).
6. An array of services (e.g., varied school/community services are available, all coordinated with the educational staff).
7. Partnerships with parents (e.g., parents are full partners in the education of their children).
8. Flexible learning environments (e.g., flexible groupings and developmentally appropriate experiences are provided to meet students' needs).
9. Strategies based on research (e.g., practices include cooperative learning, curriculum adaptation, peer tutoring, direct instruction, reciprocal teaching, social skills instruction, computer-assisted instruction, study skills training, and mastery learning).
10. New forms of accountability (e.g., there is less emphasis on standardized tests and more on assessment to monitor progress toward goals).

11. Access (e.g., adaptations, modifications, and assistive technology ensure access).
12. Continuing professional development (e.g., staff members continue to improve their knowledge and skills).

Many professionals agree on the value of integrating students with disabilities into general education classroom settings. There is disagreement, however, as to how inclusion is implemented. Many educators believe that inclusion is most effective when the integration of students with disabilities is combined with a broader restructuring that includes multiage classrooms (Irmsher, 1996). Others recommend guidelines for "responsible" inclusion: "(1) the student and family are considered first; (2) teachers choose to participate in inclusion classrooms; (3) adequate resources are provided; (4) models are developed and implemented at the school-based level; (5) a continuum of services is maintained; (6) the service delivery model is continuously evaluated; and (7) ongoing professional development is provided" (Vaughn & Schumm, 1995, p. 264).

Research on the achievement outcomes of students with disabilities underscores the need to improve services to students no matter where they are provided (Wagner, Blackorby, & Hebbler, 1993). As the debate over how best to meet the needs of students with disabilities continues, we urge you to evaluate the effects of separate programming and integrated settings on student achievement. Tables 1.1 and 1.2 contain information about organizations and resources that focus on inclusion.

**Table 1.1**  Selected Inclusion Organizations

---

Consortium on Inclusive Schooling Practices—www.asri.edu/CFSP/brochure/abtcons.htm
ERIC Clearinghouse on Disabilities and Gifted Children—www.ericec.org
National Association of State Directors of Special Education—www.nasdse.org
National Center on Educational Outcomes—http://education.umn.edu/nceo
National Center to Improve Practice in Special Education (NCIP)—www2.edc.org/NCIP
National Information Center for Children and Youth with Disabilities (NICHCY)—www.nichcy.org
Special Education Resource Center (SERC)—www.ctserc.org
U.S. Department of Education Office of Special Education and Rehabilitative Services
  (OSERS)—www.ed.gov/offices/OSERS
Federation for Children with Special Needs—www.fcsn.org
Parent Advocacy Coalition for Educational Rights (PACER)—www.pacer.org
Parent Education and Assistance for Kids (PEAK) Parent Center, Inc.—www.peakparent.org

---

**Table 1.2**  Selected Inclusion Resources and Materials

---

Bauwens, J., & Hourcade, J. (2002). *Cooperative teaching: Rebuilding the schoolhouse for all students.* Pro-Ed.

Giacobbe, A. C., Livers, A. F., Thayer-Smith, R., & Walther-Thomas, C. (2001). Raising the academic standards bar: What states are doing to measure the performance of students with disabilities. *Journal of Disability Policy Studies, 12,* 10–17.

Goodman, G. (1998). *Inclusive classrooms from A to Z: A handbook for educators.* Teachers' Publishing Group.

Hammeken, P. A. (2001). *Inclusion: 450 strategies for success.* Paytral Publications, Inc.

Lenz, K., & Schumaker, J. (1999). *Adapting language arts, social studies, and science materials for the inclusive classroom.* Council for Exceptional Children.

Putnam, J. W. (1998). *Cooperative learning and strategies for inclusion: Celebrating diversity in the classroom.* Paul H. Brookes Publishing Co.

Rea, P. J., McLaughlin, V. L., & Walther-Thomas, C. (2002). Outcomes for students with learning disabilities in inclusive and pullout programs. *Exceptional Children, 68*(2), 203–223.

Shumm, J. S. (1999). *Adapting reading and math materials for the inclusive classroom.* Council for Exceptional Children.

Simmons, D., & Kame'enui, E. J. (1999). *Toward successful inclusion of students with disabilities: The architecture of instruction.* Council for Exceptional Children.

Stainback, S., & Stainback, W. (1996). *Curriculum considerations in inclusive classrooms: Facilitating learning for all students.* Paul H. Brookes Publishing Co.

Turnbull, A. P., Turnbull, H. R., Shank, M., & Leal, D. (2002). *Exceptional lives: Special education in today's schools* (3rd ed.). Prentice Hall.

---

**ACTIVITY 1.4**

**Part 1.** Prepare a set of questions about inclusion. Interview a general education teacher, a special education teacher, one of your professors, a principal, a parent of a child or adolescent with and without disabilities, or the superintendent of schools in your area. Share your responses in class.

**Part 2.** Form two panels, one with members who will speak in favor of inclusion and the other with members who will speak against it. Arrange to have a debate in class.

 **IMPORTANT POINTS** ◀

1. Students may receive special education services in a variety of placements, arranged on a continuum from least restrictive to most restrictive.
2. The term *least restrictive* means that, to the extent appropriate, students who have disabilities should be educated with students who do not have disabilities.
3. Students may receive special education services in general classrooms with limited or no supportive services, through consultative and itinerant services, in resource rooms, in part-time and full-time special classes, in special and residential schools, and in hospital/homebound settings.
4. The concept of inclusion has as its premise that students with special needs benefit academically and socially by being served alongside normally achieving students as opposed to being separated from them.
5. The Working Forum on Inclusive Schools identified 12 characteristics of inclusive schools: a sense of community, leadership, high standards, collaboration and cooperation, changing roles and responsibilities, an array of services, partnerships with parents, flexible learning environments, research-based strategies, new forms of accountability, access, and continuing professional development.

## NATIONAL EDUCATION AND STANDARDS-BASED REFORM

"The participation of students with disabilities in standards-based reform was mandated with the 1997 amendments to the Individuals with Disabilities Act (IDEA). IDEA (1997) requires states to include all students with disabilities in their accountability programs and to provide students with disabilities the accommodations they need to be so included" (Fuchs & Fuchs, 2001, p. 174). The Individuals with Disabilities Education Act (1997):

> assures that all children with disabilities have available to them . . . a free appropriate public education which emphasizes special education and related services designed to meet their unique needs, to assure that the rights of children with disabilities and their parents or guardians are protected, to assist states and localities to provide for the education of all children with disabilities, and to assess and assure the effectiveness of efforts to educate children with disabilities. (IDEA, 20 U.S.C.: 1400[c])

The national education reform strategy, Goals 2000: Educate America Act (1994), was signed into law representing a national framework for education reform to improve our systems, policies, standards, and most importantly, outcomes for all students. This act contained the six original goals from AMERICA 2000: An Education Strategy with the addition of two new goals (i.e., professional development and parental involvement). At the time he signed the law, President Clinton called the initiative a "new and different approach" that would establish "world class" national education standards. He asked school districts at the grassroots level to help achieve these goals. Goals 2000 appeared to include students with disabilities in the designation "all children" (see Goal 1). However, some critics feared that these goals would ignore the educational needs of students with disabilities and that the emphasis on higher standards would take the focus away from the needs of students with disabilities who are unable to meet these higher standards. Many states have operationalized the national goals in their own specific and comprehensive state education reform initiatives. Goals 2000: Educate America Act has as its premise that by the year 2000, the following would occur[1]:

### Goal 1: Readiness for school

All children in America will start school ready to learn.

### Goal 2: High school completion

The high school graduation rate will increase to at least 90%.

### Goal 3: Student achievement and citizenship

American students will leave Grades 4, 8, and 12 having demonstrated competency in challenging subject matter including English, mathematics, science, foreign languages, civics and government, economics, arts, history, and geography.

### Goal 4: Teacher education and professional development

The teaching force will have access to programs for the continued improvement of their professional skills.

### Goal 5: Science and mathematics

U.S. students will be first in the world in science and mathematics achievement.

### Goal 6: Adult literacy and lifelong learning

U.S. students will be literate and will possess the knowledge and skills necessary to compete in a global economy and exercise the rights and responsibilities of citizenship.

### Goal 7: Safe, disciplined, and alcohol- and drug-free schools

Every school in America will be free of drugs and the unauthorized presence of firearms and alcohol and will offer a disciplined environment conducive to learning.

### Goal 8: Parental participation

Every school will promote parental involvement and participation.

The reauthorization of the Elementary and Secondary Education Act (ESEA), also known as the No Child Left Behind Act, was passed by Congress in December 2001 and signed into law by President Bush on January 8, 2002. The principles for reform in this legislation include accountability for results, flexibility and local control, expanded parent options, and doing what works (Paige, 2002). In its strategic plan of 2002–2007, the U.S. Department of Education targeted six strategic goals[2]:

### Goal One: Create a culture of achievement

Emphasize the No Child Left Behind legislation and its principles.

### Goal Two: Improve student achievement

Improve achievement by putting reading first, expanding high school mathematics and science teaching, and increasing teacher and principal quality.

### Goal Three: Develop safe schools and strong character

Establish educational environments that are safe and foster good citizenship.

### Goal Four: Transform education into an evidence-based field

Enhance the quality of educational research.

---

[1]Source: U.S. Senate-House Conference, 1994.

[2]Source: U.S. Department of Education Strategic Plan, 2002–2007.

**Goal Five: Enhance the quality of and access to postsecondary and adult education**

Expand opportunities for students and the effectiveness of institutions.

**Goal Six: Establish management excellence**

Require accountability throughout the Department of Education.

Notice that the Goals 2000: Educate America Act and the No Child Left Behind Act have some elements in common such as an emphasis on student achievement, citizenship, lifelong learning, safe educational environments, and parental participation. The two pieces of legislation also have some differences. While Goals 2000 includes a focus on mathematics and science, professional development of teachers, and readiness to learn, No Child Left Behind targets reading, evidence-based research, and increased accountability. Both set high expectations for public education on the national level. Some states have adopted these national standards and others are developing their own standards (Miller, 2002). We recommend that you check with your state department of education and examine the education reform initiatives that your state has established and are being implemented in your area, and monitor the impact these initiatives are having on students with disabilities and on teacher preparation. We hope you will make this one of your responsibilities as an educator.

## PROFESSIONAL COMMITMENT

The primary international organization that represents the special education field is the Council for Exceptional Children (CEC). The mission of CEC is to improve educational outcomes for individuals with exceptionalities:

CEC, a nonprofit association, accomplishes its mission, which is carried out in support of special education professionals and others working on behalf of individuals with exceptionalities, by advocating for appropriate governmental policies, by setting professional standards, by providing continuing professional development, by advocating for newly and historically underserved individuals with exceptionalities, and by helping professionals achieve the conditions and resources necessary for effective professional practice. (Council for Exceptional Children [CEC], 2002, p.4).

Members of the special education profession are responsible for upholding and advancing certain standards for professional practice (CEC, 2003). These standards include:

1. Identify and use instructional methods and curricula that are appropriate to their area of professional practice and effective in meeting the individual needs of persons with exceptionalities.
2. Participate in the selection and use of appropriate instructional materials, equipment, supplies, and other resources needed in the effective practice of their profession.
3. Create safe and effective learning environments which contribute to fulfillment of needs, stimulation of learning, and self-concept.
4. Maintain class size and case loads which are conducive to meeting the individual instructional needs of individuals with exceptionalities.
5. Use assessment instruments and procedures that do not discriminate against persons with exceptionalities on the basis of race, color, creed, sex, national origin, age, political practices, family or social background, sexual orientation, or exceptionality.
6. Base grading, promotion, graduation, and/or movement out of the program on the individual goals and objectives for individuals with exceptionalities.
7. Provide accurate program data to administrators, colleagues, and parents, based on efficient and objective record keeping practices, for the purpose of decision making.

8. Maintain confidentiality of information except when information is released under specific conditions of written consent and statutory confidentiality requirements (p. 2).

With your acceptance of these responsibilities, you make a commitment to students with exceptionalities, their families, and the teaching profession. We hope you will give careful thought to these responsibilities.

## ✳ WHAT WE BELIEVE

Our text is centered around four beliefs:

1. There are generic, research-based instructional techniques that all teachers of students with special needs should know how to apply and evaluate.
2. These generic, research-based techniques may be used in teaching various content areas and for various ages and levels of students with mild disabilities.
3. In the 21st century, special educators will need to modify curriculum and adapt instruction as they work in collaborative partnerships with general educators, administrators, families, and other school professionals to meet the needs of students in increasingly diverse and inclusive classes.
4. As external partnerships become more critical to the success of students prior to entering school, during school, and in postschool situations, special educators will need a varied repertoire of collaborative skills to initiate and maintain these relationships.

Currently, many texts focus on math, reading, and other content areas. Instead, we thoroughly discuss research-based instructional techniques and apply them, with examples, to various content areas, levels, and settings. We believe that in most inclusive settings, special educators will be responsible for modifying curriculum and adapting instruction, while relying on general educators for their expertise in curriculum areas. We believe our text fulfills the need for pre-service and in-service teachers to have a solid foundation in effective generic methodologies. From this solid foundation, teachers, through practice and successes, will add their own adaptations to best meet the needs of individual learners, as no one method works for all students.

 **IMPORTANT POINTS** ◀

1. Participation of students with disabilities in standards-based reform was mandated with the 1997 amendments to the Individuals with Disabilities Act (IDEA).
2. Goals 2000: Educate America Act (1994) represents a national framework for education reform to improve our systems, policies, standards, and most importantly, outcomes for all students.
3. The reauthorization of the Elementary and Secondary Education Act (ESEA), also known as the No Child Left Behind Act, was signed into law in 2002 with an emphasis on accountability, local control, expanded parent options, and doing what works.
4. Although Goals 2000 includes a focus on mathematics and science, professional development of teachers, and readiness to learn, No Child Left Behind targets reading, evidenced-based research, and increased accountability.
5. A career in special education carries with it many professional responsibilities that are stated in the CEC Standards for Professional Practice.
6. In this text, we focus on research-based instructional techniques that may be used for teaching in various content areas for various levels of students. These techniques can be used by special educators to modify curriculum and adapt instruction as they

work in partnership with general educators to meet students' needs.

---

 **DISCUSSION QUESTIONS**

1. Discuss with a partner the implications of national education and standards-based reform on children and adolescents with disabilities.

2. Examine the CEC Standards for Professional Practice. Reflect on what the standards mean to you as a member of the special education teaching profession.

3. Discuss some of the common characteristics of students with special needs. Relate the characteristics to students with disabilities whom you have taught or worked with previously.

# CHAPTER 2

# BEGINNING-OF-THE-YEAR PLANNING AND ORGANIZATION

# KEY TOPICS

The Council for Exceptional Children (CEC) has defined the minimum essential knowledge and skills necessary for entry into professional practice in special education. Among the eight components of the CEC Common Core is that of "planning and managing the teaching and learning environment" (Daniels & Vaughn, 1999). The planning and organization decisions you make prior to and during the first week of school can establish the climate and set the tone for the rest of the school year. The beginning of the school year is the ideal time to establish a safe, risk-free classroom learning community where all students are welcomed, valued, respected, and supported; where they are given opportunities to be active participants in the learning process; where they know and understand the rules and expectations; and where they will experience success. "No matter how well prepared your plans are, those plans will go untaught if presented to students in a classroom that is nonsupportive and poorly managed" (Callahan, Clark, & Kellough, 1998, p. 181). Taking a proactive approach at the start of the school year, quickly establishing systems and routines, and clearly communicating expectations to students will minimize the likelihood of problems later in the year. Therefore, in this chapter we present information to guide you in your efforts to plan and manage your teaching and learning environments particularly at the beginning of the year. We focus on what you should do prior to and during the first week of school as you review individualized education programs (IEPs), develop goals and objectives for students, plan or co-plan lessons and activities in pull-out and inclusive settings, prepare for a variety of grouping practices to promote student participation, establish and communicate classroom rules, and develop schedules.

## DESIGNING INDIVIDUALIZED EDUCATION PROGRAMS AND PLANS

"The Individualized Education Program (IEP) is the cornerstone of the Individuals with Disabilities Act (IDEA), which ensures educational opportunity for students with disabilities" (Smith, 2000, p. 2). With the passage of PL 94–142 in 1975, the development of an Individualized Education Program for students with disabilities became a requirement. The 1990 amendments renamed the law the Individuals with Disabilities Education Act (IDEA) and added the requirement that plans for transition services be made part of the IEP no later than age 16.

The IDEA Amendments of 1997, PL 105–17, amended and reauthorized the Individuals with Disabilities Education Act. The 1997 IDEA amendments have placed a greater emphasis on providing access for students with disabilities to participate and progress in the general education curriculum including provision of the supports needed to enhance that participation and progress (Katsiyannis, Ellenburg, & Acton; 2000; Pugach & Warger, 2001). The 1997 reauthorization of IDEA calls for substantive participation by general education teachers as active members of IEP teams who are essential to the development and implementation of instructional strategies, interventions, accommodations, and services. The emphasis on providing access for students with disabilities to the general education curriculum has increased the attention given to the selection of appropriate accommodations that can be used in general education settings (Etscheidt & Bartlett, 1999). Furthermore, "The 1997 IDEA amendments specifically addressed the need for students with disabilities to be included in state and district-wide assessment practices (with or without accommodations or through alternate assessments)" (Katsiyannis, Ellenburg, & Acton, 2000, p. 119). In addition, the new amendments changed the age from 16 to 14 for developing a statement of transition service needs. This change emphasizes the importance of early planning and preparation by students, parents/families, and teachers. Students' IEPs should reflect the courses that relate to their desired postschool outcomes, such as business and technology courses for a student interested in computer-related employment, and should contain content that addresses postschool desires and needs. For a thorough discussion of transition from school to work and community living and a description of the Transition Individualized Education Plan (TIEP), see Chapter 12.

### Components of the Individualized Education Program

The IEP is a written plan, developed in consultation with the students' parents/families and professionals, based on information gathered from assessment (Blackhurst & Berdine, 1993). It is a road map for special education instruction, because it tells where students are going and how they are going to get there. It describes what the student needs and what will be done to address those needs. One of your essential tasks at the beginning of the year is to become thoroughly familiar with each student's Individualized Education Program. IEP forms vary by state, school district, and sometimes by category within the same district, but all must contain the following components:

1. The student's present levels of educational performance, including a statement of how the disability affects the student's involvement and progress in the general education curriculum
2. Annual goals that the student is expected to attain by the end of the year
3. Short-term objectives, which are the intermediate steps leading to the attainment of the annual goal

4. A description of special education and related services, program modifications, and supports
5. The amount of time the student spends in a general education program
6. Projected dates for initiation and duration of special services
7. Evaluation procedures and schedules for determining mastery of short-term objectives at least on an annual basis
8. Modifications needed for participation in statewide or districtwide assessments or if it is determined the student cannot participate, why the assessment is inappropriate and how the student will be assessed
9. Needed transition services (from school to work or postsecondary education) for students age 14 and older

A list of materials and techniques to reach the short-term objectives often appears on the IEP, though it is not required by law.

### Present Levels of Performance and Annual Goals

The student's present levels of educational performance and the annual goals are usually based on results from both formal and informal measures, whereas the short-term objectives are usually identified through informal measures. Formal assessment measures contain specific rules for administration, scoring, and interpretation. They are usually based on a comparison with the performance of students of the same age and grade level (that is, they are norm referenced). Informal measures do not contain rigid rules for administration, scoring, and interpretation. They may consist of inventories, observations, or criterion-referenced tests. Chapter 3 presents a detailed description of informal assessment.

In examining the sample IEP in Figure 2.1, notice that both formal tests, such as the Peabody Individual Achievement Test—Revised (Markwardt, 1989), and informal measures, such as the Brigance Comprehensive Inventory

of Basic Skills, Revised (Brigance, 1999), were administered to determine the current level of educational performance and annual goals. Turnbull, Strickland, and Brantley (1982) state that there should be three or four goals for each subject area needing remediation and that these goals should be broad enough to take a year or more to accomplish. Examples of annual goals appropriate for students with special needs are:

1. Master basic computation facts at the first-grade level.
2. Read the 220 Dolch words.
3. Apply note-taking techniques in content area classrooms.
4. Solve math problems commensurate with ability.
5. Become compliant with teacher's requests.

Notice the PIAT-R, WRAT-R, Brigance, and probes were administered to Jimmy. Additionally, Jimmy's scores on the state assessment tests are recorded in this section.

### Short-Term Objectives

Informal measures, such as the Brigance Comprehensive Inventory of Basic Skills, Revised (Brigance, 1999), and curriculum-based measures may be used to identify and evaluate the attainment of short-term objectives. IDEA requires that short-term objectives be stated in instructional or behavioral terms. For example, "Lucy is hyperactive" is not written in behavioral terms, whereas "Lucy got out of her seat 32 times during her 25-minute music class" is written in behavioral terms. A behavioral objective includes four components: the learner, the target behavior, the condition, and the criterion.

The target behavior identifies what the learner is asked to do. It should be observable and specific so it can be measured. Following are some sample target behaviors frequently found in the IEPs of students with special needs. Notice that the target behaviors are observable and measurable.

**Figure 2.1** Sample IEP

## Individualized Education Program

**Student Information**

Name: _Jimmy Smith_
School: _Enterprise Elementary School_
Date: _12/9/03_
Chronological Age: _12 yrs. 2 mos._
Date of Birth: _10/5/91_
Grade: _6_

Parent Notification (if not attending meeting) _____

| | Type of | | |
|---|---|---|---|
| Date | Attempt | By Whom | Results |
| | | | |
| | | | |
| | | | |

### Present Level of Educational Performance

| Area | Source | Date | Scores |
|---|---|---|---|
| Reading Recognition | PIAT-R, WRAT-R | 11/1/03, 10/25/03 | 5.9, 6.0 |
| Reading Comprehension | PIAT-R, Brigance | 11/1/03, 11/5/03 | 2.0, 2.0 |
| Math | WRAT-R | 10/25/99 | 2.0 |
| Addition—Whole numbers | Probe | 11/5/03 | 10 correct/5 wrong in 1 min. |
| Subtraction facts (0–9) | Probe | 11/5/03 | 8 correct/5 wrong in 1 min. |
| Vocab (context clues) | Brigance | 11/5/03 | 1.0 |

### Special Education and Related Services

| Program or Service | Amount of Time per Week | Projected Initiation Date | Anticipated Duration | Person Responsible |
|---|---|---|---|---|
| Varying Exceptionalities Resource | 5 hours a week | 12/10/03 | 12 months | VE teacher |

**IEP Developers' Signature/Title**

Eve Peabody—teacher
Lorna Smith—parent
Steve Palladino—LEA Rep.

IEP Date _12/9/03_
IEP Review Date _12/9/04_
Regular Education Hours _25 hours a week_

### Annual Goal: Improve math skills to level commensurate with ability

| Short-term Objectives/ Evaluation Criteria | Evaluation Method | Date Initiated | Date Completed |
|---|---|---|---|
| Calculate subtraction facts/70 cc, 2 ce per min. for 3 days | Teacher-designed probe | 1/15/04 | |
| Add two digits plus two digits with regrouping/80% for 3 days | Teacher-designed probe | 12/10/03 | |

### Annual Goal: Improve reading comprehension to level commensurate with ability

| Short-term Objectives/ Evaluation Criteria | Evaluation Method | Date Initiated | Date Completed |
|---|---|---|---|
| Paraphrase main idea of paragraph/95% for 3 sessions | Teacher observation | 12/10/03 | |
| Identify the meaning of two new words a week/100% | Checklist | 12/10/03 | |

1. Write the answers to subtraction facts.
2. Rephrase the main idea of a paragraph.
3. State two expectations of an employer.
4. Add a column of three one-digit numbers.
5. Name three types of mollusks.
6. Follow teacher's requests.

The condition of a behavioral objective usually relates the circumstances under which the behavior will occur. It frequently tells when or how. Following are examples of conditions:

1. Given a worksheet . . .
2. When asked to begin . . .
3. Without use of a dictionary . . .
4. Given 10 completed checks . . .
5. Using a calculator . . .

The criterion of a behavioral objective describes the minimum level of performance for mastery of the target behavior. The criterion may be expressed in terms of the following:

1. Accuracy—90%, or 15 correct.
2. Rate—15 correct in 1 minute.
3. Time—10 minutes.

Academic behaviors are usually measured in terms of accuracy or rate. To ensure mastery of an objective, an overlearning measure is frequently suggested (Alberto & Troutman, 1999). The overlearning measure requires that the student perform this behavior more than one time. Examples of overlearning include the following:

1. three days
2. four sessions
3. five attempts
4. three times
5. four trials

Now, putting all four components of a behavioral objective together along with the overlearning measure, the following examples represent behavioral objectives appropriate for students with special needs:

1. Upon request, Jerome will apply the steps of a test-taking strategy to a practice test within 40 minutes for three sessions.
2. Without prompting, Matt will write the subjects and verbs of sentences with 90% accuracy on three assignments.
3. When asked, Penny will read a passage at 150 correct words per minute with two or fewer errors for 3 days.
4. Given amounts, dates, and receipts, Melissa will complete, in writing, 10 blank checks with 95% accuracy for four sessions.
5. When asked to begin, Zita will say the names of the states and their capitals within 3 minutes for three trials.
6. Without prompting, Joe will begin the teacher's assignment within 2 minutes for three sessions.

In most cases, these components do not all appear in one short-term objective on an IEP. Instead, they are described in various sections of the IEP. For example, the behavioral objective of "Given a teacher-designed probe of 40 addition problems, Jimmy will add two digits plus two digits, with regrouping, with 80% accuracy, for three days" is found in various sections of Jimmy's IEP (see Figure 2.1). The identification of the learner (student's name) is located on the first line of the IEP. The target behavior, "add two digits plus two digits, with regrouping," is listed under the short-term objectives/evaluation criteria column. The criterion and overlearning measure, "80% accuracy, for three days," appears in the same column. The condition, "given a teacher-designed test of 40 addition problems," appears in the evaluation method column as a teacher-designed probe. Many school districts require the identification of two short-term objectives for each annual goal.

Because special education teachers are assuming more responsibility for instruction in the general education classroom in consultative and co-teaching roles, IEPs need to be modified to reflect these roles. Short-term objectives can be written for instruction that is delivered in inclusive settings. Table 2.1 provides examples in reading, study skills, and social skills. Notice how more emphasis is placed on the roles of the teachers and where each objective will be accomplished.

### Description of Services Including Amount of Time Spent in General Education

Special education and related services appropriate for each student must be included in the IEP. Special education services include direct and indirect services. Direct services are those provided by a special education teacher to the student, whereas indirect services are those provided by a special education teacher to the general education teacher. Special education teachers may provide these indirect services by helping classroom teachers identify effective instructional techniques and adapt materials. Related services, provided by specialists, include counseling, social work, adapted physical education, psychological testing, and transportation. The roles, responsibilities, and amount of time allocated for special education and related services must be clearly stated in the IEP. Figure 2.1 shows that Jimmy participates in the Varying Exceptionalities Resource room for 5 hours a week and participates in regular education for 25 hours a week.

### Initiation and Duration of Services

The projected dates for the initiation and duration of services must be indicated on the IEP. For example, Figure 2.1 shows that Jimmy will spend one hour a day in a varying exceptionalities class, beginning 12/10/03 (initiation of services), for 12 months (duration of services).

### Modifications in Statewide and Districtwide Assessments

One section on the IEP describes participation in statewide and districtwide assessments. In some cases, the student will participate in these assessments, but will need modification in the administration of the tests. There is a space on the IEP for the IEP team to describe the modifications. In cases in which the student will not participate in state and district assessments, the IEP team needs to state a reason along with a description of an alternative assessment. Figure 2.1 shows that Jimmy did not need modifications, as evidenced in the reporting of only scores on the State Comprehensive Assessment Test.

### Transition Services

The transition planning section of the IEP includes a place for the IEP team to include transition goals, academic/instructional activities, related services, community experiences, employment and adult living objectives, and functional evaluation information (see Chapter 12 for a detailed description of transition IEPs). Notice, Jimmy is only 12 so no mention of transition services appears on the IEP.

### Evaluation Procedures

Progress toward goals and objectives may be assessed by using the IEP as a tool to monitor students' progress. Teachers must specify the method, the criteria for acceptable performance, and the schedule for evaluation. When teachers use IEPs as working plans for their students, they can truly monitor their students' mastery of objectives.

## Weekly and Daily Plans

"Thoughtful and thorough planning is vital for effective teaching to occur" (Callahan, Clark, & Kellough, 1998, p. 82). Planning guides teachers for a year, a 9-week term, a day, or a lesson. It requires identification of learner needs, goals and objectives, materials, instructional strategies, and evaluation procedures. IDEA requires general educators to play a major role in relating IEP goals and objectives to the general education curriculum (Gable & Hendrickson, 1999). Therefore, be

**Table 2.1** Sample IEP Objectives for Cooperative Teaching

**Area: Reading fluency and comprehension**
**Objective: Given a trade book, the student will:**

| *What* | *Who* | *How* | *When* | *Where* |
|---|---|---|---|---|
| Read fluently 75 wpm, no errors for 3 days | General Education Reading Specialist | Cooperative Training (Team Teach) | 2 × week 45 minutes | General Education Class |
| Comprehend main ideas and details with 90% accuracy | General Education Reading Specialist | Cooperative Teaching (Compl. Instruct.) | 5 × week 1 hour | General Education Class |
| Respond orally to comprehension questions with meaningful sentences at various levels of Bloom's Taxonomy | General Education Speech/Language Specialist | Cooperative Teaching (Team Teach) | 3 × week 30 minutes | General Education Class |

**Area: Study skills in history**
**Objective: Given strategy instruction, student will:**

| *What* | *Who* | *How* | *When* | *Where* |
|---|---|---|---|---|
| Take notes with 90% accuracy that include 90% of key points | General/Special Education | Cooperative Teaching (Complementary Instruction) | 3 × week 50 minutes | General Education Class |

**Area: Interaction with Peers**
**Objective: Given small-group cooperative learning activities, student will:**

| *What* | *Who* | *How* | *When* | *Where* |
|---|---|---|---|---|
| Initiate conversation with one or more peers for 3 consecutive lessons | General Education Speech/Language Specialist | Cooperative Teaching (Supported Learning) | 2 × week | General Education Class |

Note: From "IEPs for Cooperative Teaching: Developing Legal and Useful Documents," by J. Bauwens and L. Korinek, 1993, *Intervention in School and Clinic*, 28, p. 305. Copyright 1993 by PRO-ED, Inc. Reprinted by permission.

sure you collaborate with general educators and connect the IEP to instruction as you plan classroom activities for students with disabilities.

In addition to the IEP, which is mandated by law, weekly planning is required by many school principals. Often, teachers turn in plan books on Friday for the principal's approval of the next week's lessons. When teachers write their plans for the week in a plan book, they typically include times, names of texts or materials, and page numbers. Sometimes, special and general education teachers record information such as the levels of the students in each of the curriculum materials used in the class, the groups to which they are assigned, and the names of students receiving related services. In pull-out programs, teachers list the names of students and the subjects they are assigned to in general classroom settings.

Weekly plan books do not provide teachers with specifics about presenting lessons or adequate space to add much detail, which may be a problem if there are 10 students working on different objectives. Therefore, in addition to

using a weekly plan book, resource teachers and teachers who co-teach with classroom teachers in general education classrooms need to use an additional planning format to enable them to be aware of their objectives, procedures, materials, and evaluation methods for each lesson. Figure 2.2, which contains an example of a lesson about the rainforest, includes the essential parts of a lesson. Please see Chapter 4 for a detailed discussion of lesson planning and presentation.

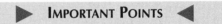

## ▶ IMPORTANT POINTS ◀

1. The planning and organization decisions you make prior to and during the first week of school can establish the climate and set the tone for the rest of the school year.
2. Establish a safe, risk-free classroom learning community where all students are welcomed, valued, respected, and supported; given opportunities to be active

**Figure 2.2** A Lesson From a Science Unit

---

**Subject:**
Science (1:45–2:30)—"The Rainforest"

**Objective:**
After instruction, the students will write in their journals three facts about the rainforest, with 95% accuracy, for 2 days.

**Procedures:**
1. Introduce the lesson by asking students if they can describe a rainforest.
2. Read *A Day in the Rainforest*.
3. Discuss the story with the students.
4. Have the students generate words from the story that describe how it feels to be in the rainforest.
5. Write their suggestions on an overhead transparency.
6. Give a 10-minute presentation on life in the rainforest.
7. Have students name things that live in the rainforest.
8. Write these on an overhead transparency.
9. Have students write in their rainforest journals three facts about the rainforest that they learned in the lesson.
10. To close the lesson, have the students share one fact that they have written about the rainforest.

**Materials:**
1. The book, *A Day in the Rainforest*
2. Overhead projector, transparencies, and pen
3. Journals

**Evaluation:**
Students will be evaluated by checking their journals to be sure that they wrote three accurate facts about rainforests.

---

## ▼ ACTIVITY 2.1

Concetta, a sixth grader, has been recommended for assistance in a pull-out program to work on spelling. Based on the following information, identify Concetta's present level of educational performance and write one annual goal and two short-term objectives for the IEP. Be sure to include evaluation procedures to determine how each short-term objective will be measured.

On the Peabody Individualized Achievement Test—Revised, Concetta had difficulty spelling words and scored on a third-grade level on the spelling subtest. When her misspellings were examined, it appeared that she had the most difficulty with vowel combinations such as ea and silent letters such as gh as in high. On an informal measure (a criterion-referenced test), Concetta again performed more like a third grader in spelling. An error analysis of her responses revealed that she had problems with the ea, oa, and ei combinations. She also misspelled words that contained gh, ph, and ght.

(Answers for this and other activities are found in the Instructor's Manual.)

participants in the learning process; have clear rules and expectations; and experience success.

3. An Individualized Education Program (IEP) is a written plan of instruction for the student, mandated by PL 94–142, amended in 1990 to the Individuals with Disabilities Education Act, and amended and reauthorized in 1997.

4. The 1997 reauthorization of IDEA calls for substantive participation by general education teachers, selection of appropriate accommodations that can be used in general education settings, the need for students to be included in statewide and districtwide assessment practices (with or without accommodations or through alternate assessments) and a change from age 16 to 14 for developing a statement of transition service needs.

5. The components of an IEP describe (a) the student's present level of educational performance, (b) annual goals, (c) short-term objectives, (d) special education and related services including the amount of time spent in general education, (e) projected dates for initiation and duration of services, (f) modifications in statewide and districtwide assessments, (g) evaluation procedures for determining mastery of each short-term objective, and (h) a description of needed transition services.

6. Information from both formal and informal assessment becomes part of an IEP.

7. In addition to the IEP, planning includes using a weekly plan book and designing specific lesson plans that include objectives, procedures, materials, and evaluation procedures.

## ORGANIZING AND MANAGING THE LEARNING ENVIRONMENT

Due to the varied and complex demands placed on special education teachers (e.g., implementing the goals and objectives of IEPs, planning appropriate learning activities, adapting instruction, and modifying materials), many tasks must be accomplished before the start of the academic year. Careful attention to these tasks eases the transitions students experience as they return to school. One of the challenges teachers face as they begin the year is organizing and managing the classroom environment. Polloway and Patton (1997) underscore the critical importance of classroom organization, which has taken on even more significance with the inclusive education movement. Greater emphasis is being placed on cooperative learning, and on the co-teaching of classes by general and special educators (Bauwens & Hourcade, 1994). Teachers must consider seating arrangements that are conducive to cooperative learning and peer tutoring, and yet minimize distractions and promote student engagement; activities and materials that help students master IEP goals and objectives; and instructional arrangements that promote student participation and academic achievement.

## Classroom Arrangement

Although the design of a classroom is secondary to instructional methodology and curriculum, evidence indicates that the physical setting may influence student behavior and attitudes (Good & Brophy, 1987; Evertson, Emmer, Clements, & Worsham, 1994). The physical arrangement of the classroom communicates important information to students about how they are expected to interact with each other and with the teacher and about how they are expected to complete tasks (Rosenfield, Lambert, & Black, 1985). For example, if you want students to interact in solving a problem, facilitate interaction by seating students at a table as opposed to seating them at individual desks in rows. We discuss the physical setting (i.e., desks in rows, tables, etc.) as related to instructional arrangements (large-group instruction, small-group instruction, etc.) extensively later in the chapter under Instructional Grouping Arrangements.

Some of the physical variables that affect the way classrooms are organized are the size of the room, the storage needs, the furniture (Lewis & Doorlag, 1991), types of equipment, type of classroom (e.g., a pull-out/resource room or a general education classroom), and the kinds of instructional activities that will be implemented. Arrange seating to avoid overcrowding and to provide for adequate personal space, keep high traffic areas free of obstacles, make sure that you can see your students and they can see you, organize and label materials and supplies so they can be easily accessed, and provide areas for large- and small-group instruction and interaction. Create a warm, inviting classroom learning community that promotes student participation and engagement. The following general suggestions will help you get started in setting up and organizing your setting.

### Learning/Interest Centers

A learning or interest center is an area within the classroom consisting of a collection of activities and materials where students may go to complete a new assignment or work on a previously taught concept (Wood, 2002). Multilevel learning centers are frequently found in general education settings at all grade levels and are an effective way to meet the needs of academically diverse students in inclusive classrooms by providing activities to accommodate many different levels of functioning and interest and offering the opportunity for students to work independently with materials on their own levels. Effective use of learning/interest centers can assist students to be more self-directed and independent. It is important to assemble materials and activities that you know are of interest to your students, have clear directions and effective methods of evaluation, and can be completed independently. Mr. Nolen set up a reading center in his classroom complete with mysteries, sports and adventure stories, magazines, newspapers, books with accompanying tapes, stories that students had written, predictable books, and multicultural literature.

### Furniture and Supplies

When teachers' desks are put off to the side, in the back, or out of the central area of the class, teachers tend to sit at them less, are more mobile, and circulate more freely around the room to monitor student progress. This helps to eliminate a long line by the side of the desk as students seek assistance. In addition, by circulating, teachers can use proximity control to keep students interested, engaged, actively involved, and alert. By moving around the room to check on students, teachers can become proactive—able to anticipate and prevent problems before they occur—instead of having to react after something has happened. In situations in which teachers float from class to class or co-teach in a general education setting, they may set up their supplies in a desk in that classroom or in a work area off to the side of the room. It is important for special education teachers to have a designated area, materials, and supplies in a co-taught classroom, first, to support their instructional efforts, and second, to affirm the important contribution they make in the general education setting.

## Equipment and Storage Space

Prior to the start of the school year, you should select and set up the equipment you will need, whether you are teaching in a resource/pull-out classroom or in an inclusive classroom. The classroom should have both desks and tables, so that individual work, group work, peer tutoring, and cooperative learning may take place. Allocate specific areas of the room for the storage of videodiscs, videotapes, CD-ROMs, computer software, manipulatives, newspapers, magazines, games, and other resource materials. Carefully label these areas so that teachers, students, substitutes, and teaching assistants can find equipment and supplies.

Teachers who are not assigned to one classroom but float from classroom to classroom or co-teach (such as when special and general education teachers work together to teach students jointly in general education settings) may need to set up equipment and supplies on a cart to make their materials mobile, or they may have designated areas within each general education classroom in which they teach. Some teachers use file boxes to organize and store their instructional materials, student folders, games, tape recorders, and manipulatives. For example, Mrs. Nestrada uses a three-tiered cart with two boxes on each shelf to teach six different classes. Although she stores additional materials elsewhere, the cart enables her to keep the most essential materials with her to use in her classes.

In some classrooms, teachers are faced with the dilemma of inadequate storage space for students' materials. There may be more students than desks. In these cases, bookshelves that have sections or cubbyholes may be used for students to store materials, such as pencils, paper, workbooks, journals, notebooks, and textbooks. In secondary classrooms, students do not usually have desks in which to store materials. They may be seated at chairs with arms that are used as the writing surface or they may sit at tables. Teachers often set up folders in which they keep student work and assignments, and sometimes code the folders by color for each class period. Students usually store their books in lockers and are responsible for bringing them to class. Therefore, storage of students' materials may not be a problem in secondary classrooms.

## Instructional Materials and Files

Prior to the first week of school, teachers should organize instructional materials so that they are readily available for students to use. When appropriate, they should be visible to students. For example, store games in see-through plastic containers so that students can find and retrieve them easily. Set up a system so that students know what materials they can use and how to access them. Callahan, Clark, and Kellough (1998) recommend arranging materials so that they are located in places that require minimal foot traffic and in a way that avoids having to line up for them. Before the school year begins, teachers should organize their own files and those files that will be used by the students so that they are easily accessible.

## Student Variables

Student variables that affect classroom organization include the number of students in the class, their age and grade levels, their learning levels, cultural and language differences, and related challenges students have (mobility, language, behavior, etc.). You may, therefore, arrange the room to accommodate students who are working at various levels and who are focusing on different content and skills by including learning centers, computers, a variety of instructional grouping arrangements, and modified curriculum materials written for several different grade levels. For example, Heron and Harris (1987) suggest that verbal communication moves across, not around, tables. Therefore, they recommend that a student with low verbal skills be seated across from a student with high verbal skills to maximize the reception of verbal messages and nonverbal cues (that is, facial expressions and gestures).

Consider cultural differences in setting up the classroom. Kitano (1987) states that few Asian Americans participate freely in group discussions. This fact is important to know as you plan your instructional activities so that you do not mistake limited participation for lack of ability. Students from cultures that are people oriented or that endorse working together for the good of the group may benefit from cooperative learning activities, group projects, and other collaborative activities. For example, Lewis and Doorlag (1991) report that the Native American culture emphasizes cooperation and group achievement and that Native American students may show a preference toward actions as opposed to words. Teachers may want to consider using physical arrangements and activities to complement various cultural preferences by including tables, peer tutoring areas, and activity areas.

## Bulletin Boards

Bulletin boards may be teacher or student created and may be used in elementary and secondary general and special education settings. Hayes (1985) suggests four types of bulletin boards: decorative, motivational, instructional, and manipulative. Hannah (1982) recommends a fifth category—informational—and we suggest a sixth, work display.

*Decorative* bulletin boards are typically designed to brighten and improve the appearance of a classroom. Examples of decorative bulletin boards are displays that say "Hello" or "Welcome" in several different languages or displays of decorative posters with themes. *Motivational* bulletin boards are used to recognize student effort and progress. For example, teachers may post charts and graphs showing student progress in mastering a particular skill. *Instructional* bulletin boards may be subject or task specific. They may be related to the curriculum and used for instruction such as a bulletin board that demonstrates the parts of an essay. *Manipulative* bulletin boards may be thought of as an enlarged version of a worksheet to be completed by actually attaching things (Hayes, 1985), such as matching the parts of speech to a list of words. *Informational* bulletin boards are used to convey information to students. They can be used for announcements, for current events, or classroom rules. *Work display* bulletin boards are used to display samples of students' work, such as original poems, essays, and short stories.

In preparing a bulletin board, Callahan, Clark, and Kellough (1998) recommend the following guidelines:

▶ Keep it simple.
▶ Focus on one main idea, concept, topic, or theme.
▶ Use illustrations to accent topics.
▶ Use short, concise captions.
▶ Consider gender and ethnic equity.

 **ACTIVITY 2.2**

Collect pictures of men, women, adolescents, and children who represent a variety of cultural backgrounds and age groups and who are engaged in both common and unusual activities. Decide how you would use these pictures to construct either a decorative or an instructional bulletin board.

## Grading and Record-Keeping Procedures

At the beginning of the school year, decide how you are going to grade student work, monitor progress, and keep records of student performance, and how you will communicate these procedures to your students. We suggest that you do this verbally, in writing, as part of the classroom rules, or in all three ways.

### Grading

Grading is an essential part of educational practice, providing feedback to students, their families, and others (Miller, 2002). More and more students with disabilities are receiving instruction in general education classrooms and, therefore, are being graded there. Grading students with disabilities is particularly perplexing in inclusive settings. In a grading survey, 368 general education teachers rated pass-fail grades and checklists as appropriate for students with disabilities (Bursuck, Polloway, Plante, Epstein, Jayanthi, & McConeghy, 1996). Both general educators (Bursuck et al., 1996) and secondary students (Munk & Bursuck, 1997) felt that grade adaptations only for students with disabilities were unfair. As a special education teacher, you may be responsible for assigning grades, you may not assign grades at all, or you may assign grades in collaboration with a general education teacher. Bursuck and others (1996) found that 50% of the general educators in their survey assumed complete responsibility for grading, whereas 40% shared grading responsibilities with special educators.

General techniques such as assigning multiple grades, contracting for grades, basing grades on a variety of assignments, factoring in growth rate, and establishing criteria for grades have been found to be effective in grading students with special needs (Gersten, Vaughn, & Brengelman, 1996; Munk & Bursuck, 1997). Written narratives could also be used to supplement the use of letter grades (Mehring, 1995). A modified grading system can be used for students with disabilities, but it must be available to all students unless the student with disabilities is taking the general education class for no credit or is not required to master the course content (Salend & Duhaney, 2002). Check with your school district to see what the grading guidelines are and whether you have the flexibility of utilizing alternative grading systems with your students.

***Assigning Multiple Grades.*** Assignments may be evaluated with multiple grades. For example, you may assign two grades for a report—one for content and one for mechanics. Giving two grades takes into consideration the ideas (content) as separate from the mechanical aspects (punctuation, spelling, grammar), which present stumbling blocks for many students with special needs. In their research, Munk and Bursuck (1997) found that general education teachers and secondary students believed that assigning separate grades for effort and product is a helpful adaptation for students with special needs. For example, Ms. Barbour assigned a grade of C for the quality of the writing of one of her student's essays and a grade of A for effort, for the time the student devoted and the research the student completed on the topic.

***Contracting for Grades.*** Contracting with students for grades based on a certain level of proficiency on IEP objectives is another suggestion (Polloway, Epstein, Bursuck, Roderique, McConeghy, & Jayanthi, 1994). In this grading procedure, you discuss short-term objectives with the students and agree on the level of proficiency to be reached by the end of each grading period. Reaching the predetermined level of proficiency results in a higher grade than not reaching it.

***Basing Grades on a Variety of Assignments.*** Miller (2002) recommends basing grades on multiple dimensions such as tests, homework assignments, projects, and extra credit work. Additionally, you have the option of determining the final grade by giving more weight to reports and homework scores than exam scores.

***Factoring in Growth Rate.*** Grading based on improvement is another adaptation that is effective for students with disabilities (Polloway et al., 1994). One of the authors based students' spelling grades, in part, on the increase in the number of words spelled correctly from the Monday pretest to the final spelling test on Friday. For example, both Jim and Jan earned an A grade. Jim, who improved by 10 words from the spelling pretest to the posttest, earned extra points, which boosted his 85% to an A grade. Jan, who improved by only one word, earned an A grade as she scored 100% on the posttest.

***Establishing Criteria for Grades.*** In addition to percentages, always make your criteria clear for the grades you give (Tiedt & Tiedt, 1986). For example, may an A paper have spelling errors? Discuss with the students the characteristics of outstanding work, average work, and poor work, and show them examples. Mr. Lucas teaches students how to take notes so that they can improve their performance in history class. As part of his teaching procedure, he shows them examples of good and poor notes. He specifies his criteria for grading notes for the content (key points of the lecture) and the technique (accurate use of a note-taking strategy).

***Using Narrative Grading.*** Mehring (1995) recommends the use of written narratives about students' academic and behavioral performances in addition to quantitative scores on the standard report card. Frequently, these written descriptions of student performance provide more meaningful and specific information to students and their families than a letter grade does. These narratives can also be used to set or adjust the student's goals (Miller, 2002).

Some effective instructional practices that support grading procedures for students with disabilities in inclusive settings are (Salend & Duhaney, 2002):

1. Communicate expectations and clear guidelines to students and families. Sharing information may be accomplished during an open house or on the Internet by posting your grading criterion and guidelines.
2. Show models of exemplary work before assigning projects.
3. Provide nongraded assignments to students first with feedback and additional instruction if necessary before grading the final product.
4. Give extra credit.
5. Calculate grades based on median, not mean, scores.
6. Involve students in the design of grading rubrics (see Chapters 3 and 7 for further discussion of rubrics).

One of the most troublesome questions for you as a teacher is whether students with special needs should fail in classes for which you have the responsibility of assigning grades. Special education teachers are supposed to provide students with an appropriate education plan. If a student is failing, the teacher should ask such questions as, Did I design an appropriate education plan? Is there something else I might do? Should I add other incentives? We feel that students should not fail in a special education setting if they truly have been provided with an individualized education program. Whatever grading system you use, be sure you explain it thoroughly to your students and that you implement it in a fair and consistent manner.

### Record Keeping

Record keeping consists of collecting and keeping information and data for instructional and/or administrative purposes (Polloway & Patton, 1997). Teachers should keep careful, written records on a daily basis regarding student performance. "The most important factor is that data are collected regularly, recorded in a systematic fashion, and then utilized to determine whether instructional modifications should be made" (Lewis & Doorlag, 1999, p. 187). Record-keeping systems may be designed prior to the start of the school year. Charts, graphs, checklists, and other forms may be developed to accompany the activities and materials that students will use in the classroom. In some classes, the record-keeping system is visible to everyone, as in Mrs. Murphy's fourth grade, where the names of the books each student has read are posted. In other cases, the record-keeping system is kept in folders, as in Mr. Russo's high school class, where math students are concentrating on probability. A checklist containing math vocabulary and rules is stapled inside each student's folder, where it is updated on a daily basis.

Teachers may develop other record-keeping systems by recording the date and score for computer activities and learning center activities; progress toward mastering specific skills; attendance records; scores on tests, homework, and other assignments; and progress in portfolios, journals, and group projects. These records may be kept in a written record book or an electronic record book (such as a computer software program, either commercially produced or teacher-developed using a spreadsheet) (Callahan, Clark, & Kellough, 1998).

Students may be responsible for some of their own record keeping. Lewis and Doorlag (1999) recommend involving students in checking their answers with an answer key and then recording or graphing the results. Mercer and Mercer (1993) suggest using self-correction tapes to provide feedback to students about their math assignments. After using such tapes, students may fill out their math record for the day (see Figure 2.3). This record keeping on the part of students provides them with immediate awareness of their performance and may

**Figure 2.3**  Math Record

Name ___Julie_____

Today I listened to tape ___#7_____

My first score was ___12/15_____

My score after corrections was ___15/15_____

lead to application of strategies to improve that performance.

Whatever record-keeping procedures you develop, be sure they reflect the instructional objectives and levels of performance designated for each student in each area of the academic and social skills curriculum. Records of student performance in pull-out and inclusive settings may be used to plan, modify, and evaluate instruction and to motivate students to greater achievement.

 **ACTIVITY 2.3**

Work with a partner to devise a way of keeping records for an individual student in a pull-out classroom and a way for keeping records for a small group of students in an inclusive classroom.

▶ **IMPORTANT POINTS** ◀

1. Due to the varied demands on special education teachers, many tasks must be accomplished before the start of the academic year.
2. One of the challenges teachers face as they begin the year is organizing and managing the classroom environment.
3. Considerations in setting up the classroom environment include attention to (a) the classroom arrangement, (b) equipment and storage space, (c) instructional

materials and files, (d) student variables, and (e) bulletin boards.

4. Grading techniques include assigning multiple grades, contracting for grades, basing grades on a variety of assignments, factoring in growth rate, establishing criteria for grades, and using narrative grading.

5. Record-keeping procedures include the use of charts, graphs, and checklists to record student progress on computer, audiotape, and learning center activities and may be kept in a written or electronic record book.

6. Whatever grading and record-keeping systems you use, be sure to explain them thoroughly to your students and their families and implement them in a fair and consistent manner.

## COORDINATING INSTRUCTIONAL AND MANAGEMENT DECISIONS

Part of beginning-year planning and organization involves making decisions about how to coordinate instruction and management. Two important decisions that may ensure a successful start to the school year include attention to creating a variety of instructional grouping arrangements and establishing management procedures such as classroom rules.

### Instructional Grouping Arrangements

Instruction may be provided in a variety of ways: large groups, small groups, one-to-one, with peers, or independently. Individualization of instruction may be achieved by using any of these instructional arrangements. As Christenson, Thurlow, and Ysseldyke (1987) point out, individualization does not limit the grouping arrangement to situations in which a student works alone or in a one-to-one arrange-

ment with a teacher. Individualization refers to "helping students succeed, to achieve a high percentage of correct responses and to become confident in his/her competence" (p. 6).

Factors influencing decisions about how to provide instruction include (a) the characteristics and needs of the students, (b) the type of learning planned—whether the teacher is teaching a skill for the first time (i.e., acquisition learning) or students are practicing and maintaining a skill that has already been taught (i.e., fluency and maintenance learning), (c) the task or activity (e.g., engaging in a dialogue about a literature selection, discussing job interviewing, building a model of the digestive system, or writing and reflecting in journals), and (d) the types of instructional methodology that are available. Callahan, Clark, and Kellough (1998) recommend that you consider the types of instructional methodology that are available, including:

▶ Cooperative learning
▶ Debates
▶ Games
▶ Laboratory experiments
▶ Multimedia
▶ Problem solving
▶ Peer tutoring
▶ Simulations
▶ Textbooks
▶ Learning centers
▶ Computer-assisted instruction
▶ Demonstrations
▶ Guest speakers
▶ Lecture/presentations
▶ Panel discussions
▶ Questioning
▶ Role playing
▶ Think-pair-share
▶ Co-teaching

Teachers should choose instructional arrangements that meet students' needs as documented in their IEPs and that address cultural and linguistic diversity.

### Large-Group Instruction

There are many opportunities for using large-group instruction. For example, you could use large-group instruction to introduce a strategy for taking notes. Lewis and Doorlag (1999) suggest providing guided practice for the whole class at once. Have the students practice taking notes by watching a videotape, while you circulate around the room to monitor use of the note-taking strategy. Other appropriate uses of whole-class instruction include the viewing of multimedia presentations, large-group discussions of content area subjects, and demonstrations. Fister and Kemp (1995) recommend the use of the Ask, Pause, Call technique during presentations to large groups. The teacher asks a question, pauses to allow students to process the question and formulate a response, and then calls on someone.

Large-group instruction is used extensively in general education classroom settings. Experience in large groups may be helpful to students as they make the transition from special to general education settings (Bos & Vaughn, 1998). In addition, special education teachers who co-teach in inclusive classrooms may share with general education teachers the responsibility for providing instruction to the whole class. Be aware that when using large-group instruction, not all of the students will learn all of the content you present. You still need to think about individual student needs. Dyck, Sundbye, and Pemberton (1997) use an Interactive Lesson Planning Model to determine the topic of a lesson, the content of the lesson, and what parts of the content can be learned by all, most, or some of the students given their varied levels and skills. This planning model, particularly useful for co-teachers, serves as a basis for differentiating activities, objectives, and assessments for students.

When providing instruction to the entire group, many teachers arrange the desks in rows. This may be appropriate when you are lecturing and making presentations through directive teaching or giving a PowerPoint presentation. When utilizing this type of arrangement, it is helpful to move around the room and to direct comments and questions to students seated in various parts of the classroom in order to keep all students engaged. Cegelka (1995) emphasizes the importance of arranging the desks so that all students can see the whole-group instructional area and yet not face areas that could distract them, such as learning center activity areas, windows, or doors.

### Small-Group Instruction

Small-group instruction is appropriate when teachers present different material to different students (Lewis & Doorlag, 1999). Small groups are frequently used in acquisition learning to teach a specific skill (Polloway, Patton, Payne, & Payne, 1989). Groups should be flexible: Sondra, Tim, Rahji, and Bertha may be grouped together for instruction in math but be members of other groups for spelling. If Bertha progresses more rapidly than the others, she is moved to another, more appropriate group.

Small-group instruction usually consists of groups of two to five students. It is used when teachers want to work closely with students, give them the opportunity to express what they know, provide them with frequent feedback, and allow them to receive feedback from other students (Vaughn, Hughes, & Moody, 2001). Small groups may also be used in cooperative teaching situations to divide the class into different skill groups. Brophy and Good (1986) suggest the use of small groups in classes that are highly heterogeneous. Small groups are often used in general education classes because of the heterogeneity of the population and thus would work well in inclusive settings. Students may be grouped for reading, math, spelling, or other academic skills.

Small-group arrangements are particularly effective for teaching academic skills. Reading is frequently taught in small groups. Small-group arrangements are also useful for cooperative learning activities (activities in which students work together and teach each other), role-playing activities, and review sessions. A detailed description of cooperative learning is provided in Chapter 8.

Weinstein (1981) suggests that teachers arrange the seating within groups so that group leaders are accessible to all members of the group and less vocal students are seated across from the more vocal leaders. For this reason, you should consider having some tables in your classroom to facilitate group work. When working with a group, some teachers prefer to seat students in a semicircle facing them in order to provide optimum feedback and attention; there is support for this grouping arrangement for low-achieving students in the area of mathematics (Carnine, Silbert, & Kameenui, 1997). Small-group instruction may be appealing to students who have language differences because they may feel more comfortable asking for clarification in a small group and because they may have more opportunity to participate.

Small-group arrangements also facilitate maintenance learning, providing students with opportunities to practice or extend a skill that was presented through direct instruction. Group projects, such as interviewing someone, writing an article for the school newspaper, or developing a budget, may be assigned to groups as extension activities to prompt maintenance and generalization of skills taught.

Small groups are not always used for purposes of direct instruction. Frequently, small groups are led by students who take turns assuming the role of the leader and guiding instruction through question asking and dialogue (Vaughn, Hughes, & Moody, 2001). In Chapter 16, we present a description of reciprocal teaching in which students assume responsibility for their own learning as they link their prior knowledge with new knowledge through questioning, summarizing, clarifying, and predicting text information. Reciprocal teaching is often used with small groups of four to seven students.

### One-to-One Instruction

Working on a one-to-one basis with the teacher allows students to ask questions, receive corrective feedback, and interact directly with the teacher, which is highly advantageous for students. Individual instruction is appropriate for students who are working on acquisition learning, having difficulty learning in a small-group setting, or needing assistance with specific aspects of assignments (Polloway, Patton, Payne, & Payne, 1989). The disadvantage of one-to-one instruction is that the special education teacher's time and attention can be focused on only one student at a time.

Teachers using one-to-one instruction must plan for the rest of the class, perhaps by including cooperative learning activities and peer tutoring. Some teachers utilize the skills of paraprofessionals or volunteers to provide one-to-one instruction to students. Other teachers ask paraprofessionals or volunteers to monitor the rest of the class while they work with individual students. Some co-teaching arrangements are conducive to one-to-one instruction. While one teacher works with most of the class, the co-teacher assists other students on a one-to-one basis (see Chapter 10 for other suggestions). In arranging the classroom, teachers can set up tables or desks away from the rest of the class for one-to-one instruction.

### Peer Tutoring

Vaughn, Schumm, Klingner, and Saumell (1995) found that students with learning disabilities prefer to work with a peer than in large groups or by themselves and are highly motivated to work in pairs. In peer tutoring, one student receives instruction from another under supervision of the teacher. Peer tutoring is effective for fluency and maintenance learning, such as practicing math facts and spelling words. Tutors may also check answers to end-of-chapter questions, provide positive reinforcement and corrective feedback, and teach or reteach specific skills to other students who need extra help. When instruction is provided through tutorial arrangements, you may want to arrange areas in the classroom for peer tutors by putting two desks together or by providing small tables set aside from the rest of the class. Peer tutoring is often combined with other instructional options, such as large- and small-group arrangements. A detailed description of peer tutoring is provided in Chapter 8.

### Independent Learning

Independent learning may include completing an activity at a learning center, viewing a multimedia presentation, writing and reflecting in a journal, preparing entries for a portfolio, using a computer, or conducting research in the library/media center. Opportunities for independent practice should be provided to students who have acquired a skill and need additional practice. It is helpful to include a self-correcting component in independent work. Independent work does not typically require the teacher's presence, so teachers should select activities that students can complete with minimal assistance (Bos & Vaughn, 1994). Thus, while some students are engaged in independent work, others work individually or in small groups with the teacher.

Classrooms may be set up to contain individual work areas where students can work quietly and independently. Students may also work independently at a table, desk, or computer workstation. The challenge for teachers is to place the individual work areas away from the more active areas of the classroom.

In summary, there are a variety of ways to arrange the classroom for instruction including whole class, teacher- and student-led small-group instruction, peer tutoring, one-to-one instruction, and independent learning. You can use any of the previously described arrangements or a combination of one or more of them,

depending on your instructional purpose(s) and the needs and characteristics of your students. Flexible grouping arrangements allow you to individualize instruction in a variety of ways. Figure 2.4 contains examples of possible arrangements for large- and small-group instruction. Notice how these groupings may be used effectively in both pull-out and inclusive classrooms, and how they allow the teacher to move around the room to provide instruction and monitor progress while keeping students interested and engaged.

 **ACTIVITY 2.4**

> Choose an elementary, middle, or high school setting and prepare a sketch of a classroom. Assume that you will have students who are involved in both acquisition learning and fluency and maintenance learning. Be sure to include evidence of the instructional arrangements (large-group, small-group, one-to-one, peer tutoring, and independent learning) you would use, as well as ideas from the section of this chapter on classroom arrangement.

 **IMPORTANT POINTS** ◀

1. An important decision that may ensure a successful start to the school year includes attention to instructional grouping arrangements.
2. Instruction may be provided in a variety of ways: large groups, small groups, one-to-one, with peers, or independently.
3. Factors influencing decisions about how to provide instruction include attention to the characteristics and needs of the students, the type of learning planned (e.g., acquisition or maintenance), the activity, and the types of instructional methodology that are available.
4. Large-group instruction is appropriate for guided practice activities, the viewing of multimedia presentations or videotapes, large-group discussion of content area subjects,

**Figure 2.4**   Large- and Small-Group Instructional Arrangements

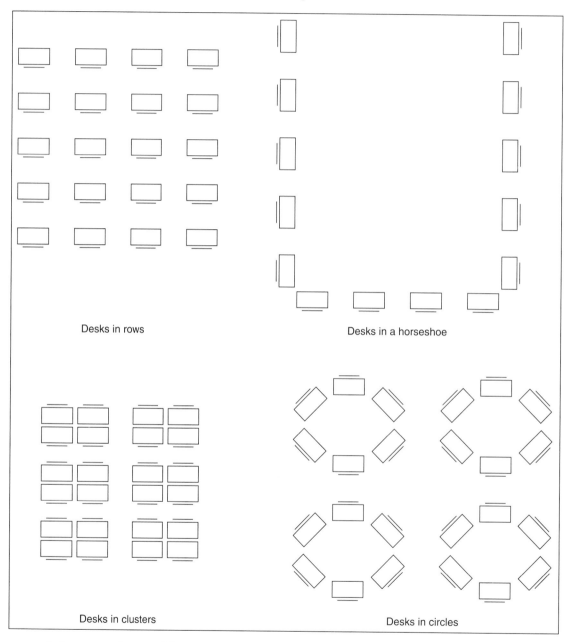

Desks in rows

Desks in a horseshoe

Desks in clusters

Desks in circles

and demonstrations and is frequently used in general education classrooms.

5. Small-group instruction is used to present different material to different students and

is effective for acquisition learning, teaching of academic skills, maintenance and generalization, and student-led activities in which students take turns assuming the role of the leader as in reciprocal teaching, cooperative learning activities, and role playing.

6. Arrangements in which teachers and students work together on a one-to-one basis are appropriate for students who are working on skills that differ from those of the rest of the class and for those who are working on acquisition learning, having difficulty in a small-group setting, or needing assistance with specific aspects of assignments.

7. Peer tutoring is effective for fluency and maintenance learning, monitoring progress, providing feedback, and teaching and reteaching specific skills to students who need extra help.

8. Independent learning may include completing an activity at a learning center, viewing a multimedia presentation, writing and reflecting in a journal, preparing entries for a portfolio, using a computer, or conducting research in the library/media center and does not typically require the presence of the teacher.

---

## Management Decisions

Many potential behavior problems may be prevented by establishing a classroom learning community built on respect and trust, selecting appropriate and motivational materials, presenting organized and motivational lessons, engaging students in learning activities, and implementing structured routines. These techniques are discussed elsewhere, so we do not repeat them here. Unfortunately, not all behavior problems can be prevented or resolved with only these instructional decisions. You must also make wise decisions concerning management options. Some of these decisions center around establishing a classroom rule system.

You will notice as you are reading this section that many of the suggestions are very teacher directed, even though we strongly encourage the use of student input in formulating the rules and the selection of choice strategies. Eventually, we feel that self-management should replace teacher direction, but this is a gradual process. Self-management strategies are discussed in Chapters 3 and 6.

### Selecting Rules

Rules let students know what you expect. Students react differently during the completion of independent assignments when the teacher expects talking in a low voice and when the teacher expects total silence. Two effective ways for you to identify class rules are to make a list of your behavioral expectations ahead of time and to ask if there are any schoolwide rules (Sprick, 1985). An examination of the list of schoolwide rules will let you know what behaviors administrators and other teachers feel are necessary for maintaining order.

Once you define your expectations, you should establish rules. Following are some guidelines:

1. *Provide opportunities for students to give input concerning the rules.* Helping to select rules gives students a sense of being a part of the decision-making process and often makes them feel more responsible for following the rules. Sprick (1981) suggests that if you want students to design their own rules, you should post temporary rules for the first 3 or 4 days, until students become familiar with the routines.

2. *Base rules on acceptable behaviors.* In deciding on the rules, keep in mind the behaviors that are expected in the general classroom setting. It may be acceptable for a student to complete work standing at a table in a pull-out setting, but this behavior may be totally unacceptable in an inclusive setting. In many school districts, there are certain rules that all students are expected to follow. If this is the case, incorporate these rules into your system. Other considerations for deciding which behaviors to

include in rules are to select those that promote the ease of functioning as a classroom community.

3. *State rules positively.* Positive rules lead to a positive atmosphere in the classroom and clue the students into appropriate behavior. "Speak politely to others by saying thank you and please" is a much better rule than, "Don't shout at others." The first rule suggests an appropriate behavior, whereas the latter just warns the students not to shout.

4. *Select only about five or six rules.* A rule cannot be invented for every slight infraction that may happen in the class. The more rules you have, the more difficult it is to enforce them consistently (Jensen, Sloan, & Young, 1988).

5. *Select rules for both academic and social behaviors.* Rules usually deal with academic behaviors, such as "Complete all assignments," or social behaviors, such as "Keep hands and feet to yourself." Often academic rules will prevent inappropriate social and affective behaviors.

6. *Relate rules to specific behaviors, but be general enough to cover many classes of that behavior.* A rule such as "Be kind to others" is general; it can cover many classes of behaviors, including "Say nice things to other students" and "Keep your hands to yourself." Thus, the use of a general rule reduces the number of rules needed. However, students may not understand what is meant by the rule if no specific behavior is identified. This problem may be solved by listing examples of specific behaviors next to the rule or by discussing and role-playing specific behaviors.

7. *Change rules when necessary.* If being unprepared for class is a problem for your third-period class, this behavior should become the focus of a new rule. If students are completing all work, it may be time to remove the rule that deals with completing all assignments. This does not mean that students no longer have to complete the

work; rather, since everyone is remembering it, a written rule is no longer necessary.

8. *Relate rules to IEP objectives.* For many students with special needs, social behavior as well as academic objectives are written in the IEP. These objectives may be added to the rules for each individual student as individual goals or, if many students have similar objectives, may become part of the group list of rules.

9. *Consider cultural differences.* In some cultures, student involvement in class is often vocal, exuberant, and physical, so students may be on task even though they are not sitting quietly in their seats. You may want to incorporate such factors into rule selection. For example, "Finish all assignments" may be a better rule than "Work quietly at your seat."

 **ACTIVITY 2.5**

Work with a partner and list five or six rules you might use in your class. Discuss how you might involve your students in developing the rules for the classroom.

### *Teaching Rules*

Once rules are selected, the next step is to teach and discuss them frequently. Particularly at the beginning of the school year, the class rules should be discussed, demonstrated, and for younger children, practiced. Adding a rationale to an explanation of the rules during the discussion is particularly effective for older students, who often are motivated if reasons for having rules are discussed (Morgan & Jenson, 1988).

The following techniques, adapted from Direct Instruction procedures (Engelmann & Carnine, 1982), are suggested for teaching rules. They include defining or describing the relevant attributes of the behavior, modeling examples and nonexamples, and asking students to discriminate between them (Morgan & Jenson, 1988). For example, with the stay-on-task rule, define for the students what "stay on task" means (e.g., "Stay on task means you write or listen or read when you work"). Next, give positive examples (e.g., "When you are doing a math paper, you are on task if you are writing down the problems, figuring out the answers, or thinking about how to solve the problem") and negative or nonexamples (e.g., "You are not on task if you are looking out the window, thinking about lunch, or talking to a friend"). Then model examples and nonexamples of on-task behaviors and ask the students to identify and explain why the behavior is an example or a nonexample of on-task behavior. In response to this question, a student may say, "You are on task because you are looking at the math book," or "You are not on task because you are looking around the room." Next, have students model the appropriate or inappropriate behavior and have others identify whether the students are displaying on-task behaviors. During this role-play activity, the students are not only practicing the rule, but also learning to evaluate behaviors.

Post the rules in the room or in individual notebooks to help students remember them. Many adolescents write the rules on a sheet of paper to keep in their notebooks. One creative student teacher incorporated the rules into a class constitution to parody the United States Constitution.

### Prompting Rules

Having rules does not mean students will automatically follow them immediately. Students often need prompts to internalize or perform behaviors independently (Rosenshine, 1990). Prompts are ways to remind students to follow the rules. For example, verbal prompts such as "Remember, raise your hand," or visual prompts, such as a finger over the lips, usually prevent talk-outs. The visual prompt of standing near the whispering students often stops off-task behavior. Other prompts include sharing expectations, peer modeling, positive repetition, and issuing either warning or choice statements. Sometimes students can remind peers to follow classroom rules.

*Sharing Expectations.* Sharing expectations is a way to explain to students what rules are in effect or what behaviors you expect for that particular activity (Sprick, 1985). Rules often vary, depending on whether the activity is to be completed by individuals or by small groups. Stating behavior rules at the beginning of a lesson is especially effective for students with problem behaviors (Emmer, Evertson, Clement, & Worsham, 1994).

An example of sharing expectations about behaviors appears in these sample instructions given to secondary students: "Today, we begin our study of the Roman Empire. As we discuss the beginning of Roman civilization, please remember to listen to others' ideas without interruptions, to copy the notes from the board, and to participate in the discussion." With many elementary students, you must share your expectations before academic and nonacademic activities. For example, "Bernice, remember, when we stand in line, we keep our hands to ourselves, we face the door, and we do not talk."

*Peer Modeling.* Peer modeling may also serve as a prompt for following rules (Alberto & Troutman, 1995). To use peer modeling, praise students who are following the rule by identifying specific behaviors (e.g., "Good, Jason, you are standing quietly in line") and ignore the student who is not (e.g., ignore Rashonda). Then, when the student displays the appropriate behavior, praise him or her (e.g., "Good, Rashonda, that's the way to stand quietly in line").

*Positive Repetition.* Positive repetition is similar to peer modeling in that you first tune in to positive behaviors of the students who are following the rules. At the same time, however, you repeat the directions or instructions you gave (Canter & Associates, 1986). For example, if Jane, a middle school student, is refusing to follow your directions to take out her sentence writing book and turn to page 45, ignore Jane and say to

Ramone, "Thank you, Ramone. I can see you have your sentence writing book out. I appreciate your turning to page 45, Towanda. This side of the room is ready to begin."

Praising other students instead of tuning in to the inappropriate behavior of a student is difficult even for seasoned teachers. The natural reaction to this type of situation is to focus on the deviant behavior immediately, instead of praising the students who are following the rules. Deviant behaviors can make teachers fearful that their authority is being questioned and that they are losing control. Yet being positive as a first step is frequently sufficient to stop inappropriate behavior. In addition, praising teaches students that teacher attention, often a powerful motivator (Alberto & Troutman, 1999), may be secured through appropriate behaviors instead of inappropriate behaviors.

***Issuing Warning Statements and Choice Statements.*** We recommend the use of warning statements and choice statements only after you have tried to change the behavior by positively attending to the appropriate behaviors of other students. If, after praising others, you find that a student is still not following the rule, you may want to use a warning or a choice statement. A warning statement alerts the student to the rule infraction. For example, "You are forgetting our rule to listen to others, Sam. This is a warning," lets Sam know that he needs to display appropriate behavior immediately. Warning statements are often used with younger children.

With a choice statement, you present the appropriate behavior that relates to the rule and some sort of unpleasant option to the student, for example, "Sally, you are breaking Rule 4. Either remember to raise your hand (rule) or leave the group (option). It is your choice."

Once you issue a choice statement, give the student an opportunity to think about the choice. Move out of the student's vicinity to avoid a direct confrontation and continue with other activities. That way, a student can save face and

even mumble nasty things out of your hearing range (or, at least, you can pretend not to hear them). Be certain always to acknowledge an appropriate choice in some way, such as "I see you've made a good choice, Sally. Thank you."

In issuing choice or warning statements, you should remain calm and speak in a quiet, firm voice. Lower your voice at the end of a warning statement. Be aware of nonverbal behaviors, such as eye contact. When issuing a warning statement, many teachers point a finger at the student, which is a clue to the student that he or she is upsetting the teacher. Instead, if your hands are resting at your sides, you convey an air of confidence.

Colvin, Ainge, and Nelson (1997) suggest that teachers give students a list of options privately when they break a rule. With this strategy, teachers focus students' attention on ways to solve the problem, instead of focusing on noncompliance. For example, options for Sally, who is not raising her hand, may include: "Sally, talking out is not appropriate. You may raise your hand when you need help, go on to the next problem until I can help you, or reread the directions."

The type of prompt given depends on the type of behavior, the time of the year, and the cultural background of the student. You would not administer a choice statement for behaviors that are physically detrimental to a particular student, other students, the teacher, or school property. Samantha cannot be given a choice if she is hitting Jim. You must stop her immediately. Typically, more prompts are given at the beginning of the year until students become familiar with the rules. Finally, public critique of behavior may cause discomfort for students from certain cultural groups. Be aware of this possibility as you work with your students.

***Involving Students.*** Sometimes other students can assist in reminding their peers to follow classroom rules. A group contingency combined with peer tutoring effectively increased the math and reading skills of at-risk African

▼ **ACTIVITY 2.6**

Three people are needed to participate in this activity. One will be the teacher, another the student, and the third will be the observer. Be sure to change roles so that each person has a chance to be the teacher, the student, and the observer. The observer is to evaluate the teacher's use of a choice statement by marking an X under yes or no for each statement on the following checklist. The student is telling the teacher that he is not going to do his math (disobeying the rule to follow teacher directions) and is trying to involve the teacher in a confrontation. The teacher should use a choice statement.

| Observer Checklist | Yes | No |
|---|---|---|
| 1. Did the teacher remain calm? | | |
| 2. Did the teacher speak in a firm, quiet voice? | | |
| 3. Did the teacher maintain eye contact? | | |
| 4. Did the teacher use her or his hands appropriately? | | |
| 5. Did the teacher state the appropriate behavior and the option in the choice statement? | | |
| 6. Did the teacher repeat the choice idea by saying, "It is your choice" or "It is your decision"? | | |
| 7. Did the teacher give the student some time to think about it? | | |
| 8. Did the teacher acknowledge selection of the appropriate choice? | | |

American students in an after-school program (Gardner, Cartledge, Seidl, Woolsey, Schley, & Utley, 2001). The group contingency required the third- through fifth-grade students to work quietly to earn a group reward of a fruit snack and juice. The 90-minute period was divided into intervals. An audiotape would chime randomly at the end of approximately 5 minutes. If all students were on task when the tape chimed, the class received a mark. Fifteen marks were required to earn the group

reinforcer. Through role-playing and examples and nonexamples, the 10 students were taught to discriminate on-task behaviors and how to correct their peers' off-task behaviors. Students gave prompts such as "Please work quietly," or "Come on, man, help the group out by working quietly" (p. 7) to remind their peers to stay on task and then praised those students who complied with the directive. After two unsuccessful peer corrections, an adult corrected the student. If the student continued to refuse, the offending student lost more reinforcers such as a loss of recreation or star for the educational period. The frequency of this occurring was about once every other week.

### Enforcing Rules

The next step is to decide what you are going to do when students follow rules and when they do not. You may want to use specific praise or positive attention intermittently to call attention to students who are following the rules, and then award certificates or free time at the end of the week based on particular criteria.

Specific praise statements identify the praiseworthy aspects of students' behaviors. When using a specific praise statement, include a description of the specific behavior the student is demonstrating and the student's name, for example, "I like the way you are working quietly, Terri" for the young student and "That was a good decision when you ignored Hugo's remark, Josh." For many adolescents, positive public praise from a teacher is unpleasant or embarrassing, as they don't want to be singled out from their peers (Sprick, 1985). Thus, you may want to praise adolescents in private or praise the group effort instead of individuals. This is also true for various cultural groups who prefer quiet, private, specific praise.

Specific praise and positive attention may be interwoven into your daily routine; neither is time consuming. Attending to the student with a raised hand and ignoring the one shouting out requires no extra time. Stopping at secondary students' desks to compliment them for staying on task during independent practice activities is appropriate for students who enjoy being praised or singled out for teacher attention in private (Sprick, 1985).

What are your options when, even after prompting, a student continues to break the rules? Usually, the options are (a) withholding something the student likes, or (b) presenting the student with something he or she doesn't like. Many teachers withhold points, privileges, or free time from students who do not follow the rules; others write referrals or require students to eat lunch alone. Canter (1979) recommends a hierarchy of consequences, such as writing the student's name on the board for the first rule infraction, withdrawing 5 minutes of recess time for the next, and referring the student to the principal for the third. He further states that a severe rule infraction (such as a fight) warrants an immediate severe punishment, such as referral to the principal.

Whatever consequence you use, remember to remain calm and follow through. Some students try to talk teachers out of the consequence, such as "Oh, Mr. Jones, please don't send me to the principal's office. I'll do my work now." A teacher who does not follow through at this time is teaching students that they can wait to do their work until the teacher threatens to take them to the office, and then they can talk the teacher out of taking them there. You need to follow through with the consequence, or your effort becomes just a threat.

In addition to following through with consequences, consistency is a prime consideration in enforcing rules. If "Raise your hand to speak" is a rule, then all students should have to follow it. Be careful not to fall into the trap of giving attention to a student who is shouting out because that student happens to be blurting out the correct answer. Consistency allows students to learn that there are expectations in your class accompanied by rewards for following them and consequences for not complying.

Finally, remember to provide appropriate feedback. For example, Mr. Anderson gave his secondary students the following feedback at the end of fifth period: "Most of today's class went well. All of you followed directions, copying the notes from the board, but I had to prompt you not to interrupt when someone was talking. Let's work on this during tomorrow's class."

 **IMPORTANT POINTS**

1. Guidelines for establishing rules are to incorporate student input, base rules on acceptable behaviors, state rules positively, select only about five or six rules, relate rules to both academic and social behaviors, make rules specific, change rules when necessary, relate rules to IEP objectives, and consider cultural differences.

2. Teaching rules requires defining or describing the important attributes of the behavior, modeling examples and nonexamples, and asking students to discriminate between them.

3. Prompts are used to remind students to follow the rules and include the sharing of expectations, peer modeling, positive repetition, the issuing of warning or choice statements, and involving students.

4. In sharing expectations, teachers should praise appropriate behavior, ignore a student displaying inappropriate behavior, and eventually praise that student once the behavior changes.

5. In peer modeling, teachers should praise appropriate behavior, ignore a student displaying inappropriate behavior, and eventually praise that student once the behavior changes.

6. In positive repetition, teachers should praise the appropriate behaviors by calling attention to the instructions students are following.

7. Specific praise and positive repetition may be used for students who follow the rules. Withholding privileges or presenting something unpleasant may be used for students who do not follow the rules.
8. Teachers must be consistent in enforcing rules and following through when students do not follow rules.

## SCHEDULING FOR INSTRUCTION

Scheduling is an essential part of effective teaching for special education teachers. Schedules provide structure and organization and allow teachers to accomplish the goals and objectives that they have planned for their students. Students with learning problems can benefit from the routine that systematic scheduling provides (Mercer & Mercer, 1998). Teachers should let students know what activities they are to accomplish and when they should complete them. Thus, the use of systematic scheduling may increase self-directedness and independence among students by eliminating the need to check with the teacher about each assignment.

### General Scheduling Guidelines

Polloway, Patton, and Serna (2001) underscore the importance of a carefully planned schedule: Students are intrinsically motivated, the use of schedules maximizes the appropriate use of time, and teachers can provide an educationally relevant program with appropriate transitions between instructional activities. It is important to provide students with a schedule that will maximize learning opportunities and address the goals and objectives of students' IEPs. Suggestions for teachers to follow in scheduling include:

1. Group students by level, interests, and needs.
2. Schedule opportunities for active involvement, cooperative learning, independent work, guided practice, both teacher-directed and student-led instruction, and peer tutoring.
3. Alternate preferred and less preferred activities and facilitate transitions.
4. Stress goals and objectives.
5. Emphasize the connection between what is done in the special education setting and its applications to general education classes.
6. Visit general education classrooms, consult with teachers, and co-plan with other members of the educational team (counselors, school psychologists, administrators, teachers, paraprofessionals, and other specialists).
7. Facilitate scheduling of students from pull-out to inclusion settings.

Special education teachers vary in the amount of time they spend providing direct services (working with students) and indirect services (working with other professionals). Some also plan time for assessment of students as part of their schedule. Your assigned roles and responsibilities affect your schedule and the schedules of your students.

### Scheduling in Elementary Schools

As teachers develop schedules in elementary schools, they should use the following information in making instructional decisions: (a) each student's needs, which can be prioritized and taken from the IEP; (b) the amount of time the student is supposed to work in the special education setting; (c) the amount of time the student is scheduled in other settings; and (d) the schedules of general classroom teachers.

#### Consultative Services and Cooperative Teaching

Many students who have special needs are capable of functioning in inclusive settings with modifications and adjustments made by their teachers. These modifications and adjustments are accomplished through collaborative consultation between special and general educators. Special education teachers provide indirect services by participating on school-based assistance teams and by helping general education teachers modify the curriculum, develop and adapt materials, and assess students' academic and social behavior. Chapter 10 provides a detailed description of collaborative consultation.

At other times, special education teachers are called on to provide direct services in the general education classroom. These services may involve co-teaching, that is, working with classroom teachers to co-teach students in inclusive classrooms. When both special and general education teachers share the responsibility for providing instruction, they should plan schedules together.

### Resource/Pull-Out Programs

Scheduling in the elementary resource/pull-out program can be time consuming and challenging because students usually participate in multiple settings with several different teachers. Scheduling is typically accomplished in cooperation with general classroom teachers and others (such as speech/language pathologist, counselor, etc.). Students attend the pull-out program for part of the day to work on specific academic and social behaviors identified in their IEPs and spend the rest of the time receiving instruction in the general education classroom and/or in various related services. Because students attend pull-out programs for varying amounts of time, teachers are faced with many challenges in scheduling students for instruction. For example:

1. Students may range in age from 6 to 14.
2. Students may have varied and specific needs.
3. Students may be functioning on many different levels.
4. General classroom teachers may have preferred times for sending students to the pull-out program.

5. Communication with many general classroom teachers may be difficult and time consuming.
6. Locating materials appropriate for many levels, ages, and interests may be challenging.

Despite the difficulties in scheduling students in a pull-out program, special education teachers may develop effective schedules by following a few guidelines:

1. Collect the schedules of all teachers who have students with mild disabilities assigned to their classrooms.
2. List the academic and social skill areas with which students need help.
3. Group students by area of need, making an effort to keep primary and intermediate students separated.
4. Plan individual and group times to keep class size reasonable and instruction workable.
5. Revise the original schedule until it works.

In addition to providing direct services to students in a pull-out program, you will also need to consult with general education teachers. This is important because of the responsibility for students that is shared between special and general education teachers and because you will want to reintegrate your students into the general education classroom to the extent that is appropriate. This requires close communication and collaboration. Table 2.2 provides an example of an elementary pull-out program schedule.

## Scheduling in Secondary Schools

At the secondary level (middle school, junior high school, and high school), special education teachers may serve as consulting teachers and co-teachers in general education classrooms or they may provide instruction in a pull-out program.

### Consultative Services and Cooperative Teaching

Special education teachers at the secondary level fulfill the roles of consulting teachers the

**Table 2.2**  Elementary Pull-Out Program Schedule (One Week)

| | Monday | Tuesday | Wednesday | Thursday | Friday |
|---|---|---|---|---|---|
| **8:00–8:30** | Problem-solving committee meeting | Consult with classroom teachers | Consult with classroom teachers | Consult with classroom teachers | Consult with classroom teachers |
| **8:30–9:30** | Work with 1st, 2nd, and 3rd grade students (Teacher-directed instruction in reading) | (Learning Centers) | (Teacher-directed instruction in comprehension) | (Process writing) | (Teacher-directed instruction in comprehension) |
| **9:30–10:30** | Work with 4th and 5th grade students (Listening) | (Comprehension monitoring) | (Summarization) | (Comprehension monitoring) | (Paraphrasing) |
| **10:30–11:15** | Co-teach in 3rd grade | Co-teach in 4th grade | Co-teach in 5th grade | Co-teach in 1st grade | Co-teach in 2nd grade |
| **11:15–12:00** | Assessment | Adapt materials | Assessment | Adapt materials | Assessment |
| **12:00–12:30** | Lunch | Lunch | Lunch | Lunch | Lunch |
| **12:30–1:00** | Work with 4th and 5th grade students in math (Small group) | (Small group) | (Computer) | (Learning center) | (Small group) |
| **1:00–1:30** | Work with 2nd and 3rd grade students in language arts (Small group) | Games | (Small group and self-correcting materials) | (Computers) | (Small group) |
| **1:30–2:30** | Assist in general classrooms on "as needed" basis in content area subjects (science, social studies, health) | | | | |
| **2:30–3:00** | Planning/Consulting | | | | |
| **3:00** | Dismissal | Dismissal | Dismissal | Dismissal | Dismissal |

same way that elementary special education teachers do. Services to students with special needs may be both direct and indirect. However, secondary schools are usually larger, which means there are more teachers to work with, more schedules to work around, and more subject area classes to deal with. Special education teachers may co-teach with classroom teachers in general education classrooms. For example, Mr. Jessup teaches an outlining strategy to a science class to help the students organize the content Mrs. Lange presents in science. He also works with her in adapting some of the material in the textbook. Table 2.3 provides an example of a middle school teacher's block schedule. In the first period language arts program, Mr. Fletcher uses the first 10 minutes of class for attendance, general directions, orientation to the day's activities, and a brief review. He spends the next 30 minutes of class providing direct instruction and guided practice to students. The next 30 minutes are devoted to small groups, where students work cooperatively to complete assignments. The final 15 minutes of class are used for whole class discussion, in which students report the results of their group work. The final 5 minutes is use for wrap up activities. In addition to teaching language arts, Mr. Fletcher co-teaches and consults with classroom teachers and adapts materials.

### Resource/Pull-Out Programs

Students at the secondary level may attend resource/pull-out programs for assistance in academic skills, social skills, job-seeking skills, learning strategies, and leisure skills (Schumaker & Deshler, 1988). Resource teachers at the secondary level are responsible for providing direct services to students and may also be responsible for assessment of students. In addition, they may have consulting responsibilities, such as working with teachers to adapt materials and instruction. They often work with guidance counselors to schedule students into their classes and into select general education classes. Secondary schools operate with fixed class periods that are approximately 50 minutes long. Good and Brophy (1984) suggest that the first 8 minutes of class be used for review, the next 20 minutes for teacher presentation and guided practice, and the next 15 minutes for independent practice.

Mrs. Hefter uses the first 5 minutes of class for attendance, general directions, orientation to the day's activities, and a brief review. She spends the next 20 minutes teaching her students how to monitor errors in their written work and providing guided practice. Then the students spend 15 minutes in independent practice with feedback. The next 10 minutes are allocated to addressing pressing individual student needs, such as clarification of an assignment from a general education class, organization of notes and materials from a content area classroom, or a quick review for a test or report from a general education classroom. These final few minutes of class are also spent giving a post organizer, such as previewing the next day's class schedule, reinforcing work completed, reporting progress toward class or individual student goals, and announcing schedule changes. By scheduling this way, Mrs. Hefter has effectively used all of the class time and met her objectives and curricular responsibilities while providing time for individual student needs (Table 2.4).

Many secondary teachers of exceptional students use a folder system. Students come into their classrooms, get their folders, and examine the schedule in the folder. This gives them a preview of the activities for the class period. While some students are receiving teacher-directed instruction, others complete work in their folders or work with a partner or a small group. Some teachers rotate students in and out of learning centers or cooperative learning activities. When not involved with other instruction, the teacher circulates around the room, providing instruction to individuals and groups, monitoring progress, and giving feedback and reinforcement.

Like pull-out program teachers at the elementary level, these teachers at the secondary level wear many hats. They must fulfill consulting responsibilities with general education teachers, be curriculum and materials specialists, have knowledge of secondary diploma options and

**Table 2.3** Middle School Teacher's Block Schedule—Consultative Services in General Education Classrooms

| | Monday | Tuesday | Wednesday | Thursday | Friday |
|---|---|---|---|---|---|
| First Period 9:00–10:32 | Language Arts (7th Grade) | Language Arts (7th Grade) | Language Arts (7th Grade) | Language Arts (7th Grade) | Language Arts (7th Grade) |
| Second Period 10:36–11:46 | Co-Teach Social Studies (8th Grade) | Co-Teach Social Studies (8th Grade) | Co-Teach Social Studies (8th Grade) | Co-Teach Social Studies (8th Grade) | Co-Teach Social Studies (8th Grade) |
| Second Period (Continued) 11:46–12:23 | Lunch | Lunch | Lunch | Lunch | Lunch |
| Third Period 12:27–1:55 | Adapt Materials for Content Teachers | Adapt Materials for Content Teachers | Adapt Materials for Content Teachers | Adapt Materials for Content Teachers | Evaluate and Select Software Programs |
| Fourth Period 1:59–3:20 | Learning Strategies (7th Grade) | Learning Strategies (7th Grade) | Learning Strategies (7th Grade) | Learning Strategies (7th Grade) | Learning Strategies (7th Grade) |
| 3:20 | Dismissal | Dismissal | Dismissal | Dismissal | Dismissal |

**Table 2.4**  Secondary Schedule—Learning Strategies Class (One Class Period)

| | |
|---|---|
| 8:00–8:05 | ▶ Take attendance.<br>▶ Announce next week's exam schedule.<br>▶ Explain activities for class period. |
| 8:05–8:25 | ▶ Review previous lesson in error monitoring.<br>▶ Teach students how to detect and correct punctuation errors in paragraphs.<br>▶ Use overhead projector and handouts (cue cards).<br>▶ Have students take turns practicing on overhead projector and orally as a group. |
| 8:25–8:40 | ▶ Hand out paragraph worksheets.<br>▶ Have students work independently to detect and correct punctuation errors.<br>▶ Circulate to monitor and check work. |
| 8:40–8:50 | ▶ Check with students on regular class assignments, homework, etc.<br>▶ Recap day's activities and preview tomorrow's lesson on detecting and correcting spelling errors. |
| 8:50 | ▶ Dismissal |

the courses students must have to graduate, possess good public relations skills, and be prepared to help students make the transition from school to work and adult living.

Students with special needs may receive instruction in math, English, science, and other subjects from a special education teacher in a resource setting. Materials are available to present the same subject matter that is covered in a general education class, but with less emphasis on reading. This is done by modifying the format of the materials and the assignments to be completed. Therefore, students with special needs may take a class called Oceanography, which parallels the class that other students take, but they complete it using modified texts and adapted curriculum materials.

## Students Who Need More Time

Despite all your efforts at scheduling, you will find that it is next to impossible to plan one schedule and expect it to work for all students. Some students need more time than others to complete assignments. This becomes problematic in inclusive classrooms, as the same students always seem to be the last to finish or may not finish at all. For students who show a willingness to work hard but who need more time because of a learning problem, limited English proficiency, or other factors, we recommend the following strategies adapted from Callahan, Clark, and Kellough (1998) in combination with our own ideas.

1. Learn as much about the student as you can.
2. Adjust your instruction to the student's preferred learning style.
3. Use all modalities when you teach.
4. Help the student learn content in small, sequential steps with frequent checks for understanding.
5. Use frequent positive reinforcement (verbal and written).
6. Check readability level of materials.

7. Adapt instruction and modify materials if needed.
8. Maximize the use of cooperative learning, peer tutoring, role play, student-led group activities, and hands-on activities.
9. Be less concerned about the quantity of content coverage and more concerned with the student's understanding of the content that is covered.
10. Teach study skills, strategies, and survival skills (such as listening strategies, test–taking strategies, teacher-pleasing and class participation skills, and time-management skills).
11. Use peer pairing for support and to enhance learning.

## Efficient Use of Time

In observation of 230 elementary students with mild disabilities, Rich and Ross (1989) found that noninstructional time such as transitions, wait time, free time, snacks, and housekeeping accounted for almost 3 hours of the school day. An examination of 52 high school programs for students with learning or mental disabilities indicated that the students spent an average of 24% of their time in nonacademic activities (Rieth, Polsgrove, Okolo, Bahr, & Eckert, 1987). Since research shows that time spent in academic learning tasks increases achievement, you should schedule the day to maximize student involvement in direct learning activities. As a teacher, you can control the time dimensions of housekeeping, transition, and allocated time by the way you schedule.

### Housekeeping Time

Housekeeping time is the time spent in performing such routine chores as taking attendance, collecting homework assignments, and writing on the board. If they are well organized, these activities make a class run smoothly. If they are not managed correctly, these activities can cause behavior problems and loss of valuable teaching time. Housekeeping questions that need to be resolved include the ways students are to turn in work, sharpen pencils, ask for assistance, and get permission to leave the classroom. If you spend time planning routines, you will spend less time on housekeeping activities during class, thus maximizing instructional time.

### Transition Time

Transition time involves changing from one activity to another or from one setting to another. Again, valuable teaching time may be lost without smooth transitions. For young students, role-playing transition times, such as moving from the desk to the reading group, is helpful. Posted schedules make both secondary and elementary students aware of subject changes. Teachers who circulate throughout the room to answer questions and monitor students' behavior promote more on-task behavior during transition times (Englert & Thomas, 1982). Frequently, much time is lost in transition from pull-out programs to the general education classroom. Incentives are often necessary to motivate students to arrive on time. Extra points, public posting of the names of on-time students, and on-time clubs with special privileges are effective solutions for late arrivals.

### Allocated Time

Allocated time is the amount of time assigned to various instructional activities (e.g., reading groups and independent work) and noninstructional activities (e.g., the completion of IEPs and consultations with classroom teachers). Effective schools allocate more of their time to learning tasks than ineffective schools do (Thurlow, Christenson, & Ysseldyke, 1987).

Sargent (1981) collected data for 60 days from 30 resource teachers serving students with mild disabilities in five different states and found that most of the time was allocated to and spent on direct instruction (51.48%) and preparing for instruction (16.38%). A number of studies found that time spent in teacher-directed instruction is the best single predictor of achievement (Leinhardt, Zigmond, & Cooley, 1981; Sindelar, Smith, Harriman, Hale, & Wilson, 1986; Stallings, 1980). Achievement is low when students are assigned a lot of seatwork to do independently (Medley, 1979) or are taught with curriculum packages (Squires, Huitt, & Segars, 1983). In fact, time spent in independent instructional activities, such as silent reading, was unrelated to achievement for elementary students with mental or learning disabilities (Sindelar, Smith, Harriman, Hale, & Wilson, 1986). Secondary and elementary students achieve more when at least 50% of the school day is spent in direct instruction (Stallings, 1980). Thus, you need to schedule your day so that most of the time is allocated to teacher-directed instruction.

 **ACTIVITY 2.7**

Brainstorm with three other people to develop more time-saving ideas dealing with housekeeping, transition, and allocated time.

 **IMPORTANT POINTS**

1. Considerations in scheduling include (a) group students by level, interests, and needs; (b) provide opportunities for active involvement, cooperative learning, independent work, guided practice, teacher- and student-led instruction, and peer tutoring; (c) alternate preferred and less preferred activities and facilitate transitions; (d) stress goals and objectives; (e) emphasize the connection between special and general settings; (f) allot time for consultative work; and (g) facilitate scheduling of students from pull-out to inclusion settings.

2. Consultative services at the elementary and secondary level include indirect services (working with teachers) and direct services (working with students) in the inclusive setting.

3. Tips for scheduling in the elementary school include (a) identifying student needs, (b) attending to the amount of time that students should spend in general and special education, and (c) examining the schedules of classroom teachers.

4. Pull-out program scheduling at the elementary level requires attention to general education classroom schedules, the needs of students, grouping arrangements, and flexibility.

5. Secondary schools operate with fixed class periods that include review, teacher presentation, controlled practice, and independent practice.

6. For students who need more time to complete assignments, teach using all modalities; check frequently for understanding; use positive reinforcement; adapt instruction and modify materials; use cooperative learning, peer tutoring, role playing, student-led group activities, and hands-on activities; focus on understanding of content; teach study skills, strategies, and survival skills; and use peer pairing.

7. Housekeeping time is the time spent taking attendance, passing out papers, and writing on the board.

8. Transition time is the time spent changing from one activity or setting to another.

9. Allocated time refers to the amount of time assigned to various instructional activities, such as group work, independent work, completion of IEPs, and consultative services. Most of the teacher's

time should be allocated to direct instruction.

---

 **DISCUSSION QUESTIONS**

1. A parent of a student in a general education class questions how a student with disabilities who is included in that class can receive a grade of 'A.' How would you explain this to the parent?

2. Discuss when you would use the following instructional arrangements in your classroom: large group, small group, one-to-one, peer tutoring, and independent learning. Draw a sketch of your classroom to reflect the instructional groupings you would use.

3. Defend the statement, "Thoughtful and thorough planning is essential for effective teaching and learning to occur."

# CHAPTER 3

# INFORMAL ASSESSMENT

W e begin the chapter by discussing some of the changes in assessment brought on by the reauthorization of the Individuals with Disabilities Act Amendments. Assessment is an important component in the reauthorization of IDEA, both in the ruling that students with disabilities will be included in district and state assessments and in the encouragement of functional behavior assessment as a means to address problem behaviors of students with disabilities (see Chapter 1).

Then, we discuss the different types of informal assessments that teachers in their classroom or in a co-teaching situation can create and implement to ensure individual accountability. In the special education field, we use different types of informal assessment. Criterion-referenced tests, precision teaching, curriculum-based measurement, and error analysis all suggest systematic data collection procedures and have a history of use in special education. The informal assessments of portfolios, interviews, and checklists have less systematic data collection procedures. Portfolios are often identified as authentic assessments. Authentic assessments are based on the constructivist paradigm with its emphasis on "assessing real-life processes and accomplishments" (Heshusius, 1989, p. 412). The authentic assessment approach is fairly new to the special education field, and the effectiveness is still uncertain, even though it is being implemented in a growing number of large-scale assessment programs at district and state levels. For example, the states of Kentucky and Maryland use portfolios in alternative assessment procedures (Kleinert, Haig, Kearns, & Kennedy, 2000).

Teachers may use these data collection procedures to plan programs for students and to monitor their effectiveness. The informal measures may also be linked to state standards and used in both pull-out and inclusive settings. They may be used alone or in combination with other assessments. For example, interviews, checklists, and error analysis may be used with all the other informal measures discussed in the chapter. We conclude the chapter with ways to involve students in data collection procedures.

## ASSESSMENT COMPONENTS OF IDEA AMENDMENTS OF 1997

As we stated at the beginning of the chapter, students with disabilities must be included in state assessments, often with accommodations or alternate assessments if they cannot participate in state and districtwide assessment programs. The core academic subject areas of math, science, social studies, and language arts are typically being assessed in statewide assessment programs and many districts link the standards to graduation, funding, and pass-fail rates (e.g., high stakes testing) (McLaughlin, Nolet, Rhim, & Henderson, 1999; Wood, 2002). Interesting, IDEA 1997 does not mandate how the scores of students with disabilities will be used in district and state measures of accountability (Kleinert et al., 2000), only that results must be made available to the public with the same frequency and detail as those of students without disabilities (OSEP, 2002). In fact, much leeway is given to states in meeting the requirement to include students with disabilities in the assessment system.

Most of the students we discuss in this text will be involved in state assessments with accommodations. Some accommodations used with basic standards testing in reading and math include extending the time, allowing frequent breaks during testing, and administering the test in small groups or in separate settings (NCED, 1997). However, according to Wood (2002), accommodation strategies are most commonly decided by states and not teachers, so you must be aware of the accommodations allowed in your district.

Another emphasis in IDEA 1977 that affects assessment is the mandate that the "IEP Team shall in the case of a child whose behavior impedes his or her learning or that of others, consider, when appropriate, strategies, including positive behavioral interventions, strategies, and supports to address that behavior" (IDEA, 20 U.S.C. (section) 1414 (d)(3) (B) (i)). The ruling allows IEP teams to decide the behaviors that constitute the need for interventions and if the behaviors are impeding a student's learning (Drasgow & Yell, 2001). These problem behaviors may include verbal and physical abuse, noncompliance, disruptive behaviors, property destruction, and aggression (Drasgow, Yell, Bradley, & Shriner, 1999). To arrive at the appropriate interventions, a functional behavior assessment (FBA) is conducted.

Additionally, a behavior intervention plan (BIP) must be created by the IEP team for students who have been referred to alternative placements, suspended from school for more than 10 school days in a school year, and placed in an alternative setting for a weapon or drugs offense (Chandler, Dahlquist, Repp, & Feltz, 1999; Gartin, & Murdick, 2001). Because teachers will not be conducting FBAs or making decisions about interventions for problem behaviors alone, we just include a basic description of FBAs and their use with students with mild disabilities.

FBAs require the following:

▶ identification of problem behavior (e.g., Jim runs out of class)
▶ analysis of the frequency, duration, and intensity of the target behavior (e.g., event recording for 5 days finds that the behavior occurs on the average of three times from 9 A.M. to 12 A.M. a day)

▶ description and analysis of the antecedents and consequences of the behavior (e.g., when teacher introduces centers, student runs, and teacher chases after student)

▶ hypothesis of the purpose the behavior is serving (e.g., to get teacher attention)

▶ selection of positive supports or behavior intervention plans (BIPs) for the appropriate behavior that achieves the same function as the inappropriate one (e.g., before introducing centers, the teacher has Jim come to the front and model how to go to centers quietly; she then praises Jim for appropriate modeling)

▶ collection of data on the effectiveness of the intervention in changing behavior (e.g., event recording for 30 days and then intermittent event recording for 6 months). (Chandler et al., 1999; Gartin & Murdick, 2001; Drasgow & Yell, 2001)

Reid and Nelson (2002) reviewed 14 studies of FBA procedures used with students with learning disabilities and emotional/behavioral disorders in school settings. They report promising results of the FBAs to decrease inappropriate behaviors, but that more research needs to address the maintenance of appropriate behaviors over time. Some other findings include:

1. Problem behaviors were related to escape (task too difficult) or attention (peer or teacher) in a majority of the children.
2. There is insufficient data to assess the practicality of FBA in school settings because direct service providers such as teachers and other IEP members were not instrumental in conducting the FBAs in any of the studies.
3. Simple curriculum modifications such as student selection of academic activity, moderation of task difficulty, student participation in preferred activity or task, and the addition of prompts resulted in improvements of behavior.

 **ACTIVITY 3.1**

Interview a special education teacher to find out the FBA procedures of a school district or county near your home.
(Answers for this and other activities are found in the Instructor's Manual.)

## PORTFOLIO ASSESSMENT

Portfolios are "purposeful, collaborative, and self-reflective collections of student work" generated during the instructional process (McRobbie, 1992, p. 2). Many states, such as California, Kentucky, Maryland, Michigan, Pennsylvania, and Vermont, incorporate portfolios into their general education assessment procedures (Kerka, 1995; McRobbie, 1992; Wolf, 1989). Moreover, software programs such as the Superschool Portfolio Assessment Kit II (2002, for Windows and Macintosh, http.//www.superschoolsoftware.com), and the Grady Profile (1995, for Macintosh only, http://www.aurbach.com) are now available to help teachers and students organize and monitor portfolios.

Portfolios have both advantages and disadvantages (Bietau, 1995; Carpenter, Ray, & Bloom, 1995; Kerka, 1995; Rivera, 1995; Schutt & McCabe, 1994; Wesson & King, 1996). Advantages include (a) a variety of ways to measure progress and to demonstrate what learners can or cannot do, (b) the incorporation of student ownership and self-reflection, (c) the measurement of both process and product, (d) the linkage to real-life situations, and (e) the emphasis on students' strengths. Disadvantages include (a) the amount of time required, (b) the lack of reliable scoring procedures, (c) the lack of empirical evidence of effectiveness, (d) cost efficacy, and (e) subjective assessment.

An examination of literature in the special education field shows that portfolio assessment is receiving more attention as an alternative assessment for students with disabilities (Cohen & Spencimer, 1998; Howell, Fox, & Morehead, 1993; Elliott, 1998; Rueda & Garcia, 1997; Wesson & King, 1996). Currently, portfolio assessment does not have much of an empirical basis for use with students with disabilities. Salend (2000) recommends the use of portfolios in inclusive classrooms for all students as portfolios may easily be tied to the annual goals and standards of the general education curriculum.

Although there are no typical portfolios, common characteristics include (a) a range of work over time, (b) teacher-assigned work (teachers often determine the number and type of pieces), (c) student-selected work, (d) a student introduction of why a particular piece of work was selected, and (e) a student summary of what was learned from the selection and reflections on compiling the portfolio (McRobbie, 1992; Wolf, 1989). We recommend the following steps in creating a student portfolio: (a) plan the focus (Valencia, 1990), (b) select the content (Valencia, 1990), (c) select the times for adding materials (Jongsma, 1989), (d) design scoring procedures (Popham, 1997; Goodrich, 1996–97), (e) teach students to self-assess and reflect, and (f) arrange periodic conferences (Miller, 1995).

## Plan the Focus

To prevent the portfolio from becoming a hodge-podge of papers, Valencia (1990) suggests that the teacher focus on the key goals of instruction. McRobbie (1992) recommends general goals and specific subject-area goals. For example, a general goal is for students to reflect on their work, whereas a specific subject-area goal in language arts is for students to show progress in summarizing a story theme. Cohen and Spencimer (1998) recommend a focus on academic progress and students' self-understanding for middle school students and a focus on career planning and graduation requirements for secondary students. Wesson and King (1996) suggest

that affective behaviors are also appropriate for the portfolio focus. We recommend the selection of goals and short-term objectives based on students' IEPs.

## Select the Content

Portfolios may contain, among other items, samples of students' work in all content areas (Flood & Lapp, 1989; Valencia, 1990), notes on social studies or science fair projects (Paulson, Paulson, & Meyer, 1991), students' periodic self-evaluations (Flood & Lapp, 1989; Valencia, 1990), student- and teacher-generated progress notes (Valencia, 1990), pictures or videotapes of a student's project (Wesson & King, 1996), a student-generated list of books and genres read each month (Flood & Lapp, 1989), and community service projects (Cohen & Spencimer, 1998). Wesson and King (1996) report that videotapes, instructor observations, self-observations, and home progress reports serve as content for a behavior portfolio. The key is selecting a variety of materials to depict a student's progress (Jongsma, 1989). You may wish to include originals, copies, or summaries of the materials. For example, the student-generated monthly lists of books could be summarized into one list. McRobbie (1992) also suggests that students organize the portfolio with a table of contents, a letter of introduction that explains its organization, dates on all examples, a short explanation of the selection of each piece of work, and references.

## Select Times for Adding Materials

Wolf (1989) schedules monthly student checks for his eighth-grade students. At this time, the students remove some papers and keep those that best exemplify their progress. Schutt and McCabe (1994) suggest that students with learning disabilities keep two portfolios: a short-term one for works in progress and a long-term one for final products.

## Design Scoring Procedures

Rubrics are scoring guides that are frequently used in portfolio and other authentic assessments. They have three features, which are referred to with different terms depending on the source: (a) criteria, evaluative criteria, or standards; (b) levels of quality or performance; and (c) quality definitions or indicators (Anderson & Reilly, 1995; Kerka, 1995; Marzano, Pickering, & McTighe, 1993; Popham, 1997). For our discussion, we will refer to these three features as criteria, levels, and indicators. Criteria describes the major components that need to be present. For example, criteria for a language arts portfolio may include neatness, mechanics, clarity, organization, and vocabulary. Popham (1997) recommends using only three to five criteria.

Levels identify the degree to which the performance meets the criteria, for example, highly acceptable, acceptable, or not acceptable. Goodrich (1996–97) suggests that teachers use such terms as "Yes, Yes but, No but, No" to assist students in the understanding of levels. Indicators identify the specific requirements for each level and criteria. For example, an indicator for the criteria of mechanics and the level of highly acceptable may be that the student has written a paper with no spelling errors, total subject and verb agreement, no grammar errors, and complex sentence structures.

Analytic and holistic scoring strategies are another feature of a rubric. An analytic scoring rubric is often used for diagnostic purposes, is specific, is frequently in matrix form, and designates a score for each criterion (Marzano et al., 1993). A holistic rubric promotes an overall impression of a student's performance, is broad and general, is frequently in hierarchical form, and designates one score for the product (Marzano et al., 1997). You may use either or both scoring strategies.

Rubrics make teacher expectations clear, show students how to reach the expectations, and assist students to evaluate quality (Goodrich, 1996–97).

Table 3.1 presents a partial scoring rubric with the various features identified. Using the sample holistic math rubric, Jimmy may score a 4 or Competent on his entire math portfolio. Using the sample analytic math rubric, Jimmy may score a 3 or Highly Acceptable in problem solving and a 2 or Acceptable in communication. Check the Web site www.teach-nology.com for rubrics designed for reading skills, paragraph writing, behaviors, and oral expression.

## Teach Students to Self-Assess and Reflect

Often, students are directed to self-assess and reflect in portfolios. Students with disabilities have problems with this type of metacognitive task (see Chapter 6). To assist a student in self-reflection, you may either use the rubric or you may identify questions for the students to answer and then model your answer to these questions. For example, Mr. Jordan identifies three questions: (1) What is characteristic about this new piece of work I am including in my portfolio? (2) What has changed between my old work and my new work? (3) What remains to be done? He then presents two pieces of his own work and models out loud his answer to the questions before he asks the students to do the same with their works.

## Arrange Periodic Conferences

Regular sessions for portfolio discussions between teachers and students should be scheduled throughout the year (Farr, 1989; Valencia, 1990). Wesson and King (1996) suggest monthly reviews and a check of one portfolio a week. During a conference, you should discuss a student's progress (Valencia, 1990), plans for inclusion of other pieces for the portfolio (Valencia, 1990), and the student's thoughts about the portfolio. Ask such questions as, "What is your favorite thing?" "Why did you organize the portfolio the way you did?" (Farr, 1989). Asking these types of questions assists students in self-reflection.

**Table 3.1** Partially Completed Sample Rubric for Math Portfolio

### SAMPLE HOLISTIC MATH RUBRIC

<u>Superior Performance (6)</u>

**Task accomplished** in an exceptional manner, superior **problem-solving** skills, apparent knowledge of **underlying concepts** throughout the task, rigorously employed and innovative **appropriate strategies**, logical and thorough **reasoning**, accurate **computations**, **directions** followed, and responses **communicated** clearly and effectively.

<u>Proficient Performance (5)</u>

**Task accomplished** in a proficient manner, effective **problem-solving** skills, apparent knowledge of **underlying concepts**, employed **appropriate strategies**, logical **reasoning**, accurate **computations**, **directions** followed, and responses **communicated** effectively.

<u>Competent Performance (4)</u>

**Task accomplished** in a competent manner, satisfactory **problem-solving** skills, frequent apparent knowledge of **underlying concepts**, frequently employed **appropriate strategies**, mostly accurate **computations**, **directions** followed, and responses **communicated** reasonably well.

### SAMPLE ANALYTIC MATH RUBRIC

|  | <u>Highly Acceptable (3)</u> | <u>Acceptable (2)</u> | <u>Not Acceptable (1)</u> |
|---|---|---|---|
| ***Problem Solving*** | Superior reasoning in problem solving; Answers justified; Valid conclusions drawn; Reasonable predictions made | Satisfactory reasoning in problem solving; Most answers justified; Conclusions usually valid; Usually reasonable predictions | Very limited reasoning in problem solving; Answers often not justified; Many conclusions invalid; Predictions generally unreasonable |
| ***Communication*** | Clear and consistent language, including terminology and symbolism to communicate the problem-solving approach | Generally appropriate language, including terminology to communicate the problem-solving approach in a satisfactory way | Limited language, including terminology to communicate the problem-solving approach in a marginal way |

<u>underline</u> = levels

**bold** = criteria

regular print = sample indicators

Adapted from http://www.ebe.on.ca?DEPART/RESEAR/RUBRIC.HTM, January 1998

## ✦ INTERVIEWS

Another type of informal assessment includes interviews in which students are asked to share their thought processes. It is important to establish rapport and provide a safe, secure environment, where students can risk being wrong without penalty. An interview may proceed in the following manner. First, you instruct the student, "Kari, please complete these problems (e.g., 85 + 19, 67 + 18, 34 + 17) out loud so I can hear how you figure them out." As Kari is calculating the problems, she replies, "Well, 85 plus 19 means to add. Five plus 9 is 14, and 8 plus 1 is 9. So the answer is 9-1-4 [nine, one, four]." She proceeds with similar explanations and mistakes in the other two problems.

In analyzing Kari's thought processes and her answers, you find that she knows that *plus* means to add and she knows the addition facts. She also knows to begin in the ones column, but she does not know place value and the regrouping process, nor does she monitor her computation by checking to see whether the answer of 914 makes sense.

Sometimes, interviews are accompanied by recommended questions for the teacher to ask the student, as in the following spelling interview (Baskwill & Whitman, 1988). To measure spelling using this procedure, select a list of 20 words from either the spelling or reading text that the student is using in the inclusive setting. To introduce the task in a nonthreatening manner, tell the student that you are really looking for a better way to teach spelling and that it doesn't matter how many mistakes the student makes. Next, give the words in isolation. Then give the same words in context. Add definitions if the student requests them.

Sit down with the student and go over the list together, asking such questions of the student as, "Which words do you think you spelled correctly?" "Which ones aren't you sure about?" "Why did you decide on this particular spelling?" "How else could you have tried to spell this word?" "If this word is incorrect, how could you find the correct spelling?" (Baskwill & Whitman, 1988). Remember that with the interviewing technique, assess both error patterns and strategies.

## ⅄CHECKLISTS

The use of checklists may provide insight into the ways in which students approach tasks and the types of errors they make. You may also use checklists to gain information concerning any subject area, to find out about interests, or to monitor a student's progress in an inclusive setting. Checklist items are frequently phrased

positively to assess what a student can do instead of emphasizing the problems. You may complete checklists using work samples (see Figure 3.1) or during observations. You may use the checklist found in Figure 3.2 to evaluate written expression as this teacher did in evaluating the work sample in Figure 3.1.

Students may also use self-assessment checklists to monitor their work. For example, you may have students answer whether they identified the relevant information, selected the correct steps, calculated the problems correctly, and verified their results as they solved word problems.

A way to use checklists as communication devices for inclusive settings is to ask the general education teacher to monitor specific behaviors during the class and to have the students return the checklist to you. Behavior and academic achievement items are often included on checklists. Some checklists even have a place for the students or teachers to write in homework assignments (see Figure 3.3). Many special education teachers include the return of checklists among their classroom rules and provide consequences for return and nonreturn of checklists.

 **ACTIVITY 3.2**

Design a checklist for students to use to help them reflect on the content of their portfolios.

 **IMPORTANT POINTS** ◀

1. With the reauthorization of IDEA (1997), students with disabilities must be included in state assessments, often with accommodations, or be given alternate assessments if they cannot participate in state and districtwide assessment programs.

2. FBAs require (a) identification of problem behavior; (b) analysis of the frequency,

**Figure 3.1** A Student's Work Sample

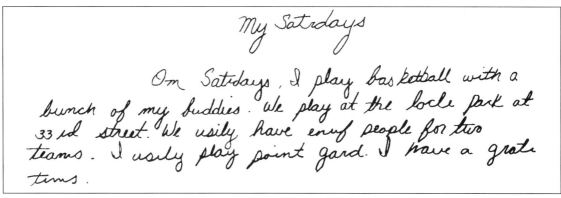

duration, and intensity of the target behavior; (c) description and analysis of the antecedents and consequences of the behavior; (d) hypothesis as to the purpose the behavior is serving; (e) selection of positive supports or behavior intervention plans (BIPs) for the appropriate behavior that achieves the same function as the inappropriate one; and (f) collection of data on the effectiveness of the intervention in changing behavior (Chandler et al., 1999; Gartin & Murdick, 2001; Drasgow & Yell, 2001).

3. Simple curriculum modifications on BIPs such as student selection of academic activity, moderation of task difficulty, student participation in preferred activity or task, and the addition of prompts resulted in improvements of behavior (Reid & Nelson, 2002).

4. Portfolio assessment is the collection of samples of the physical ongoing evidence of a student's progress.

5. Teachers must make decisions concerning the focus, the content, the scoring, the teaching of students to self-assess and

**Figure 3.2** Scoring of the Student's Work Sample in Figure 3.1

1. Is the student able to write a topic sentence?
   Yes.
2. Is the student able to write supporting sentences?
   Yes, rest of sentences relate to topic.
3. Does the student use descriptive words?
   No, limited adjectives—"point, great."
4. Is the student able to use a variety of sentences (simple, compound, complex)? No, all simple.
5. Does the student use dialogue? None used.
6. Are there many mistakes in grammar? None.
7. Is the story organized?
   Yes, it begins with a topic sentence and has details and a closing.
8. Are there many spelling errors?
   Yes, 10 out of 40 words.

**Figure 3.3** Teacher Monitoring Checklist

| | First | | Second | | Third | | Fourth | | Fifth | | Sixth | |
|---|---|---|---|---|---|---|---|---|---|---|---|---|
| **Periods** | **Y** | **N** | **Y** | **N** | **Y** | **N** | **Y** | **N** | **Y** | **N** | **Y** | **N** |
| Came on time | ✓ | | | ✓ | ✓ | | ✓ | | | | | |
| Brought supplies | ✓ | | | ✓ | ✓ | | ✓ | | | | | |
| Followed directions | ✓ | | ✓ | | ✓ | | ✓ | | | | | |
| Completed work | ✓ | | ✓ | | ✓ | | ✓ | | | | | |
| Grade on assignment | B | | C *(late work)* | | C | | B | | | | | |
| Teacher initials | gEO | | JMP | | RC | | BO | | | | | |
| Homework assigned | None | | Page 91, 1–22 | | Page 102, 12–45 | | None | | | | | |

reflect, the times for adding materials, and the arranging of periodic conferences.

6. Rubrics are scoring guides that include the three features of criteria (e.g., mechanics), levels (e.g., highly acceptable), and indicators (e.g., no spelling errors).
7. In interview assessment, students are often asked to share their thought processes.
8. Teachers may use checklists to gain information concerning subject areas, to identify students' strengths and interests, and to monitor behaviors in inclusive settings.

## ▲ ERROR ANALYSIS

The analysis of students' errors helps you to focus instruction. For example, if you find that Paul correctly calculates all facts except those involving the basic addition facts of 9 (i.e., 9 + 1 through 9 + 9), you know you must teach just these addition facts. Errors also provide insights into how students think and reason (Heshusius, 1989). Error analysis may be combined with all informal assessments.

Before using error analysis, you should consider language differences. Many experts argue

that language differences, especially those dealing with phonemes, or sounds, should be of concern only if they impair meaning (Ortiz & Polyzoi, 1989; Saville-Troike, 1976). For example, if a Hispanic student reads *easy* as "iysi" or an African American student reads *they* as "dey," but each understands the content of the message, you should note these substitutions as language differences and not reading errors. Remember, varieties of English are equally effective and valid forms of communication (Grossman, 1994). Some common language differences found in Black English include omission of the *s* suffix (e.g., "The girl play" or "I have two penny"), the use of *be* as a main verb (e.g., "He be busy"), and the deletion of contracted forms of *is* and *are* (e.g., "He here" or "They here") (Gollnick & Chinn, 1990; Washington & Miller-Jones, 1989). Spanish speakers often omit the *s* suffix, (e.g., "four bell" for "four bells"), trill the *r* when two *r*'s are together (e.g., "sorrrel for sorrel"), and pronounce the following sounds the same: *sh* and *ch, s* and *z, n* and *ng, b* and *v, d* and *th, y* and *j, t* and unvoiced *th,* unvoiced *th* and *s.* Native Americans rarely use final consonants; omit articles *a, an,* and *the;* and have difficulty with prepositions (e.g., "get on car" for "get in the car") (Gollnick & Chinn, 1990; Walker, 1987). Many Asian Americans have difficulty pronouncing *sh, ch, r, x, l,* and *j* (Chan, 1987; Chinn & Plata, 1987).

## Reading

In the *Qualitative Reading Inventory,* Leslie and Caldwell (1990) discuss the following decoding errors: (a) omissions (the student omits words when reading), (b) substitutions (the student substitutes a similar word that often makes sense in the sentence), (c) insertions (the student adds words), and (d) reversals (the student reverses letters or phrases). Leslie and Caldwell do not count repetitions (repeating a word or phrase when reading), hesitations (pausing longer at some words when reading), or omissions of punctuation (e.g., not pausing at the end of a sentence) as errors because scoring is unreliable for such factors, and repetitions and hesitations do not alter the text's meaning. In another common error, called an aided word, the teacher supplies the word for the students (Mercer & Mercer, 2001).

Reading comprehension errors frequently include mistakes in text-explicit, text-implicit, and script-implicit comprehension (Pearson & Johnson, 1978). Table 3.2 contains examples

that measure each of these areas of comprehension. Text-explicit comprehension, also termed *literal comprehension,* requires the reader to recall information specifically found in a selection. When you ask students to identify the main characters, or actions of the main characters, or to sequence events, or recall significant details, you are checking text-explicit comprehension. Question 1 in Table 3.2 is an example, because students should find the answer directly in the first sentence of the paragraph.

Text-implicit comprehension, also referred to as *inferential comprehension* (Tindal & Marston, 1990), requires the reader to interact with information that is implied and not found directly from any one source in the passage. Forming opinions, predicting the next event in a story, and identifying the influence of the setting on the actions of the main character in a story are examples of text-implicit comprehension. Question 2 in Table 3.2 checks this type of comprehension, because the reader must assimilate the information from more than one sentence.

In script-implicit comprehension questions, the reader must use the information from the text and provide additional personal information (Tindal & Marston, 1990). Undoubtedly, a person who is not familiar with the sport of basketball will not answer Question 3 correctly.

---

**Table 3.2**   Sample Comprehension Errors

---

A student reads the following paragraph:

> There were 25 seconds left in the championship basketball game. The winner of the game would be high school state champion. The score was tied 98 to 98, but no one could believe that the Tigers were in contention. After all, the tallest player of the team was only 6'5", the height of the shortest player of the opposition team, the Braves. But the Tigers had been deadly on the 3-point plays and had not missed a free throw.

After reading the paragraph, the student responded to the following sample questions:

1. How much time was left in the game? *Answer:* Twenty-five minutes. (text-explicit error)
2. What was the main idea of the paragraph? *Answer:* There was only a little time left in the game. (text-implicit error)
3. Why is height such an advantage when playing basketball? *Answer:* I don't know. (script-implicit error)

---

This type of comprehension question is generally difficult for students who lack the necessary background experiences.

## Spelling

Common spelling errors include omission of silent letters (e.g., *clim* for *climb*) and sounded letters (e.g., *cimb* for *climb*), phonetic substitutions (e.g., *clime* for *climb*), letter reversals (e.g., *cilmb* for *climb*), addition of letters (e.g., *climbe* for *climb*), words with apostrophes (e.g., possessives and contractions), and rule overgeneralizations (e.g., add an *s* for plurals such as *deers* for *deer*) (Evans, Evans, & Mercer, 1986; Salvia & Hughes, 1990). Spelling is often a problem area for many students with disabilities.

## Math

Roberts (1968) identified the following math error categories: (a) wrong operation (the student selects one operation, such as subtraction, when another operation, such as addition, should have been selected), (b) obvious computational error (the student incorrectly recalls a basic number fact $7 + 8 = 16$, instead of 15), (c) defective algorithm (the student employs the correct operation and knows the basic number facts but does not use the correct process or procedure, such as $112 - 46 = 76$, in which the student forgot to regroup in the tens place), and (d) random response (the student answers incorrectly without any apparent relationship between problem solving and the problem). Enright (1983) adds placement errors, which occur when students do not align parts of problems correctly, such as alignment of decimals. Cohen and Spencimer (1998) summarized the following word problem errors: difficulty in reading and understanding language and vocabulary, identifying relevant and irrelevant information, using all the steps for solving a problem, and performing the correct mathematical operations.

## Procedures

We recommend the following steps for analyzing errors:

1. After scoring the items, list the student errors (e.g., on the addition fact worksheet, Jan is missing $9 + 8$, $7 + 8$, $6 + 8$).
2. Make a hypothesis as to the error pattern (e.g., computational error, basic addition facts, especially the 8 facts).
3. Test the hypothesis by examining the correct problems to see if any have the same pattern (e.g., Jan calculated $6 + 4$, $5 + 6$, and $9 + 2$ correctly, so none of the correct ones involved the basic addition facts of 8).
4. If not correct, redo the hypothesis (e.g., steps 1–3 again).
5. Teach correction of the error (e.g., Jan needs to be retaught the basic addition facts of 8).

Sometimes, asking the student to think out loud helps in error analysis.

▼ ACTIVITY 3.3

Identify the following error patterns.
C = correct; X = incorrect (The student's incorrect responses are in parentheses.)

**Reading Words**

| | | |
|---|---|---|
| 1. for X (far) | 3. of X (off) | 5. fir C |
| 2. was X (w) | 4. man C | 6. top C |

**Math Problems**

| 1. | 2. | 3. | 4. |
|---|---|---|---|
| 36 | 29 | 47 | 55 |
| +19 | +68 | +16 | +79 |
| 55 C | 97 C | 63 C | (34) X |

| 5. | 6. | 7. |
|---|---|---|
| 26 | 45 | 26 |
| +87 | +65 | +13 |
| (13) X | (20) X | 39 C |

**Spelling Words**

| | | |
|---|---|---|
| 1. might X (mit) | 2. rain C | 3. run C |
| 4. flop C | 5. mine X (min) | 6. sky X (ski) |

## CRITERION-REFERENCED TESTS

Criterion-referenced tests (CRTs) measure the extent to which a student has mastered a skill or task based on an established criterion (Mercer, 1992). Unlike formal tests, which compare a student's performance to that of other students, a criterion-referenced test compares the student's performance to some expected mastery level. A commonly used CRT measure in special education is the *Brigance* diagnostic inventories (Brigance, 1981, 1983, 1999). The *Brigance* diagnostic inventories are multiskill batteries that contain subtests measuring skills in areas such as reading, math, employability, life skills, and spelling.

Commercial CRTs focus on hierarchies of skills found in the general education curriculum and are not specific to a school district's curriculum. For example, Brigance (1983) states that his test items are the direct result of checking the scope and sequence of the most recently published texts of several widely used series. The scope identifies the breadth of the subject matter, and the sequence identifies the sequential arrangement of the subject matter.

For example, the scope of the math curriculum for kindergarten through eighth grade, no matter the particular math series, usually includes math readiness (e.g., recognizing numerals), number facts (e.g., reciting basic facts, such as $4 \times 6$), whole numbers (e.g., adding two-digit numbers with regrouping), fractions and mixed numbers (e.g., adding fractions), decimals (e.g., reading decimals), percents (e.g., converting percents to decimals), measurement (e.g., telling time to the hour, recognizing different coins), metrics (e.g., reading Celsius temperature), and geometry (e.g., recognizing squares) (Brigance, 1981, 1983, 1999). In the sequence, math readiness skills such as rote counting are taught before basic facts, which are taught before fractions.

### Steps

We recommend the following steps: (1) select the test, (2) administer the test, (3) select the expected level of mastery, (4) identify objectives, and (5) monitor progress in CRT assessment. We discuss these steps as related to commercially produced CRTs. (For discussion of the creation of CRTs by teachers, see Jones, 2001a, 2001b.)

### Select the Test

A basic knowledge of the curriculum scope and sequence for various grade levels can help you in test selection. For example, if you are selecting reading tests to assess a first grader's reading performance, you are not likely to select a reading test that measures comprehension of colloquial and figurative expressions, because this skill is usually introduced much later. Instead, tests that measure basic sight vocabulary, initial consonant sounds, and short vowels are more appropriate, because these skills are introduced in the primary-grade reading curriculum. Most series have a scope and sequence that you can check for the various grade levels. Additionally, many school districts identify standards that students are expected to achieve at various grade levels. You may wish to select a subtest that is aligned with the particular curriculum standard.

Discussing a student's problem with the general education teacher is also helpful. For example, if Mr. Gonzalez, Jim's second-grade teacher, tells you that Jim has problems telling time, you should, as a first step, select a criterion-referenced test that measures math skills, especially one that contains items dealing with measurement of time.

 **ACTIVITY 3.4**

Susan is a sixth grader. Ms. Jones and you have decided to test her math skills because she is failing in the basic math class. Ms. Jones reports that Susan seems to miss problems dealing with the calculation of fractions. Examine the scope and sequence of a sixth-grade math text and identify some skills that you might select for testing or examine the curriculum standards identified by the district or state.

### Administer the Test

Many of the commercially prepared instruments provide guidelines for where to start and stop testing and general directions and procedures for easy and quick administration. Additionally, you may make adaptations during the testing process. For example, if you wish to hear Latasha's thoughts as she solves the math problems, you may ask her to think aloud as she writes the answers.

### Select the Expected Level of Mastery

There are no absolutes for selection of a mastery criterion. For profitable academic learning, students should maintain an accuracy level of 80% during lesson presentation and between 90% and 100% during independent practice (Christenson, Thurlow, & Ysseldyke, 1987). Some CRTs suggest mastery levels.

### Identify the Objectives

Mastery levels assist in the identification of objectives. For example, if you expected Sharon to score 80% on a reading comprehension test but she scored only 60%, you should target reading comprehension for remediation. Furthermore, you should examine the specific questions that Sharon missed. Did she miss questions that required her to order and sequence events, or did she miss questions that required her to remember significant details?

### Monitor Progress

Usually, teachers monitor mastery of the objectives at the end of the year using the same CRT. The results of this posttest are often recorded on the IEP.

## Sample Plan

We have presented the steps for using a CRT, but to help you better understand the process, we relate Consuela's experience to each of the steps.

1. *Discuss the student's problem with the general education teacher.* In a conference, Consuela's fifth-grade teacher indicates that Consuela has problems reading words with silent letters and two or more syllables.

2. *Check the curriculum scope and sequence of the subject area and grade level.* A check of the reading scope and sequence from Consuela's classroom text shows that silent letters, prefixes, suffixes, and syllabication are word analysis skills that students should master by fifth grade. Additionally, the school district identifies these skills in the performance standards for the state assessment exam.

3. *Select a CRT.* Consuela's teacher selected the *BRIGANCE Comprehensive Inventory of Basic Skills—Revised* (CIBS-R) (Brigance, 1999) because it measures all of the skills found in the classroom text.

4. *Administer the CRT.* The teacher administered the following tests from the *Brigance:* (a) phonetic irregularities to check silent letters, (b) suffixes, (c) prefixes, and (d) division of words into syllables.

5. *Decide on a criterion of mastery.* The teacher selected 95%.

6. *Compare the student's performance to the mastery level.* Consuela reached the established criterion on phonetic irregularities (silent vowels) only. She did not reach mastery on the tests dealing with reading suffixes and prefixes, nor was she able to apply the rules for syllabication.

7. *Identify short-term objectives for initial instruction.* (a) Presented with a list of 50 words, Consuela will read words containing the suffixes *-ous, -ment, -ation, -ward,* and *-ist* and the prefixes *de-, mis-,* and *fore-* with 90% accuracy and (b) presented with a list of two-syllable words, Consuela will apply the syllabication rules dealing with like consonants between two vowels (*bot\tom*) and unlike consonants between two vowels

(*con\form*) to divide the words with 90% accuracy.

8. *Monitor progress.* The teacher plans to test Consuela at the end of the year, unless the teacher feels that Consuela has reached the short-term objective before then.

 **ACTIVITY 3.5**

---

Write a short-term objective in reading based on the following performance on a test of phonograms. The criterion for acceptable performance is 90%. Correct = +. Error = −.

The teacher asks the student to read the common phonograms:

| | | |
|---|---|---|
| 1. ail + | 2. ble − | 3. ing + |
| 4. tion − | 5. ell + | 6. ter − |
| 7. ick+ | 8. et + | 9. ide − |
| 10. est− | | |

---

 **IMPORTANT POINTS**

1. Language differences should be considered as errors only if they impair meaning.

2. In reading, decoding errors include omissions, substitutions, insertions, reversals, and nonresponses, whereas comprehension errors include problems with text-explicit, text-implicit, and script-implicit comprehension.

3. Common spelling errors include omission of silent letters and sounded letters, phonetic substitutions, letter reversals, addition of letters, words with apostrophes, and rule overgeneralizations.

4. Math errors include wrong operation, obvious computational error, defective algorithm, random response, and word problems.

5. The following steps are recommended for analyzing errors: (a) list the student errors;

(b) make a hypothesis as to the error pattern; (c) test the hypothesis by examining the incorrect problems to see if any of these have the same pattern; (d) if not correct, redo the hypothesis; and (e) teach correction of the error.

6. The items on a CRT are often based on curriculum scope (the skills or content taught at various grade levels) and sequence (the order in which the skills are taught) from many texts.

7. In selecting a CRT, special education teachers often consult the general education teacher, a curriculum scope and sequence, and district and state standards.

8. The student's performance is compared to the criterion for acceptable performance (mastery) to arrive at a short-term objective.

9. The same test is administered before and after instruction (pre and post) to monitor student progress.

## PRECISION TEACHING

Precision teaching is a precise and systematic way to measure student performance in academic skills at both the elementary and secondary levels. Although precision teaching is not a specific teaching strategy, it helps you decide on and evaluate the effectiveness of instructional strategies. Precision teaching has demonstrated effectiveness in both inclusive and resource room settings (Lovitt, Rudsit, Jenkins, Pious, & Benedetti, 1985; Stump, Lovitt, Fister, Kemp, Moore, & Schroeder, 1992). Keel, Dangel, and Owens (1999) recommend it as one of the effective strategies to use for students with mild disabilities in inclusive classrooms.

Using rate of response, precision teaching emphasizes direct and continuous measurement of behavior (West, Young, & Spooner, 1990). Rate is the number of behavior movements divided by the number of minutes observed. In precision teaching, the average number of correct and incorrect responses per minute is calculated. The underlying principle is that a skill is mastered only if it can be performed both accurately and quickly. A student who is able to take notes at 30 words a minute will be more successful in an inclusive setting than one who is just as accurate in writing words but can transcribe only 10 words a minute.

A time limit of 1 minute is specified for measuring most academic skills, although the time limit may vary according to the amount of curriculum measured and student characteristics. For example, 3 minutes may be used when addition, subtraction, multiplication, and division facts are measured at once, compared with 1 minute when measuring addition facts alone. Fifteen seconds may be used for students who are highly distractible and cannot focus on a task for 1 minute (Binder, Haughton, & Eyk, 1990).

▼ **ACTIVITY 3.6**

Try an experiment. Time yourself for 15 seconds and, with your usual writing hand, write the numbers 1 through 9 as fast as you can, starting with 1 again when you reach 9. How did you do? Can the numbers be read? Count how many numbers you wrote by counting each digit. You probably found this skill to be both accurate and fluent. Now, reverse hands and do the same task for 15 seconds. How are your numbers this time? They can probably be read, but how many digits did you write in the 15 seconds? Unless you are ambidextrous, you probably wrote more digits the first time. If a professor told you that you could take notes with your nonwriting hand only, your accuracy would be somewhat affected, but your fluency would be more affected, and you would miss many notes.

## Steps

The steps to precision teaching lead to planning and monitoring decisions and include: (a) pinpoint the behavior to be taught, (b) design or select a probe, (c) take a baseline, (d) select an aim, (e) decide whether the skill is appropriate, (f) write an objective, (g) decide on an intervention, (h) teach and test, (i) graph scores, and (j) monitor progress. A discussion of each step follows.

### Pinpoint the Behavior

Pinpointing is choosing a behavior to change. In precision teaching, each behavior is counted, so the behavior must be repeatable and observable, and it must have a beginning and end (White & Haring, 1980). The skill of reading initial consonant clusters is appropriate to pinpoint. This skill is repeatable, as words requiring initial consonant clusters may be read again and again. It is observable, as you may listen while the student reads. Finally, each initial consonant cluster has a beginning and an end. Other appropriate pinpointed behaviors are spelling words, writing letters, and saying letter sounds.

"Betty is intelligent" is not an appropriate behavior for pinpointing, as it does not meet the three requirements. How is intelligence repeated? How do you observe intelligence? Where does it begin and end?

### Design a Probe

Once the skill is pinpointed, you can either design an informal test, called a probe, or use commercial probes. Commercial probes may be secured from the following sources:

▶ Clearinghouse/Information Center, Bureau of Instructional Support and Community Services, Florida Board of Education, 325 West Gaines St., Room 628, Tallahassee, FL 32399-0400. http://myfloridaeducation.com

▶ Beck, R., Conrad, D., & Anderson, D. (1995). *Basic Skill Builders Handbook.* Longmont, CO: Sopris West.

If you plan to design your own probe, you should first allow a standardized count in order to assess the skill accurately. To ensure a standardized count, the student must have freedom and opportunity to move (White & Haring, 1980). To allow the student freedom to move, design the probe so that you do not place physical constraints on the student. For example, if you use flash cards to test basic sight words, you are probably interfering with how fast the student can read the words, because the student's performance depends, in part, on how quickly you manipulate the cards. Thus, changes in performance during assessment may be due to your dexterity in presenting the flash cards. You are less likely to interfere with a student's freedom to move if you use a typed list instead of flash cards.

Opportunity to move requires that students never run out of problems to complete. (Remember, a 1-minute time limit is usually imposed.) White and Haring (1990) argue that an overabundance of items allows for a more accurate picture of the student's performance, because it avoids ceiling effects. For example, if there were 12 problems on the probe on Monday and Sam answered all 12 correctly and then there were 20 problems on the probe on Tuesday and Sam answered all 20 correctly, you might conclude that Sam made

progress when comparing his raw scores of 12 and 20. However, in reality, Sam's performance on Monday was limited by the number of opportunities he had to show his knowledge. In addition, inclusion of more items than a student can possibly finish within the particular time prevents rote memorization of the answers (Howell & Morehead, 1987).

Having more items on a probe than students can possibly finish does not mean including 140 different words or math facts. Ten words or 10 facts may be repeated 14 times to reach 140, or 2 words or facts may be repeated 70 times. See Table 3.3 for an example of a sight word probe. Notice that even though there are 80 total words on the sample probe, there are only 20 different words, repeated 4 times. Thus, a student is actually being assessed on 20 words, not 80.

Once you have decided the content of the probe, you should identify the input and output channels for measurement (Hefferan & Diviaio, 1989). Input channels are the ways in which a student receives the information. In a school setting, input channels are usually visual or auditory. The student either sees the information when reading a text or hears the information when listening to the teacher read the text. Output channels are the ways in which a student expresses information. In a school setting, this is often done with an oral or written response; for example, the student either says the answer to a math question or writes the answer.

**Table 3.3**   Sight Word Probe

| about | after | be | five | its | must | seven | there | well | sleep | (10) |
|-------|-------|-----|------|-----|------|-------|-------|------|-------|------|
| call | from | him | let | old | upon | ask | cold | why | around | (20) |
| after | five | must | there | sleep | from | let | around | upon | cold | (30) |
| about | be | its | seven | well | call | him | old | ask | why | (40) |
| around | why | cold | ask | upon | old | let | him | from | call | (50) |
| sleep | well | there | seven | must | its | five | be | after | about | (60) |
| about | call | after | from | be | him | old | its | let | five | (70) |
| upon | must | ask | there | cold | well | why | around | sleep | must | (80) |

The input and output measures may vary for any task; for example, you may test a student's addition skills by presenting a worksheet of addition problems. This is a visual (*see*) input as the student looks at the problems on the worksheet. However, you can change this input to an auditory (*hear*) input simply by reading the problems from the worksheet instead of giving the paper to the student. In the same way, the output measure can be either a *say* response, if the student responds by orally telling you the answer, or a *write* response, if the student responds by writing the answer.

When designing a probe, you should select the channels that are used most often to perform the skill in the classroom. For instance, in inclusive elementary classrooms, reading instruction usually involves students taking turns reading selections orally, so the channels of see and say are appropriate for measuring reading skills at this level. However, the channels of see and write are probably more appropriate at the secondary level, where reading in the content areas often consists of students reading silently and then answering questions. In both elementary and secondary classes, math instruction typically involves paper-and-pencil performance, so see and write are appropriate channels for measuring math skills.

The identification of the input and output channels leads to decisions concerning how to teach. For example, if Juan performs better on a hear/say spelling probe than on a hear/write one, you may suggest to Ms. Mueller, his second-grade teacher, that she allow Juan to spell the words orally to a volunteer in the back of the class during the traditional Friday spelling test. The last information to record on the probe is the cumulative score for each row of problems (see Table 3.3).

### Take a Baseline

To take a baseline, you administer the same probe at least three times without teaching. For most academic skills, this administration takes a minute. It is a good idea to tell the student that it is impossible to finish all of the problems but to do them as quickly as possible. If the student hesitates for more than 2 seconds on any item, tell the student to proceed to the next item. It is also important to stress to the student to be as accurate as possible.

Because the probe always contains more problems than a student can complete within the time frame, it is permissible to change the starting point during each session. For example, if Latoya finishes the last problem in the second row during the first baseline session, have her begin the second baseline session with the first problem in the third row. By doing this, you may expose her to all of the problems during the baseline, and you may use the same sheet. Alternatively, you may wish to staple a transparency to the probe sheet and instruct students to write with nonpermanent pens. That way, you still may use the same sheet repeatedly. A squirt bottle filled with water and a cloth makes the transparency easy to clean. For accurate timings, you may use a stopwatch or a cassette tape that has recorded time signals (Hefferan & Diviaio, 1989).

If the probe does not require a written student response, as in the area of reading, mark the student's errors on a follow-along sheet, which is just a copy of the student's probe. Again, to conserve paper, laminate the follow-along sheet or staple a transparency to it.

### Select an Aim

Just as in criterion-referenced assessment, you select a mastery level, which shows that the student has learned the skill for automatic application to different situations and is ready to proceed to a different skill. In precision teaching, the mastery level is expressed in terms of an aim, which consists of correct responses (count correct or cc) and error responses (count error or ce) per minute (a rate measure), with an overlearning component (more than one session). A sample precision teaching aim is 80 correct responses and 2 error responses (80 cc/2 ce) per minute for three sessions.

Before discussing the different techniques for calculating an aim, we need to describe the scoring procedures. You score items differently following precision teaching procedures than you do normally. For example, to score reading you frequently count sounds, letters, or words, and to score spelling, you count letters. To score math problems, you count each digit so $25 + 42 = 67$ is scored as two correct answers. Conversely, the problem $25 + 42 = 87$ results in one correct answer (the 7) and one wrong (the 8). Items on a probe are scored only as far as the student progresses. Thus, a student who finishes only 10 of 50 problems on a probe is not penalized for failing to complete all 50 problems as only the 10 completed problems are scored. Skipped problems are usually counted as errors only to where the student finished.

You may calculate a precision teaching aim by using performance standards, peer assessment, student baseline, or the adult/child proportional formula (Eaton, 1978; Haring & Gentry, 1976; Koorland, Keel, & Ueberhorst, 1990). We detail the procedures for the first three as we have found these most useful. For information on the adult/child proportional formula, see Koorland, Keel, and Ueberhorst (1990). Traditionally, two or less per minute is often selected as an appropriate error score (Koorland et al., 1990).

The Precision Teaching Project in the Great Falls Public Schools (1981) suggests performance standards (see Table 3.4). These standards are based on the performance of students who have demonstrated mastery of the skill and are reported as the number correct within 1 minute.

Table 3.5 describes the calculation of an aim using the various procedures. Remember, the idea of an aim is to set a mastery criterion so that the student generalizes the skill at various times

**Table 3.4**   Suggested Performance Standards

| *Pinpoint* | *Standard* |
| --- | --- |
| **Reading** | |
| See/Say Isolated Sounds | 60–80 sounds/min. |
| See/Say Phonetic Words | 60–80 words/min. |
| Think/Say Alphabet (forward or backward) | 400 + letters/min. |
| See/Say Letter Names | 80–100 letters/min. |
| See/Say Sight Words | 80–100 words/min. |
| See/Say Words in Context (oral reading) | 200 + words/min. |
| See/Say Words in Context (silent reading) | 400 + words/min. |
| Think/Say Ideas or Facts | 15–30 ideas/min. |
| **Spelling** | |
| Hear/Write Dictated Words | 80–100 letters/min. |
| Hear/Write Dictated Words | 15–25 words/min. |
| **Math** | |
| See/Write Numbers Random | 100–120 digits/min. |
| Think/Write Numbers (0–9 serial) | 120–160 digits/min. |
| See/Say Numbers | 80–100/min. |
| Think/Say Numbers in Sequence (count by's) | 150–200 +/min. |
| See/Write Math Facts | 70–90 digits/min. |

and in various settings. You are hoping that when the student reaches the aim of 80 correct and 2 incorrect digits a minute on an addition probe, he or she will be able to add at home or during the math class on Friday. If you find that a student meets the aim but then forgets the skill 2 days later, you probably did not set an appropriate mastery level.

### Determine the Appropriateness of the Skill

As a general rule, a student must have at least five correct responses (cc) and not reach the aim for two of the three sessions of baseline

▼ **ACTIVITY 3.7**

Practice setting an aim for Damion, a seventh grader, for the pinpointed behavior of see/say science vocabulary words such as centimeter, volume, and cylinder (see Table 3.5).

1. Use the performance standards found in Table 3.4. (Select the one that is closest to the pinpoint of see/say science words in isolation.)
2. Use a peer performance standard: Jason, 60 science vocabulary words a minute; Sally, 70 science vocabulary words a minute; Jenni, 92 science vocabulary words a minute.
3. Use student baseline scores: Monday, 30 correct words a minute; Tuesday, 35 correct; Wednesday, 20 correct.

(White & Haring, 1976) for a skill to be considered appropriate for teaching. If the student makes fewer than five correct responses, the skill is probably too difficult. If the student reaches the aim, the skill is too easy.

When the student makes fewer than five correct responses, you may either slice back or step down on the curriculum scope and sequence (White & Haring, 1980). To slice back, simply cut the curriculum into smaller pieces; for example, use a probe of 0 through 4 multiplication facts to replace the probe of 0 through 9 multiplication facts. To step down, select an easier skill in the curriculum scope and sequence. For example, the student still does poorly on 0 through 4 multiplication facts, so the teacher decides to assess the student's knowledge of addition facts, an easier skill. You should take another baseline if you change the amount of curriculum or the skill.

The rule of five correct responses for selection of an appropriate skill is not absolute. White (1980) reports that some students with no correct responses during the baseline still learn the skill once instruction begins. Teachers of students with speech and language problems have told us that their students are able to progress much faster and maintain interest when they score at least 15 or more correct responses during the baseline.

If you can't apply the rule of five correct responses to the performance of a particular student, begin teaching and monitoring the student's progress. If the student makes little progress, the skill is probably too difficult and you should either slice back or step down the curriculum.

### Identify the Objective

The objective consists of the input and output channels, the pinpointed behavior, and the aim. For example, Consuela will see/say (input/output channels) initial consonant clusters in words (pinpointed behavior) at 70 cc and 2 ce per minute for 3 consecutive sessions (aim).

### Decide on an Intervention

Although precision teaching may be used with any intervention, guidelines for the selection of a strategy are linked to the learning stages of acquisition, fluency, and maintenance or proficiency (see Chapter 2). Usually, anyone who learns a new skill, whether driving a car or recalling multiplication facts, proceeds through these three stages. In the first stage, acquisition, the driver attempts to keep the car in the correct lane between the middle line and the shoulder, while the math student tries to answer problems such as 4 + 5 accurately. Modeling, immediate feedback, questioning, and direct instruction are effective strategies for the acquisition stage.

In the next stage, fluency, the student is making few errors and is concentrating on pace or speed. At this stage, the driver is no longer worried about keeping the car on the road in the proper lane (accuracy) but is attempting to

**Table 3.5** Calculation of Aims for the Pinpoint of See/Say Words in Fifth-Grade Reader

### PERFORMANCE STANDARD

| *Procedures* | *Examples* |
| --- | --- |
| 1. Find the skill in the performance standards most like the one on the probe. Look under the *Pinpoint* heading. | The pinpoint of See/Say words in fifth-grade reader is most like the See/Say words in context (oral reading). |
| 2. Select the suggested standard under the *Standard* heading. | It is 200+ words/min. So student's aim is 200 cc/2 ce per minute. |

### PEER ASSESSMENT

| *Procedures* | *Examples* |
| --- | --- |
| 1. Administer the probe for 1 minute to three students who perform the skill appropriately. | Peter: 100 words correct in 1 minute. Rosa: 150 words correct in 1 minute. Amy: 134 words correct in 1 minute. |
| 2. Find the average of the peers' scores. | 100 + 150 + 134 = 384 <br> 384 ÷ 3 = 128 cc <br> So student's aim is 128 cc/2 ce per minute. |

### STUDENT BASELINE

| *Procedures* | *Examples* |
| --- | --- |
| 1. Administer the probe for 1 minute to student for 3 days. | Student scored the following words correct on the three days of baseline: <br> Monday: 50 cc <br> Tuesday: 60 cc <br> Wednesday: 40 cc |
| 2. Find the average of the three baseline assessments. | 50 + 60 + 40 = 150 ÷ 3 = 50 |
| 3. Take the average score times 2. | 50 (average score) × 2 = 100 <br> So student's aim is 100 cc/2 ce per minute. |

drive more than 10 miles an hour (fluency) while remaining in the proper lane. The math student is trying to answer 4 + 5 before a second passes. Flash cards, drill activities, and reinforcements are frequently recommended for this stage (Haring & Eaton, 1978).

The final stage, maintenance or proficiency, is reached when the aim (both cc and ce) has been obtained. The teaching strategy is to move to another skill because the student has mastered the content. Now, the driver drives on the freeway at the speed limit and the math student

adds accurately and quickly. Table 3.6 presents a summary of the decision-making procedures involved in determining the appropriateness of the skill, identifying the learning stage, and deciding on the intervention.

### *Teach and Test*

Each day, after instruction is completed, you administer the same probe to monitor the effectiveness of the intervention. Remember, if you are worried that the student will memorize the answers, you may require the student to start at

**ACTIVITY 3.8**

Look at the results of Jan's baseline performance in the following skill area. Then determine whether the skill is appropriate to teach, define the learning stage, identify the short-term objective, and describe an intervention. Explain the reasons for your answers. The first one is done for you.

**See/Say Consonant Sounds**

Session 1: 60 cc, 2 ce

Session 2: 65 cc, 3 ce

Session 3: 70 cc, 1 ce

(This skill is too easy; Jan reached the mastery level of 60 to 80 sounds per minute as suggested on the performance standards of "See/Say Isolated Sounds." Since the skill is not appropriate for instruction, no short-term objective should be identified. The learning stage is maintenance because the aim is reached, so move the student to the next skill.)

**See/Say Short Vowels**

Session 1: 20 cc, 10 ce

Session 2: 24 cc,  7 ce

Session 3: 20 cc,  8 ce

different items each day as long as the student started at different items during the baseline sessions.

### Graph the Scores

Once you record a raw score, you must convert it into a count per minute (rate) for display on a semilogarithmic chart or graph. In a semilogarithmic graph, the distances between the lines are adjusted proportionally. Proponents of this type of graph argue that a change from 10 to 20 is the same proportionally as a change from 20 to 40; both are a doubling.

Many teachers graph data on a standard celeration chart (SCC) (Lindsley, 1990). Other teachers use adaptations of the SCC, such as the ABC–5 chart (Figure 3.4). We explain how to chart data using the ABC–5 graph. The vertical lines on the ABC–5 graph are called day lines (Hefferan & Diviaio, 1989). You can chart behaviors from Sunday through Saturday for 11 weeks, or 77 days. The short, dark marks at the top of the chart are Sunday lines, an easy way to locate the beginning of the week. The horizontal lines are often referred to as number lines (Hefferan & Diviaio, 1989).

On the ABC–5 graph, we are able to count from 0.1 to 500 counts per minute. The graph is rarely marked above 300, because few behaviors

**Table 3.6** Decision Making With Precision Teaching

| Is the skill appropriate? | Why? | What is the learning stage? | Why? | What is the teaching intervention? |
|---|---|---|---|---|
| Yes | 5 or more are correct. Aim not met | Acquisition | 5 to 19 correct in a minute | Direct teaching Give immediate feedback |
| Yes | 5 or more are correct. Aim not met | Fluency | 20 or more correct and 10 or fewer wrong in a minute | Drill and practice Use reinforcers |
| No (too easy) | Aim reached | Maintenance | Reached mastery level | Go on. Take baseline on the new skill in the scope and sequence. |
| No (too hard) | Less than 5 correct | Preacquisition | Scored less than 5 | Slice back or step down |

may be accomplished at more than 300 counts a minute. Notice that there is a one-to-one correspondence between the numbers 0.1 through 10. However, from 10 to 100, the numbers proceed 10, 15, 20, and then skip in increments of 10 until 100. The count continues 100, 150, 200, 300, 400, and 500. Therefore, to chart counts between 10 and 500, you must estimate.

You are probably wondering why it is necessary to have a count of 0.1 or 0.2 on the graph. Remember, only rate is recorded on the graph, so to record a score of two items missed during a 10-minute probe, you must divide the 2 by the 10, which results in 0.2 incorrect responses per minute.

Steps for charting include (1) complete the student information, (2) mark the record floor, (3) mark the aim, (4) record the raw data, (5) convert the raw data to counts per minute, (6) chart correct and incorrect responses per minute, (7) identify ignored and no-chance days, and (8) connect data points.

1.  *Complete the student information.* Identify the name and age of the student, the pinpointed behavior, and the aims at the bottom of the graph.

2.  *Mark the record floor.* The record floor identifies the amount of time that you administer a probe. Record floor figures are found on the right side of the graph. Notice that with the ABC–5 graph, you can administer a probe from 0.2 minutes, or 12 seconds, to 10 minutes. Mark the record floor by drawing a horizontal line through each week at the appropriate minutes.

3.  *Mark the aim.* Mark the aim on the graph by finding the acceptable performance criteria of correct and error responses per minute on the count lines. The count correct part of the aim is frequently marked with a horizontal line and arrows pointing upward. The count error part of the aim is frequently marked with a horizontal line and arrows pointing downward.

4.  *Record the raw data.* Enter the raw scores in the data boxes at the right of the ABC–5 graph. Enter the correct raw data at the top and the error raw data at the bottom for each day that assessment occurred.

5.  *Convert the raw data to counts per minute.* Before you record data on the graph, you must convert each raw score to a count per minute, dividing the score by the number of minutes. Thus, to record a student's score of 3 incorrect responses in 5 minutes, you would first divide 3 by 5, then locate 0.6 on the chart. To show a 0 count, mark the data point just below the record floor. A count of 1 always falls on the record floor line.

6.  *Chart correct and incorrect responses per minute.* Use a dot (.) to mark the correct responses per minute and an *x* to mark the incorrect responses per minute. To mark the correct responses on the chart, locate the first day you administered the probe on the day lines. Then locate the count on the number lines. Follow the lines until they intersect and place a dot at the intersection. Follow the same procedures to chart incorrect responses, only place an *x* at the intersection.

7.  *Identify ignored and no-chance days.* Before you connect any of the data points, consider no-chance days and ignored days. No-chance days are days when you do not have an opportunity to assess the student, such as over the weekend or during an absence. Ignored days are days when you have an opportunity to assess the student but decide not to. Code IG for ignored and NC for no-chance in the raw data boxes. Do not connect data points across no-chance days, but do connect across ignored days. If there are many no-chance days, frequent absences may be the reason the student is not progressing. If there are many ignored days, the student may not be progressing due to the infrequency of data collection.

8.  *Connect data points.* Connect the correct data points and then connect the error data points. Do not connect data points across

no-chance days or phase change lines. Phase change lines (vertical lines) denote whenever something is changed, for example, a change in intervention, pinpointed behavior, or mastery aim. Always draw a phase change line between the last session of baseline and the first day of intervention to note that teaching has started. Once you have connected all the data points, you will have a learning picture. Figure 3.4 presents a pictorial summary of all the charting procedures.

▼ **ACTIVITY 3.9**

Chart the following data from a precision teaching assessment on a semilogarithmic graph.

*Behavior:* See/write addition facts with sums 0–18.

*Aim:* 80 cc, 2 ce.

*Observation time:* 1 minute.

*Baseline:*

Monday—10 cc, 10 ce.

Tuesday—15 cc, 10 ce.

Wednesday—5 cc, 15 ce.

*Intervention:*

Thursday—20 cc, 10 ce.

Friday—20 cc, 8 ce.

Monday—24 cc, 8 ce.

Tuesday—Ignored.

Wednesday—30 cc, 0 ce.

### Monitor Progress

Now that you have charted the data, it is time to decide whether the intervention plan is effective and whether the student is making progress. You can do this subjectively, by eyeballing the data, or objectively, by comparing the data to an *expected* level of progress (White & Haring, 1976) or an *actual* level of progress (Fuchs, Fuchs, & Hamlett, 1989).

*Subjective Evaluation.* Subjective evaluation requires an examination of the direction of the correct response data points and the incorrect response data points and a comparison of the student's performance during the baseline and intervention. Effective learning pictures have in common that the correct data points are moving up toward the count correct aim, the error data points are moving down toward the count error aim, and both are improvements on the baseline. In Figure 3.5, we show effective learning pictures.

In each of these examples, during intervention, the correct data points are moving up toward the correct aim and the error data points are moving down toward the error aim. Student C displays a common pattern of a quick gain once instruction begins. This gain is apparent when you compare the last data point of the baseline with the first one of intervention. Student A displays the best learning picture. This student had more incorrect responses than correct during the baseline and more correct responses than incorrect during the intervention. Thus, the intervention was very effective, as it resulted in a picture totally different from the baseline. When you see such pictures, you should continue with the intervention, because they indicate the intervention is working and the student is progressing (Hefferan & Diviaio, 1989).

In ineffective learning pictures, the correct data points and error data points are moving away from the aims or are stagnant (Hefferan & Diviaio, 1989). Often, a comparison with the baseline shows that there is not much difference in progress. Figure 3.6 displays some ineffective learning pictures.

Student A is not progressing, because the correct data points have flattened out. When you see three consecutive sessions of flat data, it is an ineffective picture. Student B is not progressing either, because correct responses are decreasing and incorrect responses are increasing. Note, too, that for Student B, incorrect responses remain higher than correct responses during the intervention. If you consider the

**Figure 3.4** Summary of Steps for Charting

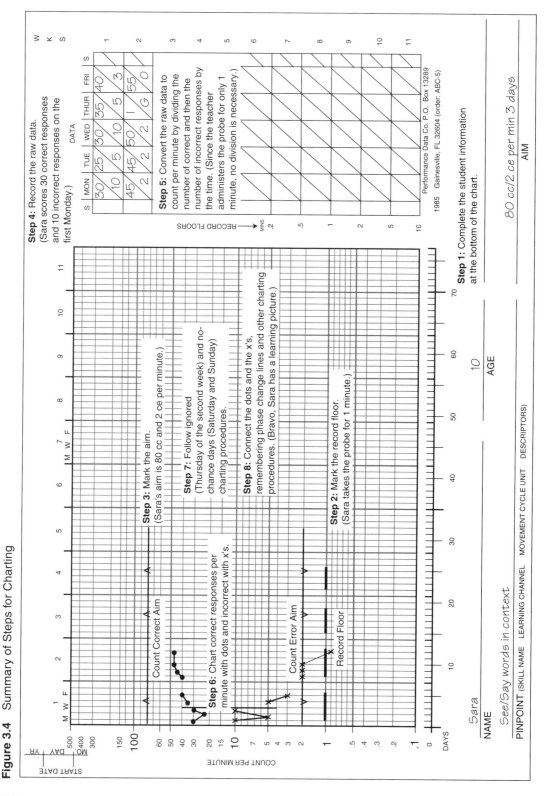

80

**Figure 3.5** Effective Learning Pictures

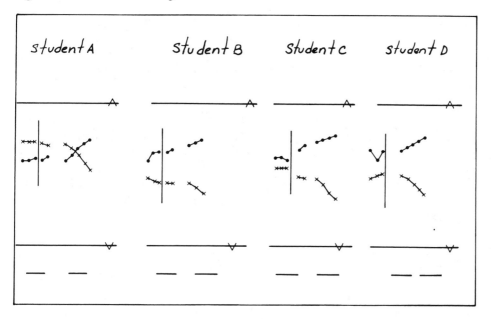

**Figure 3.6** Ineffective Learning Pictures

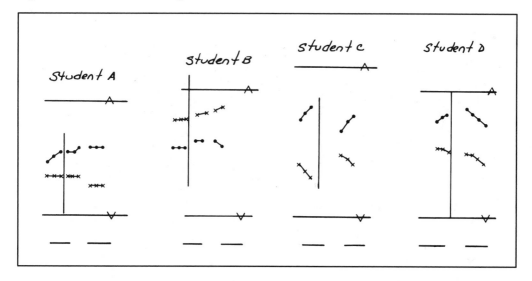

intervention data only, you may think that Student C's picture is effective, because the correct data points are ascending and the error data points are descending; however, when you look closer, you see the correct data points are lower and the error data points are higher than they were at baseline. In Student D's picture, the error data points are decreasing, but so are the count correct data points. When you see pictures like these, you should change your intervention or make other program changes (e.g., take multiple timings and average the score or change the goal), because the student is not making adequate progress.

Sometimes, the data do not present a clear picture of progress, especially when there is much fluctuation. In these cases, an objective evaluation is much more effective.

***Objective Evaluation.*** In objective evaluation of a student's progress, you analyze data trends and make changes following certain decision rules. Data trends use either *expected* or *actual* rate of student progress. When you measure *expected* rate of student progress, you have a preconceived date and aim in mind that a student must meet to show progress. When you measure *actual* rate of student progress, you do not have a preconceived date or aim in mind; instead, you rely on student behavior (the number of correct

responses per minute during intervention) to evaluate performance. See Figures 3.7 and 3.8 for a description of the procedures and the decision-making rules.

Fuchs, Fuchs, and Hamlett (1989) found that teachers who evaluated progress using *actual* student performance produced more achievement gains than did a control group of teachers who monitored progress with end-of-unit math tests, unsystematic observations, and workbook and worksheet performances. However, teachers who evaluated progress using *expected* student performance did not produce more achievement gains than did the control group.

## Sample Plan

Now that we have discussed all of the steps to precision teaching separately, we bring the steps together to write an instructional program for Rosa, a ninth grader.

▼ **ACTIVITY 3.10**

Examine the two students' charts below and tell whether you would plan to make changes based on the learning pictures. Try using both objective and subjective evaluation.

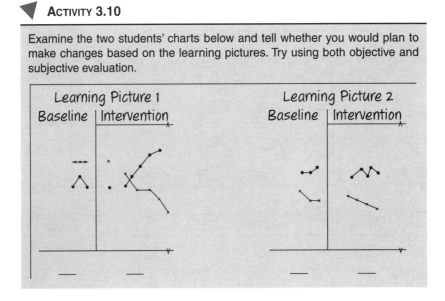

**Figure 3.7**   Steps for Drawing a Celeration Line Using Aimline Procedures (Expected Rate of Progress)

1. Select an aim rate for the student to master the aim, and mark it on the graph.

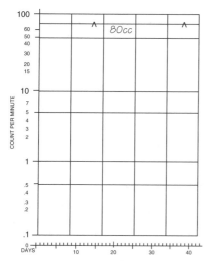

2. Select a date for the student to master the aim, and draw a line through the aim rate. Circle where they intersect; this is the end mark.

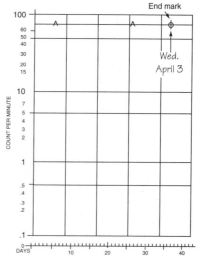

3. Record the baseline data on the graph.

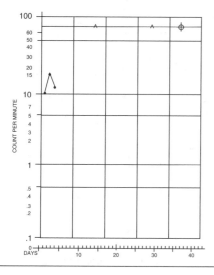

4. Find the mid-day during the baseline (the mid-day comes in the middle of three baseline sessions), and draw a vertical line through it.

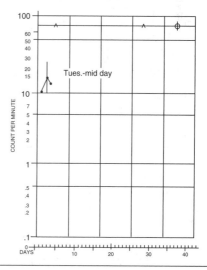

**Figure 3.7**  *Continued*

5. Find the mid-rate during the baseline (the middle count) by ranking the data points in order. If data points are the same, select that number. Draw a horizontal line through it.

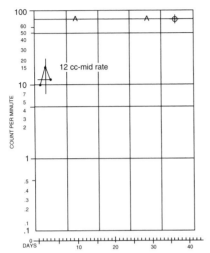

6. Put a circle where the lines intersect. This is the start mark, where the celeration line begins.

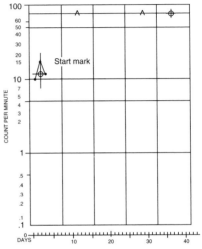

7. Connect the start mark with the end mark. The celeration line connects the two points.

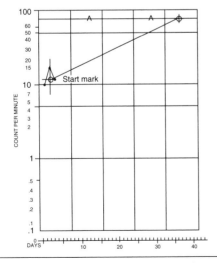

8. Chart the counts per minute during the intervention.

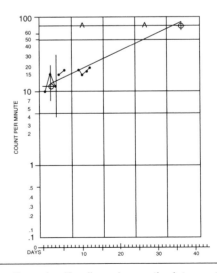

Decision Rule: If there are three consecutive data points below the celeration line, change the intervention, do multiple timings, change the goal, or make other changes.

**Figure 3.8**  Steps for Drawing a Celeration Line Using the Quarter-Intersect Method (Actual Rate of Progress)

1. Take intervention data for 7 days.

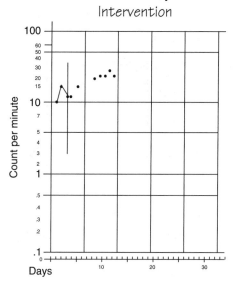

2. Divide the seven data points evenly.

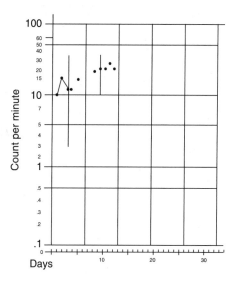

3. Mark the first three points as side A and the last three as side B.

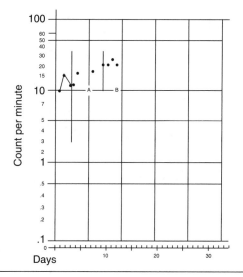

4. Find the mid-rate and the mid-day of side A.

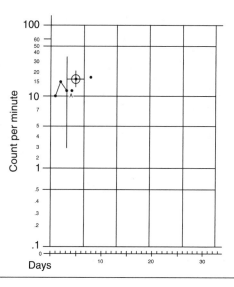

**Figure 3.8** *Continued*

5. Find the mid-rate and the mid-day of side B.                    6. Connect the two sides with a celeration line.

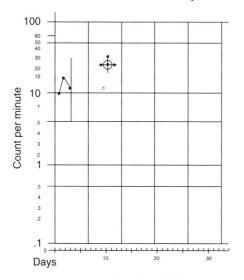 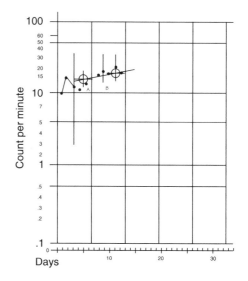

*Decision Rules*
(a) Continue the intervention with an increasing celeration line.
(b) Change the intervention with a flat celeration line.
* (c) Change the intervention with a decreasing celeration line.

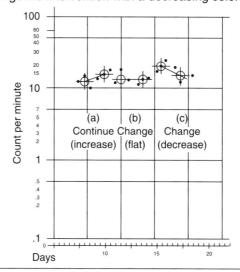

*Instead of changing the intervention you may take multiple timings and calculate an average or change the goal.

1. *Pinpoint a behavior.* After a discussion with the general classroom teacher or based on Rosa's IEP or an examination of the district standards, Ms. Kornig determines that Rosa was having problems simplifying fractions to lowest terms.

2. *Select a probe, input and output channels, a time, and scoring procedures.* The teacher-designed probe contains 40 different problems, like 4/12 and 8/20. Each of the problems is repeated once, for a total of 80 problems. Rosa takes the probe for 1 minute using the see/write channels, because she is expected to perform the skill in an inclusive setting as a paper-and-pencil task. Ms. Kornig counts each digit of the answer (e.g., 1/4 counts as two digits) only to where Rosa stops.

3. *Take a baseline.* Rosa scores 10 cc (count correct) and 5 ce (count error) responses on Day 1, 10 cc and 10 ce on Day 2, and 15 cc and 9 ce on Day 3.

4. *Select a mastery aim.* Ms. Kornig selects an aim of 70–90 correct digits and 2 incorrect digits per minute for three sessions based on the performance standard chart skill of "See/Write Math Facts" (Table 3.4).

5. *Determine the appropriateness of the pinpoint.* Examining the baseline scores, the skill is appropriate for Rosa, because she has at least five correct responses and has not reached her aim.

6. *Write a short-term objective.* The objective is "Presented with an 80-item probe, Rosa will see/write fractions to lowest terms at 80 cc and 2 ce per minute for 3 consecutive days."

7. *Select the intervention.* Because Rosa is in the acquisition stage (she scored 5–19 correct responses), Ms. Kornig plans to use modeling of the simplification procedures as a teaching intervention.

8. *Begin teaching and testing.* Every day, after a 10-minute teaching session, Ms. Kornig administers the same probe that was administered in baseline.

9. *Graph scores.* Rosa graphs her scores to create a learning picture.

10. *Monitor progress.* Ms. Kornig decides to measure progress using the *actual rate* of progress, drawing a celeration line after 7 days of data collection. She plans to change the intervention if Rosa is not making progress.

 **IMPORTANT POINTS**

1. In precision teaching, behaviors that are repeatable and observable and that have a beginning and end are pinpointed.
2. Probes should not interfere with a student's opportunity or freedom to respond and are administered for three days without any intervention to collect baseline data.
3. From the baseline data, appropriateness of the skill, learning stage, and instructional strategies are decided.
4. The acquisition stage requires a score between 5 and 19 correct; the fluency stage, 20 or more correct and 10 or fewer errors; at the maintenance stage, the aim is met.
5. In subjective evaluation, a learning picture is effective when the correct data points are moving up to the count correct aim, the error data points are moving down to the count error aim, and both are improvements over the baseline.
6. Objective evaluation requires the drawing of celeration lines based on either the *expected* rate of student change or the *actual* rate of student change.
7. A decision rule states that a change is needed when a student scores three consecutive data points below the celeration line for the *expected* rate of change.
8. Decision rules state that a change is needed when a celeration line for the *actual* rate of change is flat or decreasing.
9. Teachers may change the intervention, take multiple timings, or select a different goal when a student is not progressing.

## CURRICULUM-BASED MEASUREMENT

Curriculum-based measurement (CBM) is a measurement and evaluation system developed at the University of Minnesota Institute for Research on Learning Disabilities by Deno, Fuchs, Mirkin, and their colleagues (Deno, 1985). Curriculum-based measurement is a type of curriculum-based assessment (Fuchs, Fuchs, & Hamlett, 1989) that considers accuracy and time. CBM employs brief, frequent assessment based on the student's classroom curriculum and provides teachers with a technique for monitoring progress (Frisby, 1987). Thus, if the school district has adopted a specific reading series, material for assessment is selected from the series texts. This ensures that students are assessed on skills that have been or will be taught. The matching of assessment and instructional materials is also recommended for students with cultural and linguistic differences. Such students often perform better when they are tested on material that is presented in the classroom (Fradd & Hallman, 1983; Hoffer, 1983; Sugai, Maheady, & Skouge, 1989).

The systematic procedures of CBM demonstrate technical adequacy and validity, are well-supported in the special education literature (Elliott, 1998), and have been effectively used in inclusive settings (Salend, 2000). Like precision teaching, CBM uses frequent, direct measurement of academic performance in reading, math, spelling, and the writing curriculum. However, CBM focuses on general outcomes measured over time, whereas precision teaching involves mastery measurement of subskills of the curriculum (Fuchs & Deno, 1991). For example, in spelling, a precision teaching probe may contain only silent *e* spelling words and once students meet mastery on that skill, another probe is created with a different spelling skill. Instead, with CBM procedures, alternate probes of 20 words randomly selected from the 400 words in the second-grade curriculum are created; some of

these words contain silent *e* spelling words. Thus, CBM is measuring student performance across the entire yearlong curriculum. Fuchs and Deno (1991) note that this general outcome approach to assessment is more attuned to holistic and integrated learning outcomes. We first discuss the administration and scoring procedures for reading, spelling, math, and written expression.

### Reading

Of the reading measures created by Deno and colleagues, we discuss oral reading fluency per minute and the maze procedure. Both are supported in the research as reliable and valid measures of reading performance (Eliot & Fuchs, 1997; Fewster & MacMillan, 2002; Good & Jefferson, 1998; Madelaine & Wheldall, 1999).

To measure a student's oral reading fluency, ask the student to read three passages, each for 1 minute, from various reading texts. These passages should be approximately 100 words in length for young students and 300 words in length for older students. Select one passage from the beginning, one from the middle, and one from the end of various grade-level texts. Be careful to select prose paragraphs without much dialogue or many proper nouns or unusual words (Deno, Mirkin, & Wesson, 1984).

To begin the assessment process, instruct the student to read the passage as quickly as possible. If the student hesitates on a word for more than 2 seconds, say the word and tell the student to go on. Time the selection for only 1 minute (Salvia & Hughes, 1990). While the student is reading each passage, mark the student responses on a follow-along sheet. Count the words read correctly and incorrectly by the student through the last word read for each passage, and rank the number to find the median scores. Words misread (e.g., *house* for *horse*), words omitted (e.g., leaving out *horse*), words reversed (e.g., *was* for *saw*), and phrases reversed (e.g., *the beautiful, wild horse* for *the wild, beautiful horse*) are counted as errors. Misread proper nouns, self-corrections, and insertions (e.g., adding the word *the* to the phrase *the wild "the" dark horse* instead of *the wild, dark horse*) are not counted as errors (Tindal & Marston, 1990).

Another reading task frequently used in CBM procedures is the maze task or closure task, which permits testing of students in group settings (Shin, Denon, & Espin, 2000). The maze probe presents a reading selection with every seventh word deleted after the first sentence. The deleted word is replaced with three multiple-choice alternatives, one correct word and two clearly incorrect words. During the 3-minute reading session, students select one of the three alternatives to fill in the blank correctly.

 **ACTIVITY 3.11**

Select a 100-word passage from a third grade text. With a partner, create a maze task. Remember to delete every seventh word after the first sentence and replace with three alternative words for students to select.

## Spelling

Spelling measures typically include 20 words. Lists are randomly selected from either the spelling series used in the district or basal readers (Deno et al., 1984; Marston & Magnusson, 1985). Begin by dictating words for 2 minutes, directing the student to write as many letters of each word as he or she can. Give about 10 seconds to spell each word and do not present any new words in the last 3 seconds of the test (Deno & Fuchs, 1987).

Score the test by counting the number of correct letter sequences within the 2-minute sample. Counting correctly spelled words by letter sequences usually results in one more count than the number of letters; for example, the word *agent* consists of six possible correct letter sequences: one before *a*, because the student knew where to

start (beginning to $a = +1$); one from *a* to *g* ($+2$); one from *g* to *e* ($+3$); one from *e* to *n* ($+4$); one from *n* to *t* ($+5$); and one after *t*, because the student knew where to end (*t* to end $+6$) (White & Haring, 1976). Thus, *agent* is marked in the following manner: $^{+1}a\ ^{+2}g\ ^{+3}e\ ^{+4}n\ ^{+5}t\ ^{+6}$.

## Math

Curriculum-based measurement for math consists of multiple tests of the types of problems found in the year's curriculum (Fuchs, Fuchs, Hamlett, & Stecker, 1991). Thus, you are measuring a student's performance on the entire math curriculum over time.

You administer the various 25-item tests, directing the students to proceed as quickly as possible. As in precision teaching, score the sample by counting each correct digit. Fuchs, Fuchs, Hamlett, and Whinnery (1991) recommend a test time of 1 minute for Grade 1, 1.5 minutes for Grades 2 and 3, 3 minutes for Grade 4, 4 minutes for Grade 5, and 5 minutes for Grade 6. Others recommend a 2-minute time limit (Shinn, 1989).

## Written Expression

CBM measures for written expression consist of three story starters or topic sentences (Deno, Marston, & Mirkin, 1982). An example of a story starter is, "The score was tied. As the soccer ball rolled in front of my feet, I . . . ." An example of a topic sentence is, "He went shopping at Wal-Mart."

You may either read or write the story starter or topic sentence for the student. Administer the three story starters or topic sentences at one sitting or at three sittings. Give the student a minute to think about the story, 3 minutes to complete the stories, then count the number of words in each story. Do not count numbers (Deno & Fuchs, 1987).

Determining what constitutes a word is a teacher decision. Salvia and Hughes (1990) suggest considering grade level and linguistic backgrounds in scoring words. They recommend counting misspelled words as words for older students (e.g., *summer* spelled *sumar*) and counting any letter sequence that can be identified as a word for younger students (e.g., *summer* spelled as *sum*). For children whose first language is not English, they suggest counting word sequences that are acceptable translations of the native language.

## Steps

Now that we have discussed the assessment procedures, we identify the steps you may follow to use CBM for planning and monitoring student progress. We provide examples from the area of reading.

### *Administer and Score the Probe and Select Instructional and Mastery Standards*

We have already discussed the administration and scoring procedures, so we concentrate on discussion of the instructional and mastery standards. Instructional standards often determine the grade level of the materials appropriate for instruction. Mastery standards identify the goals students must reach to show that they have learned the information. Fuchs and Shinn (1989) caution that further research is needed as to the technical adequacy of the determination of instructional and mastery standards. Therefore, this information serves as a guideline. Many school districts are establishing their own instructional and mastery standards for CBM measures. See Table 3.7 for suggestions from the literature concerning instructional and mastery standards.

EXAMPLE: Mr. Smith administered probes from the first-, second-, and third-grade curriculum to Manu, who was in third grade. Based on the suggested instructional standards for third grade (see Table 3.7), Mr. Smith selected an instructional standard of 30 wpm with less than 7 errors. He then instructed

Manu to read the three third-grade passages as quickly as possible for a minute each and ranked his median reading score, which was 10 correct words and 17 errors. This score was below the instructional standard, so Mr. Smith then administered selections from the second-grade reader. Manu read 25 wpm correctly with only 2 errors on the first passage of the second-grade text, 35 wpm correctly with only 3 errors on the second passage, and 30 wpm correctly with 2 errors on the third passage. A ranking of the number of words per minute correct (25, 30, 31) resulted in a median score of 30 wpm correct. Thus, Mr. Smith began instructing Manu in the second-grade text.

### *Write an Annual Goal and Short-Term Objectives*

Deno, Mirkin, and Wesson (1984) recommend that teachers compare the instructional and mastery standards along with the IEP review date to write an annual goal and short-term objectives. Fuchs, Fuchs, and Hamlett (1989) recommend that teachers or students select ambitious mastery goals for the best results.

EXAMPLE: Mr. Smith, with Manu's input, selected the mastery standard of 50 words per minute with less than 7 errors (see Table 3.7 for second-grade level). Based on this information, Mr. Smith wrote the following annual goal: "When placed in Reader 2 of the Houghton-Mifflin series, Manu will increase his reading from an instructional standard of 30 wpm correct to a mastery standard of 50 wpm correct, with less than 7 errors before the next IEP review." Next, Mr. Smith subtracted the instruction standard from the mastery with the result that Manu would have to read 20 more words by the end of 12 weeks, the date of the IEP review. Because Mr. Smith was measuring Manu's reading progress weekly, he arrived at the following short-term objective: "Every week, when presented with a random selection from the Houghton-Mifflin second-grade reader, Manu will read aloud with

**Table 3.7** Suggested Instructional and Mastery Standards

| | *Instructional Standards* | *Mastery Standards* |
|---|---|---|
| **Reading (1-minute sampling)*** | | |
| 1st & 2nd grade | 11 to 20 wpm<br>10 to 30 wpm, <7errors | 50 to 70 wpm |
| 3rd–6th grade | 41 to 50 wpm<br>30 to 60 wpm, <7errors | 70 to 100 wpm |
| **Spelling (2-minute sampling)** | | |
| 1st & 2nd grade | 20 to 30 correct letter sequences (cls) | 60 to 80 cls |
| 3rd–6th grade | 40 to 59 correct letter sequences | 80 to 140 cls |
| **Math (time varies based on grade level)** | | |
| 1st grade | 11 or fewer correct digits | Weekly increase of one digit |
| 2nd grade | 12–22 | |
| 3rd grade | 23–30 | |
| 4th grade | 31–46 | |
| 5th grade | 47–60 | |
| 6th grade | >60 | |
| **Written Expression (3-minute sampling)** | | |
| 1st grade | Student's median | 14.7 words |
| 2nd grade | score of 3 samples | 27.8 words |
| 3rd grade | | 36.6 words |
| 4th grade | | 40.9 words |
| 5th grade | | 49.1 words |
| 6th grade | | 53.3 words |

*Deno, Fuchs, and Marston (2001) identify mastery standards of an increase of 2 wpm per week for beginning readers and an increase of 1 wpm per week for Grades 2–6.

(From the works of Deno, Mirkin, & Wesson, 1984; Fuchs, Hamlett, & Fuchs, 1990; Fuchs & Shinn, 1989; Hasbrouck & Tindal, 1992; Marston, Dement, Allen, & Allen, 1992; Marston & Magnusson, 1985)

an average increase of about 2 wpm correct (20 divided by 12)."

### Teach and Test

During teaching and testing, parallel assessment forms are given to the student at least once a week. Do not allow the student to practice the material before assessment. Wesson (1987) suggests that teachers select 10 pages from the beginning, middle, and end of each assigned text for measuring reading progress. The text and 30 slips of paper with page numbers written on each slip are then placed in a container. A student randomly selects a slip of paper, turns to the page number in the assigned text, reads the passage, and initials the back. Once a student has read and initialed the slip three times, he or she can no longer use that page as a measure of reading progress.

EXAMPLE: Mr. Smith instructed Manu from the second-grade text and selected parallel passages for monitoring Manu's progress. He assessed Manu once a week with 1-minute samples.

### Graph the Scores

Data is charted on an equal interval graph. An equal interval graph is a linear graph in which the distance between lines occupies equal space; that is, the distance between 5 and 10 is the same as the distance between 10 and 15 and between 15 and 20. It's probably the graph that you used in school. Fuchs, Hamlett, and Fuchs (1990) have designed a software program, *MBSP: Monitoring Basic Skills Progress,* which contains graded reading passages, spelling lists, and arithmetic probes. Students enter responses on the computer, and the computer graphs the data.

EXAMPLE:   Mr. Smith helps Manu chart his scores on an equal interval chart. They chart the results after the scoring of each probe.

### Evaluate Progress

Fuchs, Fuchs, and Hamlett (1989) recommend that teachers consider both the *expected* and *actual* rate of student change to evaluate intervention effectiveness. Their software program, *Monitoring Basic Skills Progress* (Fuchs, Hamlett, & Fuchs, 1990), displays aimlines and regression lines. The program also communicates the appropriate intervention decision. Additionally, the software conducts a skills analysis of students'

**Figure 3.9**   CBM Decision Rules

(a) Change the intervention or goal if the regression line (actual rate of change) is lower than the aimline (expected rate of change).

(b) Raise the goal if the regression line is steeper than the aimline.

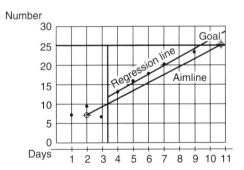

(c) Continue with the intervention if both celeration lines are the same.

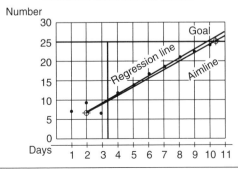

The aimline is drawn using aimline procedures and the regression line is drawn using quarter-intersect procedures.

responses to the test items (Fuchs, Fuchs, Hamlett, & Whinnery, 1991). Allinder (1996) found that special educators who knew the measurement systems and the software, scheduled frequent assessments, examined students' graphs, implemented decision rules, and had adequate planning time produced more significant math gains. See Figure 3.9 for a sample of the decision rules used to evaluate progress.

EXAMPLE: Based on the decision rules, Mr. Smith finds that Manu is making good progress.

As we discussed the various informal assessments, we attempted to point out some of the similarities and differences. Table 3.8 shows a comparison of the various informal assessments.

▼ **ACTIVITY 3.12**

You have decided to assess the written expression performance of Latoya, a sixth grader, who has a mild disability. Describe the steps you would follow in planning and monitoring using curriculum-based measurement.

**Table 3.8** Comparison of Various Informal Assessment Measures

| | Criterion-Referenced Tests | Precision Teaching | Curriculum-Based Measurement | Portfolio |
|---|---|---|---|---|
| Administration | Individual/Group | Individual/Group | Individual/Group | Individual (work selected by student) |
| Content | Curriculum scope and sequence | Curriculum scope and sequence | Classroom texts | Work samples |
| Mastery measure | Percent | Rate Reading—words per minute Math—digits per minute Spelling—letters per minute | Fluency Reading—words per minute Math—digits at varied times Spelling—letters in 2 minutes Written expression—words in 3 minutes | Varies |
| Uses | Identify goals, objectives | Identify goals, objectives, learning stages, teaching strategies | Identify goals, objectives, materials | Identify objectives |
| | Measure progress with pre- and posttests | Measure progress with repeated measurement | Measure progress with repeated measurement | Measure progress with rubrics |
| Assesses | General outcomes, Skills | Skills | General outcomes, Skills | Skills, Strategies, Interests |
| Setting | Pull out, inclusive classes | Pull out, inclusive classes | Pull out, inclusive classes | Pull out, inclusive classes |

## INVOLVING STUDENTS IN DATA COLLECTION

Student involvement in data collection increases motivation and makes them feel more responsible for their own learning, plus it often saves teacher time. If you decide to incorporate precision teaching or CBM procedures, teaching students to grade their own probes and to chart the results promotes active student participation in the learning process. Research shows that self-graphing maintains students' performance at high levels (McDougal & Brady, 1998; Trammel, Schloss, & Alper, 1994).

Wesson (1987) suggests setting up a measurement station in the class to involve the students. Place all materials, such as pencils or pens, a stopwatch with an audible beep, a tape recorder, assessment materials (probes or texts), direction sheets, answer sheets, and graphs, at the center. It is best to file the answer sheets, graphs, probes, and texts in a box for easy access. The direction sheet should contain step-by-step directions, explaining how to use any equipment. For example, Bott (1990), in giving directions for collecting oral reading samples, tells the students to "find the cassette tape labeled with your name, rewind it to the beginning, and press the record and play buttons down at the same time" (p. 287) to assist students in using a tape recorder. You may arrange the probes and texts according to subject areas. Schedule the students at the measurement station and assign them to the assessment materials based on their IEP objectives. Have the students proceed to the center, select the required assessment materials identified on their schedules, follow the assessment procedures, chart the information, and return all materials to their proper places.

Goodrich (1996–97) suggests that students help create scoring rubrics. She recommends that teachers show and discuss examples of good and poor work. From these examples, students list criteria, levels, and indicators. She then suggests they use the rubrics for peer and self-assessment. For example, eighth-grade students in cooperative groups identified the following criteria for their language arts portfolios: neatness, range of characteristics, effectiveness of story, use of unusual vocabulary, and sharpness of ideas and arguments. They then added the levels of "Yes; Yes, but; and Not Quite." They next defined indicators of a "Yes" level for neatness to include minimal erasures on the paper, straight margins, page numbers, proper heading, and legible handwriting. Lastly, they defined the other indicators.

Diaries and logs are other ways for students to participate in their evaluation (Baskwill & Whitman, 1988). Students may identify a list of writing skills they have mastered under "Things I Can Do in Writing" in their writing diaries (Calkins, 1986; Graves & Stuart, 1985). These lists are updated monthly. In learning logs, students enter what they have learned in any subject area. The students date and compile the logs in a notebook. Logs indicate whether students can describe what they have learned, relate isolated ideas, and recognize relevant information (Baskwill & Whitman, 1988). For example, at the end of each day, Ms. Anderson has her students write one thing they learned and how they felt about the day in their logs.

Self-monitoring of academic and social behaviors is another way to involve students in data collection. McDougal and Brady (1998) found that self-monitoring along with other self-management strategies increased math performance and engaged time of students with disabilities in inclusive settings. To teach students with special needs to monitor their own progress in an inclusive setting, use the following steps compiled from those suggested by many practitioners (Anderson-Inman, 1986; Frith & Armstrong, 1986; Hughes, Ruhl, & Peterson, 1988; Osborne, Kosiewicz, Crumley, & Lee, 1987).

1. *Define the behavior for monitoring.* Behaviors selected for self-monitoring should be easily identified as having occurred or not occurred. Behaviors such as turning in homework assignments, raising hand to speak, writing headings on papers, and bringing paper and pencil to class are appropriate for self-monitoring.

2. *Teach students to discriminate the behavior.* Model examples and nonexamples of the behaviors and then ask students to discriminate between them.

3. *Design the form for data collection.* On the form, be sure to include the behaviors, dates, and key for coding. See Figure 3.10 for an example of a form. This form was used with secondary students to count how often history homework was turned in on time.

4. *Demonstrate how to record using the form.* Model how to record on the form and explain the scoring code.

5. *Use a time routine.* Scheduling a specific time for students to complete the forms increases the chances that students will remember to monitor the behaviors when you are not around. Schedule the time for monitoring as close to the completion of the task as possible.

6. *Use teacher reliability checks.* A reliability check is easier if the student is monitoring a paper-and-pencil type of task, which leaves a permanent record. For example, a quick check of the general education teacher's grade book will let you know whether the student is correctly monitoring the turning in of history homework on time. Many times, teachers reward students when their counts match. Actually, checking the use of the form is more important than checking accuracy. After all, the objective is for students to monitor their own progress.

7. *Introduce self-monitoring in one inclusive class setting first, and then generalize to others.* Anderson-Inman (1986) reports that allowing students to decide when and where to use the self-monitoring form makes them feel more committed to using it. Perhaps next a secondary student may want to monitor the turning in of math homework on time.

▼ **ACTIVITY 3.13**

Identify three ways to involve students with special needs in data collection at either the elementary or secondary level.

**Figure 3.10**  Student Monitoring

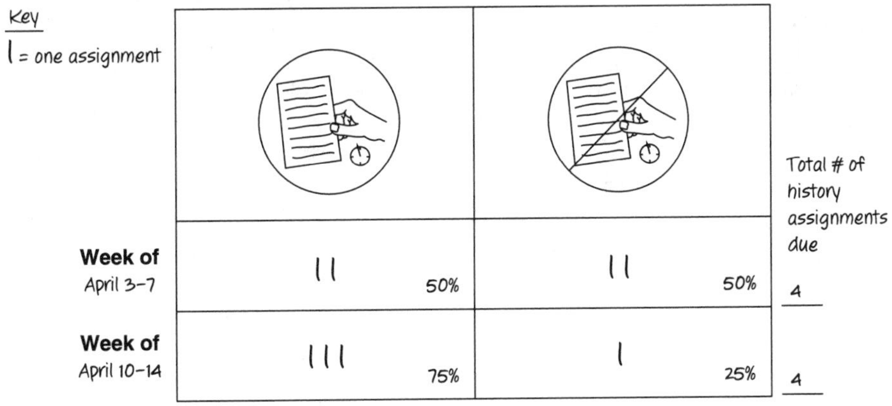

| Key<br>ǀ = one assignment | | | Total # of<br>history<br>assignments<br>due |
|---|---|---|---|
| **Week of**<br>April 3–7 | ǀ ǀ          50% | ǀ ǀ          50% | 4 |
| **Week of**<br>April 10–14 | ǀ ǀ ǀ        75% | ǀ            25% | 4 |

**IMPORTANT POINTS**

1. Curriculum-based measurement uses classroom materials for assessment, measures performance using fluency, and compares a student's score with suggested instructional and mastery standards or criteria.

2. The oral reading fluency measure requires a student to read passages for 1 minute from various reading texts to determine the instructional reading level (the grade level for instruction), and the maze procedure requires students to select the appropriate word from a choice of three words to fill in the blank correctly.

3. The spelling measure requires students to write as many spelling words as they can in 2 minutes and is scored by counting letter sequences.

4. In math assessment, sample problems from the whole-year's math curriculum are selected and scored by counting the number of digits correct.

5. In written expression assessment, students are given three story starters or three topic sentences and instructed to write a story for each within 3 minutes.

6. Once the students are assessed, the teacher selects mastery standards and writes IEP goals and short-term objectives based on suggested guidelines.

7. Decision rules are based on a comparison of *expected* rate of student change (an aimline) and the *actual* rate of change (a regression line).

8. Decision rules state that teachers should change their intervention when a regression line is lower than the aimline or when a regression line is steeper than the aimline.

9. Critical components of CBM include measurement frequency, goal ambitiousness, compliance with decision rules, and adequate planning time (Allinder, 1996).

10. Student involvement in data collection increases motivation and makes them feel more responsible for their own learning, plus it often saves teacher time.

11. Students may be involved in collecting, scoring, and charting probes; in designing rubrics; and in compiling diaries and logs.

12. To initiate student involvement in monitoring their own behaviors, teachers should define the behavior, teach students to discriminate the behavior, design the form for data collection, demonstrate how to use the form, use a time routine, use reliability checks, and introduce the monitoring gradually.

 **DISCUSSION QUESTIONS**

1. Discuss some of the difficulties encountered in establishing and maintaining a monitoring system such as Precision Teaching and Curriculum-Based Measurement. Brainstorm some solutions.

2. Discuss ways to involve students with special needs at both elementary and secondary levels in data collection procedures.

3. Present the pros and cons of using CBM compared to portfolio assessment.

# CHAPTER 4 ⋆⋆

# THE INSTRUCTIONAL CYCLE

## Key Topics

In Chapter 1, we referred to a general instructional framework for making decisions about teaching students with special needs. This framework includes planning the lesson, presenting the lesson with guided practice and feedback, providing for independent practice, and evaluating the effectiveness of the lesson. We discussed beginning-of-the-year planning and organization in Chapter 2, and in this chapter, we examine some of the decisions teachers must make in the daily teaching process. In the daily planning phase, teachers make decisions about IEPS, instructional arrangements, instructional language, instructional time, motivation, and subject content. In presenting the lesson, they make decisions about strategies for presenting new subject content, activities for practice, positive and corrective feedback, and summarization of the content. With questioning and feedback, they evaluate how the lesson is proceeding and the necessity of making changes. During independent practice activities, teachers decide on activities that reinforce the content presented and ways to generalize the information. After the lesson, they make evaluative decisions concerning student performances and the necessity of reteaching the content. They also reflect and self-evaluate. Teacher effectiveness research supports this instructional cycle (Berliner, 1984; Brophy, 1979; Christenson, Ysseldyke, & Thurlow, 1989; Englert, 1984; Rosenshine, 1995; Rosenshine & Stevens, 1986).

We feel this instructional cycle provides a useful framework whether a teacher follows the reductionist or constructivist paradigm. For example, during the lesson presentation, a teacher may present the subject matter (reductionist paradigm) or encourage a classroom dialogue (constructivist paradigm). In a review

*Effective Teaching By*

of validated practices for teaching mathematics to students with learning disabilities, Miller, Butler, and Lee (1998) reported that no matter the intervention—whether direct instruction, strategy instruction, self-regulation, etc.—instructional procedures followed a modeling, guided practice, feedback, independent practice, and evaluation cycle.

## PLANNING

The IEP is crucial in planning instruction, as students' needs and characteristics are considered. A student's annual goals and short-term objectives form the foundation for planning. We discussed creating IEPs in Chapter 2 and developing annual goals and short-term objectives from assessment data in Chapter 3. Consequently, we do not discuss them again in this chapter. Moreover, instructional arrangements (e.g., large group, small group, peer tutoring, and individual instruction), which are also considered in the planning stage, are not discussed in this section, as they are discussed in other chapters. This section focuses instead on the teacher decisions involved with instructional language, instructional time, motivation, and content.

### Instructional Language

Providing clear, explicit instructions is a strategy related to positive academic achievement (Coker, Medley, & Soar, 1980; Fisher et al., 1980; Rosenshine, 1983). Yet many teachers have problems communicating instructions to students who have special needs, especially students from diverse language backgrounds (Wohlge, 1983). To give directions, you must gain the attention of the students, examine the syntax and semantic content of the message, give visual cues, rephrase instructions, use comprehension checks, and select appropriate vocabulary.

A first step in giving directions or beginning instruction is to make certain that everyone is

 **ACTIVITY 4.1**

This is a quick check of your instructional language. First, find a cooperative friend and sit your friend with his or her back to you. Now, describe the following figures to your friend and have him or her draw them:

To make the task even more realistic, do not allow your friend to ask questions (students with special needs tend not to ask questions to clarify misunderstanding) (Bryan, Donahue, & Pearl, 1981). How did you and your friend do? Chances are that you did not achieve perfect communication. (Answers for this and other activities are found in the Instructor's Manual.)

listening. This is easier said than done. Sometimes, teachers are in such a hurry to teach a concept that they forget that John isn't going to learn it if he is asleep or is talking to Susie. A verbal cue such as "Listen" or "Look at me," followed by silence and then praise for the students who are attending can ensure that all are listening. "May I please have everyone's attention?" followed by "Thank you" is appropriate for secondary students. This cue is particularly effective when stated while standing close to a nonattending student. Other effective cues are silently standing in front of the room until all are quiet at the secondary level and gesturing with one finger in front of the lips for silence at the elementary level.

Syntax and semantics are also considerations for instructional language. An active sentence, such as "The boy hit the ball," is easier to understand than a passive sentence, such as "The ball was hit by the boy" (Wiig & Semel, 1984). Watson, Northcutt, and Rydele (1989) suggest avoiding idiomatic expressions, such as "busy as a bee," when instructing English language learners. Simple sentences are recommended for students whose ability to understand instructional language lags behind their understanding of social language (Wohlge, 1983). Wiig and Semel

(1984) suggest a sentence length of not more than 8 to 10 words.

Visual cues also help students understand instructional language. Simply writing the number 74 on the board clarifies the direction "Turn to page 74 in your math book." Writing the major points of a lecture on a transparency makes the lecture easier for secondary students to follow. Likewise, repeating a direction in a different way often helps students comprehend instructional language. For example, "Locate all the adjectives and underline them in the 10 sentences," can be rephrased as, "Find the descriptive word, or adjective, in each of the sentences and then underline it." These two suggestions are particularly effective for giving instructions to bilingual students with disabilities (Gersten & Woodward, 1994).

Comprehension checks are a necessity when working with students who have special needs. Specific questions are more effective than are general questions (Rosenshine & Stevens, 1986). "Are there any questions?" often results in silence, even though the students do not understand the task, whereas the question, "Robert, what are you to do first?" clarifies whether Robert understands the task and lets you know whether or not you should repeat it. Additionally, specific questions give students opportunities to listen to information again. Frequent comprehension checks are particularly recommended for bilingual students with disabilities (Gersten & Woodward, 1994). We discuss more about comprehension checks later in the chapter.

Vocabulary selection is another important consideration for instructional language. Wiig and Semel (1984) suggest the use of only five unfamiliar vocabulary words per lesson for students with language and learning disabilities. Gersten and Baker (2000) report that words that convey key concepts, are of high utility, and are meaningful should be selected when teaching English language learners. Marker words (such as "remember" or "the first step is" or "this is important") and voice emphasis assist poor

listeners (Alley & Deshler, 1979; Burns, 1980). Brigham, Scruggs, and Mastropieri (1992) report that animated facial expressions, frequent eye contact, expressive and varied voice tones, dramatic body movement, and overall energy had positive effects on attention, behavior, achievement, and attitudes of students with mild disabilities in junior high school classes.

 **ACTIVITY 4.2**

Work with your partner again and notice the improvement in your instructional language and your friend's performance as you describe these four figures:

## Instructional Time

Instructional time is usually divided into time allocated to various instructional activities (allocated time) and time that students are engaged in academic tasks (Greenwood, 1991). In Chapter 2, we discussed allocated time, so here we concentrate on engaged time. Academic learning time (ALT) is the amount of time that students spend engaged in successful completion of relevant learning activities (R. Wilson, 1987). It is closely linked to achievement in elementary students (Fredrick & Walberg, 1980) and students with disabilities (Sindelar, Smith, Harriman, Hale, & Wilson, 1986), including those from culturally diverse backgrounds (Gettinger & Fayne, 1982). Yet, Lago-Delello (1998) reports that kindergarten and first-grade students at risk for the development of serious emotional disturbance spend significantly less time academically engaged than do their peers.

Time on task varies, depending on the special education setting and the instructional techniques. Rich and Ross (1989) report that elementary students in resource room settings have higher levels of on-task behavior than do those in special classes and special schools. They also observed that students spent about 90% of the time on task during teacher instruction and only 60% during seatwork activities. Greenwood (1991) reports that high socioeconomic status (SES) students in suburban schools spent more instructional time in academic-oriented instruction than did low SES students in urban schools.

Presenting shorter and more frequent lessons per hour, using appropriate positioning and eye scanning to monitor the class, and reinforcing appropriate behavior facilitate student task involvement (Englert & Thomas, 1982). Additionally, the instructional technique of peer tutoring promotes more on-task behavior for students with disabilities (Greenwood, 1999). In one research study, students with mild mental retardation and students without disabilities in an inclusive spelling class spent from 5 to 10 minutes more academically engaged during peer tutoring than during teacher-led instruction (Mortweet et al., 1999). We discuss peer tutoring extensively in Chapter 8.

Sometimes students are off task because they are waiting for teacher assistance or for other students to finish assignments. Listing alternatives, such as "go on to the next problem" or "ask for help from your assigned partner," may keep students on task (Olson, 1989). Designing help signs for younger students to place on their desks or having older students take a number for help may decrease the tendency of students to discontinue work because they have their hands raised as they wait for assistance (Olson, 1989). Other times students may be off task as they finish assignments before the period ends. Instead of giving them more of the same work, you may provide (a) a free time area or learning center with games or listening activities; (b) a technology center with software programs and CD-ROMS; (c) magazines such as *National Geographic, People, Seventeen,* and *Hot Rod* for students to read at their desks; (d) social areas in the room for quiet talk (especially appropriate for secondary students who enjoy peer inter-

action); (e) self-selected worksheets to complete for extra credit; and (f) 3-by-5-inch index cards with creative, enjoyable tasks, such as reading to a stuffed animal or calculating the area of the teacher's desk, for students to complete.

Off-task talk prevents on-task behavior. For example, in answer to a question, students sometimes talk about a personal experience that is totally unrelated to the task. To redirect the student to the task at hand and to maintain the momentum or pace of the lesson, you may state that what the student has said does not have anything to do with the topic ("This doesn't relate to our topic. Remember, we are talking about electricity.") or suggest that the topic should be talked about at a later time ("I know that's important, but let's talk about it later."). Of course, you must remember to discuss the topic later if you have promised to do so.

For academic progress to occur, students must not only be on task, but also achieve at a high accuracy level. When answering questions or participating in practice connected with presentation of new material, students should achieve an accuracy level of approximately 80% (Christenson, Thurlow, & Ysseldyke, 1987; Englert, 1984; Wilson, 1987). Christenson, Thurlow, and Ysseldyke (1987) recommend a success rate between 90% and 100% during independent practice and review.

Kounin and his colleagues (Kounin, 1970; Kounin & Gump, 1974; Kounin & Obradovic, 1968) identified several teacher behaviors that decrease noninstructional time and increase appropriate behaviors and time on task. These behaviors, with examples, are explained in Table 4.1.

 **ACTIVITY 4.3**

Meet with three peers and develop three ideas for dealing with students who finish work early at the secondary level and three ideas for the elementary level.

**Table 4.1**  Ways to Increase Instruction Time and Decrease Off-Task Student Behaviors

| Behaviors | Definition | Example |
|---|---|---|
| Withitness | Constant awareness of what is going on in classroom. Selecting the correct inappropriate behavior, stopping it before it escalates, and offering alternative behaviors. | The teacher sees Mike is about to throw a spit ball at Jane and comments, "Mike, please continue—we're on the third paragraph." |
| Overlapping | Attending to more than one situation at a time. | The teacher is teaching a reading mastery lesson when Sally approaches with a question. As part of the class routine Sally knows to sit in the help chair next to the teacher. A few minutes later, the teacher tells the reading group students to practice reading to each other. She then helps Sally quickly and returns to the reading group, praising them for reading so well together. |
| Movement: Smoothness | Staying on track (not reacting to or interjecting irrelevancies). | During the science demonstration, the teacher, instead of listening to Jim's story about what he did last night, quickly states, "We need to talk about science now," and refocuses the attention of the students onto the science demonstration. |
| Movement: Smoothness | Absence of flip-flop or dangle; i.e., starting an activity, stopping it, and then returning to original or dropping it altogether. | Instead of starting the science lesson and then assigning the spelling homework she had forgotten during spelling class, the teacher makes a note in her science text. After science is completed, she reviews homework for the day and includes the spelling words. |
| Movement: Slow Down | Keeping lessons moving briskly, avoiding staying on a topic too long or fragmenting. | When the teacher sees that Tim has his feet in the aisle, she quickly moves toward Tim and taps his leg as she continues with the lecture, as opposed to the teacher who says, "I see some children with their feet in the aisle. Keeping feet in the aisle is dangerous as other students may trip over them. . . ." |
| Group Attention | Taking action to ensure students are attending to task. | The teacher varies individual and group responses or avoids a predictable pattern for calling on students. |
| Group Attention | Encouraging students to participate at all times, even during individual responses. | While Hector works a division problem on the overhead, the rest of the students complete the problem at their desks. |
| Accountability | Letting students know their participation will be monitored. | The teacher circulates as students read to each other. |

## Motivation

As a teacher, you will be faced with the challenge of motivating your students. Offering structured choices relative to curriculum content and procedures can be motivational (Adelman & Taylor, 1983). Even simple choices of whether to do the odd- or even-numbered problems or when to do various worksheets may motivate reluctant adolescents. You may schedule a variety of activities for student selection during independent practice. You may also offer a variety of ways for students to demonstrate their knowledge. One of the most common responses in education is a paper-and-pencil response, which requires students to answer questions on dittos, workbook pages, or at the end of a chapter (Rieth, Polsgrove, Okolo, Bahr, & Eckert, 1987). But students can present their knowledge in other ways as well. In Figure 4.1, we present a sample choice sheet designed for secondary students. The sheet lists different ways to exhibit content knowledge. You may instruct students in how many activities to complete and let them choose the activities. The variety of choices considers the learning styles, interests, and diversity of students. There is also a self-choice option.

Motivation is further enhanced when learning is personally relevant (Good & Brophy, 1984). Explaining why it is necessary to learn the material and applying the objectives to real life are adaptations that teachers can easily make to motivate students (Adelman & Taylor, 1983). "We are studying about business letters because next week we will be writing to the embassies of various countries to ask for information" is an example of giving relevance to the study of business letters. Adding personal relevance is also achieved by linking a student's prior knowledge to the new knowledge. For example, "Jim visited Mesa Verde over the summer so he saw one of the land forms, mesas, that we are studying today. What did you notice about the mesas, Jim?" The consideration of students' personal interests in

the selection of materials motivates secondary students (Zigmond, Sansone, Miller, Donahoe, & Kohnke, 1986). Driver's training manuals, newspapers, sports stories, or student-selected materials are often more reinforcing than a standard secondary text.

Making a commitment to learning and setting goals give students a sense of participation in the learning process. One of the techniques used in the learning strategies curriculum model from the University of Kansas Center for Research on Learning is to ask adolescents to make a commitment to learning a new strategy

**Figure 4.1** Sample Choice Sheet for Secondary Students

Name _____

Date _____

I will do _____ of these to show I understand the

material found in Chapter _____ of

_____ .

_____ 1. Take a test.

_____ 2. Design a technology presentation of the major points.

_____ 3. Write a summary and answer the questions at the end of the chapter.

_____ 4. Tape a summary and the answers to the questions at the end of the chapter.

_____ 5. Complete _____ worksheets.

_____ 6. Discuss the major points with two peers over a tape recorder.

_____ 7. Complete a notebook of major facts.

_____ 8. Your option as approved by the teacher

_____ .

(The following numbers are required by all

_____ .)

before you introduce it. The self-advocacy strategy of the learning strategies curriculum increased adolescents' participation in setting their own goals during IEP conferences (VanReusen & Bos, 1994).

Some teachers even write individual student contracts. In these contracts, students often set their own goals. We have found that students frequently set unrealistic goals, such as "completing 100 problems in a minute" or "scoring 100% on all spelling tests." Therefore, it is helpful to share common performance standards with the students to instill realistic expectations of success. In Figure 4.2, we present a sample contract for a secondary student. The student typed his responses using a word processing program.

In a discussion of the literature concerning motivation for adolescent low achievers, Mercer and Mercer (2001) note the benefit of student involvement. While teaching a secondary basic science class, Ms. Moore motivated students with special needs by asking for student volunteers to lead the class in a discussion of science questions. Before the science discussion, she had written the questions on transparencies and the answers on a piece of notebook paper. Each

volunteer took turns sitting on the teacher's high stool at the front of the class and acting as the teacher. The acting teacher read a question and called on a student to read the section of the textbook that contained the answer. The acting teacher then showed the transparency with the question printed on it, called on a different student for the answer, and wrote the answer on the transparency using the teacher's model. Some of the students led lively discussions and wrote their own answers; others just followed the procedures.

Task-attraction and task-challenge behaviors motivate students to become involved in lesson presentations (Florida Performance Measurement System, 1984). Task attraction is teacher behavior that "expresses or shows genuine zest for a task" (p. 157). Task challenges are statements that indicate "to the students that an exercise or activity will be hard to do" (p. 157). Enthusiastic statements, such as "This next activity is going to be fun" (task attraction), or challenging statements, such as "This is a very difficult concept" or "You'll need your thinking cap on for this one. Hope I don't fool you" (task challenge), are easy to incorporate into a lesson.

**Figure 4.2** Academic Contract

Math Contract

Objective I Will Be Working On:
I will learn to add, subtract, multiply, and divide like fractions and reduce the answers to the lowest terms.

Materials and Techniques:
Participation in teacher-directed lessons during the weeks of November 1-29. Completion of all worksheets and assigned activities.

Goal:
90% on at least 1/2 of the worksheets and activities.
80%-90% on the unit exam.

I have selected the goal and feel it is one I can achieve.

Signed _____ *Juan H.*_____
        (Student)

The fooler game is a task-attraction activity designed to motivate elementary students to pay attention during lesson presentations. Demonstrated by Engelmann during a Distar reading program workshop (personal observation, Chicago, 1978), it involves a game with the teacher playing against the class. First, write sounds, facts, words, or other items on the board. Then explain to the class that they will play a fooler game to practice a particular skill. Continue with, "In this game, I'm going to try to fool you. If I fool you, I get a point, but if I don't, the class gets a point. I'm going to write some letters on the board and tell you the sound. You have to tell me whether I'm right or wrong. Remember, I'm going to try to fool you, so I won't always say the correct sound. Let's see if I can fool you." Then, point to the letter *i* and say, "This is *aa*. Right?" If children say no, reply, "What sound? Yes, a point for you." If the children answer incorrectly, reply, "No, it's *ii*. What sound?" and then, following student repetition of the correct sound, say, "A point for me." Engelmann adapted components of this game into his Direct Instruction reading program.

Ms. Gaines plays a similar game during guided practice of writing skills with her primary class of students with special needs. After teaching the correct printing of a letter, she writes the letter on the board, sometimes correctly and other times incorrectly, and asks each student to tell her whether the letter is correctly printed. If the student is correct, the class gets a point; if not, the teacher does.

A classroom reinforcement system may motivate students to reduce disruptive behaviors and increase academic efforts (Sprick, 1985). A system that many of our student teachers and beginning teachers find effective is a lottery reinforcement system adapted from the Assertive Discipline program (Canter & Associates, 1986). To set up the lottery system, identify the behaviors that you wish to reinforce, then give the students slips of paper when they display these appropriate behaviors. Have the

students write their names on the slips of paper and place them in a container. At the end of the week, draw two names. Have the two winners then draw cards to determine what they have won. Each card should have a number from 1 to 7, representing the number of the reinforcers, except for one card, which says that the student wins all seven prizes. In Table 4.2, we show a lottery system designed to increase the academic performance of a class of secondary students.

 **IMPORTANT POINTS** ◀

1. Teachers enhance instruction when they gain the attention of the students, examine the syntax and semantic content of the message, give visual cues, rephrase instructions, use comprehension checks, and select appropriate vocabulary.
2. Short, active sentences that do not contain idiomatic expressions are easier for students to understand.
3. Comprehension checks involve asking specific questions instead of general ones and require students to repeat the information.
4. Marker words and voice emphasis to stress important points help students comprehend instruction.
5. Academic learning time is the amount of time students spend engaged in successful completion of relevant learning activities.
6. Time on task is influenced by setting (e.g., students in resource rooms spend more time on task than do those in special classes or schools) and instructional strategies (e.g., students spend more time on task during teacher-directed presentations and less time during seatwork activities) (Rich & Ross, 1989).
7. Providing students with alternatives for what to do when waiting for assistance from the teacher or waiting for others to finish their work decreases the amount of time

students spend not engaged in academic activities.

8. For profitable academic learning time, students should maintain an accuracy level of 80% during lesson presentation and between 90% and 100% during independent practice.

9. Offering choices, making learning personally relevant, asking students to make commitments and set goals, actively involving students, making task-challenge and task-attraction comments, and implementing a reinforcement system motivate students to achieve academically and to display appropriate behaviors.

---

**Table 4.2**  Lottery Motivation Example

You will earn chances for the room lottery held every Friday by:

▶ Returning homework on time.
▶ Bringing in paper and pencil.
▶ Participating in class.
▶ Scoring 80% or above on assignments.
▶ Turning in assignments.

The homework and paper-and-pencil tickets will be given out at the beginning of class. All other tickets will be given out at the end of class. Write your name on the tickets and drop them into the lottery container.

On Friday, two winners will be drawn. Being a winner entitles you to draw a card to determine which prize you have won. Each card has a number from 1 to 7, representing the numbers of the prizes. However, one card allows you to win all seven prizes.

---

## Subject Matter

According to Meier (1992), state and local education agencies usually determine the broad content of required courses and subjects, local school district administrators and teachers determine the specific subject area content, and individual teachers usually determine the content for a particular day or lesson. As a special education teacher, you may teach or co-teach all subject areas, so you need to be certain you are knowledgeable of the subject matter.

### *Selection of Subject Matter*

With the passage of the 1997 Amendments to the Individuals with Disabilities Education Act (IDEA, Public Law 105-17), the curriculum for students with disabilities is now aligned with the standards of the general education curriculum. Spurred by Goals 2000, Educate America's School Act (see Chapter 1), states and local districts have developed content (knowledge and skills of a particular subject matter) and performance standards (ways for students to demonstrate proficiency in knowledge and skills of a particular subject matter) to define the knowledge base in subject matter areas. All states have developed standards for mathematics, science, social studies, and language arts (McDonnell, McLaughlin, & Morrison, 1997). Some states outline general goals, whereas other states specify standards that identify what students must demonstrate at various grade levels. In the state of Florida, student performance standards are identified for four grade clusters: PreK–2, 3–5, 6–8, and 9–12 and organized into strands (across seven subject areas), standards (expected learning achievement), and benchmarks (learner expectations at end of grade) (Beech, 1997). For example, a benchmark for students in PreK–2 to meet the reading standard of "the student uses reading processes effectively" is "students are expected to predict what the content of the text will be from its title or illustrations" (Beech, 1997, p. 7). The benchmark for students in grades 6–8 to meet the same reading standard is "students are expected to predict the content, purpose, and organization of the text based on their background knowledge and their knowledge of text structure" (Beech, 1997, p. 7). Many states and districts link standards to graduation from high school for the general education population and the special education population (McLaughlin, Nolet, Rhim, & Henderson, 1999). McLaughlin and colleagues (1999) caution that small, discrete behavioral objectives may be useful only for daily planning, but teachers must learn to align content and instruction across grade levels to prepare students with disabilities to pass the curriculum standards. Thus, the standards serve as guidelines for lesson planning, so be certain to check your district's standards.

Once you have identified the standards, teachers' manuals, written for both special and general education curriculum, can assist in the daily selection and sequencing of subject matter. The manuals may also include ideas for motivation, critical thinking questions, enrichment activities, reteaching tips, activities for English-language learners, and a list of typical student errors.

In some popular commercial curriculum programs used in the teaching of students with special needs, such as *Reading Mastery* (Engelmann & Bruner, 1988), *Skills for School Success* (Archer & Gleason, 1989), and the *Learning Strategies* curriculum (Deshler & Schumaker, 1986), the subject matter is clearly specified and the lessons are scripted.

In addition to teachers' manuals, students' ideas and background information may provide a resource for the selection and sequencing of content. In an example from the Foxfire approach used with students with disabilities, the teacher presents the objectives mandated by state or district standards and the IEP, but students develop their learning experiences and negotiate how the objectives are to be achieved (Ensminger & Dangel, 1992).

Whether you use a manual or students' ideas and background information, you must analyze the subject matter to determine whether students have the necessary prerequisite skills to master the new material. In the planning stage, you should ask yourself if the students might have difficulty with the new information because

it builds on information that they are lacking. For example, Miller and Milam (1987) found that students with learning disabilities had difficulty mastering the new content of division because they had difficulty with subtraction or multiplication. A systematic way to sequence skills is to complete a task analysis.

### Task Analysis

Task analysis involves breaking down a task or objective being taught into simpler components. To perform a task analysis, you must identify "the terminal behavior, list the necessary prerequisite skills and list the component skills in sequence" (Alberto & Troutman, 1999, p. 277). Prerequisite skills are skills that students must master *before* they can be taught a terminal behavior. In the previous division example, students were unsuccessful at mastering division problems (the terminal behavior) because they could not subtract or multiply accurately (prerequisite skills). They may also be unsuccessful because you have not identified the component skills that must be mastered *on the way* to reaching the terminal behavior. The component skills may be either parallel or sequential (Desberg & Taylor, 1986). Parallel component skills have no sequential order; that is, it doesn't matter which component skill you teach first. Skills are sequential if their order is invariant; that is, each component skill cannot be mastered unless the previous one has been mastered. For example, if the terminal behavior is to discriminate between mass and weight, it doesn't matter whether you teach students to define *mass* or *weight* first (parallel component skills). However, you must teach students the definition of *mass* and *weight* before you can teach them to discriminate between the concepts (sequential component skills).

Thus, when you are planning a lesson, you need to consider prerequisite and component skills. For example, let's say that your objective involves teaching Heather to multiply accurately problems with percents, such as $25\% \times 33$. In your plan, you need to make certain Heather knows the prerequisite skills of multiplying two-digit times two-digit problems with and without regrouping. Thus, you should begin the lesson by having her multiply two-digit times two-digit problems, such as 15 × 24. By including such problems, you automatically check whether she knows the multiplication process, addition process, multiplication facts, and addition facts, the prerequisite skills required for success. The next step in your planning is to think about the component skills: "What steps should I teach first?" Performing the task yourself shows that Heather must convert the percents to decimals (25% = .25), multiply (.25 × 33), and then place the decimal point in the proper place in the answer (8.25). Now, you know the steps that may need prompting for successful completion of the task.

If you are planning to assign a commercial worksheet or lesson from a commercial text for the students to work on independently, a task analysis may identify the content to emphasize during instruction. For example, from the commercially prepared worksheet in Table 4.3, Ms. Monti decided that she had better emphasize the following capitalization rules during her lesson presentation:

1. Capitalize the beginning of a sentence (Sentences 2 and 6).
2. Capitalize the pronoun *I* (Sentence 3).

**Table 4.3** Capitalization Worksheet

*Directions*: Circle the capitalization errors below in the nine sentences.

1. Look at the old Car with the shiny hubcaps.
2. they did a fun activity in class.
3. Yesterday i went to see dr. jones.
4. did you like the movie *gremlins*?
5. Chicago is a City in Illinois.
6. monkeys are funny to watch at the zoo.
7. We went to see mother.
8. Do you know dr. smith, the dentist?
9. I really enjoyed reading a *wrinkle in time*.

3. Capitalize the names and titles of persons and things (Sentences 3, 4, 8, and 9).
4. Capitalize the word *mother* when it is used as a substitute for a name (Sentence 7).
5. Do not capitalize common nouns (Sentences 1 and 5).

 **ACTIVITY 4.4**

Using task analysis, identify the capitalization rules that students must know to complete these two sentences successfully.

1. We have left our airline Tickets at home.
2. Sunfa did not like the movie roger rabbit.

### Types of Subject Matter

The academic subject matter found in classrooms typically falls into the categories of basic concepts or skills, concepts, rules, laws, lawlike principles, and value judgments (Engelmann & Carnine, 1982; Florida Performance Measurement System, 1984). Within basic concepts or skills, we add verbal associations (facts with only one correct answer such as names of state capitals) and related facts or verbal chains (days of the week) from the work of Kameenui and Simons (1990). Basic concepts or skills may be found in any subject area. Rules are often found in reading, spelling, grammar, and math content; laws in the natural sciences; and lawlike principles in social studies. Value judgments are often found in social skills and self-help content.

As you are planning, correct identification of the types of subject matter leads to the correct selection of the content that you should directly teach or elicit from the students. For example, when teaching the subject matter of concepts, you need to include the definition, examples, nonexamples, attributes, and comparisons when you present the lesson. Then, to be certain that students really understand the concept, you must ask them to identify whether new illustrations are examples of the concept or not

(Beech, 1997). In her lesson about proper nouns, Ms. Sully presented the definition of "A proper noun is the name of a particular person, place, or thing," examples of proper nouns such as "Bill, the Grand Canyon, and Saturday," nonexamples of proper nouns such as "boy, canyon, day, and jump," and attributes such as proper nouns are capitalized. She also compared proper nouns to common nouns. Then she asked students to identify which of the following were proper nouns: desk, Milwaukee Bucks, purple, girl, Sally. See Table 4.4 for specific guidelines concerning subject matter types.

### Complexity of Subject Matter

Controlling task difficulty is an effective strategy for teaching reading and writing to students with learning disabilities (Vaughn, Gersten, & Chard, 2000). One way to control task difficulty is to present concepts in small steps. For example, after performing a task analysis on counting coins, Ms. James taught the students (1) to count pennies and had them practice that step, (2) to count nickels and had them practice that step, (3) to count pennies and nickels and had them practice that step. She preceded in small steps until the students were able to count coins from quarters to pennies.

Proponents of the constructivist model feel that teachers should refrain from breaking tasks into small steps, because that results in a lack of meaning (Poplin, 1988; Heshusius 1989). Instead, they recommend that teachers use scaffolding strategies to decrease the complexity of subject matter and preserve the meaning. With scaffolding, a teacher supports and guides learners in taking the risk to achieve a task just beyond the learner's capabilities. The teacher provides supports until the student can achieve the task independently. For example, to decrease the subject matter complexity involved in counting coins, Ms. Wolfe did not break the subject matter into small steps as Ms. James did. Instead, she decided to present all the coins at once and to provide students with a cue card, which reminded them to sort and count coins in

order from largest to smallest and of the value of each coin.

### Count

Quarter—25 cents

Dime—10 cents

Nickel—5 cents

Penny—1 cent

 **ACTIVITY 4.5**

**Part 1.**

You are teaching Jim how to round numbers as one of his IEP objectives involves rounding numbers. You plan to teach the rule: "When you round off a number, you should compare it to 5. If the number is higher than 5, you round up. If the number is lower than 5, you round down." Identify the content or subject matter that you should teach. Hint: Check the information found in Table 4.4 under Rule.

**Part 2.**

Use scaffolding to decrease the complexity of the rounding rule found in Part 1 of this activity.

### Instructional Alignment

Instructional alignment is the amount of congruence among the objectives, instructional procedures, and evaluation procedures of a lesson (Cohen, 1987). What you intend to teach should match what you teach and what you assess (West, Idol, & Cannon, 1989). An example of nonalignment is found in the following lesson. The teacher, Ms. Harper, planned to teach students to identify adjectives. During the lesson, she asked students to circle the adjectives in each sentence, and then during evaluation, she required them to write sentences with adjectives. Ms. Harper has matched the objective to the instructional procedures, but not to the evaluation procedures. Requiring students to write a sentence with *beautiful* in it (the evaluation task) is more difficult than her objective of requiring students to circle the adjective in a sentence, as in, "The

**Table 4.4**  Types of Subject Matter

**What Content to Include When You Are Teaching**

Basic Concepts or Skills—Simple facts, verbal chains, or verbal associations
    *The color red* (simple fact)
    Examples—*red apple, red block, red truck*
    Nonexamples—*blue truck, blue block, green square*
    Or
    *The days of the week* (verbal chains)
    Examples—*Sunday, Monday, Tuesday, Wednesday, Thursday, Friday,* & *Saturday*
    Nonexamples—January, February, March
    Or
    *States and capitals* (verbal associations)
    Examples—Sacramento, California; Denver, Colorado
    Nonexamples—Sacramento, New Mexico; Denver, Rhode Island
Concepts—Abstract or generic idea
    *Verb* (example)
    Definition—*A verb is a word that indicates action or state of being*
    Examples—*run, jump, is,* and *are*
    Nonexamples—*girl, man,* and *to*
    Attributes—*Verbs often follow subjects*
    Comparisons—*A verb doesn't name a person, place, or thing like a noun does.*
    Identify new examples—*Over–no*
                           *Smile–yes*
Rule—A prescribed guide for action
    *A capitalization rule* (example)
    Rule identification—*Begin a sentence with a capital letter.*
    Application items—*the boy is my friend and off the chair*
    Justification of the rule—*Tell why the rule was or was not used.*
Laws or Principles—Explanation of physical behavior
    *Movement of electricity* (example)
    Law identification—*Electricity can pass through a closed circuit only.*
    Cause and effect—*If the circuit is closed, then electricity can pass through.*
    Application items—*Experiment with wires and a battery cell to turn on a light bulb.*
Lawlike Principles—Explanation of human or animal behaviors
    *Camouflage* (example)
    Principle identification—*Animals use camouflage to hide from their enemies.*
    Cause and effect—*If a chameleon thinks an enemy is near, it will turn the color of its surroundings.*
    Application items—*Discover other animals and ways they camouflage themselves.*
Value Judgment—Evaluation of the value of things
    *Pam's behavior was appropriate* (example)
    Development of criteria—*Calm voice, polite*
    Identification of facts—*Pam asked, "May I please borrow a pencil?"*
    Comparison—*Calm voice—Yes*
                        *Polite—yes*

beautiful girl is crying." To correct this nonalignment, Ms. Harper should require students to identify adjectives in sentences during evaluation. Cohen (1987) finds that students with academic difficulty have problems with lack of instructional alignment.

112 CHAPTER 4

**ACTIVITY 4.6**

Decide whether each of the following items are aligned and then change them if they are not:

1. The teacher taught the students to reduce fractions and included problems such as 2/4 = 1/2, 4/6 = 2/3, 5/20 = 1/4 in her lesson presentation. She then passed out a worksheet with the following direction of "Convert the problems into mixed numbers" and problems such as 20/7, 14/5, and 10/3.

2. The teacher taught the students to describe a reptile. To evaluate whether they could describe a reptile, she placed the students in groups and had them make a list of dangerous and friendly reptiles.

▶ **IMPORTANT POINTS** ◀

1. Task analysis requires the identification of prerequisite skills, component skills, and terminal behaviors or objectives.

2. Prerequisite skills are skills that students must master *before* they can master the terminal objective. Component skills are skills that must be mastered *on the way* to mastering a terminal objective.

3. Definitions, examples, nonexamples, attributes, comparisons, and identification of new examples are usually presented when teaching concepts; examples and nonexamples are used when teaching basic concepts or skills.

4. The use of examples, nonexamples, and the defense of whether or not a rule applies are necessary in teaching rules.

5. When teaching laws and lawlike principles, effective teachers state and discuss cause and effect and lead students in applications.

6. Development of criteria is necessary in the teaching of value judgments.

7. When students are first learning a new skill, effective teachers decrease the complexity of materials by presenting a number of small, sequenced steps or by using scaffolding procedures.

8. With scaffolding, a teacher supports and guides learners in taking the risk to achieve a task just beyond the learner's capabilities.

9. Instructional alignment is the amount of congruence among the objectives, instructional procedures, and evaluation procedures of a lesson (Cohen, 1987).

10. Students with academic difficulty have problems with lack of instructional alignment (Cohen, 1987).

## PRESENTATION

Archer and Isaacson (1990) divide lessons into three parts: opening, body, and closing. To these areas, we add guided practice and feedback. Of course, feedback is given throughout the lesson presentation.

### Opening

To teach students, you must *gain their attention.* Sometimes, this is done by verbally cueing the students with "Look at me" for young students or "I need everyone's attention" for older ones. Sometimes, nonverbal cues, such as silently waiting in front of the room or flicking the light switch, are used. Hunter (1981) recommends an anticipatory set as a way to cue attention and open a lesson. An anticipatory set is a statement or an activity that introduces the content and motivates students to learn. For example, one of our student teachers dressed up like a pilgrim to lead a discussion of the first Thanksgiving.

Once you have everyone's attention, Rosenshine and Stevens (1986), in their summary of the teacher effectiveness research, suggest beginning a lesson with a *short review of prerequisite skills.* We previously discussed the use of task analysis to identify prerequisite skills. *Relating the current lesson to previous lessons* is also recommended when introducing a new skill to students with special needs (Cohen, 1986; Englert, 1984; Goodman, 1985). For example, a review of the definition of a paragraph from the previous lesson should precede a new lesson dealing with various kinds of paragraphs.

An *overview* or preview of the instructional activities quickly informs the students of the day's events. For example, Ms. Maddalozzo begins her lesson, "Today we are going to spend time discussing some major holidays in November. First, we will discuss the information, then we'll do a few of the items together on the worksheet, and then you will do a few items alone. After we finish with the worksheets, we will do an activity involving a holiday in November."

An introduction that is especially effective for students with problem behaviors is *sharing expectations* concerning the behavior rules of the lesson (Borg & Ascione, 1982; Englert, 1984; Evertson & Emmer, 1982; Rosenberg, 1986). Sharing behavioral expectations is particularly important at the beginning of the year and when new students enter a program. Mr. Phillips begins his lesson with, "I expect everyone to listen politely while other students read. If a reader makes a mistake, I will correct the student."

Other opening strategies include *sharing rationales* (Archer & Isaacson, 1990; Palincsar & Brown, 1989; Schumaker & Sheldon, 1985) and discussing situations where the skill may be used (Palincsar & Brown, 1989; Schumaker & Sheldon, 1985). Duffy, Roehler, and Rackliff

(1986) found that sharing the objective of a lesson and relating its importance to real life motivated readers who were reading one or more years below grade level. Rationales, such as "This lesson should help you read the back of a cereal box," influenced the amount of information that the low achievers remembered from the lesson. Describing the benefits of using different learning strategies in school, for employment, and in general also motivated secondary students with mild disabilities (Lenz, Alley, & Schumaker, 1987).

Because students come to school with prior information, *activating background knowledge* is an effective way to open a lesson (Palincsar & Brown, 1989; Rosenshine & Stevens, 1986). One of the techniques to use to activate this prior knowledge is prediction (Langer, 1984; Ogle, 1986). With prediction, the teacher is creating a group background knowledge base.

In Figure 4.3, we present a form for using prediction in preparation for reading an article about Christa McAuliffe, the first teacher scheduled to make a shuttle flight. The first two columns are completed with the students before reading and the last after the students have read the article. Notice that in the first column, guided by the teacher, the students discuss what they already "Know" from their background experiences and create a group knowledge base. In the "Think You'll Learn" column, students examine titles, pictures, and captions to make predictions about the

**Figure 4.3** Prediction Form

| What Do You . . . | | |
|---|---|---|
| **Know?** | **Think You'll Learn?** | **Know You Learned?** |
| She was a teacher. | How she trained for the flight? | |
| She died in an explosion of the shuttle. | Why she wanted to be an astronaut? | |
| She had to compete to be selected to join the crew. | How many children she had? | |
| She was married. | What classes she taught? | |

content. The last column, "Know You Learned," requires students to compare their predictions to the events described. For students from different cultural backgrounds, Ruiz (1989) suggests a variation of the prediction routine. In her variation, the teacher identifies the major idea of the selection, asks the students to relate any similar experiences, and then asks the students to predict what will happen in the story.

For students who may not have the necessary prior knowledge to understand text information, Hasselbring (1998) recommends the use of *anchoring activities* to help build backgrounds. Anchoring is using real-world situations to develop meaningful knowledge (Bransford, Sherwood, Hasselbring, Kinzer, & Williams, 1990). For example, in the *Young Explorers* multimedia reading program, teachers show a videotape of the story before they expect students to read the text (Hasselbring, Goin, Taylor, Bottge, & Daley, 1997). Brown (1991) recommends bringing in concrete objects, showing a film, or role-playing to help build background information for the Native American student.

 **ACTIVITY 4.7**

### Part 1.

For a group of elementary students with special needs, decide how you would open a lesson with the following objective: When presented with two-digit numbers and asked to round them off to the nearest 10, students will round off the numbers at a rate of at least 20 digits correct and no more than 2 digits incorrect per minute for three sessions.

### Part 2.

For a group of secondary students with special needs, decide how you would open a lesson with the following objective: When presented with a paragraph from a history text, students will paraphrase the content with 100% accuracy.

## Body

Modeling, teacher–student dialoguing, scaffolding instruction, lecturing, questioning, and guided practice may occur during the body of a lesson when new information is presented (Christenson, Ysseldyke, & Thurlow, 1989; Deshler & Schumaker, 1986; Palincsar & Brown, 1989; Larkin, 2001). Peer-mediated instruction may also occur in the body and during guided practice. See Chapter 8 for a detailed discussion of various peer-mediated instruction. We also include a discussion of feedback here, even though feedback permeates a lesson.

### *Modeling*

Modeling is defined as a "teacher's active performance of a skill" (Haring & Eaton, 1978, p. 25). Teacher modeling is recommended when students are just acquiring a skill (the acquisition stage). Teachers may model the steps to a problem or use think-alouds. In think-alouds, teachers model their thought processes. Think-alouds are frequently used in teaching learning strategies. Modeling is effective for all levels and ethnic groups of students with special needs (Cohen, 1986; Englert, 1984; Graham, 1985; Rivera & Smith, 1988).

An example of modeling the steps of a problem is found in Mr. Clarke's oral introduction to long division: "The first step to work the problem 365 divided by 5 is to ask if 3 can be divided by 5. It cannot, so 36 will have to be divided by 5. Thirty-six divided by 5 is about 7, because 7 times 5 is 35. The next step is to subtract 35 from 36, which yields a remainder of 1. One cannot be divided by 5, so bring down the 5, which makes the number 15. Fifteen divided by 5 is 3. The answer is 73." Of course, Mr. Clarke is drawing a visual model of each step of the problem on the board as he completes each step verbally.

Duffy, Roehler, and Rackliff (1986) described a think-aloud for low-achieving readers. In this think-aloud, teachers talk about their thought processes and the steps to the strategy. We have modeled the following think-aloud after theirs.

> Mr. Clarke begins: Today, I'd like to share with you a strategy I use when I come to a word that I don't know when I'm reading. I'll think out loud so you can hear my thoughts.
>
> **First**, I read the unknown word in the sentence. The weather forecaster said there will be snow flurries. I know I've heard the word *flurries* before, but I don't know what it means.
>
> My **second** step is to see if there are any other words in that sentence that can help me figure out the word. The word before *flurries* is *snow*, so it has something to do with snow. Hm. It may mean it's going to snow a lot or it may mean it isn't going to snow much.
>
> The **third** step is to read more of the sentences. OK, I'll read on. The next sentence says, "When the little boy heard the weather report, he became angry, because he wanted to build a snowman."
>
> The **fourth** step is to use any background information. I think that sentence can help me figure the word out, because I know that you have to have a lot of snow to build a snowman. My brother and I used to make snowmen all the time.
>
> The **fifth** step is to guess at the meaning. Now I bet I know what *flurries* means. I think it means light snow.
>
> The **last** step is to substitute the meaning and reread the sentences. Let me go back and check. "The weather forecaster said there will be snow flurries or light snow. When the little boy heard the weather report, he became angry, because he wanted to build a snowman." Yep, I'm right.

▼ **ACTIVITY 4.8**

Take the example of Mr. Clarke's long division and change it to a think-aloud modeling procedure.

## Teacher–Student Dialoguing

In reciprocal teaching, Palincsar and Brown (1984) teach students to generate their own questions and to ask questions of others as they compose a dialogue to learn new information (see Chapter 6). After writing the following two-syllable words (chimney, open, coaster, intend, and today) on the overhead, Mr. Leonard asks the students if they think these words are alike in any way. No student replies so Mr. Leonard continues with, "Any idea of how we might go about figuring it out?" One of the student replies, "Maybe, we should look at individual letters." Another student says, "Maybe, we should try to say the words and that would help." The teacher asks, "Any other ideas?" "Which one do you think we should try?" The class decides, as a group, to pronounce the words and see if that will help. The teacher asks if anyone would like to read the first word. The dialogue continues in the same manner until the class concludes that the commonality is that the words contain two parts and that the parts are called syllables.

## Scaffolding Instruction

Previously in the chapter, we discussed how scaffolding can decrease the complexity of subject matter. In this section, we describe some scaffolding procedures that can be used in the body of the lesson. Remember, in scaffolding, teachers assist and support students until students can complete the task independently. Hogan and Pressley (1997) suggest that teachers assist students through prompting, questioning, modeling, telling, and discussing. Rosenshine (1990) recommends the use of procedural facilitators and anticipation of students' errors as specific scaffolding strategies.

Procedural facilitators may include hints or prompts, cue cards, and half-done examples. Listing the steps of rounding hundreds, beginning with the first step of "Look at the number in the ten's position" provides hints to students. Montague and Leavell (1994) used grammar cue cards to improve the quality and length of stories by junior high students with learning disabilities. The cue cards contained key words such as *where, when, characters, problem and plan*, and *story ending*. These key words reminded students to include this information in their stories. Half-done examples provide questions or statement starters, such as "That doesn't sound right because *cold* means _____," for students to complete.

In anticipating student errors, effective teachers point out the material that is easily misunderstood. For example, Mr. Anderson, in discussing the spelling of *all right*, mentioned that most students forget that it is two words and spell it as *alright*. It may be difficult to anticipate mistakes at first, but with experience you will begin to recognize content that may prove particularly troublesome for students.

Foorman and Torgesen (2001) describe a scaffolding procedure that directly shows children who are at risk for reading difficulties the thinking or process necessary to complete a reading task successfully. First, the student is presented with a reading task (read the word *emergency*). When the student makes an error or doesn't know how to proceed (reads the word *emergency* as *emercy*), the teacher asks a question that "focuses the child's attention on a first step in the solution process, or that draws attention to the required piece of information" (p. 209). For example, you are correct on the first part of the word *emer*, let's look at this part, *gency*. "Any idea?" The child responds again. The questioning and prompting continue until the student discovers the information without being told directly.

### Lecturing

Often, at the secondary level, especially in an inclusive classroom, teachers present information through the lecturing technique. During lecturing teachers should limit their amount of talk, because research shows that active student involvement is essential during lesson presentation (Christenson, Ysseldyke, & Thurlow, 1989; Schumaker, Nolan, & Deshler, 1985). There-

fore, the three-statement rule (Schumaker, Nolan, & Deshler, 1985)—the teacher will make no more than three statements without having a student make a response—is essential to remember.

Some effective adaptations to ensure that students with disabilities are engaged during a lecture is to use the instructional-pause procedure, think-pair-share routine, Numbered Heads Together (NHT; Kagan, 1992), guided note taking, and visual aids. The instructional-pause procedure and NHT involve the teacher interacting with students in groups. Sparks (2000) lists the use of visual aids during lecturing as an effective strategy for teaching Native American students.

In the instructional-pause procedure, the teacher lectures and then allows time for student discussion. During the brief discussion, the students may identify the main idea and important points and predict the next section of the lecture, or they may share notes and review information. In a secondary social studies class, the following co-teaching instructional-pause procedure was established. The general educator, Mr. Green, lectured for 10 minutes, then had the students repeat the important points in small peer groups for about 3 minutes while he and the special education teacher monitored the comments of the various groups. Both teachers then listed the major points on an overhead projector, asked questions of the groups to summarize the relevant features of the lecture, and clarified any misunderstandings that they heard while monitoring the group discussions.

In the think-pair-share routine, the teacher asks students in pairs to think about the topic for a minute, discuss it, and then share their ideas with the rest of the group. Mr. Green and his co-teacher could just as easily incorporate this routine during the social studies class.

To use NHT, teachers divide students into hetergeneous learning teams and have students number themselves 1 to 4. The teacher continues to lecture and asks questions. After asking a question instead of calling on one student, the teacher directs the students to put their heads together to arrive at the best answer and to make certain that everyone in their group knows and understands the answer. The teacher then randomly calls on different students to respond (all 3s tell the answer). Other class members then argue or expand on the answer. When NHT was used in a third-grade social studies class and a sixth-grade science class, students with and without disabilities performed better on exams and had higher on-task rates than those in whole-group instruction (Maheady, Harper, & Malette, 2001).

With guided note taking, students are actively involved during a lecture as they complete a teacher-prepared handout to assist them in taking notes from the lecture. The guided note handout consists of cues and spaces for students to write key facts, concepts, and important relationships while the teacher is lecturing. For example, guided notes concerning the taxes levied by the British on the colonists may include a statement that says:

1.  To increase revenue, the British decided to levy _____ on the colonists. Some of the products taxed were
    a.  _____
    b.  _____
    c.  _____

Guided notes resulted in the taking of more accurate notes and in improved quiz scores for middle and secondary students with disabilities (Heward, 1994). Heward (1994) recommends that guided notes include the use of consistent cues (lines, bullets, etc.), more than a simple fill-in-the-blank format, daily quizzes as a follow-up activity, and minimal student writing, along with the inclusion of all facts, concepts, and relationships that students must learn. In Chapter 9, we discuss guided notes in detail with more examples.

With PowerPoint and other publishing technology, teachers can easily prepare visual aids listing the important points of a lecture.

The students may either copy notes from the prepared transparencies or receive copies of the prepared transparencies. For example, Ms. Montgomery prepared a PowerPoint presentation to correlate with her lecture on the effects of global warming. She also provided students with copies of the transparencies in a student packet that contained three slides per page (handouts—3 slides per page option of the print command of the PowerPoint program). Then, students added any extra points that came up during the discussions.

### Questioning
Teachers use questioning during lesson presentation to elicit student involvement (Engelmann & Carnine, 1982), to foster cognitive learning (Florida Performance Measurement System, 1984), to reinforce concepts, and to monitor and adjust instruction (Christenson, Ysseldyke, & Thurlow, 1989).

Teachers may also teach students to generate their own questions. In summarizing the critical findings in a synthesis of research conducted with students with learning disabilities, Vaughn, Gersten, and Chard (2000) report that directed response questioning or teaching students to generate their own questions while reading, solving math problems, or composing an essay produced a strong impact on student learning. Teaching students to self-question is discussed extensively in Chapter 6 under metacognition and other cognitive strategies.

***Involving Students.*** Questioning students is a way to increase their academic responding time. Academic responding time is the time that students spend making active, overt responses. It is positively related to achievement (Greenwood, Delquadri, & Hall, 1984). Even though teacher questioning can effectively involve all students, minority and low-achieving students are not given as many opportunities to respond in class as other students (Reid, 1986; Stanley & Greenwood, 1983). Teachers advance the following reasons for not calling on low achievers: to protect the student from embarrassment, to prevent a slowdown of the lesson, and to ensure that everyone will hear a good answer (Christenson, Thurlow, & Ysseldyke, 1987). To ensure that every student is given an opportunity to respond to questions, you may call on students in a fixed order or put each student's name on an index card, which you flip once the student is called on. Another strategy to involve all students is to call on students with disabilities first whenever you ask a question with many parts. For example, a question such as "What were the three causes of the uprising?" is easier for a student to answer when first asked than after other students have responded with two causes.

***Fostering Cognitive Learning.*** A number of studies (Englert, 1984; Goodman, 1985) demonstrate that it is best to use low-level, fast-paced questions that produce many correct responses and elicit the involvement of students with special needs when teaching basic concepts or skills. These low-level questions generally fall into the knowledge domain of Bloom's taxonomy of cognitive development (1956). Use of only low-level questions (recall questions) hinders the development of higher-level thinking skills (Meier, 1992). Higher-level thinking skills include comprehension, application, analysis, synthesis, and evaluation (Bloom, 1956). Asking students to list the effects of the Civil War is an example of a low-level recall question; asking students to compare and contrast the effects of the Civil War on the northern states as opposed to the southern states is an example of a high-level question. See Table 4.5 for some key words to assist in asking different levels of questions based on Bloom's taxonomy and adapted from the work of Morgan and Saxton (1994).

 **ACTIVITY 4.9**

Using the sample question stems found in Table 4.5, write questions for each of the levels about the movie *Star Wars Episode II—Attack of the Clones* or about one of your favorite books.

***Reinforcing and Repeating Information.*** Teachers also use questioning to reinforce and repeat information (Engelmann & Carnine, 1982). For example, Mr. Pratt asked these two questions to reinforce the fact that three-fourths of the earth is covered with water: (a) "How much of the earth is covered with water?" and (b) "Three-fourths of the earth is covered with what?" With

**Table 4.5**   Sample Question Stems Based on Bloom's Taxonomy

1. Knowledge
     Who, what, when, and where
2. Comprehension
     What is the main idea . . . ? What is meant by . . . ?
3. Application
     How would you . . . ? What would happen if . . . ?
4. Analysis
     Why? What was the author's purpose in . . . ?
5. Synthesis
     Do you suppose that . . . ? What if . . . ?
6. Evaluation

     Which is better . . . ? What do you think . . . ? Would you tend to agree that . . . ?

these questions, the fact that three-fourths of the earth is covered with water is repeated. Repetition is frequently recommended for bilingual students with disabilities (Gersten & Woodward, 1994).

***Monitoring and Adjusting Instruction.*** Specific questions, such as "What is the next step in the operation, Bob?" or "What kind of punctuation marks do you use at the end of a sentence?" serve as checks of comprehension and enable you to monitor and adjust instruction. The answers to specific questions will inform you if you should reteach concepts or skills or change the content of the lesson. If the students cannot answer the questions, you should reteach the concept instead of continuing with a new one. Rosenshine and Stevens (1986) identify three errors teachers frequently make in monitoring for understanding: (1) asking a general question (e.g., "Do you understand?") and then assuming, if there are no questions, that everyone understands; (2) calling only on volunteers, who usually know the answers, and assuming that other students know the answers, too; and (3) asking only a few questions. An effective routine is to ask specific questions after giving instructions or directions.

***Nonacademic Questioning.*** Nonacademic questions frequently disrupt the flow of a lesson (Florida Performance Measurement System, 1984) and may lead to noncompliant behavior. Remember, an academic focus increases academic learning time, which results in higher achievement for students with special needs. For example, during her experience in a primary setting with students with special needs, a student teacher asked a 7-year-old student, "Joey, will you read the next two paragraphs?" to which he replied, "No, let Jamey do it." Now the student teacher was faced with another problem. This type of response to a nonacademic question is not unusual for noncompliant students. A nicely stated command, "Please read

the next two paragraphs, Joey," is a better way to proceed.

***Wait Time.*** Two types of wait time are connected with questioning. One involves the amount of time a teacher waits for a student's response after asking a question. The other concerns the amount of time a teacher waits after a student's response to ask another question. Rowe (1974) investigated both types of wait time in elementary science classes and found that teachers waited an average of 1 second for a student's response after asking a question and 0.9 seconds after a student's response before asking another question. When teachers increased the amount of wait time, students responded with longer answers, volunteered answers more frequently, and even initiated more questions. Teachers who use appropriate wait time are more flexible, ask a greater variety of questions, listen more carefully to answers, expect more of students, and demonstrate more genuine interest (Rowe, 1987).

In a review of wait-time research, Tobin (1987) stated that a 3- to 5-second wait time enhanced achievement in all content areas with all levels of students, kindergarten through 12th grade. Wait time is also important for bilingual students who have language-processing difficulties (Watson, Northcutt, & Rydele, 1989).

The suggestion to increase wait time may seem to contradict the instructional procedure of asking many questions that require quick, short student responses when teaching basic skills. It certainly is not appropriate for a teacher to wait 5 seconds when asking a child what sound a short *a* makes. Tobin (1987) suggests that the amount of wait time is a function of the type of question. He contends that low-level cognitive questions require less wait time and high-level questions require more. This is a logical explanation of the difference between the results of the wait-time research, which shows achievement enhanced by a 3- to 5-second pause after questioning, and the teacher-effectiveness research, which shows that a brisk pace of teacher questioning and a high frequency of accurate student responses are effective for teaching basic skills.

 **ACTIVITY 4.10**

Change the following ineffective questioning techniques to effective ones:

1. A secondary teacher asks, "Sarah, why is this an example of a narrative paragraph? What is the relevant cue? How can you tell?"
2. A primary teacher asks, "Do you understand?" after reading the directions of the activity to the students.

 **IMPORTANT POINTS**

1. Effective ways to open a lesson include the use of an anticipatory set, a short review of either prerequisite skills or previous lessons, an overview, sharing expectations and rationales, activating background knowledge, and anchoring activities.
2. Modeling may involve orally presenting the steps to a problem.
3. In think-alouds, teachers share their thought processes.
4. Instructional-pause procedures, think-pair-share routines, guided notes, and visual aids are suggested to insure more active student participation during lecturing.
5. Questioning is used to elicit active student involvement, to foster cognitive learning, to reinforce concepts, to monitor, and to adjust instruction.
6. Procedural facilitators are prompts that help students when they begin to learn a skill.
7. Teaching students to generate their own questions produced a strong impact on student learning (Vaugh, Gersten, & Chard, 2001).

8. Low-level, fast-paced questions produce many correct responses and elicit much student involvement when teaching basic skills, whereas high-level, slow-paced questions are generally required in the teaching of higher-level cognitive thinking.
9. Specific questions, such as "What is the next step in the operation, Bob?" serve as checks of comprehension and enable teachers to monitor and adjust instruction.
10. Nonacademic questions frequently disrupt the flow of a lesson and may lead to noncompliant student behavior.
11. Wait time refers either to the amount of time a teacher waits for a student's response after asking a question or the amount of time a teacher waits after a student's response to ask another question.

## Guided Practice

Guided practice is active participation directed by the teacher. After presenting subject matter, the teacher leads the students in practice of the information. Often, guided practice is alternated with teacher modeling and demonstration, so that presentation and practice appear as one (Rosenshine & Stevens, 1986). A common practice routine in general education classrooms is to call on one student to demonstrate the answer to a problem on the board while other students watch. To increase the active participation of and extra practice for all students, simply have the other students complete the problem at their desks. One of our interns supplied her students with small individual chalkboards. You may also use peer tutoring or cooperative learning instructional formats during guided practice (see Chapter 8).

Guided practice activities should always align with the objective of the lesson and actively involve the students. For example, if the objective of the lesson is to write a descriptive sentence, then guided practice activities should involve students in writing descriptive sentences, not identifying which of two sentences is a descriptive one. During guided practice, effective teachers provide prompts, check for understanding, repeat and rephrase lesson content, provide examples and nonexamples, and give feedback (Gettinger & Fayne, 1982; Good & Grouws, 1979; Rosenshine & Stevens, 1986). Often, a teacher continues with guided practice until students reach a mastery level, usually 80% (Brophy, 1980).

Guided practice activities may include repeated readings, repetitive routines, and choral responding practices. In repeated readings, the teacher first reads the selection. Then the students read it in unison. Next, the teacher and students reread together, and, finally, the students read it alone. In a comparison with worksheets, repeated readings resulted in improved reading rate and comprehension for students with special needs (Henk, Helfeldt, & Platt, 1986; O'Shea & O'Shea, 1988; O'Shea, Sindelar, & O'Shea, 1985). Suggestions for repetitive routines for both elementary and middle school students with special needs include telling students to "Repeat the rule with your eyes closed," "Whisper the rule to a neighbor," and "Say it with your right hand raised."

Choral responding is an effective strategy for providing practice for students with disabilities (Heward, 1994; Sainato, Strain, & Lyon, 1987). Choral responding was more effective than turn taking in teaching sight words to elementary students with learning disabilities or mild mental disabilities (Sindelar, Bursuck, & Halle, 1986). The normal choral responding routine is to ask a question or model a response, pause, cue students to respond together, and give feedback (see "Reading Mastery" in Chapter 7). For example, after telling students that an adjective tells which, what kind of, or how many, the teacher signals, pauses, and asks, "Everyone, what does an adjective tell?" Then all the students respond and the teacher acknowledges with feedback, "Absolutely correct, a perfect answer." Notice in the preceding example that a cue word, *everyone*, was used to

elicit the group response. If a cue word is not used, the fastest and brightest students often blurt out the answers, defeating the purpose of the choral response. Interspersing choral responses with individual responses tends to keep students actively involved. Heward, Courson, and Narayan (1989) recommend the use of choral responding when a short and specific answer is required and when presenting information at a fast pace.

Response cards may be used instead of oral choral responding. Studies found that elementary and middle school students with or without disabilities participated more, scored higher on quizzes, and preferred response cards as compared to hand raising and one-student-at-a-time recitation in answering teachers' questions during math, social studies, and science classes (Gardner, Heward, & Grossi, 1994; see Heward, 1994, for master and doctoral studies results; Narayan, Heward, Gardner, Courson, & Omness, 1990). Ms. Otto used 3-by-5-inch cards in a nonverbal guided practice activity involving adjectives and adverbs for middle school students. She passed out two cards to each student and had them write *adjective* on one card and *adverb* on the other. She also made two cards for herself. She read a sentence written on the transparency (e.g., "The dilapidated window shutter was flapping wildly in the breeze."), asked a question (e.g., "What part of speech is *dilapidated*?"), followed with a pause, then cued the students to respond in unison (e.g., "Now"). Upon hearing the cue word, the students held up one of the cards. At the same time, she held up her adjective card so students could compare their answers with hers.

With this immediate feedback, it is not so embarrassing for students to have an incorrect answer, because they usually correct it before their peers notice. With a quick glance, the teacher can identify students who looked at others' cards for the answer or who were holding up the incorrect card. Such a format for eliciting active participation is particularly effective when teaching bilingual students (Watson, Northcutt, & Rydele, 1989).

Heward (1994) recommends "pinch" cards with multiple answers instead of a single set of cards. Students respond by holding up the card and then pinching the correct response with either the thumb and forefinger or with a colored clothespin. In the previous example, Ms. Otto may have had students write *adverb* and *adjective* on one card and then pinch with a clothespin the correct response.

You may also wish to preprint some general cards such as Yes/No or True/False that students can use for any curriculum. Whatever type of response cards you may choose to use, model several question-and-answer trials first, elicit many responses during a short time period of about 5 or 10 minutes, provide cue words such as *everyone*, give specific feedback based on the majority response, repeat items missed, and allow students to look at their peers' response cards (Heward, Gardner, Cavanaugh, Courson, Grossi, & Barbetta, 1996).

 **ACTIVITY 4.11**

Correct the following mistakes made by two student teachers.

1. A student teacher was teaching a reading lesson to primary students with special needs by calling on one student to sound out 10 words, then calling on another student to sound out 10 words.
2. A student teacher was teaching a math lesson to a group of five middle school students. He spent the first 20 minutes lecturing to the students.

## Closing

Frequently, the lesson ends with (a) a review of the information presented (Archer & Isaacson, 1990; Schumaker, 1989), (b) a preview of the future use for the information (Archer & Isaacson, 1990;

Schumaker, 1989), (c) a statement of expectations (Archer & Isaacson, 1990; Schumaker, 1989), (d) a cue to chart progress or self-evaluate (Palincsar, 1986b; Schumaker, 1989), and (e) an introduction of the independent work (Archer & Isaacson, 1990) plus generalization activity. Following is an example of each feature.

### Review

Students or teachers may review the major points of the lessons with summaries or by asking questions, for example, "Today we discussed the three types of sentences. What was the first type of sentence, Shari?" or "Shari, please summarize what you learned today." One of our interns led students in a listing of major points under the column, "What Did We Learn Today?" Another intern had students enter major points in their learning journal at the end of each math lesson.

### Preview

Teachers frequently use previews to tie together information. "Today we prepared our published books. Tomorrow we will visit the retirement home and read them to our grandparent partners."

### Expectations

You may either summarize how students met your behavior expectations or what they may expect as a result of their new knowledge. For example, one of our student teachers, in commenting on behavior expectations of the tenth graders, noted: "You all really listened today. You remembered to write down the major points and you listened to others' comments without interruptions. Thank you."

### Self-Evaluation

You may have students monitor their own progress using any of the procedures discussed in Chapter 3. In the self-advocacy strategy, VanReusen, Bos, Schumaker, and Deshler (1994) have students keep track of their mastery of the strategy using goal dates and completion dates.

### Introduce the Independent Practice Activity

You should discuss the directions of the activity and then check for student comprehension of the directions. Remember, "Do you understand?" is not an effective question. Also, build in generalization activities that include the use of the information in the natural setting. For example, in a lesson on nutrition, have students keep track of what they eat for breakfast for a week and then have them sort the foods into groups such as dairy, etc.

## Feedback

Feedback often proceeds in the following cycle: teacher asks a question or elicits a response, students respond, teacher evaluates answer and gives feedback (Pressley et al., 1996). Teachers give feedback by acknowledging, amplifying, rephrasing, and correcting (Anderson, Evertson, & Brophy, 1979; Florida Performance Measurement System, 1984).

### Acknowledgment

Acknowledgment involves telling a student that an answer is correct or wrong, such as "Yes, that is correct" or "No, that is not correct." Acknowledgment also involves the use of specific praise. Specific praise requires specification of the appropriate behavior. It is not merely "Good," but "Good reading" or "Good remembering." Stating a specific behavior (reading, remembering) helps students recognize why they are receiving positive statements from you. They know the exact behavior that earned the positive statement. In response to a general statement like "Good boy," a student may think, "Oh, yes, I read well," or "Oh, the teacher must be in a good mood today." Many students with special needs have problems connecting a behavior with the praise when the behavior is not specified. Soldier (1989)

recommends praising a Native American's efforts rather than the product. Positive comments are extremely important for students who are at risk. In an examination of 16 first- and second-grade general education classrooms, Lago-Delello (1998) discovered that teachers gave more negative comments to students at risk for emotional disturbance than to students not at risk.

Positive comments may also be made in the feedback of written products. Marking the correct items in color or writing positive comments on the paper ("Excellent printing," "Great idea") take a little more time, but they help students view school more positively.

### Amplification and Rephrasing

Amplification is expansion of a student's response by either the teacher or another student, such as "Yes, Jim, you are correct. We do multiply to solve that problem and the reason we do that is . . . " or "Yes, Sue, that is a good start. Now, Pat, would you explain it further?" Amplification is used during the teaching of learning strategies to help students discriminate between good and poor student modeling of the teacher's think-alouds (Schumaker, 1989). Rephrasing is often used to emphasize the steps or methods used to arrive at a correct answer (e.g., "Yes, Jimmy, you first divide and then you multiply.") or to repeat the relevant points of a lesson (e.g., "Yes, that's correct, the rule is *i* before *e* except after *c*.") (Anderson, Evertson, & Brophy, 1979).

### Correction

Correcting a wrong response usually follows a supply or scaffolding format, or adaptations of them. A teacher who employs the supply format simply supplies or has another student supply the correct answer. For example, after a student's incorrect response, you or another student model the correct one ("No, the word is *heat*." or "Susie, please read the word."), lead the student ("Let's say it together."), and test the student ("Now, you read the word."). Alternatively, you may just model and test, as in "No, the word is *heat*. What word?" (Engelmann & Carnine, 1982; Meyer, 1986).

With the scaffolding format, the teacher follows up the question with more questions, prompts, and hints "to probe students' understandings and as a guide for individualized instruction, rather than for evaluation only" (Pressley et al., 1996, p. 142). For example, now you may suggest a strategy ("Is this a word that can be sounded out?") or provide information that the student can use to deduce the correct answer ("Try using the silent 'e' rule to sound out the word."). With either format, the process should end with the student responding with the correct answer (Collins, Carnine, & Gersten, 1987).

 **ACTIVITY 4.12**

> **Student Teacher 1** asked a third-grade student to make up a sentence with the word *me*. The student said, "*Me* am happy," Provide a correction using the supply format; using a scaffolding format.
>
> **Student Teacher 2** responded, "That's correct," when a student answered the question of why the astronauts are weightless in space by saying that there is no gravity. Provide a rephrasing type of feedback to emphasize the effect of gravity. Provide a specific praise acknowledgment statement.

## INDEPENDENT PRACTICE

When students are making few errors during guided practice, they should move to independent practice activities (Rosenshine & Stevens, 1986). Independent practice activities are completed by students with minimal teacher assistance. Independent practice should result in fluency, maintenance, and generalization of skills. Teachers must design generalization activities, as students with disabilities often have a difficult time relating content they are learning to other settings and situations. For example, if you are teaching the job-related social skill of giving compliments appropriately, you may assign an activity that requires students to record each time they give compliments at home for 1 week.

Independent practice is not to be confused with a student's interacting with a worksheet. Ineffective teachers often expect students to learn too much from worksheets (Medley, 1979; Rieth, Polsgrove, Okolo, Bahr, & Eckert, 1987; Rosenshine & Stevens, 1986; Squires, Huitt, & Segars, 1983). It is appropriate to use worksheets or dittos during independent practice, but only to reinforce a concept that has already been taught. Remember, independent practice should relate to objectives and guided practice activities, even though new examples are provided. For example, if the objective of the lesson is to identify possessive nouns, then students should practice the identification of possessive nouns during both guided and independent practice activities.

A success rate of 90% to 100% is suggested for independent practice of basic skills for effective learning (Christenson, Thurlow, & Ysseldyke, 1987). To ensure a 90% success rate, give instructions telling what you expect during the independent activity and, if necessary, adapt the activities. Wong, Wong, and LaMare (1982) caution against the use of general instructions like "Read the assignment carefully." Instead, to promote optimal learning and on-task behavior, they suggest that teachers inform students of the specific objectives of the assignment. In working with students from the African American culture, Kuykendall (1992) recommends that teachers set aside a few minutes for the stage-setting behaviors often practiced by these students before they begin an assignment. These stage-setting behaviors, which are applicable for all students, include "pencil sharpening, rearranging posture, checking paper and writing space, asking for repeat directions, and even checking perceptions with their neighbors" (Kuykendall, 1992, p. 63).

Teachers may adapt the directions or content of worksheets for independent practice. (Refer to Chapter 5 for an extensive discussion of ways to adapt materials.) They may also complete the first problem on the worksheet with the students.

Instead of sitting at their desks, effective teachers circulate and give extra help and individual feedback during independent practice (Brophy & Evertson, 1977). But if you need to spend more than a few minutes explaining a problem to a student, you should probably reteach that lesson. Beginning teachers often run into management problems during independent practice because they spend too much time with one student or they position themselves with their backs to the other students, making it impossible to monitor behaviors.

## EVALUATION

The last step in the instructional framework is to evaluate whether students have learned the skills, strategies, and content of the lesson. Evaluation procedures should be aligned with the lesson objectives, guided practice, and independent practice. For example, if the objective of the lesson is to teach students to write descriptive sentences, then students should practice writing descriptive sentences during guided and independent practice activities and be evaluated on how well they write descriptive sentences.

In Chapter 3, we discussed different ways to monitor student progress. The procedures of precision teaching, curriculum-based measurements, and alternative assessments are just as effective for individual lesson evaluations. For example, Mr. LaRue has students chart the number of words they read correctly during the reading story. Ms. Smythe observes the strategies students use in solving math problems as she moves from one student to another during independent practice. Ms. Gonzalez uses oral questions to check comprehension. Some general evaluation guidelines are to specify the criteria, vary evaluation methods, and teach students to self-evaluate and reflect on the teaching episode.

## Specify the Criteria

Students need to know how you plan to evaluate them. One way to share evaluation expectations is to use expert products (Rosenshine, 1990). With expert products, you present the students with a project that you feel demonstrates the quality of work you expect. M. J. Johnson (1991) noted that a completed expert project assists Native Americans, who frequently do not exhibit risk-taking behaviors and are hesitant to complete unstructured assignments. Asking a student to make a copy of a well-done project for later use in other classes is easy to do.

Another way to specify criteria is to prepare a holistic or analytic scoring rubric (see Chapter 3). Archbald (1992) adds the feature of assigning percentages to each of the standards in a rubric dealing with the scoring of written essays. For example, the organization standard of the essay accounts for 30% of the total score, the sentence structure standard for 25%, usage accounts for 20%, mechanics for 20%, and format for 5%. Now, students know that a high-level score of 5 on the sentence structure standard not only meets the indicator of "sentences are complete and varied in length and structure" but also is worth 25% of the final essay grade. Check the Web site www.teach-nology.com for examples of rubrics for paragraph writing, basic reading skills, oral expression, and behavior.

One of our student teachers presented students with an evaluation sheet as they began an assignment. Before he divided students into cooperative groups to write a report about Ohio, he presented them with a checklist of items such as (a) Did you describe three of the major occupations of the state? (12 points) and (b) Did you write complete sentences in the two-page report? (10 points). Thus, he shared with his students the information he expected to see on the report and the importance of including it. He also listed the point value for each question on an exam or quiz and taught students to spend more time answering the questions worth more points.

## Vary Ways to Evaluate

Teachers frequently use worksheets or pencil-and-paper tests to evaluate performance. There are many other ways for students to show that they know the information. You may allow students to give an oral report, complete a homework project, or prepare a portfolio. In the section on motivation, we presented a sample choice sheet for secondary students to select ways to demonstrate their knowledge. When you give students choices as to ways to share information, you are providing for the different learning styles of students, which makes the experience more meaningful. Evaluation should be linked to meaningful and relevant tasks.

## Teach Students to Self-Evaluate

In Chapter 3, we discussed strategies to teach students to self-evaluate as they monitor their progress in the general education classroom setting and as they complete their portfolios. Self-evaluation is an important aspect of authentic evaluation, as evidenced in its use in portfolio assessment, learning logs, and journals. One of our interns required her secondary students in a pull-out setting to complete a daily journal entry. During the last 15 minutes of class, the students independently or in a small group answered the questions: (a) What did you learn today? and (b) Do you have any concerns? She then responded to the entries and used their concerns to reteach any confusing information during the next day's lesson.

Another intern and her primary students listed items for students to evaluate before turning in written assignments. The students answered yes or no to these items on a separate sheet of paper and then attached the paper to their required assignments: (1) Did I use my best handwriting?, (2) Did I remember to write my name and date on the paper?, (3) Does my paper look neat? and (4) Is my paper free of dirt marks?

## Complete a Self-Evaluation

Effective teachers frequently reflect on the teaching episode (Costa & Garmston, 1994). The use of videotapes, cognitive coaching, student evaluations, and self-questioning are multiple ways of gathering data for reflection. Some questions that you may wish to ask for reflection are: (a) What did I want to have happen? (b) Is what happened different? (c) What strategy was particularly effective today? (d) What strategy didn't work as well as I thought? (e) How should I change what happened? and (f) What did I learn that I may use in the future?

As discussed previously, teachers constantly monitor the effectiveness of the teaching strategies as the lesson is progressing. However, no matter how carefully a teacher has planned, there are some days that lessons do not go as expected. Some things that can be done when this happens is

1. Change the grouping structure directing students to work with partners in completing the task or worksheets, pairing students who understand with those who do not.
2. Stop the lesson and review what was discussed the day before or move on to a different subject area or activity.
3. Before assigning independent work, give a couple of problems for students to complete. Assign independent work to those students who completed the problems correctly on their own, but continue instruction with those students who did not complete the problems correctly.
4. Tell the students that the lesson doesn't seem to be going well and ask if they have any suggestions.

5. Pass out worksheets that review previously taught skills.

6. Pass out 3-by-5-inch index cards with creative, enjoyable tasks, such as reading to a stuffed animal or calculating the area of the teacher's desk, for students to complete, based on IEP objectives. Additionally, check the information under motivation in this chapter and the information concerning behavioral decisions in Chapter 2.

 **IMPORTANT POINTS** ◀

1. Guided practice is teacher-led practice that must be aligned with the objective and independent practice. Examples of guided practice activities are repeated reading, repetitive routines, and choral responding.

2. Frequently, lessons close with a review of the information presented, a preview of the future use for the information, a statement of expectations, a self-evaluation measure, and an introduction of the independent work.

3. Feedback involves responding to students' answers and correcting students' errors.

4. Acknowledgment involves telling a student that an answer is correct or wrong.

5. Specific praise requires specification of an appropriate behavior and an evaluative word, such as *good.*

6. Rephrasing is often used to emphasize facts that make an answer correct or the steps or methods used to arrive at a correct answer.

7. Amplification is an expansion of a student's response by either the teacher or another student.

8. Correction procedures often consist of either a supply format or a scaffolding format.

9. Independent practice activities should relate to objectives and guided practice activities and reinforce previously taught information, even though new examples are provided. Generalization activities are also introduced during independent practice.

10. Instead of sitting at their desks, effective teachers roam around the classroom to give extra help and individual feedback during independent practice.

11. Evaluation procedures should be aligned with the lesson objectives, guided practice, and independent practice.

12. Some general guidelines to follow in evaluation are to specify the criteria, vary evaluation methods, teach students to self-evaluate, and reflect on the teaching episode.

## LESSON PLAN

As a way of summarizing the parts of the instructional cycle, Figure 4.4 contains a sample lesson plan. Notice that a short explanation is given in parentheses after each section of the plan.

 **DISCUSSION QUESTIONS** ◀

1. Discuss how you plan to involve **all** your students actively during lesson presentation.

2. Research shows that motivation is further enhanced when learning is personally relevant for students. Describe how you plan to make learning personally relevant for your students.

3. Discuss why it is necessary to identify subject matter as laws, rules, etc.

4. Describe how you would use the teacher–student dialogue technique to teach the difference between an equilateral and isosceles triangle.

**Figure 4.4** Sample Lesson Plan

*Objective:* When presented with an independent practice sheet of 10 fractions, students will write equivalent fractions with 90% accuracy. (Fractions were identified on each of the students' IEPs.)

*Subject Matter Content:*
For presentation: Concept
        Definition—Equivalent fractions are fractions that name the same number (from text, *Applying Mathematics,* 1986, Laidlaw Brothers, p. 538.)
        Attribute—Equivalent fractions are equal.
        Examples—$\frac{1}{2} = \frac{2}{4} = \frac{4}{8} = \frac{8}{16}$, $\frac{1}{4} = \frac{2}{8} = \frac{4}{16}$, $\frac{1}{8} = \frac{2}{16}$, $\frac{2}{4} = \frac{4}{8} = \frac{8}{16}$, etc.
        Nonexamples—$\frac{1}{2} = \frac{3}{4}$, $\frac{1}{4} = \frac{3}{8}$, $\frac{1}{8} = \frac{4}{16}$, $\frac{2}{4} = \frac{7}{8}$, etc.

For review: Basic concept/skill—write fractions from pictures. Examples—see Transparency A.
        Basic concept/skill—identification of fraction kits

Curriculum standard: Students in grades 3–5 are expected to recognize and generate equivalent forms of commonly used fractions, decimals, and percents in the understanding numbers standard.

**(Since this is a concept, a definition, examples, nonexamples, and attributes were identified. Teacher reviewed prerequisite basic concepts/skills. See Step 4 of the plan and Transparency A. The curriculum standard was adapted from the National Council for Teachers of Mathematics Standards, 2001.)**

*Questions:*
    How many eighths are in one-half? How many fourths are in one-sixteenth?
    Why aren't $\frac{3}{4}$ and $\frac{7}{8}$ equivalent fractions?
    What does *equivalent* mean?
    Are $\frac{1}{2}$ and $\frac{2}{4}$ equivalent fractions?
    Why are these fractions equal?
    How can you prove that the fractions are equal?

**(Notice, the teacher identified both low- and high-level questions.)**

*Feedback:*
    Correct—You certainly know how to find equivalent fractions, well done, (name). You are absolutely correct, $\frac{1}{2}$ does equal $\frac{2}{4}$.
    Incorrect—What was the first step? What fraction pieces do you think you need?

**(Notice, the teacher plans to use specific praise and amplification for correct answers and a scaffolding strategy for incorrect.)**

*Ideas If Plan Is Not Working:*
        Do more Think-Alouds and modeling with the students drawing more examples on a blank transparency similar to those found on Transparency A, assign two students to work together on the independent practice sheet, or complete the independent practice sheet as a class.

*Materials:*
    Math Journal
    Teacher Fraction Kit (same as students' kits, but made from transparencies, produced by a graphics software program and color printer)
    Students' Fraction Kits made from construction paper:
        One sheet of yellow construction paper represents 1 whole.
        One sheet of green construction paper cut into 2 equal pieces represents halves.
        One sheet of blue construction paper cut into 4 equal pieces represents fourths.
        One sheet of orange construction paper cut into 8 equal pieces represents eighths.
        One sheet of purple construction paper cut into 16 equal pieces represents sixteenths.

**Figure 4.4** Continued

**Transparency A** with pictures for review (Students must write the fraction from the picture.)

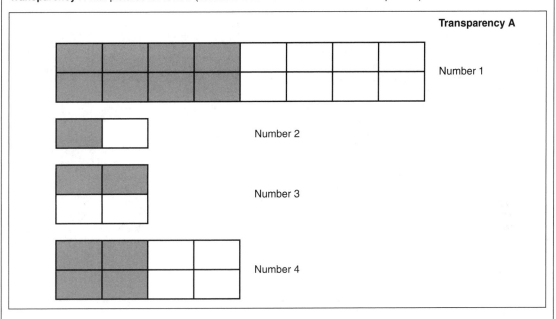

**Transparency A**

Number 1

Number 2

Number 3

Number 4

Transparency B, which has the definition of equivalent fractions written on it.

**Transparency B**

Definition—Equivalent fractions are fractions that name the same number.

Independent Practice Sheet—(Of course, all of the materials would be in larger print for the actual lesson.)

**Independent Practice Sheet**

Directions: Convert the fractions into equivalent fractions:

1. ½ = /4      2. ¾ = /8      3. $^6/_{16}$ = /8      4. ²⁄4 = /8      5. ⅝ = /16

6. ¼ = /16      7. ²⁄16 = /8      8. ⅝ = /4      9. ⁴/₁₆ = /8      10. ¹⁰⁄₁₆ = /8

*Lesson Presentation*

Opening:
1. Overview: "Today we will talk about equivalent fractions and use our fraction kits to explore equivalent fractions. We'll start off working problems together, then you will work with a partner, and then alone on identifying equivalent fractions."
2. Rationale: "Why do you think we need to know about making equal fractions?"
3. Expectations: "During today's lesson I expect all of you to remain seated, to be good listeners, and to raise your hand to answer questions. I know you will enjoy class today."

**Figure 4.4** Continued

4. Review: "But, first, let's quickly review writing fractions and our fraction kit values."
   a. Show Transparency A and have students write down fractions on a sheet of paper. Then check with unison response, "Everyone, what is this fraction?" Give feedback.
   b. Hold up yellow construction paper and ask, "What do we call the yellow pieces of our fraction kit, everyone? Blue? Purple? Orange? Green?"

**(Notice, the teacher selected overview, rationale, expectations, and review as components to use to introduce this lesson. She cued with "Everyone" in eliciting a student response and then gave feedback.)**

Body:

5. After review, state and show the definition of equivalent fraction (Transparency B). Ask students questions about the definition. (Emphasize that they are equal parts of the whole.) Have students copy the definition into their math journals.
6. Model doing an equivalent fraction using Transparency A, Example 2, and fraction kit. "Let's see, I've identified that fraction as ½ so I need to find all the fractions equivalent to ½. Let me start by pulling out my green ½ pieces from my fraction kit. Now, I'll pull out my fourth pieces, the blue ones from the kit. How many fourth pieces do I think equal the ½ piece? Hm, let's try 3. Nope. That doesn't work. They do not fit on top of each other. So ½ doesn't equal 3 pieces of the fourths or ¾. Let's try 2 pieces. They fit fine. So ½ equals ²⁄₄. So ½ and ²⁄₄ are equivalent fractions; they cover an equal portion of the whole. They are equal." (Write ½ = ²⁄₄ on the board.)
7. Do another example (Write ½ = ⁄₈ on the board.), asking students questions as they watch you, beginning with, "Now, I wonder if I can find an equal number of eighths to equal ½. What should I do first, Jack?"

   **(The teacher employed a think aloud type of modeling and then involved students in the modeling process.)**

Guided Practice:

8. Have students take out their fraction kits. "Let's see if you can find an equal number of sixteenths. (Write ½ = ⁄₁₆ on the board.) What should you do first? Yes, start with your green or half sheet."
9. Do two more examples (⁸⁄₁₆ = ⁄₂, and ¾ = ⁄₈), asking the students questions.
10. Divide the students into pairs, having one student show one fraction with the kit and another student the equivalent fraction. Model with two students first, "Jim and Jason are partners. They are working the problem of ⁸⁄₁₆ = ⁄₈. Jason, show us ⁸⁄₁₆ with your fraction kit. Now, Jim, take out your eighths. What do you do now?" (Remember, to have students write both fractions.)
11. Circulate while students are working five more examples (taken from the examples listed in subject matter).
12. Call on each group to write one of the problems, explaining and showing how they got their answers. Then have all students copy the five examples into their Math Journal underneath the definition.

   **(The teacher used peer tutoring, discussion, and teacher monitoring.)**

Closing:

13. "Let's do a quick review. What is the definition of an equivalent fraction? How do you use your fraction kit to find an equivalent fraction?"
14. Share with students how they met expectations set at the beginning of the lesson.
15. Have students write what they learned from today's Math Lesson in their Math Journal.

   **(The teacher asked questions and had students reflect on the lesson.)**

*Independent Practice:*

16. Have the student helper pass out the worksheets. Go over the directions and do the first problem with the students. Remind the students that they may use their fraction kits. (See Independent Practice sheet in Materials section of plant.)
17. Have students interview parents to see how they use equivalent fractions. Write up the results for the 5 points extra credit.

   **(The teacher made certain students understood the task using comprehansion checks and completing the first problem. Additionally, the teacher attempted to connect the lesson to real life experiences.)**

*Evaluation:*

18. Circulate as the students are completing the worksheets. Plan to reteach the lesson to any student who scores less than 90%.

# CHAPTER 5

# INSTRUCTIONAL MATERIALS

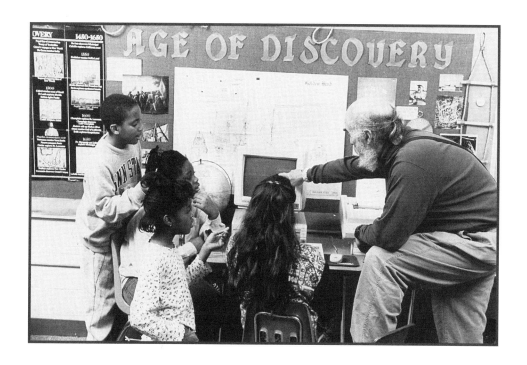

The instructional materials you use are the nuts and bolts of your instructional program, the vehicles through which instruction is delivered. If your students are to achieve success in the classroom, the materials they use must produce appropriate learning outcomes, motivate them, and hold their interest. The increased diversity among students in today's classrooms necessitates the use of adaptations to increase the likelihood that students will experience success in school (Miller, 2002). In school districts where state-adopted textbooks and materials are used, teachers should be adept at modifying and adapting materials. Udvari-Solner (1997) recommends that general and special education teachers collaborate to design adaptations and accommodations as part of the curriculum. In districts where they are given choices in the selection process, teachers should be skilled in the selection, analysis, and development of materials. In this chapter, we present ways to select, analyze, adapt, and develop instructional materials along with strategies to modify/adapt tests.

## SELECTING INSTRUCTIONAL MATERIALS

The selection of appropriate instructional materials and activities is part of the process of individualizing and planning instruction for students. Many commercially produced instructional materials are available for use with students who have special needs. The suggestions in this section and throughout the chapter are appropriate for teachers to use with students with special needs who are receiving instruction in general education inclusive classrooms as well as in pull-out programs.

### Factors Influencing the Selection of Instructional Materials

Remember to exercise care in your selection of instructional materials. Attention to individual learner needs, interest and motivation levels of materials, opportunities for social interaction, and diversity increases the probability of success with commercially produced instructional materials.

#### Student Needs

In choosing materials, you should consider the fact that you will work with students who have a wide variety of needs, abilities, and individual differences and you will be addressing these needs, abilities, and differences in both general and special education settings. Instructional materials should be compatible with diverse learning and presentation styles; adaptable to a variety of disabilities; include supplementary items such as software, manipulatives, and games; allow for monitoring of student progress; and be developmentally, culturally, linguistically, age, and interest appropriate for students.

#### Motivation and Interest

Motivation is an important factor to consider when you select materials for your students. Materials that are age appropriate, interesting, appealing, and related to real life are likely to be used by your students, particularly when you have given consideration to cultural backgrounds, gender, and interests. For example, some students benefit from using high-interest, low-level vocabulary materials that are age and interest appropriate. Secondary students are often motivated by functional materials that relate to real life.

Many elementary students enjoy reading themselves or listening to others read commercial materials called predictable books (see Table 5.1). According to Rhodes and Dudley-Marling (1996), "books are predictable when they enable students to quickly and easily predict what the author's going to say and how the author's going to say it based upon their knowledge of the world" (p. 108). Rhodes (1981) has identified the characteristics that make books predictable: (a) a match between the content and the reader's experiences; (b) rhythmical, repetitive patterns; and (c) familiar, well-known stories. You may select books with characters, cultural backgrounds, and themes your students can easily relate to. You can choose books with repetitive patterns, such as *Alexander and the Terrible, Horrible, No Good, Very Bad Day* (Viorst, 1972) or *Brown Bear, Brown Bear, What Do You See?* (Martin, 1970), and books with which most of your students may be familiar, such as tall tales or folktales. You may include many of the typical American folktales, such as *Paul Bunyan, A Tall Tale* (Kellogg, 1984), and tales from other countries, such as the Asian legend *A Song of Stars* (Birdseye, 1990) and the Chinese tale *The Empty Pot* (Demi, 1990).

#### Social Interaction

Teachers may use instructional materials, both commercial and teacher-made, to foster social interactions through peer tutoring, learning center activities, role playing, group projects, and cooperative learning activities. Interpersonal skills are important for school and community adjustment (Lovitt & Harris, 1987; Schloss & Schloss, 1987; Schloss, Schloss, & Harris, 1984;

**Table 5.1** Predictable Books

Aardema, V. (1981). *Bringing the rain to Kapiti Plain*. New York: Dial.
Ahlberg, J., & Ahlberg, A. (1978). *Each peach pear plum*. New York: Scholastic.
Barrtt, J. (1980). *Animals should definitely not act like people*. New York: Atheneum.
Bishop, C., & Wiese, K. (1938). *The five Chinese brothers*. New York: Coward, McCann & Geoghegan.
Brand, O. (1970). *When I first came to this land*. New York: Putnam's Sons.
Burke, C. L., & Harste, J.C. (1983). *All kinds of cats*. Worthington, OH: School Book Fairs.
Carle, E. (1969). *The very hungry caterpillar*. Cleveland: Collins World.
Christian, M. B. (1973). *Nothing much happened today*. Reading, MA: Addison-Wesley.
de Paola, T. (1981). *Now one foot, now the other*. New York: Putnam's Sons.
Dodd, L. (1985). *Hairy Maclary*. Milwaukee, WI: Gareth Stevens.
Durrell, J. (1985). *Mouse tails*. New York: Crown.
Galdone, P. (1985). *Cat goes fiddle-i-fee*. New York: Clarion.
Hines, A. (1984). *Come to the meadow*. New York: Clarion.
Hoguet, S. R. (1983). *I unpacked my grandmother's trunk*. New York: Dutton.
Kalan, R. (1981). *Jump, frog, jump!* New York: Greenwillow.
Leydenfrost, R. (1970). *The snake that sneezed!* New York: Putnam's Sons.
Lobel, A. (1984). *The rose in my garden*. New York: Greenwillow.
Martin, B. (1970). *Brown bear, brown bear, what do you see?* New York: Holt, Rinehart, & Winston.
O'Neill, M. (1961). *Hailstones and halibut bones*. Garden City, NY: Doubleday.
Perme, D. (1982). *Joshua James likes trucks*. Chicago: Children's Press.
Plume, I. (1980). *The Bremen-town musicians*. Garden City, NY: Doubleday.
Satchwell, J. (1984). *Odd one out*. New York: Random House.
Singer, M. (1981). *Will you take me to town on strawberry day?* New York: Harper & Row.
Thomas, P. (1971). *"Stand back" said the elephant, "I'm going to sneeze!"* New York: Lothrop, Lee & Shepard.
Viorst, J. (1972). *Alexander and the terrible, horrible, no good, very bad day*. New York: Atheneum.
Williams, B. (1974). *Albert's toothache*. New York: Dutton.

Schloss & Sedlak, 1986). For example, Joe and Mike, high school juniors, have been working with instructional materials that emphasize job-seeking skills. In addition to providing them with skills in finding and securing employment, the materials have given them valuable socialization experiences through role-playing the employability activities.

### *Diversity*

Instructional materials may be used to help students recognize and celebrate the diversity and variety that exists among individuals and to share information about people from different cultural backgrounds. "Students' contextual, linguistic, and gender characteristics influence how they learn" (Winzer & Mazurek, 1998, p. 327).

As you select materials, make sure that all groups are represented. Underrepresentation in instructional materials appears to occur most often for minority groups, women, people with disabilities, and older individuals (Gollnick & Chinn, 2002). Make sure to use culturally responsive instructional strategies and materials to meet the needs of students from diverse racial, ethnic, cultural, and linguistic groups (Banks et al., 2001).

In Mr. Rizzati's English class, students read and discuss books that incorporate different age groups, both males and females, a variety of cultural groups, and people with disabilities. For example, the class examined the problems of the elderly in *Grandpa and Me* (Tolan, 1978), a story about a family that has to decide what to do about their aging grandfather, who has always lived with them. The story highlights the special friendship between the grandfather and granddaughter. A particular favorite of the class was *Summer of the Swans* (Byars, 1974), a story told from the perspective of the sister of a boy with a mental disability. The story tells how the girl comes to know and understand herself better because of her brother.

*Water Sky* (George, 1987) is a story about a young man living with an Eskimo family in Alaska. There he learns the importance of whaling in the Eskimo culture. *The Black Snowman* (Mendez, 1989) describes a young African American boy who discovers the beauty of his heritage and self-worth. For a list of books about a variety of cultural groups, see Table 5.2.

## Materials Selection and the Stages of Learning

You may use a variety of instructional materials to meet the needs of your students at each of the stages of learning (see Chapter 3). At the acquisition level, materials should provide opportunities for extensive teacher participation. For example, to teach writing skills to your students, you may use materials that explain how to write a variety of sentence types and then require you to model what to do when writing sentences.

After your students have acquired skills, they need to practice them to gain fluency. Students should practice first in a controlled or guided situation under close supervision, then in independent situations. Therefore, you should select and develop a wide variety of materials and provide opportunities for extensive student involvement. Practice materials should foster participation on the part of students. You may use workbooks, magazines, practice exercises, audiotapes, software programs, and games to develop fluency in writing. In addition, you may use charts and graphs to monitor each student's progress.

After students have demonstrated fluency, you should provide instructional materials that allow them to maintain their skills. At this stage, you should provide materials that will encourage frequent use of the skills. Students with special needs can practice writing a variety of things to maintain their writing skills (such as a letter to the editor). In addition, maintenance is frequently enhanced by learning centers, where students work independently on such skills as writing different sentence types and writing reports.

The final stage of learning involves the generalization of skills across situations and settings. For example, you should help students identify the opportunities for using writing in real-life materials. Thus, you should select materials that require students to apply their writing skills to the types of writing they do in content area classes (e.g., English), on the job (e.g., taking orders), and personally (e.g., writing letters). One high school student confided to her teacher that her letters to her boyfriend were easier to write after she improved her writing skills.

 **ACTIVITY 5.1**

Examine a commercially produced instructional material for reading or literature and answer the following questions:

1. How does the material meet the needs of the students?
2. Is the material motivating and related to real life?
3. Does it provide opportunity for social interaction?
4. Does it share information about diversity?
5. Which stage of learning does it address?

(Answers for this and other activities are found in the Instructor's Manual.)

**Table 5.2**　Multicultural Literature

**African Americans**

Angelou, M. (1989). Writers' voices selected from *I know why the caged bird sings* and *The heart of a woman*. New York: Readers House.

Bryan, A. (1989). *Turtie knows your name*. New York; Antheneum.

Chocolate, D. M. (2000). *The piano man*. New York: Walker.

Cole, K. (2001). *No bad news*. Morton Grove, IL: A. Whitman.

Greenfield, E. (1989). *Nathaniel talking*. New York: Writers & Readers.

Martin, A. M. (2001). *Belle teal*. New York: Scholastic Press.

Mendez, P. (1989). *The black snowman*. New York: Scholastic.

Patterson, L. (1989). *Martin Luther King, Jr., and the freedom movement*. New York: Facts on file.

Pinkney, S. (2000). *Shades of black: A celebration of our children*. New York: Scholastic.

Porter, A. P. (1992). *Jump at the sun: The story of Zora Neale Hurston*. Minneapolis: Carolrhoda Books.

Rinaldi, A. (1996). *Hang a thousand trees with ribbons: The story of Phillis Wheatley*. San Diego, CA: Harcourt Brace & Co.

Taylor, M. D. (1997). *Roll of thunder, hear me cry*. New York: Puffin Books.

**Asian Americans**

Coatsworth, E. J. (1990). *The cat who went to heaven*. New York: Aladdin Paperbacks.

Demi. (1998). *The empty pot*. New York: Henry Holt & Company.

Huynh Quang Nhoung. (1982). *The land I lost: Adventures of a boy in Vietnam*. New York: Harper.

Kessler, L. (1994). *Stubborn twig: Three generations in the life of a Japanese American family*. New York: Dutton.

Kingston, M. H. (1990). Writers' voices selected from *China men and the woman warrior*. New York: Readers House.

Namioka, L. (1994). *Yang the youngest and his terrible ear*. New York: Bantam Doubleday Dell Books for Young Readers.

Nguyen Ngoc Bich. (1975). *A thousand years of Vietnamese poetry*. Translated by B. Raffel & W.S. Merwin. New York: Knopf.

Pittman, H. C. (1986). *A grain of rice*. New York: Bantam.

Seros, K. (1982). *Sun and moon: Fairy tales from Korea*. Winslow, WA: Holly.

*Tikki Tikki Tembo* told by Arlene Mosel (1968). New York: Henry Hott & Company, LLL.

Vuyon, L. D. (1982). *The brocaded slipper and other Vietnamese tales*. Reading, MA: Addison-Wesley.

Wells, R. (2001). *Yoko's paper cranes*. New York: Hyperion Books for Children.

Yep, L. (1995). *Thief of hearts*. New York: Harper Collins.

**Hispanics**

Aardema, V. (1979). *The riddle of the drum: A tale from Tizapan, Mexico*. New York: Four Winds.

Ada, A. F. (1995). *My name is Maria Isabel*. New York: Aladdin Paperbacks.

Anaya, Rudolto A. (1989). Writers' voices selected from *bless me, Ultima*. New York: Readers House.

Bethancourt, T. E. (1987). *The me inside of me*. Neward, DE: Lerner.

Bierhorst, J. (1986). *The monkey's haircut and other stories told by the Maya*. New York: Morrow.

Griego y Maetras, J., & Anaya, R. A. (1980). *Cuentos: Tales from the the Hispanic Southwest*. Santa Fe, NM: Museum of New Mexico.

Jagendorf, M. A., & Boggs, R. W. (1960). *The king of the mountains: A treasure of Latin American folk stories*. New York: Vanguard.

**Table 5.2**  Continued

Lattimore, D. (1987). *The flame of peace: A tale of the Aztecs.* New York: Harper & Row.
Marrin, A. (1986). *The Aztecs and Spaniards: Cortez and the conquest of Mexico.* New York: Atheneum.
Steptoe, J. (1997). *Creativity.* New York: Clarion Books.
White, C. (1976). *César Chávez, man of courage.* Champaign, IL: Gerrard.

**Native Americans**

Bierhorst, J. (1987). *Doctor Coyote: A Native American Aesop's fables.* New York: Morrow.
Carter, F. (1990). *The education of Little Tree.* Albuquerque, NM: University of New Mexico Press.
Erdrich, L. (1989). Writers' voices selected from *Love medicine.* New York: Readers House.
Esbensen, B. (1988). *The star maiden.* Boston: Little, Brown.
Freedman, R. (1988). *Buffalo hunt.* New York: Holiday.
George, J. (1987). *Water sky.* New York: Harper & Row.
Highwater, J. (1998). *I wear the morning star.* New York: Harper & Row.
Hortze, S. (1990). *A circle unbroken.* New York: Clarion.
Hudson, J. (1992). *Dawn rider.* New York: Philomel.
Hudson, J. (1989). *Sweetgrass.* New York: Philomel.
Paulsen, G. (1992). *Canyons.* New York: Delacorte.

## ANALYZING INSTRUCTIONAL MATERIALS

It is important to analyze instructional materials for their appropriateness for students before incorporating them into the instructional program. Many commercial products are not appropriate because they possess characteristics that make their use extremely difficult for students with special needs. Commercial materials, curricula, programs, and textbooks are ineffective for many reasons:

1. *The readability of text may be too difficult.* Many materials are written on a reading level that may be challenging for students with special needs. Sentences may be too long and complex, and vocabulary may be unnecessarily difficult, as in "The man, addressing the audience before him, told them that he had repented for all of his past offenses" instead of "The man told the people he was sorry for what he did."

2. *The vocabulary is often highly sophisticated.* Complex words may be used when easier synonyms would be just as effective (see preceding example). Unfortunately, when techni-

cal terms are introduced in some content materials, definitions are omitted or not clearly stated. Wiig and Semel (1984) suggest the use of only five unfamiliar vocabulary words per lesson for students who have language or learning disabilities.

3. *Too many concepts may be presented at one time.* Students with special needs benefit when concepts are introduced one at a time. Unfortunately, math materials sometimes present more than one type of problem on a page. For example, in one text we examined, the division problems ($24/8$ = ____; $38/5$ = ____; and $215/3$ = ____) required three different skills and levels of competence but were presented on the same page. Notice that the first problem can be divided evenly, the second has a remainder, and the third involves a two-digit quotient with a remainder. Each type should be mastered before the next is introduced.

4. *The sequencing of skills may be inappropriate.* Students with special needs may experience problems when skills are taught out of sequence. For instance, students should be taught initial consonant sounds before they are

introduced to the concept of consonant blends (Spache, 1982).

5. *Directions are not always clear.* Some materials use different words for the same directions, as in the case of "Circle the best answer" and "Put a line around the best answer." It is less confusing for students if directions are worded consistently on assignments and tests.

6. *There are insufficient opportunities for practice and review.* Many workbooks, textbooks, and other printed products move too quickly, failing to provide sufficient practice. For example, students should spend sufficient time learning how to subtract two-digit numbers *without* regrouping before attempting similar problems *with* regrouping. Many commercial materials do not incorporate a review of previously learned skills in practical, relevant situations. For example, once students in an employability skills class have learned the steps for job interviewing, they need to apply those skills through role-playing scenarios and videotaping. Students with special needs require practice to become fluent and to maintain a skill.

7. *Key points and terms may not be given adequate emphasis.* Printed products do not always highlight, print in bold type, print in italics, or define the most important terms and ideas. This may cause difficulty for students who do not easily identify key points and terms.

8. *Organization, format, and layout are sometimes confusing.* Printed materials do not always begin with an advance organizer or introduction of what is to come (e.g., list of objectives, key vocabulary list, outline), nor do they conclude with a postorganizer (e.g., summary, list of important points, questions). In addition, when tables, graphs, and illustrations are placed far away from the text that describes them, they may confuse students or be ignored, as the students do not see the connection between the text and the graphic aid. Imagine trying to follow an explanation of how to record checks in a check register, when the instructions are on one page and a diagram of

the check register is on another. In addition, pages may be cluttered with too much information. Crowded formats may confuse students and discourage them from even beginning a task. Students may be unable to pinpoint relevant information and screen out nonessential information when a page is overcrowded. Pages with ample white space are more student friendly.

9. *Materials may be unmotivating and uninteresting.* Some commercially produced materials simply are not appealing or interesting because of format, level of difficulty, lack of color and illustrations, subject matter, age level targeted, typeface, or lack of relevance and functionality. Thus, they may not hold the learner's attention.

10. *Materials and text are sometimes too abstract.* Some written materials contain long passages of text with no clues to the definitions of abstract vocabulary and concepts. For example, a social studies chapter on justice, democracy, and freedom may not make these concepts concrete. Another example is math material that contains the term *congruent* with no examples, definitions, or illustrations of the term.

11. *Students may be limited in their response modes.* Unfortunately, some materials require only one type of response from students. For example, a science text that provides only end-of-chapter questions limits response. In contrast, a science text that provides suggestions for experiments, topics for discussion, suggestions for group activities, ideas for field trips, and chapter questions provides a variety of ways for students to respond.

12. *A variety of ethnic, cultural, and gender groups may not be represented or they may be inaccurately represented.* Some instructional materials do not include exposure to a variety of ethnic and cultural groups and genders, thereby limiting their appeal. This omission may communicate to students that some ethnic and cultural groups are less important than others (Gollnick & Chinn, 2002). Some materials

include descriptions of people and activities that stereotype individuals in terms of culture, ethnic group, religion, gender, age, and vocational or career choice. Biases may occur within both the printed and graphic sections of materials (Baca & Cervantes, 1998). There still exists the lack of Spanish, Polish, African, and other non-Anglo names in materials, as well as feminine pronouns (Gollnick & Chinn, 2002), and Asian Americans, Latinos, Native Americans, and women are underrepresented in instructional materials (Hernandez, 2001).

A way to analyze the appropriateness of materials is to conduct a textbook analysis. The U.S. Department of Education, Office of Special Education Projects, which focused on instructional materials for students with mild disabilities, identified features that are typically examined in a textbook analysis: vocabulary, concept development, and reading level (Burnette, 1987). Analyzing a textbook as part of your selection process helps you determine the amount of repetition, review, and material that is included. You should be sure that your students can handle the concept load and that the text provides ample opportunities for your students to check their understanding. Supplementary materials may include study aids, activity sheets, and overviews. You should also make sure that the format (layout, print, graphics) is compatible with the needs of your students. By analyzing elementary and secondary textbooks for content, organization, supplementary materials, and format, you can identify elements that cause problems for students and then adapt the textbooks accordingly.

You may also want to check the readability level of your textbooks and other reading materials. Typically, readability formulas are used to evaluate the complexity of the sentences in a passage (e.g., sentence length) and the level of difficulty of the vocabulary (word length or frequency). Figure 5.1 contains the Fry Graph for Estimating Readability. You can use these steps to obtain a general idea of

the difficulty level of a passage. Although readability formulas are typically used to determine readability level, they should be used with caution and as only one means of evaluating the appropriateness of a text or reading passage. Standal (1978) recommends using a readability formula as a "general indicator of a possible range of materials" (p. 646) and a good starting point for estimating the readability of a passage.

Most readability formulas are based on sentence complexity and vocabulary and do not take into consideration other aspects of a textbook, such as the way it is organized and formatted (headings, graphic aids, important points, definitions in margins, etc.). Bailin and Grafstein (2001) refer to multiple readabilities, varying with the topic, the nature of the text, and the nature of the audience. Beals (1989) suggests that teachers should also evaluate vocabulary load, syntax, and style and recommends the following steps:

1. Determine the reading level of the student who will be using the text/material.
2. Select an easy-to-use readability formula, such as the Fry Readability Formula (Fry, 1968), to get a general estimate of readability (see Figure 5.1).
3. Examine the passages that you used to determine readability, and mark any words that the student might not understand (those that require direct instruction or use of context).
4. Analyze the syntax in the passage by identifying the basic sentence types.
5. Compare the sentence types typically used by the student (e.g., simple, compound, complex) with those found in the passage.
6. Analyze the style of the writing by looking for anything that might cause problems for the student.

By analyzing material using a readability formula to obtain a general indication of a range of materials (Standal, 1978) and assessing

**Figure 5.1** Fry Readability Formula

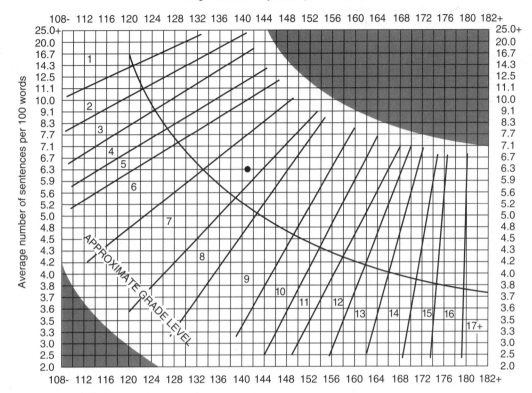

GRAPH FOR ESTIMATING READABILITY—EXTENDED
by Edward Fry, Rutgers University Reading Center, New Brunswick, NJ 08904

Average number of syllables per 100 words

**Expanded Directions for Working Readability Graph**

1. Randomly select three (3) sample passages and count out exactly 100 words each, beginning with the beginning of a sentence. Do count proper nouns, initializations, and numerals.
2. Count the number of sentences in the hundred words, estimating length of the fraction of the last sentence to the nearest one-tenth.
3. Count the total number of syllables in the 100-word passage. If you don't have a hand counter available, an easy way is to simply put a mark above every syllable over one in each word, then when you get to the end of the passage, count the number of marks and add 100. Small calculators can also be used as counters by pushing numeral 1, then push the + sign for each word or syllable when counting.
4. Enter graph with *average* sentence length and *average* number of syllables; plot dot where the two lines intersect. Area where dot is plotted will give you the approximate grade level.
5. If a great deal of variability is found in syllable count or sentence count, putting more samples into the average is desirable.
6. A word is defined as a group of symbols with a space on either side; thus, *Joe, IRA, 1945*, and *&* are each one word.
7. A syllable is defined as a phonetic syllable. Generally, there are as many syllables as vowel sounds. For example, *stopped* is one syllable and *wanted* is two syllables. When counting syllables for numerals and initializations, count one syllable for each symbol. For example, *1945* is four syllables, *IRA* is three syllables, and *&* is one syllable.

Note. This "extended graph" does not outmode or render earlier (1968) version inoperative or inaccurate; it is an extension of the earlier version. (REPRODUCTION PERMITTED—NO COPYRIGHT) vocabulary load, syntax, and style (Beals, 1989), you should be able to judge the suitability of reading materials for your students. Remember also to take into consideration the characteristics of the reader as you make your selection of materials that are reader friendly.

Numerous forms and checklists are available, both commercial or teacher-made (such as the one following), for teachers to use when analyzing instructional materials for students. You should use some type of evaluation procedure to help you decide whether to use a given material as it is, use it with modifications, or not use it at all. In addition to evaluating materials themselves, some teachers borrow or obtain sample sets of commercial materials from publishers and ask their students to try them out and provide feedback about them.

*Complete the following:*

Title: _____

Author: _____

Publisher: _____

Copyright: _____

Cost: _____

Purpose: _____

### Rate the following:

|  | Acceptable | Unacceptable |
|---|---|---|
| Directions | _____ | _____ |
| Readability | _____ | _____ |
| Sequencing | _____ | _____ |
| Interest level | _____ | _____ |
| Pace | _____ | _____ |
| Examples | _____ | _____ |
| Opportunities for practice | _____ | _____ |
| Opportunities for self-monitoring | _____ | _____ |
| Multicultural emphasis | _____ | _____ |

**Respond to the following:**

1. How would you use this material (e.g., supplementary, required, to help with generalization)? _____
2. In what type(s) of instructional arrangement(s) would you use this material (e.g., individual, group)? _____
3. Give your overall impression of the material.

 **ACTIVITY 5.2**

Select a classroom material (kit, program, game, workbook) and analyze it using the teacher-made materials analysis form previously discussed. Present the material and your findings to the class. Now, select a passage from this text or from an elementary or secondary textbook and apply the Fry Readability Formula. Discuss your results with the class.

 **IMPORTANT POINTS** ◀

1. When selecting instructional materials, teachers should be aware of individual learner needs, interest and motivation levels of materials, opportunities that materials provide for social interaction, and the level of attention to diversity within the materials.
2. Materials should be developmentally, culturally, linguistically, age, and interest appropriate for students.
3. The features of vocabulary, concept development, and reading level are usually examined in a textbook analysis (Burnette, 1997).
4. Typically, readability formulas are used to evaluate the complexity of the sentences in a passage and the level of difficulty of the vocabulary.
5. Instructional materials may be used to address the needs of students at each of the stages of learning (acquisition, fluency, maintenance, and generalization).

6. It is important to analyze instructional materials for their appropriateness with students to decide whether to incorporate them into the instructional program.

---

## ADAPTING MATERIALS

Once you have analyzed materials and identified any shortcomings, you may need to adapt the materials for use with students who have special needs. Materials should be usable under different instructional conditions with students who have varying abilities. If students experience difficulty with assignments or activities, teachers may make changes to help meet their needs. The number of students with disabilities being educated in general education classrooms is continuing to grow (National Center for Education Statistics, 2001; Fuchs & Fuchs, 1994), thus increasing the need for general education teachers to be knowledgeable about adapting materials and instruction. Unfortunately, observational studies of actual instruction provided by general education teachers to mainstream students show that few, if any, adaptations in instruction are being made (Baker & Zigmond, 1990; McIntosh, Vaughn, Schumm, Haager, & Lee, 1993). Therefore, one of the most important roles of the special education teacher is to assist general education teachers in the adaptation of materials and instruction to ensure the successful participation of students with special needs in the general classroom community.

### Instructional Materials

Instructional materials include textbooks, workbooks, worksheets, transparencies, kits with cards or written information, and software programs. Following are areas to modify and techniques that you may use to modify materials for students with special needs.

#### *Readability*

To modify the readability level:

1. Decrease the use of complex language and provide examples that explain statements (Salend, 1995a).
2. Provide outlines or study guides to accompany the text.
3. Highlight essential information.
4. Limit the amount of information on a page.
5. Make the topic sentence of a paragraph the initial sentence (Wood & Wooley, 1986).

#### *Vocabulary*

To modify vocabulary:

1. Use the marginal gloss technique. Write terms and their definitions in the margins of a textbook page (Figure 5.2).
2. Underline or highlight key terms.
3. Locate all boldface, italicized, or new concept words from the text and list them with the corresponding page number (Wood & Wooley, 1986).

**Figure 5.2** Marginal Gloss Technique

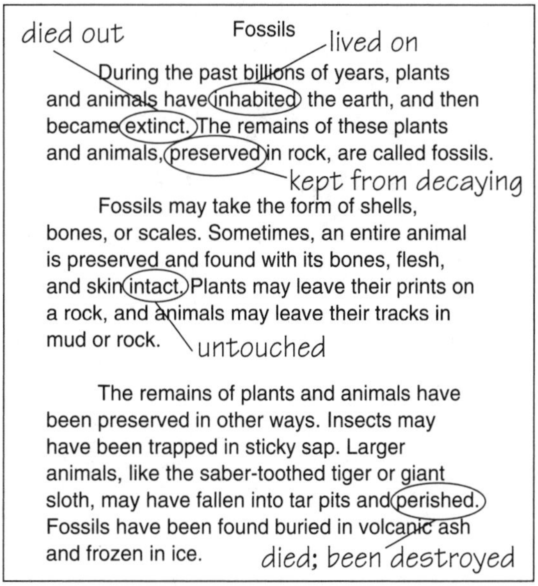
Fossils

During the past billions of years, plants and animals have inhabited the earth, and then became extinct. The remains of these plants and animals, preserved in rock, are called fossils.

Fossils may take the form of shells, bones, or scales. Sometimes, an entire animal is preserved and found with its bones, flesh, and skin intact. Plants may leave their prints on a rock, and animals may leave their tracks in mud or rock.

The remains of plants and animals have been preserved in other ways. Insects may have been trapped in sticky sap. Larger animals, like the saber-toothed tiger or giant sloth, may have fallen into tar pits and perished. Fossils have been found buried in volcanic ash and frozen in ice.

4. Record essential words, definitions, and sentences on language master cards or on audiotapes.
5. Provide vocabulary lists or glossaries with simplified definitions and use the words in sentences.

### *Presentation of Concepts*

To modify the presentation of concepts:

1. Supplement print material with concept-teaching procedures.
2. Present concepts one at a time.
3. Provide visual supplements, such as transparencies, illustrations, and diagrams.
4. Use modeling and demonstration to clarify concepts.
5. Use games, manipulatives, and hands-on activities to reinforce concepts.
6. Draw upon the different cultural backgrounds and experiences of your students to make concepts meaningful.

### *General Comprehension*

To increase understanding of materials:

1. Include prereading organizers and end-of-text summaries.
2. Provide study guides or outlines.
3. Insert stop points in text and have students summarize what they have read.
4. Include periodic reviews in the form of statements or questions.
5. Have students generate their own questions about printed materials.
6. Highlight main ideas in one color and supporting details in another. Post a key to the coding system in the classroom.
7. Give short, frequent quizzes instead of one long test.
8. Use books on tape to assist students with pronunciations and the understanding of dialects.
9. Use graphic organizers (Figure 5.3).
10. Conduct brainstorming sessions.

**Figure 5.3**  Graphic Organizer

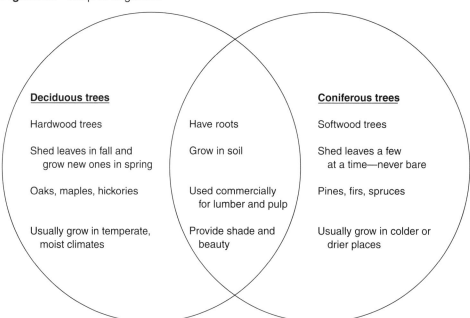

### Directions

To clarify written directions:

1. Simplify the directions.
2. Shorten the directions.
3. Use concise, boldface directions.
4. Put the words typically used in directions on language master cards.
5. Highlight the key words in a set of directions (e.g., "**Write** a *t* in the blank if the answer is **true** and an *f* if the answer is **false**.").
6. Have the students underline what they are supposed to do (e.g., "Write your answer in the blank provided for you.").
7. In a set of multiple directions, use colored dots or numbers to differentiate the separate directions (Lambie, 1980).

### Practice

To provide sufficient practice:

1. Have students move laterally before they move vertically to a new skill (e.g., have students practice multiplying one-digit numbers by one-digit numbers to mastery level before you teach them to multiply one-digit numbers by two-digit numbers).

2. Supplement practice in printed products with games, audiotapes, and manipulatives.
3. Provide repetition, review, and application of skills.
4. Provide opportunities to practice previously taught skills within learning centers.

### Manageability of Assignments

To increase the manageability of assignments:

1. Shorten assignments by cutting worksheets in half or circling even-numbered questions for students to complete.
2. Clip a piece of paper to a page so that it covers half of the page, and have the student complete the other half.
3. Draw a box around the questions that the student should answer (Figure 5.4).
4. Use bookmarks to help students locate words and keep their place.
5. Underline or highlight specific information that is being introduced or emphasized.
6. Mask out certain areas of print material to emphasize specific concepts, eliminate unnecessary visual stimuli, and encourage task performance.
7. Color-code newly introduced material, major concepts, or material to be memorized.

**Figure 5.4** Shortening an Assignment

Name _____ Date _____

*Directions: Write your answers to the subtraction problems in the space provided.*

Do the problems that are inside the box.

| 1. $5.10 | 2. $6.28 | 3. $4.43 | 4. $8.11 |
|---|---|---|---|
| −2.51 | −2.99 | −1.76 | −5.86 |
| 5. $7.56 | 6. $4.41 | 7. $9.05 | 8. $6.43 |
| −6.78 | −3.85 | −2.79 | −4.78 |
| 9. $3.10 | 10. $8.83 | 11. $6.76 | 12. $5.20 |
| −2.98 | −5.99 | −3.97 | −4.91 |
| 13. $5.84 | 14. $4.12 | 15. $8.03 | 16. $7.07 |
| −1.96 | −3.87 | −5.75 | −2.49 |

8. During presentations using PowerPoint or transparencies, indicate the important points with one symbol (e.g., highlighting or printing in boldface type) and the details with another (e.g., underlining or italicizing).

9. For students who have difficulty reading lengthy chapters, audiotape every other page. Have the student read one page and listen to the next (Lambie, 1980).

10. Allow students to begin homework in class and provide feedback to ensure that they will complete the assignment correctly when they work on it at home.

### *Organization*

To organize printed materials in a clear, consistent manner:

1. Use advance and post organizers for each activity (e.g., give students an outline or a set of questions at the beginning of a lesson and print a summary or list important points on a transparency to use for review at the end of a lesson).

2. Reorganize poorly designed worksheets to create simple, easy-to-follow layouts and formats (Figures 5.5 and 5.6).

3. Provide graphics that are clear and understandable. Be sure graphics clarify and support the printed text (e.g., give students a photocopy of a check that has been filled out so that, as they read the text, they can see where the date, amount, signature, etc., belong).

### *Response Modes*

To increase the options for student responses:

1. Allow students to tape their responses on audiocassette.

2. Provide opportunities for students to work in groups with games, flash cards, and hands-on activities in response to printed assignments.

3. Let students dictate stories, themes, and book reports.

4. Allow students to use the computer instead of writing spelling words, themes, and reports.

5. Provide role play and discussions.

6. Make materials self-correcting.

### *Motivation*

To increase motivation and interest in printed materials:

1. Use concrete examples and demonstrations to supplement printed materials.

2. Draw upon prior knowledge to make material more interesting to students.

3. Supplement text materials with nontraditional printed materials, such as newspapers, magazines, and comic books (e.g., use stories dictated by students about popular athletes and other celebrities to develop reading lessons for students).

4. Allow students to use self-correcting materials and manipulatives.

5. Use materials that interest students while simplifying vocabulary.

6. Use audiovisual aids, such as CD-ROM technology, videotapes, language master cards, and computer software to increase interest in printed materials.

7. Use think/pair/share—after asking a question, ask students to find a partner, share their response to the question, remember their partner's response, and share with the class.

8. Incorporate multicultural materials into your classroom.

### *Abstract Concepts and Materials*

To make materials more concrete:

1. Provide demonstrations.

2. Use concrete examples.

3. Present abstract concepts in the form of concept maps, graphic organizers, or webs.

4. Use role play.

5. Associate concepts with music or art.

6. Relate materials to students' cultural backgrounds and experiences.

**Figure 5.5**  Example of a Poorly Designed Worksheet

---

Name _____ Date_____

Read Chapter 5 about the rainforest and answer the following questions.

**A.  TRUE/FALSE**
   1.  Rainforests are characterized by vast, dry, sunny regions.
   2.  Destruction of the world's rainforests may affect plants, animals, and climate.
   3.  It is humid and rains almost every day in a rainforest.
   4.  Rainforests are dense forests that are found in tropical regions around the equator.
   5.  Rainforests are very heavily populated areas with many people.
   6.  The trees of a rainforest grow so close together that sunlight rarely reaches the forest floor.

**B.  Look up the following words in the Glossary of your social studies book.**
   1.  uninhabited
   2.  vegetation
   3.  tropical
   4.  frontier
   5.  agriculture
   6.  lumbering
   7.  ecologists
   8.  economy
   9.  climate
   10.  temperature
   11.  Amazon
   12.  equator
   13.  continents
   14.  minerals
   15.  extinction
   16.  humidity
   17.  minerals
   18.  petroleum
   19.  resources
   20.  carbon dioxide

**C.  Read another story or article about rainforests. Compare the information in Chapter 5 with your new article. Or write a story about a rainforest including how it would look, sound, smell, and feel.**

---

## Test Adaptations

The increase in the percentage of students with disabilities receiving instruction in general education classrooms for 80% of the day or more has implications for general education teachers (National Center for Education Statistics, 2001). Students with disabilities are spending more time with the general education curriculum, including tests. A nationwide survey of general education teachers was conducted regarding their views related to test adaptations for students with disabilities (Jayanthi, Epstein, Polloway, Bursuck, 1996). The adaptations that were rated by the teachers as being the most helpful for students were assisting students with directions during tests; reading test questions to students; and simplifying the wording of questions. The adaptations rated as the easiest to make included providing extra space for answers; open-note and open-book tests; giving practice questions as a study guide; and helping with directions during testing.

In another study, middle school students, including those with high incidence disabilities, were asked to rate each of 23 testing adaptations (Nelson, Jayanthi, Epstein, & Bursuck, 2000). Students indicated a preference for

**Figure 5.6**  Example of an Adapted Worksheet

Name _____ Date _____

**The Rainforest**

*Directions:* Read pages 43–52 in Chapter 5 of your social studies book. Then complete Parts I, II, and III about the rainforest.

---

**Part I—True/False**

*Directions:* Read each of the following statements. Write "True" in the box if the statement is true, and "False" if it is false.

[____] 1. Rainforests are characterized by vast, dry, sunny regions.

[____] 2. Destruction of the world's rainforests may affect plants, animals, and climate.

[____] 3. It is humid and rains almost every day in a rainforest.

[____] 4. Rainforests are dense forests that are found in tropical regions around the equator.

[____] 5. Rainforests are very heavily populated areas with many people.

[____] 6. The trees of a rainforest grow so close together that sunlight rarely reaches the forest floor.

---

**Part II—Vocabulary**

*Directions:* Look up the following words in the Glossary in the back of your social studies book. Write the word and its definition in your notebook.

|            List 1 |            List 2 |
|-------------------|-------------------|
| 1. uninhabited    | 1. lumbering      |
| 2. vegetation     | 2. ecologists     |
| 3. tropical       | 3. climate        |
| 4. agriculture    | 4. temperature    |
| 5. frontier       | 5. economy        |

|            List 3 |            List 4 |
|-------------------|-------------------|
| 1. carbon dioxide | 1. extinction     |
| 2. Amazon         | 2. humidity       |
| 3. equator        | 3. petroleum      |
| 4. populated      | 4. resources      |
| 5. continents     | 5. minerals       |

---

**Part III—Take Your Choice**

*Directions:* Complete *either* Choice #1 or Choice #2.

Choice #1

    1st  —  Read another story or article about rainforests.

    2nd  —  Write two things that are the same as the information in Chapter 5 of your book.

    3rd  —  Write two new things that you learned.

Choice #2

    Write a story about a rainforest including how it would look, sound, smell, and feel.

open-note and open-book tests; practice questions; multiple choice over short answer or essay questions; using a dictionary or calculator; a copy of the test for studying; and extra space for answers. As you might predict, students with disabilities and students with low achievement did show a significantly higher preference for test adaptations than did students with average or above-average achievement.

In addition to using adaptations, such as providing practice questions and giving open-note and open-book tests, we recommend that you examine your own teacher-made tests and adapt them, if needed, using these suggestions:

1. Type your tests. Tests are more legible when they are typed, not hand written, on an easy-to-see background.
2. Use a combination of uppercase and lowercase letters, which are easier to read than all capital letters (Salend, 1995a).
3. Allow students to write on the test instead of using a separate answer sheet (Salend, 2001). Leave ample extra space for answers.
4. Provide extra paper for students to work out problems, jot down an outline, or make lists of words for later reference.
5. Use separate sheets of paper (not front/back) for each page of the test to make the test easier to follow and to ensure that students do not forget to respond to every page and every question.
6. Vary the response modes by allowing students to spell words aloud to a para-educator or teacher instead of writing them; dictate written responses into a tape recorder; or use a computer instead of writing an essay by hand.
7. Use cues such as color coding, underlining, or highlighting key words in a test to alert students to specifics about the items, and arrows and stop signs at the bottom of test pages (Salend, 2001).
8. Modify the end-of-chapter questions.

    ▶ Read questions as a class.
    ▶ Ask fewer questions.

    ▶ Reword the questions in simpler terms.
    ▶ Increase response time.
    ▶ Allow students to work on some of the questions together (e.g., odd numbered questions) and then complete the remaining questions independently.
    ▶ Write the number of the page on which the response can be found next to each question at the end of the chapter (see Figure 5.7). Or next to the response in the chapter, write the number of the question, then highlight the response (Wood & Wooley, 1986). Students may actually spend more time reading the material as they look for the answer to a particular question than they might if you just asked them to read the material.

9. Teachers should consider the readability of test items when they construct tests (Salend, 1995a). Modify the readability level of a test by rewording the content, shortening sentences, and simplifying vocabulary. Adapted from Murphy, Meyers, Olesen, McKean, and Custer (1993), Table 5.3 provides an example of how to reword test items while maintaining the original intent of the questions.

Many authors have offered guidelines to use in writing or adapting test items such as multiple choice, matching, fill in the blanks, and essay. For example, for multiple-choice questions, you should present the choices vertically; avoid using

**Figure 5.7**  Chapter Questions

*Directions:* Read each question carefully. Next to each question is the page on which the answer may be found. Find the page in the chapter and look for the answer. Write your answers at the bottom of this paper.

1. What are bacteria? (*Page 16*)
2. What shape are bacteria? (*Page 16*)
3. Where do bacteria live? (*Page 17*)
4. How are bacteria harmful to us? (*Page 19*)
5. How are bacteria helpful to us? (*Page 21*)

**Table 5.3** Test Questions With Lowered Readability

**These are examples of how you can rewrite test questions to lower the readability level. Notice that the original intent of each question is maintained.**

| | |
|---|---|
| Orginal | Earthquakes are produced by what force within the earth? |
| Revised | What causes earthquakes? |
| Original | Compare and contrast the personal attributes and characteristics of Ulysses S. Grant and Robert E. Lee. |
| Rivised | How were Ulysses S. Grant and Robert E. Lee alike? How were they different? |
| Original | What is the sensation of seeing two objects when only one is viewed? |
| Rivised | What is double vision? |
| Original | Discuss the rationale of the secessionists in regard to their threat to secede from the union in 1860. |
| Rivised | Why did the southern states decide to leave the union in 1860? |
| Orginal | According to the Gadsden Purchase, the United States procured thousands of square miles of unsettled land located in New Mexico and Arizona along the southern borders of both states. |
| Rivised | The Gadsden Purchase gave the United States unsettled land along the southern border of New Mexico and Arizona. |
| Orginal | List the four primary taste sensations that are each sensitive to a particular kind of chemical stimulus. |
| Rivised | List the four primary taste sensations. |
| Orginal | Describe the three environmental conditions required for the prolific growth of mold and mildew. |
| Rivised | List three things mold and mildew need in order to grow. |
| Orginal | Crystal Thompson needs insurance for her personal belongings, but not for her residence, since she lives in an apartment. If her annual insurance premium is $63.00, what amount will she have paid in three years? |
| Revised | Crystal Thompson lives in an apartment and needs to insure her belongings. The insurance premium costs $63.00 a year (annually). How much will she pay in three years? |

words such as always, all, never; and make sure the choices are of similar length (Salend, 2001). In constructing matching items, you should list both columns on the same page. For fill-in-the-blank items, you should make the size of the blanks the same. Essay questions are frequently challenging for students because they involve reading, critical thinking, and written expression. There are some things you can do to assist students to respond to an essay item on a test that may result in a more complete and better organized response. After you write the essay question, provide subquestions and a list of key words that the student can include in the response (Salend, 2001) (see Table 5.4). Notice how by structuring the student's response with subquestions and including a key word list, you can assist the student to better analyze the question and organize a well-thought-out written reponse.

## SELECTING, ANALYZING, AND ADAPTING ASSESSMENT TECHNIQUES AND MATERIALS TO MEET THE NEEDS OF CULTURALLY AND LINGUISTICALLY DIVERSE GROUPS

Because the assessment of students from diverse racial and ethnic groups is influenced by cultural and language differences as well as by varied learning styles, Banks and colleagues (2001) recommend that teachers use multiple, culturally sensitive assessment techniques. They suggest that teachers use formative and summative strategies that include observations, oral tests, and teacher-made and standardized assessments because students acquire and demonstrate competencies in different ways.

In addition to using multiple and appropriate assessment techniques with students from culturally and linguistically diverse groups, teachers must also use meaningful and appropriate instructional materials. In some states, textbooks and other materials are adopted by the state or district, whereas in other states the teacher may have the opportunity to recommend textbooks, supplementary materials, and other printed products. Because many teachers depend on the textbook in determining the curriculum, the way in which textbooks and other printed materials are selected is vitally important in providing multicultural education (Gollnick & Chinn, 2002). Some groups such as women, minority groups, individuals with disabilities, and older persons are underrepresented in materials (Gollnick & Chinn, 2002). Teachers who are sensitive to these omissions will develop strategies for including them as part of instruction. They will use supplementary materials and discussions to overcome biases that are inherent in some instructional

**Table 5.4** Adapted Essay Question

---

**Key word list:** Funnel-shaped, cloud particles, updraft, debris, destruction, kilometers, Doppler radar, meteorologists

**Essay question:** Gigantic cumulonimbus clouds have been building overhead. The sky is dark with a strange tint of gray and green. The air has become very still and the sound of a siren can be heard. Name and describe the type of severe storm that is about to occur.

**Subquestions:** In writing your answer, discuss the following:

1. How is this type of storm formed?
2. How can this type of storm be predicted?
3. What are the possible effects of such a storm?
4. What safety measures should you take in this type of storm?

---

materials and ensure that their students are exposed to the multicultural nature of society.

It is helpful for teachers to continue to try out different materials, and adapt or supplement until they achieve an appropriate education plan for all students who are culturally and linguistically diverse (Baca & Cervantes, 1998). For example, in her history class, Ms. Andreas adapts and supplements the history textbook significantly to include the perspective of Native Americans in the study of Western expansion. Gollnick and Chinn (2002) state that textbooks typically present only one perspective and suggest that students should be given the opportunity to read more than one perspective. If the textbook presents only the U.S. government's perspective of treaties and protection, the teacher should also present the Native American perspective, which might examine the topics of broken treaties and the appropriation of lands (Gollnick & Chinn, 2002). To further illustrate this point, a text that is limited to the contributions of the European settlers in the United States does not present a balanced perspective (Gollnick & Chinn, 2002). Many students would fail to learn about the contributions of their own cultural groups in the development of their country. Such a text would have to be significantly modified or supplemented. Therefore, it is important for teachers to be knowledgeable about particular cultures and heritages and the compatibility of the cultures and heritages with selected materials and be prepared to adapt and supplement when necessary.

Ortiz (1989) recommends that teachers consider certain factors when adapting materials for students who have limited English proficiency. He suggests that teachers analyze vocabulary and syntax for verbal load and regional forms and rewrite the text if necessary. He feels that teachers should support texts with pictures, media, and action to make the content understandable. For example, Mr. Bonavidez uses videotapes and CD-ROM technology to supplement his discussion of famous inventors.

His students are able to see different parts of the United States and the world as each videotape and CD-ROM traces the origin and background of one inventor. Mr. Bonavidez provides glossaries that contain terms, definitions, and pictures to help students who are not proficient in English.

Winzer and Mazurek (1998) state that the materials teachers use have a major impact on students' cognitive and affective domains and can help develop understandings. They recommend that you include the following in your classroom:

1. Fiction, nonfiction, dual-language texts, poetry, magazines, and newspapers.
2. Books that have predictable features, invite conversation, have meaningful illustrations, support the curriculum, and are linked to the student's culture.
3. Materials that are culturally appropriate, meaningful, accurate, and in the student's language.
4. Manipulatives, technology, and bulletin boards.

 **ACTIVITY 5.3**

Locate the instructional material you analyzed in Activity 5.2 and think about the limitations you identified. Now, use some of the strategies we've presented to modify the material to make it more appropriate for students with special needs. Remember to include multicultural, age, and gender considerations.

 **IMPORTANT POINTS**

1. Materials and texts that are not appropriate for students with special needs in special or inclusive education settings may be adapted.

2. Strategies for adapting printed products include highlighting, color coding, and simplifying, among others.

3. Test adaptations include typing clear, easy-to-read tests; providing study questions; modifying the readability level; and using visual cues on the test to guide students.

4. Teachers should use multiple, culturally sensitive assessment techniques that include observations, oral tests, and teacher-made and standardized assessments (Banks et al., 2001).

5. To facilitate the effective and appropriate use of instructional materials with students who are culturally and linguistically diverse, strategies include modification of vocabulary; use of media, pictures, and glossaries; presentation of multiple perspectives; attention to gender, age, individuals with special needs, and older persons; and incorporation of supplementary materials that emphasize different languages and cultures.

## DEVELOPING MATERIALS

Some instructional materials cannot be adapted or modified to a level that is acceptable for use with students who have special needs. For example, we have worked with some math and spelling materials that required an almost complete reconstruction because of inappropriate sequencing of skills, problems with format, and print quality. Other materials have been inappropriate because of cultural or gender bias. Still other materials have introduced too much new vocabulary.

Because of such problems and others, you may choose to develop your own materials. When developing instructional materials, avoid the problems that are characteristic of ineffective commercial products. For example, design materials that provide sufficient practice, repetition, and review and consider factors that will affect the performance of your students. Consider how the learner is going to interact with the material.

The input may be auditory, with directions given on an audiotape, and the output may be written, with the student required to write something. Vary the input (auditory, visual) and output (written, verbal), depending on the activity and the characteristics of your students.

You should also attend to the complexity of the material and match it to the level of your students. Some teachers develop manipulative materials to help their students better grasp abstract concepts. The complexity of the material can also be related to the stages of learning. For example, when Ms. Roberts teaches place value to her students, she gives them popsicle sticks to help them understand the concept (acquisition stage).

As you develop materials, consider how your students will receive feedback. Some of your materials should be self-correcting, so that your students can monitor their own performance. Computers can provide automatic feedback. With other materials, you should provide positive and corrective feedback to your students.

In materials development, you should give careful consideration to the concept load of the material. This includes the number of new concepts you present at one time, the amount of practice you provide, and the rate of presentation. For example, Mr. Saunders spends a class period with his high school students going over a diagram that he developed after examining several textbooks. He consolidated into one diagram nearly everything he could find on the topic of prejudice. Concentrating on the one concept, the class defines prejudice, identifies characteristics of it, and gives examples.

In materials development, you should also consider your level of involvement with the materials and whether it is extensive (teacher-directed) or minimal (student-directed, individual, or group). Rewriting materials and then presenting them to your students (teacher-directed) will require quite an investment of your time. Giving the students self-correcting materials requires less teacher interaction and time. Finally, you should consider the affective aspects of materials, such as cultural emphasis, age bias, and gender bias.

## Development of Specific Materials

Teacher-made materials may include worksheets, folder activities, educational games, and self-correcting materials. These materials may increase the effectiveness of the overall instructional program because they ensure individualization and because they are designed to reinforce, motivate, and enhance pupil participation. For example, Marco, a third grader, had trouble learning vocabulary in its written form in his reading workbook. Ms. Micelli, his special education teacher, made him a word bank that contained the reading vocabulary on language master cards. Marco practiced his words on the language master, which presented the words to him both visually and aurally. Marco said each word aloud as he practiced and again, later, as Ms. Micelli checked him. Ms. Micelli noted Marco's progress on a chart that listed each of the words. Marco learned the words quickly because he received positive and corrective feedback and found the material interesting and motivating.

Laurie, a seventh-grade student, had just been taught a technique to improve her comprehension of reading material. Because she works successfully in groups and learns well from others, her teacher, Mr. Nohmura, grouped her with two other students to practice, repeat, and review the steps of the comprehension monitoring technique. Mr. Nohmura developed worksheets for the students to use for written practice, let them verbally rehearse the steps with one another, and then, using a teacher-made checklist, evaluated each student for mastery of the steps. Use of the teacher-made materials and attention to affective concerns, in combination with learner interactions with the materials and feedback and evaluation, increased Laurie's opportunities for success.

### Worksheets

Because many schools use worksheets, you should know how to recognize and develop effective worksheets. In developing worksheets for students, you should make directions clear and concise and be careful not to overload the page with items. Worksheets should focus on one concept at a time and provide adequate practice. Worksheets should be manageable in appearance, not overwhelming, with a clear, easy-to-follow, inviting format. In addition to developing your own worksheets, you may also need to adapt or rewrite worksheets.

Look back to the section of this chapter that discusses adaptations. Figure 5.5 contains a sample of a poorly designed worksheet. Figure 5.6 shows how that worksheet has been adapted. Notice how the poorly designed worksheet is crowded and lacks clear, specific directions. For example, there are no directions for Part A (the true/false items), there are incomplete directions for Part B (the vocabulary section), and the directions lack specificity in Part C (the written response section). The list of 20 words looks overwhelming, and the worksheet looks crowded. The adapted worksheet is easier on the eye because of the way it is organized (e.g., boxes around sections and better spacing). Introductory directions are provided and directions for Parts I, II, and III are clear and specific. Part I contains boxes in which students may write their responses, and the directions specify that students are to write *true or false*. The directions for Part II state where to write the words and definitions. The long list of 20 words has been divided into four smaller, more manageable lists. The directions for Part III clearly state that students have a choice of *two* activities for the written response question.

You can make worksheets self-correcting by printing the answers on the back, on the bottom (upside down), or along the right margin (which can be folded over to conceal them). A word of caution: If you plan to use worksheets, be sure they serve a valid purpose and are not used merely to fill time, and make sure you provide feedback to students.

### Folder Activities

File folders meet the needs of students by providing opportunities for practice and reinforcement of a wide range of skills. File folders are convenient to use and store, and teachers who float from classroom to classroom can easily transport them. Because folder activities are usually student directed, they should contain clear, concise directions. Many folder activities include some means of self-monitoring, such as access to an answer key.

Folders may be constructed to include activities that are multilevel. For example, in her preparation of a math unit, Mrs. Barkwell set up folder activities that used a restaurant menu. In one folder activity, students were asked to locate the cost of various items, such as hamburgers, soft drinks, French fries, and milkshakes. In another folder activity, students were required to order several items and compute the total cost. In still another activity, students had to figure the total cost plus tax. In a more advanced folder activity, students determined the total cost and tax, then figured out how much change they would receive from $10 and from $20. Notice how the difficulty level of the activities varied, making them appropriate for students functioning at several different levels. The activities were set up to be self-correcting, with the answers written on the reverse side (e.g., a card with a picture of a hamburger on one side and the price on the back).

### Educational Games

Educational games do not take the place of instruction, but they do provide motivating ways to help reinforce skills (Heit, 1980). By creating games, you help students attain skills and solve problems that are important to their success both in and out of school. A teacher-made game must provide (a) a clearly stated purpose, or rationale, and outcome; (b) complete yet uncomplicated directions and rules; (c) reinforcement and practice of skills already acquired; and (d) a method of monitoring and evaluating progress.

You may construct your own board game or use a commercial board. Little Kenny Publications has wipe-off game boards, cards, spinners, and game pieces available for purchase. You can use this generic equipment to create your own instructional games to support the sequential development of the academic skills your students need. The game boards can be adapted to any academic skill and content that you want to reinforce, including simplifying fractions, reviewing science vocabulary, and practicing long vowel sounds. You may also construct a spinner for a game by attaching a paper fastener to the center of a transparency. By drawing a circle on the transparency, dividing it into eighths, and writing numbers 1 through 8 in consecutive sections, you can make a generic spinner that is appropriate for use with any game and is usable with the entire class or a small group.

Cosgrove (1992) recommends creating board games from computer programs, or adapting boards from old, unused games (e.g., recycle an old game board by adding math fact questions to the game cards). Matrix boards (e.g., checkers) or a deck of cards may also be adapted (Cosgrove, 1992) to make Concentration and Jeopardy games for vocabulary and math.

### Self-Correcting Materials

Many teachers include a self-correcting component in the materials they develop because of the importance of immediate feedback to learning. Mercer, Mercer, and Bott (1984) point out some advantages of self-correcting materials:

Students avoid practicing mistakes.

Students learn better with immediate rather than delayed feedback.

Students can function independently.

Students tend to remain on task with self-correcting materials.

You can develop self-correcting materials in a variety of formats (e.g., answer on the back, audiocassette, matching, etc.). The following ideas are based on suggestions by Mercer, Mercer, and Bott (1984).

***Answer on the Back.*** You can write a problem on one side of a card and put the answer on the back. You may use such cards for math facts and their answers or for vocabulary terms and their definitions. Alternatively, you can write terms or math facts and their answers on the same side of the card. Then cut each card in half in a different zigzag pattern, so the question is on one half of the card and the answer is on the other half. That way, the two parts fit together each time your students respond correctly. You may also use this technique for the states and their capitals.

***Audiocassette.*** You can use an audiocassette to record a problem, question, or direction, then pause before dictating the answer. This self-correcting technique is also effective with spelling words, science vocabulary, and word problems.

***Matching.*** For practicing a word and its abbreviation, a math problem and its answer, or a date in history and the event that took place on that date, prepare sets of cards with a problem or question on one card and the answer on another card. Be sure the back of each pair of cards contains some type of picture completion. After students respond to the problems, they should turn the cards over. If the answer is correct, the pictures should either match or fit together to complete an object or design.

 **ACTIVITY 5.4**

**Part 1.** Develop a math worksheet on telling time for a third-grade student. Make sure the directions are clear and the worksheet is self-correcting.

**Part 2.** Develop a self-correcting activity appropriate for an elementary student (such as states and their capitals) and one for a secondary student (such as subject-verb agreement).

 **IMPORTANT POINTS** ◀

1. In developing instructional materials, it is important to provide sufficient practice, repetition, and review.
2. Key variables during materials development include the learner's interactions with the materials, the concept load, the extent of teacher involvement, and affective aspects of materials.
3. Teacher-made materials may include worksheets, folder activities, educational games, and self-correcting materials.
4. Worksheets should focus on one concept at a time, provide adequate practice, present clear and concise directions, and display an easy-to-follow inviting format.
5. File folders are convenient to use and store, are student-directed, and are often multilevel.
6. A teacher-made game must provide a clearly stated purpose, uncomplicated directions and rules, reinforcement and practice of acquired skills, and a monitoring method.
7. Self-correcting materials provide immediate feedback to learning.

 **DISCUSSION QUESTIONS** ◀

1. Provide examples to support the statement, "One of the most important roles of the special education teacher is to assist general education teachers in the adaptation of materials and instruction."
2. Discuss how you are going to provide materials in your classroom that are appropriate for culturally and linguistically diverse groups of students.
3. How do you build a classroom community and at the same time provide test adaptations for students with special needs?

# PART 2

# INSTRUCTIONAL TECHNIQUES

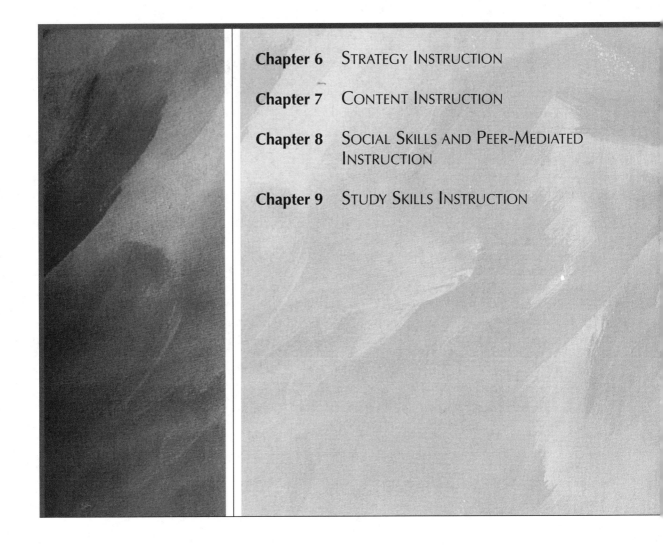

# CHAPTER 6

# STRATEGY INSTRUCTION

The adage, "Give me a fish and I eat for a day. Teach me to fish and I eat for a lifetime," exemplifies the need to teach students *how to learn*. If you teach students how to learn, then you will not have to help them prepare for every test, assist them with each report, or help them answer the questions at the end of every chapter they are assigned. In other words, you provide them with the strategies that will empower them to act independently and master skills across a variety of situations and settings. These skills may include finding the main idea in a paragraph, summarizing a passage, accessing information on their own, or writing a research paper (Rosenshine, 1990).

In this chapter, we discuss the use of cognitive strategies to teach students with special needs to become strategic information processors and problem solvers. First, we provide a discussion of cognitive strategies in general. Then we describe how cognitive strategies are taught through the use of metacognition, cognitive behavior modification (CBM), reciprocal teaching (RT), the Strategic Instruction Model (SIM), and the Self-Regulated Strategy Development (SRSD) model, all of which include aspects of both the reductionist (scientific) and constructivist (holistic) paradigms described in Chapter 1. These approaches rely on direct instruction, modeling, feedback, and active student involvement—characteristics of the reductionist paradigm. They also place an emphasis on how students think, embed instruction in meaningful contexts, and provide opportunities for students to assume responsibility for their own learning by setting their own objectives and learning from one another—characteristics of the constructivist paradigm. Metacognition, cognitive behavior modification (CBM), reciprocal teaching (RT), the Strategic Instruction Model (SIM), and the Self-Regulated Strategy Development (SRSD) model begin with the teacher assuming the major responsibility for teaching, then gradually shifting the responsibility to the students.

## COGNITIVE STRATEGIES

Cognitive strategies relate to how we process information (Lenz, Ellis, & Scanlon, 1996). They are the cognitive processes that learners use to influence learning (Mayer, 2001). For example, Joshua may use the cognitive strategy of writing a long-distance phone number five times to help him memorize it, whereas B. J. may use the cognitive strategy of clustering, so the phone number is processed as 305 452 38 10. Cognitive strategy instruction combines the elements of explicit teaching with scaffolding procedures (Ciardiello, 1998), and empowers students by giving them access to techniques or methods for acquiring, remembering, and demonstrating information in order to solve problems.

### Rationale

Students with learning problems are often described as inefficient learners who lack certain strategies, choose inappropriate strategies, or do not monitor their use of strategies (Swanson, 1991; Wong, 1991). Students with learning disabilities, mild mental disabilities, or behavior problems often fail to take an active role in their own learning and frequently fail to use strategies when approaching the complex requirements of academic tasks (Swanson, 1991; Torgesen, 1982; Wong, 1991). Others may actually use strategies but may not choose them wisely (as in repeating a long list of words over and over in order to memorize it instead of using mnemonics or visual imagery). Jones, Palincsar, Ogle,

and Carr (1987) indicate that if students do not already possess a strategy for completing certain tasks, then teaching an appropriate strategy is likely to improve achievement, especially for less proficient students. Because low-achieving students are not likely to develop cognitive strategies spontaneously, it is important to provide specific strategy instruction (Jones et al., 1987). Research has shown that students with learning disabilities benefit from cognitive strategy instruction (Montague, 1997), including the use of self-instruction (Van Luit & Naglieri, 1999). Cognitive strategies provide students with a set of self-instructional steps that assist them in addressing a specific need (e.g., writing an essay) and in learning, organizing, retaining, and expressing information. Cognitive strategies offer promise for students with mild disabilities to set goals, devise strategies, and monitor their own progress (Meese, 1994).

In addition to knowing how to use a cognitive strategy, it is important for students to know why the strategy is useful or how to evaluate its effectiveness (Billingsley & Wildman, 1990). Students need to know (1) what the strategy is for; (2) how, when, and where to use the strategy; (3) why the strategy is important and useful; and (4) how to evaluate its effectiveness (Winograd & Hare, 1988). This knowledge is critical to generalization efforts. Studies have shown that cognitive strategy training has a significant impact on academic performance when generalization of the training to natural environments occurs (Ellis, 1983; Schmidt, 1983). In other words, "the strategy must be generalizable across a variety of settings, situations, and contexts" (Lenz et al., 1996, p. 16).

### Strategic Teaching and Learning

In classroom settings where strategic teaching and learning are taking place, teachers and students think and make decisions about strategy selection, application, and evaluation. If you walked into a classroom where the teacher was using cognitive strategy instruction, you might notice the teacher (1) tailoring instruction to meet students' needs and difficulties, (2) modeling the use of strategies by "thinking aloud," (3) making sure that students understand the task and the significance of the strategy to the task, (4) actively involving students, (5) helping students create their own strategies, (6) assisting students to personalize the strategies they use, (7) providing feedback regarding students' use of strategies, and (8) gradually transferring the responsibility for teaching and learning to the students. In that same classroom you would see students (1) applying strategies to various academic content, (2) actively participating, (3) monitoring their own progress, (4) interacting with teachers and with each other, and (5) taking responsibility for their own learning through self-instruction, self-evaluation, and self-regulation.

In describing strategic teaching and learning, we borrow from the ideas of Jones and associates (1987), along with the principles of effective teaching (Englert et al., 1992). Strategic teachers:

▶ Spend time thinking/reflecting about instructional planning and teaching

▶ Focus on students' prior learning experiences

▶ Possess a wide variety of strategies and explain to students the purpose and significance of each strategy

▶ Are rich in content knowledge

▶ Know how to achieve a balance between strategies and content

▶ Understand characteristics of learners

▶ Are knowledgeable about the organization of instructional materials and curriculum

▶ Actively collaborate with their students in selecting, applying, and monitoring the use of strategies to meet specific goals

As you read the next sections on metacognition, cognitive behavior modification (CBM), reciprocal teaching (RT), the Strategic Instruction Model (SIM), and the Self-Regulated Strategy

Development (SRSD) model, notice that the strategic teaching and learning behaviors previously described are included in each of them.

Metacognition is the knowledge (awareness) and control (monitoring) that individuals have over their learning. Cognitive behavior modification (CBM) teaches self-regulation and problem solving. Reciprocal teaching (RT) involves gaining meaning from text through the use of teacher–student dialogues. Both SIM and SRSD include how to plan and complete a task, monitor progress, and make adjustments and modifications. Although there are some differences among these five approaches, the many similarities qualify each of them in the category of cognitive strategies. Each approach (1) has a set of steps or procedures, (2) uses cognitive modeling, (3) involves explicit instruction, (4) includes practice and feedback, (5) incorporates a gradual transfer of responsibility and ownership from teacher to students, and (6) promotes generalization. Table 6.1 provides a comparison of metacognition, cognitive behavior modification (CBM), reciprocal teaching (RT), the Strategic Instruction Model, and the Self-Regulated Strategy Development (SRSD) model in terms of definition, components, instructional procedures, instructional approach, and content taught. Figure 6.1 illustrates an example of a cognitive/metacognitive strategy for mathematical problem solving (Montague, 1997).

## METACOGNITION

The general knowledge (awareness) and control (monitoring) that an individual has over his or her thinking and learning is known as metacognition (Flavell, 1976; Paris, Lipson, Jacobs, Oka, Debritto, & Cross, 1982). Metacognitive strategies relate to how an individual selects, monitors, and uses these strategies (Lenz et al., 1996). Awareness, the first component of metacognition, involves a person's knowledge about his or her cognitive resources

**Figure 6.1** A Cognitive/ Metacognitive Strategy for Mathematical Problem Solving

Read (for understanding)
**Say:** Read the problem. If I don't understand, read it again.
**Ask:** Have I read and understood the problem?
**Check:** For understanding as I solve the problem.

Paraphrase (your own words)
**Say:** Underline the important information. Put the problem in my own words.
**Ask:** Have I underlined the important information? What is the question? What am I looking for?
**Check:** That the information goes with the question.

Visualize (a picture of a diagram)
**Say:** Make a drawing or a diagram.
**Ask:** Does the picture fit the problem?
**Check:** The picture against the problem information.

Hypothesize (a plan to solve the problem)
**Say:** Decide how many steps and operations are needed. Write the operation symbols $(+ - \times \div)$.
**Ask:** If I do—, what will I get? If I do—, then what do I need to do next? How many steps are needed?
**Check:** That the plan makes sense.

Estimate (predict the answer)
**Say:** Round the numbers, do the problem in my head, and write the estimate.
**Ask:** Did I round up and down? Did I write the estimate?
**Check:** That I used the important information.

Compute (do the arithmetic)
**Say:** Do the operations in the right order.
**Ask:** How does my answer compare with my estimate? Does my answer make sense? Are the decimals or money signs in the right places?
**Check:** That all the operations were done in the right order.

Check (make sure everything is right)
**Say:** Check the computation.
**Ask:** Have I checked every step? Have I checked the computation? Is my answer right?
**Check:** That everything is right. If not, go back. Then ask for help if I need it.

Note. From "Cognitive Strategy Instruction in Mathematics for Students with Learning Disabilities" by M. Montague, 1997, *Journal of Learning Disabilities, 30(2)*, p. 171. Copyright (1997) by PRO-ED, Inc. Reprinted by permission.

and the relationship between those capabilities and the demands of the task. For example, if you notice that you can study better with the radio off, you are demonstrating an understanding of how you function best in a specific situation or with a certain task. If you are aware of what you need to do to perform effectively, you may be able to regulate and control activities to solve a problem or complete a task. For example, when Rebekah observes that she is more successful in afternoon classes than in morning classes because she performs better in the afternoon, she is demonstrating metacognitive awareness.

The second component of metacognition involves self-regulatory mechanisms that enable a person to monitor, adjust, correct, and control his or her cognitive activities and task performance. For example, when you estimate the length of time it will take to complete an activity and adjust your pace to allow yourself sufficient time to finish, you are exercising control and regulating your actions. You are actively participating in the learning situation and assuming control over it. Active monitoring of cognitive activities is necessary for efficient learning (Swanson, 1991; Baker & Brown, 1980). For example, Brady has learned self-regulation by adjusting his rate when he reads different materials. He reads *The Sporting News* magazine and the daily comics quickly, but spends more time methodically reading his science textbook, looking back frequently to check his comprehension. Notice how he first demonstrates an awareness of the need to read materials at different rates (metacognitive awareness) and then exercises control over the situation by actually adjusting his reading rate with different materials (metacognitive monitoring).

## Rationale

The reason we teach metacognitive strategies to students is to influence how students interact with a learning task (Palincsar, 1986a). Metacognitive instruction is designed to empower students to assume control over their own learning and problem solving. It allows students to be more independent, to understand the purpose behind their academic assignments, and to realize the results of their actions. Metacognitive instruction is designed to promote generalization and transfer of skills across content areas and settings and is effective in teaching higher-level skills such as summarizing, paragraph writing, and self-questioning. Wong (1986) found that students who believe they are in control of their environment appear to be the most successful learners, and that therefore remedial programs for students with learning disabilities should include a metacognitive component to help them become independent learners.

▼ **ACTIVITY 6.1**

**Part 1.** Read the following passage. As you read it, try to observe what you do by asking yourself these questions, which are based on H. A. Robinson's (1975) work:

1. Do I look back at the words I have just read?
2. Do I look at each word?
3. Do I think of other things when I read?
4. Do I read and think about the meaning of every word, or do I put words together into groups?
5. Do I really know what I am reading?

When you finish reading, write down all the things you did while you were reading (activity adapted from Platt, 1987; Platt & Williams, 1988).

Beneath their feet the diesel engine thudded slowly, sending a thrust of power trembling through the deck. Across Tauranga Harbor, against the wharf at Mount Maunganui, a Japanese timber ship lifted her long black hull fretfully on the tide, dragging at the hawser with a dark, clumsy impatience. Farrer looked away, out to the harbor mouth, mentally checking off Matakana Island, impatient to be past it, as though the approaching bird sanctuary barred their passage to the open sea and the thing he knew awaited him there. The sun, still rising, spread hot, multi-fingered hands across the water. (Burns & Roe, 1985)

**Part 2.** Now that you have completed a metacognitive awareness activity, try a metacognitive monitoring activity. If you were to read this passage again, what would you do to improve your reading of it? Write down any strategies you would use or adjustments you would make. For example, would you look back? Would you adjust your pace? (Answers for this and other activities are found in the Instructor's Manual.)

## Description

Cognitive psychology is an important source of information for teachers working with students who have special needs. Using the contributions of cognitive psychology, special educators can

**Table 6.1** Comparison of Cognitive Approaches

| | Metacognition | Cognitive Behavior Modification | Reciprocal Teaching | Strategic Instruction Model | Self-Regulated Strategy Development Model |
|---|---|---|---|---|---|
| Definition | The knowledge (awareness) and control (monitoring) that individuals have over their own thinking and learning | A technique in which the teacher models his or her thinking processes while performing a task; then the student practices overtly and covertly by him- or herself | An interactive teaching strategy that takes the form of a dialogue between teachers and students to construct the meaning of text jointly | Learning *how* to learn and perform on tasks Focus on curriculum demands | An integrated approach that assists students in developing composition skills and self-regulation strategies |
| Components | Active involvement of students<br>Systematic steps or procedures<br>Cognitive modeling<br>Self-awareness<br>Self-monitoring<br>Gradual transfer of ownership and regulation<br>Generalization | Active involvement of students<br>Systematic steps or procedures<br>Cognitive modeling<br>Guided practice<br>Verbalizations<br>Overt and covert processing<br>Gradual transfer of ownership and regulation<br>Generalization | Active involvement of students<br>Systematic steps or procedures<br>Instruction in useful strategies<br>Guided interactive instruction<br>Well-informed learners<br>Readable, meaningful practice materials<br>Scaffolding<br>Cognitive modeling<br>Gradual transfer of ownership and regulation<br>Generalization | Active involvement of students<br>Systematic steps or procedures<br>Cognitive modeling<br>Overt and covert processing<br>Guided and independent practice<br>Gradual transfer of ownership and regulation<br>Generalization | Active involvement of students<br>Systematic steps or procedures<br>Cognitive modeling<br>Overt and covert processing<br>Instruction in useful strategies<br>Gradual transfer of ownership and regulation<br>Individualization of instruction<br>Criterion-based instruction<br>Generalization |

|  | Metacognition | Cognitive Behavior Modification | Reciprocal Teaching | Strategic Instruction Model | Self-Regulated Strategy Development Model |
|---|---|---|---|---|---|
| Instructional procedures | Identify task<br>Determine student's performance<br>Select a strategy<br>Teach the strategy<br>Provide practice<br>Provide feedback<br>Teach generalization | Explain strategy<br>Share rationale<br>Perform task while thinking aloud<br>Have student perform task overtly and covertly<br>Provide feedback | Teach summarizing, question generating, clarifying, and predicting<br>Read title, ask for predictions<br>Read a segment of text<br>Ask a question about content<br>Summarize/ask for elaborations<br>Discuss clarifications<br>Discuss predictions regarding next segment<br>Provide feedback | Pretest<br>Describe/obtain commitment<br>Model<br>Verbal practice<br>Controlled practice and feedback<br>Advanced practice and feedback<br>Confirm acquisition and obtain generalization commitment<br>Generalization | Develop background knowledge<br>Discuss it<br>Model it<br>Memorize it<br>Support it<br>Independent performance |
| Instructional approach | Integration of reductionist and constructivism | Integration of reductionist and constructivism | Integration of reductionist and constructivism | Integration of reductionist and constructivism | Integration of reductionist and constructivism |
| Content | Academic subjects<br>Social behaviors | Academic subjects<br>Social behaviors | Academic subjects | Academic subjects<br>Social behaviors | Academic subjects<br>Social behaviors |

Note. Adapted from Platt, J., & Olson, J., *Teaching Adolescents With Mild Disabilities*. 1997. Brooks/Cole Publishing Company, Pacific Grove, CA. Reprinted by permission.

design interventions that emphasize the maintenance and generalization of metacognitive skills and strategies (Wong, 1986). For example, a self-questioning procedure taught to students with learning disabilities resulted in systematic self-monitoring and enhanced reading comprehension (Wong & Jones, 1982). Other investigations have studied the effects of metacognitive instruction on the memory (Paris, Newman, & McVey, 1982) and written expression skills (Harris & Graham, 1994) of students with academic problems. Researchers in cognitive developmental psychology and instructional psychology have developed systematic procedures for teaching metacognitive strategies (Cooney & Swanson, 1991; Palincsar, 1982; Taylor & Beach, 1984; Swanson, 1991; Wong & Jones, 1982). Teachers may use these procedures with students who have special needs.

There are a variety of metacognitive strategies for you to use as you work with students with special needs. We can compare a student having a variety of metacognitive strategies to a good rock group that has a repertoire of hits that it can perform at a concert. Students with special needs require a number of strategies at their disposal to respond to the academic demands of the classroom. Besides knowing a variety of strategies, students need to know which strategies to use and when to use them. The members of the rock group will consider their audience and the acoustics of the facility in which they are playing (setting demands); the lighting, equipment, their voices, instruments (strengths and weaknesses); and what they are trying to accomplish at each concert they hold, such as fund-raising or plugging a new release (personal goal or objective). Students need to consider the demands and problems they encounter in the classroom, what strengths they bring to a learning activity, what typically gives them problems, and what they are trying to do, such as understand a reading passage, remember a list of words, or write a theme. Successful musicians monitor throughout the concert how they

are received by the crowd. They may decide to rearrange the sequence of hits they are performing based on the reaction of the audience, or they may resurrect some of their old classics if they get lots of requests for them or if the new ones are not getting a good reaction. You may have been to a concert that started out in a sequenced and organized manner and then noticed signals being passed among the group members to change the original plan and try something else.

Just as the rock group members monitored and made adjustments in their performance at the concert, students who are metacognitively aware and know how to regulate their learning make adjustments as they proceed through a task. Karim could not remember what he had read when he got to the bottom of the page in his history book (awareness), so he reread the page, this time pausing after each paragraph to paraphrase what he had just read (monitoring). Angel was having difficulty studying for tests at the end of a unit because she could not understand her own notes or remember what the teacher had said (awareness). She began to rewrite her notes after each class, thereby engaging in a cumulative review (monitoring). These two students were using metacognitive skills. When students possess good metacognitive skills, they are able to interact effectively with learning situations and perform independently.

 **ACTIVITY 6.2**

Give an example of a metacognitive awareness activity and a metacognitive monitoring activity.

## Implementation

Teachers initially assume the responsibility for helping students identify tasks for which they need metacognitive instruction. They begin metacognitive instruction by modeling self-regulation activities. Then, gradually, through scaffolding, they shift the responsibility to the students, who participate in applying metacognitive skills. Metacognitive strategies become student-directed when students show independent application of them, or generalization.

A review of the literature in metacognition suggests the existence of specific elements to include in metacognitive instruction. We present the following critical steps adapted from the work of Palincsar and Brown (1987) and Pressley, Borkowski, and O'Sullivan (1984), in combination with our own thoughts.

1. Identify the task.

   Example: Remembering what was read

2. Choose a strategy to facilitate completion of the task.

   Example: Inserting stop points in a text and then telling students to paraphrase what was read

3. Explicitly teach the strategy.

   Example: Modeling for students what they should do when they come to a stop point

4. Explain the benefits to be expected.

   Example: Describing that grades will improve, frustration will decrease, and reading will be easier and more fun

5. Provide guided practice.

   Example: Working through an activity with students; having them apply the strategy

6. Provide feedback.

   Example: Giving positive and corrective comments, oral and/or written, regarding consistent and appropriate use of the strategy

7. Teach students how to generalize the use of the strategy.

   Example: Showing students how to use this technique with reading materials in school (content-area subjects) and out of school (magazines, mail, written directions)

Let's take a look at a metacognitive intervention for increasing class participation. Ellis's (1989) class participation intervention (CPI) for students with special needs addresses metacognitive awareness ("Am I prepared for class?") and monitoring ("What do I already know? Can I tell three things about the topic?"). CPI consists of four parts (PREP, SLANT, RELATE, and WISE) that teach students to think ahead, think during class discussions, and think after class discussions. PREP (prepare materials, review what you know, establish a positive mindset, and pinpoint goals) activates students to prepare themselves for class discussions. During actual class discussions, SLANT (sit up, lean forward, act like you're interested, nod, and track the teacher) cues students to demonstrate appropriate nonverbal behaviors. RELATE (reveal reasons, echo examples, lasso comparisons, ask questions, tell the main idea, and examine importance) directs students to the verbal behaviors essential for class participation. WISE (were goals met, itemize important information, see how information can be remembered, and explain what was learned) requires students to think back and evaluate their participation after class is over. Figure 6.2 shows the WISE strategy for thinking after a lesson, and Figure 6.3 shows the PREP/WISE score sheet.

Ellis recommends teaching PREP and WISE together and, after they are mastered, he recommends teaching SLANT and RELATE together. Ellis specifies that the CPI strategies should be taught by (a) motivating students to learn them, (b) describing and modeling the strategies, (c) requiring verbal elaboration and then rote memorization of the strategies, (d) providing group and individual practice, and (e) periodically checking for maintenance of the strategies. He reports that students who master the CPI strategies come to class better prepared and increase academic responding during class.

**Figure 6.2** The Metacognitive Strategy for Thinking After a Lesson

---

**Think Back with WISE**

**W**ere goals met?

- Did you learn what you wanted to learn?
- Did you meet your participation goals?

**I**temize important information

- Review study guide, notes, or textbook
- Mark key information

**S**ee how information can be remembered

- Draw graphic displays
- Create mnemonic devices
- Create study cards

**E**xplain what was learned to somebody

- Use your notes to teach somebody about the topic

---

Note. From "A Metacognitive Intervention for Increasing Participation" by E. S. Ellis, 1989, *Learning Disabilities Focus*, 5(1), p. 37. Reprinted by permission.

 **IMPORTANT POINTS**

1. Cognitive strategies relate to how we process information.
2. Students need to know the purpose for a cognitive strategy; how, when, and where to use it; why it is useful; and how to evaluate its effectiveness.
3. In classrooms where strategic teaching and learning are taking place, both teachers and students are constantly thinking and making decisions related to strategy selection, application, and evaluation.
4. Metacognition is the general knowledge (awareness) and control (monitoring) that an individual has over his or her thinking and learning.
5. Metacognitive awareness involves a person's knowledge about his or her own cognitive resources and the relationship between those capabilities and the demands of the task.
6. Metacognitive monitoring involves self-regulatory mechanisms that enable a person to monitor, adjust, correct, and control his or her cognitive activities.
7. Metacognitive instruction is designed to improve student problem solving, increase student independence, promote generalization and transfer of skills, and teach higher-level skills such as summarizing and self-questioning.
8. Metacognitive teaching procedures include the following: (a) identify the task, (b) choose a strategy, (c) teach the strategy, (d) explain the benefits, (e) provide guided practice, (f) provide feedback, and (g) teach generalization.

---

## COGNITIVE BEHAVIOR MODIFICATION (CBM)

Cognitive behavior modification (CBM) involves "specific techniques that teach self-control through increased awareness of cognitive processes and knowledge of how behavior affects academic outcomes" (Swaggert, 1998, p. 235). The teacher models his or her thinking processes in performance of a task and then the student practices the teacher model, overtly with assistance, and then covertly alone. It requires the teacher to analyze the task and the thinking processes involved in performing the task. In turn, the students are active participants as they attempt to change their cognitive behaviors. Students are taught to continuously monitor their progress toward preset goals (Swaggert, 1998). Thus, students are able to regulate their own actions (Fraser, Belzner, & Conte, 1992).

Cognitive behavior modification training was first introduced by Meichenbaum and Goodman (1971) to improve the self-control of children with hyperactivity. Since then, various components of CBM have been found to be effective in

**Figure 6.3** PREP/WISE Evaluation Sheet

## PREP/WISE score sheet

Student name: _____

### PREP

**Prepare materials for class**

yes no N/A
- ☐ ☐ ☐ Textbook
- ☐ ☐ ☐ Notebook
- ☐ ☐ ☐ Pen/pencil
- ☐ ☐ ☐ Homework
- ☐ ☐ ☐ Study guide
- ☐ ☐ ☐ Other _____

yes no N/A
- ☐ ☐ ☐ Difficult areas marked on notes/book

**PREP/WISE Process Score**

# of "yes" boxes ☐

☐

Process Score _____

# categories evaluated

**Review what you know**

(at least 3 items known about topic listed)

What I already know:
1. _____
2. _____

yes no N/A
☐ ☐ ☐
3. _____

**Establish positive mindset**

yes no
☐ ☐   Positive statement about myself: _____

**Pinpoint goals**   _____

Question about the topic has been noted

I want to find out _____

yes no N/A
☐ ☐ ☐
_____

yes no N/A
☐ ☐ ☐   My participation goal is to _____
_____

Participation goals noted

### WISE

**Were goals met?**

yes no N/A
☐ ☐ ☐   Noted whether topic question had been answered during the lesson/what answer was

**Itemize important information**

yes no N/A
☐ ☐ ☐   Marked on notes/book perceptions of most important information from lesson

**See how information can be remembered**

yes no N/A
☐ ☐ ☐   Remembering devices created

**Explain what was learned to somebody**

yes no N/A
☐ ☐ ☐   Explained what was learned to someone else

I found out ☐       I still don't know ☐

I met my goal ☐       I didn't meet my goal ☐

Note. From "A Metacognitive Intervention for Increasing Participation" by E. S. Ellis, 1989, *Learning Disabilities Focus*, 5(1), p. 39. Reprinted by permission.

developing cognitive, behavior, and academic skills in students with learning and behavior problems (Ager & Cole, 1991; Hughes, Ruhl, & Misra, 1989; Meichenbaum, 1977; Nelson, Smith, Young, & Dodd, 1991; Rooney, Polloway, & Hallahan, 1985).

## Rationale

One of the premises of cognitive behavior modification is that language is thought to affect the socialization and learning processes (Vygotsky, 1962). According to Vygotsky, children first use language to mediate their actions overtly (e.g., "If I touch the stove, I will get burned."). These overt processes (thinking aloud) eventually change to covert processes (thinking to yourself), and the child no longer uses external language mediation to avoid the hot stove. Overt behavior can be changed by modifying a person's pattern of thoughts; that is, changing the way a person thinks about a task can change how he or she approaches it. For example, labeling a task as interesting or boring will often determine whether the person attacks the task vigorously or approaches it reluctantly (Mahoney, 1974). As a teacher, you can share your thought processes with students as you attempt to solve problems and complete tasks, providing a model for students to imitate. For example, Mercer and Mercer (2001) suggest that teachers model appropriate actions and language for responding to frustrating situations and dealing with failure.

The procedures used in CBM training can be adapted to fit a variety of tasks (Meese, 1994), situations, and settings. Cognitive behavior modification is effective in assisting students to remember the steps needed to solve an academic or a social problem, such as computing a long division problem or responding to peer pressure (Swaggart, 1998; Williams & Rooney, 1986). It is also a way for students to improve their self-control (Fraser et al., 1992).

## Description

Cognitive behavior modification is an approach that teaches students self-regulation and problem solving. Its essential components are cognitive modeling, guided practice, and verbal mediation.

### Cognitive Modeling

Cognitive modeling is used as the primary means of instruction (Bos & Vaughn, 1998). In cognitive modeling, you model your thoughts by thinking aloud for students as you attempt to solve an academic or a social problem. As a first step, Albion (1980) suggests that you identify the specific steps if the task deals with a skill such as dividing numbers or the generic steps if the task deals with such behaviors as being prepared for class. Once the steps are identified, you should reconceptualize them into the conversational styles of the students. For example, Ms. Williams used think-aloud procedures as she completed long division problems ("I know I can solve this problem. Let's see . . . first I divide.

Yes, that's right. Now, what do I do next? I remember . . . I multiply. Let's see, did I multiply correctly? Yes. Next, I need to subtract. Okay . . . that looks good. Now, the last thing I do is bring down the next number. This looks right . . . I knew I could do it!").

### Guided Practice

An adaptation of a training sequence developed by Meichenbaum and Goodman (1971) is usually used to teach students to imitate the teacher's verbalizations (Alberto & Troutman, 1999). The sequence proceeds from overt verbalization (in which students perform out loud the same task that was modeled by the teacher) to covert verbalization (in which students perform the task via private speech). It also moves from external guidance provided by the teacher as he or she assists the students in performing the task to internal guidance in which the students complete the steps alone.

### Verbal Mediation

Self-instruction, self-reinforcement, self-regulation, and self-evaluation are generally included individually or in combination as part of the verbal mediation procedure. Self-instruction is the use of language to mediate the completion of a task. Self-reinforcement includes selecting and administering a reinforcer, contingent on meeting some performance standard (Hughes, Ruhl, & Misra, 1989). Self-evaluation refers to monitoring the quality or acceptability of the behavior, whereas self-regulation refers to monitoring whether the strategies are working and changing them if they are not (Paris & Oka, 1986). Examples of these various components follow in our description of two different verbal mediation procedures, one recommended by Meichenbaum (1977) and Meichenbaum and Goodman (1971) and one that we and our students have found effective.

Adaptations of the verbal mediation strategy created by Meichenbaum (1977) are frequently found in studies that measure the effectiveness of cognitive behavior modification (Alberto & Troutman, 1999). The verbal mediation strategy includes the following steps:

1. *Problem definition*: "What is it I have to do?"
2. *Focusing attention and response guidance*: "Oh, proofread the paragraph I've just written."
3. *Self-reinforcement*: "Good, I'm remembering to check to see if I've capitalized everything I'm supposed to."
4. *Self-evaluative coping skills and error-correction options*: "That's okay; even if I make an error, I can go slowly." (p. 23)

You may have noticed that the last step also includes self-regulation, as students are taught how to monitor their errors and how to decrease them (in this case, "go slowly").

We have adapted a problem-solving type of verbal mediation strategy appropriate for teaching elementary and middle school students with problem behaviors (MARC, 1983).

1. *Define the problem*: "I talk out during independent practice time."
2. *Study the problem and its consequences*: "I am breaking one of the class rules. It gets me into trouble with the teacher. I don't finish my work, I don't do well on my math quizzes, and I miss important points."
3. *Make a value judgment*: "I really don't like the teacher to be angry with me. I don't like it when my friends get mad because I disturb them. I'd like to get better grades on my math quizzes. I really need to be quiet and concentrate on my work."
4. *Identify alternative solutions*: "I can count to five when I feel the urge to talk out. I can draw a picture of an open mouth with a slash through it and tape it on my desk and mark on it each time I feel the urge to talk out."
5. *Evaluate the solutions*: "If I count to five, I may just end up shouting the number out loud. If I try marking on the picture of the

mouth, I won't bother anyone and I won't be saying anything at all."
6. *Make a decision and be happy about it*: "I think I'll try the picture of the open mouth with the slash through it. I think it will work well. Yeah, that sounds good."
7. *Implement the decision and evaluate it*: "I just made the picture and taped it to my desk. Now I'll check 2 days from now to see how I did. Maybe I'll buy myself a candy bar if I have only a few marks. I really think this will help me."

A teacher who taught his students this problem-solving procedure prepared the poster shown in Figure 6.4 to cue the students to use the strategy. He hoped these reminders would assist the students in using the technique independently.

## Implementation

Like most cognitive strategies, this one should be introduced with an explanation, purpose, and rationale to implement cognitive behavior modification. Then model your strategy and elicit student participation to model the strategy overtly and then covertly. The steps, adapted from Meichenbaum and Goodman (1971) and Meichenbaum (1977), usually proceed in the following manner:

1. *Explain the technique*: "You seem to be having problems with talk-outs, Lupa. I have a neat strategy that I use whenever I am having problems. Let me show it to you."
2. *Share the purpose*: "The strategy should help you stop your talk-outs."
3. *State its value*: "Last year it helped one of my students make new friends because she listened to them when they spoke. It should help you get your work done because you won't talk out as much."
4. *Select a verbal mediation procedure*: The teacher selects the steps of the problem-solving techniques found in Figure 6.4.

**Figure 6.4**   Problem-Solving Poster

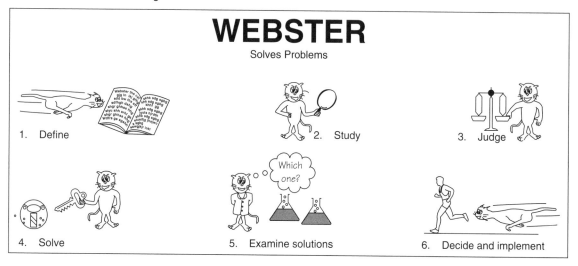

5. *Model your thoughts out loud, using appropriate vocabulary*: "Let's see . . . my first step is to define my problem. Uh, I seem to have difficulty with talk-outs." (The teacher continues modeling each of the steps of the problem-solving procedure.)
6. *Prompt and guide the student in imitating your model*: "What do you plan to do first? What are your options?"
7. *Have the student practice overtly without guidance, but with feedback*: "Lupa, you try it alone." "Well done, Lupa, you remembered each of the steps." Or, "Not quite, Lupa, you forgot to look at all the solutions."
8. *Fade overt practice*: "Whisper the problem-solving steps now, Lupa."
9. *Have the student practice the model silently*: "Practice the problem-solving steps just by thinking about them now, Lupa."

Anita Gearhart, a teacher of middle school students with behavior problems, adapted the technique into a Think Sheet (see Figure 6.5). She has the student identify the problem (My behavior), study the problem (Reasons), and suggest alternative ways to behave (Acceptable alter-

natives). We added the requirement of selecting a strategy to try the next time a similar incident occurs (Next time, I will try). She has the student take the sheet home for parent signatures.

▼ **ACTIVITY 6.3**

Design a verbal recitation procedure using self-reinforcement and self-evaluation, then give examples to implement a student's use of cognitive behavior modification procedures.

▶ **IMPORTANT POINTS** ◀

1. Cognitive behavior modification is a technique in which the teacher models his or her thinking processes in the performance of a task. The student practices overtly with assistance and eventually covertly (internalizing the procedure).
2. Cognitive behavior modification includes the components of cognitive modeling, guided practice, and verbal mediation.
3. Cognitive modeling involves modeling your thoughts by thinking aloud while

**Figure 6.5** Think Sheet

My behavior: _____

_____

_____

Rule: I will be held responsible for my own behavior (copy).

_____

_____

_____

Reasons for my behavior: _____

_____

_____

Acceptable alternatives (acceptable behavior I could have decided on):

_____

_____

_____

_____

Next time, I will try (which of the above): _____

_____

☐ I am ready to return to task.

Student _____

Teacher _____

Parent (s) _____

students watch you solve an academic or social problem.

4. Guided practice involves having students perform a task that was modeled by the teacher, first overtly (out loud) with external teacher guidance, then covertly (using private or internal speech) with internal guidance (completing the steps alone).

5. Verbal mediation involves the use of overt verbalization (thinking aloud) through self-instruction, self-reinforcement, self-regulation, and self-evaluation, which is gradually faded to covert verbalization (private or internal speech).

6. Cognitive behavior modification may be implemented by completing the following

steps: (a) explain the technique, (b) share its purpose, (c) state its value, (d) select a verbal mediation procedure, (e) model your thoughts using appropriate vocabulary, (f) prompt and guide the student in imitating your model, (g) have the students practice overtly without guidance but with feedback, (h) fade overt practice, and (i) have the student practice the model silently.

## RECIPROCAL TEACHING (RT)

Reciprocal teaching (RT) is a research-based instructional procedure designed to encourage students' active participation in lessons (Speece, MacDonald, Kilsheimer, & Krist, 1997). Like the other approaches in this chapter, reciprocal teaching concentrates on teaching students how to learn, specifically, how to gain meaning from reading text. Essentially, "reciprocal teaching is a dialogue between teachers and students for the purpose of jointly constructing the meaning of the text" (Palincsar, 1986a, p. 119). The approach helps students understand how to study and learn from a text and promotes metacognitive monitoring of comprehension (Palincsar & Brown, 1986, 1987). The instruction is teacher-directed at first, but then a student assumes the teacher's role as other students comment on the student's questions, elaborate on the student's summary, and assist in constructing meaning and predicting new information. Students take turns assuming the role of the teacher as they lead discussions using the four reading strategies of summarizing, questioning, clarifying, and predicting text information (Bos & Anders, 1990). The context in which these four strategies are learned is social, interactive, and holistic in nature (Englert & Palincsar, 1991). To move from teacher-directed to student-directed instruction, the teacher uses a scaffolding procedure, decreasing the intensity and frequency of the prompts and supports (Palincsar & Brown, 1984).

The technique is usually taught to students individually or in groups of four to seven, and the lessons last approximately 30 minutes for 20 days (Palincsar & Brown, 1986, 1988). Many of the techniques identified in the teacher effectiveness literature (see Chapter 4) are the same as those used in reciprocal teaching, and we point out the similarities in our discussion.

The value of reciprocal teaching for students with poor comprehension has been documented in the literature (Brown & Palincsar, 1989; Rosenshine & Meister, 1994). In fact, much of the research on the effectiveness of reciprocal teaching was conducted by the creators of the model with junior high students in remedial reading classes as the subjects, and expository or informational text as the reading material. The students were identified as "adequate decoders but poor comprehenders" (Palincsar & Brown, 1986, p. 775). In the studies (Brown & Palincsar, 1982; Palincsar & Brown, 1984), students improved in comprehension, measured by daily curriculum-based tests of 450-word passages and 10 comprehension questions. They also improved in comprehension of material presented in their general education classes, demonstrating that reciprocal teaching produced generalization.

Additionally, Palincsar and Brown (1989) found that reciprocal teaching was effective with first and second graders judged to be at risk for academic failure. In these studies, the teachers, instead of the students, read the text. It was found that 75% of the first-grade children achieved criterion performance on comprehension. In addition, the first-grade children attempted to apply the procedure to spontaneous discussions and were able to maintain the procedures in a follow-up study conducted when the students entered second grade.

### Rationale

The idea behind reciprocal teaching is that the teacher is teaching the students strategies that will enable them to learn how to gain information from the printed page. Once the students learn the strategies, they can apply them to different situations without the presence of the teacher. The strategies improve self-concept, because students learn to attribute their success to their ability to use the strategies and not to luck (Palincsar, 1986a). The emphasis on ensuring that the students are well informed about the procedures, purposes, and applications finds its basis in metacognition and in the premise that students with learning problems acquire information more readily when they are well informed (Duffy, Roehler, Meloth, Putnam, & Wesselman, 1986). The interactive nature of the approach, which requires a joint construction of meaning, is based on the belief that students can learn from each other (Palincsar & Brown, 1988).

## Description

The essential components of reciprocal teaching are strategies that teach students how to gain information from text, guided interactive instruction, and informed learners. The teacher instructs the students in the strategies of summarizing, questioning, clarifying, and predicting. In guided interactive instruction, control of the lesson moves from the teacher to the students. Students are informed about the procedures, purposes, and applications.

### Strategies

The teacher teaches the four strategies: summarizing, questioning, clarifying, and predicting. For the first 4 days of the procedures, the teacher teaches the students the strategies. On the fifth day, the teacher begins modeling the strategies in constructing a dialogue. For example, Palincsar and Brown (1986) suggest that you teach students to generate information—seeking questions by first asking them to generate questions concerning everyday events, such as, "If you are interested in knowing what time the afternoon movie begins, you call the theater and

ask" (p. 773). The teacher spends only about a day introducing each strategy, because the emphasis is on teaching the strategies through the interaction between teacher and students in a dialogue (Palincsar & Brown, 1986).

*Summarizing.* Summarizing involves identifying and paraphrasing the main ideas. Students are taught first to summarize the content in a paragraph or section and then to integrate the content across paragraphs.

*Questioning.* Questioning requires students to question themselves about the content. Students become more involved when they must generate questions than when they merely respond to teacher questions (Palincsar & Brown, 1986). At the beginning, students often generate questions that cannot be answered using the information presented in the text, which is a clue that they are not focusing on the text information (Palincsar & Brown, 1988).

*Clarifying.* Clarifying is discerning when there is a breakdown in comprehension and identifying appropriate strategies to restore meaning. To do this, students must know that they are not comprehending the information (metacognitive awareness). Readers who have comprehension problems often cannot discriminate when they do not understand materials, as they are more interested in decoding words than in making sense of the words (Palincsar & Brown, 1986). At first, students attribute lack of vocabulary knowledge as the cause for not understanding the meaning of a passage, so they focus on the unknown words in a selection for clarification. Eventually, however, they realize that unfamiliar ideas or difficult content may block understanding of the text, so they attempt to clarify these concepts (Palincsar & Brown, 1988).

*Predicting.* Predicting is hypothesizing the next event in the text. Students often use pictures and text structures, such as headings and italicized words, to aid them in making predictions. Predicting requires students to activate background information concerning the passage and to link that information to the author's intent. However, students who come from different cultural backgrounds often find that their background information does not relate to the classroom materials that they are using, and they have difficulty comprehending the author's message (Ruiz, 1989). For example, if you are reading a selection about plants of the desert, you probably will predict that sometime in the text the author will mention cactus. Think of the advantage for the student who has read about or visited a desert compared with one who has never encountered the desert environment before.

Predictions can also let teachers and students know when there is a breakdown in comprehension and a student's background knowledge is incorrect. Palincsar and Brown (1988) relate the example of students not using the facts of a selection to check an incorrect prediction. In reading the title and looking at the picture in the selection "Ships of the Desert," some students predicted that the author would talk about camels storing water in their humps. When asked to summarize, these same students said the author told how camels stored water in their humps, when in fact the author had stated that camels store fat in their humps. The students did not correct their prediction and, thus, didn't glean the correct meaning from the selection. They failed to use metacognitive monitoring to check their incorrect prediction.

### Guided Interactive Instruction

During guided interactive instruction, you model the use of the four preceding strategies. Remember, you have already spent 4 days teaching the strategies. During the initial modeling, you attempt to involve the students by having them answer questions, elaborate on your summary, and add predictions and clarifications (Herrmann, 1988). You gradually transfer responsibility for these activities to the students

until, eventually, you just provide feedback and coach the students through the dialogue as they interact with each other. For example, if the student discussion leader cannot generate a question, you may prompt by suggesting that the student begin the question with when. If that doesn't work, then you may modify the task by asking the student to identify a fact instead of a question. If that doesn't work, you may model the task: "I might ask the question. . ." You may also give corrective feedback using the prompt format (e.g., "I think you forgot an important point in your summary. Remember . . .") and praise for correct answers (e.g., "Good summary, James").

High-risk students frequently have difficulty constructing summarizing statements and generating appropriate questions, so during the beginning stages, you should construct paraphrases and questions for the students to mimic (Brown & Palincsar, 1982). Eventually, however, high-risk students are able to use the strategies on their own. In a comparison between student performance on the beginning dialogue sessions (when the teacher assumed most of the responsibility) and the end sessions (when the students assumed most of the responsibility), Brown and Palincsar (1982) report that nonquestions were reduced from 19% to 0%, and student responses needing clarification were reduced from 36% to 4%. Only 11% of the students' summary statements described main ideas in the beginning sessions, whereas 60% of the statements did at the end of the study.

### Informed Learners

At the beginning of every reciprocal teaching session, inform learners about the strategies they will be using, the importance of using the strategies, and ways to generalize them. In addition, inform learners of the consequences of learning the strategies. Specifying what happens when a strategy is employed leads to a better understanding of the relationship between the strategic learning and successful performance (Paris & Oka, 1986). Students must feel that the effort of learning the strategies produces success with a task (Paris & Oka, 1986). Direct and frequent measurements are suggested as a means to convince students of the worth of reciprocal teaching (Palincsar, 1986b). Frequent graphing of the results of comprehension testing, and taping of the reciprocal sessions help prove to students that the use of reciprocal teaching leads to positive consequences (Palincsar & Brown, 1984).

## Implementation

Implementation of reciprocal teaching requires careful planning and incorporation of the activities of summarizing, questioning, clarifying, and predicting into the lesson presentation. The steps for planning and presentation are adapted from the work of Palincsar and Brown (1986, 1988, 1989) and Herrmann (1988). These steps are not rigid, nor is the exact wording given for modeling, prompting, or feedback. Unlike Direct Instruction (see Chapter 7), with its emphasis on teacher control and scripted lessons, much of the learning interaction in reciprocal teaching is controlled by the students, so teacher responses cannot be specifically worded.

### *Planning*

To prepare for a reciprocal teaching session, first select text segments. Criteria for text selection are that the students can decode the material with at least 80 words-per-minute (wpm) accuracy with no more than 2 errors and that the text is representative of the materials that students read and study in the general education class (Palincsar, 1986b). Remember, most reciprocal teaching research was completed with expository or informational materials. Other planning activities include (a) generating possible predictions, (b) identifying questions, (c) summarizing each section, (d) circling difficult vocabulary or concepts, and (e) identifying supports that students will need to help them learn the information (Hermann, 1988). We present each of these activities with an example in Table 6.2.

### *Presentation*

We suggest the following steps for presentation in a reciprocal teaching lesson during the initial stages of teacher modeling and after the students have been taught the four strategy skills. We follow each step with an example of its implementation in teaching a group of middle school students with special needs. Because this is an initial lesson, the teacher is more in charge, and the students are participating mostly by answering questions generated by the teacher, elaborating on the summary, and adding predictions and clarifications. The teacher explains, instructs, models, guides the students, and praises (Palincsar & Brown, 1986). We use the plan in Table 6.2 to assist in generating the dialogue.

1. Begin with a review of the four strategies, their importance, and the context in which the strategies are useful.
2. Read the title and ask the students to predict what they will learn. For example:

   TEACHER: The title of the passage is *Langston Hughes: He Believed Humor Would Help Defeat Bigotry and Fear.* In your own words, by looking at the pictures, what do you think this story will be about?
   STUDENT 1: A man.
   TEACHER: Correct. Any other predictions?
   STUDENT 2: A black man.
   STUDENT 3: He thinks humor is powerful and can beat fear.
   STUDENT 4: I bet he's a comedian.
   STUDENT 5: No, look at the picture. He's signing autographs. I bet he's a writer.
   TEACHER: Those are excellent predictions. Let's begin.

3. Read a small portion of the text orally or have the students read it silently, depending on the group.
4. Ask a question about the content. In the beginning ask students to answer your question. Then ask if students have any

**Table 6.2** Planning Steps With Examples for Reciprocal Teaching

---

1. *Select the text segment for the first modeling.*

   *Langston Hughes: He Believed Humor Would Help Defeat Bigotry and Fear* by L. Morgan (Ed.). (Seattle, Washington: Turman Publishing Company, 1988)

   > "I've known rivers," wrote Langston Hughes in *The Negro Speaks of Rivers*, one of his best-known poems. "I've known rivers ancient as the world and older than the flow of human blood in human veins. My soul has grown deep like the rivers."
   > Langston, one of America's greatest writers, was a powerful artist. He was able to capture in his writing both the humor and sadness of life.
   > Langston had a very difficult childhood. Not long after he was born in Missouri on February 1, 1901, Langston's father James left home. James had studied law for years and learned he could not become a lawyer because he was black. Angry and bitter, James moved to Mexico to become a lawyer there. (p. 9)

2. *Generate possible predictions.*

   He was an author.

3. *Identify questions.*

   - How do you think Langston's father's leaving affected his writing?
   - Why did Langston's father leave home?
   - Why did his father have to leave for Mexico?
   - Did Langston think life was only funny?
   - What did he compare his soul to?
   - Who is Langston Hughes?

4. *Summarize each section.*

   Include who he was and why he had a difficult childhood.

5. *Circle difficult vocabulary or concepts.*

   Bigotry. "My soul has grown deep like the rivers." Effect that a difficult childhood may have on writing.

6. *Identify supports.*

   - Kendra will need help on questions.
   - All will need a prompt for prediction.

7. *Generate possible predictions for the next section.*

   It will tell more about Langston's childhood.

---

additional questions of their own to ask about the text material. For example:

TEACHER: After reading the first three paragraphs my question is, Why did Langston's father leave home?

STUDENT 1: To go to Mexico.

TEACHER: To do what?

STUDENT 1: To become a lawyer.

TEACHER: Why did he go to Mexico?

STUDENT 1: Because he was black.

TEACHER: And . . .

STUDENT 1: Oh, yeah, he couldn't practice law in this country.

TEACHER: That's correct. Does anyone else have a question to ask?

5. Summarize the section and invite elaboration from the group members. Herrmann (1988) recommends that you also explain how you arrived at the summary. For example:

TEACHER: My summary begins with the statement that Langston Hughes was a famous black writer who wrote about the humor and sadness in life. He had a difficult childhood. His father left to become a lawyer in Mexico, because he wasn't allowed to practice law in this country. This is a summary because I have included only information that we have already read.

6. Discuss any clarification that needs to be made concerning ideas or words.

TEACHER: Let me ask you something. Do you know what bigotry in the title means?

STUDENT 1: No.

TEACHER: Let's see if we can find the meaning somewhere in the text. I see an example in the story. Langston's father had to move to Mexico to practice law because he was black. This is an example of bigotry. Does anyone know what it means now?

STUDENT 4: Oh, it's when people do not like you because your skin is black.

TEACHER: Any other ideas?

STUDENT 2: Yes, bigotry means having bad feelings about someone.

TEACHER: I guess you could say that it is having bad feelings without a good reason.

7. Predict the next section of the text.

TEACHER: I think the next part of the story may be about some more unhappy childhood experiences. Anyone have another prediction?

**▶ IMPORTANT POINTS ◀**

1. The essential components of the reciprocal teaching model are strategies to teach students how to gain information from text, guided interactive instruction, and informed learners.

2. The comprehension and monitoring strategies of summarizing, questioning, clarify-

---

**▼ ACTIVITY 6.4**

Prepare a reciprocal teaching lesson identifying possible predictions, questions, a summary, and difficult words or concepts from the following selection from *Langston Hughes*. Check the plans in Table 6.2.

Carrie Hughes, Langston's mother, moved to Topeka, Kansas. She worked in a law office. Carrie wanted Langston to go to a public school that did not allow black children. She went to the school board and won her fight to place Langston in the school. Even though his mother won that fight, Langston had to struggle every day to fit in at the school. Many of the children, and one teacher especially, were mean to Langston and made fun of him. Langston later wrote about his school years in *The Big Sea*, a book about his life. [Morgan, *Langston Hughes*, Seattle: Turman Publishing Company 1988, p. 9]

ing, and predicting are taught to structure the dialogue of reciprocal teaching.

3. Teachers employ a scaffolding procedure, decreasing and adjusting support as they model the techniques, assist the students in the transfer of the technique, and move into a coaching and feedback role.

4. Careful planning includes identification of the text segment, possible predictions, questions, a summary, difficult words or concepts, and supports that students may need.

5. Presentation includes (a) sharing a brief review of the strategies, (b) reading the title for student predictions, (c) reading a small portion of the text, (d) asking questions, (e) summarizing and encouraging the students to elaborate on the summary, and (f) adding clarifications.

# STRATEGIC INSTRUCTION MODEL (SIM)

The Strategic Instruction Model (SIM), developed over the last 15 years by researchers

Donald Deshler, Jean Schumaker, and their colleagues, represents a combination of reductionist and constructivist principles (Deshler, Ellis, & Lenz, 1996). The teaching approach used in the Strategy Intervention Model has changed over the years from one of direct teaching to a combination of direct teaching and a significant amount of student involvement, participation, and commitment in the instructional process (Lenz et al., 1996). This incorporation of the direct (i.e., the teacher teaches the strategy) and indirect approaches (i.e., the teacher leads the students toward understanding and use of the strategy) has been the result of formal and informal research with students who are at risk for school failure, including those with learning disabilities (Lenz et al., 1996). The purpose of the Strategy Intervention Model is to teach students how to learn and perform academic, social, and job-related tasks so that they can cope with immediate setting demands and generalize these skills across situations and settings throughout their lives (Deshler & Schumaker, 1988). The model employs techniques that encourage students to think and act strategically in their problem solving (e.g., know what information to memorize for a test and know when an outline will be helpful).

## Rationale

As students with special needs progress through the grades, the gap widens between what they can do (their levels of functioning) and what they are expected to do (curriculum demands). By the time such students reach secondary school, the demands have increased more than their skills. Research conducted at the University of Kansas Center for Research on Learning indicates that low-achieving students, just after tenth grade, appear to plateau at about a fourth- to fifth-grade level in reading and writing and at a sixth-grade level in math (Deshler, Schumaker, Alley, Warner, & Clark, 1982). It seems appropriate

to change the curricular approach to one that teaches students how to learn, solve problems, monitor performance, and take control of their cognitive processing.

Research conducted at the University of Kansas Center for Research on Learning indicates that low-achieving students do not use effective or efficient study techniques, have difficulty completing assignments, do not organize information well, and have problems distinguishing important information from unimportant information (Alley, Deshler, Clark, Schumaker, & Warner, 1983; Deshler, Lenz, & Ellis, 1996; Lenz et al., 1996). These problems can be addressed by assisting students to select appropriate strategies, monitor their own execution of the strategies, and generalize the strategies across situations (content) and settings (school, home, work, and community).

Often, students with special needs are not actively involved in, or do not assume responsibility for, learning and applying specific strategies to help themselves acquire the skills needed to meet the demands of the curriculum (Graham, Harris, & Troia, 2000; Swanson, 1991; Torgesen, 1982). Research has shown that students with learning disabilities do not typically apply techniques to facilitate their comprehension of reading materials (Wong & Jones, 1982). However, students have shown significant improvement in performance when taught appropriate strategies (Graham, Harris, & Troia, 2000; Pressley, Brown, Van Meter, & Schuder, 1995; Swanson, 1991; Torgesen, 1977). Through strategic instruction, a teacher actively involves students in learning and gives them opportunities to set their own goals. Many low-achieving students fail to generalize the skills they have learned to new situations and settings (Ryan, Weed, & Short, 1986; Schneider, 1985; Lenz et al., 1996). The Strategic Instruction Model emphasizes mastery and includes specific procedures to promote generalization.

## Description

The Strategic Instruction Model stresses collaboration among support agents: general education teachers, special education teachers, students, parents, and administrators. Ongoing, systematic, collaborative efforts among support agents will assist in ensuring generalization. Special education teachers may be responsible for teaching strategies or co-teaching them with general education teachers in inclusive classrooms. General education teachers and parents may be responsible for cueing strategy use and reinforcing students when they apply strategies at school and home. Administrators may promote and reinforce the use of strategies on a schoolwide basis.

The Strategic Instruction Model consists of three components: a strategic curriculum (what strategies are taught), strategic instruction (how strategies are taught), and a strategic environment (how the environment is arranged to promote and enhance learning) (see Table 6.3).

### Strategic Curriculum

The strategic curriculum component consists of four types of strategies: (1) learning strategies (memorizing information, paraphrasing, test taking), (2) social skill strategies (getting along, conversational skills, problem solving), (3) motivation strategies (goal setting), and (4) executive strategies (selecting and designing appropriate strategies). Learning strategies are critical for understanding, retaining, and expressing content. Social skill strategies are needed for students to be successful in school, at home, and on the job. Motivation strategies assist students in problem solving and decision making. Executive strategies enable students to create their own strategies, monitor their effectiveness, and make the adaptations necessary to improve the strategy's effectiveness. All four types of strategies are essential for success.

In this section, we focus on strategies that deal specifically with academic content. The learning strategies curriculum is divided into three strands: (1) the acquisition strand helps students acquire information from printed materials, (2) the storage strand helps students store important information, and (3) the expression and demonstration of competence strand helps students with writing, proofreading, and organization (see Table 6.4). The learning strategies curriculum is organized in the form of a series of instructor's manuals with accompanying student activities, detailed lesson plans for teachers, and teaching materials.

### Strategic Instruction

The strategic instruction component consists of four stages that are critical to the success of the model: (1) stages of acquisition, (2) stages of generalization, (3) strategic teaching behaviors, and (4) content enhancement procedures. Table 6.5 provides a description of the stages of acquisition (Stages 1–6) and generalization (Stages 7–8) that are used to teach strategies and content to students. It is important to adhere to these stages during instruction if maximum results are to be achieved.

The strategic teaching behaviors are the critical teaching procedures that must be used throughout strategy and content instruction in order to meet the needs of low-achieving students (Kea, 1987, 1995). Strategy instruction is more effective when teachers actively involve their students and make instruction motivating and interesting. The strategic teaching behaviors include:

▶ Using advance and post organizers
▶ Communicating rationales
▶ Communicating expectations
▶ Reviewing and checking for understanding
▶ Facilitating independence
▶ Ensuring intensity of instruction
▶ Providing instructional monitoring
▶ Providing feedback
▶ Requiring mastery of learning

**Table 6.3**  Components of the Strategic Instruction Model

**Strategic Curriculum Component**

The Strategic Curriculum Component of the Strategic Instruction Model specifies *what* will be taught to low-achieving or at-risk students. This component consists of four types of strategies.

*Learning Strategies*: designed to teach students how to cope with the academic demands encountered across a variety of school, home, community, and employment settings. These learning strategies teach students how to respond to critical reading, writing, listening, remembering, and test-taking demands.

*Social Skill Strategies*: designed to teach the student how to interact appropriately across a variety of situations and settings. Strategies such as resisting peer pressure, accepting criticism, negotiating, following directions, and asking for help are included.

*Motivation Strategies*: consist of strategies that enable students to become active in planning the direction of their lives. Strategies that teach students how to set, monitor, and attain goals related to important areas of their lives and then communicate these goals to others are included.

*Executive Strategies*: designed to teach students how to solve problems independently and generalize learning. These strategies are taught to students after instruction in three to five learning strategies.

**Strategic Instruction Component**

The Strategic Instruction Component includes procedures for *how* strategies should be taught to students. In addition, it includes procedures for the effective delivery of content to low-achieving and at-risk students.

*Acquisition Procedures*: provide teachers with a sequenced set of steps for teaching the strategies to mastery.

*Generalization Procedures*: provide teachers with a sequenced set of steps for teaching and ensuring generalization and maintenance of newly acquired strategies to other settings and situations.

*Strategic Teaching Behaviors*: provide teachers with the critical teaching behaviors that should be infused throughout all steps and phases of strategy and content instruction to promote maximum learning by low-achieving and at-risk students.

*Content Enhancement Procedures*: provide teachers with routines and devices for delivering subject-matter information in a manner that can be understood and remembered by students.

**Strategic Environment Component**

The Strategic Environment Component deals with how to manage and organize educational settings and programs to promote and prompt strategic learning and performance.

*Teaming Techniques*: consist of methods related to teaching teachers, students, parents, and other professionals how to work as a team to bring about maximum student learning.

*Management Techniques*: consist of methods related to how to manage materials, time, instructional arrangements, and student behavior to promote student independence and success.

*Evaluation Techniques*: consist of systems related to evaluating student performance, program performance, and teacher performance and providing feedback to those involved in a manner that will promote student learning and success.

*Development Techniques*: consist of methods related to systematically implementing program components and developing strategies responsive to student needs.

Note. From *Students With Learning Disabilities*, 4th ed. (p. 371), by C. D. Mercer, 1992, Upper Saddle River, NJ: Merrill/Prentice Hall. Copyright 1992 Merrill/Prentice Hall. Reprinted by permission.

**Table 6.4**   Learning Strategies Curriculum

**Acquisition Strand**

Word Identification Strategy: teaches students a problem-solving procedure for quickly attacking and decoding unknown words in reading materials, allowing them to move on quickly for the purpose of comprehending the passage.

*Paraphrasing Strategy*: directs students to read a limited section of material, ask themselves the main idea and the details of the section, and put that information in their own words. This strategy is designed to improve comprehension by focusing attention on the important information of a passage and by stimulating active involvement with the passage.

*Self-questioning Strategy*: aids reading comprehension by having students actively ask questions about key pieces of information in a passage and then read to find the answers for these questions.

*Visual Imagery Strategy*: designed to improve students' acquisition, storage, and recall of prose material. Students improve reading comprehension by reading short passages and visualizing the scene which is described, incorporating actors, action, and details.

*Interpreting Visuals Strategy*: designed to aid students in the use and interpretation of visuals such as maps, graphs, pictures, and tables to increase their ability to extract needed information from written materials.

*Multipass Strategy*: involves making three passes through a passage for the purpose of focusing attention on key details and main ideas. Students survey a chapter or passage to get an overview, size up sections of the chapter by systematically scanning to locate relevant information which they note, and sort out important information in the chapter by locating answers to specific questions.

**Storage Strand**

*First-Letter Mnemonic Strategy*: designed to aid students in memorizing lists of information by teaching them to design mnemonics or memorization aids, and in finding and making lists of crucial information.

*Paired Associates Strategy*: designed to aid students in memorizing parts or small groups of information by using visual imagery, matching pertinent information with familiar objects, coding important dates, and a first-syllable technique.

*Listening and Notetaking Strategy*: designed to teach students to develop skills which will enhance their ability to learn from listening experiences by identifying the speaker's verbal cues or mannerisms which signal that important information is about to be given, noting key words, and organizing their notes into an outline for future reference or study.

**Expression and Demonstration of Competence Strand**

*Sentence Writing Strategy*: This strategy is designed to teach students how to recognize and generate four types of sentences: simple, compound, complex, and compound-complex.

*Paragraph Writing Strategy*: designed to teach students how to write well-organized, complete paragraphs by outlining ideas, selecting a point of view and tense for the paragraph, sequencing ideas, and checking their work.

*Error Monitoring Strategy*: designed to teach students a process for detecting and correcting errors in their writing and for producing a neater written product. Students are taught to locate errors in paragraph organization, sentence structure, capitalization, overall editing and appearance, punctuation, and spelling by asking themselves a series of questions. Students correct their errors and rewrite the passage before submitting it to their teacher.

*Continued*

**Table 6.4**   Continued

---

*Theme Writing Strategy*: teaches students to write a five-paragraph theme. They learn how to generate ideas for themes and how to organize these ideas into a logical sequence. Then the student learns how to write the paragraphs, monitor errors, and rewrite the theme.

*Assignment Completion Strategy*: teaches students to monitor their assignments from the time an assignment is given until it is completed and submitted to the teacher. Students write down assignments; analyze the assignments; schedule various subtasks; complete the subtasks and, ultimately, the entire task; and submit the completed assignment.

*Test Taking Strategy*: designed to be used by the student during a test. The student is taught to allocate time and read instructions and questions carefully. A question is either answered or abandoned for later consideration. The obviously wrong answers are eliminated from the abandoned questions and a reasonable guess is made. The last step is to survey the entire test for unanswered questions.

---

Note. From the University of Kansas Center for Research on Learning. Reprinted by permission.

Please note the similarities between the instructional procedures that are part of the Strategic Instruction Model and those described in Chapter 4 in our presentation of teacher effectiveness research (e.g., prompting, active student involvement, self-charting of progress, promoting generalization).

Content enhancement procedures are used to help make decisions about what content to teach and how to present it in a meaningful way. Content enhancement procedures provide teachers with planning and teaching routines and devices for presenting content in a way that can be organized, comprehended, and remembered by students. The use of content enhancement planning and teaching routines is based on the premise that students learn more effectively when:

▶ they are actively involved,
▶ abstract concepts are presented in concrete forms,
▶ information is organized for them,
▶ relationships among pieces of information are made explicit, and
▶ important information is distinguished from unimportant information.

Look ahead to Chapter 7 and examine the content enhancement planning and teaching device called the Unit Organizer. The unit organizer is a visual or graphic worksheet used by the teacher to plan, chart, monitor, and evaluate the teaching of a unit. It can be used to teach any subject, with or without a textbook. It is prepared by the teacher alone, or by the teacher in combination with the students for maximum ownership of the subject matter and topic. Frequently, it is used by the teacher as an advance organizer to introduce a unit; by students as a monitoring device to help keep up with assignments, meet deadlines, and review for a test; and by anyone who wants to see where a current topic fits in relation to other topics.

### Strategic Environment

The Strategic Instruction Model consists of four types of techniques designed to promote a learning environment that is strategic: (1) teaming techniques, (2) management techniques, (3) evaluation techniques, and (4) development techniques. Teaming techniques relate to preparing the members of the educational community (teachers, parents, students, psychologists, vocational rehabilitation counselors, and others) to work together cooperatively. Management techniques are related to managing time, materials, and the expertise and contributions of professionals in order to facilitate student learning and performance. Evaluation techniques

**Table 6.5**   The Stages of Strategy Acquisition and Generalization Developed by the University of Kansas for Research on Learning

---

**Stage 1: Pretest and Make Commitments**

*Purpose: To motivate students to learn a new strategy and establish a baseline for instruction*

Phase 1: Orientation and pretest

   Give rationales and overview

   Administer pretest

   Discuss how decisions are made

   Assess student's current learning habits

   Determine whether strategy is appropriate

Phase 2: Awareness and commitment

   Review pretest results

   Describe:

      the alternative strategy

      what is required to learn the strategy

      results others have achieved

   Ask for a commitment to learn the new strategy

   Affirm and explain the teacher's commitment

**Stage 2: Describe the Strategy**

*Purpose: To present a clear picture of the overt and covert processes and steps of the new strategy*

Phase 1: Orientation and overview

   Give rationales for the strategy

   Describe situations where the strategy can be used

   Prompt comparisons with old learning habits

Phase 2: Present the strategy and the remembering system

   Describe the overall strategic processes

   Describe the overt and covert processes in each step

   Explain the remembering system and its relationship to self-instruction

   Compare/contrast the new strategy to old approaches

   Set goals for learning the strategy

**Stage 3: Model the Strategy**

*Purpose: To demonstrate the cognitive behaviors and physical actions involved in using the strategy*

Phase 1: Orientation

   Review previous learning

   Personalize the strategy

   Define lesson content

---

*Continued*

**Table 6.5**  Continued

State expectations

Phase 2: Presentation

Think aloud

Self-instruct

Problem solve

Self-monitor

Perform task

Phase 3: Student enlistment

Prompt involvement

Check understanding

Correct and expand responses

Engineer success

**Stage 4: Verbal Elaboration and Rehearsal**

*Purpose: To ensure comprehension of the strategy and facilitate student mediation*

Phase 1: Verbal elaboration

Have students describe the intent of the strategy and the process involved

Have students describe what each step is designed to do and why it is important to the overall process

Phase 2: Verbal rehearsal

Require students to name each of the steps at an automatic level

**Stage 5: Controlled Practice and Feedback**

*Purpose: To provide practice in controlled materials, build confidence and fluency, and gradually shift the responsibility for strategy use to students*

Phase 1: Orientation and overview

Review the strategy steps

Review previous practice attempts

Discuss group progress and errors

Prompt reports of strategy use and errors

Prompt reports of strategy use or potential use

Phase 2: Guided practice

Give directions for activities

Model strategy applications

Prompt student completion of activities as teacher models

Prompt increasing student responsibility

Give clear instructions for peer-mediated practice

*Continued*

**Table 6.5**   Continued

---

**Stage 6: Advanced Practice and Feedback**

*Purpose: To provide practice in advanced materials (e.g., regular class, work related) and situations and gradually shift the responsibility for strategy use and feedback to students*

The instructional sequence for Advanced Practice and Feedback is the same as the instructional sequence used for Controlled Practice. However, this level of practice should:

Use grade-appropriate or situation-appropriate materials

Require application of the strategy to a variety of materials

Provide practice in poorly designed materials

Fade prompts and cues for use and evaluation

**Stage 7: Confirm Acquisition and Make Generalization Commitments**

*Purpose: To document mastery and to build a rationale for self-regulated generalization*

*Phase 1: Confirm and celebrate*

Assign task to confirm mastery

Congratulate student on meeting mastery (if mastery is not met, provide additional explanation, encouragement, and practice)

Discuss achievement and attribution for success

Identify ways to recognize accomplishment

Phase 2: Forecast and commit to generalization

Explain goals of generalization

Identify consequences of focusing and not focusing on generalization

Explain the phases of generalization

Prompt increasing student responsibility

Prompt commitment to generalize

Affirm and explain teacher's commitments

**Stage 8: Generalization**

*Purpose: To ensure the use of the strategy in other settings*

Phase 1: Orientation

Prompt students to:

discuss rationales for strategy use

identify settings in which the strategy might be used

discuss how to remember to use the strategy

identify cues within settings that signal use

identify materials in other settings

discuss most and least helpful aspects of the strategy

identify other strategies to combine

Construct cue cards and affirmation statements

---

*Continued*

**Table 6.5** Continued

Evaluate appropriateness of the strategy in various settings and materials

Phase 2: Activation

Prompt and monitor student application across settings

Enlist assistance of other teachers

Request feedback from other teachers

Reinforce progress and success

Prompt students to:

apply the strategy in a variety of settings, situations, materials, and assignments

set goals for the use of the strategy

develop a plan to increase application

review affirmation cards

Prompt regular classroom teachers to:

understand the strategy

identify cues that the students have been taught

provide sufficient cues for students to identify when to use the strategy

monitor whether the strategy is being used

cue use of strategy

model how to apply the strategy, if necessary

provide feedback on strategy use

Phase 3: Adaptation

Prompt students to:

describe the strategy and its parts

discuss the overt and covert processes

identify cognitive strategies embedded in the strategy

identify where these processes and strategies are required across settings

identify how the strategy can be modified

repeat application with the modified strategy

Phase 4: Maintenance

Prompt students to:

discuss rationales related to long-term use of the strategy

identify barriers to continued use

determine how they can monitor long-term use and how the teacher can help

set goals related to monitoring long-term use

determine how use of the strategy will be evaluated

identify self-reinforcers and self-rewards

Note. From *Students With Learning Disabilities,* 4th ed. (pp. 384–387), by C. D. Mercer, 1992, Upper Saddle River, NJ: Merrill/Prentice Hall. Copyright 1992 by Merrill/Prentice Hall. Reprinted by permission.

emphasize the provision of feedback to teachers and students. Finally, development techniques refer to the systematic and continued design and development of strategies and other program components to meet student needs.

## Implementation

In teaching learning strategies, you follow the stages of strategy acquisition and generalization. You begin by pretesting students and gaining their commitment to learn the strategy. You then describe and model the strategy, conduct verbal elaboration and rehearsal, provide controlled and advanced practice and feedback, administer a posttest, gain student commitment to generalize the strategy, and ensure the use of the strategy in other settings. If you follow these stages, you can teach students such strategies as error monitoring, paraphrasing, sentence writing, and word identification. The following systematic application of these stages is vital to the success of the model (see Table 6.5).

### Pretest and Make Commitments (Stage 1)
Establish the student's current level of performance and secure his or her agreement to learn a strategy. For example, after Rudy takes his pretest, he and his teacher, Ms. Olan, review the results. Perhaps Rudy notices that his written work is messy and contains quite a few capitalization and punctuation errors, or Rudy and Ms. Olan discover this together. Ms. Olan makes a commitment to help him improve and motivates Rudy to make a commitment to proofread his work by learning and applying the error monitoring strategy (Schumaker, Nolan, & Deshler, 1985).

### Describe the Strategy (Stage 2)
Discuss or elicit the rationales and benefits for learning the strategy, then carefully describe the steps of the strategy. This step was also included in reciprocal teaching and metacognitive instruction. Ms. Olan asks and then shows Rudy

how the error monitoring strategy will help him improve his grades in school, his chances for employment, and his ability to write error-free letters to his girlfriend. Then she describes and gives examples of each step of the error monitoring strategy.

 **ACTIVITY 6.5**

Use the describe stage of acquisition to teach someone to parallel park a car. Remember to include the rationale and benefits of the strategy and to describe the steps carefully.

### Model the Strategy (Stage 3)
The modeling stage is based on the premise that students learn a skill better if they see it performed, rather than just hear it described. Therefore, Ms. Olan models the steps of the strategy by thinking aloud and using self-instruction, self-regulation, and self-monitoring. For example, she says, "Let's see. I will look at this sentence to see if there are any capitalization errors. Hm, I have capitalized all of the proper nouns. Oh, I forgot to capitalize the first word in the sentence. Good, now I don't have any capitalization errors." After Ms. Olan models the cognitive processes by thinking aloud as she examines a written passage for errors, she enlists Rudy's participation in finding errors in the passage.

### Conduct Verbal Elaboration and Rehearsal (Stage 4)
The next stage consists of two parts—verbal elaboration and rehearsal. With verbal elaboration, you ask questions about the strategy and lead the student to discover how the strategy could be helpful. Ms. Olan asks, "Why do you think it is important to prepare papers that are error-free and neat in appearance?" "What do you think are the most common mistakes students make in their written work?" "In which of your classes do your teachers penalize you for

spelling, punctuation, and grammatical errors?" With verbal rehearsal, you review the steps of the strategy until the student knows them on an automatic level. For example, Rudy and Ms. Olan practice the steps to error monitoring until he has committed them to memory.

### Provide Controlled Practice and Feedback (Stage 5)

Provide ample guided practice in easy materials (controlled) until mastery is reached. Give individual feedback to reinforce efforts and avoid practice of incorrect responses. For example, Ms. Olan gives Rudy practice exercises and then provides verbal and written feedback regarding his performance of detecting and correcting errors in passages. This type of practice usually begins by having the teacher and students work together, and then with partners or in groups.

### Provide Advanced Practice and Feedback (Stage 6)

Provide advanced practice in grade-level materials found in general education classrooms while providing positive and corrective feedback. For example, Ms. Olan checks some of Rudy's work from selected general education classes and gives him feedback regarding his ability to detect and correct errors in these more difficult materials.

### Posttest and Elicit Commitments to Generalize (Stage 7)

Give a posttest to determine progress and to provide feedback. Ask students to agree to generalize use of the strategy to other settings.

### Promote Generalization (Stage 8)

After ensuring that students have acquired a strategy, teachers should focus on the stages of generalization. Although teachers should be promoting generalization throughout the teaching of a strategy, they should focus on a systematic set of generalization procedures after they have completed the stages of acquisition. For strategy instruction to be effective, students must generalize the use of strategies. The following stages of generalization provide students with the steps necessary to ensure successful transfer of skills across situations and settings.

*Orientation:* Make the student aware of the need to apply the strategy. For example, Ms. Olan and Rudy discuss where Rudy could use the error monitoring strategy, how he will remember to use it, and why it is important to use it in a variety of classes.

*Activation:* Prompt the student to use the strategy and monitor use of it. For example, Ms. Olan checks with general education teachers to see if Rudy is using the error monitoring strategy and helps Rudy set goals.

*Adaptation:* Prompt the student to examine the strategy for the cognitive behaviors he or she is using (e.g., self-questioning) and to modify the strategy to the demands of new situations. For example, Rudy and Ms. Olan work together to figure out how Rudy can use the error monitoring strategy as he takes tests.

*Maintenance:* Promote long-term use of the strategy across situations and settings. For example, Ms. Olan conducts periodic checks to see that Rudy is still using the error monitoring strategy effectively in a variety of situations (home, school, and on the job).

 **ACTIVITY 6.6**

Choose a partner to work with. Use the stages of acquisition and generalization to teach your partner to add three one-digit numbers (e.g., 5 + 2 + 3 = ___). Now switch roles and have your partner use the acquisition and generalization stages to teach you the steps in long division (e.g., 46 ÷ 8 = ___). Be sure to incorporate reductionist and constructivist principles in your instruction.

## SELF-REGULATED STRATEGY DEVELOPMENT (SRSD) MODEL

The Self-Regulated Strategy Development (SRSD) model was developed about 20 years ago for students with academic learning difficulties and has been used to teach writing strategies and self-regulation procedures to students with and without disabilities (Graham et al., 2000). Through an integrated approach, students are taught task-specific strategies for planning or revising expository or narrative text (Graham et al., 2000) and the self-regulation procedures of goal setting, self-monitoring, self-instruction, and self-reinforcement (Harris & Graham, 1996). SRSD provides a way to help students become more strategic and self-regulatory in their writing (Graham et al., 2000).

### Rationale

Many students, particularly those who exhibit significant difficulties with writing, lack self-regulation and composition strategies and skills (De La Paz, 1999; Graham et al., 2000; Graham & Harris, 2000; Harris, Schmidt, & Graham, 1997). Their compositions do not typically show evidence of planning, effort, and monitoring (Graham & Harris, 1993). Students with problems in reading and writing need structured and explicit instruction in strategies crucial to literacy (Graham & Harris, 1994). Self-regulated strategy training focuses on strategies for planning, writing, editing, and managing the writing process (Harris, Schmidt, & Graham, 1997) as well as on self-regulation strategies such as self-instruction, self-assessment, self-monitoring, and self-reinforcement. The use of Self-Regulated Strategy Development has resulted in improved writing skills of both normally achieving students and students with learning disabilities (De La Paz, 1999; Graham, Harris, MacArthur, & Schwartz, 1991). SRSD has had a significant impact on students' goal setting (Graham, MacArthur, & Schwartz, 1995), self-monitoring

(Harris, Graham, Reid, McElroy, & Hamby, 1994), organization of writing content (Sawyer, Graham, & Harris, 1992), and revising of written products (Graham et al., 1995), among others.

### Description

Self-Regulated Strategy Development is an instructional approach that directly addresses students' affective, behavioral, and cognitive characteristics, needs, and strengths (Harris & Graham, 1996). SRSD complements existing effective practices in writing; involves teachers as collaborators in the learning process through dialogues, sharing, and scaffolding; and actively engages students in writing instruction, development of their own strategies, and transfer and generalization of strategies. It is important to note that SRSD is only as explicit and supportive as is required by individual students, due to the fact that students vary in their needs for writing and self-regulation strategies. Although Harris and Graham have worked primarily with students in elementary and middle school, SRSD has also been used with high school students (Harris et al., 1997). In the area of writing, the three major goals of SRSD include:

▶ Assist students in developing knowledge about writing and powerful skills and strategies involved in the writing process, including planning, writing, revising, and editing.

▶ Support students in the ongoing development of the abilities needed to monitor and manage their own writing.

▶ Promote children's development of positive attitudes about writing and themselves as writers. (Harris et al., 1997, p. 1)

### *Characteristics of Self-Regulated Strategy Development*

Harris, Graham, and Troia (2000) indicate that five characteristics are essential for the effective implementation of SRSD. We list them here with our own descriptions and support from other researchers:

1. ***Strategies and self-regulation procedures are explicitly taught.*** Students with learning difficulties generally require direct, explicit instruction to acquire and master certain skills. Therefore, strategies are explicitly taught. Later, when students become more skilled, the level of explicitness may be adjusted so that students can be guided to discover a strategy or even create one on their own (Graham et al., 2000). Schloss, Smith, and Schloss (2001) cite the importance of making instruction explicit so that students learn efficiently with few errors, but they quote a statement from Harris and Graham: "Explicitness and structure need not equate with decontextualized learning of meaningless skills, passive learning, or the teaching of . . . basic skills as a pre-requisite to higher-order thinking and skills" (Harris & Graham, 1994, p. 238).

2. ***Interactive learning is emphasized.*** As with other types of cognitive strategy instruction discussed in this chapter, the teacher takes the initial responsibility for teaching and learning and then gradually shifts the responsibility to the students. For example, students are seen as active participants who work with each other and the teacher in goal setting, monitoring, executing, and modifying writing strategies.

3. ***Instruction is individualized.*** Instructional decisions are based on the needs of students. For example, students will vary in terms of goals, strategies, pace of instruction, amount of repetition and practice, ability to select and modify strategies, as well as many other considerations.

4. ***Instruction is criterion-based.*** Students progress through the stages at their own pace and focus on their own individual goals. As previously stated, not all students will need to work at each stage.

5. ***The SRSD model represents an ongoing process.*** New strategies are introduced and formerly taught strategies are upgraded (Graham et al., 2000). For example, a strategy that was

previously taught may have been introduced in its simplest form. Now that students have mastered it, additional steps or more complex applications are presented. Each student's developmental level as a writer and as a strategic learner must be considered. As mentioned earlier in the chapter, it is important to help students understand the meaning and significance of strategy use and assist them in making decisions about how and when to apply strategies. Teachers must be knowledgeable about each student's stage of development and how strategies can best assist them at that level.

## Implementation

In teaching SRSD, you generally follow six stages of instruction and choose from a variety of strategies. These strategies may be presented by the teacher or may be developed and/or modified by the students.

### Stages of Instruction

Although six stages are provided for the implementation of Self-Regulated Strategy Development, these stages serve only as a general guideline. In other words, some stages will not be needed by some students. Stages may be combined, modified, reordered, or revisited. For example, some students may be able to skip Stage 1, as they already possess sufficient background knowledge. Others may need to revisit Stage 3 for additional instruction or Stage 5 for additional support. The model is flexible and focuses on addressing individual needs of students. Note, for example, in Table 6.6 that some students who are learning an essay writing strategy may need to revisit Stage 5 for additional support. Perhaps, they need more help writing supporting reasons for their premise, or maybe they need additional assistance with self-regulation procedures (e.g., "Slow down and take my time. Then my work will be better."). Students set their own goals and work at their own pace. As with the

**Table 6.6**  Self-Regulated Strategy Development Instructional Stages: Using the TREE Strategy to Teach Essay Writing

**Stage 1—Develop Background Knowledge**

Find out what students already know about essays and build on it.

Look at samples of well-written essays.

Identify the effective features of these well-written essays.

Look for these features in essays they are reading in class and in essays of classmates.

Using a variety of topics, brainstorm ideas for essay parts.

**Stage 2—Discuss It**

Have an individual conference with each student to discuss their essays and identify any strategies or self-statements currently being used.

Introduce the idea of a strategy for writing essays along with the self-monitoring components of self-assessment and self-recording.

Discuss the benefits of using the strategy.

Determine each student's current performance.

Set goals.

Describe the TREE strategy (note **T**opic sentence, note **R**easons, **E**xamine reasons, note **E**nding) in an interactive session with students.

Provide strategy charts and lists of self-statements.

**Stage 3—Model It**

Model the TREE strategy while thinking out loud.

Elicit student help during modeling.

Use self-statements throughout the modeling (e.g., "What do I need to do next?" "Yes, that is a good reason. I'll write that.").

**Stage 4—Memorize It**

Have students memorize the strategy and practice using self-statements.

**Stage 5—Support It**

Collaborate with the students in supporting their use of the strategy and the self-regulation procedures.

Revisit the rationale for using the strategy and the self-statements, as needed.

Model the correction of errors in the use of the strategy and include a self-statement (e.g., "I'm going to change this supporting reason. I need to remember to follow all of the steps of the strategy so that I will write a good essay.").

Adjust the level of support as students become more proficient, gradually fading prompts or reminders.

Use goal setting and self-assessment (e.g., Have students assess their work to see if they have met their goals. Have them provide feedback to one another.)

*Continued*

**Table 6.6**   Continued

**Stage 6—Independent Performance**

Have students plan and write essays independently.

Provide positive and constructive feedback.

Encourage students to work without their strategy charts and self-statement lists.

Promote generalization of the strategy and self-regulatory procedures.

Note. Information taken from *Every Child Can Write: Strategies for Composition and Self-Regulation in the Writing Process* by K. Harris, T. Schmidt, & S. Graham (1997). In *Teaching Every Child Every Day: Learning in Diverse Schools and Classrooms* by S. Graham & K. Harris (Eds.). Cambridge, MA: Brookline Books. Reprinted by permission.

Strategic Instruction Model, procedures for maintenance and generalization are integrated throughout the six stages of the SRSD model (see Table 6.6).

### Strategies

Harris and Graham (1996) have developed writing strategies in a variety of areas that include but are not limited to planning, brainstorming, story writing, essay writing, and report writing. We provide examples of some of their strategies for assisting students with planning and writing. When teaching these strategies, remember to use the instructional stages noted in Table 6.6.

*Three-Step Planning Strategy for Story Writing.*   The teacher introduces a planning and writing strategy to students by explaining that these three steps will help them write better stories and essays. Students are asked to think about who will read the story or essay and why they are writing it. Then the students are instructed to use the SPACE mnemonic, which will help them plan what to say in their story or essay. As they write, they may think of more things to say and should be encouraged to do so.

1. Think.

   Who will read this? Why am I writing this?
2. Plan what to say.

   Use SPACE (Setting, Purpose, Action, Conclusion, Emotions)
3. Write and say more.

*Three-Step Writing Strategy.*   This strategy is similar to the planning strategy for story writing. However, this time the mnemonic, TREE, is used to help students make note of their **T**opic sentence (e.g., "My topic sentence is that it is better to be the oldest child in the family instead of the youngest."); note **R**easons (e.g., "One of my reasons is that you get privileges that your younger brothers and sisters do not get. Now, I need to think of others."); **E**xamine reasons (e.g., "Hm, I think I'll cross out the one about getting to boss the others around—that's a little weak."); and note **E**nding (e.g., "Now I need to write a good ending.").

1. Think.

   Who will read this? and Why am I writing it?
2. Plan what to say.

   Use TREE (note Topic sentence, note Reasons, Examine reasons, note Ending).
3. Write and say more.

*W-W-W or Story Grammar Strategy.*   This strategy teaches students how to write stories by focusing on seven questions that prompt the story parts. Significant improvements were noted in the quality and length of students' stories after they learned and practiced this strategy.

1. Think of a story you would like to share.
2. Let your mind be free.

3. Write down the story part reminder (W-W-W).

   Who is the main character?

   When does the story take place?

   Where does the story take place?

   *What = 2*

   What does the main character do or want to do, and what do the other characters do?

   What happens when the main character does or tries to do it, and what happens with other characters?

   *How = 2*

   How does the story end?

   How does the main character feel, and how do other characters feel?

4. Make notes of your ideas for each part.
5. Write your story—use good parts, add, elaborate, revise as you write or afterwards, and make sense.

***STOP and LIST Writing Strategy.*** The strategy of STOP (Stop Think of Purpose) and LIST (List Ideas and Sequence Them) assists students to set goals, brainstorm, and sequence when writing or performing other tasks. It can be used for completing writing assignments, planning a report, or preparing for other activities (e.g., deciding what supplies or resources will be needed for a project and in what order you will proceed, completing homework assignments).

### Evaluation Procedures

Harris, Schmidt, and Graham (1997) suggest several basic principles for assessing SRSD methods and procedures:

▶ Involve students as co-evaluators. Co-evaluation increases the sense of ownership and enriches the evaluation process. Students may use self-assessment, peer evaluation, and other reflective techniques.

▶ Consider the level of evaluation needed. Harris, Schmidt, and Graham (1997) recommend that teachers find out if students are using the strategy, whether it is having a positive effect on performance, and if students think the strategy is valuable and manageable.

▶ Assess changes in performance, attitudes, and cognition. It is important to determine changes in the quality and quantity of students' writing and any changes in attitude (e.g., enthusiasm for writing, confidence in writing abilities) and cognitive processes (e.g., spontaneous statements about writing).

▶ Assess how students actually use the strategy. It is helpful to observe students directly as they write and also to look for evidence of strategy use by examining students' written work.

▶ Assess students' use of the strategy over time and in new situations. To be sure that students are continuing to use a strategy and use it appropriately, find out how students are using and/or modifying strategies. In other words, conduct spot checks by asking students to share information about using the strategy, asking general education teachers if students are using the strategy in their class, or looking at samples of students' written work.

▶ Collaborate with colleagues during the evaluation process. It is important to collaborate with other teachers in promoting generalization and in monitoring strategy use in other classroom settings. This teamwork should result in more effective use of strategies by students and more consistent application and generalization of strategies.

▶ Use portfolio assessment procedures. We discussed portfolio assessment in Chapter 3. As it relates to SRSD, portfolio assessment is an excellent way to encourage students to engage in reflection and self-assessment of their writing and self-regulation strategies and to ensure that they are taking more responsibility for their own learning.

 **ACTIVITY 6.7**

You are an elementary level special education teacher co-teaching in a fifth-grade classroom. You have asked the students to write a theme about someone they would consider their hero. They will be reading their themes to the fourth graders. The students are having difficulty developing a quality product, one that has the essential elements of a well-structured theme and that is of sufficient length. How can you help them?

 **IMPORTANT POINTS** ◀

1. The Strategic Instruction Model (SIM) includes a strategic curriculum component (what to teach), a strategic instruction component (how to teach), and a strategic environment component (how the environment is arranged to enhance student performance).
2. The teaching approach used in the SIM includes direct teaching of strategies; significant amount of student involvement, participation, and commitment in the instructional process; application of strategies by students to classroom materials; and generalization of strategies across content areas, new situations, and various settings.
3. The Self-Regulated Strategy Development (SRSD) model is an integrated, instructional approach that assists students in

developing composition skills and using self-regulation procedures (e.g., goal setting, self-instruction, self-monitoring, self-assessment, and self-reinforcement).
4. The SRSD model directly addresses students' affective, behavioral, and cognitive characteristics, needs, and strengths.
5. The characteristics of SRSD emphasize explicit teaching, interactive learning, individualization, criterion-based instruction, and an ongoing process of learning new strategies and adding to or upgrading previously learned strategies.

 **DISCUSSION QUESTIONS**

1. Differentiate between the reductionist and constructivist elements of cognitive strategy instruction. Be sure to use examples from metacognition, cognitive behavior modification, reciprocal teaching, the SIM, and the SRSD model.
2. Explain the benefits for students when the teacher thinks aloud during instruction. Give three examples of using think-alouds in the general education classroom.
3. Work with a partner to respond to this question. You are a special education teacher and you are explaining to a general education teacher the importance of having students use self-regulation procedures such as self-instruction, self-monitoring, self-assessment, and self-reinforcement. What will you say? Now reverse roles and have your partner convince you of the importance of self-regulation, particularly for students with special needs.

# CHAPTER 7

# CONTENT INSTRUCTION

In special education, the Direct Instruction model is often used to teach academic content. This model is the basis for various popular commercial reading, math, and spelling curriculum programs such as *Distar Arithmetic, Corrective Spelling Through Morphographs, Reading Mastery,* and *The Corrective Reading Program,* all created by Engelmann and his colleagues. *Direct Instruction Mathematics* by Silbert, Carnine, and Stein (1990) and *Direct Instruction Reading* by Carnine, Silbert, and Kame'enui (1997) are also examples of the Direct Instruction model.

As we described in Chapter 1, the Direct Instruction model has its basis in the reductionist paradigm. The teacher is directly in charge of instruction: The teacher's role is to present well-structured sequences of subject matter, supervise practice, provide feedback, maintain a brisk pace, and ensure a high success rate. We follow the Direct Instruction discussion with a discussion of a combination, or balanced, approach that combines the Direct Instruction strategies and literature-based techniques. From an examination of about 28 studies dealing with whole language or phonics reading instruction, Stahl, McKenna, and Pagnucco (1994) recommend a balanced approach. The balanced approach includes open-ended tasks and self-selection (more aligned with the constructivist paradigm), plus teacher-directed explicit phonics and comprehension instruction (more aligned with the reductionist paradigm). Gersten and Woodward (1994) also recommend a combination approach for the instruction of bilingual students with disabilities.

Next, we examine the Unit Approach, which has been used in classes to teach content to students with mild disabilities (Englert, Raphael, & Mariage, 1994) and in classes for students with learning disabilities (Swicegood & Parsons, 1991). You may also encounter the Unit Approach in an inclusive setting. With the Unit Approach, students usually participate in various activities and are exposed to a variety of instructional techniques and arrangements. Depending on the structure of the unit, the Unit Approach may fall under either the reductionist or constructivist paradigm. Generally, the Unit Approach promotes meaningful contexts and establishes classroom communities. The teacher's role may vary from the direct purveyor of knowledge to that of a facilitator as students assume responsibility for their own learning.

We conclude the chapter with a discussion of teaching content using a single text. Frequently, instruction in science, social studies, health, math, and other content areas is based on the use of a single text. In her description of textbooks, Kovalik (1994) laments the importance given to them: "Parents demand that they be brought home, teachers won't start class without them, and academic departments spend months examining new texts for adoption" (xiii). Even though we agree with Kovalik's belief that textbooks are given too much importance, we do realize that many of our students with disabilities will be expected to learn from textbooks. Therefore, we discuss some adaptations that will make textbook learning more meaningful and effective.

## DIRECT INSTRUCTION

Direct Instruction (DI) is used in this chapter to refer to the structured, teacher-directed curriculum program first designed by Becker and Engelmann as a model for Project Head Start, a federally funded preschool intervention program for disadvantaged children from low-income homes. In 1967, when Head Start was extended to Project Follow-Through (an intervention program with a focus on the primary grades), Direct Instruction (with the Distar language, math, and reading programs) was retained as one of the 22 experimental models selected for evaluation (Peterson, 1987). A wealth of empirical evidence supports the use of the Direct Instruction model with children from low-income homes.

The Direct Instruction model began to be used with special education elementary students in the late 1960s with similar success, especially in the teaching of basic skills (Gersten, 1985; Gersten, Woodward, & Darch, 1986; Lloyd, Cullinan, Heins, & Epstein, 1980; Stein & Goldman, 1980). Direct Instruction has also been shown to increase the academic performance of adolescents with mild disabilities (Polloway, Epstein, Polloway, Patton, & Ball, 1986), senior high school students with reading problems (Gregory, Hackney, & Gregory, 1982), and preadolescents and adolescents with mild mental disabilities (Gersten & Maggs, 1982). Remember, as reported in Chapter 1, Direct Instruction is one of the effective interventions identified by Forness, Kavale, Blum, and Lloyd (1997) from a meta-analysis examination of special education research.

A distinct advantage of the DI model is that the scripted lessons allow adults other than teachers to use the program successfully. For example, after being trained, two volunteers presented lessons from the Direct Instruction *Corrective Reading Program* (Engelmann, Hanner, & Johnson, 1989). Combined with peer tutoring practice activities and timed repeated readings, students improved their reading scores from a pretest score of 2.4 grade level to a posttest score of 3.5 (Gardner, Cartledge, & Seidl, 2001).

### Rationale

The Direct Instruction model is based on behavioral principles. Its fundamental premise is that students must master basic academic skills before they can master higher-level cognitive skills. According to Tarver (1986), "Instruction begins with specific decoding skills and strategies and progresses in a highly structured, spiraling fashion to higher-level comprehension skills and strategies" (p. 370).

Another premise of Direct Instruction is that the best way to teach both basic and higher-level skills is to present carefully sequenced content using task analysis and mastery learning principles. In discussing the basis of *Distar Arithmetic* (Engelmann & Carnine, 1972, 1975, 1976), Gersten and Carnine (1984) posit that "all children can learn mathematics if the lesson is designed so students can understand what is being presented, if they are given adequate practice with corrective feedback and their progress through the curriculum is assessed regularly" (p. 396).

## Description

The Direct Instruction model features a well-designed curriculum and detailed instructional procedures. As described by Tarver (1986), "The curriculum design components constitute the cognitive elements of DI and the presentation components constitute the behavioral elements" (p. 369).

The curriculum features include sequential order, positive and negative examples, well-constructed formats, prompts, independent practice activities, and mastery learning. All skills are taught directly, with minimal reliance on incidental learning. Each lesson includes teacher-scripted presentations with fast-paced, repetitive formats, individual tests, and independent practice activities. Mastery tests are interspersed throughout the curriculum. The use of scripts permits teachers to focus on monitoring student performance, instead of concentrating on the use of clear instructional language and appropriate examples (Stein, Carnine, & Dixon, 1998).

The effective instructional procedures include cueing attention, modeling, eliciting overt student responding, providing immediate feedback, testing individual children, and teaching to mastery. The teacher usually presents the lesson to small groups of children.

Examples of these curriculum and instructional components may be found in a sample section of the DI lesson in Figure 7.1. The "s" sound is one of the easiest to teach so the skill appears early in the program. The visual prompt of the arrow reminds students that reading occurs from left to right and the large size of the letter focuses students' attention. The second ball cues the student to hold the sound.

The format is very specific and repetitive. The teacher (a) cues the students to attention by touching the ball, (b) models and repeats the sound twice (Items 1–3), (c) tells the students to practice the sound in unison and provides feedback (Items 4 and 5), (d) directs students to

**Figure 7.1** Sample DI Format for Teaching Sounds

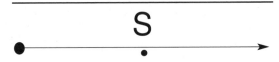

*The teacher models the sound and repeats twice.*
1. Touch the first ball of the arrow. **Here's a new sound. My turn to say it. Get ready.** Move quickly to the second ball. Hold. **sss.**
2. Touch the first ball of the arrow. **My turn again. Get ready.** Move quickly to the second ball. Hold. **sss.**
3. Touch the first ball of the arrow. **My turn again. Get ready.** Move quickly to the second ball. Hold. **sss.**
   *The teacher prompts the students to practice the sounds in unison.*
4. Touch the first ball of the arrow. **Your turn. Get ready.** Move quickly to the second ball. Hold. sss. **Yes, sss.**
5. Touch the first ball of the arrow. **Again. Get ready.** Move quickly to the second ball. Hold. sss. **Yes, sss.**
   *The teacher directs students to repeat sound until firm.*
6. Repeat **5** until firm.
   *The teacher tests individuals.*
7. Call on different children to do **4.**
   *The teacher gives feedback.*
8. **Good saying sss.**

Note. From *Reading Mastery: Distar Reading I* (p. 102) by S. Englemann and E. C. Bruner, 1988. Chicago: Science Research Associates. Copyright 1988 by McGraw-Hill, Inc. Reprinted by permission.

repeat the sound until firm to reach mastery (Item 6), (e) tests individual children (Item 7), and (e) gives feedback (Item 8). Notice, the feedback involves both acknowledgement ("Yes, ssss") and specific praise ("Good saying sss"). This same format with similar wording continues from lesson to lesson whenever a new sound is introduced. Other well-constructed formats introduce different skills.

## Use

Many school districts have adopted the previously discussed commercial programs for Direct Instruction in reading, spelling, math, and language. Thus, you may find a kit with a teacher's manual, student workbooks, and other materials in the classroom. Although you should try to follow the scripted teacher presentation, Gersten, Carnine, and Woodward (1987) discovered that immediate correction of student errors and the number of correct student responses were linked to student success more often than was following the script word for word.

Even if Direct Instruction commercial programs are not available, it is possible to incorporate the curriculum design features and instructional procedures into a lesson. For example, Darch and Gersten (1986) incorporated Direct Instruction procedures as they used an advance organizer with high school students with learning disabilities. They used a well-constructed format, carefully worded definitions, and carefully selected examples to open the science lesson. The format consisted of (a) the teacher reading the item, (b) the teacher cueing responses, (c) the students reading the item in unison, and (d) the teacher asking fast-paced questions of the students after several items were read to check comprehension. The scripted lesson began:

**Information about Ocean Currents**

I. A current moves like a river.
   A. Water moves in parts of the ocean. These are called ocean currents.

B. These currents can be very wide—sometimes as wide as 100 miles.

TEACHER: Today we are going to learn about ocean currents and how these currents can affect the weather on land. Everybody look at I. A current moves like a river. Say that.
STUDENTS: A current moves like a river.
TEACHER: Everybody look at IA. Water moves in parts of the ocean. These are called currents. Say that.
STUDENTS: Water moves in parts of the ocean.
TEACHER: Touch IB. These currents can be very wide—sometimes as wide as 100 miles. Say that. . . . Let's review what we have covered so far. Everybody, can an ocean have currents?
STUDENTS: Yes.
TEACHER: Do these currents move?
STUDENTS: Yes.
TEACHER: Everybody, how wide can these currents be?

(Darch & Gersten, 1986, p. 238)

 **ACTIVITY 7.1**

Use Direct Instruction procedures to continue to teach the lesson written by Darch and Gersten. Be certain to include feedback comments, unison or choral responding, visual prompts, individual tests, mastery learning, and a repetitive format. Teach from the following information found on a transparency:

**Examples of Ocean Currents and How Weather on Land is Affected**

II. Ocean currents that start in the tropical temperature zone are warm.
   A. The Gulf Stream is an example.
   B. The current starts in a tropical temperature zone.
   C. The Gulf Stream is a warm current.
   D. It makes land warmer. (Darch & Gersten, 1986, p. 238)

(Answers for this and other activities are found in the Instructor's Manual.)

## BALANCED INSTRUCTION

In general education, many teachers are finding success with a balanced instruction approach that combines literature-based and basal reading programs (Foorman & Torgesen, 2001). In this section, we share a balanced instruction program that has been used in special education settings. The program integrates Direct Instruction commercial reading programs with the whole language or literature-based model (Hefferan & O'Rear, 1991). Called BALANCE (*Blending All Learning Activities Nurtures Classroom Excellence*), the program promotes the use of Direct Instruction, precision teaching, quality literature, the writing process, and integrated subjects to enhance the teaching of skills. The program has been used by special education teachers in pull-out settings. A sample BALANCE lesson on the unit theme "Accepting Myself and Others" proceeds in the following manner:

### Day 1, 50-minute period

| | |
|---|---|
| *10 minutes:* | Read *Leo the Late Bloomer* (a trade book)—use Preview and Predict. |
| *5 minutes:* | Do character chart of Leo. |
| *20 minutes:* | Teach Reading Mastery Lesson 11—use Preview and Predict, model reading, and modify questions from teacher's guide. |
| *5 minutes:* | Do character chart of Arf. |
| *5 minutes:* | Do precision teaching timing with partners. |
| *5 minutes:* | Introduce writing assignment, which students complete on their own. Draw a picture of yourself in a place where you like to spend time. |
| *Homework:* | Reading Mastery Lesson 11 Take-Home (Hefferan & O'Rear, 1991, p. 1). |

Prediction, a character chart, and writing assignments add the balance to the Direct Instruction components of the Reading Mastery lesson and precision teaching. Science Research Associates/McGraw-Hill, the publisher of many Direct Instruction commercial materials, also publishes a series of Direct Instruction resource guides that correlate literature to Reading Mastery Plus. The supplemental product, *Language Through Literature* (SRA/McGraw-Hill, 2002) helps children make the connection between basic skills and literature.

Some of our student teachers have adapted the reading of stories from the Direct Instruction curriculum programs of Reading Mastery and Corrective Reading. These adaptations, many of which consider literature-based strategies, include:

1. Have students practice reading with a partner before taking turns to read the story.
2. Read a poor reader's part first and then have him or her paraphrase and then read it.
3. Rephrase, or have the students rephrase, the story at stopping points.
4. Review the previous day's section of the story before starting today's.
5. Remind students that some words, like *mopper,* are not used that frequently and have students substitute other, more commonly used words or phrases, such as *janitor.*
6. Expand on a story theme with creative activities.

We want to spend a little more time discussing Suggestion 6, "expand on a story theme with creative activities," as expansion activities lead to inclusion of the two effective strategies of student choice and open-ended tasks. Art and drama activities are easy to add to the Direct Instruction Curriculum of Reading Mastery and Corrective Reading. One of our interns had students participate in their own treasure hunt after reading about a treasure hunt in their Corrective Reading text. The teacher divided the students into cooperative groups to plan the hunt. One group drew the map, one wrote the clues and hid the treasure, and one group formulated a search plan and then searched for the treasure. They then dictated their experiences to the teacher, who published their accounts in a class book. Throughout the week, they selected one of the accounts to read during the reading class. Another intern had students make puppets of their favorite characters from the stories they read that month. They made a puppet stage from a refrigerator box and then presented the plays to other classes.

Writing activities are also easy to correlate to the Direct Instruction curriculum. Experience stories may be completed after each class period. For example, Ms. Phillips has her students retell the story they read each day. As they are retelling it, she transcribes the story on chart paper. The children then read the story and several are selected to draw a picture to go with the story. The next day, Ms. Phillips begins class by having the students read their own story as a review before reading the new part of the story. Depending on the students, you may want them to write their own story or even think of their own endings.

Ms. Anderson had her children create big books from literature selections that were correlated to a particular theme from the Reading Mastery curriculum. A Big Book is usually made after children are quite familiar with a story. The children retell the story, and the teacher prints one or two sentences at the top of each 12-by-18-inch piece of light cardboard until the children's version of the story is complete. Then the children, either individually or in small groups, draw illustrations that correspond to the text on each page. A cover page with the title and author and a preface page that explains why the children selected the story to retell are also included (Herald-Taylor, 1987). The pages are sequenced by the children and then bound with a heavy-duty stapler or bookbinding tape.

 **ACTIVITY 7.2**

Return to the Direct Instruction lesson teaching the "s" sound (Figure 7.1). Add some activities to make the lesson more balanced.

 **IMPORTANT POINTS**

1.  The Direct Instruction model is demonstrated commercially in such programs as *Distar Arithmetic, Spelling Through Morphographs, Reading Mastery,* and *Corrective Reading Program* created by Engelmann and his colleagues and *Direct Instruction Mathematics* (Silbert, Carnine, and Stein, 1990).

2.  Research demonstrates that DI is effective in teaching basic skills to students from ethnically diverse cultural backgrounds and students with disabilities at both elementary and secondary levels.

3.  The DI model has both cognitive and behavioral components (Tarver, 1986).

4.  The curriculum features include sequential order, positive and negative examples, well-constructed formats, prompts, independent practice activities, and mastery learning.

5.  The effective instructional procedures include cueing attention, modeling, eliciting overt student responding, providing immediate feedback, testing individual children, and teaching to mastery.

6.  Gersten, Carnine, and Woodward (1987) discovered that immediate correction of student errors and the number of correct student responses were linked to student success more often than was following the script word for word.

7.  Balanced instruction combines literature-based and basal reading programs.

8.  As used in special education, balanced instruction integrates Direct Instruction and literature-based materials.

This big book was designed by primary-age students with special needs.

## THE UNIT APPROACH

The Unit Approach integrates subject matter with a topic, theme, or interest area. With the Unit Approach, teachers can also emphasize higher-order thinking skills linked to standards-based reforms. These higher-order thinking skills may include authentic problem solving, project-based learning, experimentation, prediction, evaluation, and application. For exam- ple, instead of teaching students about electricity by having them read page by page in the science text, you may promote higher-order thinking by having students complete a unit on electricity. Students may calculate the average cost of the school's electric bill for the past 6 months and problem solve how to reduce the cost, set up an experiment demonstrating the idea of a circuit, or predict the different types of power that may replace electricity in the future.

Mastropieri and Scruggs (1994) posit that students with disabilities are less likely to encounter difficulties with language and literacy demands with a hands-on science approach that includes manipulative activities and thematic units instead of a text-oriented one. Roser, Hoffman, and Farest (1990) found that literature units contributed to improved language arts and reading test scores on the California Test of Basic Skills for second graders at risk, many of them from the Hispanic culture. Thematic units were part of a school-based literacy learning project that improved the reading and writing performance of students with mild disabilities over that of a control group (Englert, Raphael, & Mariage, 1994).

The Unit Approach is also recommended for integrating multicultural content into the curriculum (Banks, 1987; Grant & Sleeter, 1989; Tiedt & Tiedt, 1986). For example, if you are teaching a unit dealing with different shelters, it is easy to include such diverse cultural elements as shelter on a reservation and shelter in a ghetto. A unit on folktales may include a selection of tales of African origin, such as *Mufaro's Beautiful Daughters* by John Steptoe (1987); tales of Native American origin, such as dePaola's (1983) *The Legend of the Bluebonnet*; and tales of Hispanic origin, such as Belpre's (1973) *Once in Puerto Rico*; and tales of Asian American origin such as *Tikki Tikki Tembo* told by Arlene Mosel (1968).

## Rationale

The Unit Approach is based on the premise that students learn and assimilate information by actively participating in a variety of activities. Current brain research shows us that the brain does not process information in a step-by-step, one-item-at-a-time process, but by continuously multiprocessing information and emotions through all of our senses at the same time (Stanciak, 1997). Integration of information promotes real purposes and audiences for language, factors important in learning (Rhodes & Dudley-Marling, 1988). Furthermore, units are motivational because they can take advantage of

a student's special interests, natural curiosity, experiences, and cultural background and incorporate student choice.

## Description

In a teacher-prepared unit, the teacher decides the topics and information to be presented. In a teacher-student-prepared unit, the teacher generally selects the topic but guides the students in their selection of the content and ways to learn the information. In a student-prepared unit, the students decide the topic, ways to learn the information, and how much time to spend on a topic. Units may contain activities centered around different themes, content areas, learning styles, or multiple intelligences.

### *Units Related to Themes and Content*

Thematic units are organized around themes, which state a point of view or perspective, not topics (Shanahan, Robinson, & Schneider, 1995). For example, a theme may be, "we need to respect individual differences," whereas a topic is a subject, such as "transportation." Often, teachers then integrate that theme into math, reading, and other academic content.

Lewis (1993) suggests the organization of units around the areas of cognition, self-help, expressive language, receptive language, gross motor, fine motor, socialization, and preacademics for preschool; writing, speaking/listening, science/health, reading comprehension, word recognition, arithmetic/mathematics, and humanities for elementary; and social studies, English, math, geography, humanities, science, and foreign language/cultures for secondary. Englert, Raphael, and Mariage (1994) arrange their units around the four levels of literacy: "(a) performative literacy (e.g., decoding and printing facility); (b) functional literacy (the use of literacy for interpersonal exchange); (c) informational literacy (literacy used to communicate and acquire knowledge); and (d) epistemic literacy (literacy in pursuit of creative, exploratory, and evaluative purposes)" (p. 3). Swicegood and Parsons (1991) created a unit that integrated speaking, listening, reading, and writing around the theme of offshore petroleum exploration for adolescents with learning disabilities.

Created at the University of Kansas Center for Research on Learning, "The Unit Organizer Routine is a teaching method used to introduce a unit of content to a diverse group of students" (Lenz, Bulgren, Schumaker, Deshler, & Boudah, 1994, p. 5). In *The Unit Organizer Routine*, the teacher and students create a graphic worksheet to identify the important content and relationships of a unit. For example, the Unit Organizer contains (a) key words to identify the theme;(b) lines and labels to help students see connections; (c) schedules of assignments, topics, tasks, activities; and (d) a list of questions (see our example shown in Figure 7.2).

Three different teaching routines accompany the visuals: one for introducing the unit (**Cue**), one for daily instruction (**Do**), and one for follow-up (**Review**) (Lenz et al., 1994). In the **Cue** routine, the teacher explains the purpose of the unit organizer and how it will assist the students in learning the information. Then, the teacher distributes copies of the unit organizer with the Current Unit and Unit Schedule completed [see (1) and (2) in Figure 7.2]. In the **Do** step, the teacher (a) leads the students to link the current unit with the previous and the future units by eliciting summarization and prediction and how all units are related [see (3), (4), and (5)]; (b) leads students in recognizing the major areas, the connecting words, and a summary of unit content [see (6)]; (c) has students identify the relationships to assist in understanding the unit and identifying the information they will need for passing an exam [see (7)]; (d) helps students construct good self-test questions based on the relationships [see (8)]; and (e) relates the content to the assignments and activities listed in the unit schedule. In the **Review** step, the teacher reiterates the purpose and how to use the unit organizer as a review for the exam, as a basis for

expanded maps, and as a reminder of the organization and relationships of the unit content. The reader is referred to the Content Enhancement Series (Edge Enterprises, 1994) on unit organization for further information.

An additional part that some teachers like to use is the Expanded Unit Map, which is completed as the unit is taught and expands on the major topics and subtopics. We present our example of a partially completed Expanded Unit Map dealing with cold deserts in Figure 7.3. Notice, in our example, the topic of cold deserts is expanded on to include more information (see Figure 7.2). When the Unit Organizer Routine was used in secondary science and social studies general education classes, both students with and without learning disabilities increased their scores on unit tests 10 percentage points over baseline (Deshler, Schumaker, Lenz, Bulgren, Hock, Knight, & Ehren, 2001).

### Units Related to Learning Styles and Multiple Intelligences

Even though research concerning learning styles and brain hemisphere preferences is controversial (Dunn, Griggs, Olson, Beasley, & Gorman, 1995; Kavale, Hirshoren, & Forness, 1998; Snider, 1992), this approach provides teachers with a model for individualizing instruction and honoring diversity. Thinking about learning styles and multiple intelligences reminds us to present information in a variety of ways and to provide students with choices of ways to demonstrate their knowledge.

*The 4MAT System.* In the 4MAT system for preparing a unit, McCarthy (1987) recommends correlating subject matter to the learning styles and brain hemispheric preferences of students. The four learning styles are imaginative (Type 1), analytic (Type 2), common sense (Type 3), and dynamic (Type 4). According to McCarthy, the imaginative learner needs personal involvement in the learning experience and learns through social interaction; the analytic learner wants to know what experts think and learns by

**Figure 7.2** Unit Organizer

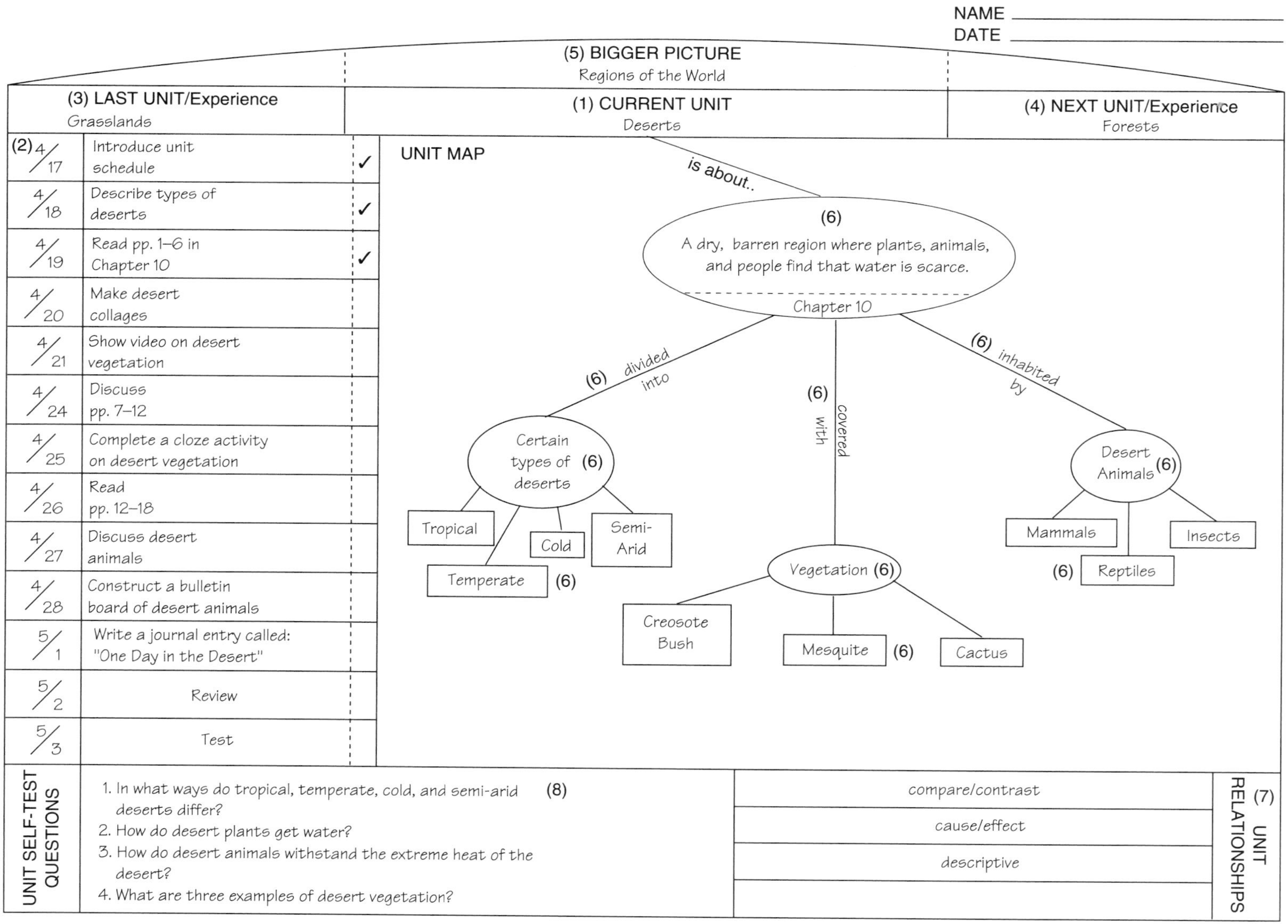

Note. The Unit Organizer is an instructional tool developed and researched at the University of Kansas Center for Research on Learning (Bulgren, Schumaker, & Deshler, 1988). Reprinted by permission.

208

**Figure 7.3** Expanded Unit Map

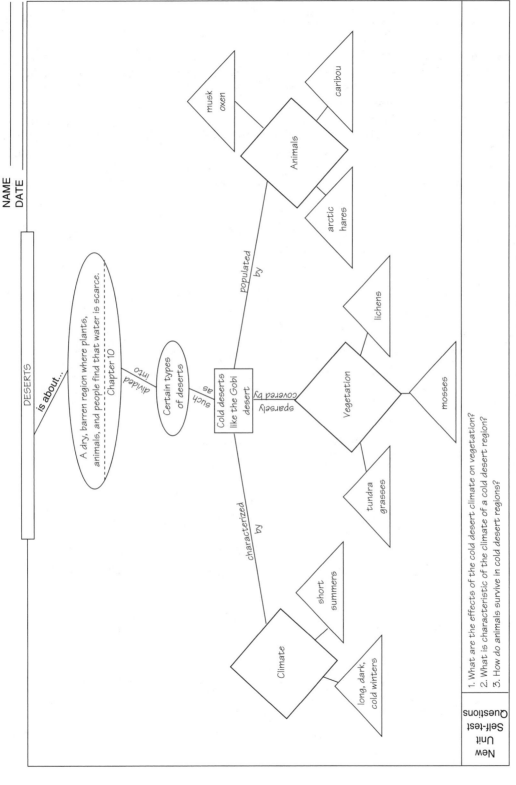

Note. The Expanded Unit Map is an instructional tool developed and researched at the University of Kansas Center for Research on Learning (Bulgren, Schumaker, & Deshler, 1988). Reprinted by permission.

209

thinking through ideas; the common sense learner wants to know how things work and learns through hands-on activities; and the dynamic learner enjoys being involved with a variety of activities and learns through self-discovery. In an examination of brain hemispheric preferences research, McCarthy finds that some individuals process information in a nonverbal global manner (right hemisphere); some in a linear, sequential, logical manner (left hemisphere); and some show no preference. Thus, the teacher organizes information with a specific type of learner in mind, using either a logical, step-by-step format (left hemisphere) or an overview presentation (right hemisphere). Unit activities and the teacher's role vary depending on learning styles and hemispheric preferences. The teacher's role also changes during the unit from direct teaching to becoming more of a facilitator. See Figure 7.4 for a sample

**Figure 7.4**   Sample 4MAT Unit

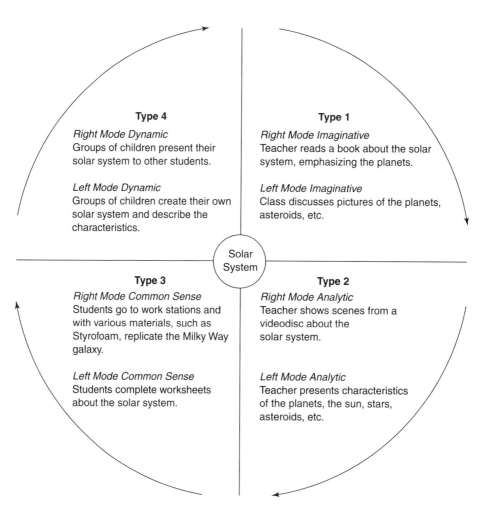

of the activities one of our interns planned for a solar system unit based on this model.

***Multiple Intelligences.*** Gardner (1983) posits the existence of multiple intelligences that enable people to solve problems. These intelligences are verbal/linguistic, logical/mathematical, visual/spatial, musical/rhythmic, body/kinesthetic, interpersonal, and intrapersonal. Verbal/linguistic is related to words and language; logical/mathematical is related to numbers and the recognition of abstract patterns; visual/spatial includes the ability to create mental images; musical/rhythmic is related to recognition and sensitivity to rhythms and beats; body/kinesthetic includes physical movement and body awareness; interpersonal relies on relationships and communications; and intrapersonal centers on metacognition and inner awareness (Lazear, 1991).

In a 1997 interview, Gardner added an eighth intelligence, naturalistic intelligence (Checkley, 1997). He defines this intelligence as "the human ability to discriminate among living things (plants, animals) as well as sensitivity to other features of the natural world (clouds, rock configurations)" (p. 12). He notes that botanists and biologists exhibit a great deal of naturalistic intelligence.

Building on Gardner's theory, Maker, Nielson, and Rogers (1994) devised a thematic curriculum that considers multiple intelligences, problem types, and cultural diversity. With a unit theme of "Connections" and the topic of Native Americans in North Carolina, they devised different activities that, they feel, are appropriate for each intelligence:

A. *Verbal/linguistic:* Read a road map of North Carolina. List the Native American place names on the map.

B. *Logical/mathematical:* Compute the number of miles Cherokees walked per day during the Trail of Tears.

C. *Visual/spatial:* Trace the route of the Trail of Tears on a modern-day map.

D. *Musical/rhythmic:* Find a recording of Native American music and share it with your classmates.

E. *Body/kinesthetic:* Demonstrate a Native American game that teaches the skills of hunting.

F. *Interpersonal:* Identify the problems specific Native American groups have had with settlers in North Carolina. Which was the most severe? Why?

G. *Intrapersonal:* Choose your favorite event(s) from *Knots on a Counting Rope.* Show in some way the role you would play in the event(s) (p. 15).

Gardner (1995) believes that multiple intelligence theory may enhance education by (a) presenting concepts in a variety of ways, although he cautions that not all topics may be approached via the intelligences; (b) cultivating more than verbal/linguistic or logical/mathematical intelligences, which comprise the focus of most school curricula; and (c) personalizing education with the emphasis on children's strengths. He also believes that most people possess all intelligences at various competence levels.

 **ACTIVITY 7.3**

With a colleague, discuss the various ways to organize a unit. Then select one of the ways and design some activities.

## Planning

The suggestions for planning a unit are a compilation of ideas from Englert, Raphael, and Mariage (1994); Pappas, Kiefer, and Levstik (1990); Rhodes and Dudley-Marling (1988); Swicegood and Parsons (1991); Weaver, Chaston, and Peterson (1993); and our own experiences. Although there is not a single correct way to create a unit, we suggest the following steps: (1) select the unit theme or topic, (2) brainstorm ideas, (3) group ideas into categories, (4) identify general goals, (5) identify specific objectives, (6) develop activities to meet the objectives, (7) evaluate the objectives and activities, and (8) compile a list of resources. The steps are not always sequential, as sometimes it is easier to identify the activities before the objectives.

### Select the Unit Theme or Topic

The selection of the unit theme or topic is often dictated by district curriculum guides, which list required topics and objectives in social studies, language arts, science, history, health, and other subject areas for various grade levels. Swicegood and Parsons (1991) suggest that teachers first give an overview of the possible topics that address the curricular objectives and then let students participate in the selection of the topic.

Roser, Hoffman, and Farest (1990) used children's literature to select unit themes or topics. They selected and grouped 10 children's books that focused on character traits and the ways these traits made characters special into the unit topic, "Being Different Is Being Special" (p. 556). Rhodes and Dudley-Marling (1988) suggest, "The topic can be selected because the teacher knows that it will inspire students' interests and meet some of their needs, or because the students themselves have suggested the topic or revealed a great interest in it during another instructional experience" (p. 93).

### Brainstorm Ideas

After selection of the general theme or topic, the students and teachers list everything that comes to mind. This brainstorming creates a collective group knowledge with equal access to information and a common vocabulary for all (Englert, Raphael, & Mariage, 1994). With young children, you may wish to show pictures or a book to elicit brainstorming.

During this process, you may want to think of your students' IEP objectives, current resources, interests, and literature books. For example, the topic of *time* may elicit a list of hours, minutes, clocks, days, nights, calendar, movement, and

the book, *A Wrinkle in Time.* Hours and minutes may be related to your students' IEP objectives of telling time.

### Group Ideas into Categories

Next, take these ideas and develop them into semantic maps or webs with categories that show relationships (see Figure 7.5). For example, students in the Early Literacy Program talked about snapping, poison, and box turtles, which were categorized under different kinds of turtles (Englert, Raphael, & Mariage, 1994). Another example shows simple clocks, manual clocks, and mechanical clocks mapped under "measuring time" (Pappas, Kiefer, & Levstik, 1990). The software program of Inspiration may assist in the creation of semantic maps (Inspiration Software, Inc., 7412 SW Beaverton, Hillsdale Hwy., Suite 102, Portland, OR 97225; 1-800-877-4292). Students and teachers continue to update the map or web as students secure more information and check the accuracy of their brainstormed ideas. This, then, leads to the identification of goals and objectives.

 **ACTIVITY 7.4**

> Brainstorm with another student ideas concerning global warming. Then draw a semantic map with the ideas grouped into categories.

### Identify General Goals

General goals present an overall picture of what you wish the students to accomplish and learn. A general goal for a unit on time may be "to help students understand the role of time in history."

### Identify Objectives

Behavioral objectives specify the learner, condition, criterion, and target behavior (see Chapter 2). They describe outcomes that can be measured and correlated with the categories and the major goals of the unit. For example, an objective for the general goal just discussed

**Figure 7.5** Sample Semantic Map

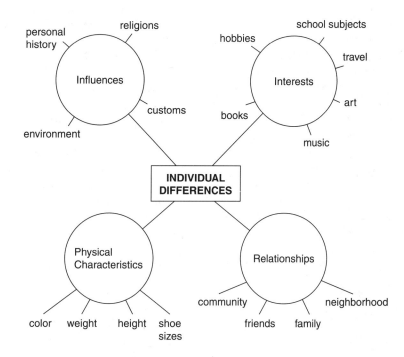

may be, "Following a discussion of ways time was measured over the centuries, the students will build a water clock and use it to tell time at 100% accuracy." Students may wish to develop their own objectives based on the questions that they would like answered.

### Develop Activities and Learning Experiences

Ideas for activities may come from suggested experiments and enrichment activities found in teachers' manuals, your own creativity and experiences, or again, from student interest. Activities may be tied to subject areas, literacy stages, themes, learning styles, and multiple intelligences, as discussed in the description section. Englert and Mariage (1996) suggest that students now transform their ideas into written or oral reports after they use the semantic map to make decisions about the relevant ideas and the relationships of the ideas. Swicegood and Parsons (1991) include speaking and listening activities (such as debates and role-plays), reading activities (such as constructing tree webs),

and written expression activities (such as keeping journals and diaries) for their secondary unit on offshore petroleum exploration.

Weaver, Chaston, and Peterson (1993) recommend dividing the students into cooperative groups, based on their interests. Students then research the topic and decide on the activities. One of our interns used this procedure in a co-taught health class on substance abuse. After weeks of researching information, one group wrote a play about the dangers of smoking. Another group presented posters dealing with statistics on teenage substance abuse and a comparison with their own school from interviews and surveys that they had conducted. A third group videotaped a day in the life of a teenage substance abuser, as role-played by a member of the group, emphasizing the effects on work, school, and relationships. After researching the causes of substance abuse, a fourth group wrote 10 two-minute infomercials dealing with handling peer pressure and how to help a friend who may be having difficulties.

Students' presentation of information may be enhanced through the use of desktop publishing programs that integrate text and graphics, such as *The Writing Center* (The Learning Company), *The Bilingual Writing Center* (The Learning Company), *Kids Work Deluxe* (Davidson), *Creative Writer* (Microsoft), *Print Shop Deluxe 12* (Broderbund), and *Kidspiration* (Inspiration Software). Please check the Web site www.learningneeds.com for a more thorough description of many of the programs.

Many times, teachers plan a culminating activity to tie together the information and understandings the students have developed in a unit. For example, after studying about Mexico, students in a co-taught inclusion class invited parents and members from other classes to visit the various booths designed by each cooperative group. Visitors were treated to sample foods in the food booth, dramatizations in the arts booth, oral reports in the government booth, and visual displays in the lifestyles booth. The culminating activity was so motivating to one student who was essentially a nonreader that he volunteered to read one of the group-prepared reports. He had memorized the report, but pretended to read from the typed project.

### Evaluate Objectives and Activities

Swicegood and Parsons (1991) recommend both quantitative (product) and qualitative (process) evaluation procedures. Some of their examples of quantitative procedures include evaluating the amount of work, scoring writing mechanics, and comparing work samples over time. Some of their examples of qualitative procedures include audiotaping class participation, judging debates, and scoring writing holistically. Barnes (1993) recommends that both teachers and students reflect on the product and process. Here again, rubrics may be used to score student projects. For example, in the co-taught health class, the students and teachers created a rubric to evaluate the drug abuse projects (see Table 7.1). Remember, one group created a

play; one, a poster and interviews; one, a videotape; and one, infomercials. The teacher then brought in two projects from the previous year and students evaluated the projects with the rubric, which helped them understand the teacher's expectations. The teacher then used the rubric to evaluate the student's projects.

### Compile a List of Resources

Because no single text is used in the Unit Approach and because you want to include many activities when presenting the information, you must compile a list of resources. Englert, Raphael, and Mariage (1994) had their students list additional sources of information with the following results: "Ask brothers and sisters, look in books, look on the book cover, library, dictionary, encyclopedia, ask parents, and look in books at home" (p. 11). To this resource list, we add CD-ROMs, such as *Eyewitness Children's Encyclopedia: School Version CD-ROM* (Dorling Kindersley), *The Golden Book Encyclopedia* (Jostens Learning Corporation), *Encarta Encyclopedia Deluxe* (Microsoft), and *Steck Vaughn Interactive Science Encyclopedia CD-ROM* (Steck Vaughn). In Table 7.2 we provide sources for ordering free materials.

Sometimes, students may secure supplemental materials. One teacher, who organized the social studies curriculum into units with various countries as topics, had the students write to the embassies located in Washington, DC, for information about each country. Frequently, embassies send addresses of other places to write to for free materials as well as free pamphlets about their countries. At the beginning of the school year, this same teacher had parents identify any special skills or topics they or their friends might share from a list of planned unit topics for the coming school year. Other sources for prepared units may be found in Table 7.3. In addition, innumerable sites for units may be found on the Web. For example, the Web site, www.ask.com, turned up a list of over 100 sites for thematic units. We adapt examples from

**Table 7.1**   Holistic Rubric for Drug Abuse Project

---

### *Superior (5)*

The information on drug abuse was clearly stated and accurate. The project was well-organized. The information presented was relevant to the targeted audience and easily understood. The project contained minimal grammar and spelling errors. The project was creative and it was evident that all members participated.

### *Good (4)*

The information on drug abuse was somewhat confusing, but accurate. Most of the project was well-organized, but sometimes the focus was lost. The information presented was relevant to the targeted audience, but it was a little difficult to understand. There were minimal grammar and spelling errors. The project was creative and all members participated, although some appeared to do more work than others.

### *Fair (3)*

Some of the information on drug abuse was confusing and inaccurate. The project tended to lose focus for much of the time. Most of the information was relevant to the targeted audience, but it was difficult to understand. There were many grammar and spelling errors. The project was creative, but it appeared that only some members participated.

### *Poor (2)*

Most of the information on drug abuse was confusing and inaccurate. The project did not appear to have a focus. The information was not relevant to the targeted audience and was difficult to understand. The project appeared to be incomplete. There were many spelling and grammar errors. It appeared that only some of the members participated.

---

**Table 7.2**   Sources for Ordering Free Materials

---

*Educator's Guide to Free Materials*
Educator's Progress Service, Inc.
214 Center St.
Randolph, WI 53956
(*Phone*: 920-326-3126)

*Free Stuff for Kids*
Meadowbrook Publishers
Distributed by Simon & Schuster
1230 Avenue of the Americas
New York, NY 10020
(*Phone*: 800-223-2336)

*The Kid's Address Book*
by Michael Levine
Putnam Publishers Group
405 Murray Hill Pkwy.
East Rutherford, NJ 07073
(*Phone*: 800-631-8571)

---

Pappas, Kiefer, and Levstik's theme of wash and wear to summarize the steps to unit preparation (see Figure 7.6).

 **ACTIVITY 7.5**

Develop a unit based on themes, content, 4MAT, or multiple intelligences. Be sure to identify the major goal, categories, objectives, activities, and evaluation.

## THE SINGLE-TEXT APPROACH

In some inclusive settings, teachers rely on the textbook for instructing students. Frequently, the instruction proceeds with students taking turns reading paragraphs orally or reading the text silently and answering questions. For some

**Table 7.3**   Sources for Prepared Units

*Multicultural Teaching: A Handbook of Activities, Information, and Resources* by Tiedt & Tiedt (1986)
   The authors suggest ideas for various multicultural units.

*The 4MAT System* by McCarthy (1987)
   Sample elementary unit topics—living and nonliving things
   Sample middle-school-level topics—probability and energy
   Sample secondary-level topics—due process and respiration/breathing

*ITI: THE MODEL: Integrated Thematic Instruction* by Kovalik (1994)
   The author identifies research, basic information to be learned, activities, and resources for weekly and monthly units, based on brain-compatible learning and brain research.

*www.teach-nology.com*
   Unit themes include computers, countries, science, social studies, holidays, language arts, math, seasonal, and many other topics for grades K–12. Within each unit are lesson plans, download sites for background information, hands-on activities, interactive sites, clip art, photos and other resource materials, and worksheets to customize.

*www.thesolutionsite.com*
   The site contains thematic units with lesson plans developed for K–12 grades by the West Virginia TurnKey Solution Project via a U.S. Department of Educational Technology Innovation Challenge Grant. Teachers created the units, which identify learner outcomes, national standards, related technology, and activities that require more student involvement in learning.

*www.sbcss.k12.ca.us/sbcss/specialeducation/ecthematic*
   The site contains early childhood thematic units for students with special needs. The units incorporate technology and center on fine and gross motor development, language development, preacademic development, sign language, and other areas of early childhood development. Software may be downloaded from the site and lists of support media, including videos, may be found. The units were designed through a technology grant program supported by the San Bernardino County Schools, Special Services, Special Education Division.

students with disabilities who have reading, organization, memory, and attention problems, these instructional strategies are ineffective. Adaptations should be made before, during, and after lesson presentation. We present adaptations dealing with a health lesson on skin, hair, and nail care, taken from *Decisions for Health, Book One* (Bernstein, 1997), a textbook written for students with special needs. We feel these adaptations require minimal teacher time and are easy to implement.

### Before Instruction

Content-area texts frequently include chapters with independent practice items. As a first step, you need to examine the practice items and ask

yourself the following questions: (a) How are the items presented? (b) Are there enough items? (c) Are the independent practice items aligned with the objectives and content of the lesson and with students' needs and objectives? (d) What do I need to emphasize in the lesson so that my students will successfully complete the items? (e) Does the student text cover the information that my students need to complete the independent practice items successfully?

EXAMPLE:  Ms. Robinson read the four-page Chapter 6 of the health text and examined the independent practice items. She found that there were **four vocabulary** items, **six comprehension** questions, and **six analogy** questions. The **vocabulary** items were fill-in-the-blank that

**Figure 7.6** A Sample Unit

**Step 1.** Select a topic or theme.

Example: wash and wear

**Step 2.** Brainstorm ideas.

Example: drip dry, washing machines, rocks, ringers, cotton, pioneers, cave dwellers, keeping clean, safety clothes, dress-up clothes, working clothes, playing clothes, nylon, wool, sewing machines, hand, etc.

**Step 3.** Group ideas into categories.

Example: Types of clothes people wear—safety, dress-up, work, play

What clothes are made of—nylon, wool, cotton

Ways to wash—rocks, washing machines, hand, ringers

How clothes are made—sewing machine, by hand

How what we wear has changed—cave dwellers, pioneers

**Step 4.** Identify the general goals.

Example: Students will develop an understanding that fibers go through many changes to make clothes.

**Step 5.** *Identify the specific objectives.

Example: (A) After listening to the book, *Charlie Needs a Cloak* (dePaola, 1974), the children will illustrate the various steps of making Charlie's cloak with 100% accuracy.

Example: (B) Given a piece of material, students in groups of three will illustrate at least three changes the material must go through to make a hat. The only criterion is that students must illustrate three changes.

(*Note: Sequencing is listed in the IEP objectives for four students with disabilities in the inclusive class. Additionally, Objective B is promoting higher-level thinking skills and cooperation.)

**Step 6.** Develop activities and learning experiences.

Example: To go with (A), the teacher reads the book and discusses the steps of making Charlie's cloak. The teacher then presents students with four pictures, and she and the students practice putting them in order on the felt board. For independent work, some students are given a blank sheet of paper and they draw their pictures in order for making Charlie's cloak, while some select the teacher-made worksheet with the four pictures. If they selected the teacher worksheet, they then cut and paste them in order to make their own picture chart.

Example: To go with (B), the teacher divides students into groups of three and gives each group a sample of material and tells them to illustrate the steps the material must go through to make a hat. She tells them there are no right or wrong answers, but they must illustrate three steps.

**Step 7.** Evaluate objectives and activities.

Example: (Objective and Activity A) Teacher observes the student working and then she checks students' pictures for correct sequencing. She discusses incorrect responses.

Example: (Objective and Activity B) Teacher observes students working in groups, reminding the students to draw at least three steps and encouraging all to participate. Each group shares the illustrations. All ideas are applauded by the class.

**Step 8.** Compile a list of materials and resources.

Example: Books such as *Mrs. Wishy-Washy* (Cowley & Melser, 1981), *The Five Hundred Hats of Bartholomew Cubbins* (Geisel, 1938). Visitors such as a seamstress. Centers with looms to make potholders; with paper bag vests that can be decorated with various materials; with pictures of articles of clothing that they must sort into work, play, safety, and dress-up clothes. Pictures of three-dimensional objects that show different ways to wash items. Field trips to department stores and museums that have exhibits featuring pioneer clothes, cave dweller garments, and garments through the ages.

required students to select the correct word from three choices [e.g., Pimples form when blocked _____ become infected (moles, pores, glands).]. The **comprehension** questions gave the students the answers and required them to write the questions (e.g., You shouldn't squeeze blackheads or pimples because this can spread acne. Why _____). In the **analogy** questions, students selected a word from a group of words to finish each sentence (e.g., Shampoo is to hair as _____ is to skin (oil, acne, sun, soap).

After rereading the chapter, she decided to increase the **vocabulary** items to 10 on the independent practice sheet. To emphasize the problems and care of the skin, hair, and nails, she replaced the comprehension activity with 10 **comprehension** questions, such as, "Why shouldn't you squeeze a pimple or blackhead?" that the students had to answer. She eliminated the **analogies,** as she felt they were not important to her objectives and were not aligned with the information found in the text.

## During Instruction

To introduce the lesson, you may wish to ask students questions to bring in their background information, to list important key points or vocabulary, to complete a **K** (Know Already) –**W** (Want to Learn) –**L** (Learned) (Ogle, 1986) activity, to bring in concrete objects, to act out simulations, or to preview the lesson by attending to the pictures or vocabulary terms. For example, one of our student teachers brought in Native American artifacts to introduce a chapter on the Plains Indians. Another student teacher had all the students measure their heart rate, run in place for 2 minutes, and then measure their heart rate again to introduce a chapter on physical fitness.

Frequent adaptations in the body of the lesson include the use of guided notes, instructional pausing, vocabulary simplification, concrete objects, paraphrasing, questioning, and graphic organizers. We discussed guided notes and instructional pausing procedures in other sections of the text, so we do not discuss them again here. Paraphrasing and questioning involve turn-reading, but stopping after a few paragraphs are read and then either the teacher or student paraphrases what was read (paraphrasing) or either the teacher or student asks questions after the previously read material (questioning). Some examples of graphic organizers are presented in Figure 7.7. More examples of graphic organizers are presented in Chapter 9.

EXAMPLE: To open the lesson, Ms. Robinson used the **K** column of the **K-W-L** procedure and asked students what they already knew about skin, hair, and nail problems and cures. Students looked at the pictures and titles in the text to add ideas. She then directed student attention to the words that they needed to know for successful completion of the independent practice items.

Ms. Robinson next used the instructional pause procedure: one student read two paragraphs and then the students in groups of three discussed the main idea and two details. One of the groups then shared their ideas with the class. Ms. Robinson wrote the main idea on a transparency and students wrote it in their health journal. In her discussion of the details, she referred to the word on the board and listed a short definition or a key word (e.g., bacteria—tiny living things that can lead to sickness; glands—oil and sweat). She also decided to use a graphic organizer for each of the topics, for example:

| Hair | |
|---|---|
| Problems | Cures |
| | |
| | |
| | |

To close the lesson, she used the **L** column of the **K-W-L** procedures and had students tell what they had learned about hair, skin, and nail problems and cures as she wrote the information on an overhead. She then asked them to compare this information to what they listed in the **K** column at the beginning of the lesson. The students then completed the adapted worksheet of 10 vocabulary items and 10 comprehension questions.

 **ACTIVITY 7.6**

Select a chapter from a content-area text and design two graphic organizers.

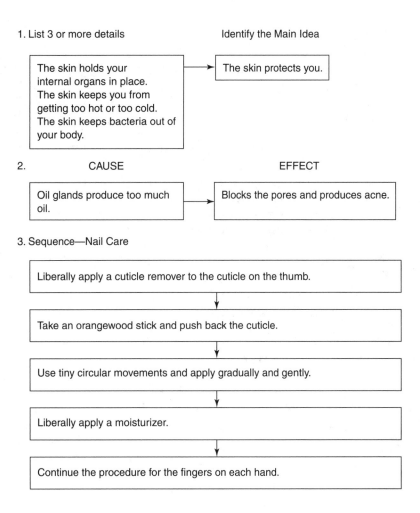

**Figure 7.7** Sample Graphic Organizers

1. List 3 or more details — Identify the Main Idea

The skin holds your internal organs in place. The skin keeps you from getting too hot or too cold. The skin keeps bacteria out of your body. → The skin protects you.

2. CAUSE → EFFECT

Oil glands produce too much oil. → Blocks the pores and produces acne.

3. Sequence—Nail Care

Liberally apply a cuticle remover to the cuticle on the thumb.

Take an orangewood stick and push back the cuticle.

Use tiny circular movements and apply gradually and gently.

Liberally apply a moisturizer.

Continue the procedure for the fingers on each hand.

## After Instruction

Teachers now select activities that reinforce, enrich, generalize, or apply the information. Brown (1991) recommends that these activities build on students' interests, skills, and talents and that they include written, oral, and visual experiences. We like to emphasize generalization activities at this time, as generalization of new information or skills is such a problem for students with disabilities.

Example: Ms. Robinson then gives a homework assignment that requires students to interview peers or parents to see how they care or certain skin, hair, and nail problems. Each group writes a list of five questions and then presents the list to the entire class. Students may select any five questions for their interviews.

 **ACTIVITY 7.7**

With a colleague, design another generalization activity concerning problems and care of the skin, hair, and nails.

**IMPORTANT POINTS**

1. The Unit Approach integrates subject matter with a topic, a theme, or interest areas.

2. The Unit Approach is known for integration of multicultural content into the curriculum, active student participation, and motivational aspects.

3. A unit may incorporate activities to correspond with various subject areas, themes, learning styles, or multiple intelligences.

4. In planning a unit, select the unit theme or topic, brainstorm ideas, group ideas into categories, identify general goals, identify specific objectives, develop activities to meet the objectives, evaluate the objectives, and compile a list of resources.

5. Unit topics may be selected from curriculum guides, classroom texts, children's literature, and students' interests.

6. Objectives identify specific behaviors and correlate with the categories and major goals of the unit and relate to students' IEP objectives.

7. Activities and learning experiences should relate to the unit objectives, require student participation, and provide for various instructional arrangements.

8. Teaching content with a single text requires various adaptations, such as changing or adding more practice items, using guided notes or instructional pausing, simplifying vocabulary, adding concrete objects, paraphrasing, questioning, and using graphic organizers.

**DISCUSSION QUESTIONS**

1. Opponents of the Direct Instruction model frequently assert that the lessons are boring and not motivating to the students due to the constant repetition and controlled vocabulary. How might you respond to such criticism?

2. Discuss the various types of units.

3. What are some effective adaptations that you may make if you are using a single text for content instruction?

# CHAPTER 8

# SOCIAL SKILLS AND PEER-MEDIATED INSTRUCTION

In the early days of American education, when one-room schoolhouses were prevalent, the practice of older students instructing younger students was often a necessity, as the teacher usually taught four to eight grades (Allen, 1976). Today, teachers are again turning to the idea of students working with and instructing each other to meet the needs of the diverse population in inclusive classes. Cooperative goal structures are emphasized as students work together to accomplish goals and to create collaborative learning communities.

In this chapter, we examine some peer-mediated strategies that focus on students helping others learn. In particular, we concentrate on peer tutoring and cooperative learning, as both are recommended as effective strategies for inclusive settings (Johnson & Johnson, 1996; King-Sears & Bradley, 1995; Lag-Delello, 1998; Maheady, Harper, & Malette, 2001; Slavin, 1988a; Vaughn, Klinger, & Bryant, 2001). These peer-mediated strategies can accommodate the wide range of cultural, linguistic, and academic diversity found in the current inclusive classroom.

Peer tutoring involves students working together, whereas cooperative learning usually occurs in groups of three or more. Peer tutoring and cooperative learning draw from both the reductionist and constructivist paradigms. Once the procedures are directly taught, the teacher's role changes to that of a facilitator, and the students participate in classroom communities. However, before we discuss these peer-mediated strategies, we spend time discussing social skills. Teachers must teach social skills before and during peer-mediated instruction for effective learning to occur (Allsopp, 1997; Cohen, 1994).

223

## SOCIAL SKILLS

As discussed in Chapter 1, many students with special needs display inappropriate social skills. The lack of social skills tends to isolate these students from their peers, prevent positive interactions with teachers, and limit successful transitions to the world of work. Meta-analysis of social skills training finds only a modest effect for both students with learning disabilities and students with emotional disabilities (Kavale & Forness, 1995; Kavale, Mathur, Forness, Rutherford, & Quinn, 1997). Some possible explanations for the modest effect of social skills training may be intervention vagueness, imprecision in assessment procedures, lack of generalization of social skills, absence of a conceptual framework, and questionable social validity of social skills (Mather & Rutherford, 1996). Additional factors include the lack of intensive training as most of the studies in the meta-analysis report an average time of 30 hours in social skills training and the lack of matching interventions to social skills deficits (Gresham, Sugai, & Horner, 2001). As with all intervention strategies, the individual teacher should rely on data collection procedures to monitor the effectiveness of social skills training (see Chapter 3), as one cannot argue with the necessity of teaching social skills to students with special needs.

### Identification of Social Skills

An examination of the literature finds varied definitions of social skills. McFall (1982) conceptualized a two-tiered model of social competence and social skills. According to his model, social competence involves the overall effectiveness of social behavior. A person who is socially competent perceives and interprets social situations and knows how to modify behavior when the situation changes (Chadsey-Rusch, 1986). Social skills are the specific strategies (accepting criticism, initiating conversation) and tactics that students use to negotiate daily social tasks.

Kavale and Forness (1995) discuss three types of social deficits—skill, performance, and self-control:

1. A skill deficit exists when a student has not learned the skill.
2. A performance deficit occurs when the student knows the skill but doesn't perform it due to a problem with motivation or discrimination (Smith, 1995). Students who are unmotivated do not perform the skill unless they are provided external motivation, while students with discrimination deficits are skilled and motivated, but don't know when to exhibit the skill.
3. Self-control deficits result when a student displays behaviors that interfere with the acquisition and performance of appropriate social skills. These behaviors include impulsivity, distractibility, hyperactivity, etc. (Smith, 1995).

Gresham, Sugai, and Horner (2001) identify three social skills deficits: social skill acquisition deficits, performance deficits, and fluency deficits. Additionally, they recommend the selection of various interventions and settings based on the identification of the deficit (see Table 8.1).

With these various ways of conceptualizing social skills, how does a teacher decide which social skills will promote the behaviors necessary for effective peer tutoring and cooperative learning practices? You may check two sources: the empirical literature and consumer preferences (Walker, Schwarz, Nippold, Irvin, & Noell, 1994). In a review of the literature, offering encouragement and assistance, accepting compliments and criticism, taking turns, listening to what others are saying, avoiding sarcasm and criticism, and presenting a positive and friendly manner are frequently mentioned as skills that promote the behaviors necessary for effective peer tutoring and cooperative learning (Nelson, 1988; Mathes, Fuchs, Fuchs, Henley, & Sanders, 1994). To these skills, Wolford, Heward, and Alber (2001) add recruiting positive attention and instructional

**Table 8.1** Matching of Interventions to Social Skills Deficits

| Social Skills Deficit | Definition | Intervention | Setting |
|---|---|---|---|
| Acquisition | Absence of knowledge to execute skill or failure to discriminate which behaviors are appropriate for different situations | Modeling, coaching, behavioral rehearsal, feedback on performance | Small group |
| Performance | Skill is present but students fail to execute it | Manipulation of antecedents such as teaching strategies (e.g., peer tutoring) or consequences (e.g., contingency contracting) | Naturalistic (e.g., classrooms, playgrounds) |
| Fluency | Skill is present and student wants to perform, but executes an awkward performance | Behavioral rehearsal and feedback for performance | Small group or natural settings |

feedback from peers for students with learning disabilities to have success in peer tutoring and cooperative learning situations.

Leffert, Siperstein, and Millikan (2000) emphasize that teachers need to teach students with mental retardation not only discrete observable social behaviors, but also underlying social-cognitive skills, as these students frequently have difficulty participating in cooperative groups (Pomplun, 1997). Students with mental retardation often have difficulty interpreting cues regarding intentions of others and selecting effective social strategies (Leffert et al., 2000).

A survey of consumer preferences involves social validation of whether a skill is valued by the individuals in a particular setting. Students who display socially valued behaviors are more likely to be reinforced and accepted by peers. Walker and colleagues (1994) identify compromising, assisting, cooperating, and contributing to achievement of a valued outcome as behaviors that are highly preferred by peers and lead to peer acceptance and popularity. Nelson (1988) lists smiling, making eye contact, asking for help, sharing, and saying "thank you" as behaviors that have a high probability of being reinforced by peers. Thus, you may wish to interview your students to identify the social skills that they feel are necessary for peer tutoring or cooperative learning to work.

Knapczyk and Rodes (1996) suggest that teachers look at the setting demands and the social behavior of students who display appropriate skills. Greenwood (1996) followed this suggestion as he examined the behaviors of effective students during peer-tutoring sessions and found that they provided more encouragement and praise to their peers. It is also extremely important to make certain that students understand the meaning of the social skill. For example, Christensen (1992) prepared the poster in Figure 8.1 to make certain students understood what was meant by encouragement.

**Figure 8.1**  Sample Social Skills Poster for Peer-Mediated Strategies

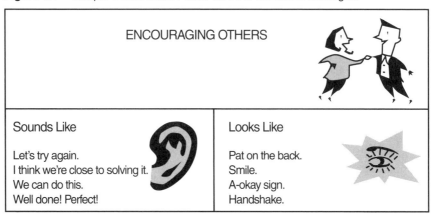

Note. Adapted from Marge Christensen (1992). *Motivational English for At-Risk Students: A Language Arts Course That Works,* Copyright 1992 by the National Education Service, 1252 Loesch Road, Bloomington, IN 47404, Telephone: 800-733-6786. Reprinted by permission.

## Social Skills Interventions

Social skills interventions generally fall into two areas or combinations of the two areas of skill-based approaches and problem-solving approaches (Walker et al., 1994). Smith (1995) recommends a skill-based approach for students who demonstrate skill deficits and a problem-solving approach for students who demonstrate performance deficits or self-control deficits. The skill-based approach adheres to the effective teaching strategies mentioned in Chapter 4: (a) teaching definition, steps, and rationale; (b) modeling; (c) presenting examples and nonexamples; (d) scheduling opportunities for students to practice the skill; (e) prompting; (f) giving feedback; (g) providing contingent reinforcement; and (h) teaching generalization of the skill. The problem-solving approach frequently teaches students to identify their feelings, tell what is happening, decide on a goal, identify alternative responses, envision possible outcomes for each response, select the best solution, decide on one solution, emit the behavior, and self-evaluate for future problem solving (Elias & Tobias, 1996). Whether using

the skill-based approach or the problem-solving approach or elements of both, teachers should directly teach social skills, provide practice opportunities, integrate social skills with other curriculum, and emphasize generalization of the skills to other settings.

 **ACTIVITY 8.1**

Select a social skill other than encouragement and design a poster to help students remember the definition.

(Answers for this and other activities are found in the Instructor's Manual.)

### Directly Teach Social Skills

As with academic skills, students with disabilities have difficulty learning social skills incidentally. Teachers should directly teach the skills and then use scaffolding (prompting) to facilitate social skills performance. Adolescents with learning disabilities (LD) were successfully trained to directly teach social skills to their peers with LD (Prater, Serna, & Nakamura, 1999). Prater and colleagues (1999) report that students taught by peers acquired the social skills of contributing to discussion, giving positive feedback, and accepting negative feedback faster than those students taught the same skills by the teacher. However, those students in the teacher-led class maintained the skills for a longer time. Interestingly, whether the students were taught by peers or a teacher, the most difficult social skill to acquire was accepting negative feedback, a necessary skill for successful peer-mediated activities.

Elias and Tobias (1996) recommend teaching students problem-solving strategies by using questioning techniques. They suggest that open-ended questions, such as "What happened? What were you trying to do? How are you feeling? What was the other person doing? What happened before this?" (p. 24) assist students to become competent and independent thinkers. For the resistant or younger child, they suggest teaching students to make choices, such as "Were you trying to keep the toy for yourself?" or "Did you just want to play with it a little longer?" A two-question rule is used to encourage children to think. For example, before putting children into cooperative groups, you may ask them to think about these questions: "How do you plan to show you do not agree with your partner's idea? What are some words you could start with?" The idea is to lead students to reflect on their own behaviors.

Rosenthal-Malek (1997) used six 10-minute daily instruction periods to teach her preschool children self-interrogation questions, such as "What will happen if _____?" to develop social skills. She asked each child to repeat the questions, she then wrote the questions on the board, and she developed games for application of the questions.

Modeling social skills is another effective way to teach social skills directly. Teachers or other students may model the skill. Often the skill is modeled in an appropriate manner and then in an inappropriate manner, and students must discriminate between them. For example,

Ms. Trailer modeled the appropriate way to disagree with a peer and then the inappropriate way. The children designed their own evaluation to help discriminate the appropriate example from the inappropriate.

Elias and Taylor (1995) suggest the use of videos to teach social skills. They first show a segment of a television program or a movie. Then they ask students to discuss the main characters, the problems they have, their expressed feelings, the character's goals, their solutions, the roadblocks, the plan, and evaluation of the plan. Instead of using a movie, Ms. Fearis videotaped each cooperative group for 5 minutes and then presented the tape to the students and asked them to pinpoint any problems they saw that the group was having, brainstorm some solutions, vote on one solution, and agree to try the solution the next time the group met.

Directly teaching social skills using literature is another effective strategy (Cartledge & Kiarie, 2001; Morris, 2002). Select books that include the social skill you are planning to teach, that are not dominated by violence, that include brief stories, that are culturally diverse, that present males and females in nonstereotypical ways, and that have minimal text with repetitive refrains for young children and students who are not skilled readers (Cartledge & Kiarie, 2001). Two sources to check for literary sources are the Web site http://www.carolhurst.com and the book *Cultural Diversity and Social Skills Instruction: Understanding Ethnic and Gender Differences* by Cartledge and Milburn. The Web site describes award-winning books correlated to social skills such as how to handle bullies. Activities and links to related books are described. Each chapter in the Cartledge and Milburn book identifies sample books for various social skills (Cartledge & Kiarie, 2001).

### Provide Practice Opportunities

Practice for social skills frequently occurs during role playing. Role playing allows students to identify and learn skills and to solve problems in a group context with impersonal materials. During role playing, an effective teacher provides prompts and feedback. Many commercial social skills curriculum kits provide role-playing suggestions (see Chapter 12). However, you or your students may generate the role-playing situations. At the end of one of the peer-tutoring sessions, Ms. Bright had students role-play how to give corrective feedback, as she noticed many tutors were having problems correcting their peers in an effective manner.

Another effective strategy is to provide students with mnemonics to cue students to remember and practice a skill. The SLAM (McIntosh, Vaughn, & Bennerson, 1995) strategy does just that. After skills instruction, teachers may use SLAM to remind students how to handle negative feedback: "**S**top whatever you're doing. **L**ook the person in the eye. **A**sk the person a question to clarify what he or she means. **M**ake an appropriate response to the person."

### Integrate Social Skills With Other Curriculum

If you use peer tutoring and cooperative learning groups frequently in your class, it is easy to integrate social skills, as both arrangements incorporate academic and social skills. The writing process also promotes the use of social skills, especially if you have students evaluate each other's work. During student feedback and evaluation of other students' writings, Zaragoza (1987) teaches her students to react positively to each other's work through the simple steps of TAG: "(a) **T**ell what you like, (b) **A**sk questions, and (c) **G**ive ideas" (p. 293).

Elias and Tobias (1996) suggest that social problem-solving frameworks may be applied to language arts, social studies, and health. For example, a "Book Talk" format brings problem-solving ideas into language arts for young readers:

My character's problem is . . . .

How did your character get into this problem . . . ?

How does the character feel?

What does the character want to happen?

What questions would you like to be able to ask the character you picked, one of the other characters, or the author? (p. 109)

### Generalize Social Skills

Students with disabilities have great difficulty in generalizing new information to other situations and settings (Rivera & Smith, 1997). Therefore, you must incorporate generalization strategies into your teaching of social skills. Skills that possess social validity are often easier to transfer, as they are maintained by naturally occurring behaviors, such as peer approval and attention. Prompting social skill use throughout the day and giving homework assignments are two strategies that often assist students to generalize behaviors. In her primary, inclusive, literacy-based classroom, Burke (1993) provides an example of the former by immediately attending to a social problem through the use of "Blue Chairs." Students who are involved in the conflict move to a separate part of the room and follow these procedures:

1. Only people who are part of the problem sit in the Blue Chairs.
2. No touching, yelling, or name calling.
3. One person tells his/her feelings at a time. "I feel _____, because _____." The other person must wait his/her turn. There are no interruptions.
4. The people who are part of the problem must solve the problem. Each person must be satisfied with the solution. (p. 84)

The teacher acts as a mediator, prompting students to remember the steps and making suggestions if the students are having difficulty resolving the problems. The teacher then leaves and allows the students to continue the process independently.

Salend, Jantzen, and Giek (1992) found that a peer confrontation system was effective in modifying inappropriate verbalizations and low levels of on-task behavior for students with mild disabilities. Whenever the 8- through 10-year-olds displayed either behavior during the language arts classes, the teacher initiated the procedure by asking the group to respond to these questions: "_____ seems to be having a problem. Who can tell _____ what the problem is? Can you tell _____ why that is a problem? Who can tell _____ what he/she needs to do to solve the problem?" (p. 214). The teacher verbally praised appropriate responses to the questions and verbally praised the student who had been confronted for accepting and displaying the alternative suggested by the group. Twelve of the 13 students reported that they felt the teacher should continue the intervention, even though some felt it was embarrassing to be singled out. An adaptation is to direct the confrontation to the group and not a single subject; for example, "Our group seems to be having a problem . . . ."

Teachers may give homework assignments for students to generalize social skills in addition to academic skills. Ms. Holt noticed that students were not demonstrating encouraging behavior to each other during group work. Using peer confrontation procedures, the group defined the problem and discussed how to show more encouragement to others. Ms. Holt then gave the students a homework assignment to complete for their social skills journals (see Figure 8.2). Chances are with the peer-mediated strategies of peer tutoring and cooperative

learning, social skills instruction will become an integral part of your curriculum.

 **ACTIVITY 8.2**

Describe a social skills generalization activity that you plan to use in your classroom.

 **IMPORTANT POINTS**

1. Meta-analysis of social skills training finds only a modest effect for both students with learning disabilities and students with emotional disabilities (Kavale & Forness, 1995; Kavale, Mathur, Forness, Rutherford, & Quinn, 1997).
2. Social skills may be conceptualized in many ways: McFall (1982), social competence and social skills; Kavale and Forness (1995), skill deficit, performance deficit, and self-control deficit; Gresham, Sugal, and Horner (2001), social skill acquisition deficits, performance deficits, and fluency deficits.
3. Surveying the literature and interviewing significant peers and adults are two ways to identify social skills for instruction.
4. Some social skills that have been identified for effective peer tutoring and cooperative learning to occur include: (a) recruiting

**Figure 8.2** Homework Entry for Social Skills Journal

Date: *January 1, 2003* _____ Name: *Jason C.* _____

Practice Skill: *Encouragement* _____

Where I did it: *At home* _____

What I did: *I told my brother that he really was a good drawer and I knew he'd draw a good map.* _____

How I felt: *Good. Happy.* _____

How it worked: *Good. He smiled at me. And Mom told me that I was being thoughtful.* _____

positive attention and instructional feedback from peers for students with learning disabilities (Wolfred et al, 2001); and (b) interpreting cues regarding intentions of others and selecting effective social strategies for students with mental retardation (Leffert et al, 2000).

5. The skill-based approach for teaching social skills involves teaching the definition, steps, and rationale; modeling; presenting examples and nonexamples; scheduling opportunities for students to practice the skill; prompting; giving feedback; providing contingent reinforcement; and teaching generalization of the skill.

6. The problem-solving approach teaches students to identify their feelings, tell what is happening, decide on a goal, identify alternative responses, envision possible outcomes for each response, select the best solution, decide on one solution, emit the behavior, and use their self-evaluation for future problem solving (Elias & Tobias, 1996).

7. Whichever approach is used, teachers must directly teach social skills, provide practice opportunities, integrate social skills with other curriculum, and emphasize generalization of the skills to other settings.

---

# PEER TUTORING

Peer tutoring consists of one student acting as a tutor, or the person who transmits the information, and one student acting as the tutee, or the person who receives the information. A tutor may be the same age as the tutee (same-age tutoring) or a different age (cross-age tutoring). Students may also assume reciprocal roles: sometimes as a tutor and sometimes as a tutee.

Peer tutoring enjoys much empirical support in the field of special education for students with mild disabilities in both elementary and secondary grades in all subject areas (Durrer & McLaughlin, 1995; Utley, Mortsweet, & Greenwood, 1997). Peer tutoring was identified as one of the promising interventions from a meta-analysis of special education research (Forness, Kavale, Blum, & Lloyd, 1997). In summarizing the research on peer tutoring, Kalkowski (2001) reports its effectiveness for low-achieving, limited-English-speaking, learning disabled, behaviorally disordered, and other at-risk populations in both academic and affective areas and at all age/grade levels.

Not only is peer tutoring effective for students, but both teachers and students appear to like peer tutoring (Greenwood & Delaquadri, 1995; Mastropieri, Scruggs, Mohler, Beranek, Spencer, Boon, & Talbott, 2001; Mathes, Grek, Howard, Babyak, & Allen, 1999). Students prefer it over teacher-led and student-regulated activities (Maheady, Harper, & Mallette, 2001). Danville High School in Kentucky has offered an elective course in peer tutoring for 11th and 12th graders to tutor students with moderate and severe disabilities since 1983 (Longwill & Kleinert, 1998).

## Rationale

The rationale behind the use of peer tutoring is that the procedures promote more active student responding, a direct link to higher achievement. Students have more opportunities to correct errors, are given immediate feedback, and are exposed to more social and academic support than in teacher-mediated instruction (King-Sears & Bradley, 1995; Utley, et al., 1997). Furthermore, peer tutoring is another way to accomplish individualized instruction, because instructional material may be matched to the learner's interest and ability. Peer tutoring is also an effective way to reinforce concepts previously taught by the teacher. A peer who has similar experiences and is closer to the developmental age of the tutee can often interpret the teacher's ideas or content in the child's language. Last, peer tutoring is an economical and teacher-friendly way to accommodate the wide range of cultural, linguistic, and academic diversity found in the current inclusive classroom.

## Description

Within peer tutoring, we examine instructional procedures that involve two peers working together, such as Reciprocal Peer Tutoring (Fantuzzo, King, & Heller, 1992) and the Reciprocal Peer Revision Strategy (MacArthur, Schwartz, & Graham, 1991). Additionally, we present models that involve peers working together as part of a team, such as ClassWide Peer Tutoring (CWPT; Delquadri, Greenwood, Stretton, & Hall, 1983), and Peabody Peer-Assisted Learning Strategies (PALS; Mathes et al., 1994). We select these particular models to describe, as they are supported in the literature for their effectiveness for students with mild disabilities and students at risk (Utley et al., 1997).

### *Reciprocal Peer Tutoring*

The routine for Reciprocal Peer Tutoring (RPT) includes 20 minutes of peer tutoring, followed by 7 minutes of testing to teach math and spelling skills. Teachers use modeling and instructional prompts to teach students to follow specific techniques for acting as partners and for managing their own group reward contingencies (Heller & Fantuzzo, 1993). We describe the math tutoring procedures (Fantuzzo et al., 1992; Fantuzzo, Davis, & Ginsburg, 1995). Students are paired randomly in same-age dyads and work with flash cards selected for them individually, based on their scores on a math pretest. They also select their rewards and performance goals from teacher-prepared options. Sometimes students begin the procedures by completing a 5-minute multiplication drill, while other times they begin by reminding themselves of their individual and group goals. The tutoring format proceeds in the following manner:

A. Peer teacher presents flash card with answer and strategy on back to student.
B. Student completes problem on a worksheet that is divided into sections (Try 1, Try 2, Help, and Try 3).
C. If student is correct, peer teacher praises and presents next problem.
D. If student is wrong, peer teacher provides structured help (strategy on back of card) and personal suggestions.
E. Student attempts problem again in Try 2 section.
F. If still incorrect, the peer teacher completes the problem, explaining the procedures in the Help section on the worksheet.
G. Student attempts to solve problem again in Try 3 section.
H. At the end of 10 minutes, students change roles.
I. Both students take a 16-problem quiz.
J. Students grade each other's quizzes using an answer sheet.
K. Students compare their team score with the team goal.
L. If the score exceeds the team goal, the students score a "win."
M. After a certain set of "wins," the team earns the predetermined reward.

### *Reciprocal Peer Revision Strategy*

The Reciprocal Peer Revision Strategy combines strategy instruction and peer interaction. MacArthur, Schwartz, and Graham (1991) designed the highly structured approach to teaching revision skills, which are usually taught more informally in the process approach to writing instruction. The teacher introduces the peer editing strategy, shares its importance, teaches the steps and rationale for each step, models the steps, and provides practice opportunities. At the conclusion of the teacher instruction, pairs of students work together in a structured routine to improve composition writing.

The routine requires the peer editor to (a) listen and read along as the peer author reads; (b) tell the peer author the main idea of the paper and the part liked best; (c) reread the paper, take notes, and address whether the material is clear and is written with enough details; and (d) discuss suggestions with the peer author. Both students complete Steps (a) and (b) as a peer editor and as a peer author. At Step (c), each student works independently on each other's composition. Students ask two questions during this step: "(1) Is there anything that is not CLEAR? and (2) Where could more DETAILS and information be added?" (MacArthur et al., 1991, p. 203). They then discuss the suggestions (Step d), and each student revises his/her composition. At the second meeting, they discuss revisions that they made and complete a checklist that concentrates on four types of errors: complete sentences, capitalization (beginning of sentences), punctuation (end-mark), and spelling. The students with learning disabilities in the strategy group made more revisions and produced papers of higher quality with peer support than those who did not participate in the Reciprocal Peer Revision Strategy.

### ClassWide Peer Tutoring

Initially developed by researchers to work with poor, culturally diverse children, the second phase of the Juniper Garden Children's Project extended the program to special education settings (Greenwood & Delquadri, 1995). Since then these procedures have demonstrated effective results in both pull-out and inclusive classrooms for students with and without disabilities (Greenwood, 1999). Although many different versions of ClassWide Peer Tutoring (CWPT) are evident in the literature, certain core components are usually incorporated into the various adaptations. These core components include direct teacher presentation of new material to be learned, teacher monitoring of the tutoring process, whole-class instructional activity, explicit presentation formats for peers to follow, active student responding, reciprocal roles in each session, teams competing for the highest team point total, contingent point earning, systematic error correction strategies, public posting of stu-

dent performance, and social awards for the winning team (Greenwood & Delquadri, 1995; Greenwood, 1996). Teachers explain the tutoring methods, model the procedures, have students role-play the procedures, and then give students feedback regarding their performance (Maheady & Harper, 1991). When ClassWide Peer Tutoring procedures were instituted in a health education class, the entire class was trained for 15 minutes a day for three consecutive days using role playing and feedback (Utley, Reddy, Delquadri, Greenwood, Mortweet, & Bowman, 2001).

We describe the use of CWPT in a secondary social studies inclusive classroom (Maheady, Sacca, & Harper, 1988). However, CWPT has been just as successful with elementary-age students and in math, reading, and spelling.

Maheady, Sacca, and Harper (1988) instituted the following CWPT approach in an inclusive secondary social studies class using study guides developed by the general and special education teachers. On Monday and Tuesday, the general education teacher presented the material; on Wednesday and Thursday, the peer tutoring occurred; on Friday, the students took a quiz during class time. Students with disabilities were paired with general education students. The pair was assigned to one of two teams by randomly drawing colored squares. The students then contributed points to each team as the teams competed with each other. The team membership stayed the same for 2 weeks.

During the 30-minute peer tutoring sessions, the tutor dictated the study guide questions to the tutee, who wrote and said the correct answer. The tutors gave feedback: either "that's right" or "wrong" and the correct answer. Tutees earned three points for each correct answer. When tutees gave an incorrect answer, the tutors instructed them to write the correct answer three times and awarded two points instead of three. After 15 minutes elapsed, the students reversed roles and continued with the same procedures.

The teachers' roles were also structured. Each teacher moved around the classroom and awarded up to 10 bonus points to tutors for following the presentation format. The individual scores of tutor and tutee were totaled for the daily team scores and posted on a chart in front of the class. On Friday, an individual quiz was given, and each student earned five team points for each correct answer. The winning team was announced following the weekly quiz.

A common complaint of teachers in using CWPT is the amount of time that it takes for the score-reporting process and the planning. A computerized system is available that provides support to teachers in both these processes (Greenwood et al., 1993). The computerized system was used successfully with English-language learners in five first- through fifth-grade classrooms to increase sight vocabulary and spelling words (Greenwood, Arreaga-Mayer, Utley, Gavin, & Terry, 2001). Other concerns are increased noise levels, complaints about partners, and cheating on point counts (Maheady, Harper, & Mallette, 1991).

 **ACTIVITY 8.3**

Share ideas with another student for correcting some of the common complaints of teachers in using CWPT procedures.

### Peabody Peer-Assisted Learning Strategies

In the Peabody Peer-Assisted Learning Strategies (PALS), also referred to as the Peabody ClassWide Peer Tutoring procedure, the reading strategies of summarization, main idea identification, and prediction are combined with peer interactions (Mathes et al., 1994). Teachers directly instruct the students in the key procedures of the tutoring process and in the strategies. Mathes and colleagues (1994) recommend that teachers teach each of the strategies separately for a week at a time. The teachers model the procedures and give students practice in them.

Once the students are trained in the strategies and the tutoring procedures, PALS typically occurs for three 35-minute periods each week for 15 weeks (Mathes et al., 1994; Fuchs, Fuchs, Mathes, & Simmons, 1996). Each strategy takes about 10 minutes, and the rest of the time is spent on taking out and putting materials away and for transition time between strategies. Readers of various levels work together and assume reciprocal roles. Teachers rank order their students and then split the class into high and low performers. The top-ranked student in the high-performing group is then matched to the top-ranked student in the low-performing group until all students from each group are paired (Mathes et al., 1994). Pairs may read from different texts.

Each pair is then assigned to one of two teams. Individuals earn points for their teams and then at the end of the week, the teacher's and each student's points are totaled, and the winning team is announced. Teachers may give points to students for following the procedures correctly and for exhibiting cooperative behaviors. The winning team receives applause from the other team. After 4 weeks, new peers and teams are assigned. In Table 8.2, we outline the specific format for peer teaching of the reading strategies.

There are also PALS procedures for math and group story mapping and writing. Developed for students in Grades 2–8, the PALS procedures are being expanded to kindergarten, first, and high school in the area of reading (Fuchs et al., 2001; Mathes et al., 1999). The kindergarten and first-grade PALS feature beginning literacy skills such as phonological awareness, whereas the high school program differs in frequency of changing partners from 4 weeks to every day, use of tangible reinforcers, and reading materials that apply to students' lives.

**Table 8.2**   Peer Teaching of Reading Strategies

*Partner Reading* (Mathes et al., 1994)

The instructional format for partner reading is:

5 minutes—Best reader reads orally while worse reader tutors.

5 minutes—Worse reader reads the same passage.

1 or 2 minutes—Worse reader retells in sequence what is read.

After the retell sequence, partners reward themselves 10 points if they feel they have worked hard and tried their best.

The routine for correction of word recognition errors for each student is:

Peer teacher says,"You missed this word. Can you figure it out?" Pauses 4 seconds (p. 45)

If correct, student rereads sentence.

If incorrect, peer teacher says, "That word is ____" (p. 46).

Student rereads the word and then the sentence.

Peer teacher rewards a point for each sentence read correctly, no matter the trials.

The routine for the retell sequence is:

Peer teacher says, "What did you learn first?" "What did you learn next?" (p. 46)

If incorrect or the student can't remember, the peer teacher provides the information.

*Paragraph Shrinking* (Fuchs et al., 1996)

The instructional format for paragraph shrinking is:

5 minutes—Best reader orally reads one paragarph.

Worse reader prompts tutee to recall main idea by reading cue cards:

"Who or what was the paragraph mainly about? Tell the most important thing learned in the paragraph" (p.10).

Best reader identifies main idea with not more than 10 words.

Worse reader awards 1 point for correct who or what, 1 point for main idea, and 1 point for shrinking the statement to 10 words.

5 minutes—Worse reader reads next paragraph.

Best reader prompts worse to recall main idea with the same questions.

Best reader assigns points.

The routine for correction for each student is:

Incorrect answer, peer teacher says, "Try again."

Still incorrect answer, peer teacher says,"Read the paragraph silently and try again."

Still incorrect answer, peer teacher provides the answer.

*Prediction Relay* (Mathes et al., 1994)

Prediction Relay is introduced after the students become better at summarizing and identifying the main idea.

The instructional format for prediction relay is:

5 minutes—Best reader makes a prediction about content, reads half page, confirms or disconfirms prediction, summarizes content in 10 words or less, makes a new prediction about next half page, and continues with routine until 5 minutes are up.

Worse reader decides if answers are correct and assigns 1 point for each step, totaling 4 points.

5 minutes—Roles reverse and same procedures are followed.

▼ **ACTIVITY 8.4**

Choose one of the peer-tutoring models and describe how you plan to use it.

## Implementation

Teachers must carefully plan peer-tutoring activities. Decisions must be made about selecting objectives, selecting tutor and tutees, preparing materials, determining schedules and selecting sites, planning the presentation format, training tutors, monitoring progress, and evaluating the tutoring session. Many of these decisions will be made for you if you select any of the models we have just described. See Table 8.3 for a description of how each model addresses some of these decisions.

### Selecting Objectives

Your first step in deciding to institute peer tutoring is to formulate the objectives of the peer-tutoring program. Usually, basic academic skills are taught directly, and positive social interaction is achieved indirectly. IEPs are a good source of objectives for peer tutoring.

Delquadri, Greenwood, Whorton, Carta, and Hall (1986) designated the following target behaviors as appropriate for peer-tutoring selection: "answering comprehension questions; practicing in reading workbooks; practicing spelling word lists; practicing math facts; and practicing words, their meanings, and definitions" (p. 536). Objectives may also include the teaching of strategies such as revision, paragraph shrinking, and others.

### Selecting and Matching Students

In a meta-analytic review of grouping practices and reading outcomes for students with learning disabilities and behavior disorders, Elbaum, Vaughn, Hughes, and Moody (1999) report that peer tutoring was an effective grouping whether students with mild disabilities acted in a reciprocal role (both tutor and tutee) or in a tutee role; however, with cross-age tutoring, students with disabilities perform better when they are the tutors. Furthermore, they report that students with disabilities benefit from tutoring younger students at least a grade level below them. You may wish to change your pairing every 3 to 4 weeks and more frequently if you are working with high school students to counteract frequent absences.

### Preparing Materials

Either the student or you may prepare the materials depending on the objective. If you target spelling words as the objective for peer tutoring, the tutor may just use the class text. If you select memorizing math facts, the tutor may write each fact on a 3-by-5-inch card. If the objective is studying for a test, you should prepare a study guide. For a shared reading objective, you may guide tutors in selecting a book for the session. Administration of a pretest and the selection of 10 missed items comprised the content for math tutoring sessions designed by Miller, Barbetta, and Heron (1994). Monitoring sheets may also be prepared by the tutors or by you. This step requires substantial time initially, but materials may be reused. Additionally, written copies of the correction procedures or cue cards for strategies may assist students in remembering the tutoring procedures.

Checklists are also effective reminders of essential behaviors. Ms. James prepared the following list for her students: (a) I have all the materials, (b) I have examined the materials, (c) I plan to _____ when my student says something wrong, (d) I know when to say, "Good answer," and other positive things, (e) I will remember to smile, and (f) I will count to five to give my tutee a chance to answer after I ask a question.

### Determining Schedules and Selecting Sites

The popular length of a tutoring session is 30 minutes two or three times a week for 5 to 7

**Table 8.3** Comparison of Peer-Tutoring Models to Assist in Teacher Decision Making

| Models | Selecting Content as Pertains to Our Descriptions (Objectives) | Matching Students | Preparing Materials | Determining Schedules & Sites | Planning Presentation Format | Training Tutors | Evaluating Sessions |
|---|---|---|---|---|---|---|---|
| Reciprocal Peer Tutoring | Math facts | Paired randomly; Same age; Reciprocal roles | Flash cards with answer and strategy to solve problem on back of cards; Worksheet divided into Try 1, Try 2, & Try 3 | 20 minutes for tutoring; 7 minutes for test | Tutee gets three tries to answer problem, gets feedback from tutor for each try following specific procedures; Change role at end of 10 minutes; Both take exam; Earn points for team and then earn reward | Teachers train students to act as partners and to manage their own group reward contingencies through modeling and instructional prompts | Quizzes; Team scores; Goals |
| Reciprocal Peer Revision Strategy | Written expression | SLD students with non SLD; Reciprocal roles | Individual written assignments; Checklist of four types of errors | None specified | Assumed roles of peer editor and peer author; Both listen to each composition, tell main idea, and what like; Use questions such as "Is there anything that is not CLEAR?" and "Where could more DETAILS and information be added?" to assist in revision | Teachers teach strategies through rationale, modeling, practice, and comparison to students' previous work; Students view and discuss a videotape of two students following the presentation format | Amount of revisions and quality of papers |

236

| Models | Selecting Content as Pertains to Our Descriptions (Objectives) | Matching Students | Preparing Materials | Determining Schedules & Sites | Planning Presentation Format | Training Tutors | Evaluating Sessions |
|---|---|---|---|---|---|---|---|
| ClassWide Peer Tutoring | Social studies | Students with disabilities to students without disabilities; Same age; Reciprocal roles | Study guide questions. Cue cards for prompting of procedures | Teacher-directed instruction for two days, peer tutoring (30 minutes) of practice activity for two days, quiz on fifth day | Tutor read study guide question while tutee wrote answer; Tutor awarded points for each correct answer; Tutors gave feedback as either, "That's right" or "That's wrong"; Change role at end of 15 minutes; Individual points totaled for team; Team scores posted | Teachers explain, model, role-play tutoring procedures, and give students feedback on their performances in the role-playing episodes | Bonus points for following presentation format; Individual scores; Team scores |
| Peabody Peer-Assisted Learning Strategies | Reading | Heterogeneous matching by ability highs to lows; Reciprocal roles; Changed after four weeks | Reading texts | Three 35-minute periods each week for 15 weeks | For reading, 10 minutes is spent in teaching each strategy; Best reader reads first or employs the strategy first for 5 minutes, then roles are reversed; Tutor asks specific questions for each strategy; Correction procedures are specified for each strategy; Individual points totaled for team; Team scores posted | Teachers teach students key procedures of the tutoring process and the strategies; Each strategy is taught separately through modeling and practice | Bonus points for following procedures correctly and for exhibiting cooperative behaviors; Individual scores; Team scores |

weeks, with about 15 to 20 minutes for the actual student contact time (the rest of the time is spent organizing materials). The site should be a place where the tutors and tutees can work together undisturbed. If you use any of the reciprocal peer procedures, tutoring is scheduled as part of the class routine, so there is no problem with site selection; students may just be instructed to move their desks together. Two unsatisfactory areas for peer tutoring are outside the school building and in the hallways, where distractions tend to be excessive.

### Planning the Presentation Format

You may decide on the presentation format or you may ask for student input. You may wish to select or adapt any of the well-researched models that we discussed previously (e.g., CWPT, PALS), where students assume reciprocal roles, or you may adapt those models with only one student acting as the tutor. Remember, you should identify how the tutor retrieves and returns materials, presents the information, gives feedback, and monitors the progress of the tutee. You may even wish to script the procedures. In a case study of a student with behavior disorders, Fulk and King (2001) scripted the correction procedure for the tutor to help the child with behavior disorders accept correction without argument. This is an excellent idea as many students often have trouble with correction, especially accepting negative feedback (Prater et al., 1999).

Yasutake, Bryan, and Dohrn (1996) report that attribution statements such as "You're getting smart because of your hard work" for correct responses and strategy statements such as "Try to sound out the word" for incorrect responses were of benefit to students with mild disabilities and those at risk for special education referral. Both tutors and tutees in third through eighth grade perceived themselves more positively in academic and affective performance than those students who did not receive the same type of feedback.

### Training Tutors

Once you have decided on the presentation format, you must train your tutors to follow the format and to display appropriate teaching behaviors (Warger, 1990). These behaviors include waiting for the response instead of immediately telling the answer, avoiding sarcasm and criticism, and proceeding in a positive, friendly manner.

You should plan an orientation session in which you share the purpose, responsibilities, general guidelines, and expected outcomes of the tutoring session (Lazerson, Foster, Brow, & Hummel, 1988). This is also a good time to teach the tutors how to set up and put away the tutoring materials (Schuler, Ogulthorpe, & Eiserman, 1987).

Following the orientation session, you should model the presentation format including correction procedures, guide the students in their imitation of the model, and point out the important behaviors. In a co-teaching situation, modeling is frequently presented with one teacher acting as the tutor and the other as the tutee. Role-playing positive interactions and negative interactions and having students discriminate between the two are essential.

### Monitoring Progress

You should collect academic and social data to document the progress of both tutors and tutees. This data may be particularly helpful to answer any parent concerns about the tutoring process (Durrer & McLaughlin, 1995). It is helpful to have the tutors chart the progress of the tutee. For example, the tutor may count and chart the number of words the student reads correctly each day or the number of addition facts the tutee answers correctly. Be sure to monitor and praise tutors for following the procedures.

### Evaluating the Tutoring Session

Both tutors and tutees should evaluate the tutoring session. After each session, you should give tutees forms to mark whether they learned anything and how the session went. See Figure 8.3 for a sample elementary evaluation form.

**Figure 8.3** Elementary
Evaluation Form

Tutee Form

Date: _____

Name: _____

| | 😊 | 😐 | ☹️ |
|---|---|---|---|
| I liked working with my tutor. | | | |
| I liked the materials. | | | |
| I liked what we did. | | | |
| I learned something. | | | |
| I want to be tutored next week. | | | |
| My tutor let me think of the answer by myself. | | | |

Maher (1984) suggests support conferences for tutors to discuss group concerns and meetings with the teacher individually if necessary. Gartner and Riessman (1993) suggest an assigned time for both tutors and tutees to meet and reflect on their tutoring experiences. In Figure 8.4, we present feedback forms for tutors to complete.

### Informing Significant Others

You should be certain to notify parents of peer-tutoring programs. Parents need to understand when their children come home and talk about working with other students. Tell them why, when, and how tutoring will be used. It is important to indicate that you are still responsible for teaching the children and to document that their children are continuing to learn.

 **ACTIVITY 8.5**

With a partner, design a peer-tutoring system for elementary, middle school, or secondary students with mild disabilities. Identify the objective, plan the presentation format, and describe how you are going to notify and inform parents.

 **IMPORTANT POINTS**

1. Peer tutoring may consist of one student acting as a tutor, or the person who transmits the information, and one student acting as the tutee, or the person who receives the information, or students may assume reciprocal roles.

**Figure 8.4** Tutor Feedback Form

Tutor Form

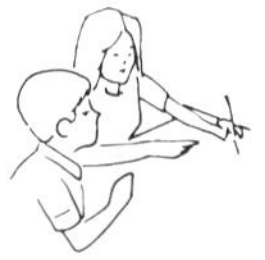

Date: ____________________

Name: ____________________

My tutee learned: ____________________

He/She made ___ many ___ some ___ few mistakes

| | Yes | No |
|---|---|---|
| He/She seemed to like the sessions. | ___ | ___ |
| I enjoyed the sessions. | ___ | ___ |
| I used praise. | ___ | ___ |
| I paused after I asked a question. | ___ | ___ |

Next week I plan to: ____________________

2. Reciprocal Peer Tutoring (Fantuzzo et al., 1992), Reciprocal Peer Revision Strategy (MacArthur et al., 1991), ClassWide Peer Tutoring (CWPT; Delquadri et al.,1983), and Peabody Peer-Assisted Learning Strategies (PALS; Mathes et al., 1994) are peer-tutoring models supported in the literature for their effectiveness for students with mild disabilities and students at risk (Utley et al., 1997).
3. Reciprocal Peer Tutoring involves students paired randomly in same-age dyads and self-selection of rewards and performance goals.
4. In the Reciprocal Peer Revision Strategy, strategy instruction and peer interaction are combined to teach written revision skills.
5. The core components of ClassWide Peer Tutoring include (a) direct teacher presentation of new material to be learned, (b) teacher monitoring of the tutoring process, (c) whole-class instructional activity, (d) explicit presentation formats for peers to follow, (e) active student responding, (f) reciprocal roles in each session, (g) teams competing for the highest team point total, (h) contingent point earning, (i) systematic error correction strategies, (j) public posting of student performance, and, (k) social awards for the winning team (Greenwood & Delquadri, 1995; Greenwood, 1996).
6. The Peabody Peer-Assisted Learning Strategies involve the teaching of both academic skills and strategies in reading, math, story mapping, and writing.
7. The steps for implementing peer-tutoring procedures consist of (a) selecting objectives, (b) selecting and matching students, (c) preparing materials, (d) determining schedules and selecting sites, (e) planning the presentation format, (f) training tutors, (g) monitoring progress, (h) evaluating the tutoring session, and (i) informing significant others.

8. Tutors must be taught to follow a lesson presentation format, wait for a response, and avoid sarcasm and criticism.

9. Peer tutoring is effective for low-achieving, limited-English-speaking, learning disabled, behaviorally disordered, and other at-risk populations in both academic and affective areas and at all age/grade levels (Kalkowski, 2001).

## COOPERATIVE LEARNING

Like peer tutoring, cooperative learning relies on peers working together to solve problems or share information. But cooperative learning groups consist of teams of three or four students working together to master academic tasks or content to meet individual and group goals, rather than just two students as in peer tutoring. The students are usually of varying ability levels, races, and ethnic groups. Slavin and his colleagues and Johnson and Johnson have studied cooperative learning extensively.

The effectiveness of cooperative learning with students with disabilities is equivocal in the research literature (Tateyama-Sniezek, 1990). The difference in the research findings may be due to the nature of the student population, to the task requirement, or to the instructional practice. Brandt and Ellsworth (1996) found cooperative learning effective in increasing academic performance and attendance and in decreasing discipline problems of adolescents with learning disabilities from diverse cultures. However, O'Connor and Jenkins (1996) judged that cooperative practices were only effective for 40% to 44% of third- through sixth-grade students with learning disabilities. They found that students with learning disabilities required more help and contributed less to the group activities than those students without disabilities.

Students with behavior disorders, those with visual disabilities, and those with mental disabilities participate less in the group process (Cohen,

1994; Pomplun, 1996). When students with behavior disorders and students with mental disabilities were members of the cooperative group, the group listened less to each other during a fifth-grade state science assessment (Pomplun, 1997).

Cohen (1994) suggests that participation may be related to the task, with more participation of students with disabilities in open-ended, nonroutine tasks that do not have one correct answer such as projects or experiments. Open-ended, nonroutine tasks may promote more participation, in part, because students may participate in many ways such as "asking questions, making suggestions, listening, agreeing, criticizing, and explaining" (Pomplun, 1997, p. 50). Different instructional practices may also result in the equivocal research findings. The instructional processes of individual accountability and group rewards are required for positive effects (Stevens & Slavin, 1991). Teacher behaviors that promote effective cooperative learning procedures include (Johnson & Johnson, 1996; O'Connor & Jenkins, 1996; Slavin, 1984, 1985, 1988a, 1988b):

1. Public identification of students who demonstrate cooperative behaviors
2. Validation of low-status students' contributions to the group process
3. Insistence that all students participate
4. Direct instruction of cooperative behaviors and strategies
5. Repeated review and reinforcement of group cooperation
6. Monitoring of cooperative behaviors
7. Explicit explanation of expectations for group process and individual products

Two common special education practices that seem to defeat the effectiveness of cooperative learning are differential assignments and teacher assistance. O'Connor and Jenkins (1996) found that students with disabilities participated more in cooperative learning groups when their assignments matched those of their peers and that teachers who provided more assistance to students with disabilities or joined the cooperative learning group interfered with peers working together.

## Rationale

Cooperative learning is proposed as a way to ensure successful inclusion of students with special needs (Johnson & Johnson, 1996; Slavin, 1988a) based on the premise that students who work together tend to come to like each other (Johnson & Johnson, 1980). A long tradition of research in social psychology "has shown that people working for a cooperative goal come to encourage one another to do their best, to help one another do well, and to like and respect one another" (Slavin, 1988b, p. 8). Cooperative learning also provides more opportunities for students of all abilities to participate and engage in class activities. As discussed in Chapter 4, time on task is positively related to achievement (Greenwood, 1999).

Cooperative learning also relies on peer pressure, a powerful reinforcer for adolescents in particular (Alberto & Troutman, 1999). Urging other students to complete a task for the good of the group frequently motivates reluctant adolescents. Similar to peer tutoring, cooperative learning, when effective, is an economical and teacher-friendly way to accommodate the wide range of cultural, linguistic, and academic diversity found in the current inclusive classroom.

## Description

Our discussion centers around models of cooperative learning that have been shown to be effective with students with mild disabilities and appear in the special education literature. They were selected because they have been used or we feel could easily be implemented in inclusive classrooms and are detailed enough that they may be implemented. They include ClassWide Student Tutoring Teams (Harper, Mallette, Maheady, & Brennan, 1993), Cooperative

Homework Teams (O'Melia and Rosenberg, 1994), and Collaborative Strategic Reading (Klinger & Vaughn, 1996). We also include the Jigsaw Approach (Aronson, 1978) and Learning Together (Johnson & Johnson, 1991) because we have used these strategies in our own classrooms and have observed their effectiveness in special education classrooms. Many of these models are based on the work of Slavin and Johnson and Johnson. The discussion of cooperative learning models is not meant to be exhaustive.

### ClassWide Student Tutoring Teams

A combination of Slavin's competitive teams programs and the CWPT model, the ClassWide Student Tutoring Teams (CSTT) requires team members to play a game (Harper et al., 1993; Maheady, et al., 2001; Utley et al., 1997). For example, in a math class, the teacher assigns one student with high math ability, one student with low math ability, and two students with average math ability to each table (Harper et al., 1993). At each table is a folder with the task (e.g., study guide, math problems, etc.), answer sheet, paper and pencils, and deck of cards. The cards contain numbers on them that correspond to the items. Students take turns at being the teacher. The first peer teacher draws a card and reads the corresponding question from the study guide. Each student then writes an answer. The peer teacher checks each answer against the answer sheet and awards five points. If an answer is not correct, the peer teacher gives the correct answer, shares strategies, and awards two points to the students after they successfully write the answer two times. The teaching responsibility is then moved to the next student and the procedures are repeated. The classroom teacher gives bonus points to teams who follow the steps and who demonstrate appropriate interactions. After 20 or 30 minutes, the teacher tallies individual points and converts them into team points, which are displayed on laminated scoreboards within the classroom.

The most improved team is recognized, the teams that reached the preset criterion are recognized, and the most outstanding team members are recognized (Utley et al., 1997). The three- to four-member team composition is usually changed every 4 to 6 weeks.

### Cooperative Homework Teams

Based on the guidelines of Slavin's Team-Accelerated Instruction, O'Melia and Rosenberg (1994) designed a Cooperative Homework Teams (CHT) model for secondary students with learning disabilities. The model uses peer teams to grade and make corrections on individual homework assignments. At the end of each math period, the teacher assigns the students eight computation and two story problems. The next day, after opening activities, the CHT groups meet for 10 minutes. Each day, a different student assumes the role of the checker. The checker in each group checks the other students' homework assignments using teacher-made answer sheets, then reports the grades to the teacher and returns the papers to the team members for review and corrections. Students help each other correct the errors before they return the papers to the teacher.

The teacher awards daily points based on the completion of the assignment and the percentage of correct answers. The teacher then converts the mean individual scores to mean team scores and presents certificates to those teams who exceed a certain criterion set by the teacher. With CHT in effect, seventh- and eighth-grade students with mild disabilities completed more homework assignments and increased their accuracy scores (O'Melia & Rosenberg, 1994).

### Collaborative Strategic Reading

Collaborative Strategic Reading (CSR) combines components of reciprocal teaching (see Chapter 6) and cooperative learning structures. CSR can be used effectively with different reading programs (literature-based, basal, and balanced), different texts (expository and narrative), and various student populations (students with learning disabilities, students without disabilities, bilingual students, and students at risk for reading difficulties) in inclusive settings (Klinger & Vaughn, 1996; Vaughn, Klinger, & Bryant, 2001).

Using think-alouds, teacher and student modeling, practice, and feedback, teachers directly teach students the four strategies of preview, click and clunk, get the gist, and wrap-up in a whole-class setting before students are assigned to groups. In the preview strategy, students examine headings, bold words, pictures, and so on to make predictions before reading and to activate a "group" background knowledge. If background knowledge concerning a particular topic is limited, Vaughn and colleagues (2001) suggest that the teacher continue to employ the preview strategy with the class as a whole, instead of assigning students to small groups. Click and clunk involve a self-monitoring strategy that students employ as they are reading. The reader "clicks" along with no difficulty in understanding the content and vocabulary, but "clunks" when comprehension breaks down. Students in the group employ fix-up strategies when clunking occurs. Cue cards are given to the students to help them remember some fix-up strategies. Some groups may need teacher assistance at this point. The strategy of get the gist requires students to rephrase the main idea in 10 or fewer words after every two paragraphs. At the end of the selection, the students ask and answer questions to summarize the most significant ideas about the entire passage using the wrap-up strategy. See Figure 8.5 for a more detailed discussion of these strategies.

Once students are taught these strategies and the cooperative procedure, four or five students are randomly assigned to heterogeneous groups. To ensure the participation of all students, the specific roles of leader, clunk expert, announcer, encourager, reporter, and time keeper are

**Figure 8.5**  The Four Strategies of CSR

Before Reading
   Examine headings, bold words, pictures, and so on
1. Preview (2–3 minutes)
   a. Brainstorm: What do we already know about the topic?
   b. Predict: What do we expect to learn?

During Reading
   Self-monitor understanding after two paragraphs and then at the end
2. Click and Clunk
   a. Keep reading if we understand the content (click).
   b. Were there any words or concepts that were hard to understand (clunks)?
   c. Use fix-up strategies to fix the clunks:
       (1) Reread the sentence and look for key ideas to help you understand the word.
       (2) Reread the sentence with the clunk and the sentences before or after the clunk
           looking for cues.
       (3) Look for a prefix or suffix in the word.
       (4) Break the word apart and look for smaller words.
3. Get the Gist (answer in 10 words or less)
   a. What is the most important person, place, or thing?
   b. What is the most important idea about the person, place, or thing?

After Reading
4. Wrap-Up
   a. Ask questions and answer them:
           Why do you think that?
           How were _____ and _____ the same? How were they different?
           What do you think would happen if _____?
           What do you think caused _____ to happen?
           What might have prevented the problem of _____ from happening?
           What are the strengths and weaknesses of _____?
           What are some other solutions for the problem of _____?
   b. Review
           Write answer to question, What did we learn in Learning Log, and share entry
           with class.
   c. Ask questions that begin with what, when, where, why, and how.

Note. Adapted from Figure 1 by Klinger, J. K., & Vaughn, S. (1998). Using collaborative strategic
reading. *TEACHING Exceptional Children, 30*(6), 32–37. Reprinted by permission.

assigned (Klinger & Vaughn, 1998). The leader tells the group what to read next and what strategy to apply. The leader asks the teacher for assistance if needed. The clunk expert uses the cue cards to remind students of the fix-up strategy when a word or concept is not understood. The announcer makes certain all students participate and listen to each other. She or he calls on different students to read or share ideas. The encourager gives feedback, praises behavior, encourages students to help each other, evaluates how well the group cooperated, and gives suggestions for improved cooperation. The reporter reports the main ideas of the group to the rest of the class and shares a question the group has generated. The time keeper sets the timer for each portion of CSR and makes certain the group moves on to the next activity. Teachers may take over the role of the leader and time keeper to speed up the procedures (Klinger & Vaughn, 1998; Vaughn et al., 2001).

Roles are assigned for a day or longer and cue sheets are provided to prompt students to remember their responsibilities. For example, the cue sheet reminds the encourager to tell two things that went well with the group and then asks, "Is there anything that would help us do even better next time?" (Klinger & Vaughn, 1998, p. 36) Teachers monitor the group interactions and provide assistance when needed.

Learning logs monitor student progress and suggest follow-up activities. Students are directed to write down the most important ideas that they learned from the day's reading assignment. They then take turns sharing their entries with the rest of the class. Materials that have one main idea in a paragraph, provide cues for prediction, and help students connect information are conducive to strategy application. Klinger and Vaughn (1998) recommend that teachers select brief, nonfiction articles such as those found in *Weekly Reader* or *Junior Scholastic* when first instituting CSR procedures.

 **ACTIVITY 8.6**

With a partner, compare ClassWide Student Tutoring Teams, Cooperative Homework Teams, and Collaborative Strategic Reading on the following components: teacher's role, student's role, correction procedures, individual accountability, and group rewards.

### The Jigsaw Approach

In the jigsaw format (Aronson, 1978), each member of the jigsaw group becomes an expert in some aspect of the task or material and teaches the others what he or she knows. For example, in preparing a report or answering a worksheet about the life of Martin Luther King, Jr., each student in the group may select to study one aspect of Reverend King's life. Once each student has mastered the specific content, he or she shares the information with the rest of the group. Then the group as a whole combines the individual information for the final project, whether it is a report or a worksheet about King's life.

The idiom of jigsaw is appropriate for this technique, for each student has a puzzle piece (e.g., Hector has information concerning Reverend King's childhood and Lashonda has information concerning King's educational background) that must be joined together with the puzzle pieces of the other students before it is possible to complete the entire puzzle (a report on the life of Martin Luther King, Jr.). But student absenteeism can be a problem in the jigsaw approach. If Hector is absent, he cannot contribute the information concerning Reverend King's childhood. Slavin (1988b) suggests assigning two students from each group to the same subtopic (Hector and Kendra would both be assigned to gather information concerning Reverend King's childhood) or selecting an activity that may be completed during one class period if absenteeism is a problem.

A variation of the jigsaw technique is a "counterpart" group (Aronson, 1978). In this adaptation, all students working on a particular subtopic meet together. After sharing information on this subtopic, they rejoin their original group members and complete the report.

### Learning Together

In Learning Together (Johnson & Johnson, 1991), students pool their knowledge and skills to create a project or complete an assignment often in the areas of social studies and science. These groups are informally structured and usually are organized for a specific task. Noddings (1989) recommends complex tasks such as projects and experiments to increase student participation. For example, Pomplun (1997) describes one such project where fifth-grade students with and without disabilities participated in the Kansas Science Assessment and were assigned a collaborative activity of completing a study. Groups of three, four, or five students were required to develop a hypothesis, study their hypothesis, and reach a conclusion concerning results. For example, with the topic of water waste, each group had to develop a hypothesis as to one cause of water waste, study the cause, and develop one solution.

## Implementation

You should follow certain steps when implementing cooperative learning procedures, especially if you are planning to use the less-specific procedures of Jigsaw and Learning Together. Planning is essential for cooperative groups to succeed.

### Specifying Objectives

Specify both academic and collaborative objectives. You may emphasize collaborative objectives (such as all students need to know how to do the work and students need to help each other learn). Slavin (1988a) insists that the group objective must be important to the group members and suggests that awarding certificates, free time, or bonus points for appropriate group participation may motivate each group member to cooperate.

### Assigning Students to Groups

It is recommended that you assign students of various ethnic backgrounds and ability levels to each group (Johnson & Johnson, 1986; Slavin, 1988a). In an inclusive class, make certain that students with special needs are evenly distributed among the different groups. O'Connor and Jenkins (1996) emphasize that this step is extremely important, as students with disabilities need peers who are both willing and compassionate. Much of the research that shows positive effects for stu-

dents with special needs has combined two students who are performing the skill or task at a low level and two who are performing the skill at a higher level in each group (Slavin, 1984; Slavin, Stevens, & Madden, 1988). The recommended size of a group is three to five members (Johnson & Johnson, 1986). To ensure the cohesiveness of the team, Slavin (1988b) stresses that you should make clear to the students that "putdowns, making fun of teammates, or refusing to help them are ineffective ways for teams to be successful and not acceptable kinds of behavior" (p. 52).

### Deciding Team Schedules

As with anything new, you should first try the cooperative learning approach with one class or in one area. Students may stay on one team from 4 to 10 weeks. However, if teams do not work out, reassign the students after 3 or 4 weeks (Slavin, 1988b). The idea is to give every student an opportunity to work with all students in the classroom.

### Arranging the Room and Materials

Group members should be close together and groups should be far apart (Schniedewind & Salend, 1987). Johnson and Johnson (1986) recommend a circle arrangement to accommodate student communication. Such an arrangement allows students to share and discuss materials and to maintain eye contact. The physical arrangement must allow clear access for the teacher. Each group also needs an area to store materials or the group project. One teacher bought square laundry baskets that each group decorated and used for the storage of their materials. The decorations were removable to accommodate the frequent changes in group membership.

### Guaranteeing Individual Accountability and Participation

Teachers must make certain that each member is participating in the group and that the project or activity is not being completed by only one or two students. Individual point assignments in CSTT, specific role assignments in

CSR, and individual grades and homework assignments in CHT insure individual accountability and participation.

Johnson and Johnson (1986) recommend assigning the roles of checker, accuracy coach, summarizer, elaboration seeker, and reporter, so that each group member has a specific responsibility. The checker makes certain that all students can understand the information. The accuracy coach corrects any mistakes in another member's explanation or summary. The summarizer restates major conclusions or answers of the group. The elaboration seeker asks members to relate material they previously learned. The reporter writes down the information or completes the worksheet. Remember, Klinger and Vaughn (1998) incorporate a cue sheet in the CSR procedures to prompt students to remember the responsibilities of their assigned roles. Assigning a specific role to students is particularly important for cooperative learning activities in an inclusive setting as, often, students with disabilities are left out if no particular role is assigned to them.

Another way to ensure individual accountability and participation is to select only one student's product to represent the group effort (Johnson & Johnson, 1986). Of course, this selection is kept secret until the end of the project. Salend and Allen (1985) ensure participation of all students by limiting the number of times each student may talk. Before the group activity, each member is given a certain number of tokens. Each time a student addresses the group, he or she must surrender a token. Once all of the tokens are used, the student may no longer address the group. A final technique for ensuring group participation is to limit the amount of material given to the group (Slavin, 1988a). If only one worksheet is given to the group, then four members cannot complete the worksheet individually.

### Teaching and Role-Playing Cooperative Behaviors

Just placing students with disabilities in cooperative groups is not effective unless they are directly taught the strategies and cooperative skills. In the CSR model, Vaughn and colleagues (2001) note that much explicit teaching with modeling and practice is needed before students are assigned to groups. As discussed at the beginning of the chapter, many students with disabilities must also be taught social skills before they can effectively participate in cooperative groups.

For students with mild disabilities, role-playing such cooperative behaviors as "use a quiet voice," "stay with your group," and "say one nice thing to everyone in your group" (Putnam, Rynders, Johnson, & Johnson, 1989) is necessary, because many of these students have an inability to relate to others in socially appropriate ways. Research shows that students with disabilities can be taught the social skills for successful group participation (Prater et al., 1999; Wolford et al., 2001). You should model cooperative behavior first. Then have students role-play appropriate and inappropriate ways to show cooperation and evaluate whether the demonstrated behavior is an example of cooperative or uncooperative behavior. Continue to review appropriate cooperative behaviors whenever you plan to form cooperative groups.

You may also use games to teach cooperative behaviors. Cooperative games require players to cooperate in order to overcome some obstacle. For example, Cartledge and Cochran (1993) created a circular game board with the goal that everyone must complete the entire circle before time ran out. Thus, students helped each other complete the game as they raced against time. Students were reinforced for their cooperative interactions instead of win-lose behaviors. Sapon-Shevin (1986) described a nonelimination musical chairs game. The object was to keep everyone in the game as the chairs were eliminated. The children had to find ways to make room for more and more children. The verbal behavior during the game was of a cooperative nature: "Come sit on/with me," or "Make room for Johnny" (p. 284).

For older students, a checklist of cooperative behaviors for students to self-monitor is often useful. Examples may include (a) I listened to others' opinions, (b) I complimented a person's idea in the group, (c) I spoke in a pleasant voice, (d) I didn't get angry if my ideas weren't used, and (e) I made constructive comments when I thought another student's idea was outrageous or not appropriate.

### Monitoring Cooperative Behaviors

Once you have taught the concept or given directions for the required activity or project and modeled cooperative behavior, your role becomes that of a monitor. You monitor each member's cooperative behavior, keep the group on task, and intervene when necessary to provide task assistance. For young students, praise the sharing or helping behaviors publicly (Putnam et al., 1989) with such comments as "Sunny shared her article with Juan. She was being very cooperative." Your comments should also include validation statements, such as "Matt has the correct idea. He is on target," directed to students with disabilities who are often perceived as incompetent by peers.

One teacher instituted a system for students to self-monitor everyone's participation in the cooperative learning group. On a grid of names of team members and question numbers, one student placed a yellow Post-it note next to a student's name when he or she participated. Strategy cards with a list of questions can remind students to monitor participation and understanding: Am I listening to group members? Do I understand the directions and goal? If not, ask others in the group; if not, ask teacher? Am I helping group members? (Goor, Schwenn, Elridge, Mallein, & Stauffer, 1996). Students using the cards made more on-task comments and were better able to explain the main idea of the group discussion.

### Evaluating Both the Product and the Process

You should evaluate both the product and the process of the group. In the jigsaw or group project approaches, you may elect to grade the group project or the individual student's project selected to represent the group work. Some teachers, when they know what individual members have contributed, grade the students' individual contributions in addition to assigning a group grade. Another strategy is to average the group grade with the individual student's grade. For example, if Joe scored 10 points on his individual project and his group scored 20 points, his final score would be 15.

According to Slavin (1988a), the group grade should be based on an average of the performances of all of the students. Johnson and Johnson (1986) suggest using different criteria to evaluate the project of a student with special needs, giving bonus points to the groups that have members with special needs. Some teachers also give grades for the group process. Remember, Slavin (1988b) recommends giving points to the students for appropriate participation. Even if you don't grade the process, you and the students should evaluate how the group functioned. See Table 8.4 for a sample evaluation form. In fact, you may want to have students role-play problem areas and possible solutions for evaluation of the process.

### Recognizing the Group Effort

Certificates and scoreboards are used to recognize group effort in CHT and CSTT, respectively. In Table 8.5, we present a checklist of decisions you need to make before you use cooperative learning techniques. Remember, teachers make instructional decisions and monitor their effectiveness.

 **ACTIVITY 8.7**

With three other students, solve the problems Mr. Hernandez encountered when working with cooperative groups. First identify the problem, then describe a solution.

1. Sam is frequently absent during the jigsaw procedure.
2. Rupert monopolizes the group discussion.
3. Only two of the four members of the Tiger Team are completing the projects.

**Table 8.4**   Student Evaluation of Cooperative Session

What was learned in the group today? _____
_____

Describe an example of cooperative behavior (a helpful action).
• You did _____
_____

• Others did _____
_____

Describe an example of uncooperative behavior (not a helpful action).
• You did _____
_____

• Others did _____
_____

Change the uncooperative behaviors to cooperative ones.
_____
_____

The completion of this sheet is worth 10 points toward your grade.

---

**Table 8.5**   Teacher Checklist

1. Specify group objective.
   Academic:
   _____
   Motivated to attain by:
   _____ a. Points
   _____ b. Certificates
   _____ c. Free time
   _____ d. Praise
   _____ e. Homework pass
   _____ f. Other

2. Specify other group objective.
   Collaborative:
   _____
   Motivated to attain by:
   _____ a. Points
   _____ b. Certificates
   _____ c. Free time
   _____ d. Praise
   _____ e. Homework pass
   _____ f. Other

3. Select model
   _____ a. CSTT
   _____ b. CHT
   _____ c. CSR
   _____ d. Jigsaw
   _____ e. Learning Together
   _____ f. Own Creation

4. Assign students.
   _____ a. Even number of girls/boys
   _____ b. Two high-level/two low-level

   _____ c. Special students divided
   _____ d. Students of various cultures/interests divided
   _____ e. Random

5. Decide team schedule.
   Time Frame:
   _____ a. No. of weeks
   _____ b. No. of days

6. Arrange room materials.
   _____ a. Clear access for teacher
   _____ b. Storage for materials

7. Guarantee individual accountability.
   _____ a. Grade individual quizzes or projects
   _____ b. Assign roles
   _____ c. Select one student's project
   _____ d. Tokens
   _____ e. Other

8. Have students evaluate their own cooperative behaviors.
   _____ a. Complete student evaluation form
   _____ b. Answer questions

9. Evaluate the students' work.

   | The product: | The process: |
   |---|---|
   | _____ a. Points | _____ a. Points |
   | _____ b. Grades | _____ b. Grades |
   | _____ c. Other | _____ c. Other |

10. Recognize the group effort.
    _____ a. Bulletin board
    _____ b. Newsletter
    _____ c. Other

**IMPORTANT POINTS**

1. Cooperative learning groups consist of teams of three or four students who work together to master academic tasks or content.
2. The effectiveness of cooperative learning with students with disabilities is equivocal in the research literature (Tateyama-Sniczek, 1990).
3. In ClassWide Student Tutoring Teams (CSTT), students earn points for their teams by answering questions in a gamelike format.
4. In Cooperative Homework Team (CHT), peer teams are used to grade and make corrections on individual homework assignments.
5. Cooperative Strategic Reading (CSR) combines components of reciprocal teaching (see Chapter 6) and cooperative learning structures to teach reading comprehension.
6. In the jigsaw approach, each student has a piece of the puzzle, which must be combined with all the other students' pieces to produce a group report or project.
7. In the learning together format, students pool their knowledge and skills to create a project or complete an assignment, such as a chart on objects that sink or float.

8. To implement cooperative learning, the following steps are recommended: (a) specify objectives, (b) select the model, (c) assign students to groups, (d) decide team schedules, (e) plan room and material arrangements, (f) guarantee individual accountability and participation, (g) role-play cooperative behaviors, (h) monitor cooperative behaviors, (i) evaluate both the product and the process, and (j) recognize the group effort.

 **DISCUSSION QUESTIONS** ◀

1. With the increased emphasis on academic standards, defend the incorporation of social skills objectives in your curriculum.
2. When Lashonda went home and told her mother that she was teaching Susanna how to add during math class, her mother immediately called you to complain. She commented that you are the teacher and her child is not. How would you respond to this criticism of peer tutoring?
3. Describe how you would teach the social skill of handling corrections or negative feedback in a cooperative group structure.

# CHAPTER 9

# STUDY SKILLS INSTRUCTION

School settings present many challenges for students with special needs, particularly in view of the inclusion of students with mild disabilities in general education settings. Students are expected to arrive at school on time with their materials, prepared to listen, participate, and respond. During a typical school day, students in K–12 settings may be asked to acquire new content; demonstrate understanding and mastery of the content through completion of tests, projects, or other assignments; demonstrate good work habits; and perhaps work with several school professionals who may have different expectations and requirements and whose teaching styles may vary. Students with special needs may have problems meeting these expectations because they lack strategies for organizing and remembering information (Day & Elkins, 1994; Wood, 2002), taking tests (Hoover & Rabideau, 1995), and listening (Hoover, 2001). It has been suggested that integrated study skills programs be provided throughout students' schooling and as lifelong skills (Hoover & Patton, 1995) to help students meet these expectations. The purpose of this chapter is to present study skills and strategies that will assist students with special needs to acquire information, organize it, and express it.

## RATIONALE FOR STUDY SKILLS INSTRUCTION

"Study skills are those competencies associated with acquiring, recording, organizing, synthesizing, remembering, and using information and ideas" (Hoover, 2001, p. 423). They typically include listening, note taking, outlining, textbook usage, test taking, reference skills, and others that are needed for success in academic (e.g., science class) and nonacademic (e.g., the workplace) settings (Platt & Olson, 1997). In other words, study skills assist students to acquire, retain, and express knowledge (Mercer & Mercer, 2001). Utilization of study skills may lead students with special needs to exhibit more active learning styles and to demonstrate proactive approaches to academic tasks. Incorporation of study skills instruction into the curriculum may help students attribute their learning successes to the systematic selection and application of study strategies instead of luck or the assistance of others. Study skills represent the key to independent learning by helping students acquire and use information effectively (Bos & Vaughn, 2002).

Because evidence suggests the need for study skills in elementary and secondary settings for students with special needs (Hoover, 1997), we recommend the introduction of study skills instruction at the elementary level followed by continuous instruction and monitoring throughout middle and high school. Systematic instruction in study skills can show students the relationship between their approach to a learning task and the result of that approach (e.g., using a mnemonic device to memorize a list of words may facilitate memorization of that list better than simply repeating the words in the list). The application of study skills and strategies may, therefore, increase the independent functioning of learners.

## COMPONENTS OF STUDY SKILLS INSTRUCTION

For study skills instruction to be effective, teachers must be aware of the components that contribute to its success. The following five criteria derived from Paris (1988) should be included in study skills instruction. These criteria are similar to the critical features of strategy instruction that we presented in Chapter 6. Notice how the teacher's role may incorporate elements of both the reductionist and constructivist paradigms, which we introduced in Chapter 1. For example, it is recommended that study skills instruction be direct, informed, and explanatory with the teacher providing instruction in small, sequential steps (i.e., reductionist). However, notice also, that the teacher may engage students in dialogue following the modeling of various study skills, thus allowing students to draw their own conclusions about the usefulness of study skills (i.e., constructivist). The teacher can also seek elaboration of students' initial responses (Brooks & Brooks, 2001) in regard to what strategies they already employ and what strategies might be helpful for them to try (i.e., constructivist). The five criteria for inclusion in study skills instruction include:

1. *Study skills should be functional and meaningful.* Identify your students' needs and determine the study skills that would be most effective in meeting those needs. For example, if Jesse is required to memorize lists of terms for his fourth-grade health class, you may want to teach him a mnemonic strategy to help him memorize material and prepare for tests. Suppose Jesse has to memorize the parts of the digestive system. He may make a list with all the parts and then look at the first letter of each of the words. Perhaps they spell a word, or maybe he can make a sentence out of them.

2. *Students should believe that study skills are useful and necessary.* Your students must be convinced that study skills are important, necessary for success, worth using, and effective in solving problems; therefore, it is helpful to demonstrate to your students that their current methods may not be effective and to explain the rationale for each specific strategy (Alley & Deshler, 1979). For example, Mr. Waldo asked his students to take

notes on one of his math lessons. When he evaluated their notes with them, he pointed out any shortcomings or ineffective practices that he noted. He elicited from the students the rationale for taking effective notes and had them suggest situations in which they might need to use this skill. One student mentioned she could use it in her social studies class, and another said that it would help him as a reporter for the school newspaper. Then Mr. Waldo presented some effective note-taking techniques to the class. By first demonstrating how note-taking techniques are useful and necessary, he was able to motivate and interest the students in note taking.

3. *Instruction should be direct, informed, and explanatory.* According to Rosenshine (1983), instruction should include (a) presenting material in small steps, (b) focusing on one aspect at a time, (c) organizing the material sequentially for mastery, (d) modeling the skill, (e) presenting many examples, (f) providing detailed explanations for difficult points, and (g) monitoring student progress. For example, in their instruction of report writing, Ms. Tartaglia and Ms. Dearden took their co-taught fifth-grade class to the media center and modeled the steps that they wanted the students to follow as they used reference materials. They provided several different topics and modeled the steps sequentially for each one. They spent time teaching the students how to use the automated card catalog or similar computer system before they assigned them topics to look up. Then, as the students worked through the steps they had modeled, the two teachers carefully monitored their progress. Remember to provide opportunities for the practice of study skills and monitor student use of study skills (Hoover & Patton, 1995).

4. *Instruction should demonstrate what study skills can be used, how they can be applied, and when and why they are helpful.* For example, Mr. Johansen, working with his high school students on test taking, taught the students study skills to apply when taking tests. Next, he elicited from the students when and why the study skills would be helpful (content classes, job seeking, and taking the driver's test, or the test for the military). Finally, he showed the students how to apply the study skills to each of the situations they had identified.

5. *Instructional materials must be lucid and enjoyable.* The materials you use as part of study skills instruction must be motivating, meaningful, relevant, and easy to understand. For example, working with a group of fifth graders in a general education classroom, Ms. Barnhart incorporated information about the students into a lesson that showed them how to use the graphic aids in textbooks. She taught her fifth-grade students to read graphs by graphing several topics of their own choosing—the students' birthdays, their favorite movies and television shows, and their interests and hobbies. These activities were instrumental in holding student interest and attention.

Because we believe the preceding components of effective study skills instruction should be included in the teaching of all of the study skills presented in this chapter, we do not mention them each time a new study skill is introduced. However, we urge you to incorporate them into your instruction. We hope that you will look back frequently at this section of the chapter as you reflect on how you will teach study skills to students.

## ACQUISITION OF INFORMATION

As mentioned in Chapter 1, students with special needs often have difficulty with reading, mathematics, oral and written language, attending, and organizing. Therefore, they must be taught techniques to help them acquire the skills and content expected of them. In this section, we present strategies for listening, taking notes, and comprehending.

### Listening

Students spend approximately two thirds of their time in school in listening-related activities (Gearheart, Weishahn, & Gearheart, 1995). In fact, listening skills are needed to complete most academic tasks or requirements (Hoover & Patton, 1995). Students with special needs should be made aware of the fact that listening is more than hearing words, and it may require practice and training (Carlisle & Felbinger, 1991; Masters & Mori, 1993). Listening can be improved through systematic teaching and practice (Devine, 1987). The following suggestions are provided for students who have difficulty listening effectively, have developed poor listening habits, do not attend to relevant stimuli, or are inattentive.

1. Make sure students are seated where they can listen, attend, and concentrate.

2. Use verbal and nonverbal cues at the beginning of and throughout a lesson to get attention (e.g., standing at the front of class, making eye contact, using a phrase that signals you are ready to begin).

3. Alert your students before they listen to a class presentation that there will be at least one factual error in the presentation. Ask the students to write down the error(s) after the information has been presented (Wallace & Kauffman, 1986). For example, during a presentation on the size, population, major cities, and important industries of New Jersey, Mr. Feldman erroneously identified the capital as Newark. We recommend telling the students what the error is if they cannot identify it themselves.

4. Prior to a lecture or presentation, list the five most important points of the talk on the chalkboard, an overhead projector, or a handout. Then ask your students to listen for those five points and arrange them in the correct sequence before the conclusion of the presentation (Devine, 1981).

5. Periodically, stop your presentation and ask students to construct summary statements (e.g., "The subject of a sentence tells whom or what the sentence is about;" "Stacy constantly struggled with her own feelings because she was torn between her Chinese and American cultures").

6. Show a videotape containing subject matter that is interesting and age appropriate. Ask the students to listen for specific information, such as the speaker's intent; definitions of certain words and how context affects them; factual information; the general theme; or the multiple perspectives that were generated by the subject matter. You may stop the videotape at any time to ask questions about the content or ask for predictions of what will happen next. For example, Mr. Johnson showed a series of videotapes to his students about the lives of four African Americans who made great contributions to our country: (a) Paul Lawrence Dunbar, (b) Booker T. Washington, (c) Dr. Martin Luther King, Jr., and (d) Dr. George Washington Carver. He periodically stopped the videotape to ask open-ended questions and to give his students a specific fact to listen for.

7. Ask your students to listen to television or radio advertisements and explain how the advertisers are trying to influence listeners to buy their products. For example, some advertisers ask celebrities to advertise and endorse their products, others use catchy tunes, and some tell about the money you will save. This listening activity may be done in the classroom or as a homework assignment (Lerner, 1985).

Listening is essential for students both in their schoolwork and in their overall development and transition to independent living (Hoover & Patton, 1995). Students need to learn how to listen effectively and practice the skill of listening just as they practice other skills. It is never too late to learn how to listen.

 **ACTIVITY 9.1**

During your next class lecture, note all of the verbal and non-verbal cues that the instructor utilizes. Compare these to what other class members identify.

(Answers for this and other activities are found in the Instructor's Manual.)

# Note Taking

The inclusion of students with learning problems in general education classrooms where they must meet the demands of that environment, combined with the fact that college is a viable option for many students with learning disabilities, has increased the need for learning how to take notes during class presentations (Czarnecki, Rosko, & Fine, 1998; Deshler, Ellis, & Lenz, 1996). In general education settings, high school teachers spend at least half of their class time presenting content through lectures (Putnam, Deshler, & Schumaker, 1993). Although many students without disabilities develop note-taking skills on their own (Beirne-Smith, 1989), many students with learning disabilities may not develop note-taking skills or may evidence deficient note-taking skills (Suritsky & Hughes, 1996). "Many students in inclusive settings have difficulty taking notes because of their inability to organize ideas or concepts, distinguish main points, or transfer information from written or oral formats" (Wood, 2002, p. 435). Therefore, many of them do not take notes in class. You may need to convince your students of the importance of taking notes. One effective way is to make them aware of what they currently do during a lecture or class presentation. For example, Ms. Malone presented information on the recycling of products as a way to protect the environment. She asked her students to take notes during her presentation, using the activity as a pretest to show the students that improvement might be needed. After instruction in note-taking techniques, she used the activity as a posttest to show the students their improvement in note taking.

Pauk (1989) found that non–note takers forget 80% of a lecture within 2 weeks. Therefore, it is important for you to teach note taking directly and to reinforce its use. Many strategies are available to improve note taking, although "no evidence indicates that any one technique is consistently superior to another" (Devine, 1981, p. 173). You may want to show your students a variety of ways to take notes so that they can find the ways that are effective for them.

## Guided Notes

In Chapter 4, we introduced the topic of guided notes as an effective adaptation to ensure that students with disabilities are engaged throughout a lecture. For students who have difficulty taking notes, it is helpful to begin with guided notes, because students do not have to generate all of the notes themselves. Guided notes are the skeleton outlines that contain the main ideas and related concepts of a lecture, including designated spaces for students to complete as the lecture/presentation occurs (Lazarus, 1991, 1996). They are prepared by the teacher to guide students through a lecture, presentation, or reading assignment (Schloss, Smith, & Schloss, 2001). Guided notes assist students who have mild disabilities participate actively in note taking, follow along with the sequence of the lecture/presentation, and write useful notes for later review (Lazarus, 1991). First, the teacher provides the students with a structured outline of a class presentation (Shields & Heron, 1989). As the teacher presents the information, the students follow the outline and fill in missing words, underline key words, and mark the important points. The advantages of guided notes include their applicability across subject areas and settings, their emphasis on the major points of a topic, their assistance with retention of information, and the opportunities for student involvement (Kline, 1986).

Shields and Heron (1989) recommend including three components in a set of guided notes, as illustrated by this example of a presentation on ecosystems:

1. *Key terms.* ecology, ecosystem, atmosphere, hydrosphere, geosphere, biosphere, ecosphere, energy, matter, and organisms.
2. *Two brief paragraphs that provide definitions of the terms and explain the key concepts.* For

example, the goal of *ecology* is to discover how air, water, soil, and organisms work and how they sustain themselves.

3. *Several questions that the student must answer after reading the notes.* What is an ecosystem and what are its most important living and nonliving components? What roles do different organisms play in an ecosystem, and how do they interact?

Figure 9.1 contains an example of another approach to using guided notes. This example illustrates what a teacher might give to students at the beginning of a lecture/presentation. Notice that the student's copy of the guided notes contains main ideas and key concepts and follows a specific sequence. It contains a minimal amount of information, giving students maximal opportunities and flexibility to respond (Lazarus, 1996). Note how Lazarus (1996) includes cues (e.g., blanks, labels, etc.) along with a review tally so that students can self-record how many times they review their own notes. Figure 9.2 contains an example of the teacher's completed notes on transparencies or PowerPoint, which may be shown to students before the lecture/presentation to introduce and provide an overview of a lesson/unit and communicate the expectation that students will complete their own notes. The completed notes

**Figure 9.1** Student's Copy of Guided Notes with Cues and Review Tally

Review Tally

Chapter 20

Cell Reproduction

I.  All life starts out as a _____ ____.

    A.                  ----------------------

    B.

II.  _____ _____ are formed by _____ _____.

III.  Types of cell division.

    A.  Mitosis—DEFINITION:

        1.  Mitosis is used for replacement of:

           a.

           b.

           c.

           d.

           e.

        2.

        3.

Note: From "Flexible Skeletons, Guided Notes for Adolescents with Mild Disabilities" by B. D. Lazarus, *Teaching Exceptional Children*, 28(3), 1996, 38. Copyright (1996) by The Council for Exceptional Children. Reprinted by permission.

**Figure 9.2** Teacher's
Transparencies with
Completed Guided Notes that
Correspond with the
Students' Copies

Chapter 20

Cell Reproduction

I. All life starts out as a <u>single</u> <u>cell.</u>

   A.  single cells ------------------------ millions of cells

   B.  Humans have millions of cells.

II. <u>New</u> <u>cells</u> are formed by <u>cell</u> <u>division.</u>

III. Types of cell division.

   A.  Mitosis—DEFINITION: process of cell division in which two cells are
              formed from one cell.

      1. Mitosis is used for replacement of:

         a.  red blood cells

         b.  skin cells

         c.  muscle cells

         d.  root tips

         e.  leaf cells

      2. Before cells divide, the cell parts are copied so the result is two
         identical cells.

      3. Mitosis is a series of steps.

Note: From "Flexible Skeletons, Guided Notes for Adolescents with Mild Disabilities" by B. D. Lazarus, *Teaching Exceptional Children*, 28(3), 1996, 38. Copyright (1996) by The Council for Exceptional Children. Reprinted by permission.

may be shown to students during and after a lecture/presentation so that students may monitor the accuracy of their own work and so that teachers can provide immediate feedback regarding students' notes. After the lecture/presentation, the completed notes may be used to review the material together as a class or in small groups.

### The Five-Step Method for Taking Lecture Notes
The five-step method for taking lecture notes (Bragstad & Stumpf, 1987) includes the following:

1. *Surveying.* Many teachers give an advance organizer or preview of what they are going to cover. Students can take notes on these points, thereby alerting themselves to what to expect during the lecture.

2. *Questioning.* Encourage your students to have a questioning attitude to help them focus on what is happening in the presentation. They may ask themselves, What is the main idea of this presentation? What am I supposed to know when the speaker is finished? What is being said about the topic? Effective ways to teach students to have a questioning attitude during a lecture presentation include (a) modeling question asking for them and (b) setting up role plays so that they can practice with each other.

3. *Listening.* Encourage students to employ listening strategies to help them listen carefully for content, cues, organization, main points, and supporting statements.

4. *Organizing.* Have your students determine how you are organizing the information being

presented. Perhaps you use the chalkboard, an overhead projector, or handouts to organize content. If you do not provide these clues, your students may listen for verbal cues to organization, such as, "The most important point to remember is . . . " or "Note this . . . " You may also repeat important points or say them slowly with emphasis and then a pause.

5. *Reviewing and revising.* As soon after the lecture or presentation as possible, your students should review their notes. In this way, they can add, change, or delete material while the information is still fresh in their minds. Encourage your students to conduct frequent cumulative reviews of their notes. By going back over that day's notes along with all previous notes after each class session, your students will be committing the material to memory.

### Two- and Three-Column Methods of Note Taking

Two- and three-column methods of note taking provide opportunities for students to interact with content. The two-column method (Bragstad & Stumpf, 1987) may be varied and modified for individual purposes. With this system, students divide their papers into two sections by drawing a line from top to bottom, thus forming two columns. The narrower column is used to record the teacher's ideas as presented in class. The wider column is used after the lecture to write questions or to summarize the major points and ideas. For example, Ms. Tuttle asked one of her students to read the following information about bats while she took notes using the two-column method.

> Today we are going to talk about bats. Bats are classified as mammals—a group of vertebrates that include people, dogs, and mice. Like all mammals, bats nurse their young on milk. Like most mammals, they bear living young and have hair on their bodies. However, in one way, bats are different from all other mammals, because bats can fly! Bats fly through the air with wings. . . .

Ms. Tuttle shared with the class what she wrote in each column. First, she filled out the "Teacher's Comments" column by writing down information from the presentation in the form of key words. Next, she filled out the "Student's Summary Statements and Questions" column with words, phrases, and sentences that clarified what she had written under "Teacher's Comments." It is helpful if teachers give students class time to fill in their summary statements and questions (see Figure 9.3), so that students can remember how the information in the two columns is related. They can also use this time to connect the information in their textbook to the notes in class by jotting down additional material from the text.

Some students prefer to have a third, narrow column to define key terms or to paraphrase material from the class presentation. Students in Ms. Tuttle's class preferred a third column to write the definition of terms (e.g., mammals—any of the group of vertebrate animals, including humans, that nourish their young with milk) and to paraphrase information (e.g., Bats are like other mammals except that bats can fly).

### Additional Note-Taking Tips

In teaching note taking to students, you should model effective note taking. Bragstad and Stumpf (1987) suggest playing a tape of a lecture and, while the class is watching, taking notes on an overhead projector so that the students see what you write. At the conclusion of the demonstration, you and your students can discuss the note-taking techniques that you utilized.

You should provide your students with ample practice in note taking before asking them to take notes in general education classes. Devine (1981) recommends using how-to-do-it presentations, such as how to change a tire, how to look up a word in the dictionary, or how to make a peanut butter sandwich. Have your students take notes as you present one of these topics.

Bragstad and Stumpf (1987) suggest giving students a set of notes that contains errors.

**Figure 9.3** Two-Column Method of Note Taking

| Teacher's Comments | Student's Summary Statements and Questions |
|---|---|
| *Bats* <br> – Mammals <br>   • Bats <br>   • People <br>   • Dogs <br>   • Mice <br> – Nurse young <br> – Bear living young <br> – Have hair on bodies <br> – Fly | –All of these animals are classified as mammals. <br><br><br> –How are bats like all other mammals? <br><br><br> –How are bats different than other mammals? |

Then have the students work in groups to correct the errors and to improve the notes. Remember to provide positive and corrective feedback to students, so that they will know what they did well and will be aware of exactly where the errors were. To reinforce the importance of taking notes, Devine (1981) recommends having a note-taking contest in which main ideas and supporting details are each worth a specified number of points. Then have the students calculate the scores of the different sets of notes. You may also specify other aspects to look for in a set of notes, such as underlining of key points or defining of technical vocabulary in the margins, and then ask the students to judge which notes contain all of the important elements.

Czarnecki, Rosko, and Fine (1998) developed two note-taking strategies for middle and high school students with special needs. The first, CALL UP, was designed for students to use while they are taking notes in class. The second, "A" NOTES, was created for students to use when reviewing notes after a lecture/presentation. They developed these strategies so that students with special needs participating in inclusive settings would be able to take notes in their general education classes. After instruction, both teachers and students reported greater competency in taking notes (Czarnecki et al., 1998).

### CALL UP

**C**opy from board or transparency.

**A**dd details.

**L**isten and write the question.

**L**isten and write the answer.

**U**tilize the text.

**P**ut it in your own words.

### A NOTES

**A**sk yourself if you have a date and a topic.

**N**ame the main ideas and details.

**O**bserve ideas also in text.

**T**ry margin notes and use SAND strategy.

**S**tar important ideas.

**A**rrange arrows to connect ideas.

**N**umber key points in order.

**D**evise abbreviations.

**E**xamine for omissions or unclear ideas.

**S**ummarize key points.

In addition to teaching one or more of the previous note-taking strategies, you may wish to share the following general note-taking tips with your students to help them organize, understand, and retain information for later recall (Platt & Olson, 1997).

1. Before going to class, review notes from the previous class, review vocabulary, read assigned pages, and think about the topic that will be covered.
2. Use a looseleaf notebook so that you can keep notes, handouts, and tests in order and together. You can take out materials, add materials, and move them around as needed.
3. Divide your notebook into different sections for each class, or use a different notebook for each class.
4. Bring materials to class each day (pens, pencils, highlighters, calculator, etc.).
5. Sit in front where you can see and hear, away from distractions, and pay close attention.
6. Write the name of your class and the date at the top of the paper and number each page.
7. Write on only one side of the paper.
8. Write quickly but clearly and legibly. Do not write everything the teacher says—just key words and phrases.
9. Write a main idea. Then indent details under the main idea in outline form. Add an example of your own or one of the teacher's. Skip a line or two before moving to another idea.
10. Leave a blank column on your paper to record your own questions and ideas. Take advantage of pauses in the presentation to make your own notes.
11. Put a question mark by items that you do not understand or that you need more information about, and ask the teacher for clarification.
12. Put a blank where you missed a word and check on it later.
13. Use a marking system to distinguish main ideas from details and examples, perhaps by drawing a box around main ideas and underlining, highlighting, or color coding certain items.
14. Use abbreviations:
    e.g. = example    p = page      # = number
    > = greater than  < = less than  vs = versus
15. Listen and look for verbal and nonverbal cues.
    ▶ Points that are repeated
    ▶ Key points ("The most important point to remember is . . .")
    ▶ Definitions
    ▶ A change in the speaker's volume, rate, and posture
    ▶ Gestures used to emphasize points
    ▶ Information that is written on the board, overhead, or PowerPoint presentation
    ▶ Use of absolute words (all, always, never, none, best)
    ▶ Words and phrases that signal or alert you to something:
      — In conclusion        — In summary
      — Finally              — For example
      — The opposite of      — Remember
16. After class, fill in any missed information, and ask the teacher to clarify anything you did not understand.
17. Make sure your notes are organized chronologically along with supporting handouts.
18. As soon as possible after class, examine your notes and check to see how they support, supplement, and/or explain the information in your textbook.

19. Review your notes before the next class. Cumulative review assists with understanding, retention, and test preparation.

20. Compare your notes to those of a peer and check for accuracy and consistency, consulting your textbook if necessary.

 **IMPORTANT POINTS** ◄

1. Study skills assist students to acquire, record, organize, remember, and use information.

2. The components of effective study skills instruction include: (a) study skills should be functional and meaningful; (b) students should believe that study skills are useful and necessary; (c) instruction should be direct, informed, and explanatory; (d) instruction should demonstrate what study skills can be used, how they can be applied, and when and why they are helpful; and (e) instructional materials must be lucid and enjoyable.

3. Teachers can help students develop better listening skills by (a) using verbal and nonverbal cues, (b) alerting students to listen for factual errors in a presentation, (c) listing the five most important points of a lesson and directing the students to listen for those points, (d) asking students to listen for certain information as they view a videotape, (e) having students listen to advertisements to determine how consumers are being influenced to buy products, and (f) using a pause procedure to assist students with recall of information.

4. Guided notes are the skeleton outlines that contain the main ideas and related concepts of a lecture, including designated spaces for students to complete as the lecture/presentation occurs (Lazarus, 1991, 1996).

5. Guided notes consist of a teacher-prepared, structured, sequenced outline of a class presentation. Students follow along, fill in missing words, underline or write key words, and mark important points.

6. A five-step method of taking notes includes (1) surveying, (2) questioning, (3) listening, (4) organizing, and (5) reviewing and revising.

7. The two- and three-column methods of note taking provide students with opportunities to interact with content.

8. General note-taking tips for students include following an outline, using abbreviations, listening and looking for cues, leaving blanks where you missed something, using a marking system to distinguish main ideas from details and examples, and organizing notes chronologically.

## Comprehension

To succeed in content classes, students with special needs are expected to acquire information from textbooks and from material presented orally in lectures (Faber, Morris, & Lieberman, 2000), class discussions, demonstrations, and student presentations (Herr, 1988). However, "many secondary students with disabilities have difficulty in reading from content area textbooks" (Schloss et al., 2001, p. 266). Because your students may lack a systematic approach to comprehending content material, or have difficulty reading and comprehending text, you must provide specific strategies to help them structure their efforts. In this section we present study skills and strategies that will improve comprehension such as the use of advance organizers, mapping, concept teaching, and textbook usage.

### *Advance Organizers*

An advance organizer is material that is presented "in advance of, and at a higher level of generality, inclusiveness, and abstraction than, the learning task itself" (Ausubel & Robinson, 1969, p. 606). Advance organizers may be verbal or written statements, activities, or illustrations that assist students in identifying and understanding essential information in a learning activity (Munk, Bruckert, Call,

Stoehrmann, & Radant, 1998). Used at the beginning of a lesson, advance organizers are used to orient students to the content to be presented (Salend, 2001).

An advance organizer may consist of an activity for obtaining student attention, a statement of the lesson objectives, a confirmation of the teacher's expectations, or a presentation of a graphic organizer (Putnam & Wesson, 1990). Mr. Row used a written advance organizer in the form of a handout to introduce a lesson on the parts of a story. The first part of the handout contained the lesson objectives, and the second part listed the parts of a story and then identified them in an actual story. While co-teaching with a general education teacher, Mr. Dunn used a verbal and visual advance organizer to introduce a lesson on rocks. He began by showing the students a display of different kinds of rock formations and then said, "Today we are going to learn about the three types of rocks: igneous, sedimentary, and metamorphic. Tell me what you already know about these three types of rocks and make some predictions about them now that you have seen and touched them." In both of these classrooms, the teachers used advance organizers to provide clues to important information that they wanted their students to acquire and to inquire about.

### Mapping

Mapping is making a word picture of ideas. It involves structuring information on a topic into categories using a graphic or web (Bulgren & Lenz, 1996). Maps may have boxes, arrows, lines, or other figures; they are visual representations that show relationships among conceptual ideas. Mapping is an excellent method for acquiring information from printed materials. It enhances comprehension, allows students to think about the relationships among concepts and ideas, and facilitates the condensing of material to be studied.

A type of mapping technique that promotes comprehension of reading content involves the use of a character web. A character web is a type of map that allows students to study characters, their traits, and examples of those traits. Figure 9.4 contains a character web that the teacher and class co-constructed about Big Anthony, a character in *Strega Nona* by Tomie dePaola. This is a delightful folktale about an elderly woman with special, magical powers and the young man who takes care of her and helps her with her house. When Strega Nona leaves him alone with her magic pasta pot, Big Anthony is determined to show the townspeople how it works. The story goes on to describe what happens when Big Anthony tries to show off for the town instead of listening to Strega Nona. Note how the use of this web with second graders enhances their understanding of the story and opens up opportunities for lessons in character and career education. After initial instruction in how to develop a character web, students can construct them independently, with a peer, or in a cooperative group.

### Concept Teaching

Concept teaching possesses many of the same characteristics as mapping. The Concept Mastery Routine, which utilizes Concept Diagrams (Bulgren, Deshler, & Schumaker, 1993), is effective for helping students acquire information. This teaching routine is particularly useful in facilitating the comprehension of content material (e.g., science, social studies, history). It requires the teacher to select and become familiar with textbook or unit content before initiating instruction with students.

The Concept Mastery Routine, developed at the University of Kansas Center for Research on Learning, consists of (a) a visual device called a Concept Diagram (see Figure 9.5), (b) a set of linking steps used to develop the Concept Diagram (see the seven steps listed below and represented by the acronym CONCEPT), and (c) instructional procedures that help the teacher cue the students to use the Concept Mastery Routine, interact with the students in completing the Concept Diagram, and review

**Figure 9.4**  Character Web

| CHARACTER | TRAITS | EXAMPLES |
|---|---|---|
| Big Anthony | Likeable | He means well and tries hard to do the right thing. |
| | Lazy | He wanted the magic pasta pot to do his work for him. |
| | Show-off | He bragged that he could make the magic pasta pot work. |
| | Poor Listener | He did not listen to Strega Nona about how to make the magic pasta pot work. |

understanding of the concept. For a detailed description of this teaching routine, please contact the University of Kansas Center for Research on Learning in Lawrence, Kansas 66045. Bulgren, Schumaker, and Deshler (1988) successfully assisted general education teachers in using Concept Diagrams with students with learning disabilities and with other students by using the following procedures (CONCEPT):

1. *Convey the targeted concept.* Name a word or phrase that represents a category or idea. *Example:* cooperation.
2. *Offer the overall concept.* Explain the category into which the targeted concept can be grouped. *Example:* a way to do tasks.
3. *Note key words.* List words or phrases that are related to the concept. *Examples:* sports team, lab partners in science, rewards, two or more people, no competition.
4. *Classify characteristics as always, sometimes, or never present.* For each word or phrase that is classified as a characteristic, decide whether it is always, sometimes, or never present. *Example:* two or more people— always-present characteristic of cooperation; study—sometimes-present characteristic of cooperation; only individual—never-present characteristic of cooperation.
5. *Explore examples and nonexamples.* Decide which words or phrases represent examples

or nonexamples. *Examples:* lab partners in a science class—example of cooperation; a person playing golf—nonexample of cooperation.

6. *Practice with a new example.* Generate your own examples and nonexamples of the concept. These are words or phrases that were not on the original key word list. *Example:* construction team—example of cooperation; movie theater audience—nonexample of cooperation.
7. *Tie down a definition.* Use the always-present characteristics and the overall concept to form a definition. *Example:* Cooperation is a way to do tasks that involves two or more people with shared goals, tasks, rewards, and responsibilities.

The preceding information is plotted in Figure 9.5. The sixth step, practice with a new example, gives you and your students the opportunity to generate additional examples and nonexamples. For example, in Figure 9.5 you will note that + (yes) or 0 (no) is used to decide whether *students in a math class* is an example or a nonexample of *cooperation*. An example has all the always-present characteristics, none of the never-present characteristics, and possibly some of the sometimes-present characteristics. A nonexample lacks at least one of the always-present characteristics or has at least one of the

**Figure 9.5** Concept Diagram

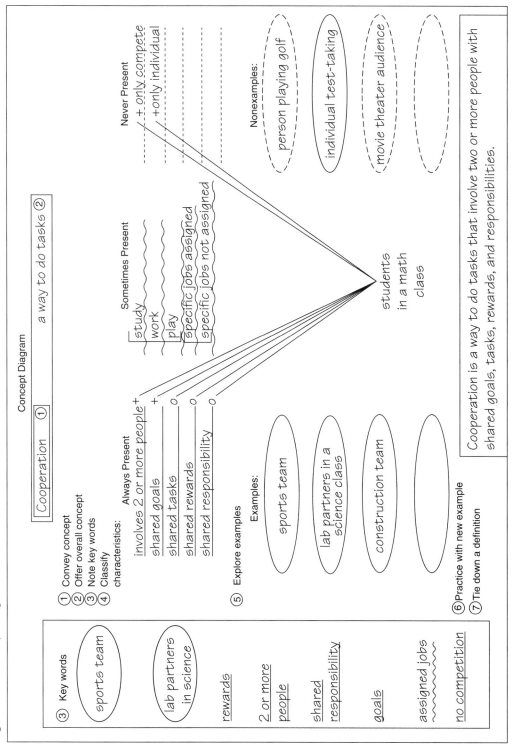

Note: The Concept Diagram is an instructional tool developed and researched at the University of Kansas Center for Research on Learning (Bulgren, Schumaker, & Deshler, 1988). It is a teaching device designed for teachers to use as they teach content information to classes containing diverse student populations. It is a data-based teaching instrument found effective when used with a planning routine, as well as a teaching routine that combines cues about the instruction, specialized delivery of the content, involvement of the students in the cognitive processes, and a review of the learning process and content material (Bulgren, Deshler, & Shumaker, 1993). Reprinted by permission.

never-present characteristics. *Students in a math class* is a nonexample, because it meets these criteria. Remember, the Concept Mastery Routine is intended to be dynamic, with a great deal of teacher and student interaction with the concept being studied. The Concept Diagram has not been shown to be an effective tool if it is simply distributed to students. Like mapping, concept teaching routines help students comprehend content material. Concept Diagrams condense material into manageable chunks and facilitate the acquisition of information.

 **ACTIVITY 9.2**

Select one of the following concepts and develop a concept diagram: conservation, democracy, pollution.

### Textbook Usage

Almost 44% of the information that students are responsible for learning is contained in textbooks but is not discussed in class (Zigmond, Levin, & Laurie, 1985). Students with special needs frequently encounter problems when trying to read, use information, or locate it in textbooks. Many secondary students with disabilities experience difficulty reading (Schloss et al., 2001) and comprehending content area textbooks (Meese, 1994). Thus, strategies in textbook usage provide valuable assistance, particularly to students who are expected to use textbooks independently in general education classes. We present suggestions for previewing textbooks, surveying textbooks and textbook chapters, and using graphic aids.

***Textbook Previewing.*** Davis and Clark (1981) indicate that by focusing on 10 specific aspects of a textbook, students concentrate on the fewest number of words that contain the greatest amount of information. After previewing these

10 components, your students will know a great deal about the textbook (Davis & Clark, 1981):

1. Title
2. Introduction
3. Summary
4. Pictures and maps
5. Chapter questions
6. Subtopic titles
7. First paragraphs following topics
8. First sentences of paragraphs
9. Special print
10. Bold print

***Textbook and Chapter Surveying.*** Prior to using a new textbook, a valuable activity for your students to perform is surveying that textbook. This allows the students to become familiar with the parts of a textbook: table of contents, preface, glossary, appendix, bibliography, and index. This activity may be performed in small groups, thus encouring students to ask questions of each other, or individually.

After a textbook is surveyed and students become familiar with its contents, surveying a chapter may be performed. This allows students to predict from the title and their prior knowledge what the chapter is about, turn headings into questions, identify study aids (e.g., bold print, italics, graphs, and charts), and divide the chapter into manageable sections. Class discussions, cooperative learning activities, and class presentations may facilitate sharing information about the chapter before the students read and study it. These discussions and activities allow students to test their initial hypotheses regarding the chapter content. Another way to survey a chapter is to use the chapter survey routine called TRIMS (Schumaker, Deshler, & McKnight, 1989):

**T**itle

**R**elationship

**I**ntroduction

**M**ain parts

**S**ummary

**Table 9.1**   Surveying a Textbook and Chapter

**Surveying Your Textbook**

1. Name of textbook _____

2. Author (s) _____

3. List two things you can tell about the book by its title. _____
_____

4. List three points that the author makes in the introduction. _____
_____

5. Look at the table of contents. List three things you know about the textbook by reading the chapter titles.
_____
_____

6. Does the textbook contain an index, glossary, and appendix? If so, how will you use each of them?
_____
_____

**Surveying a Textbook Chapter**

1. Title of chapter _____

2. List two things that the chapter title suggests. _____
_____

3. Read the first and last paragraphs and the boldface headings in the chapter. What do you think the author wants you to learn? _____
_____

4. What graphic aids does the chapter contain?

| | |
|---|---|
| —— maps | —— italics |
| —— graphs | —— questions |
| —— charts | —— definitions |
| —— illustrations | —— bold print |
| —— diagrams | —— other |

5. What other clues does the chapter have that might help you understand it?_____
_____
_____

An important part of TRIMS involves identifying the common relationship structures and signal words associated with these relationship structures (Bulgren & Lenz, 1996). These include listing, compare/contrast, cause/effect, and general/specific. These structures are organized on a worksheet that the teacher and students can use to complete a TRIMS of the chapter. For a thorough description of the procedures involved in using TRIMS, consult the work of Schumaker, Deshler, and McKnight (1989).

Table 9.1 illustrates textbook and chapter surveying. If students know how to use a textbook and are aware of how to read and study individual chapters, they are more apt to interact with the content presented. This interaction may promote more independent functioning in both pull out and inclusive settings.

**ACTIVITY 9.3**

Utilize the form in Table 9.1 to survey this text-book and one of its chapters.

***Graphic Aids.*** Many students with learning problems do not automatically activate and utilize strategies to help them acquire information from text (Stanovitch, 1986; Torgesen, 1982). This problem is intensified in the content areas because of the prevalence of inconsiderate text (e.g., a text that lacks structure, unity, coherence, and audience appropriateness) (Armbruster & Anderson, 1981; Schloss et al., 2001). For students to be successful in content classes, teachers must present information in a clear and organized manner (Dye, 2000). The use of graphic aids may alleviate the problems inherent in content area textbooks, and may assist teachers to organize material for students. Graphic aids may take the form of a table of contents, chapter headings, tables, a glossary, an appendix, a bibliography, or an index, as well as maps, semantic webs, Venn diagrams (see Figure 5.3), graphs, illustrations, or other visual displays. These graphic aids help students gather clues about the content of the text and organize facts so that they are easy to understand.

Traditionally, students with problems in academic areas have demonstrated greater difficulty managing abstract writing concepts that teachers have not explicitly taught to them (Berninger, Abbott, Brooks, Vaughan, & Graham, 1998). We recommend that you specifically teach the use of each graphic aid rather than assume that your students know how and when to use them to acquire information, and that you include the critical features of strategy instruction presented at the beginning of the chapter. For example, Mr. Alonzo taught beginning map skills to his primary students by drawing a map of the neighborhood around the school. He showed the students

how to use the compass rose (the symbol that has lines or arrows that point in the four main directions on the map). He gave them many opportunities to practice by asking them questions such as, "If you wanted to walk from East Main Street in front of the school to Spruce Street behind the school, in which direction would you walk?" Next, he showed them how to use the distance scale (1 inch = 3 miles) on the map to determine the distance between streets and between stores. After modeling how to figure distance with the distance scale and a ruler, he asked them questions such as, "If I live on Bellvedere Street and I want to walk to school, how far will I have to walk?"

In large part, gains made by students with special needs have been linked to the use of a specific type of graphic aid, the graphic organizer (Griffin, Malone, & Kame'eui, 1995; Robinson & Keiwra, 1995). The graphic organizer is a visual representation that shows relationships, and serves as a means for organizing material to be learned. There are many varieties of graphic organizers. Alvermann (1983) suggests using a modified graphic organizer: a tree diagram that contains empty spaces to represent missing information for students to fill in while reading their textbooks. It focuses attention on what is important in the textbook and secures the students' involvement by requiring them to search for the missing information (see Figure 9.6)

Merkley and Jefferies (2001) recommend following specific guidelines when using graphic organizers in instruction. We present their instructional guidelines with our own examples from Figure 9.6.

1. *Verbalize relationships (links) concepts expressed by the visual.* ("Notice, the graphic organizer describes the different types of mollusks with examples.")

2. *Provide opportunity for student input.* ("Should we add any other examples of mollusks?")

**Figure 9.6**  Tree Diagram

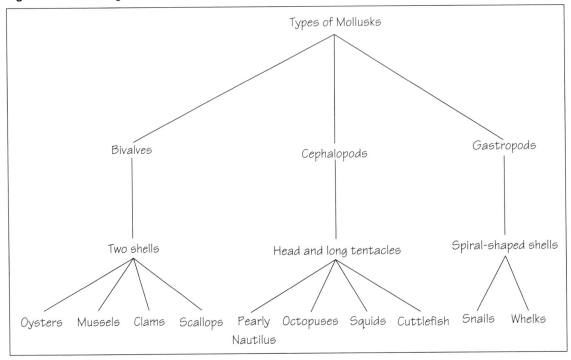

3. *Connect new information to past learning.* ("How would you compare mollusks to the types of sea life that we studied in the last section?")

4. *Make reference to the upcoming text.* ("As you read, look for the three types of mollusks and be ready to tell something about each one.")

5. *Seize opportunities to reinforce decoding and structural analysis.* ("Remember that the letters "ph" make the sound that "f" makes. Look at cephalopods. If you have trouble pronouncing a word, try dividing it into syllables.")

Once you have taught the use of graphic aids, be sure to provide opportunities to practice. For example, Dye (2000) constructed an organizer to use for a lesson about flight, which compared the early attempts at flight made by people in the United States with those made by people in Europe. She left some blank spaces on the graphic organizer so that students could add to it as the lesson progressed.

Initially, the teacher may assume responsibility for constructing the graphic organizer in order to assist students with the understanding of concepts, the meaning of vocabulary, the relationship among terms and ideas, and the organization of textbook material. Eventually, students will be able to construct these diagrams in collaboration with the teacher and, finally, on their own. To construct a graphic organizer, you should follow these steps adapted from Alvermann (1983):

1. *Choose the portion of a textbook chapter* (e.g., a few pages) *that you are ready to teach next.* Let's continue to use the topic of mollusks, which we introduced with our discussion of graphic organizers (see Figure 9.6).

2. *Write down the words that represent your topic* (e.g., types of mollusks).

| | | |
|---|---|---|
| mantle | clams | cuttlefish |
| bivalves | scallops | tentacles |
| oysters | cephalopods | gastropods |
| pearly nautilus | octopuses | mussels |
| whelks | snails | squids |

3. *Arrange the words in a tree diagram to show their relationship to the concept* (e.g., types of mollusks). You may need to add or delete words to connect terms and ideas and to clarify relationships. We added *two shells* to describe *bivalves, head and long tentacles* to describe *cephalopods,* and *spiral-shaped shells* to describe *gastropods.* We deleted *mantle.*

4. *Draw your tree diagram on the board or overhead transparency to discuss with the students.* We recommend giving each student a copy. If you use a modified graphic organizer (a tree diagram with some empty spaces), students must have a copy so that they can supply the missing information.

5. *Demonstrate for the students how the information on the diagram simplifies, clarifies, and relates to the information in the textbook.*

▶ **IMPORTANT POINTS** ◀

1. An advance organizer is used at the beginning of a lesson to orient students to the lesson and the content to be presented.

2. An advance organizer may be verbal or written and may consist of an activity for obtaining student attention, a statement of the lesson objectives, a confirmation of the teacher's expectations, or a presentation of a graphic organizer.

3. Mapping is a word picture of ideas and involves structuring information into categories using a graphic or web.

4. Maps are visual representations that show relationships among concepts.

5. A character web is a type of map that allows students to study characters, their traits, and examples of those traits.

6. The Concept Mastery Routine consists of selecting the targeted and overall concept; selecting key words or phrases; identifying characteristics as always, sometimes, or never present; identifying examples, nonexamples, and new examples; defining the concept; and plotting this information on a Concept Diagram.

7. A textbook may be previewed by attending to the title, introduction, summary, pictures and maps, chapter questions, subtopic titles, first paragraphs following subtopics, first sentences of paragraphs, italics, and bold print.

8. Graphic aids, the parts of a textbook that provide clues to content and assist in organizing facts, include the table of contents; chapter headings; maps, graphs, and other illustrations; tables; glossaries; appendices; bibliographies; indexes; semantic webs; and Venn diagrams.

9. A graphic organizer is a visual representation that shows relationships, and serves as a means for organizing material to be learned.

## ORGANIZATION AND MEMORIZATION OF INFORMATION

In this section, we present strategies that relate to how students organize and memorize information. We describe mnemonic and general memory strategies, underlining and highlighting, and study guides.

### Memory Strategies

Memory plays an important part in the academic success of students. Memory skills affect the organization and storage of information for later retrieval. Memory skills are among the most commonly reported areas of weakness among students with learning disabilities (Mastropieri & Scruggs, 1998) and students in special education and remedial classes (Scruggs

& Mastropieri, 1984). Students with disabilities may have difficulty memorizing information for tests, presentations, and written work (Ashbaker & Swanson, 1996). Consequently, it is important to teach specific strategies that will enhance memory skills.

### Specific Mnemonic Strategies

Mnemonic strategies are systematic strategies to facilitate the organization, storage, and retrieval of information (Masters & Mori, 1993). *Mnemonics* comes from a Greek term and refers to the art of improving memory by using formulae or other aids (Bragstad & Stumpf, 1987). The following mnemonic strategies may be helpful to students who have difficulty with remembering.

***Keyword Method.*** The keyword mnemonic method has been used successfully for learning and recalling information (Mastropieri, Scruggs, & Levin, 1986b; Mastropieri, Scruggs, Levin, Gaffney, & McLoone, 1985); remembering foreign language vocabulary (McLoone, Scruggs, Mastropieri, & Zucker, 1986); and remembering abstract English vocabulary (Mastropieri, Scruggs, & Fulk, 1990). Additionally the keyword method has been used in teaching history and science to students with learning disabilities (Scruggs, Mastropieri, Levin, & Gaffney, 1985; Veit, Scruggs, & Mastropieri, 1986).

The keyword method is a mnemonic strategy that assists in the retention of facts by using auditory and visual cues as well as visual imagery (Mastropieri, 1988). It employs the steps of recoding, relating, and retrieving. In recoding, an unfamiliar word is associated with a familiar, acoustically similar keyword. The relating element allows the learner to link the keyword to the actual word through a picture or image. Finally, the retrieving component enables the learner to call to mind systematically the original word (Mastropieri, Scruggs, & Levin, 1986a). For example, Mastropieri (1988) suggests that to learn the word *apex*, you recode it to a word that sounds similar, like *ape*. This is a good key-

word for students who are familiar with the concept of ape. Next, relate the keyword, *ape*, by creating an image of the keyword and the definition of the word *apex*. Since *apex* means highest point, you would picture an ape at a highest point. A good interactive image may be an ape (possibly King Kong) sitting on the highest point of something, for example, the Empire State Building. To retrieve the word *apex* and its definition, you would tell the student to think of the keyword, think back to the picture, and state the definition. It is important to consider students' experiential and cultural backgrounds when choosing keywords. You want to be sure to include concepts with which they are familiar.

***Pegword Method.*** A method for learning and remembering a list of items is the number rhyme, or pegword, method. A pegword is a rhyming word for the numbers from 1 to 10:

1. Bun            6. Sticks
2. Shoe           7. Heaven
3. Tree           8. Gate
4. Door           9. Vine
5. Hive          10. Hen

To learn a list of words, you create an image that associates the number 1, the word *bun,* and the first word on the list of items to be learned. For example, if you wanted to remember the five senses (sight, hearing, smell, taste, and touch), you would picture (1) a large bun wearing glasses, (2) a shoe with big ears, (3) a tree with an oversized nose sniffing its blossoms, (4) a door with an open mouth licking its lips, and (5) a beehive with long arms extending from its sides that were getting stung by bees because they kept touching the hive. This technique utilizes the visualizing and associative potential of the learner to help aid memory.

***Other Mnemonic Aids.*** Although mnemonic aids are not to be used as a substitute for studying and understanding, they may provide useful cues for students who are required to memorize lists, items, causes, laws, or equations. Some commonly used mnemonics are suggested:

1. Directions (north, east, south, west)— *N*ever *e*at *s*oggy *w*affles
2. Parts of the atom (proton, electron, neutron, shell)—*PENS*
3. Colors of the spectrum (red, orange, yellow, green, blue, indigo, violet)—*Roy G. Biv*
4. Time changes—Spring forward, fall back
5. Coordinating conjunctions (for, and, nor, but, or, yet, so)—*fan boys*

 **ACTIVITY 9.4**

Develop a mnemonic strategy for each of the following situations:

1. Teach a fifth grader to memorize the following parts of speech: noun, verb, adverb, adjective, preposition, conjunction
2. Show a ninth grader an effective way to memorize the following types of trees: spruce, oak, willow, sycamore, elm, palm, maple.

## Underlining and Highlighting

Some study strategies help students organize information by physically altering the text or material. Underlining is one of the most popular and frequently used study strategies (Anderson & Armbruster, 1984) and is accomplished by drawing a line under the important text. Highlighting is accomplished by going over the text with a transparent marker. Particularly useful with consumable materials, underlining and highlighting may facilitate studying by isolating the information to be recalled (Blanchard, 1985) and may help focus student attention on the most significant information (Echevarria & Graves, 1998). This is particularly helpful in an inclusive setting for students who have difficulty with vocabulary and for English-language learn-

ers. You should underline only after you have read the material by going back and picking out a few words (not whole sentences) that summarize the author's main point (Murphy, Meyers, Olesen, McKean, & Custer, 1996). Effective underlining identifies the main ideas and supporting statements in a passage and conveys the same meaning as the entire passage (Raygor, 1970). For example, consider the following passage that Ms. Rodriguez used with her students:

Every now and then, a *moving light* may appear in the *night sky*. That light may be a *comet*. A comet has a *head* and a *tail*. The *head* of the comet is *made up of* a large cloud of *gases called* the *coma*. The *tail* actually *forms when* the cloud of *gases* is *blown back* by the wind.

Notice that the same meaning is conveyed when you read the entire passage and when you read only the underlined portions. The results of many of the studies conducted in the area of underlining (Anderson & Armbruster, 1980; Johnson & Wen, 1976; Rickards & August, 1975) suggest that teachers should do the following:

1. Give preunderlined material whenever possible.
2. Provide training in effective underlining.
3. Encourage students to underline important general ideas.
4. Remind students that with underlining, less is more.
5. Encourage students to use the time saved by underlining to study the material.

For example, Ms. Rodriguez frequently gives handouts to her students to accompany their fifth-grade science textbook chapters. Her handouts contain sections that she has underlined prior to assigning the chapter. This has helped her students focus on important concepts, key terms and their definitions, study questions, and other elements that she wants them to study in preparation for a quiz or test. Sometimes, she passes out handouts that have not been underlined and models for her students what they should underline. She uses cognitive modeling techniques to demonstrate by saying, "I am going to underline *moving light* and *night sky* because it is important to know that comets move and that we can see them against the dark sky at night. I will underline *comet, head,* and *tail* because I need to remember that a comet has a head and tail. I am going to underline *head made up of gases called coma* so that I will remember what the head is composed of. That sounds as if it might be a test question."

After modeling for her students, she gives them another handout and asks them to practice underlining the way she has shown them. When Ms. Rodriguez began this procedure, her students tended to underline almost everything on a page, but after repeated practice, the amount of underlining decreased and was limited to the most essential information.

## Study Guides

Study guides help students organize visual (e.g., reading assignment, chalkboard, PowerPoint presentation, laboratory work) and auditory (e.g., lecture and audiotape) information. They help students develop a plan for reviewing and studying information (Wood, 2002). By directing attention to specific points, study guides provide organized ways to view videotapes or listen to audiotapes. They are also valuable to students as a tool for reviewing for tests.

Study guides may be used with elementary and secondary students before, during, and after instruction. A child in the elementary grades may benefit from a guide illustrating the four steps in long division or an outline with the names of the five parts of a friendly letter and an example of each. Mario, a second-grade student, was given a study guide with the five short vowels (*a, e, i, o, u*) on it. Next to each vowel was a picture that represented the sound that the vowel made (apple, elephant, igloo, octopus, umbrella). Bonita, a fifth-grade student, received the following guide prepared by her teacher:

| | |
|---|---|
| *Topic* | Writing four types of sentences |
| *Terms* | Declarative, interrogative, exclamatory, and imperative |
| *Definitions* | Declarative: a sentence that states or declares something. Interrogative: a sentence that asks a question. Exclamatory: a sentence that expresses emotion or surprise. Imperative: a sentence that gives a command or order. |
| *Examples* | Don ran all the way home from Bob's house. (declarative) Do you think I could have left my notebook in school? (interrogative) I'll never do that again as long as I live! (exclamatory) Close the door. (imperative) |

Riegel, Mayle, and McCarthy-Henkel (1988) recommended different levels of study guides depending on a student's reading level. Table 9.2 illustrates three different types of study guides. The *independent* study guide includes critical information and is appropriate for students who have good reading and study skills, know how to use an index, can skim and scan for information, and can make inferences (Riegel et al., 1988). The *prompted* study guide includes critical information and prompts (e.g., page numbers) to help students locate the information. The *directed* study guide identifies, provides prompts for, and defines critical information.

Students at the secondary level may profit from a listing of (1) title or subject, (2) purpose, (3) key vocabulary and definitions, (4) a brief outline of subject matter, (5) questions, and (6) text references with pages. For example, Leroy needed to prepare for a test on Japan. Utilizing the six elements just listed, his teacher, Ms. Delgado, developed a study guide to help structure his studying and organize the information.

1. *Title/Subject* The island of Japan
2. *Purpose* To describe the environment of Japan and the way of life of its people

**Table 9.2** Independent, Prompted, and Directed Study Guides

### Sample Independent Study Guide

*Define the following terms:*
1. Axis
2. blitzkrieg
3. neutral
4. isolation

*Answer the following questions:*
1. What happened on December 7, 1941?
2. Describe two factors that contributed to war in Europe.

### Sample Prompted Study Guide

*Define the following terms:*
1. Axis (page 123)
2. blitzkrieg (page 130)
3. neutral (page 129)
4. isolation (page 125)

*Answer the following questions:*
1. What happened on December 7, 1941? (page 132)
2. Describe two factors that contributed to war in Europe. (pages 121 & 122)

### Sample Directed Study Guide

*Define the following terms:*
1. Axis (page 123)—Germany and its allies
2. blitzkrieg (page 130)—lightning warfare
3. neutral (page 129)—to take no side between nations at war
4. isolation (page 125)—a belief that a nation should not become involved in foreign (other countries') problems

*Answer the following questions:*
1. What happened on December 7, 1941? (page 132) The Japanese bombed Pearl Harbor, Hawaii.
2. Describe two factors that contributed to war in Europe. (pages 121 & 122) Economic factors and political conditions contributed to war in Europe.

*Note:* From *Beyond Maladies and Remedies: Suggestions and Guidelines for Adapting Materials for Students With Special Needs in the Regular Class* by R. H. Riegel, J. A. Mayle, & J. McCarthy-Henkel, 1988. Novi, MI: RHR Consultation Services. Reprinted by permission.

3. *Key vocabulary and definitions*

| | |
|---|---|
| *bonsai:* | potted plants and trees kept small through specific cultivation techniques |
| *monsoon:* | a periodic wind that reverses direction seasonally |
| *archipelago:* | a body of salt water interspersed with numerous islands |
| *typhoon:* | a tropical cyclone that occurs in the western Pacific |
| *tsunami:* | a huge wave caused by an underwater disturbance |

4. *A brief outline*
   I. Climate
   II. Population distribution
   III. Landforms
      A. Mountains
      B. Plateaus
      C. Plains
   IV. Natural resources
   V. Life in Japan
      A. Urban
      B. Rural

5. *Questions* What are the advantages and disadvantages of Japan's location? What are Japan's greatest natural resources? Describe urban and rural life in Japan.

6. *Text references*
   *World Cultures*, pages 56–67
   *Japan Today*, page 34 and pages 117–129

A couple of weeks after Leroy has become used to the format of the study guide, Ms. Delgado will leave some blanks in his study guide and require him to fill in these sections, increasing his involvement with the material. Perhaps he will supply some of the definitions, generate some questions about the topic, or fill in parts of the outline.

Students at both elementary and secondary levels may benefit from study guides to assist them with school or home reading assignments. For example, Ms. Donahue gave her students a reading assignment on wild plants and animals and prepared a study guide to accompany their reading (see Table 9.3). Notice how Ms. Donahue made this reading assignment meaningful by developing a study guide to accompany it.

**Table 9.3**   Study Guide to Assist With Reading Assignments

**Questions to Guide Your Reading About Wild Plants and Animals**
*Directions*: Read this study guide before you begin reading the material or responding to the questions.

1. The main idea can be found in the first paragraph. Write it in your own words. (p. 68)

2. Read pp. 68–73 and then stop and write in your own words two major points the author is making. Now read pp. 74–79 and do the same.

3. Terms you should know are: (pp. 68–79)

| | |
|---|---|
| extinct | wildlife management |
| species | wildlife refuges |
| depleted | ethics |
| resources | predator |
| endangered | poaching |
| threatened | migration |

Be prepared to use them meaningfully in a class discussion.

4. What wild plants and animals are in danger of becoming extinct? Six are listed on pp. 70–75.

5. The author gives three reasons why we should not let these endangered species die. Write them and give one of your own. (Hint: Think about our speaker from the Audubon Society as well as the debate we had in class.)

6. Make sure you read the captions under the pictures. They give excellent descriptions of the California condor, snow leopard, whooping crane, black-footed ferret, Florida manatee, and black lace cactus.

7. Write down any words that you are unsure of and bring them to class. Remember first to use context clues and the glossary in the back of the book to help figure them out.

8. Think about what you have read and how this material relates to the previous unit on land and water resources. List at least two things in the previous unit that helped you with this unit.

Study guides may take many different forms, depending on the age of the student, the purpose of the guide, the subject matter, and the needs of the students. They provide an excellent way to facilitate the organization of information for students with special needs in inclusive settings.

 **ACTIVITY 9.5**

Select a chapter from this textbook and develop a study guide for it. Switch with someone else. How would his or her guide assist you in reading the chapter? In preparing for a test on the chapter? Critique the guide, using some or all of the suggestions given in the chapter. Now have the other person do the same for yours.

 **IMPORTANT POINTS**

1. To organize and remember information effectively, students may use memory strategies, underlining or highlighting techniques, and study guides.
2. Mnemonic strategies are strategies that facilitate the organization, storage, and retrieval of information.
3. The keyword method uses auditory and visual cues as well as visual imagery to enhance memorization; the pegword method utilizes a number rhyme technique to assist in memorizing a list of items.
4. Underlining and highlighting help students organize information to be studied by physically altering the material.
5. Effective underlining identifies the main ideas and supporting statements and conveys the same meaning as the entire passage.
6. Study guides help students organize information presented visually (in reading assignments, on the chalkboard, in a PowerPoint presentation, in laboratory work) and auditorily (through lectures and audiotapes or videotapes).

7. Independent study guides include critical information and are appropriate for students who have good reading and study skills, know how to use an index, can skim and scan for information, and can make inferences. Prompted study guides include critical information and prompts; directed study guides identify, provide prompts for, and define critical information.

## EXPRESSION OF INFORMATION

In this section, we present study skills and strategies that relate to how students express information. Students are expected to possess skills that will enable them to demonstrate their knowledge and mastery of content in school. Therefore, in this section, we provide techniques to improve two skill areas important for success in school and later at work and in life: (1) test preparation and test taking and (2) report writing and presentation.

### Test Preparation and Test Taking

Most students are required to take tests before they enter elementary school, during the elementary and secondary years in school, and before they leave high school. Even though students spend their school years taking quizzes, unit tests, minimum competency tests, and state assessments, they are not necessarily proficient at doing so. Students with special needs encounter problems preparing for and taking tests because of difficulties with organization, comprehension, memory, task completion within time limits, studying, self-confidence, and test-wiseness.

Just as you prepare your students in computation, handwriting, and theme writing, you may also prepare them to take tests. After all, your students are tested in every aspect of the curriculum, from reading to vocational skills. We present several suggestions to help your students improve their skills in test taking. Studying the content, using the study skills previously mentioned in this chapter (e.g., listening, note taking, memory techniques, study guides), and using these test-taking tips should help your students improve their performance on tests. The following suggestions, adapted from the work of Bos & Vaughn (1998, 2002), Bragstad & Stumpf (1987), and Mercer and Mercer (2001), may assist your students before they take a test, during the completion of a test, and after a test is returned.

### Before the Test

You may teach some general and specific strategies to help students prepare for a test. The specific strategies include **EASY**, **RCRC**, and the use of flash cards.

*General Strategies.* Students typically need to spend a significant amount of time trying to comprehend and retain information in order to take tests (Hughes, 1996). Therefore, it is extremely important for them to have good test preparation skills that they can use across content areas and in a variety of situations and settings. Following are some general procedures you may suggest to your students as they prepare for a test.

1. *Keep reviewing.* Students should review after each class, week, or section. A spaced or cumulative review is more effective than a massed review of the information just before a test. You may suggest that your students keep a study log to help keep up with information. The study log may contain things to do, such as review prior work, rewrite notes, or highlight important information.

2. *Determine the specifics about the test.* Suggest that your students find out the following from the teacher: date of test, sources to be studied (e. g., text, notes, presentations), and types of questions (e. g., objective, essay), and time allowed.

3. *Guesstimate about the test.* Prompt your students to use past tests and quizzes, clues

from their teachers, and brainstorming with other students to predict questions on the test. This will help them allocate study time more efficiently.

4. *Think positive thoughts.* Encourage your students to tell themselves that they will do well because they have studied the right sources of information, prepared for specific types of questions, and thought about how to allot their time.

*Easy.* Ellis and Lenz (1987) developed a strategy for students to use independently to prepare for tests by organizing and prioritizing information.

> **E** = **Elicit** "Wh" questions (who, what, when, where, why) to identify important information.
>
> **A** = **Ask** yourself which information is the least troublesome.
>
> **S** = **Study** the easy parts first and the hardest parts last.
>
> **Y** = Say "**Yes**" to self-reinforcement (p.99).

*RCRC.* Archer and Gleason (1994) have developed the **RCRC** strategy that students can use independently to prepare for tests by verbally rehearsing information from class presentations, notes, handouts, and textbooks.

> **R** = **Read.** Read a section of material from the textbook, notes, or handouts and read it again.
>
> **C** = **Cover.** Cover the material so you cannot see it.
>
> **R** = **Recite.** Tell yourself what you have read.
>
> **C** = **Check.** Uncover the material and check to see if you are right.

*Flash Cards.* McCarney and Tucci (1991) suggest putting information to be learned for tests on flash cards using a who, what, where, when, how, and why format. The questions are written on one side, with the answers written on the back, and may be prepared by the teacher, a teaching assistant, or the students themselves. Students can study independently or with a partner. This technique can be adapted for younger children by using pictures instead of words. Our example shows a sample of the flash cards a fifth-grade teacher had his students use to study for a test on a unit about heroes and heroines.

### Who

*Front:* was Molly Pitcher?

*Back:* Molly Hays McCauley (Called Molly Pitcher) was a heroine of the Revolutionary War.

### What

*Front:* did she do to help the soldiers during the Revolutionary War?

*Back:* She cooked for and fed the soldiers and the wounded during the Revolutionary War.

### Where

*Front:* was she born?

*Back:* She was born in New Jersey.

### When

*Front:* did she live?

*Back:* She lived from 1754 to 1832.

### How

*Front:* did she earn her nickname, Molly Pitcher?

*Back:* She got her nickname by carrying pitchers of water to the wounded during the Battle of Monmouth. They called, "Molly, pitcher!"

### Why

*Front:* was she proclaimed a heroine at the Battle of Monmouth?

*Back:* She fought side by side with the soldiers by loading and firing cannons during the Battle of Monmouth.

## During the Test

You may teach some general and specific strategies to assist students during a test. We discuss some general strategies first followed by a discussion of the specific strategy of **SCORER.**

*General Strategies.* Following are some techniques you can suggest your students use as they actually take a test:

1. *Situate yourself where you can concentrate.* If seats are not assigned, remind the students to choose one that will allow them to concentrate. For some it will be in the back and for others in the front—away from friends, noise, or other distractions.

2. *Survey the test.* Suggest that the students take a few deep breaths before starting. They should then put their names on their tests and look over the entire test before beginning. This will help them decide how much time to spend on each section and how the points are allocated. If this is not clear to them, they should ask the teacher.

3. *Complete the test.* Alert the students to read the directions carefully and to respond as directed, since failure to do so may result in a loss of points. They should answer the easy questions first (to earn points quickly and gain confidence) and place a mark by each question that they are unsure of. Then they can go back later to the questions they left unanswered. Unless there is a penalty for guessing, they should answer all of the questions, even if they must guess.

4. *Review the test.* Remind the students that after they have completed the test, they should look it over again. They should have followed the directions, answered all of the questions, and put their name on the test. They should check to see if their writing is legible and all words are spelled correctly. Caution the students to change an answer only if they are absolutely certain it is incorrect.

*Scorer.* Carman and Adams (1972) designed a technique called **SCORER** for students to use when they take tests. We discuss each step of the SCORER technique in detail to assist students in using the test taking strategies.

1. **S**chedule time
2. **C**lue words
3. **O**mit difficult questions
4. **R**ead carefully
5. **E**stimate answers
6. **R**eview the work

***Schedule Time.*** Students should begin their test by looking it over and planning how much time they will spend on each section. They can determine this by identifying the items that are easy and difficult for them, the point values of items, and how many items are on the test.

***Clue Words.*** Students should look for clue words in multiple-choice and true–false items. Words like *never, none, every, always, all*, and *only* are "100 percent words," which imply that the response is true 100 percent of the time (Pauk, 1989). In most cases, students should avoid choosing responses that contain these words in multiple-choice items, and should answer *false* to true–false items containing these words.

***Omit Difficult Questions.*** A good rule of thumb in taking tests is to answer the questions you know first and mark the ones you do not know. Come back later to the marked questions. Sometimes a question that a student has already answered on the test contains information that will help with an abandoned item.

***Read Carefully.*** It is important that students read directions and test items carefully so they will not miss points because they did not follow the directions, answer the actual question, or answer all parts of a question.

***Estimate Answers.*** Carman and Adams (1972) suggest that students performing mathematical calculations should estimate the answer before performing the calculation in order to avoid careless errors. Mercer and Mercer (1998) sug-

gest that if guessing is not penalized, students should eliminate obvious choices and make their best guess.

***Review the Work.*** Students should go back over the entire test to make sure they have followed directions accurately, answered all abandoned items, and responded to all questions.

Lee and Alley (1981) found that junior high students with learning disabilities demonstrated significantly improved unit test scores using the **SCORER** approach. Ritter and Idol-Maestas (1983) used **SCORER** with high school students with mental disabilities and found the students who received instruction in **SCORER** performed better than the control group on content tests.

### After the Test

Following are some of the suggestions you can give to your students after they turn in their tests. Have the students systematically analyze their test-taking strengths and weaknesses.

*Directions:* This is an analysis of your test-taking performance. Please mark *Yes* or *No* for each of the following statements.

|  | **Yes** | **No** |
|---|---|---|
| 1. Studied for test | | |
| 2. Put name on paper | | |
| 3. Surveyed test | | |
| 4. Decided order to do test | | |
| 5. Read and followed directions | | |
| 6. Answered easy questions first | | |
| 7. Marked/left difficult questions | | |
| 8. Went back to unanswered questions | | |
| 9. Answered all questions | | |
| 10. Proofread test | | |

### Managing Instructional Language and Terms

Tests and quizzes are accompanied by directions that contain key words requiring students to respond in a specific way. It is vital for students to have a clear understanding of these words in order to complete short-answer and essay questions accurately. Several authors have identified

**Table 9.4** Instructional language of Tests

| | |
|---|---|
| Apply | Using examples, explain how an idea or concept would work. |
| Compare | Show similarities and differences of two or more things. |
| Contrast | Highlight just the differences of two or more concepts. |
| Define | Provide a general description of the concept. |
| Discuss | Provide a more detailed description, including pros and cons. |
| Evaluate | Discuss the concept, including your opinion and the facts to support the opinion. |
| Explain | Tell why something occurred. |
| Illustrate | Use examples, including diagrams and pictures, to explain your idea further. |
| Justify | Offer reasons and provide facts to support your statements. |
| Outline | Condense material into major topics with their subpoints underneath. |
| Relate | Show the connection between several thoughts and ideas. |
| Solve | Arrive at a desired outcome using facts and knowledge. |
| State | Offer main point without providing details. |
| Summarize | Bring knowledge together with emphasis on main points only. |

commonly used terms (Bos & Vaughn, 2002; Pauk, 1989; Reigel, et al, 1988), which we have listed in Table 9.4. To check for understanding of these terms, Bos and Vaughn (1994) recommend asking students to respond to test items that use different instructional language. This enables students to see how varying the instructional language varies their responses. Consider the different responses you would get to the following two instructions: *Define* autocratic. *Discuss* autocratic.

## Report Writing and Presentation

Students are frequently required to express information through the writing and presenting of reports. This begins in elementary school, with children in the primary grades using show-and-tell activities and writing and illustrating simple stories and with students in the intermediate grades creating short stories, book reports, and themes. Students in middle and high school express themselves in writing (through theme writing, journal writing, and preparation of written reports and research papers requiring extensive use of references) and orally (through the presentation of themes, reports, and research papers).

It is helpful for students to have a time line to follow in the development of a paper or report. Some teachers ask for a topic, outline, and first draft by specific dates. These deadlines may be planned cooperatively with students, thus involving them in setting their own goals. You may want to instruct your students in how to do the following:

1. *Choose a topic.* When possible, topic choices should reflect student interests. For example, Mr. Bruno wanted his elementary students to write a report in his science class. He gave his students several choices of topics (e.g., the greenhouse effect, environmental pollution, depletion of resources, waste disposal) to motivate them to do the research and prepare the report. With choices, students had more involvement in the assignment from the start.

2. *Use reference materials in the media center* (e.g., Reader's Guide, encyclopedia, fiction and nonfiction, and technology resources—World Wide Web, CD-ROMs, videodiscs, software, etc.). It may be necessary to demonstrate for students how to locate reference materials and use them effectively. Some teachers take their classes to the media center during class time to review how to use the automated card catalog

and conduct a search on the Internet, and to introduce the students to current Web sites that may be helpful to their research. Ms. Taylor took her tenth-grade students to the media center to give them guided practice in using reference materials and technology resources. She showed them how to make a card or create a file on line for each reference they used. This helped them later as they put together their bibliographies.

3. *Prepare an outline ( for organization and prioritization) and submit it for approval.* Many teachers require their students to submit outlines of their reports prior to the preparation of the actual report. This is an excellent way to monitor the progress of your students and to guide them in organizing and expressing themselves. For example, Mr. Tseng helped two of his students sequence the events of the Civil War by changing the order of the items on their outlines.

4. *Write and submit a thesis statement.* Your students should begin with a thesis statement and make sure that all of their information contributes to and supports that thesis. Show your students how to write a sample thesis statement such as, "Insects have an effect on people and the environment." Then list several facts about insects, and ask your students to decide which statements contribute to the thesis.

▶ Insects have three body regions: the head, thorax, and abdomen.
▶ Insects are the largest class of organisms, including three-fourths to five-sixths of all known types of animals.
▶ Some insects transmit diseases to humans, plants, or animals.
▶ Some insects feed on crops and stored products.
▶ The expense in combating insects and the cost in loss or damages is at least $4 billion per year.
▶ Insects play an important role in soil improvement.

This step helps your students organize their writing so that what they write relates to and supports the thesis statement.

5. *Prepare a rough draft of the report.* Many teachers require a rough draft of a report as a monitoring device. They assign points or credit to emphasize its importance in the preparation of a report. Suggestions, adjustments, and corrections can result in an improved final product. For example, out of a possible 300 points, Jeremy received 30 points for his outline, 90 points for his rough draft, 15 points for his bibliography, and 110 points for his final report.

6. *Prepare a bibliography.* Your students should include a list of the references and resources they used in completing their reports. This task is made easier when they make a card for each of their references as they find them.

7. *Develop a final copy of the report.* By incorporating any changes suggested during the rough draft stage of the report preparation, students have the opportunity to earn the maximum points possible. If students voice reluctance with "doing the report twice," remind them that their work will be more complete and polished and more likely to earn them a better grade when they complete the final copy.

8. *Proofread all work.* Some teachers award extra points when students turn in perfect papers because this indicates that they have proofread their work.

9. *Submit the paper or give the report orally.* You may require a written paper or an oral report as a final product. Either way, it is helpful for students to follow a well-sequenced, systematic set of procedures. Smith, Boone, and Higgins (1998) suggest that students may want to share their reports with students in other schools, states, or countries by posting it to a school or classroom Web site. This is an excellent way for students to receive feedback about their work from a variety of sources and to disseminate their research and writing to others.

Whether your students are presenting the information orally or in writing, they should follow the preceding steps. You may want to give your students the nine points listed above in the form of a checklist. Let this form serve as a monitoring tool for your students as they complete each stage of the presentation or the report.

**ACTIVITY 9.6**

Part I. Evaluate your test-taking skills. Think of the last test you took. How many of the suggestions for what to do before, during, and after taking a test did you follow? What are your favorite types of test items to answer? What are your least favorite? Which, if any, part(s) of SCORER did you use? What aspects of your test-taking performance do you think you should change? Be specific.

Part 2. Practice writing a thesis statement. List several facts about the topic, including both extraneous and relevant issues. Justify which ones relate to the thesis statement and which ones do not.

## PUTTING IT ALL TOGETHER

We have included a wide variety of study skills in this chapter. Now, it is up to you. Schloss, Smith, and Schloss (2001) state that students who have not been taught study skills will not learn them on their own. Students need to be specifically taught study skills and stagies in listening, note taking, outlining, test taking, report writing and other areas, so that they can meet the expectations of general education settings (i.e., to acquire, organize, remember, and express information). We urge you to use the critical features of study skills instruction that we presented at the beginning of the chapter for every study skill you teach. Remember that *study skills should be functional and meaningful; students should believe that study skills are useful and necessary; instruction should be direct, informed, and explanatory; instruction should demonstate what study skills can be used, how they can be applied, and when and why they are helpful;* and *instructional materials must be lucid and enjoyable* (Paris, 1988). These critical features represent the keys to the successful implementation of a study skills program, and it is the teacher's role to ensure that they are implemented.

> **IMPORTANT POINTS** ◀

1. Techniques to use before taking a test are to review using a study log, determine specifics about the test, guesstimate about the test, and think positive thoughts.
2. Techniques to use during a test are to sit where it is possible to concentrate, survey the test, complete the test, and review the test.
3. A suggestion to use after taking a test is to analyze test-taking performance, including strengths and weaknesses.
4. Short-answer and essay questions contain instructional language that is important to understand in order to respond accurately to questions.
5. Specific test-preparation strategies include EASY, RCRC, and the use of flash cards that follow a who, what, where, when, how, and why format, and an effective test-taking strategy is SCORER.
6. The steps for developing an oral or written report are to choose a topic, use reference materials, prepare an outline, write a thesis statement, prepare a rough draft, prepare a bibliography, develop a final copy, proofread all work, and submit or give the report.

 **DISCUSSION QUESTIONS** ◀

1. Justify the inclusion of study skills instruction in an already overcrowded curriculum.
2. Describe what you would include in a study skills program in elementary, middle, and high school.
3. Why do you think some students leave high school without a repertoire of study skills to enhance their success in postsecondary education? What can be done about it?

# PART 3

# FACTORS AFFECTING INSTRUCTION

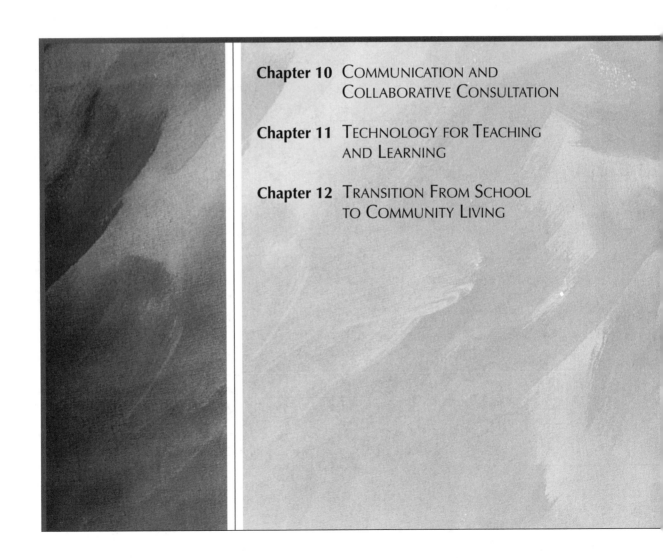

# CHAPTER 10

# COMMUNICATION AND COLLABORATIVE CONSULTATION

The field of special education is undergoing many changes. Major reform efforts and legislation (see Chapter 1) have focused on redefining and restructuring the relationship between general and special education. Among the recommendations for this restructuring and redefining of relationships are that general and special educators increase their collaborative efforts in planning and providing instruction to students with disabilities in inclusive settings (Kamens, 1997). Increasing numbers of students with special needs are receiving services in general education classrooms, so that the question is no longer *what* to teach, but *where* to teach (Baker & Zigmond, 1995). To provide successful experiences for students with special needs, teachers need to become more involved in collaborative planning and problem solving (Voltz, Elliot, & Cobb, 1994). According to Bondy and Brownell (1997), "teachers and other members of school communities are increasingly recognizing the need for collaboration" (p. 112). Collaborative interactions are occurring in inclusionary schools, where students previously excluded from their neighborhood schools are now included in general education classrooms (Friend & Bursuck, 1996; Stainback, Stainback, & Stefanich, 1996). It has become more the norm than the exception that teachers of children and adolescents with special needs are working less in isolation and more as members of an educational team. Thus, the ability to communicate and collaborate with other members of a team (general classroom teachers, administrators, paraprofessionals, other direct- and related-service providers, and families) may have a significant impact on the quality of services that special educators provide for their students.

"Good communication skills are a prerequisite for collaboration. If we cannot communicate effectively with our colleagues and others, a collaborative relationship is not possible" (Pugach & Johnson, 1995, p. 62). Therefore, in this chapter, we begin with the topic of communication, share strategies for effective communication, and present specific techniques to use with parents/families. We also provide the rationale for collaborative consultation, describe the options for implementing collaborative consultation, and share with you some of the barriers to collaborative consultative interactions along with suggestions for overcoming or preventing them. Finally, we provide recommendations for planning and implementing paraprofessional programs, and leave you with some final thoughts about collaborating with other partners in the school and community.

## COMMUNICATION

The importance of communication skills has been well documented in the literature (Bos & Vaughn, 2002; Olson & Platt, 2000; Thomas, Correa, & Morsink, 1995). We believe that communication is the key to effective working relationships with teachers and other members of the school team and is essential for successful interactions with parents/families. Dettmer, Thurston, and Dyck (2002) state that people spend 70% of their day communicating in one form or another (i.e., listening, speaking, and writing), and therefore, good communication among special educators, general educators, and parents is essential to the success of students with special learning needs in the general education classroom.

### Factors to Consider in Communication

Because communication is vital to your success as a professional, we hope that you will consider skills in communication to be as important as skills in subject-area content; strategies for planning, teaching, and assessment; classroom management; and adapting materials and instruction. Attention to the following will assist you in building rapport, respecting and accepting differences, and building and sustaining productive partnerships with others.

### Nonverbal Skills

Eighty-five percent of communication is primal, nonverbal communication (Crisis Prevention Institute, 1983). Nonverbal communication is essentially all communication other than the spoken or written word. It is an important component of communication. When there is a discrepancy between a person's verbal and nonverbal message, people more often attend to the nonverbal message (Argyle, 1975; Mehrabian, 1969). If a friend of yours says everything is fine, but has a scowl on his face, do you really want to ask if you can borrow his car? Nonverbal communication consists of proxemics, kinesics, and paraverbal components.

***Proxemics.*** Proxemics refers to personal space, or the amount of distance you need to feel comfortable in your interactions with others. It is an imaginary circle that surrounds your body and is your comfort zone. When others cross it, you become uncomfortable. If you have ever worked with students who have behavior problems, you know that many problems develop because these students frequently do not respect the personal space of others.

Culture influences a person's comfort zone. Many Asian Americans require more personal space and are uncomfortable with the physical closeness of a teacher, whereas people from the Hispanic culture frequently need less personal space (Briganti, 1989). Most Arabs and southern Europeans stand closer when they talk than do Indians, Pakistanis, northern Europeans, and African Americans (Baxter, 1970; Watson, 1970). The personal space you are comfortable with is often influenced by the sex, age, race, and size of the other person. Do you stand closer to an unfamiliar female or male? Anxiety also plays a part in personal space. A person who is anxious usually requires more personal space. When communicating with parents during a conference, you may want to place the chairs so that there is room for the parents to move and adjust their comfort zone.

*Kinesics.* Body language, such as posture and gestures, also conveys a message. Again, cultural effects are evident in this nonverbal communication. For some cultures, looking down, not at the teacher, is a sign of respect. Many Native Americans avoid eye contact (Simpson, 1982), as do many Asian Americans, who are taught that avoiding direct eye contact conveys respect (S. Chan, 1987). Many individuals from Hispanic (Briganti, 1989) and African American cultures (Grossman, 1994) teach children to lower their heads and not maintain eye contact when they are being reprimanded. In fact, eye contact with authority figures is frequently a sign of disrespect in the African American culture (Gilliam & Van Den Berg, 1980; Grossman, 1994).

It is important when communicating with other professionals and parents/families to maintain a supportive stance. A supportive stance requires physical positioning so you are not sitting or standing directly in front of a person. Many people equate a straightforward position with an authoritarian figure, which may decrease verbal communication (Crisis Prevention Institute, 1983). Instead of sitting or standing in front of someone, try sitting or standing to the side.

*Paraverbal Communication.* The tone, volume, and cadence of your voice are involved in paraverbal communication. Paraverbal communication is what your dog understands, causing it to hop around when you say, "Let's go for a walk," or hide when you say, "It's bath time." It's the type of communication that interfered with the first speech you ever had to give in front of a large, unfamiliar audience. Remember the sweaty palms and the quaking voice?

▼ **ACTIVITY 10.1**

You will need the help of a friend for this activity. With about 7 feet between you, stand directly across from your friend. Looking at your friend, have him or her walk toward you. Hold your hand out and say stop when you begin to feel uncomfortable. Now reverse roles. Was your friend's personal space different from your own? Try the same experiment without the stop cue when you are with people you do not know as well. Did your comfort boundary change? Did it differ from theirs? Did the person move back as you approached? Did your comfort boundary change? Did it differ from theirs?

(Answers to this and other activities are found in the Instructor's manual.)

Being a good, responsive listener is essential for effective communication. Dettmer, Thurston, and Dyck (2002) offer two comments by humorists in regard to listening:

"It takes six letters of the alphabet to spell the word *listen.* Rearrange the letters to spell another word that is a necessary part of responsive listening (Did you get *silent?*).

In the middle of listen, the *t* doesn't make a sound." (p. 134)

Other suggestions for desirable nonverbal communication skills are found in Table 10.1.

### Verbal Skills

The verbal skills of active listening, rephrasing, open-ended questioning, and summarizing are powerful during communication (FDLRS East, 1982; Roberds-Baxter, 1984; Turnbull & Turnbull, 1986). Coupled with nonverbal skills and the avoidance of educational jargon, they can lead to productive communication sessions.

*Active Listening.* Many teachers use active listening. In active listening, you communicate to others that you are interested in what they have to say, will work to understand what they

**Table 10.1**  Nonverbal Communication Skills

| *Desirable* | *Undesirable* |
| --- | --- |
| **Facial Expressions** | |
| • Direct eye contact (except when culturally proscribed)<br>• Warmth and concern reflected in facial expression<br>• Eyes at same level as client's<br>• Appropriately varied and animated facial expressions<br>• Mouth relaxed; occasional smiles | • Avoidance of eye contact<br>• Eye level higher or lower than client's<br>• Staring or fixating on person or object<br>• Lifting eyebrow critically<br>• Nodding head excessively<br>• Yawning<br>• Frozen or rigid facial expressions<br>• Inappropriate slight smile<br>• Pursing or biting lips |
| **Posture** | |
| • Arms and hands moderately expressive; appropriate gestures<br>• Body leaning slightly forward; attentive but relaxed | • Rigid body position; arms tightly folded<br>• Body turned at an angle to client<br>• Fidgeting with hands (including clipping nails, cleaning pipe)<br>• Squirming or rocking in chair<br>• Slouching or placing feet on desk<br>• Hand or fingers over mouth<br>• Pointing finger for emphasis |
| **Voice** | |
| • Clearly audible but not loud<br>• Warmth in tone of voice<br>• Voice modulated to reflect nuances of feeling and emotional tone of client messages<br>• Moderate speech tempo | • Mumbling or speaking inaudibly<br>• Monotonic voice<br>• Halting speech<br>• Frequent grammatical errors<br>• Prolonged silences<br>• Excessively animated speech<br>• Slow, rapid, or staccato speech<br>• Nervous laughter<br>• Consistent clearing of throat<br>• Speaking loudly |
| **Physical Proximity** | |
| • Three to five feet between chairs | • Excessive closeness or distance<br>• Talking across desk or other barrier |

Note: From *Direct Social Work Practice: Theory and Skills*, Third Edition, by Dean H. Hepworth and Jo Ann Larsen. ©1990 by Wadsworth, Inc. Reprinted by permission.

mean, and are comfortable with the feelings underlying their message. You echo what others say, including their emotions, and they can either confirm or correct the accuracy of your understanding. For example, if a parent or professional says, "I just can't understand why Janet is the way she is!" an active listening response is, "You sound very concerned about

Janet." Active listening allows parents and professionals the freedom to express their feelings, to feel accepted, and to accept themselves (FDLRS East, 1982).

***Rephrasing.*** When you rephrase, or reframe, what parents and professionals are saying, you are attempting to use your own words to restate the speaker's message (FDLRS East, 1982). Unlike active listening, in which you concentrate on both the affective and cognitive parts of the message, in rephrasing you concentrate on the meaning, or cognitive part. For example, look again at the speaker's message, "I just can't understand why Janet is the way she is!" A possible rephrasing response is, "You are having difficulty understanding Janet's problems." With this response, you are not attempting to describe the feeling (e.g., concern), but the cognitive part of the message. Rephrasing changes the words to help parents and professionals hear what they are saying and perhaps approach their problems from a different perspective.

***Open-Ended Questioning.*** Open-ended questions encourage parents and professionals to share information and participate more. They typically begin with *how, what,* and *tell me about* (Bos & Vaughn, 2002). The questions may be unstructured (e.g., "What do you think about Hector's program?") or structured, which limits the responses (e.g., "What have you found that works with Susan when she begins to cry?") (Turnbull & Turnbull, 1986). According to Hepworth and Larsen (1990), open-ended questions may take the form of a polite command (e.g., "Tell me how the notes are working with Jock.") or an embedded question (e.g., "I'd like to know how the notes are working with Jock."). This doesn't mean that you should never ask a closed-ended question, such as "Do you feel Lashonda is making progress?" or "Does Lashonda frequently appear tired?" Such questions are useful for finding factual information, but a preponderance of these questions limits discussion.

***Summarizing.*** To summarize, simply restate what the parents or professionals said, highlighting the major points. Summarization helps to acknowledge that a topic has been exhausted and that the major points are understood.

 **ACTIVITY 10.2**

**Part 1:** A parent has said that she is upset that you are allowing the other children to pick on her daughter. Write down two active listening statements and an open-ended question in response to this comment.

**Part 2:** The third-grade teacher comments that she has to spend too much time helping Camille when she is in her classroom. Write down two active listening statements and an open-ended question in response to this comment.

 ▶ **IMPORTANT POINTS** ◀

1. Communication is the key to effective working relationships with teachers and other members of the school team, and is essential for successful interactions with parents/families.
2. Seventy percent of the day is spent in communicating (listening, speaking, writing).
3. Eighty-five percent of communication is nonverbal.
4. Nonverbal communication includes proxemics (personal space), kinesics (posture and gestures), and paraverbal components (tone, volume, and cadence).
5. Nonverbal behaviors such as proxemics are influenced by a person's culture (e.g., Hispanics often require less personal space than Asian Americans and African Americans).
6. Effective verbal communication skills include active listening, rephrasing, open-ended questioning, and summarizing.

7. Active listening involves echoing the cognitive and affective components of a verbal message.
8. Rephrasing involves restating the cognitive component of a verbal message.
9. Open-ended questioning such as "How is sending the note home working with Vivian?" tends to foster active interchanges.
10. Summarizing requires highlighting the major points of an interaction.

## COMMUNICATION AND COLLABORATION WITH PARENTS/FAMILIES

"Parents are an integral part of efforts to improve student performance, their insights critical to educational change" (Hernandez, 2001, p. 82). Interactions among parents/families and school professionals result in benefits to both students and family members (Hoover-Dempsey & Sandler, 1997). Parents are able to assist their children at home, and children and adolescents benefit from increased opportunities to learn. Teachers and school systems also benefit from increased family involvement because teachers learn more about their students through the wealth of information that families can contribute, and attitudes toward schools are enhanced through home–school collaboration (Dettmer et al., 2002).

Involving family members in the education of students with disabilities is not only educationally sound, but also mandated by law (Salend, 2001). The Individuals with Disabilities Education Act (IDEA) Amendments of 1997 strengthened parent participation in decision making and in resolving home–school disputes, by including family members in the educational process (National Information Center for Children and Youth with Disabilities, 1997).

Families of students with special needs face the typical challenges of child rearing and, in addition, must cope with the issues involved with a child with a disability (Blalock, 2001). Additional characteristics of families, such as the increasing number of women in the workforce, a reliance on day-care centers and extended family members (Olson & Platt, 1996), the number of single-parent families (Ascher, 1987), ethnic/cultural identities, and employment patterns (Wehmeyer, Morningstar, & Husted, 1999) make it imperative for teachers to be sensitive and responsive to family issues. Encouraging parents to visit school; increasing the frequency of communication by making phone calls, sending home positive notes, e-mails, or newsletters; and using telephone answering machines for recorded messages are just a few techniques that encourage a collaborative relationship between the school and family members (Blalock, 2001; Haring, Lovett, & Saren, 1991; Minner, Beane, & Prater, 1986).

The foundation for any collaborative effort between families and school personnel is based on clear, open communication. "What may appear to be a lack of home cooperation may actually be a problem in communication" (Kroth & Edge, 1997, p. 106).

We hope you will incorporate the verbal and nonverbal communication skills mentioned earlier in the chapter in your interactions with family members. Throughout this chapter, and the entire text, the terms *families* and *parents* are used interchangeably, and may refer to mothers, fathers, stepparents, foster parents, aunts, uncles, grandparents, guardians, older siblings, and others.

### Barriers to Communication

Unfortunately, not all communication with family members has been positive. To encourage school–home collaboration, you must be aware of some of the barriers to communication as well as ways to manage conflict. Sonnenschein (1981) identified attitudes of professionals that interfere with communication with parents/families. These include the beliefs that parents are helpless, that parents are responsible for the child's conditions, that parents' opinions are not worthwhile, that parents are pushy or adversarial, and that parents and professionals should not become overly friendly. A belief particularly attributed to family members from minority cultures is that they lack interest in their child's development (Rounds, Weil, & Bishop, 1994). As Harry (1992) explains, this belief is exacerbated by the fact that some cultures stress respect for and deference to authority, which interferes with active participation at IEP and other meetings. The National PTA conducted a survey of PTA presidents to determine why more families are not getting involved in their children's education and found the following reasons: lack of time, difficulty understanding the system, language and cultural differences, transportation difficulties, problems arranging child care, and feelings of intimidation and not being welcome (Kroth & Edge, 1997).

A first step in communicating with parents is viewing parents as partners, showing trust and respect, and having empathy for their problems. An attitude of respect and trust is particularly important when working with parents from various cultural groups (S. Chan, 1987; Johnson, 1987; Olion, 1989). Lack of respect from teachers and other school personnel is often mentioned as one of the reasons for infrequent involvement with their child's educational program (Marion, 1981).

Imagine what it would be like to have a child with you all day who is in constant motion or has frequent temper tantrums and to worry constantly about how that child will function as a productive adult. The Native American saying, "Oh, Great Spirit, grant that I may not criticize my neighbor until I have walked a mile in his moccasins," reminds us to consider the perspectives and experiences that parents bring to the communication process. Remember, the parent is the child's first teacher.

## Crisis Confrontation

Communicating with a parent who is upset is never easy, even for veteran teachers. If you know that communication with a particular parent has the potential to become quarrelsome, you may wish to first practice with other people what you plan to say and ask them for feedback (Roberds-Baxter, 1984). But how do you handle communication when you are surprised by an irate parent? The Crisis Intervention Institute (1983) recommends the following procedures for handling verbal, aggressive behavior.

1. *Stay calm.* Trying to remain calm when a parent is shouting at you is easier said than done. Wanting to shout back or to escape is normal. Breathe deeply or think a pleasant thought before you engage in conversation.

2. *Isolate the parent.* Remove the parent from the public area. There is no need for others to be involved, and it is often difficult to change an attitude when others are observing. For example, you might say, "Ms. Herman, I'm sorry you're upset about Joe's test score. Let's go to my classroom, so I can get his test and we can sit down and talk." Remember to use the nonverbal behaviors of a calm, steady, low voice and a supportive stance.

3. *Listen and be aware of nonverbal cues.* Remember the nonverbal postures specified in Table 10.1. Look for nonverbal cues, such as relaxation of the shoulders, to show that the parent is moving from an anxious stage and is ready to listen and discuss the problem rationally.

4. *After listening to the complaint, attempt to restate the parent's comment.* Restating what the parent said gives you time to think and possibly break the parent's pattern of irate communication. For example, "I can see that you are upset with Joe's grade because you feel the test was unfair and I'm picking on him." You may even agree with part of the criticism (e.g., "I know this was a difficult test").

5. *Question for specifics.* When you question for specifics, try to promote a rational reaction to the problem and show that you are willing to

look at the problem from the parent's viewpoint. Open-ended, structured questions are often the best (e.g., "I have the test. Let's see what questions you feel were unfair."). Avoid making judgmental comments like, "Ms. Herman, you are so wrong."

6. *Keep communication simple.* Refrain from long explanations until the parent has calmed down. An anxious person is usually not ready or willing to listen to others. Spend more time listening than talking.

7. *Try not to take the action personally.* Do not automatically assume that the parent dislikes you. People lose control for many reasons besides personal animosity, including displaced anger, loss of personal power, confusion, fear of the unknown, attention getting, or psychological or physical disorders (Crisis Prevention Institute, 1983). Think of the reasons people lose control and try not to take the comments personally.

8. *Be assertive.* This is a step we have added in preparing our students to deal with verbal aggression. If Ms. Herman continues to scream, attempt to reschedule the conference with an assertive comment, "Ms. Herman, I appreciate your concern and I would like to resolve the problem with you, but it is difficult to do right now. Let's reschedule for tomorrow morning." Or "Ms. Herman, we don't seem to be able to resolve this. Sometimes, it helps to talk to another person. Why don't you come in tomorrow and we'll talk with the principal, Ms. Martinez, and maybe she can help us with our discussion."

*Do not promise what you cannot do.*

## Parent/Family-Teacher Conferences

"The very nature of the educational process makes the relationship between home and school an important one" (Hernandez, 2001, p. 82). Communication with parents/family members can be strengthened by improving parent/family-teacher conferences (Salend, 2001). Effective communication skills should be practiced during conferences with family members. In a longitudinal survey conducted by Harry, Allen, and McLaughlin (1995), parents of preschool special education students from the African American culture identified four deterrents to participation: inflexible scheduling, limited conference time, emphasis on documentation rather than parent participation, and role structure of professionals as authoritarians. Hopefully, we will avoid these deterrents with the following suggestions for successful parent/family-teacher conferences. These conferences generally include three steps: (a) planning the conference, (b) conducting the conference, and (c) following through after the conference. We present a checklist identifying procedures for these three steps in Figure 10.1. The procedures were adapted from the University of New Mexico/Albuquerque Public Schools Center for Parent Involvement.

### Planning the Conference

Because many parents feel that a parent-teacher conference signifies some sort of problem (Flake-Hobson & Swick, 1984), be specific about the purpose of the meeting in addition to specifying the date and time. You may notify parents of the parent-teacher meeting by a note or by phone. A phone call provides an opportunity for the parents to ask questions and for you to check their understanding of the purpose of the meeting. If you are working with families from diverse cultures, Hyun and Fowler (1995) suggest that you encourage the parents to invite other people who are important to them to the conference.

Before the conference, review the student's folders, gather examples of work, and prepare materials, including a skeleton script of what you are planning to say. Scripting the content allows you to check your communication to determine whether it is free of educational jargon, to organize your thoughts, and in many cases, to listen carefully to the parents (because you have planned the important points you want

**Figure 10.1** Conference Checklist

**Planning the Conference**
_____ 1. Notify
  • Purpose, place, time, length of time allotted
_____ 2. Prepare
  • Review student's folder
  • Gather examples of work
  • Prepare materials
_____ 3. Secure co-teacher's input, if appropriate
_____ 4. Script important points you wish to make
_____ 5. Arrange environment
  • Select site
  • Choose comfortable seating
  • Eliminate distractions

**Conducting the Conference**
_____ 1. Build rapport
  • Welcome
  • Introduce yourself and others
  • Describe roles of all individuals at conference
_____ 2. Preview meeting
  • Purpose
  • Time limitations
  • Note taking
  • Emphasize importance of parents' input
_____ 3. Share information
  • Use open-ended questions
  • Use active listening/rephrasing
  • Discuss strengths, concerns, and solutions
  • Pause once in a while
  • Look for nonverbal cues
_____ 4. Complete parent-conference form
_____ 5. Summarize information
  • Review high points
  • Schedule other meetings or follow-ups
  • Thank them for taking the time to come and
    for their contributions

**Following Up on the Conference**
_____ 1. Review conference with student, if appropriate
_____ 2. Share information with other school personnel,
    if needed
_____ 3. Mark calendar for planned follow-up
_____ 4. File parent-teacher form

to mention). A script also allows you to check with other teachers to obtain their input. In a co-teaching situation, it is essential that you meet with the general education teacher ahead of time for his or her input. In fact, you may want to sit down together and complete the script.

Educational jargon often interferes with communication. If you must use educational jargon, define or give examples of the terms. For instance, if you use the term *short-term objective,* add a definition, "the small steps students must master to reach a goal," or an example, "Jason must master the short-term objective of changing percentages, such as 70%, to decimal numbers, such as 0.70, before he can figure out sales tax."

When scripting the content, include student strengths, your concerns, and possible solutions. Remember the cultural implications of solutions. For example, in many cultures, such as Asian American (Chinn & Plata, 1987), Latino (Briganti, 1989), and Native American (Walker, 1988), child rearing is shared by grandparents or others who live in the home. Therefore, consistency in helping children and adolescents with disabilities can be achieved only if whole families agree to participate in the intervention.

Another consideration in offering solutions is to recognize that some resources may not be available to the parents. For example, Johnson (1987) cautions that it is not appropriate to suggest that a child play with water at home, if water must be hauled to the home. For these reasons, it is important to secure parent input concerning solutions; the ones you write during the planning should never be etched in stone. A sample script appears in Figure 10.2.

A final part of planning is selection of the environment for the conference. Try to use the classroom. There, you have immediate access to the files, plus the setting serves as a reminder of things the student said or did and that the purpose of the meeting is to discuss educational goals (Stephens, Blackhurst, & Magliocca, 1988). Be certain to provide all participants with adult-sized chairs. Spend time before the meeting relaxing. Roberds-Baxter (1984) recommends that you visualize yourself before the conference as being nondefensive, assertive, listening, and showing confidence.

**Figure 10.2** Sample Script

Student's Name  _Bill_

Grade  _Ninth_

1. *Strengths* (Check vocabulary.)
   • Participates in discussions.
   • Makes insightful comments that often describe the point the author is trying to make.
   • Is a leader during cooperative learning groups. (Cooperative learning groups involve students of different ability working together on a project.) For example, Bill helps organize the other students by suggesting how they might all work together, asking such questions as, Who wants to draw the graph? and Who wants to look up the information in the encyclopedia?

2. *Concerns* (Check jargon and specific examples.)
   • Bill is constantly late for his first-period history class, which is resulting in a failing grade.
   • His ninth-grade class teacher and I kept a record of the number of times late the past 3 weeks—late 11 of 15 days an average of 20 minutes each day. On time about 1 day a week.
   • Bill says he oversleeps or he rides with a friend who oversleeps.
   (Ask parents if they have any idea why he is late.)

3. *Possible Solutions* (Initiate by asking parents if they have any solutions. If none, ask them about each of the following and see if they think any one would work.)
   • Bill rides the bus instead of riding with a friend.
   • Set up a home reinforcer system. At the end of the week the teacher will call the parent. If Bill is on time 3 out of 5 days, he can go to the football game or dance or out on Friday night. If not, he stays home.
   • Bill and both teachers write out a contract. If Bill is on time 3 out of 5 days, he earns the negotiated reinforcer at school, such as leading a small-group discussion with materials provided by the teacher.

## Conducting the Conference

Establishing rapport, previewing the conference, sharing information, and summarizing the information are ingredients for successful completion of a conference. We also recommend the completion of a conference form during the conference to serve as a written verification of the content. A completed form dealing with the problem of Bill's being late for class is found in Figure 10.3. Beginning with

Possible Solutions, the information was completed with the input of family members.

***Establishing Rapport.*** Greeting parents at the door is a way to add to the comfort of parents from diverse cultures (Kuykendall, 1992). Begin the conference by introducing yourself and any other individuals, indicating their responsibilities. Be certain to address the parents respectfully. Hyun and Fowler (1995) suggest using greeting words in the family's language. Perl (1995) suggests you begin the conference with small talk and something nonalcoholic to drink to help relax parents. If you are part of a co-teaching situation and the general education teacher and you are both present, the person who contacted the parents should take charge. If you are in charge, remember to ask opinions of your co-teacher as well as the parents as you conduct the conference. Arrange adult seating for the parents and place your chair next to the parents and not directly across from them.

***Previewing the Conference.*** At this time, state the purpose of the meeting, identify time limitations, and emphasize to the parents their importance in providing input and solutions. If you plan to take notes, inform the parents and ask them if they would like a copy. Take notes openly, so that they can see what you are writing (Turnbull & Turnbull, 1986). If you are going to complete a conference form similar to that in Figure 10.3, show and explain the form.

***Sharing Information.*** In sharing information, remember to use open-ended questions, active listening, and rephrasing. Make every attempt to involve the parents actively. In many cultures, parents are passive receivers of information in school matters. For example, in the Asian culture, schooling is viewed as the responsibility of the school (Chinn & Plata, 1987). In the Hispanic culture, parental involvement in school matters is not expected or encouraged (Echevarria-Ratleff & Graf, 1988). The inclination to be a passive receiver of information is

**Figure 10.3**  Conference Form

---

Parent-Teacher Conference Form

Student's Name:  Bill Jacobs                               Grade: 9th

Date:  10/12

Place:  Milton High School

*Purpose:* To discuss Bill's lateness to his first-period history class, which is resulting in a failing grade. Tardy 11 out of 15 days the past 3 weeks. On time 4 out of 15 days, about once a week.

*Possible Solutions:*

| Solutions | Evaluation |
|---|---|
| 1. Parents will talk with Bill. | Question effectiveness. |
| 2. If late for more than two days during the week, he must ride the bus the entire week. | Negative, too long of a punishment. |
| 3. If on time for three days during the week, Bill's father will take him out to drive the car on Saturday. | Positive, must do every week. |
| 4. If on time for three days a week for five or six weeks, Bill's father will take him to a professional football game. | Positive, six weeks' time. |

*Solution Selected: #4*
Bill's parents feel he will work for football and they want him to take driving lessons at school. His teachers will make up a chart for Bill, so he can see his progress.

*Follow-Up Procedures:*
Ms. Gonzalez will call Bill's parents on Tuesday and Thursday to report Bill's progress.

*Signatures:*   Diane Jacobs      (parent/s)
                Linda Gonzalez    (teacher)

---

also often found in the Native American parent, whose culture promotes a reluctance to share information with authorities (Johnson, 1987).

Always start on a positive note, mentioning the strengths of the student. Next, move to the concerns, using specific examples or work samples. You may want to ask parents if they see similar behavior at home. Once your concerns are thoroughly discussed, move to possible solutions, asking for parent input. Throughout the conference, remember to listen to the parents, refrain from interruptions, and give the parents many opportunities for input. If you do not understand what a parent is saying, ask the parent for clarification (Hyun & Fowler, 1995). Wait for the parents to respond before adding another point: In some cultures, it is impolite to interrupt others. For example, in some Native American tribes, it is an unwritten rule that an individual waits for the speaker to finish talking before saying anything (Johnson, 1987).

*Summarizing the Information.* Before concluding the conference, review the major points, including the concerns and the solution agreed upon. Schedule any future meetings, phone calls, or follow-through plans. Be certain to thank the parents for their ideas and contributions, and offer to send them a copy of your notes or the conference form.

### Following Through After the Conference

If you are planning to review the conference with the student, you should mention this at the end of the parent conference and ask the parents for their permission, or summarize what you plan to say. If you need to share the information with other professionals, remember that any written information that is shared with other school personnel must be revealed to parents upon request (Morgan & Jensen, 1988). Finally, be certain to file the conference form and follow up on any of your responsibilities. For example, the solution agreed on for Bill's tardiness requires the teacher to contact the parents twice a week.

 **ACTIVITY 10.3**

> Examine the description below and script the information using the script in Figure 10.2 as an example. Include strengths, concerns, and possible solutions.
>
> > Rosa is having problems turning in her homework. She keeps telling her fifth-grade teacher and you that her younger brother rips it up or that she forgets it, but it is finished. At this time, her grade is a *D* due to her incomplete homework assignments. She is able to score *Bs* and *Cs* on the weekly quizzes.

 **IMPORTANT POINTS**

1. Interactions among families and school professionals result in benefits for students, family members, teachers, and school systems.
2. The Individuals with Disabilities Education Act (IDEA) of 1997 strengthened parent participation in the educational process.

3. Treating parents/families with respect and having empathy for their problems may remove communication barriers.
4. During a crisis confrontation, teachers should stay calm, isolate, listen, restate, question, keep the communication simple, view it as not personal, and be assertive.
5. Parent-teacher conferences involve (a) planning the conference, (b) conducting the conference, and (c) following through on the conference.
6. Before the conference, review the student's folders, gather examples of work, and prepare materials, including a skeleton script of what you want to say.
7. During a parent-teacher conference, a teacher should establish rapport; preview the meeting; share strengths, concerns, and possible solutions; and summarize the conference content.
8. Prior to concluding the conference, review the key points, including the concerns agreed upon.
9. Schedule a follow-up to the conference.

## COLLABORATIVE CONSULTATION

In a dynamic field that is constantly undergoing reform, school professionals continue searching for alternative methods to serve students with special needs. An alternative that is continuing to receive increased attention and support is that of collaborative consultation. Collaborative consultation originates from a triadic model (Tharp, 1975; Tharp & Wetzel, 1969). The triadic model consists of three components: (a) the target (T), or student with a problem; (b) the mediator (M), or someone who has the ability to influence the student; and (c) the consultant (C), or someone with the knowledge and skills to work with the mediator. Idol, Paolucci-Whitcomb, and Nevin (2000) indicate that consultants and mediators may be general education teachers, special education teachers, speech patholo-gists, principals, paraprofessionals, parents, or other members of the educational community. Correct use of the model results in participa-tory decision making, collaborative solutions to carefully specified problems, and shared responsibility for outcomes. Special education professionals refer to this as collaborative con-sultation. According to Idol, Nevin, and Paolucci-Whitcomb (2000):

> Collaborative consultation is an interactive process that enables people with diverse exper-tise to generate creative solutions to mutually defined problems. The outcome is enhanced, altered, and produces solutions that are different from those that the individual team members would produce independently. The major out-come of collaborative consultation is to provide comprehensive and effective programs for students with special needs within the most appropriate context, thereby enabling them to achieve maximum constructive interaction with their nonhandicapped peers. (p. 13)

In collaborative consultation, participants such as general and special education teach-ers, families, students, administrators, para-professionals, school counselors, employers, and speech pathologists serve as consultants in their respective areas of expertise, so that all participants have the opportunity to share their knowledge and skills (Blalock, 2001). Through this collaborative effort, it is possi-ble to exchange information about a student's strengths and weaknesses and to identify potential teaching strategies and curricular adaptations that could prove beneficial (Knackendoffel, 1996). Successful resolution of problems is dependent on the skills of the collaborators. Because most educators may not possess a strong background in collabora-tive strategies, it is recommended that they receive training in order to serve in collabora-tive roles (Berdine & Cegelka, 1995; Idol, Nevin, & Paolucci-Whitcomb, 2000).

## Rationale and Need for Collaborative Consultation

Collaboration between special and general edu-cators is viewed as an essential component in the success of students with disabilities who are being served in general education classes (Dettmer et al., 2002; Pugach & Johnson, 1995; Voltz & Elliot, 1997). Today, special educators must operate as part of a team in many aspects of their roles, such as planning, placement, assessment, instruction, and monitoring progress, necessitating greater collaboration among school professionals and others (Blalock, 2001). "Effective collaborative consultation relies on the parity and equity of contributions from all collaborators" (Idol, Nevin, & Paolucci-Whitcomb, 2000, p. 13). Friend and Cook (2000) have identified several characteristics of collaboration, including the following: Collaboration is voluntary, requires parity among participants, is based on mutual goals, depends on shared responsibility for par-ticipation and decision making, requires the sharing of resources and accountability for out-comes, involves trust and an appreciation of dif-ferences in interpersonal styles, and builds a sense of community.

Studies have revealed that the use of collabo-rative consultation has resulted in (1) improved student outcomes, (2) the effective instruction of students with special needs in general education classrooms, (3) a reduction in the number of stu-dents referred for special education, (4) support for the implementation of the collaborative con-sultation model, and (5) improved mutual problem solving, sharing of knowledge, and communication among general and special edu-cators (Gable, Young, & Hendrickson, 1987; Givens-Ogle, Christ, Coleman, King-Streit, & Wil-son, 1989; Saver & Downes, 1991). Support for consultation among general educators was shown in a survey by Myles and Kasselman (1990) in which half of the teachers surveyed reported using collaborative consultation, even though a formal consultation program was not available in their schools. Kamens (1997) found that collaborative activity increases job satisfaction and self-esteem, promotes better working relationships, and contributes to professional development. When teachers collaborate, they tend to become more knowledgeable about their fields, become more involved in school decision making (Sindelar, Griffin, Smith, & Watanabe, 1992), and improve their skills and those of their students (Elliott & Sheridan, 1992). According to Dynak, Whitten, and Dynak (1997), teaching should not be an isolated act; elementary education, special education, and content-area teachers should collaborate as part of their regular school day. Educators should be interdependent and make use of each other's knowledge and expertise (Lieberman, 1995).

 **ACTIVITY 10.4**

Collaboration is a major topic of discussion in education today. Using some aspect of collaboration as your topic, locate an article in a professional journal, a paper that was presented at a national meeting, or an education or special education Web site and report your findings to a peer or in a small group at your next class meeting.

 **IMPORTANT POINTS**

1. The ability to communicate and collaborate with members of a team (general classroom teachers, administrators, paraprofessionals, other direct- and related-service providers, and families) may have a significant impact on the quality of services that special educators provide for their students.
2. Collaborative consultation is an interactive process that enables people with diverse expertise to generate creative solutions to mutually defined problems (Idol, Nevin, & Paolucci-Whitcomb, 2000).
3. Studies have revealed that the use of collaborative consultation has resulted in (a) improved student outcomes, (b) the effective instruction of students with special needs in general education classrooms, (c) a reduction in the number of students referred for special education, (d) support for the implementation of the collaborative consultation model, and (e) improved mutual problem solving, sharing of knowledge, and communication among general and special educators.
4. Collaborative activity increases job satisfaction and self-esteem, results in better working relationships, contributes to professional development of teachers, and improves the skills of students (Kamens, 1997).

## Options for Implementing Collaborative Consultation

Several options or models have been found to be effective in the implementation of collaborative interactions (i.e., mutual problem solving and shared decision making) among professionals. They include teacher assistance teams (Chalfant & Pysh, 1989; Chalfant, Pysh, & Moultrie, 1979), prereferral intervention (Blackhurst & Berdine, 1993; Graden, Casey, & Christenson, 1985; Winzer & Mazurek, 1998), coaching (Costa & Garmston, 1994; Knackendoffel, 1996; Showers, 1990), consulting teacher (Idol, 1986, 1988; West & Cannon, 1988), and cooperative teaching (Bauwens, Hourcade, & Friend, 1989; Bauwens & Hourcade, 1997).

Teacher assistance teams and prereferral interventions are examples of a team approach to problem solving. Members of these teams range from general education teachers to special education teachers, counselors, social workers, or other members of the school community. In these two approaches, the intent is to work collaboratively through formal, structured stages to solve problems and make decisions about students. These approaches tend to reduce the number of inappropriate or unsuitable referrals for special education placement (Blalock, 1997), provide support to students (Bos & Vaughn, 1994), and expand the instructional alternatives that teachers have at their disposal (Olson & Platt, 2000). The coaching, consulting teaching, and cooperative teaching options for implementing collaborative consultation usually involve close collaboration between general and special education teachers in actual classroom settings.

### Teacher Assistance Teams

Teacher assistance teams (TATs) are support systems for teachers (Chalfant & Pysh, 1989; Chalfant et al., 1979). Such teams provide opportunities to brainstorm solutions to problems and exchange ideas, methods, and techniques for developing instructional alternatives to help students referred to the team (Hayek, 1987). The philosophy behind TATS is that classroom teachers have the skills to teach students with learning and behavior problems by working together in a problem-solving, collaborative manner. Teacher assistance teams are composed of general education teachers and function to help the referring teachers resolve problems. The use of TATS has resulted in benefits to students, their families, and professionals (Chalfant & Pysh, 1989; Chalfant et al., 1979). Pysh and Chalfant (1994) emphasize the importance of providing time for teams to meet and ensuring that teams receive external reinforcers when they meet outside of their daily activities.

*Teacher Referrals.* A teacher who is having difficulty with a student submits a referral to the team. The referring teacher describes the student's performance, strengths, and weaknesses; the interventions already attempted; and other pertinent information, such as health history or assessment results.

*Reviews of Referrals.* The team coordinator reviews the referral and asks the team members to read it prior to a team meeting so that the team members may devote the meeting time to actual problem solving (Chalfant & Pysh, 1981).

*Requests for Specific Information.* The team coordinator responsible for the case may need to contact the referring teacher for clarification of information submitted or for additional information, may observe in the classroom if necessary, and develops a problem-interaction diagram that summarizes the concerns (Chalfant & Pysh, 1989).

*Classroom Visits.* It may be helpful if one of the team members observes the student in the classroom. This team member may collect additional pertinent information through observation of the student and the environment.

*Problem-Solving Meetings.* The TAT meeting lasts for 30 minutes and includes the following steps recommended by Chalfant and Pysh (1981):

1. Reach a consensus about the nature of the problem.
2. Negotiate one or two objectives with the referring teacher. Be sure that the objectives specifically state the behaviors the student should achieve.
3. Brainstorm alternatives.
4. Select the methods the referring teacher would like to try and define the methods.
5. Assign responsibility for carrying out the recommendations (who, what, when, where, how).
6. Establish a follow-up plan for continued support and evaluation.

*Recommendations.* The meeting should result in recommendations for the referring teacher to implement, recommendations for informal assessment for the teacher or a team member to complete, or a referral for special help.

### Prereferral Intervention

Prereferral intervention refers to "a systematic set of activities in which students believed to be at risk for school failure are evaluated with regard to their learning and educational needs as well as their abilities" (Blackhurst & Berdine, 1993, p. 51). Prereferral intervention is designed to prevent inappropriate placements in special education and to help general classroom teachers interact effectively with students who have special needs. Implemented in a highly collaborative manner (Welch, Judge, Anderson, Bray, Child, & Franke, 1990), prereferral intervention focuses on instructional and behavioral interventions as opposed to testing and placement. In other words, it involves the use of interventions with students who have diverse needs outside of special education (Baca & Almanza, 1991). Some professionals dislike the use of the term *prereferral*, as it implies that referral to special education is imminent (Graden, 1989; Pugach & Johnson, 1989). The term *intervention assistance teams* is used by some to describe a team approach to assisting teachers with students, prior to considering referral for special education (Friend & Cook, 2000; Graden, 1989; Whitten & Dicker, 1995).

Through prereferral interventions, teachers gather data on a student's learning and behavior, design a support system to assist the student in general classrooms, and adapt curriculum and modify the classroom environment (Winzer & Mazurek, 1998). Thus, prereferral intervention has two areas of emphasis: problem solving and adaptations/modifications. Problem solving involves collaborative consultation among members of a school-based problem-solving team to which referrals are sent and whose members suggest instructional interventions. Adaptations and modifications are recommended when students' needs are not being met in the existing classroom setting. Studies

conducted on prereferral interventions demonstrated that schools could reduce referrals and testing for special education, and increase the use of consultation (Graden, Casey, & Bornstrom, 1985; Gutkin, Henning-Stout, & Piersal, 1988; Safran & Safran, 1996).

Table 10.2 contains examples of modifications for prereferral recommended by Winzer and Mazurek (1998). Look back at Chapter 5 for additional suggestions of how to adapt materials for students with special needs in inclusive settings. Graden, Casey, and Christenson's (1985) model includes both problem solving and adaptations. They suggest that intervention begin at the point of initial referral and recommend a prereferral system comprised of six stages: four in the prereferral process and two in the referral/assessment of eligibility process, if needed.

***Stage 1: Referral for Consultation.*** The classroom teacher requests assistance from a consultant (such as a school psychologist, a social worker, a special education teacher, or a counselor) or seeks assistance from a school-based problem-solving and screening team (school psychologist, other classroom teachers, special education teacher, principal, social worker, counselor).

***Stage 2: Consultation.*** The consultant or team collaborates with the classroom teacher to define the problem, explore intervention strategies, try them, and evaluate the outcomes. If the intervention attempts are successful, the process ends. If they are not, the process moves to a third stage.

***Stage 3: Observation.*** During the observation stage, additional information is collected through observation of the student and the environment. Then alternate intervention plans are implemented and evaluated. At Stages 2 and 3, the participants must specify the roles and responsibilities of those implementing the plan. For example, the school psychologist may be responsible for observing the

**Table 10.2**   Modifications for Prereferral

| | |
|---|---|
| **Materials modifications** | Make materials self-correcting.<br>Highlight critical features.<br>Block out extraneous elements. |
| **Instructional modifications** | Use mnemonic devices.<br>Shorten directions.<br>Provide mediators.<br>Use advance organizers.<br>Preface all remarks with a title or the main idea of the lesson.<br>Use cognitive learning strategies. |
| **Cues, feedback** | Provide more prompts.<br>Use corrective feedback.<br>Provide visual cues. |
| **Management** | Use contingency contracts.<br>Change seating.<br>Use cooperative strategies.<br>Use peer tutoring. |
| **Content** | Slow pace; use wait time. |
| **Grouping** | Use learning centers. |
| **Test taking** | Teach test-taking skills. |
| **Study** | Teach study skills.<br>Note all assignments on a special bulletin board. |
| **Psychosocial** | Use the following:<br>Counseling<br>Support groups<br>Social services<br>Crosscultural counseling |

Note: From Winzer, M.A., and Mazurek, K.M., *Special Education in Multicultural Contexts*. 1994. Prentice Hall, Upper Saddle River, NJ. Reprinted by permission.

student, the classroom teacher may be responsible for collecting work samples and performing an error analysis, and the special education teacher may be responsible for adapting instructional materials.

*Stage 4: Conference.*   At this stage, a conference is held with a child review team to communicate the results of interventions and make decisions. This team comprises some of the school resource people mentioned in Stage 1 (school psychologist, general classroom teachers, spe-

cial education teachers, etc.). All information is reviewed and the team makes recommendations to continue the interventions, try alternative interventions, or refer the student for consideration for special education placement.

*Stage 5: Formal Referral.*   At this stage, the student may be referred for an educational assessment. Information previously gathered and interventions tried during the previous stages can be vitally important. The team members may want to ask themselves what additional data are necessary to make a decision. They may want to reexamine student work samples, records of assignment completion, observations of classroom behavior and participation, screenings of academic skills, and modifications made in the classroom. Further assessment could include curriculum-based assessment, criterion-referenced testing, and additional observation measures.

***Stage 6: Formal Program Meeting.*** A formal meeting of the child study team is held to review information from the first five stages. The team discusses alternative placements and services and writes IEP goals, if appropriate.

***Cultural and Linguistic Diversity as Factors in the Prereferral Process.*** Students with limited English proficiency and students from culturally diverse backgrounds tend to be overrepresented in special education and remedial classes (Winzer & Mazurek, 1998). One reason may be that language and cultural characteristics may be interpreted as disabilities instead of differences. The prereferral process should include considerations related to the education of multicultural populations.

Ortiz and Garcia (1989) developed an eight-step prereferral process for preventing inappropriate referrals of Hispanic students to special education. Their prereferral system addresses very specific questions that include but are not limited to the following:

1. Is the student experiencing academic difficulty?
2. Is the curriculum known to be effective for language minority students?
3. Has the student's problem been validated?
4. Is there evidence of systematic efforts to identify the source of difficulty and take corrective action?
5. Do difficulties continue in spite of the programming alternatives?

Although Ortiz and Garcia (1989) provide this prereferral process to use with Hispanic students, it may be used effectively with members of other language minority and multicultural populations as well. For an extensive discussion of how to adapt referral and assessment processes for culturally and linguistically diverse students who may have learning disabilities, consult the work of Ortiz (1997).

### Coaching

Another model found to be effective in implementing collaborative interactions among teachers is that of coaching. Although different terms have been used for coaching, such as cognitive coaching, peer coaching, and others, it typically refers to individuals engaged in helping one another to improve their skills or practices or to learn something new. Cummings (1985) defines coaching as the process of giving teachers structured feedback about the practices they used in a lesson. In the school community, coaches may be teachers, administrators, or other school professionals. In an examination of studies on coaching, Showers (1990) reports that approximately 80% of teachers who were in coaching programs implemented new teaching strategies compared with approximately 10% of uncoached teachers.

Collaborative interactions between general and special education teachers and the learning outcomes of their students may be enhanced through coaching. Coaching typically involves observations of instructional practice, followed by discussions and reflections on that practice by the coaching partners. The coaching partners usually identify and focus on a specific instructional practice with which the teacher is experimenting (Showers, 1985). The coaching partners, or teachers, may also use the coaching relationship to share with each other methods for adapting instruction and materials, suggestions for checking student understanding during lesson presentations, specific teaching techniques, ideas for classroom management, methods for teaching various content areas, and strategies for monitoring student progress. Successful coaching relationships depend on trust, openness, mutual learning, and a willingness to change.

"Cognitive coaching is a nonjudgmental process—built around a planning conference, observation, and a reflecting conference" (Costa & Garmston, 1994, p. 2). During the planning conference, the partners identify what the teacher is going to work on, establish what one teacher will observe the other teacher do, and prepare or rehearse the lesson. For example, Ms. Johnson (general education teacher) selected her instructional language, and specifically, her questioning strategies, as an area that she wanted to improve. She asked her coaching partner, Ms. Washington (special education teacher), to give her some suggestions for phrasing her questions so that her students would raise their hands instead of calling out the answers and so that more students would respond to questions instead of the same few students each time. She also asked Ms. Washington to listen carefully to the questions she asked during the lesson and to check how long she waited for students to respond (wait time). The teachers developed sample questions at various levels of difficulty that could be used during the lesson. They practiced how to allow sufficient wait time after asking a question.

During the observation, Ms. Johnson taught the lesson and Ms. Washington observed by jotting down the questions that Ms. Johnson used and recording the amount of time that she gave for students to respond. During the observation stage of coaching, "the intent is to cast the teacher in the role of experimenter and researcher and the coach in the role of data collector" (Costa & Garmston, 1994, p. 21). Notice that the process is nonjudgmental and highly collaborative, with both teachers committed to solving the problem.

The reflecting conference is held after the observation. The coach may want to organize or revise the notes and data taken during the observation before sharing them with the teacher. During the reflecting conference, coaches usually ask teachers to share their impressions of the lesson, thereby encouraging them to judge their own performance. It is important for teachers to reflect on the relationship between their own actions and student outcomes. It is very difficult for teachers to change their actions or behaviors when they are not aware of them.

In our example, after examining the data that Ms. Washington collected, Ms. Johnson may decide that the way she phrased her questions had a direct impact on how her students responded during the lesson and that providing sufficient wait time after asking questions definitely resulted in more students responding. The reflecting conference may be used by the teacher to reflect about the lesson that was just observed and to plan for future lessons based on new learnings resulting from the coaching experience. During this conference, the partners should also evaluate the coaching experience and devise ways to strengthen it.

### Consulting Teacher

Consulting teaching is "a process for providing special education services to students with special needs in which special education teachers, general education teachers, other school professionals, or parents collaborate to plan, implement, and evaluate instruction conducted in general classrooms for the purpose of preventing or ameliorating students' academic or social behavior problems" (Idol, 1986, p. 2). As a service delivery system, the pure consulting teacher model is one of indirect service to students (Idol, 1986; Lilly & Givens-Ogle, 1981). As a problem-solving process, it is meant to be highly collaborative, with general and special education teachers working as partners in planning instruction.

The intent of the consulting teacher model is to provide general classroom teachers with the skills necessary to instruct students who have special needs. In other words, the goal is not to relieve general classroom teachers of the responsibility for instructing students with mild disabilities and other low-achieving students

(Huefner, 1988). Idol (1988) feels that consultation should support, not supplant, general education programs.

West and Cannon (1988) surveyed individuals in 47 states to identify the competencies essential for consultation and found that the highest ratings were given to interpersonal skills, personal and professional attitudes and beliefs, and personal qualities. Reeve and Hallahan (1994) report that the technical skills associated with effective teaching of students with disabilities were not included in West and Cannon's (1988) survey, and they question whether communication and compatibility are sufficient for successful collaboration when the ultimate target is student outcomes. We suggest that consulting teachers should possess excellent listening, interpersonal, communication (verbal and nonverbal), problem-solving, and teaming skills, as well as effective technical skills (e.g., task analysis, content enhancement, direct instruction, questioning).

The role of the consulting teacher requires knowledge of large- and small-group instruction, familiarity with the general education curriculum, ability to adapt and modify materials and instruction, flexibility, and expertise in working with others. For example, a high school teacher was concerned that the readability level of her history textbook was too high for many of her students, that the text failed to represent the contributions of different cultural groups to the development of the United States, and that it did not present a balanced perspective. She worked with the consulting teacher in the development of materials to supplement the text. They used videotapes, books that represented different ethnic groups, and reference materials from the media center and Web sites. Consulting teachers may also design curriculum units, participate in prereferral systems, and co-teach with general classroom teachers.

As part of their Teaming Techniques series, Knackendoffel, Robinson, Schumaker, and

Deshler (1992) focus on basic communication skills, the problem-solving process, partnership-building skills, and the instructional principles needed in decision-making situations. They use a problem-solving worksheet that provides general and special education teachers with a systematic method of collaborating to solve student problems. Thurston (1987) uses the POCS method of problem solving in which general and special education teachers cooperatively complete a worksheet with the POCS steps for problem solving (problems, options, consequences, and solutions). This method promotes collective thinking in generating viable alternatives for students with special needs.

Figure 10.4 contains an example of a cooperative planning guide, which employs the four steps in consultation. Notice that the form was completed cooperatively by the special education teacher, Judy Hernandez, and the classroom teacher, Don Whitley. They began by defining the problem. Through an exchange of information including listening, questioning, and clarifying, they were able to target Marcus's problem—he does not pay attention in science class and this affects his performance on tests and projects. Second, they analyzed the problem. They did this by listing (a) the factors in the classroom that might be contributing (e.g., the class is primarily lecture), (b) the behaviors of the student that might be contributing (e.g., he doesn't write anything down), and (c) the strengths of the student (e.g., he learns well from visuals). As you can see by examining Figure 10.4 they learned a great deal about Marcus by using environmental variables and student strengths and weaknesses to analyze his problem.

Third, they implemented a plan. They did this by first generating and then prioritizing several recommendations. They also decided who would be responsible for carrying out each recommendation. For example, their first priority was to award points to Marcus for coming to class prepared, with the science teacher assuming the responsibility for implementing this. The next priority was to teach Marcus to take notes. The special education teacher assumed responsibility for this.

Finally, they determined how they would evaluate the plan. They did this by deciding how they would fulfill their roles and responsibilities. For example, the science teacher kept a daily

**Figure 10.4** An Example of a Cooperative Planning Guide

Cooperative Planning Guide

Student's Name: Marcus Wyler
Date: 11/10

1. Define the problem:

   Marcus doesn't pay attention in science class and this affects his performance on tests and projects.

2. Analyze the problem:
   a. List the factors in the environment that may be contributing to the problem
      • The pace is fast.
      • The class is large.
      • The class is primarily lecture.

   b. List the behaviors of the student that may be contributing to the problem
      • He doesn't come to class prepared with pencil and paper.
      • Ho doesn't watch when information is put on the board.
      • He doesn't write anything down, so he probably doesn't study.

   c. Discuss the student's strengths
      • He likes working with peers.
      • He has excellent attendance.
      • He learns well from visuals.

3. Implement a plan:
   a. List and prioritize five recommendations
      • Award points for coming prepared. (1) D.W.
      • Present material on transparencies when possible. (4) D.W.
      • Cue him when to write something down.(3) D.W. & J.H.
      • Teach him to take notes. (2) J.H.
      • At the end of class, review the key points of the presentation and let him compare his notes to a peer's. (5) D.W.

   b. Go back and write the initials of the person responsible for implementing each recommendation next to that recommendation

4. Evaluate the plan:
   For each recommendation listed in 3(a), specify how it will be monitored and evaluated
      • Science teacher will keep a record of points earned.
      • Special education teacher will check notes for technique and science teacher for content.
      • Science teacher will keep track of the effectiveness of cueing.
      • Science teacher and special education teacher will check notes for evidence of material presented on transparencies.
      • Science teacher and special education teacher will check notes for key points.

Special education teacher: Judy Hernandez
Science teacher: Don Whitley
Comments: Let's meet next Thursday after school to review Marcus's progress.

record of the points Marcus earned by coming to class prepared. The special education teacher agreed to evaluate Marcus's notes for technique, and the science teacher assumed responsibility for checking the notes for content.

The consulting teacher may use any of the previously mentioned methods for collaborative problem solving. The key is to use teamwork and shared decision making to create, implement, and evaluate realistic alternatives for students.

### Cooperative Teaching

Given the increased diversity in today's public school classrooms, it is essential to develop alternative forms of service delivery within the general education setting. Cooperative teaching has emerged as an effective way to facilitate the inclusion of students with diverse needs (Bauwens & Hourcade, 1997; Friend & Cook, 2000). According to Bauwens, Hourcade, and Friend (1989), "Cooperative teaching, or co-teaching, refers to an educational approach in which general and special educators work in a co-active and coordinated fashion to jointly teach academically and behaviorally heterogeneous groups of students in educationally integrated settings (i.e., general education classrooms)" (p.18). In co-teaching, cooperative planning and instructing are emphasized. Both the general and special education

teachers are present in the classroom and assume responsibility for instruction. Roles and responsibilities are determined on the basis of the strengths and skills of the teachers.

By combining the planning and teaching skills of general and special education professionals in a cooperative arrangement, it may be possible to achieve successful reintegration of students with special needs into general education classrooms. Most general education teachers are skilled in content and curriculum and in providing instruction to large groups, whereas most special education teachers are adept at analyzing and adapting materials and are knowledgeable in special teaching methodologies. In planning instruction, general educators typically identify a theme or topic related to district or state competencies and then develop activities, whereas special education teachers, who are accountable for student mastery of IEP objectives, focus on student learning first and then generate activities to help students meet the objectives (Dyck et al., 1997). Figure 10.5 illustrates the interaction of curriculum content (the specialty of general education) and specialized methodology (the specialty of special education) to produce a more effective instructional situation through cooperative teaching (White & White, 1992).

**Figure 10.5**  Interaction Curriculum Content

| Regular Education | Collaborative Teaching | Special Education |
|---|---|---|
| Content knowledge<br>Curriculum objectives<br>Curriculum materials<br>Content resources support<br>Content development<br>Curriculum sequence<br>Learning environment | Shared teaching<br>Evaluation<br>Classroom management<br>Student supervision<br>Team problem solving<br>Communication skills<br>Response to change<br>Professional growth<br>Social and emotional needs addressed | Knowledge of each disability<br>Individual learning styles<br>Adaptation of curriculum<br>Learning strategies<br>Modifications to learning environment<br>Legal issues<br>Motivational techniques |

Note: From "A Collaborative Model for Students With Mild Disabilities in Middle Schools" by A. E. White and L. L. White, 1992. *Focus on Exceptional Children*, 24(9), p. 7. Copyright 1992 by PRO-ED. Reprinted by permission.

In our world of specialists, we need to be careful that the contributions of general education teachers are not overlooked. Pugach and Johnson (1989) describe a presentation that they observed by a collaborative team of two general educators and one special education teacher. After the team had shared their collaborative efforts, members of the audience commented on how much the general education teachers must have learned from working with the special education teacher. The special education teacher asked the audience why they didn't ask her about all the things she had learned from the general education teachers. We hope you will think about this as you work collaboratively with classroom teachers—for the learning is reciprocal.

Figure 10.6 lists some of the tasks that special education teachers may perform as co-teachers to help students with special needs succeed in regular classrooms. Of course, both teachers should provide input into the appropriateness of these tasks for a given situation.

Bauwens, Hourcade, and Friend (1989) recommend three approaches to co-teaching—team teaching, supportive learning activities, and complementary instruction—and suggest that, at times, two or more of these approaches may occur simultaneously in the classroom.

**Figure 10.6** Possible Tasks of the Special Education Teacher in Cooperative Teaching

**Lectures and Presentations**
1. Provide visuals.
2. Prepare study guides and chapter outlines.
3. Use modeling and demonstration.
4. Prepare glossaries.
5. Teach note taking.

**Textbooks and Other Printed Materials**
1. Physically alter printed material.
   a. Insert stop points in text.
   b. Use marginal gloss.
   c. Highlight.
   d. Underline.
2. Tape-record printed material.
3. Have the students develop their own end-of-chapter questions.
4. Teach the use of mnemonic devices.
5. Show the students how to preview a textbook and chapter.

**Interest and Motivation**
1. Use story starters.
2. Alternate listening and doing activities.
3. Allow students to demonstrate knowledge in a variety of ways (e.g., writing, telling, making, working with a partner or group).
4. Provide written feedback.
5. Use calculators, games, word searches, puzzles, audiovisuals (videotapes, language master cards, slides, and filmstrips).
6. Develop learning centers.
7. Develop self-correcting materials.

**Teacher Assistance**
1. Cooperatively plan lessons and activities.
2. Help teachers locate and adapt materials.
3. Monitor student progress (academic and social).
4. Help grade assignments.

*Team Teaching.* In the team teaching approach, general and special educators share the responsibilities for planning and presenting content to students (Friend & Cook, 2000). At times, one teacher may take the lead for some aspect of instruction, such as teaching the steps for a bill to become a law. At other times, the other teacher takes the responsibility for part of a lesson, such as instructing students in how to interpret the graphics in their social studies texts. Knackendoffel (1996) refers to team teaching as teaching in concert with each other. The decision of who teaches what depends on the preferences, training, and strengths of the teachers (Snell & Janney, 2000).

Mr. Milaki (special education teacher) and Mr. Webster (sixth-grade teacher) jointly planned a social studies lesson for the sixth grade. Mr. Milaki began the lesson by using direct instruction to introduce new vocabulary to students. Mr. Webster presented the lesson content using the overhead projector to emphasize key points and show examples. Both teachers monitored student attention to, and acquisition of, the social studies content. In addition to this example, Bauwens and Hourcade (1997) suggest other ways of team teaching such as (a) dividing students into two heterogeneous groups to receive similar instruction, but in smaller groups, (b) having one teacher present the content while the other moves around the classroom to monitor student progress, (c) having one teacher present content while the other poses questions, and (d) having one teacher present content while the other conducts a review for those who need it.

*Supportive Learning Activities.* In this approach to cooperative teaching, both general and special education teachers plan and present content (Bauwens & Hourcade, 1997). General education teachers present the essential content, and special education teachers are responsible for designing and implementing supplementary and supportive learning activities (Bauwens, Hourcade, & Friend, 1989). Both teachers are present during instruction to monitor student performance.

For example, Ms. Parrish (classroom teacher at the high school level) presented a lesson on the different forms of government. She described the forms of government, provided examples, and discussed characteristics. She asked the students several questions to check their understanding of the material. After she finished her presentation, Ms. Ramirez (special education teacher) organized the students into cooperative learning groups and asked them to describe how their history class would be run under a democracy, dictatorship, or parliamentary government. Ms. Ramirez also planned a trip to the media center later in the week to examine some supplementary materials on the topic. Through cooperative teaching, these teachers provided their students with the essential content as well as supplementary and supportive activities to reinforce, enrich, and supplement the content.

Additional ways of using supportive learning activities include (a) dividing students in two groups with each teacher presenting content to that group, then dividing students into peer-tutoring teams to tutor each other; (b) having one teacher provide small-group instruction while the other monitors the rest of the class; and (c) breaking the class into four groups while the two teachers rotate around the class to provide support or supplementary information (Bauwens & Hourcade, 1997). A final way to use supportive learning activities is by having one teacher work with the majority of the class while other students work at learning centers with the second teacher monitoring and supporting their efforts.

*Complementary Instruction.* Students in intermediate grades, middle school, and high school may have difficulty with some of the skills necessary for school success, such as organization, studying, test taking, report writing, use of reference materials, and note taking. In the complementary instruction approach to cooperative teaching, general education teachers assume the responsibility for presenting specific content (e.g., science), while special education teachers instruct students in how to access that content by teaching strategies (note taking and test taking) (Bauwens & Hourcade, 1997). Complementary instructional activities are typically worked into a classroom schedule as mini-lessons (Bauwens & Hourcade, 1997).

For example, Ms. Ruiz (special education teacher) spent the first 12 minutes of science class instructing students in note taking. She had the students divide their papers into two columns. Next, she showed them how to write the science teacher's key words and points on the left side of the page during the teacher's presentation. Then she showed them how to summarize the teacher's notes and jot down questions on the right side of the page after the presentation. While Mr. Peterson (science teacher) presented some information on ecosystems, Ms. Ruiz took notes so that she would have a model to show the students later. Mr. Peterson stopped about 20 minutes before the end of class so that he and Ms. Ruiz could circulate and give feedback to the students about their note-taking content and technique. Then Ms. Ruiz showed her notes to the class on the overhead projector. With this type of cooperative teaching, students are presented with strategies to access content directly and, therefore, generalization is facilitated.

## Barriers to and Ingredients of Effective Collaborative Consultation

Although collaboration has many benefits as a service option, a number of barriers may interfere with its effectiveness (Bondy & Brownell, 1997; Idol, 1988; Mitchell, 1997; Tindal, Shinn, & Rodden-Nord, 1990). In this section, we discuss some of the barriers to collaboration and provide suggestions for overcoming them.

1. PROBLEM: *Insufficient time and overwhelming caseloads*

   Lack of time is frequently cited as a barrier to developing interactive relationships (Pugach & Johnson, 1995; Tindal et al., 1990) and may

▼ **ACTIVITY 10.5**

Read the following scenario. Work with a partner to complete the scenario using the cooperative planning guide in Figure 10.4.

TENTH-GRADE TEACHER: Beth, thanks for stopping in. I have a problem I need help with.

SPECIAL EDUCATION TEACHER: What seems to be the problem?

TENTH-GRADE TEACHER: Some of the students with learning problems who are included in my third-period class can't seem to write a theme. Every time I assign one, they fail.

SPECIAL EDUCATION TEACHER: What is it about the assignment that is giving them trouble?

TENTH-GRADE TEACHER: Well, they can't seem to write enough. Actually, they can't even write a variety of sentences. In fact, they don't always write complete sentences.

SPECIAL EDUCATION TEACHER: I can see this is a real problem for you. Let me see if I understand the situation. They are having trouble writing themes because they don't know how to write a variety of sentences and sometimes their sentences aren't correct.

TENTH-GRADE TEACHER: Right. I thought maybe you could help me.

be one of the greatest obstacles to collaborative consultative efforts (Idol, 1986). Because of the demands of multiple roles and responsibilities, some teachers state that consultation is just one more thing to do (Evans, 1980; Idol-Maestas & Ritter, 1985; Nowacek, 1992).

SOLUTIONS:

In situations in which cooperative teaching has been implemented, time has not been found to be a problem, perhaps because with more efficient communication, duplication of instruction to students with mild disabilities is minimized (Bauwens et al., 1989). Furthermore, as teachers gain more experience with the roles of consulting teacher and co-teacher, responsibilities may become more evenly distributed. Teachers who participate as members of collaborative consultation teams, as they do in prereferral intervention and teacher assistance teams, may initially find the procedures time consuming; however, with increased use, these structured procedures may expedite decisions about students. Finally, school administrators can play an important part in easing the time and scheduling problems of teachers. Administrators may help alleviate the time problem by providing adequate planning and scheduling time for teachers and by assigning concurrent preparation periods to those who need them. West and Idol (1990) report several strategies for increasing consulting time that have been successfully used in elementary and secondary settings. We present an adapted version of their work in Table 10.3.

2. PROBLEM: *Lack of administrative support*

Lack of administrative support was found to be the major barrier to developing and

**Table 10.3** Strategies for Increasing Consulting Time

1. Have the principal or other support staff member teach a period each day on a regular basis.
2. Cluster students for independent assignments and study activities in large rooms with fewer staff supervising.
3. Ask a business or community organization that has adopted your school to supply a permanent floating (no cost) substitute.
4. Use teaching assistants or volunteers to supervise at lunch and as classes change.
5. Ask the principal to assign a specific time each week for professionals to collaborate.
6. Use part of regularly scheduled in-service days for collaborative teams to meet, or designate a half day each month without students (third Monday afternoon of each month) to use for collaboration.

Note: "Collaborative Consultation in the Education of Mildly Handicapped and At-Risk Students" by J.F. West and L. Idol, 1990, *Remedial and Special Education, 11*(1), p.30. Copyright 1990 by PRO-ED, Inc. Reprinted by permission.

implementing consultation efforts between general classroom and special education teachers (Nelson & Stevens, 1981). Administrative support is necessary for effective consultation programs (Idol-Maestas & Ritter, 1985) and for designing and implementing consultation efforts (Phillips & McCullough, 1990).

SOLUTIONS:

School administrators can create a climate in which collaborative consultation is valued. Their involvement in promoting consultation, controlling caseloads, providing adequate time for consultation, financing programs, facilitating teachers' efforts, breaking down barriers, and addressing implementation issues is crucial to the success of consultation-based programming. Teachers should share their ideas and suggestions for how to schedule cooperative planning time with their principals, provide incentives and support for teachers engaged in consultation, and solve implementation issues. Active involvement of teachers in planning and decision making helps increase collaboration (Rozenholtz, Basler, & Hoover-Dempsey, 1985) and ensures ownership (Duke, Showers, & Imber, 1980) and implementation (Fullan & Pomfret, 1977). When administrators include teachers from the initial planning stage through implementation and evaluation, they significantly increase support for new programs. Platt and Olson (1997) provide the following suggestions for school administrators:

▶ Promote a climate that is conducive to collaboration.
▶ Take a leadership role in promoting collaborative consultation, and model collaboration for faculty and staff.
▶ Have a clear understanding of the basic principles of collaborative consultation and facilitate similar understanding by others (by providing speakers, written information, visits to other sites, and ample opportunities for dialogue).

▶ Develop an awareness of probable road-blocks to consultative efforts and effective solutions for managing them.

▶ From the beginning, include faculty and staff in participatory planning and decision making and secure their ownership.

▶ Provide necessary staff development training for all participants.

▶ Know how to plan, finance, implement, and evaluate collaborative consultation.

▶ Provide incentives and support for professionals engaging in collaborative consultation. (p. 174)

3. PROBLEM: *Differences in background and areas of expertise*

Historically, the roles and responsibilities of special and general educators have been different. Phillips and McCullough (1990) cited a lack of understanding between general and special educators in regard to each other's roles. In fact, general and special education teachers may have very different priorities. According to Glatthorn (1990), "the special education teacher is more often concerned with one student and how learning might be individualized; the classroom teacher worries about the entire class and how overall achievement might be advanced. The special education teacher tends to be concerned with developing a wide range of learning and coping skills; the classroom teacher focuses on academic skills and content" (p. 307). The beliefs general and special educators have about each other may pose barriers to collaboration (Bondy, Ross, Sindelar, & Griffin, 1995) and may cause each to question the credibility of the other.

SOLUTIONS:

The options for implementing collaborative consultation, such as consulting teacher or co-teacher, may reverse negative attitudes, misunderstandings, and resistance. Combining a professional who possesses knowledge in curriculum, content, and large-group instruction with a professional who is skilled in adapting instructional materials and implementing effective teaching strategies may enhance the progress of all students. Once teachers experience the power of collaboration, they will not view their differences as weaknesses, but as strengths. The competencies presented in Table 10.4 are derived from the work of Friend and Cook (1992); Idol, Paolucci-Whitcomb, and Nevin (1994); Little (1982); and Platt and Olson (1997). They represent the types of technical skills and personal qualities that are likely to facilitate effective collaboration for all professionals regardless of field, background, and training.

4. PROBLEM: *Lack of knowledge about collaborative consultation and the change process*

Training is necessary to deal effectively with change in the educational setting. Pre-service and in-service teachers should be given opportunities to develop these skills, as most individuals do not develop them automatically.

SOLUTIONS:

As we mentioned earlier in the chapter, training in collaboration is a must if we expect teachers to serve in collaborative roles (Berdine & Cegeika, 1995; Erchul & Conoley, 1991; Gersten, Darch, David, & George, 1991). Comprehensive training programs should be available at pre-service and in-service levels for general and special education teachers and school administrators. For teachers, the training should include, but not be limited to, clarification of roles, consultation skills, techniques for adapting to change (Idol, 1988), and peer coaching skills. For administrators, training should include, but not be limited to, role and responsibility clarification, techniques for implementing change, awareness of barriers to implementation, strategies for promoting and implementing school consultation (Idol, 1988), and coaching skills.

**Table 10.4**  The Top 10 Technical Skills and Personal Qualities of Effective Collaborators

| *Technical Skills* | *Personal Qualities* |
|---|---|
| *Effective collaborators typically know how to* | *Effective collaborators typically are* |
| 1. Manage resistance | 1. Respected by others |
| 2. Facilitate change | 2. Socially competent |
| 3. Resolve conflict | 3. Warm, sensitive, understanding |
| 4. Adapt curriculum and instruction | 4. Flexible |
| 5. Use principles of effective instruction | 5. Risk-takers |
| 6. Manage the learning environment | 6. Knowledgeable and experienced |
| 7. Use effective communication skills | 7. Good listeners |
| 8. Monitor student progress | 8. Confident |
| 9. Work as a member of a team | 9. Able to think on their feet |
| 10. Engage in problem solving | 10. Energetic |

Note: From Platt, J., and Olson, J., *Teaching Adolescents With Mild Disabilities*, 1997, Brooks/Cole Publishing Company, Pacific Grove, CA. Reprinted by permission of Wadsworth Publishing Company.

Studies indicate that people move through specific stages when adapting to change. Hall and Hord (1984) report seven stages: (1) awareness ("I'm really not involved that much."), (2) informational ("Tell me more."), (3) personal ("What is my role going to be?"), (4) management ("How will I implement this?"), (5) consequence ("Let's see how this is going to impact . . ."), (6) collaboration ("By cooperating on this we can . . ."), and (7) refocusing ("This has worked well, but I have a suggestion for making it even better."). Teachers and administrators need training in consultation-based programming and in adapting to change. Once consultation-based programming has been established, ongoing training and support are essential to maintain it. Effective support strategies include observation, practice, experimentation, feedback, formation of support teams, and peer coaching (Joyce & Showers, 1983).

5. PROBLEM: *Differences and difficulties in communication*

Special education teachers may use a communication code not easily understood by general education teachers. Teachers of students with special needs may use abbreviations such as LRE, IEP, FAPE, WRAT, ITP, CRT, and CBM, unaware that classroom teachers may not understand them. This may pose a major barrier to effective communication (Stamm, 1980).

SOLUTIONS:

Use a shared language to communicate about students and school-related activities. This may help strengthen the bond that should exist among professionals who share responsibility for the same students. Suggestions for enhancing communication include:

▶ Using a common language that is easily understood by all participants (avoiding jargon, abbreviations, and vocabulary specific to one person's experiential background, but not to others') (Platt & Olson, 1997).

▶ Using effective communication techniques, which we described earlier in the chapter, such as active listening, reflective statements, nonverbal techniques, questions, and adequate verbal space.

▶ Showing respect for others' knowledge, valuing their expertise, and pooling the talents of all team members (Platt & Olson, 1997).

▶ Developing an attitude of shared ownership for ideas and activities, and assuming joint responsibility, accountability, and recognition for problem resolution (Phillips & McCullough, 1990).

 **ACTIVITY 10.6**

Examine the following statements made by general education teachers about collaborative consultation. In a group, brainstorm ways of responding to these concerns:

1. "I don't have time for all those meetings. I have too much to do."
2. "When will I plan with the special education teacher? She has planning during sixth period and I have it during fourth."
3. "I don't understand all those terms they use in special education."
4. "There's too much paperwork. How will I keep up?"
5. "How will these collaborative consultation procedures help my students?"

 **IMPORTANT POINTS** ◄

1. Options for implementing collaborative consultation include teacher assistance teams, prereferral intervention, coaching, consulting teacher, and cooperative teaching.
2. The teacher assistance team is a support system for teachers that provides opportunities for brainstorming solutions to problems in order to develop alternatives for students referred to the team.
3. In prereferral intervention, a consultant or team collaborates with a teacher to define a problem, explore intervention strategies, try them out, and evaluate the outcomes.
4. Coaching involves individuals helping each other improve skills or practices through self-reflection.
5. Cognitive coaching is a nonjudgmental process that includes a planning conference, an observation, and a reflecting conference.

6. Consulting teaching is conducted in general education classrooms and involves providing support services to teachers and students to prevent or ameliorate students' academic or social behavior problems.
7. Co-teaching is an approach in which general and special educators work together and jointly teach academically and behaviorally heterogeneous groups of students in educationally integrated settings.
8. Barriers to effective collaborative consultation include insufficient time and overwhelming caseloads, lack of administrative support, differences in background and areas of expertise, preparation in collaborative consultation and the change process, and differences and difficulties in communication.
9. Ingredients of effective collaborative consultation include administrative support, teams, peer coaching, and use of a shared language with general educators.

# COLLABORATION WITH PARAPROFESSIONALS

Today's teachers are asked to work with increasingly diverse learners in their classrooms including students with disabilities who have a wide range of needs (Stanovich, 1996) and second-language learners who pose challenges for school personnel to provide links between home and school languages and cultures (Miramontes, 1990). The efforts in special education to expand services to students with disabilities by including them in general education classrooms along with changes in the Individuals with Disabilities Act (IDEA) have prompted increased participation of paraprofessionals as facilitators of instructional and behavioral support (Wadsworth & Knight, 1996; Wallace, Shin,

Bartholomay, & Stahl, 2001) and members of the educational team.

## Definitions

According to the National Joint Committee on Learning Disabilities (NJCLD, 1999):

> Paraprofessionals are employees who, following appropriate academic education/instruction and/or on-the-job training, perform tasks as prescribed, directed, and supervised by fully qualified professionals. Job titles for paraprofessionals may include terms such as "aide," "assistant," "associate," "paraeducator," "instructional assistant," and "classroom aide," among others. The intent of using paraprofessionals is to supplement not supplant the work of the teacher/service provider.(p. 24).

Pickett (1986) has defined a paraprofessional as "a person whose position is either instructional in nature or who delivers direct services to students and/or their parents; and who serves in a position for which a teacher or another professional has ultimate responsibility for the design and implementation of individual education programs or other services" (p. 2). Therefore, in addition to the job titles given in the NJCLD definition, the paraprofessional could also be a job coach, recreation aide, mental health worker, human service technician, or home or community liaison (Blalock, 1991). Throughout the text, we use the terms *paraprofessional*, *paraeducator*, and *assistant* interchangeably, as we do *professional*, *teacher*, and *service provider*.

## Growth of Paraprofessionals

Over the last several years, the substantial growth in the use of paraprofessionals in special education has had a positive impact on the delivery of services to students with disabilities (Blalock, 1991; Pickett, 1988). A typical urban district is likely to employ 80% of its paraprofessionals in special education and related services with the remaining hired in bilingual, remedial, and general education (Blalock, 1991). Pickett (1996) indicates that, among the many reasons for employing paraprofessionals, the main reason is to improve the quality of education and other services to students and their parents/families.

The phenomenal growth rate of paraprofessionals has been attributed to (a) the high marks that paraprofessionals have received in serving exceptional students (Frith, Lindsey, & Edwards, 1981; Killoran, Templeman, Peters, & Udell, 2001); (b) the ability of paraprofessionals to work with a wide range of exceptionalities in a variety of settings (Frith & Lindsey, 1980; Stanovich, 1996; Wadsworth & Knight, 1996); (c) the improvement of teacher–pupil ratios (Skelton, 1997), thus providing a cost-effective manner to extend the impact of professionals (Blalock, 1991); (d) the changing roles of paraprofessionals from performing routine clerical and housekeeping tasks to providing instructional support, assisting with functional assessment activities, administering tests, and observing and documenting student performance (Blalock, 1991; Evans & Evans, 1986; Miramontes, 1990); and (e) the introduction of various reform initiatives and/or legislation such as the Individuals with Disabilities Education Act (IDEA) mandating that states provide services to students in the least restrictive environment and provide transition services; Goals 2000: Educate America Act of 1994 requiring states to set professional development standards for educational personnel; and Title I of the Elementary and Secondary Education Act of 1994, which has guidelines for the preparation of teaching assistants (Pickett & Gerlach, 1997). Case (1986) found that 98% of paraprofessionals interviewed believed that their presence in the classroom enabled teachers to attend better to the individual needs of students. This was supported in another study that illustrated that paraprofessionals feel they make a positive difference in special education classrooms and that teachers are satisfied with their performance (Frank, Keith, & Steil, 1988). Some paraprofessionals have reported having full responsibility for planning, supervising, and evaluating students receiving special education services (Stahl & Lorenz, 1995).

Unfortunately, although paraprofessionals have a great deal to offer, their skills are not always accurately identified or utilized to enable them to contribute in a meaningful way (McKenzie & Houk, 1986). Training and supervision have been informal, haphazard, or nonexistent (French, 2001; Hilton & Gerlach, 1997), and placement decisions have not always been made systematically. Blalock (1991) reports that many schools are not providing training at all for paraprofessionals, which is contrary to what is recommended in the literature. Furthermore, pre-service and in-service programs rarely prepare teachers to work with paraprofessionals in a manner that will result in improved student performance (Wallace et al., 2001), nor do they provide instruction in supervision (NJCLD, 1999). Therefore, it is necessary to examine ways to improve current practices and maximize the positive effects that these important members of the educational team can have on students.

## Planning Paraprofessional Programs

There are certain aspects that merit consideration in best utilizing the skills and talents of paraprofessionals to meet the needs of teachers and students. They include matching skills with needs, utilizing paraprofessionals with culturally and linguistically diverse populations, and defining role expectations/responsibilities.

### Matching Skills With Needs

From time to time, you may overhear special education teachers discussing their needs, such as "I could really use some help assisting students with their computer searches" or "I am trying to get my class checked out on their job application and job interview competencies, but it's impossible to do by myself." You may also hear a general education teacher say "I like the idea of including students with disabilities in my classroom, but it would be helpful to have assistance in monitoring student progress and providing more immediate feedback." A paraprofessional should be placed with a teacher whose needs and expectations match the skills of the paraprofessional (McKenzie & Houk, 1986). Frank, Keith, and Steil (1988) found that paraprofessionals need to possess different competencies based on the educational setting in which they are working.

The activities assigned to a paraprofessional should be determined by a teacher or service provider based on the education, skills, and interests of the paraprofessional (NJCLD, 1999). McKenzie and Houk (1986) suggest the use of an inventory to be completed by both the teacher and paraprofessional. Teachers can use the inventory to identify the types of support they need, and paraprofessionals can use it to indicate their skills and interests. In this way, a paraprofessional who is skilled at the modification of materials and the adaptation of lessons is assigned to help a teacher make these kinds of adjustments, whereas someone with effective instructional skills and good rapport with students is assigned to a teacher who needs someone to go over vocabulary with the students, monitor progress during practice activities in an inclusive setting, or help students review for tests. Those with skills in monitoring, collecting data, and providing feedback could assist with the reintegration of students to general education classrooms or help students make the transition into work settings. Special education teachers who are co-teaching with general education teachers could enlist the assistance of a paraprofessional in preparing study guides, tape-recording portions of textbooks, and developing supplementary activities. Figure 10.7 contains an inventory that we have adapted from the work of McKenzie and Houk (1986).

**Figure 10.7**   Inventory of Paraprofessional Skills and Teacher Needs

---

Name _____   Date _____

*Directions:*   Listed below are tasks that a paraprofessional may perform. If you are a paraprofessional, mark with a "P" those activities/duties that you feel you could conduct. If you are a teacher, mark with a "T" those areas in which you would like to use a paraprofessional.

**Instructional Support**
1. ____ Reinforce concepts already presented by the teacher, collaborate with teacher in planning and scheduling.
2. ____ Develop materials (e.g., study guides, chapter outlines).
3. ____ Supervise independent or small-group work.
4. ____ Modify written materials, adapt lessons to address specific learning needs.
5. ____ Assist students with projects or assignments.
6. ____ Help students with computer assignments.
7. ____ Practice vocabulary with second-language learners.
   ____ Other. Please describe.

**Behavior Management Support**
8. ____ Assist teacher in implementing classroom management strategies.
9. ____ Monitor and record student progress.
10. ____ Provide feedback.
   ____ Other. Please describe.

**Assessment Support**
11. ____ Correct and grade assigned activities.
12. ____ Observe and record academic behavior and progress.
13. ____ Observe and record social behavior.
14. ____ Administer informal assessments, such as unit tests and criterion-referenced measures.
   ____ Other. Please describe.

**Classroom Organization**
15. ____ Make instructional games.
16. ____ Develop and manage learning centers.
17. ____ Prepare displays.
18. ____ Locate instructional materials.
19. ____ Assist in daily planning.
20. ____ Make bulletin boards.
   ____ Other. Please describe.

**Clerical and Other Support**
21. ____ Prepare materials.
22. ____ Take attendance.
23. ____ Record grades.
24. ____ Check and maintain equipment.
25. ____ Supervise during non-instruction time (e.g., bus, recess).
   ____ Other. Please describe.

---

Note: Adapted from "Paraprofessionals in Special Education" (p. 249) by R. G. McKenzie and C. S. Houk, 1986, *Teaching Exceptional Children,* 19(4). Reprinted by permission.

### Utilizing Paraprofessionals With Culturally and Linguistically Diverse Populations

Teachers are expected to possess the knowledge, skills, and experience to be effective with students from increasingly diverse cultural, linguistic, and socioeconomic backgrounds (Ortiz & Garcia, 1989; Stanovich, 1996). Therefore, it is helpful to have a paraprofessional who can work effectively with culturally and linguistically diverse groups and can speak multiple languages. Miramontes (1990) recommends the selection and training of paraprofessionals who can provide links between the students' home and school languages and cultures, make home visits, act as translators at staffings, and serve as tutors to help with special education interventions.

Paraprofessionals can and have assisted non-English-speaking students and students from culturally diverse backgrounds (Miramontes, 1990). One of the authors of this textbook set up a program that utilized volunteers to work individually and in small groups with students to teach them to speak English. Through the volunteers, the students were able to share some of their culture, language, and customs with their peers. It is an asset to have an assistant who can explain in two languages something about the diversity within cultures and who can create learning activities compatible with student characteristics and interests.

Another way to involve assistants in ensuring that students from culturally and linguistically diverse backgrounds succeed is to have them develop multisensory teaching aids, such as games, computer programs, and multimedia in which material can be learned in a variety of ways. Assistants may also help you monitor diversified grouping patterns, such as cooperative learning and peer tutoring. These instructional arrangements allow more students to participate, regardless of their cultural and linguistic backgrounds.

### Defining Role Expectations and Responsibilities

The lack of a clear job description appears to be one of the problems most commonly experienced by paraprofessionals. In fact, the greatest frustration between professionals and paraprofessionals is the lack of specificity regarding roles and responsibilities (Blalock, 1993). According to Frith and Mims (1985), "Paraprofessionals who possess a realistic perception of what is expected of them are more likely to perform admirably and to be more satisfied with their work" (p. 226). Teachers should clearly specify what the teaching assistant is expected to do within the areas of instruction, behavior management, assessment, classroom organization, and clerical support. As you can see from Figure 10.8, a paraprofessional can accomplish many tasks in the special education setting and in the general education classroom. The key is careful communication of tasks, roles, expectations, and responsibilities.

Carefully specifying role expectations and responsibilities may also help prevent the awkward situation of a teaching assistant who tries to assume a supervisory role. Regularly scheduled conferences in which you and your assistant talk about student progress, clerical activities, development or modification of materials, and scheduling are ideal for reviewing and clarifying the assistant's assignments and responsibilities. Some teachers prepare a written schedule each day for their assistants, in order to clarify roles and responsibilities. Praising and reinforcing your assistant for performing agreed-upon assignments is an effective way to ensure that these, and not other, assignments are carried out.

## Implementing Paraprofessional Programs

There are several things to consider when organizing a paraprofessional program. To implement the program effectively, you should include orientation and training, clarification of expectations, scheduling, communication, feedback, and evaluation.

### Orientation and Training

Before beginning employment as a paraprofessional, Blalock (1991) recommends that individuals attend an orientation to learn about the

**Figure 10.8**   Example of a Paraprofessional's Schedule

| | Monday | Tuesday | Wednesday | Thursday | Friday |
|---|---|---|---|---|---|
| 8:00–8:30 | Plan with special education teacher. | → | | | |
| 8:30–10:30 | Assist with small-group instruction in reading in pull-out program and monitor independent work. | → | | | |
| 10:30–11:30 | Monitor student progress in 4th-grade language arts class. | Monitor student progress in 5th-grade math class. | Monitor student progress in 3rd-grade reading class. | Monitor student progress in 2nd grade in process writing. | Monitor student progress in 1st-grade reading class. |
| 11:30–12:30 | Make study guides for 5th-grade social studies class. | Make reading games for 3rd-grade class. | Adapt materials in science for 4th-grade class. | Adapt materials in social studies text for 5th-grade class. | Make chapter outlines for 6th-grade math class. |
| 12:30–1:00 | Lunch | → | | | |
| 1:00–2:00 | Assist teacher in monitoring cooperative learning groups in math in pull-out program. | Assist in whole language in pull-out program. | Assist in math in pull-out program. | Assist in whole language in pull-out program. | Assist in math in pull-out program. |
| 2:00–2:45 | Work one-to-one with specific students in pull-out program. | → | | | |
| 2:45–3:15 | Assist in supervising peer-tutoring arrangements in 6th grade. | Check student folders in pull-out program. | Assist in supervising peer-tutoring arrangements in 6th grade. | Check and update files in pull-out program. | Assist in supervising peer-tutoring arrangements in 6th grade. |
| 3:15–3:30 | Meet with special education teacher to review and plan. | → | | | |

types of programs, individuals who will be served, roles and responsibilities, and physical sites. Lindsey (1983) suggests that paraprofessionals attend an initial meeting with other members of the school faculty and staff. Such a meeting should include the following activities: (a) introductions, (b) definition of the paraprofessional's role, (c) distribution of information about assessment and instructional techniques, (d) audiovisual presentations, (e) simulations, and (f) a question-and-answer session. An initial session may include discussions about confidentiality, rules, and school procedures. Then a general orientation from a building-level administrator may occur, followed by specific training by a teacher or other service provider.

Training is necessary at the outset and on an ongoing basis (Blalock, 1991; Demchak & Morgan, 1998; Hilton & Gerlach, 1997; Wadsworth & Knight, 1996). Training may be provided in the classroom by the teacher and in separate training workshops as needed. Separate training sessions may focus on topics such as how to work with culturally diverse populations, work in co-teaching situations, teach learning strategies and study skills, implement cooperative learning activities, use effective questioning, or work effectively in inclusive settings. Lindsey (1983) suggests providing ongoing in-service activities to maintain the diagnostic, instructional, and interpersonal relationship competencies of the paraprofessional and recommends monthly staff meetings to provide support.

### Clarification of Expectations

Once a teacher and paraprofessional clarify expectations, they should decide on (a) the specific tasks the paraprofessional will complete (e.g., collecting data on students' knowledge of multiplication facts), (b) the skills necessary to accomplish the tasks (e.g., charting and graphing), and (c) any training or modeling of strategies that would help the paraprofessional complete the tasks (e.g., strategies for monitoring students' performance). For example, if a paraprofessional were going to help a teacher make data-based decisions about a student's learning by using precision teaching to monitor progress, he or she would need specific training or instruction in how to use it. McKenzie and Houk (1986) suggest developing a plan that specifies the skills a paraprofessional must have in order to accomplish the tasks assigned. The plan should indicate exactly how the paraprofessional will acquire the skills, such as through on-the-job training, in-service workshops, or by reading information on the topic.

### Scheduling

Once identified, the tasks or job descriptions may be written on a task sheet (Salvia & Hughes, 1990) or schedule (see Figure 10.8). Daily and weekly schedules are helpful in clarifying assignments and structuring the activities of an assistant. This is an important point: What is written

down is more likely to be accomplished than what is just mentioned. You may have encountered this when you made a to-do list in the morning compared with when you had ideas in your mind of things you wanted to do that day. On which day did you accomplish more?

The responsibilities of a paraprofessional should change as the classroom needs change. For example, during the month of September, Ms. Hernando's students were preparing for a young author's conference to be held in October. Ms. Hernando's teaching assistant, Ms. Talbot, helped students write stories, complete illustrations, prepare them in final form on the computer, and bind them in covers. During late October, Ms. Talbot helped students prepare for their end-of-the-quarter exams. She made sets of review cards with questions on the front and answers on the back. Her responsibilities changed because the needs of the students and classroom changed.

### Communication and Feedback

"On-going communication between professionals and paraprofessionals is vital to their collaborative relationship and to positive educational outcomes for students" (Demchak & Morgan, 1998, p. 13). It is important for professionals and paraprofessionals to schedule regular meetings (Blalock, 1991) each day if possible (Kahn, 1981). The meeting can be used to discuss student progress, make modifications and adjustments in instructional and behavior management programs, or revise the paraprofessional's job responsibilities.

Professionals should make a point of providing both positive and corrective feedback to their paraprofessionals. Ms. Brizo provided positive feedback to her paraprofessional, Ms. Grant, by reinforcing her work on the many multicultural activities she had developed as part of their learning center on famous American poets. On another occasion, when they were having a weekly planning session, Ms. Brizo noticed that Ms. Grant had left out some information on a chapter outline that she had been developing for some of the sixth graders. Ms. Brizo showed Ms. Grant a new technique to use in pulling the essential information out of a chapter. Ms. Grant used the technique to rework the outline, and Ms. Brizo gave her feedback and reinforcement for her work.

### Evaluation

Effective programs for paraprofessionals include an evaluation component. Paraprofessional competence is often documented through performance evaluations, direct observation, work samples, and videotapes (Killoran, Templeman, Peters, & Udell, 2001). The greater the specificity of the assistant's duties and the greater the structure in identifying the tasks in writing, the easier it is to evaluate performance. If paraprofessionals are to provide services to students with special needs, then teachers must provide them with adequate training and supervision, clarify their roles, schedule their time effectively, and give them ample feedback and recognition.

For readers who desire a more in depth study of paraprofessionals, we refer you to the work of Anna Lou Pickett and Kent Gerlach. Anna Lou Pickett is the Director of the National Resource Center for Paraprofessionals in Education and Related Services in New York, and Kent Gerlach is at Pacific Lutheran University in Tacoma, Washington.

## COLLABORATION WITH OTHER PARTNERS

Throughout this chapter, we have focused on collaboration with parents/families, general educators, and paraprofessionals. However, a variety of other partners are critical for the success of school and community programs (Blalock, 1997). These partners include administrators (e.g., principals, assistant principals), other teachers or specialists (e.g., Chapter 1, bilingual, transition specialists),

 **ACTIVITY 10.7**

**Part 1:**   You are a teacher of students with special needs at the elementary level. Several of your students are integrated into general education classrooms for math and reading. Make a list of the ways you would utilize the skills of a paraprofessional to help these students in the general education classroom.

**Part 2:**   You are a teacher of secondary students with special needs. You work with your students in school in the morning and in the community by supervising them on the job in the afternoon. In what ways could you utilize a paraprofessional in these situations?

related service providers (e.g., speech/language pathologists, counselors, school psychologists, occupational and physical therapists, and assistive technology specialists), community and state agency personnel, and job coaches. The key to success in working effectively with these and other partners is through communication and collaboration. Many of the techniques and procedures we have suggested that you use with teachers, paraprofessionals, and parents/families will work effectively with these partners as well. In particular, see our suggestions for administrators in the section of this chapter on barriers to and ingredients of effective collaboration. In addition, we have included an example of the desired qualities of an exemplary collaboration inspired by the work of Hunt (1995). We believe that these seven suggestions (Table 10.5) can be used in collaborative interactions with all partners.

 **IMPORTANT POINTS** ◀

1. The use of paraprofessionals in special education has grown substantially, and this growth has positively affected the delivery of services to students with special needs.

**Table 10.5**  Desired Qualities of
an Exemplary Collaboration

1. Unconditional support based on shared goals, mutual decision making with the agreement to disagree.
2. Positive attitudes and interactions combined with mutual respect among partners/collaborators.
3. Shared responsibility and no-fault teaming.
4. A total commitment by the partners to resolve problems/conflict.
5. Team spirit that is enhanced by building on existing strengths and skills of partners.
6. Professional development and support of partners to learn and grow.
7. Ongoing, positive interactions with the community.

2. A paraprofessional, sometimes called a teaching/educational assistant or paraeducator, is a person who either instructs or delivers direct services to students and/or their parents, and who serves in a position for which a teacher or other professional has ultimate responsibility for the design and implementation of IEPs and other services.
3. The use of paraprofessionals is to supplement, not supplant, the work of the teacher/service provider.
4. In planning paraprofessional programs, it is important to (a) match the skills of the paraprofessional with the needs of the teacher, (b) examine ways to utilize the skills of paraprofessionals in working with culturally and linguistically diverse populations, and (c) clearly define role expectations and responsibilities.
5. Implementation of paraprofessional programs should include (a) orientation and training, (b) clarification of expectations, (c) scheduling, (d) communication and feedback, and (e) evaluation.
6. A variety of other partners are critical for the success of school and community programs, including administrators, other teachers or specialists, related service providers, community and state agency personnel, or job coaches.

 **DISCUSSION QUESTIONS** ◀

1. Discuss the impact of coaching on collaborative interactions among teachers, administrators, and other school professionals.
2. Give examples of the verbal and nonverbal communication skills that you, as a teacher, feel would be most effective in the following situations:
   a. The planning conference, the observation, and the reflecting conference involved in cognitive coaching.
   b. A feedback session with a paraprofessional.
   c. A meeting with parents who are concerned about their child's progress.

# CHAPTER 11

# TECHNOLOGY FOR TEACHING AND LEARNING

*by Colleen Klein and Dan Ezell*

## KEY TOPICS

The use of technology is widespread in classrooms at all levels—as a tool for teachers to develop, monitor, and provide instruction and as a tool for students to access and engage in learning. Today technologies play a critical role in the education of all students, including students with disabilities. Technology can offer students with disabilities alternative ways to showcase their capabilities and can provide teachers with tools to enhance their instruction and support student learning (Lewis, 2000). Unmotivated students suddenly become interested in the task of writing a friendly letter when given the option of using a word processing program and adding graphics. Students whose spelling problems interfered with their writing skills are suddenly turning in papers free of spelling errors.

The purpose of this chapter is to focus on technology as a tool for students and teachers. We first examine the legislation that promoted the use of technology. We next discuss technology tools as powerful enablers that help students access curriculum, engage in learning, meet required outcomes, and transition to the workplace. Then, we discuss technology tools as an integral part of the curriculum to support effective instructional interventions. Finally, we describe assistive technology tools that make a positive impact on the lives of children and adolescents.

We include computers, videocassettes, and the Internet plus assistive technology devices in our discussion of technology applications. Roblyer (1989) suggests that teachers use technology in the curriculum when the content or skills (a) are difficult for students to understand, (b) present hurdles such as too much calculation or handwriting that interfere with or are irrelevant to the main objective of the lesson, (c) require extensive homework, and (d) are tedious or uninteresting.

A caveat in writing any chapter on technology is the impossibility of presenting current information, as technology is always changing. Two months later, that powerful computer is no longer so powerful, as another computer is on the market with more RAM (random access memory) and faster processor speeds (megahertz). The Internet site that last month provided you with valuable lesson plans and information has disappeared. Please remember this caveat as you read the chapter and continue to stay current by reading professional journals, participating in professional organizations, visiting new Web sites, and taking technology classes.

## TECHNOLOGY LEGISLATION

Legislation was instrumental in promoting the use of technology tools for children and adolescents with disabilities. PL 99–457, Part G of the Education for All Handicapped Children Act of 1986, authorized the Technology, Educational Media, and Materials Program for Individuals with Disabilities to research and develop technology tools for students with disabilities (Hauser & Malouf, 1996). PL 100–407, the Technology-Related Assistance for Individuals with Disabilities Act (Tech Act) of 1988 was designed to enhance the availability and quality of assistive technology (AT) devices and services to all individuals and their families throughout the United States (Behrmann, 1995). The Assistive Technology Act of 1998 (AT Act), PL 105–394 (S.2432), replaced the Tech Act and created discretionary activities for states to fund, such as alternative financing systems to increase access to assistive technology. In addition, provisions of the AT Act included promoting public awareness; providing technical assistance, training, and outreach; and promoting interagency collaboration.

The Technology Education and Copyright Harmonization Act of 2002 (TEACH Act) allows teachers and faculty to use copyrighted materials in the "digital classroom" without prior permission from the copyright holder as long as certain measures are met. Additional information about the inclusions and exclusions of the TEACH Act may be found at http://www.ala.org/washoff/teach.html. See Table 11.1 for a summary of legislation affecting assistive technology.

## TECHNOLOGY AS A SUPPORT FOR THE CURRICULUM

In an adaptation of Means' (1997) classification scheme for technologies, we suggest the broad categories of traditional, exploratory, tool, and communication applications. Although these categories are not mutually exclusive, they highlight the differences in instructional applications.

### Traditional Applications

Tutorial, drill and practice, simulation, and problem solving are examples of traditional applications of software. This use of software represents the traditional view of learning where information is transmitted to the student.

#### *Tutorial Programs*
Tutorials are designed to teach new concepts and skills. They may be simple to very complex in design. They may be linear, with all students completing the same program, although the pace may be different for each student. More complex programs may offer multiple branching opportunities, with different responses taking students to different parts of the program for review, remediation, or advanced information. Good interactive tutorials can provide students with disabilities the kind of individual instruction that matches learner needs to a specific concept or skill.

#### *Drill and Practice Programs*
Drill and practice programs give students opportunities to practice skills and concepts.

**Table 11.1** Federal Legislation that Applies to Assistive Technology

| *Legislation* | *Date* | *Basic Content Related to Assistive Technology (AT)* |
|---|---|---|
| Rehabilitation Act 93–112 | 1973 | Reasonable accommodations and LRE mandated in federally funded employment and higher education—AT devices and services required |
| Vocational Rehabilitation Act, section 504 | 1973 | AT can be used as an accommodation to allow individuals with disabilities who are not in special education programs to take part in activities |
| Education for All Handicapped Children Act (EHA) 94–142 | 1975 | Reasonable accommodations and LRE are extended to all school age children, IEP mandated, AT plays a major role in gaining access to educational programs |
| Preschool and Infant/Toddler Program (amendments to EHA) | 1986 | Reasonable accommodations and LRE are extended to children ages 3–5, expands emphasis on educationally related assistive technologies |
| Technology-Related Assistance for Individuals with Disabilities Act (Tech Act) 100–407 | 1988 | First federal legislation directly related to assistive technology, stresses consumer driven services and systems change, Section 508 extended to all states |
| Reauthorization of the Rehabilitation Act | 1990 | Formally adopted the same definitions and terminology as IDEA, also mandated that rehabilitation technology be seen as "a primary benefit" to be included in the IWRP |
| Americans with Disabilities Act (ADA) 101–336 | 1990 | Provisions including assistive technology are recognized in the areas of public accommodations, private employment, transportation, and telecommunications—extends 503, 504, and 508 to all citizens |
| Individuals with Disabilities Education Act (IDEA) 101–496 | 1990 | Specifically defined assistive technology devices and services as well as carefully delineating how they apply to education |
| IDEA Amendments | 1997 | Assistive technology needs must be considered during the discussions involving a student's IEP—an indication during these discussions that AT might be needed leads to an evaluation of needs |

Note: Adapted from Judith P. Sweeney (2002) http://www.onionmountaintech.com/PDF files/ATLaws. pdf Reprinted by permission.

Good drill and practice programs offer corrections, hints for improvement, and even simple reteaching. They provide immediate feedback and do not allow students to make the same mistakes over and over again. When well designed and used as an integral part of the curriculum, drill and practice programs can help students with disabilities gain fluency in required skills. When poorly designed and used without instructional planning, drill and practice programs can be an inappropriate use of a powerful computer and a student's academic time.

### Simulation Programs

Simulation programs offer students opportunities to see the consequence of their choices. These programs model reality and allow students to use their skills to make decisions and solve problems in a safe learning environment. Well-designed simulation programs provide some of the authentic experiences students need to succeed outside school (e.g., vocational, education, and transition). They may provide opportunities for instruction in settings that may not generally be available in schools.

### Problem-Solving Programs

Problem-solving programs generally give students practice in identifying a problem, finding alternative solutions, selecting appropriate strategies, and evaluating results of the decisions made. Students may need to collect information, take notes, discover patterns, make generalizations, chart data, apply strategies, use inductive or deductive reasoning, or create a product. Some of these programs encourage students to work together in pairs or teams. Problem-solving software can offer students with disabilities the opportunity to develop and apply the higher-order thinking skills that are required for success in school and in the world of work. Although it is critical that students have the prerequisite skills for using the program, teachers need to remember that students with disabilities may be capable of solving more complex problems than their mastery of basic skills indicates.

## Exploratory Applications

Exploratory application software allows the student to navigate through a program and select information for learning. Examples are electronic encyclopedias, atlases, and multimedia databases of animals, plants, people, places, and

things. Today, the ability to access and manage information is a required skill for success in school and in the world of work.

## Tool Applications

These programs include the familiar applications like the word processor, database, and spreadsheet. Here, the technology facilitates the performance of such tasks as writing, organizing, and presenting information. All students and teachers need tools. Students with disabilities may need special tools or need to use common tools in a special way. Technology tools provide access to the curriculum, offer alternative experiences for learning, allow students to demonstrate performance, and provide alternative options for assessment.

## Communication Applications

These applications allow students to send and receive information from anywhere in the world. They include interactive distance learning, e-mail, and electronic field trips. As more schools are connected to the Internet, students with disabilities are getting the opportunity to participate in the technologies that can minimize differences.

 **ACTIVITY 11.1**

Describe when you might use a tutorial program with students and when you might use an exploratory application with students. Share your ideas with a partner.

(Answers for this and other activities are found in the Instructor's Manual.)

## TECHNOLOGY AS A TOOL FOR STUDENTS

Technology advancements such as the widespread availability of digital materials and rapid computer networks coupled with universal design principles are making the general education curriculum more available to students with special needs. The Center for Applied Special Technology (CAST) and the National Center to Improve the Tools of Educators (NCITE) at the University of Oregon have pioneered the application of the principle of universal design to learning. The premise of universally designed learning (UDL) is that instructional materials can be designed so that learning goals may be achieved by individuals, no matter their disability, cultural background, or experiential background.

With technology, accommodations such as reading the text to students, highlighting important words or phrases, controlling the speed of presentation, changing print size, presenting advance and post organizers, and allowing students to record compositions may be built into a text, instead of added as an afterthought. With these accommodations, students with disabilities may interact successfully with the general education curriculum and are no longer stigmatized because they are using different texts or materials than used by their peers without disabilities.

Two software programs that use the principles of universal design are Wiggleworks (Scholastic) and the ULtimate Reader(Universal Learning Technology). With Wiggleworks, an early literacy software program, the text may be enlarged, read aloud, and highlighted, and students may express themselves by typing, drawing, recording, and other ways. With the ULtimate Reader software, any text may be digitized and loaded into the program. Created by CAST, the program provides many accommodations such as adding spoken voice and visual highlights to the electronic text. With the text in digital form, students may accomplish the traditional task of answering questions at the end of the chapter by dragging and dropping whole paragraphs for use in the answer, allowing more time for instruction in higher-order thinking skills. To learn more about UDL, visit the Center for Applied Special Technology (CAST) (http://www.cast.org) or ERIC/OSEP

Special Project for the ERIC Clearinghouse on Disabilities and Gifted Education(ERIC EC) for a topical brief on universal design principles (http://ericec.org/osep/recon5/re5cov.html).

Technology may assist students with mild disabilities in organization, the writing process, productivity, accessibility to reference materials, and cognitive assistance (Lahm & Morrisette, 1994). Each of these areas has a wide range of technology available, from low-tech tools to more sophisticated tools that may require the use of a computer.

## Organization

Your students may benefit from low-tech electronic organizers that are commonly available in office supply and major discount stores. These small, portable planners, referred to as personal digital assistants (PDAs), and the more advanced ones that are referred to as handheld computers can help compensate for poor organizational skills, illegible handwriting, and memory deficits. Students can use a variety of inexpensive PDAs and handheld computers to keep track of homework assignments or due dates for projects, write to-do lists, store short notes or spelling words, consult a calendar, or set an alarm as a cue to perform some task such as stopping to check for understanding. The Web site http://www.k12handhelds.com/apps.php lists 101 educational uses for the handheld computer and has case studies of how teachers are using them in the classroom.

 **ACTIVITY 11.2**

Go to the web site http://www.k12handhelds.com/ apps.php and list 5 education uses for the handheld computer.

High-tech organization tools enable your students to organize and communicate their thoughts with story webs, character charts, tree diagrams, time lines, and other graphic organizers. Two examples of high-tech organization tools are the software programs of Inspiration (Inspiration) and TimeLiner (Tom Snyder Productions). Inspiration allows students to create a picture of ideas or concepts in a diagram (see Figure 11.1). Using TimeLiner, students can print out a visual display of critical dates on a time line.

One of our student teachers assigned students to organize their personal histories or life maps using TimeLiner and then to relate their own time lines to events in American history.

## The Writing Process

Videocassettes, computers, digital cameras, and the Internet are invaluable tools to assist stu-

**Figure 11.1**  Sample Graphic Organizers From Inspiration Software

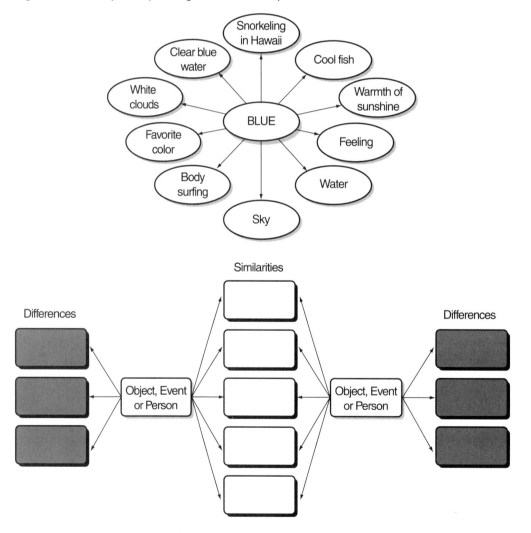

Note: From Inspiration Software, 7412 SW Beaverton, Hillsdale Hwy., Suite 102, Portland, OR 97225. Reprinted by permission.

dents with disabilities in the steps of the writing process: prewriting, writing, editing and revising, and publishing.

In the **prewriting** stage, instead of reading resource books or magazines, students may collect information by clicking on a link to a Web site, viewing a video, using pictures from digital cameras, or inserting a CD-ROM or DVD. For example, in Ms. Zelk's class, students used digital pictures they had taken during a field trip to assist in constructing a story.

In the **writing** stage, instead of paper and pencil, students may use word processing, word predictions, and abbreviation expansion programs. Even young children can begin to use word processors such as ClarisWorks for Kids (Apple Computer, Inc.), Word (Microsoft), and Kid Works 2 (Knowledge Adventure). Using the "Write" command of Wiggleworks software(Scholastic), students may type, record, or place words from a word list into their composition to assist in the writing stage.

Word prediction and abbreviation expansion help students with disabilities compose text and overcome problems with word recall, spelling, and keyboarding. For example, in word prediction, students enter the beginning letters of a desired word. The program produces a list of predicted words that begin with that letter. For example, if the student enters "th," a predicted list might look like:

1. them        4. think
2. then        5. thing
3. their       6. this

When students see or hear the word that they want from the list, they enter the corresponding number, and the word is added to their text. If the word is not on the list, students keep typing the next letter until the word appears.

In programs with abbreviation expansion, a long word or phrase can be coded using a few consonants. When the word or phrase is needed, students type the code, and the full word or phrase is entered into the text. For example, if

Jim is writing a story about Tyrannosaurus rex and doesn't want to type out the word each time, he can type in a code such as TYR, and the full name (Tyrannosaurus rex) will appear in the body of the text. Co:Writer (Don Johnston, Inc.), TypeIt4Me by Riccardo Ettore (Shareware), E Z Keys (Words +, Inc.), and Telepathic II (Madenta Communication, Inc.) are word prediction programs that allow for abbreviation expansion and may be used in conjunction with any word processors.

Students who are struggling with reading or writing may use "talking" word processors during the writing stage. Such programs as Write: Out Loud (Don Johnston, Inc.), Intellitalk II (IntelliTools), and Kid Works Deluxe (Knowledge Adventure) help students make critical connections among saying, writing, and reading words. Students of all ages can enter their own words into the program, hear the computer say them, and print them out to be read.

A technology solution that may help some students overcome difficulties related to the physical process of writing is the portable keyboard. It is a low-cost and lightweight alternative to a computer. Students may type on the portable keyboard conveniently at their desks without laboriously having to go through the process of physically writing letters and words. Several models are available, including the AlphaSmart, DreamWriter, Laser PC6, and the QuickPad. The student turns the keyboard on, does some typing, and turns it off. The system saves several files, which allows for students to share the keyboard. The files will load into any computer word processing file by attaching a cable from the portable word processor to the computer. The student can then use spell check and other features of the word processing software.

AlphaSmart has launched a new affordable laptop alternative called the Dana. The Dana features Palm OS operating system and includes a full-size keyboard and screen. Just like a Personal Digital Assistant you can enter data by writing with the Dana stylus directly on the screen, or, like the AlphaSmart, you can use the keyboard. All Palm applications are compatible, and the Dana is expandable to add memory and devices. The Dana can print to your printer and easily synchronizes data with a computer just like a PDA. The writing stylus feature will be most beneficial to students who have difficulty using traditional keyboards.

Smith, Boone, and Higgins (1998) suggest that during the **revision** and **editing** stages, students paste their word processed story into a Web publishing program called Home Page (Claris Corporation). Next, they select graphics and create a hypertext link to other Web sites. They also e-mail their draft to other students or to experts for help in the revising process. In their example, Smith and colleagues (1998) relate how Billy, at this stage, selects the word *skull* from his story and links the word to a Web site that has a picture of a dinosaur's head. When the teacher and his peers read Billy's story, they may click on the underlined word *skull* and see the close-up picture of the head of the dinosaur from another Web site. Spelling and grammar check programs are also invaluable at this step.

The **publishing** stage provides for an exciting use of technology. Smith and colleagues (1998) suggest that students now establish a Web site address, or URL, and register the story for international access.

A publishing alternative is to use software programs that create a multimedia presentation such as HyperStudio (Knowledge Adventure), PowerPoint (Microsoft), and LinkWay (IBM). Students may use these programs to build interactive presentations that combine text, graphics, sound, animation, and movie clips to present ideas and information. Students create a stack of screens or slides that are interrelated and cross-referenced by hot spots or buttons on each card (Ray & Warden, 1995). Students may easily program buttons to perform functions such as move to another card, play a sound, play a QuickTime movie, play a videodisc or CD-ROM, start an animation, keep a running test score, or direct

an Internet browser to open a specific home page or site on the Internet. For example, Sherry published her story about dinosaurs using HyperStudio. On her first card, she located a button on her dinosaur picture. A click on the button took the reader to a QuickTime movie of a dinosaur eating.

Many other software programs are available that make the writing process motivational. EasyBook Deluxe (Sunburst) allows students to make double-sided books by writing and illustrating each page. Clicker 4 (Crick Software) can be used from preschool through adulthood for writing, reading, communicating, and making multimedia presentations and is adaptable for use with students who have physical and/or sensory disabilities. Hollywood High (Theatrix) lets adolescent students write a script with 10 characters and 20 places designed to reflect typical high school hangouts, including a mall, the arcade, or the beach.

 **ACTIVITY 11.3**

Jorge has trouble writing and spelling, so he dislikes both. He seldom finishes his written work, and although he thinks clearly, his thoughts seldom find their way to paper. Jorge has become discouraged and frustrated with school. He frequently shows his frustration by misbehaving. His attention span is short. Discuss the technology tools that you would use to help Jorge in writing and that would motivate him to succeed.

## Productivity Tools

Students with disabilities need to use productivity tools to become independent lifelong learners. An ever-increasing number of productivity tools is available to enable your students to work effectively in all subject areas. They may be handheld devices like the Bookman Speaking Merriam Webster Dictionary and Thesaurus from Franklin Learning Resources. Students type in a word, such as *enuf*, and see the word, *enough,* on the screen and hear the word pronounced. Students can also store the word in a customized list to practice for a spelling test. Optional headphones eliminate classroom noise and provide privacy.

Other handheld devices include calculators or spreadsheet programs. Simple calculators perform rote tasks while students use higher-order thinking skills to solve real math problems. Graphing calculators may help students who are visual learners "see" abstract algebraic concepts. Talking calculators may assist students who transpose digits to verify the sequence of their numbers.

For students with special needs, "an electronic spreadsheet helps students organize their math problems and print them out so they can be read. Since computers do most of the calculations, students can only get the correct answer by understanding how to set up the problem, a key thinking and problem-solving skill" (Male, 1988, p. 68). The Cruncher (Davidson & Associates) is a full-featured, easy-to-use spreadsheet for young children through adults. It includes tutorials to introduce students to spreadsheet functions and enables students to add sound effects and animation to their work in addition to reading text and numbers out loud.

There are many opportunities to learn to work with spreadsheets in any classroom. Using a spreadsheet, a student can keep track of expenses for a field trip or project. The student can estimate expenses item by item, calculate the actual total, and compare the differences. A unit on weather yields many statistics that can be stored, sorted, calculated, and analyzed. Hypotheses can be tested. Which month has the hottest average temperature in Arizona? Is it the same month as it is in Alaska? Are warm months windier than cool months?

Many students who have poor math skills have excellent abilities to recall and interpret sports statistics. Spreadsheets may be used to record statistics from the daily paper, make comparisons, and predict outcomes. Who will have the best batting average? Which team had the most touchdowns at the end of the season? Students can also use spreadsheets to manage their allowances and prepare personal budgets or keep statistics during simulations.

## Reference Material Tools

As we discussed in the prewriting stage of the writing process, technology has given students other ways to gain information in addition to the library book. The explosion of CD-ROM technologies has made electronic access to encyclopedias, atlases, dictionaries, and other reference materials a common occurrence in school media centers and classrooms. Most of the electronic encyclopedias provide basic information on a wide range of topics. They may contain a speech output option where the program will read selected passages to students. Most offer Internet links to Web sites for additional information.

To select effective reference materials, you should check such features as the reading comprehension level of the material; the ease of searching for information; the ability to cut and paste pictures and text into a word processor; and the use of video, sound, animation, charts, and illustrations to bring content alive (see Chapter 9). If your students cannot access the reference material because they cannot read the passages (and the program will not read it to them), you can use a tool such as the ULtimate Reader (Universal Learning Technology). Remember, this program allows students to import the text from CD-ROMs or other files and have the text read to them.

## Cognitive Assistance Tools

Many technology tools are available to help students develop and improve cognitive and problem-solving skills. Well-designed, multimedia systems support students in learning both basic and more complex literacy skills. Videotape technology was effective in teaching students with disabilities problem-solving skills (Elias & Taylor,

1995), and videodisc technology increased the math skills of secondary students with mild disabilities (Woodward & Gersten, 1993).

Through multimedia presentations students see the text and hear it read aloud. Simultaneous presentation of written words and sounds assists students in building decoding skills. An example of this technology is the interactive book. With an interactive book, students can follow the highlighted text as the passage is read. Then they can click on individual words to hear them pronounced. They can also explore the engaging hot spots on each page. For example, in *Just Grandma and Me* by Mercer Mayer (Broderbund), the student can click on the cow to see and hear it moo.

The Peabody Learning Lab, a multimedia software program developed for middle school students from disadvantaged backgrounds who have reading and spelling problems, enlists a virtual tutor (Melvin) to take students through a series of skill-development activities in reading, spelling, and writing. First, the students watch a segment of a video, which gives them some background for their upcoming reading. After students view the video, they may either read a related text passage, with Melvin helping them with individual words, or they may ask Melvin to read the passage slowly (word by word) or fluently (sentence by sentence) to them (Hasselbring, Goin, Taylor, Bottge, & Daley, 1997). In a 2-year pilot study of the Peabody Learning Lab Program, the average vocabulary and reading comprehension scores of 376 students improved significantly (Hasselbring et al, 1997).

One of the suggestions Broome and White (1995) make for the use of videotapes in classrooms serving youth with behavioral disorders is to give students practice to self-monitor their behaviors. Students view the tape, tally appropriate and inappropriate behaviors, use a scale to evaluate their behaviors from 1 to 5, and reinforce themselves for successful performance. Salend (1995b) suggests the use of

videotapes to prepare students with disabilities for inclusive settings. Students may view segments of an inclusive class and discuss the general education teacher's expectations, rules, and routines.

In a videodisc lesson of Mastery Fractions (System Impact), students first view a 3-minute presentation of the concept of reducing fractions with computer graphics and narration. The videodisc program then presents a set of two to four guided-practice problems. Each set is a still frame, and students in cooperative groups can use the remote to advance the frame (Woodward & Gersten, 1993). Secondary students with mild disabilities improved math performances with this program.

 **ACTIVITY 11.4**

Describe how can use the following technology tools and tell how they may assist students with disabilities. The first one is completed for you.

1. a word prediction program (This program is used for students with spelling problems as they can enter the beginning letters of the word that they do not know how to spell and then the program will produce a list of possibilities.)
2. Dana
3. a multimedia presentation such as Hyperstudio and EasyBook Deluxe
4. an electronic spreadsheet
5. the ULtimate Reader

 **IMPORTANT POINTS**

1. Legislation such as PL 99–457 and PL 100–407 have been instrumental in promoting the use of technology tools for children and adolescents with disabilities.

2. Roblyer (1989) suggests that teachers use technology in the curriculum when the content or skills (a) are difficult for students

to understand, (b) present hurdles such as too much calculation or handwriting that interfere with or are irrelevant to the main objective of the lesson, (c) require extensive homework, and (d) are tedious or uninteresting.

3. An adaptation of Means' classification scheme includes the broad categories of traditional, exploratory, tool, and communication technology applications.

4. The premise of universally designed learning (UDL) is that instructional materials can be designed so that learning goals may be achieved by individuals, no matter their disability, cultural background, or experiential background.

5. With technology and universal design principles, accommodations such as reading the text to students, highlighting important words or phrases, controlling the speed of presentation, changing print size, presenting advance and post organizers, and allowing students to record compositions may be built into a text, instead of added as an after-thought.

6. Authentic uses of technology provide students with experiences that include features such as (a) supporting the use of technology for tasks that are similar to tasks performed by workers in nonschool settings, (b) integrating technology into activities that are a core part of the classroom curriculum, and (c) treating technology as a tool to accomplish a complex task.

7. You may use low- and high-level technology to assist students with mild disabilities in organization, the writing process, productivity, accessibility to reference materials, and cognitive assistance (Lahm & Morrisette, 1994).

8. Technology greatly enhances the prewriting, writing, revising and editing, and publishing stages of the writing process.

9. Word prediction and abbreviation expansion programs help students with disabilities compose text and overcome problems with word recall, spelling, and keyboarding.

10. Students who have difficulty with mathematics may manipulate numbers and perform complex calculations using productivity tools such as spreadsheets.

11. Videotapes, videodiscs, and multimedia systems support students in learning both basic and more complex literacy skills.

---

## SOFTWARE SELECTION

Thousands of software programs are available for teachers and students to use. Many schools or districts purchase site licenses for software packages for everyone to use. The daunting task is to match the appropriate software to the curriculum and students' needs. Komoski (1995) recommends seven steps to responsible software selection:

***Step 1—Analyze Needs:*** The major question to ask here is whether the computer is the most appropriate medium to meet the instructional goals and objectives or if other strategies are more efficient.

***Step 2—Specify Requirements:*** Questions here involve analyzing learners' characteristics and needs and matching the software to these characteristics and needs. Komoski (1995) also recommends thinking about compatibility of software to current hardware, user friendliness, and access to technical support. For new multimedia programs in which students are developing their own presentations, questions may include: How easy is the program for students to use? Can students incorporate the elements they need to produce an effective presentation? What is the learning time required? Does the program work consistently well so that the students don't have downtime when the program crashes?

*Step 3—Identify Promising Software:* Sources such as *Closing the Gap* and *Technology and Learning* frequently provide listings of software appropriate to a particular subject area or unit of instruction. The Technology and Media Division of the Council for Exceptional Children also includes information about computer software in its journal. These sources and others frequently present ideas for integrating computers into the curriculum and for using application programs in the classroom.

Another source for finding software is software advertisements. You should carefully examine the advertising claims about the effectiveness or the content of software, as believing all of the claims may lead to disappointment. Remember, software producers are not likely to identify the poor qualities or limitations of the program in an advertisement.

Komoski (1995) recommends that teachers join a listserv on the Internet and post questions to other teachers about software. For example, "I am a teacher of students with behavior disorders and I want to find an interactive software program that teaches a fourth-grade student to handle temper tantrums" may lead to many suggestions.

*Step 4—Read Relevant Reviews:* Software reviews are reports of evaluations by experts. However, even a piece of software that has received a good review may not be appropriate for a particular situation or student. It is important to consider the needs, strengths, and weaknesses of students as well as the expert's viewpoint of the software.

*Step 5—Preview Software:* Many companies now let you download a demonstration version of their software from their Web site that you can preview before you decide to purchase it. The most effective way to preview software is to watch students as they interact with the program.

*Step 6—Make Recommendations:* At this step, Komoski (1995) suggests teachers complete an

evaluation form (see Table 11.2 for a sample one) and also keep a record of the optimal uses for the piece of software.

*Step 7—Get Post-Use Feedback:* Accountability requires a check that the software program is meeting the instructional goals and objectives identified in Step 1 and the needs of the students.

The following are additional criteria to consider when selecting software for students with special needs (Lewis, 1993; Powers, 1986):

1. *Flexibility:* Can the software be used by many students? Can it be used by a single student many times? Does the software offer a large variety of formats and contexts to facilitate the acquisition of new skills and maintain learner attention?

2. *Student or teacher control of the presentation of the materials:* Can students work at their own pace? Is the rate of movement through the program response controlled rather than time controlled? Can the response time be set at a very slow rate appropriate for the students? Can the rate be increased in small increments?

3. *Number of problems or length of lesson:* Can you control the number of problems presented so that students are challenged but attention is maintained? Are students able to stop a program and continue it later from the same point?

4. *Type of feedback:* Does feedback include an indication of correct responses, incorrect responses, and reasons why a response is incorrect? Does the feedback compare an incorrect response with the correct response? Is feedback intermittent and varied? Does the program refrain from negative feedback? Are prompts and hints provided?

5. *Program content:* Is the software built on clearly specified learning objectives? Is the reading level of information presented in the program carefully controlled and specified in the program manual? Do supplementary materials that provide extensive and varied practice accompany the software? Do the content and

**Table 11.2**  Software Evaluation Form

Title _____ Date _____
Publisher _____
Address _____
Subject Area _____ Grade Level _____ Price _____
Directions: Place a check mark under Y if yes, N if no, or NA if not applicable.

| | Y | N | NA |
|---|---|---|---|
| **Appropriateness:** | | | |
| • Age | ⎯ | ⎯ | ⎯ |
| • Interest | ⎯ | ⎯ | ⎯ |
| • Level | ⎯ | ⎯ | ⎯ |
| **Hardware Considerations:** | | | |
| • Compatible with computer | ⎯ | ⎯ | ⎯ |
| • Sufficient memory | ⎯ | ⎯ | ⎯ |
| • Color monitor required | ⎯ | ⎯ | ⎯ |
| • Peripherals required (printer, mouse, etc.) | ⎯ | ⎯ | ⎯ |
| **Documentation:** | | | |
| • Manual provided | ⎯ | ⎯ | ⎯ |
| • Additional materials included (worksheets) | ⎯ | ⎯ | ⎯ |
| • Adaptations suggested | ⎯ | ⎯ | ⎯ |
| **Program:** | | | |
| • Content interesting | ⎯ | ⎯ | ⎯ |
| • Content accurate | ⎯ | ⎯ | ⎯ |
| • Information up to date | ⎯ | ⎯ | ⎯ |
| • Information free from stereotypes | ⎯ | ⎯ | ⎯ |
| • Content well organized | ⎯ | ⎯ | ⎯ |
| **Interaction:** | | | |
| • Active participation required of learner | ⎯ | ⎯ | ⎯ |
| • Varying levels of difficulty available | ⎯ | ⎯ | ⎯ |
| • Learner control of presentation rate | ⎯ | ⎯ | ⎯ |
| • Learner control of exit function | ⎯ | ⎯ | ⎯ |
| • Feedback provided | ⎯ | ⎯ | ⎯ |
| • Concepts and skills reinforced | ⎯ | ⎯ | ⎯ |
| **Technical Considerations:** | | | |
| • User friendly | ⎯ | ⎯ | ⎯ |
| • Sound optional | ⎯ | ⎯ | ⎯ |
| • High-quality graphics | ⎯ | ⎯ | ⎯ |
| **Record Keeping:** | | | |
| • Reporting of scores option | ⎯ | ⎯ | ⎯ |
| • Capable of printing out scores | ⎯ | ⎯ | ⎯ |

the presentation meet the needs of the students? Do they fit the curriculum?

6. *Screen design:* Is the screen display simple and uncluttered? Is color used to add interest, motivation, and complement the content? Are relevant stimuli clearly identified and emphasized through flashing, underlining, color, or contrast? Are graphics utilized to provide realistic and concrete illustrations of abstract concepts?

## INTERNET

The Internet is a network of computers throughout the world that are connected to each other to share information. By the year 2005, some estimate the number of Internet users worldwide will exceed the one billion mark (United States Internet Council, 2000). In this section, we discuss general information, instructional use, professional development, and safeguards of the Internet.

### General Information

To connect to the Internet, your computer must have available a minimum of 8—preferably, 16—megabytes of RAM (random access memory) and a very fast processor (Heflich, 1998). Many schools have access to the Internet either through local area networks (LANs) or through modems and telephone lines. An Internet service provider (ISP) connects you to the Internet. Many school districts have a dedicated computer that has been assigned as a gateway (ISP) to connect to the Internet for their teachers, staff, and students. Information on the Internet is basically organized by a Web site of individual Web pages that pertain to a similar subject. Browsers (software programs such as Netscape Navigator and Microsoft Internet Explorer) allow you to move from page to page and site to site. Netscape Navigator is available on the Internet and is free to educators, whereas Microsoft Internet Explorer is bundled with the Windows operating system (Heflich, 1998).

On the Web page, you may see some text that is highlighted in different colors or highlighted and underlined. By clicking your mouse on this highlighted text, you are automatically connected to different pages or sites. All Web pages at a site have addresses or URLs (uniform resource locators). For example, if you wish to go to the Council for Exceptional Children (CEC) Web site, you would type the URL of http://www.cec.sped.org/ in the location box and find information concerning CEC divisions and other special education information. In Table 11.3, we describe some popular Web sites.

Let's say that you do not have a specific site in mind, but you want to explore a general topic. You can access directories such as Yahoo or Yahooligans (a directory for children ages 8 to 12) or such search engines as AltaVista or Google to find sites that contain information concerning your topic.

### Instructional Use

Learning on the Internet is occurring on a daily basis in many classrooms across the nation. As advances are made in technology, the selection of information on the Internet steadily increases. Materials may be downloaded from the Net to enhance lessons. For example, one special education intern in a co-teaching setting downloaded the production graph from the M & M Corporation. The students then compared their class graph of the various M & M colors to the company's production graph. Wissick and Gardner (1998) recommend the Internet for designing thematic units. They give an example of how the topic of whales quickly leads to various sites, information, and integrated activities. The Educator's Toolkit (http://www.eagle.ca/~matink/) and Thematic Units (http://www.ed.sc.edu/caw/toolboxtheme.html) are two sites that provide a hotlist of sites grouped thematically (Wissick & Gardner, 1998). WebQuests, virtual tours and field trips, and

**Table 11.3**  Sample Internet Sites

| Site Name | Internet (URL) Address | Description |
|---|---|---|
| AskEric | http://ericir.syr.edu | Lesson plans for all levels and content, education information, search engine for educational professional literature |
| ATEN | http://www.aten.scps.k12.fl.us | Resources and links for assistive technology |
| BCK2SKOL Lessons | http://www.sc.edu/bck2skol/fall/fall.html | Lessons on using the Web and search engines |
| Busy Teachers' WebSite K–12 | http://www.ceismc.gatech.edu/busyt/ | Materials, lesson plans, class activities, interactive Web projects for students |
| Classroom Connect | http://www.classroom.net/ | Site for K–12 educators and students |
| Education World | http://www.educationworld.com/ | Lesson plans, templates, professional information |
| About Learning (4MAT) | http://www.aboutlearning.com/ | Information on teaching/ learning, lesson exchange |
| Internet Island—Miami Science Center | http://www.miamisci.org/ii/ | Teaches students to use the Internet via a story |
| Multicultural Pavilion | http://curry.edschool.virginia.edu/go/multicultural/teachers.html | Links to multicultural sites |
| The Online Books Page | http://onlinebooks.library.upenn.edu/ | Source of online books and out of copyright ones |

Note: Site addresses may change without notice. If you are unable to find the site, use Web search engines and search by subject area(s).

research projects are other ways to incorporate the Internet into classroom instruction.

Created by Bernie Dodge with Tom March in 1995, WebQuest is an inquiry-oriented activity in which most or all of the information used by learners is drawn from the Web. WebQuests are designed to use learners' time well, to focus on using information rather than looking for it, and to support learners' thinking at the levels of analysis, synthesis, and evaluation (Dodge, 1995). A visit to the Web site at http://edweb.sdsu.edu/webquest/matrix.html finds a variety of WebQuests in different grade levels and content areas. For example, a click on the content area of ART and Music for Grades K–2 finds three WebQuests. A click on one of the three WebQuests, *World of Puppets*, results in seven pages of notes to teachers, a suggested lesson sequence, and Internet plus more traditional resources. Using these Internet resources, students visit different countries to find out about their puppets. Then Internet links are provided to assist students in making their own puppets and creating a puppet play.

Even though typical WebQuests may be used successfully for all students, some accommodations and modifications may be necessary for students with special needs. Vocabulary may need to be modified by hyperlinking difficult vocabulary words to their definitions. This will give the children an easy and quick way to look up words they do not know. More prompts may also be needed to assist students in completing the projects. Additionally, Hines and Hall (2000) recommend the following accommodations for students with special needs: (a) design simple backgrounds with few distractions, (b) use a consistent page layout, (c) create large buttons for easy navigation, and (d) leave plenty of white space to increase readability. If you plan to design your own WebQuests, the Web site http://edweb.sdsu.edu/ outlines steps for you to follow.

Virtual tours or field trips allow students to visit places they have never before visited without leaving the classroom. Even though virtual tours and field trips are not the same as actual travel experiences, Roblyer and Edwards (2000) suggest that virtual field trips give students a chance to discover new places worldwide and share their experiences with others. Virtual tours and field trips also give students access to places they otherwise could not go, such as to the sun, to the moon, or to a planet. Virtual tours and field trips involve active learning and encourage student interaction and collaboration.

Teachers can save time by using premade tours available on the Internet. Students can take a tour of the White House (http://www.whitehouse.gov/history/whtour/), the mall of Washington, DC (http://ahp.gatech.edu/dc_map.html), the South Pole (http://astro.uchicago.edu/cara/vtour/pole/), or the nine planets (http://seds.lpl.arizona.edu/billa/tnp/).

Teachers can get ideas for lesson plans on virtual field trips such as a tour of Antarctica (http://www.education-world.com/a lesson/lesson042.shtml), download a virtual permission slip (http://www.field-guides.com/PermissionSlip.pdf), or browse through some examples at (http://www.sesd.sk.ca/teacherresource/virtual tour/virtualtours.htm).

Teachers may also develop their own virtual tours or field trips to match their instructional content. Specific Web sites can be arranged so students can journey from site to site, adding meaning to teachers' lessons. Students can experience the site through virtual pictures or video. Some software allows the user to manipulate pictures of objects in a museum so that they can look at the object from all angles. Even if the students were to visit a museum, they wouldn't be allowed to pick up or touch a valuable artifact. The other way virtual tours are useful is in performing tasks such as dissecting a virtual frog or other scientific experiments that may be too costly or too dangerous to perform in a classroom setting.

Students can also use the Internet to enhance their research skills. Teachers can guide students to specific Internet sites to locate information on particular research questions. Since many students with disabilities have difficulty with organization, software programs such as Research Assistant for Students and Teachers (Visions Technology in Education) can be a valuable tool to assist students in gathering and organizing information and storing it on the computer. Research Assistant for Students and Teachers references the sources in a bibliographical format after the student plugs in the necessary information.

In searching the Internet for information for research purposes, students need to be aware of specific strategies and tools to locate their own Web sites for their particular research topic. Students should be taught Boolean terminology, which can enhance their search endeavors. Boolean operators such as *and, or,* and *not* between key words will provide the students with more efficient searching power.

Through these Internet connections, students and teachers are able to tap into resources previously unavailable. There are online dictionaries, encyclopedias, databases, picture databases, movie clips, sound clips, and chat rooms with subject-area experts.

## Professional Development

The Internet enables educators to access current, up-to-date information from professional organizations; listservs and Usenet Newsgroups may provide support and encouragement to teachers. Professional organizations, such as the Council for Exceptional Children (CEC) maintain Web sites that house a wealth of information concerning professional development opportunities in exceptional education and information on disabilities.

Listservs provide forums for discussing topics with people who have similar interests (Lewis, 1998). People subscribe to a listserv, read messages, and send messages to the listserv (Morgan, 1997). Usenet Newsgroups are an electronic bulletin board system that consists of discussion forums on thousands of topics (Morgan, 1997). Using e-mail, teachers can interact with other professionals in solving everyday problems. For example, Terry Perkins (Mosca & Perkins, 1997) relates how she requested help for 10 students with emotional disabilities and learned of curriculum guides, lesson plans, and behavior systems from colleagues via a Usenet Newsgroup.

The Internet may also enhance background information for many special educators who may feel at a disadvantage in subject matter knowledge in a co-teaching setting. For example, when Mr. Sams, the special education teacher, was co-teaching a unit on the American Revolution with Ms. James, the history teacher, he decided to upgrade his subject knowledge by checking the Internet for information on famous generals of the revolution.

## Safeguards

Although many schools have enlisted the aid of software that helps create a safer Internet environment, students can still get to sites that are not appropriate. It is important to teach students "Net safety" in the same manner that they are taught drug safety and stranger safety

(Bakken & Aloia, 1998; Goldstein, 1998). Some general precautions to teach students are that they should (a) let teachers know if any e-mail message or Web site information is inappropriate or makes them feel uncomfortable, (b) not believe everything that is on the Internet, (c) not give out personal information, and (d) not agree to meet anyone face-to-face (Bakken & Aloia, 1998; Goldstein, 1998). We want to reiterate the idea of evaluating carefully what you find on the Internet. Anyone can put information on the Internet without having it checked for accuracy, validity, or appropriateness. In fact, Caruso (1997) relates the story of how one of her seventh graders built his own Web site on computer repair and network consultation.

 **ACTIVITY 11.5**

**Part 1.**   Find two Internet sites and tell how you might use the information in your class. Share your site with a peer.

**Part 2.**   Using the Internet, download a demonstration version of a talking word processor such as Write: Out Loud from Don Johnston, Inc. Describe the features of the program and its advantages for students who have reading and writing problems.

**Part 3.** Using the WebQuest Web site, http://edweb.sdsu.edu/webquest/matrix.html, select one of the WebQuest examples and describe at least three accommodations that can be made for students with disabilities.

 **IMPORTANT POINTS**

1. Komoski (1995) identifies the following steps for analyzing software: (1) analyze needs, (2) specify requirements, (3) identify promising software, (4) read relevant reviews, (5) preview software, (6) make recommendations, and (7) get post-use feedback.

2. By the year 2005, some estimate the number of Internet users worldwide will exceed the one billion mark (United States Internet Council, 2000).

3. Several ways in which the Internet can be used to enhance student instruction include WebQuests, virtual tours and field trips, and research projects.

4. WebQuest is an inquiry-oriented activity in which most or all of the information used by learners is drawn from the Web.

5. Even though virtual tours and field trips are not the same as actual travel experiences, Roblyer and Edwards (2000) suggest that virtual field trips give students a chance to discover new places worldwide and share their experiences with others.

6. Students should be taught Boolean operators such as *and, or,* and *not* between key words for more efficient searching power.

7. Some general precautions to teach students are to let their teachers know if any e-mail message or Web site information is inappropriate or makes them feel uncomfortable, and to not believe everything that is on the Internet, give out personal information, and agree to meet anyone face-to-face (Bakken & Aloia, 1998; Goldstein, 1998).

## TECHNOLOGY AS A TOOL FOR TEACHERS

As technology becomes more common in the classroom, teachers are looking beyond school boundaries for new and innovative ways to integrate and infuse that technology into the curriculum (Craig, 1997). As previously discussed, online access to the Internet is helping teachers bring boundless resources to the classroom. Technology applications that can be used as a tool or a communication vehicle (word processing, spreadsheet, drawing program, network) can support any curriculum and can be fully assimilated into a teacher's ongoing core

practice (Means, Blando, Olson, Middleton, Moroaco, Remz, & Zorfass, 1993).

When instruction incorporates concept-based, integrated curricula and focuses on relevant issues, problems, and ideas, learning acquires a new depth (Erickson, 1995). When such instruction is paired with telecommunications and technology, students make the connection between academics and the world outside the classroom. This relevancy has a lasting impact on student learning. In the previous section, we included a discussion of the Internet. Therefore, we do not repeat the information on the application of the Internet for instruction here.

## Planning

Good planning is critical to successful instruction. Because any word processing program allows you to enter, edit, format, print, and save text, you can easily produce lesson plans that are professional-looking, easily revised, and available when you need to retrieve them. By using a template, which is like filling in a blank form, you can develop a format that meets your needs and simplifies entering new lessons. Or you may want to develop a simple database of lesson plans. A database will allow you to categorize your plans according to such areas as content, objectives, developmental level, themes, and instructional strategies. Integrated programs such as AppleWorks (Apple Computer, Inc.), Microsoft Works, and Microsoft Word will allow you to pursue either option.

You may prefer to use a graphic organizer, such as Inspiration (see Figure 11.1), which allows you to map or diagram your lesson plans. This is a powerful tool for planning and developing integrated thematic units. A demonstration copy of the program is available from Inspiration at their Web site (www.inspirationsoftware.com).

## IEP Generation

Another popular use of technology in classrooms with students who have special needs is developing and producing Individualized Education

Programs (IEPs) (Krivacska, 1986; Maddux, 1986; Male, 1988, 1997). You can use your own word processor or database to enter, store, retrieve, and modify your required form, or you can use an IEP generation program. However, more and more districts and states are developing their own computerized IEPs or customizing commercial products to meet federal, state, and local requirements, curriculum objectives, and standards. Computerized IEPs offer the ability to enter data and edit without retyping. Larger systems may provide access to databases of annual goals and objectives, resources that have been correlated to local curriculum, and assessment data. They also allow generation of a variety of reports (Male, 1988, 1997). It is important to remember that IEPs should be written by teams of people, and computerization should not reduce the individualization of the process (Krivacska, 1986; Maddux, 1986).

## Record Keeping and Classroom Management

Technology can help you manage your classroom. You can improve your record keeping by using a simple spreadsheet program or a spreadsheet template that is available with some integrated programs for educators, such as AppleWorks, Microsoft Works, and Microsoft Word. You may be interested in a comprehensive classroom management program that includes grading, seating charts, and lesson plans, such as the one from Excelsior Software.

Programs are also available for sampling language and testing readability. Many schools are using programs like the Accelerated Reader (Advantage) to track what books students are reading and to measure comprehension of the material they read. It is important to examine informal or formal assessment programs for appropriateness to current curriculum goals and instructional practices.

Because the thinking behind how we deliver and measure learning is changing, digital or electronic portfolios for students are becoming more common as tools for assessment in many schools. The Grady Profile Portfolio Assessment (Aurbach, 1993) allows teachers to track students' work samples in scanned images, sounds, full-motion video, graphics, text data, and other information pertinent to the students' educational history (see Chapter 3 for more information about portfolio assessment). An example of an entry in an electronic portfolio is found in Figure 11.2. Check the Web site www.aurbach.com for more information.

The PowerPoint program may also be used to create portfolios. You may easily include the literature-based portfolio components within a PowerPoint presentation. Once completed, you can burn the PowerPoint portfolio collection on a CD. Within the PowerPoint presentation you can include pictures, video clips, voice recording of the child, charts, scanned student work samples, and much more just as you can with commercially made electronic portfolio software. We have found that taking a picture of the students' work samples using a digital camera is easier than using a scanner to scan the work sample. We have also found that the difference in quality between scanning and using the digital camera is minimal.

You can also save your PowerPoint presentation using the Autorun CD Project Creator Pro, which will allow the parent/guardian to view the PowerPoint presentation on any computer without having the PowerPoint software or a presentation reader (see the Web site, www.soniacoleman.com for more information). Many parents may have the technology skills to go to the Internet and find a free presentation reader to download, but using the Autorun CD Project Creator Pro will eliminate this step. The parent can simply place the CD in the computer and wait 30 seconds and the child's portfolio collection will appear. You can opt to set the presentation to automatically scroll if you do not want the parent to have to click to go to the next slide. Encourage the parents to go to the

**Figure 11.2**  Electronic Portfolio Entry

---

### Einstein's Academy for the Advancement of Science and Violin Middle School Division

**Demo-Student, Ann**                                              **Work Sample—Graphic**

**Assignment**                                                          Draft
The student was asked to explain some math problems.          X Final
The goal of the exercise was to assess the student's              Typical
ability to verbalize the operations performed.                    Atypical
                                                                X Printing
                                                                   Cursive

| **Legend** |
| --- |
| − = performance does not meet expectation |
| √ = performance meets expectation |
| + = performance exceeds expectation |

**Title:** 3/02/94—math problems
**Evaluator:** Ms. A. Nelson
**Skill-Set:** Mathematics
**Date:** 9/25/98

Student  Parent  Teacher                                        Ann

+                       +       Explanation shows math           2) $(5^3 + 25) + (50 + 50) = 250$
                                understanding
+                       +       Explanation is accurate          3) $7 \cdot 6^3 - (42 - 36) - 150 = 1,356$
+                       +       Explanation is thorough          4) $9 \cdot 3 - 9 \div 3 + 3 = 27$
                                                                 5) $6 \cdot 3 \div 2 + 2^2 = 36$

**Reflections**
My teacher asked me to give an example of my best math
work this quarter and write a complete explanation. I picked
these problems because they show that I know how to write
long problems. I know that you are supposed to do the work
inside the parentheses before you follow the signs outside
them. Then you do multiplication first before the adding to get
the right answer. I know how to use an integer (that's the little
number three up in the air by the 5 in problem #2). That
means to multiply that number by itself three times. Another
word for that is cubed. If that number is a 2, it's called
squared. You do this cubing or squaring first before you
multiply. So here's the order you should go in if you get a
problem like this. First look at stuff in parentheses and get
those answers done. If there's an integer do that the very first.
Then follow the math directions outside the parentheses. Do
times and dividing first, then add or subtract. You'll get the
right answer every time!

**Miscellaneous Remarks**
This is the first semester report for all students at Einstein. We the faculty hope you like our new output format. It is
part of our new student profile system.

**Notes**
3/6/94 Ann shows understanding of the process of grouping and order of operations. She also understands squaring
and cubing. I'd like her to learn to use the word "operation." Alice Nelson.

---

Note: Grady Profile Portfolio Assessment Software(1998). Aurbach & Associates, Inc.; St. Louis, MO.
Reprinted by permission.

local library or other community facilities if they do not have a computer at home. We have found that many parents are excited to view their child's work electronically.

In addition, you may use videotaping in the classroom setting. Videotaping may be used to document academic and behavior growth during the year and assist students in assessing their own behaviors and learning. Videotapes may also be used to inform and involve families in monitoring their child's IEP goals and increase their knowledge of daily activities their child encounters in the classroom (Hundt, 2002).

It is extremely important that teachers obtain written permission from the families of their students prior to using videotaping. We would suggest that you develop your own form in addition to the permission form routinely sent to parents at the beginning of the year that is generally housed in the school office. The form should specifically address the purpose and use of the videotaping to prevent any misunderstandings. Of course it goes without saying, children whose families object to videotaping should be excluded from this process.

## Presentation Tools

You may use a combination of graphics, text, sound, and video to introduce new topics, deliver necessary information, explain examples, demonstrate problems, and review previously covered material. Your computer presentations can be viewed by individual students or small groups or you can project them for larger groups. In fact, Middleton, Flores, and Knaupp (1997) recommend the elimination of one-student, one-computer thinking and the use of a high-end machine with a projection device that can involve an entire classroom of students in problem-solving and other interactive software.

PowerPoint software has been predominately used as a presentation tool. Many teacher pres-

entations include real pictures, sound, and colorful graphics that enhance their presentations. We feel teachers should continue this effective instructional method, but should also explore creating Interactive PowerPoint activities that are student directed and provide student choices.

Interactive PowerPoint presentations, intended for use by an individual student or small group of students, allow students to navigate through the lesson by clicking on various hyperlinks. For example, a vocabulary word within the text may be linked to a definition slide or a picture slide with an explanation of the vocabulary word. Content may be further explained or examples added using hyperlinks. Action Buttons that have the forward arrows or backward arrows help students navigate from slide to slide.

The teacher may easily modify the lesson to include the specific learning needs of the student by allowing students to select hyperlinks. Individual students who know the definition will probably not click on the hyperlink. Thus, every student need not click on each hyperlink.

The more sophisticated you become in creating interactive PowerPoint presentations, the more options you will be able to provide your students. You can create learning tracks that will be tailored to the individual level of your students based on the options selected by the students.

You can develop slides that check for understanding. These slides can ask questions using multiple-choice options. If the child answers the question incorrectly, you should link it to a feedback slide that will then be linked to review slides. If the student answers the question correctly, the slide should be linked to a feedback slide that would then be linked to the rest of the new material to be learned. It is important to have several review slides that emphasize the important points. We also suggest that you end interactive PowerPoint activities with a multiple-choice interactive quiz.

In addition, the use of sound, colorful graphics, and real pictures can enhance the overall lesson. Caution: Because the PowerPoint software is designed to advance to the next slide with the click of the mouse, some students may be tempted to repeatedly click the mouse without using the Interactive Action Buttons. As a precautionary measure, the teacher should create dummy slides that would direct the child to click the Action Button to return to the appropriate slide (e.g. "Johnny, you are on the wrong slide. Do not click the mouse repeatedly. Please return to the lesson by clicking the arrow below.") Some teachers choose to attach an alarm sound to the dummy slides so when the student repeatedly clicks the mouse, the sound alerts the teacher that the student is merely clicking the mouse and advancing out of sequence. When the teacher hears the sound, he/she can quickly go to the computer and get the student back on track.

Creating interactive PowerPoint activities may be accomplished following some simple steps. Different versions of PowerPoint have various menu options, but the following outlines the basic steps that should work for all versions. **Hint:** Create and save all of your slides before you attempt to make them interactive.

Steps to create hyperlinked Action Buttons within the PowerPoint are:

1. From the PowerPoint menu, click AutoShapes.
2. From the AutoShapes menu, click Action Button and then select the appropriate Action Button for your activity (e.g. forward arrow button or backward arrow button).
3. Move the cursor to the PowerPoint slide and then left click the mouse, hold and then drag the mouse to create the Action Button to the size you desire and then release the left mouse click. **Hint:** The larger the Action Buttons, the easier it is to navigate.
4. After you release the left mouse in Step 3, an Action Settings box will appear. In the Action

Setting box locate the "Hyperlink to:" option. This is where you will select the slide that you wish to be linked. You can scroll down the slide options by clicking the arrow that is next to the "Hyperlink to:" option. You can hyperlink to the previous slide, first slide, last slide, or other slides. After you select the slide to be linked, click OK.

**Note:** If you want to select the slide based on the title of the slide, click on the word *slide* and then the titles will appear. Click on the slide title you want to be linked and then click OK.

Alternative to Steps 3 and 4: After you have clicked on AutoShapes, selected the Action Button and move your cursor to the slide, you can right (instead of left) click the mouse, hold, and drag to create the size of the button. Then click the hyperlink option, click Place in this Document and then select the slide you want to be linked.

Steps to hyperlink a word within the text to a slide within the PowerPoint are:

1. Highlight the word to be linked.
2. Right click the mouse.
3. Select the hyperlink option.
4. Click Place in this Document.
5. Select the slide for linkage.
6. Click OK.

**Note:** If Step 2 does not work, try pressing the control key and k after highlighting the word. Then, at the hyperlink option, fill in the Named Location in File box with the number of the slide for linkage or click on Browse and select the slide title. After you have created all of the interactive links, be sure to run the PowerPoint show and check the accuracy of all the links prior to using with your students.

DVD-video players and laser disc/videodisc players connected to a television monitor can also present graphics and sounds. For example, one of our student teachers used a videodisc to supplement her lecture on sea animals to her high school students. Checking in the teacher's guide that accompanied the videodisc, she found lists of images and video clips to enhance her presentation. She then entered a sequence of the frame numbers into the computer's database using a software program (Bar'N'Coder, Pioneer) and printed out the list. While she was lecturing to her students about the various animals, she passed a pen-shaped scanner over one of the barcodes and showed related pictures, such as a picture of crabs eating.

 **ACTIVITY 11.6**

Create two slides with PowerPoint and insert Action Buttons to hyperlink the slides.

## Preparation of Classroom Materials

Technology can enhance instruction by helping you prepare materials for your classroom environment and curriculum. Technology today allows teacher-made materials such as worksheets, tests, certificates, templates, games, and learning cards to be created with ease and style.

Computers can help you generate worksheets that match student needs for practice of skills and concepts. Programs such as Worksheet Magic (Teacher Support Software) allow you to produce a variety of creative formats, including crossword puzzles, scrambled words, word searches, and secret codes. Math Worksheet and Fraction Worksheet Generator (S & S Software) will help you develop pretests, posttests, and practice problems to meet individual student needs. Problems can be printed horizontally or vertically, with or without answers, with the procedure being shown, or with an example problem. Many software programs offer interpretation of test results, information management of test results and data, report writing, and generation of goals, objectives and instructional strategies (Male, 1997).

You can create certificates, awards, banners, signs, bookmarks, and bulletin board signs to enhance your themes, and instructional activities on such programs as Print Shop Deluxe

(Broderbund) and PrintMaster Gold (Mindscape). Colored paper or color printers will add to the appearance of your products.

With desktop publishing programs you can add a professional polish to instructional materials and reports. Templates for newsletters in many word processing programs will allow you to add columns, rules, boxes, and shading to your work. Programs like the Student Writing Center (Learning Company) and the more professional PageMaker (Adobe) will offer more publishing options. You can find templates on the Internet for letters, forms, certificates, and seating charts, saving you the time normally spent in developing these items from scratch. A popular Web site for teacher templates is http://www.educationworld.com.

Interactive file folder games may be created to meet the individual needs of students. Technology is a great resource to help create games. Once you know the content you want to teach, a new game is merely a few clicks of the computer mouse from creation. You may use word processing software, such as Microsoft Word, to integrate various graphics and clip art. A variety of font colors and sizes enhances the overall appearance of the games, and the AutoShapes options and WordArt options add colorful detail. In addition, software such as Inspiration, KidPix, Kidspiration, and BoardMaker picture symbols may be used in designing games. Teachers may also use the Internet to download clip art items to meet the goal of the game or download actual photographs of items that can be used to help the games provide authentic learning.

For students with lower cognitive skills, the teacher may use the digital camera to take pictures of the children's faces. The teacher may then cut out the faces of the children and use them as the game pieces. This helps the children locate their game piece as they navigate along the game board. Using the students' actual pictures will also keep them more interested and motivated to play the game. We encourage teachers to actively involve the children in helping develop the games. This involvement will enhance the feeling of student ownership in their learning.

In addition to interactive file folder games, teachers may create learning cards, which present information to be learned in a self-correction card format. The content is presented with the answers. Usually learning cards include pictures to enhance the learning process, but they may be used without pictures. Learning card templates may be created using Microsoft Word. Once you have a general format saved, you may easily insert various content into the template. The content to be learned should guide how you present it on the learning card and can be placed in the format of your preference. To create the template, you will need to become familiar with the Text Box feature on the Microsoft Word software. An example of the learning card format may be found in Figure 11.3. Follow these simple directions to begin developing your learning card template:

1. From the pull down menu click on Insert.
2. Scroll down and click on Text Box.
3. Drag the Text Box to the desired place on the page.

4. Right click on the Text Box and then click on Format Text Box, which will give you many preferences including the thickness and colors of the Text Box lines.

An important point to remember is that technology should enhance the content, not distract from it. The first step should always be to review the objectives to be taught and then explore one of the technology tools to see whether it can enhance the learning. Never start with a technology tool and then try to find content to fit into the tool. When the latter occurs, there is a high risk of using a wonderful technology tool without a content match. More importantly, there is a higher risk of introducing objectives out of sequence. A teacher may be tempted to select an objective that is out of sequence in order to integrate the new technology in the lesson. It is easy to get sidetracked with the motivational aspect of new technology, but if teachers are enticed by the newest technology tool without first looking at the content, many difficulties may follow and technology may distract instead of enhance the learning process.

## Learning Card

**Florida Black Bear**

**Interesting Facts about the Florida Black Bear**

- Florida Black Bears tend to be shy and reclusive.
- Never has a human been killed by a Florida Black Bear.
- The Florida Black Bear is an omnivore and enjoys a wide variety of foods, including berries, acorns and fruits.
- The Florida Black Bear weighs between 150-350 pounds.
- Male Florida Black Bears are much larger than the females.
- The Florida Black Bear lives in woods and swamps.
- Some Florida Black Bears have a white band of fur across their chest.

**Figure 11.3**   Learning Card Template

**IMPORTANT POINTS** ◀

1. Technology assists teachers in planning, IEP generation, record keeping and classroom management, lesson presentation, and material preparation.
2. It is important to remember that IEPs should be written by teams of people, and computerization should not reduce the individualization of the process (Krivacska, 1986; Maddux, 1986).
3. The Accelerated Reader program and electronic portfolios are samples of technology application for record keeping and classroom management.
4. It is extremely important that teachers obtain written permission from the families of their students prior to using videotaping.
5. Middleton, Flores, and Knaupp (1997) recommend the elimination of one-student, one-computer thinking and the use of a high-end machine with a projection device that can involve an entire classroom of students in problem solving and other interactive software.
6. Interactive PowerPoint activities should be designed so that students can easily navigate through the lesson by clicking on hyperlinks placed throughout the slides, which are linked to slides that further explain or provide additional examples of the content.
7. Software programs are available to assist teachers in preparing individualized worksheets, tests, certificates, templates, games, and learning cards.
8. The first step in using technology should be to review the objective for the lesson and then explore one of the technology tools to see whether it enhances the objective.

## ASSISTIVE TECHNOLOGY

Assistive technology addresses the special tools that students with disabilities must have to access curriculum, engage in learning, meet required outcomes, and transition successfully to the workplace. Assistive technology augments student learning by providing the tools, devices, and services necessary for circumventing particular learning problems or physical disabilities.

According to Hasselbring (1998), "assistive technology provides powerful tools for students with disabilities to become an integral part of schools and the community. Access to the assistive technology services and devices can remove barriers, unmask abilities and create opportunities for increased independence and inclusion for children and adults, regardless of the severity of their disability. Assistive technology provides avenues for people to increase expectations and to stretch their imaginations toward a future filled with possibilities" (p. 2).

When people think of assistive or adaptive technology, they think of high-tech devices such as Stephen Hawking's speaking keyboard. Most adaptations are more mundane and address issues such as relocating the on/off button of the computer or pressing two keys at once or picking up a disk to slide into the drive. A pencil grip would qualify as assistive technology if it assists a student with writing problems to write better! It is technology that allows the student to do something that he/she would not be able to accomplish otherwise.

As discussed previously, legislation promoted the use of assistive technology in the classroom (see the Technology Legislation section at the beginning of the chapter). The definition of assistive technology includes both devices and services.

### Assistive Technology Devices

Section 300.5 of IDEA defines assistive technology devices as "any item, piece of equipment or product system, whether acquired commercially off the shelf, modified, or customized, that is used to increase, maintain, or improve functional capabilities of individuals with disabilities" [20 U.S.C. Chapter 33, Section 1401 (25)]. This definition is broad and includes many of the modifications, adaptations, and accommodations made to help a student participate in a Free Appropriate Public Education (FAPE). As discussed previously, the devices may range from low technology to high technology. With this definition, assistive technology does not have to be electronic or mechanical.

A useful source of information on assistive devices is the ABLEDATA Web site at http://www.abledata.com. The ABLEDATA site contains detailed descriptions of approximately 29,000 assistive technology products from over 2,000 different manufacturers.

## Assistive Technology Services

IDEA defines assistive technology service as "any service that directly assists an individual with a disability in the selection, acquisition, and use of an assistive technology device" [20 U.S.C. Chapter 33, Section 1401(25)]. Specifically, this service must include (a) evaluating an individual's assistive technology needs; (b) purchasing, leasing, or providing for acquisition of devices; (c) selecting, designing, adapting, maintaining, repairing, or replacing devices; (d) coordinating therapies, interventions, or services; (e) providing training and technical assistance for the individual and/or family; and (f) providing training and technical assistance for professionals. School districts are responsible for helping individuals with disabilities select and acquire an appropriate assistive technology device and assist in training them to use it.

Students, parents, and professionals together decide on the assistive technology needs of an individual student. Professionals who may be included are the teacher, speech therapist, occupational therapist, physical therapist, and any other person who works with the student.

## Modifications

As we discussed previously, assistive technology may also include simple, low-tech modifications. Simple modifications are sometimes all that is needed to allow a student to use the computer software program. Some students may benefit from the use of bright stickers to code keys that are frequently used with a program. You may use word processing or graphics software to produce some special help cards for use at the computer. These cards can list frequently used commands or summarize directions in large, clear print with illustrations. Using screen capturing features of the computer allows you to print or download the image that appears on the screen. You can use screen capturing features to produce flash cards, prepare transparencies and task cards for a computer program, display and file exemplary work, and incorporate actual software graphics into student-produced presentations.

When considering the use of assistive technology, it is important to start simple. Teachers should begin with simple, inexpensive low-tech options first to prevent wasting extra time and money on high-tech solutions. If the low-tech options are successful, excessive time, money, and effort have not been lost. One option for teachers in trying low-tech solutions is the LoTTIE Kits—Low Tech Tools for Inclusive Education (Onion Mountain Technology, Inc.). These kits contain a collection of low-tech, easy-to-use assistive technology tools. LoTTIE Kits contain tools such as colored filters, pencil grips, hand-held devices, raised paper, and rubber letter and number stamps. These tools allow the teacher to conduct informal assessments by trying out simple devices prior to trying more expensive ones. In addition to the tools, the kits also include notebooks detailing the contents along with strategies for using the low-tech tools. All of these simple, low-tech tools are stored in a handy carrying container for ease of use —all at your fingertips at a moment's notice. A variety of LoTTIE Kits are available, including the basic kit as well as one specifically designed for literacy and one specifically designed for math. A fourth kit is also available, designed specifically for occupational therapists and teachers for informal writing assessment for grades K–12. This kit includes a variety of paper (lined, grid, colored, NCR) and different writing tools as well as a booklet with product information and strategies for use.

The operating systems of computers have accessibility features either built in to the system software or available at no cost. These features provide simple modifications that make using the computer more accessible to students. The features were designed primarily for individuals with motion-related disabilities who may have difficulty using the computer keyboard or mouse, for individuals who prefer visual feedback in place of sounds, and for some low-vision students. However, many of these features make the computer more user friendly for other students as well. The terminology for these features may vary from one computer system to another, but the accessibility features are offered in most of the system software.

Both the Macintosh and Windows operating systems include built-in controls that make standard functions simpler for individuals with special needs. For example, Ms. Perez slows down the speed at which the mouse pointer moves for Kimberly, who has some eye–hand coordination difficulties. More examples of built-in controls appear in Table 11.4.

Many programs give you and your students the option of using various peripheral devices to enhance instruction or provide the student with special access to use the program. Adapted standard computer input devices include different sizes of a mouse or a trackball, and different size or different key layouts of keyboards. Other examples include keyguards, touch-sensitive screens, alternate or adapted keyboards, switches, and voice entry systems.

Students usually respond to instructional software programs by typing on the computer keyboard. **Keyguards** reduce the possibility of hitting the wrong keys as students attempt to enter information. Keyguards fit over the regular computer keyboard and have holes cut out for the individual to access the keys on the keyboard with a finger, stylus, or stick. Keyguards may also have a latching key on certain function keys, such as the shift or control. With **touch-sensitive screens** (e.g., Touch Window, Edmark), students use a finger or stylus for input. To make a selection, the student simply points at the computer screen with a finger or a special penlike device. This often allows students who have fine-motor problems, inaccurate keyboard skills, or problems with spelling to complete programs without frustration.

**Alternative or adapted keyboards**, such as IntelliKeys (Intellitools) and Discover:Board (Madentec) offer input methods that can be customized to a student's needs. Many of the same features that are system accessibility fea-

**Table 11.4** Sample Operating Systems Built-In Controls

These built-in controls include:
- The capability of switching from mouse control to keyboard control using the numeric keypad
- Control of the speed at which the mouse pointer moves
- Allowance for control key combinations to be pressed consecutively rather than simultaneously
- Use of the keyboard keys to select menu functions
- Adjustment of icons for size, spacing, and title next
- Change of the background screen color
- Custom features for controlling your mouse, trackball, or operating system
- An audible cue to tell when either the Caps Lock, Num Lock, or Scroll Lock keys have been made active or inactive
- A visual alert for persons with hearing disabilities or for those who are too easily distracted by the alert sounds

tures are also included in these alternate keyboards. Most of these alternate keyboards have software that allows you to make customized overlays for the keyboards that will correspond to the specific software that the student is using.

The use of on-screen keyboards is an alternative input method that is software and hardware controlled. A graphical representation of the keyboard is displayed on the computer screen to allow individuals who cannot type with a standard keyboard to enter text using a pointing device (e.g., mouse, switch, or trackball).

Software devices such as Adaptive Firmware Card (Apple IIE and IIGS), Discover:Kenx (Macintosh), and DADA (IBM and compatibles) allow **switch activation** and a communication device to act in place of the computer keyboard. With switch activation, the software that comes with the specific device displays the computer keyboard. A switch activation signals the computer to start scanning the on-screen keyboard by row, column, or individual character. The scan can be customized for rate of scanning and activation as well as for different placements of characters on the on-screen keyboard. The simplest communication device activates a switch for selecting an actual object, whereas more advanced devices use intricate symbol codes to produce words on a display or for voice output.

**Voice entry systems** allow students to enter information into the computer simply by speaking into a microphone attached to the computer. Voice entry software is available as an alternative input system. Some computer systems have built-in systems providing voice access to the functions of the computer, but do not necessarily allow voice input of data. An individual may give a voice command, such as "Computer, open hard drive," and other commands to control the computer functions. However, the individual cannot tell the computer to enter the data. Instead, specific voice input software, such as Dragon NaturallySpeaking, ViaVoice, or PowerSecretary, can be installed to provide for

data input. These programs are fairly sensitive to voice discrepancies of different students. Therefore, they must be programmed to be used by one student at a time and in a fairly quiet environment. For some students with written expression problems, voice input can expedite the entering of text. To be successful, individuals who use voice input must have a fairly high cognitive level as well as extreme patience in working with the software.

An assistive technology continuum may help you in selecting the type of assistive devices to use (see Figure 11.4). To use the continuum, the teacher or IEP team identifies the task (e.g., reading), the needs (e.g., comprehension), and the environment (e.g., classroom). Next, the teacher or IEP team selects the tech tools beginning with low-tech tools (e.g., reading guides) to mid-tech tools (e.g., audio books) to high-tech tools (e.g., text readers) until the student is successful. For further information on a variety of low-tech tools and their implementation, visit http://www.onionmountaintech.com.

Not all communication devices interface with the computer. These devices fall into a category of augmentative and alternative communication.

**ACTIVITY 11.7**

With a colleague, list five modifications that you may make for your students using assistive technology.

## AUGMENTATIVE AND ALTERNATIVE COMMUNICATION

Augmentative and alternative communication provides a method of communication for students whose speech is not fluent or understandable enough to communicate effectively. Communication devices include such things as symbol systems, manual communication boards and wallets, electronic communication

**Figure 11.4**   The Assistive Technology Continuum

## *The Assistive Technology Continuum*
### *Devices to try if a student has problems with*

| Tasks | Needs | Environments |
|---|---|---|
| reading | faster work | classroom |
| writing | legible, understandable work | resource/study hall |
| spelling/grammar | comprehension | therapy |
| communication | same work as everyone else | home |
| worksheet completion | modified, shortened, parallel work | community |
| math | visual/graphic/auditory presentations | |
| mapping | independent work | |
| note-taking | fine motor practice | |
| organization/planning | sharing of knowledge | |
| learning another language | correct grammar/spelling | |

**Problems** ━━━━━━━━━━━━━➤ **Success**
                                                    **Independence**

| Low Tech Tools | Mid Tech Tools | High Tech Tools |
|---|---|---|
| specialized pens/pencils/crayons/markers/grips | tape recorders | alternative keyboard/alternative cursor control |
| specialized erasers, correction tapes | digital recorders | word processing |
| raised line paper, grid paper, colored papers | calculators | word prediction |
| highlighters, highlighter tapes | spell checker, dictionary/thesaurus (talking) | brainstorming, graphic organization |
| color coding | dedicated word processor | spell checker, grammar checker |
| Post-It notes, flags, arrows | electronic organizer | word banks (on-screen, overlays) |
| colored filters, page overlays (clear acetate sheets) | audio books | text readers |
| NCR paper | music (tapes/CDs) | on-screen math, computer calcuators |
| reading/writing guides | electronic eraser, stapler | communications devices/software |
| slanted surfaces, dycem, copy holder | mini-book lights | internet access |
| white board, markers, crayons | switch operated toys and appliances | CD reference (maps, encyclopedias) |
| magnetic letters, tactile letters | | CAI |
| magnifiers | | environmental control devices |
| rubber stamps, labels | | |
| specialized measuring and cutting tools | | |

Note: Judith P. Sweeney (2002). Onion Mountain Technology, Inc. http:www.onionmountaintech.PDFfiles/banner.pdf. Reprinted by permission.

devices, speech synthesizers, and communication enhancement software.

Augmentative and alternative communication (AAC) is the supplementation or replacement of natural speech and/or writing. AAC is thought of as a process of assessing and providing a variety of symbols, strategies, and techniques to assist people who are unable to meet their communication needs through natural speech and/or writing. Frequently, professionals and parents think that assistive technology (AT) and AAC are synonymous. It is important to remember that AAC is a process, whereas assistive technology refers to the tools used to assist individuals with functions and activities. We do not discuss AAC in depth here, as the students with disabilities whom we address in this text very rarely use these methods for communication.

**IMPORTANT POINTS**

1. Assistive technology addresses the special tools that students with disabilities must have to access curriculum, engage in learning, meet required outcomes, and transition successfully to the workplace.
2. Examples of assistive technology range from a high-technology solution such as a speaking keyboard to a low-technology solution such as a pencil grip.
3. Legislation has encouraged the use of assistive technology in the classroom.
4. Teachers should begin with simple, inexpensive low-tech options first to prevent wasting extra time and money on high-tech solutions that may not be necessary.
5. The LoTTIE Kits provide teachers with a good source of low tech, easy-to-use assistive technology tools.
6. The operating systems of the computers have had accessibility features either built in to the system software or are available at no cost that provide simple modifications that make using the computer more accessible to students.
7. Some operating system modifications include keyguards, touch sensitive screens, alternative or adapted keyboards, switches, and voice entry systems.
8. Augmentative and alternative communication is a process, whereas assistive technology refers to the tools used to assist individuals with functions and activities.

 **DISCUSSION QUESTIONS**

1. Given the budget constraints placed on schools, make a case for expenditures in the area of technology, perhaps at the expense of other types of instructional materials.
2. Predict how students with special needs and their teachers will be using technology 5 years from now.
3. Describe how you will use technology to enhance your roles in teaching and learning.

# CHAPTER 12

# TRANSITION FROM SCHOOL TO COMMUNITY LIVING

*by Sara C. Pankaskie*

Children with disabilities grow up. They grow up to become adolescents and adults with disabilities. One of the critical turning points in the lives of young people is the transition from secondary school to the world of postsecondary education, employment, and life in the community as an adult. Developing independence, examining one's talents and interests, deciding on a career path, and pursuing either employment or additional schooling are just some of the challenges that all youth in transition face. In addition to these challenges, students with special needs face unique challenges (Wagner & Blackorby, 1996). They are unemployed at a higher rate than peers without disabilities, tend to drop out of school before graduation, are involved with the criminal justice system to a higher degree, and often are living in a dependent situation for a longer period of time (Edgar, 1988; Wagner & Blackorby, 1996). The education reform movement has made these challenges more intense.

The purpose of this chapter is to provide you with information and strategies to help adolescents with special needs make a successful transition from school to adult life. We begin the chapter with a summary of some of the best practices in transition found in the literature. Then we suggest activities for students during early school years to prepare them for the more intense transition programming during the late middle and high school years. As part of this, we define and describe career education and discuss high-stakes testing. We address the legal requirements for transition planning under the Individuals with Disabilities Education Act (IDEA), including other federal laws related to transition, and information about the transition

IEP. Next, we provide guidance in developing and maintaining linkages with families, with other people and agencies within the school, and with other people and agencies in the larger community. In the last section of the chapter, we suggest some practical programming and teaching approaches so you may assist students with special needs to complete high school, become employable, and emerge as independent and productive young adults. There are two main values underlying this chapter. One is that student and family involvement are critical for successful transition. The other is that transition is not a postschool experience. Instead, transition can be thought of as everything we do with and for students while they are in school to help them succeed in their postschool lives.

## BEST PRACTICES IN TRANSITION

The transition literature suggests many "best practices" in the area of transition from school to community living. Unfortunately, many of these best practices have not been substantiated by empirical, student outcomes research (Greene & Albright, 1995; Johnson & Rusch, 1993). A meta-analysis of various studies (Kohler, 1993) found that of the many practices thought to be critical, only four had been substantiated through data-based studies of student outcomes. These four are vocational training, parent involvement, paid work, and social skills training. However, there were several more practices that were strongly implied to be critical. These were interagency collaboration, individualized plans/planning, community-based instruction, community-referenced curriculum, follow-up employment services, integration, and vocational assessment. Other areas that are considered important for students who plan to continue their education at colleges, universities, or vocational-technical schools include self-awareness and advocacy (Adelma & Vogel, 1990; Aune, 1991; Blalock & Patton, 1996; Brinkerhoff, 1996; McGuire, Hall, & Litt, 1991), social-interpersonal (Aune, 1991), independent living (Brinkerhoff,

Shaw, & McGuire, 1992), and academic preparation (Aune, 1991; HEATH Resource Center, 1990; McGuire et al., 1991).

## PREPARING FOR TRANSITION

Preparing for the many roles we will have as adults is a gradual process. A desirable long-term goal for all children and adolescents is for them to become productive members of society. Because children and adolescents with special needs may require a longer time to attain this goal, there are activities parents and teachers may do at school and at home to set the stage for the more direct and intense transition experience that will occur later in high school. We suggest activities for pre-kindergarten, elementary, and middle school.

### Pre-Kindergarten

1. Design activities that encourage children to become more independent.
2. Involve children in activities that build self-esteem and self-direction.
3. Take young children into the community so they may see and learn about many possible careers and lifestyles.
4. Spend time talking to children about what they might like to do when they grow older.
5. Model a good work ethic and a joy of productive engagement.

### Elementary Years

1. Assign jobs to students within the classroom (or at home). Encourage completion of work in a timely and accurate manner.
2. Notice and praise good grooming and hygiene.
3. Encourage parents to participate in the "Take Your Child to Work Day."
4. Show films, bring in guest speakers, or visit different work sites where people with and without disabilities from different career fields are employed.
5. Encourage students to talk about what jobs they might like.

### Middle School

1. Complete vocational aptitude and interest inventories for each student.
2. Address transition service needs on the IEP.
3. Identify adult agencies from whom students may need assistance in the future.
4. Engage students in career exploration activities. Become familiar with high school exit options and the advantages and disadvantages of each.

## Career Education

*Career education* is a term that was introduced into American education in 1971 (Brolin, 1995). It has been defined in several ways, but the basic concepts remain the same: career education is an *ongoing* process that *infuses* an emphasis on careers in *all subjects, K–12*. It includes employment and job-specific training as well as training in areas that prepare the student for many adult roles. Career education develops within stages:

### Grades K–5: Self- and Career Awareness

Self-, career, and technology awareness activities are infused into the curriculum.

### Grade 6: Personal Assessment and Technology Literacy

At this age, most students continue the process of assessing their academic, physical, and social/emotional strengths and weaknesses. They should have intense technological literacy instruction.

### Grades 7 and 8: Career Orientation and Exploration

During this period, students identify broad goals to work toward. Four-year plans for grades 9–12 are developed with input from the students, families, and school personnel.

### Grades 9–12: Academic and Specialized Skills Development

During high school, students attain the competencies necessary to go on for further education, training, and employment. This is done through academic programs and vocational programs and through applied learning in the community.

### Postsecondary: Skills Development and Career Advancement

Career education is not a process that ends with high school. Many students choose to go on for further education or training either immediately after high school or at some point as adults.

Many elements of career education are found in functional curriculum, supported employment, and other transition-related programs. One of the best known and most widely used curricula is the Life Centered Career Education (LCCE) curriculum (Brolin, 1993). LCCE is a K–12 curriculum model that focuses on what an individual needs to know to function in society. It incorporates the basic tenets of the career education concept and provides teachers with a scope and sequence around which to teach children and young adults of all ages. A useful addition to the original LCCE, which targets students with mild disabilities, has been an edition of the LCCE for students with moderate disabilities.

 **ACTIVITY 12.1**

Reexamine the description of career education. Write down the things you did in kindergarten, elementary, middle, and high school that you think helped prepare you for the transition from school to the "real world." Who provided or helped you with these experiences? What other experiences might have been helpful?
(Answers for this and other activities are found in the Instructor's Manual.)

## High-Stakes Testing

Current school reform efforts, including stricter high school graduation requirements will have a powerful effect on the paths students take to attain a high school diploma. High-stakes requirements are of particular concern for students with disabilities (Johnson, Stodden, Emanuel, Luecking, & Mack, 2002; Bakken & Kortering, 1999; Blackorby & Wagner, 1996; Thurlow, Ysseldyke, & Anderson, 1995). The changes in graduation requirements are just a part of the larger movement to increase standards and accountability; however, local and state policy makers often seem unsure about how to include students with disabilities in the new and rigorous high school graduation requirements (NASBE, 1997).

Findings of studies in this area indicate general conclusions about graduation requirements of students with and without disabilities. Among these were (a) states are raising expectations for graduation, (b) choices in exit options are available to students in most of the 50 states, (c) states that have flexible graduation requirements are likely to have multiple paths to graduation, (d) the most common type of modification for students with disabilities is modified coursework, (e) not all states use IEP completion as a way for students with disabilities to meet graduation requirements, and (f) states who administer graduation exams as a requirement for graduation have more exit options for students but are less flexible in standard diploma requirements (Guy, Shin, Lee, & Thurlow, 1999).

Teachers and parents want to know how they can help with this important new challenge. Some of the most important assistance and advocacy should take place early in a student's academic career. Once students are assigned to a self-contained classroom or a modified curriculum, their chances of mastering the competencies associated with a standard diploma are small. If a diploma with an academic emphasis is not possible, then students should seek a graduation option that includes increased opportunities for meaningful employment training and experiences (Patton, Polloway, & Smith, 1996; Thurlow & Johnson, 2000).

## PLANNING FOR TRANSITION

One of the goals of the original landmark federal legislation, PL 94-142 Education for All Handicapped Children's Act, was to increase the personal independence and productivity of persons with disabilities through the provision of educational programming (Kruelle v. New Castle County School District, 1981). Although studies show some improvement in the employment percentages for students with disabilities after they had been out of school 3 to 5 years, they still lag substantially behind their peers without disabilities in all areas. Thus, the trend of unsuccessful postschool outcomes continues in spite of increased efforts over several years (Blackorby & Wagner, 1996; Wehman, 1993).

### The Individuals With Disabilities Education Act and Transition

In 1990, PL 94-142 was amended and became the Individuals with Disabilities Education Act or IDEA (PL 101-476). IDEA required schools to address the transition needs of students in the Individualized Education Program (IEP) to help them plan for life after high school. The law contained a specific definition of transition services and mandated that all IEPs address needed transition services no later than age 16 and annually thereafter. IDEA defined transition services as follows:

> Transition services are a *coordinated set of activities* for a student, designed within an *outcome-oriented process,* which promote movement from *school to postschool* activities, including postsecondary education, vocational training, integrated employ-

ment (including supported employment), continuing and adult education, adult services, independent living, or community participation. The coordinated set of activities shall be *based upon the individual student's needs, taking into account the student's preferences and interests,* and shall include *instruction, community experiences,* the development of *employment* and other *post-school adult living* objectives, and, when appropriate, acquisition of *daily living skills* and *functional vocational evaluation.*(IDEA, PL 101-476)(italics added for emphasis by the authors)

The 1997 amendments to IDEA (PL 105-17) made small but important changes to the part of the law addressing transition from school to community living. The new amendments added language requiring that "beginning at age 14 and updated annually, each student's IEP must include a statement of the transition service needs under applicable components of the child's IEP that focuses on the child's courses of study" (Sec. 300.347 (b)(i)). In a subtle way, this requirement differs from the requirement at age 16 to have "a statement of needed transition services including interagency linkages." The new requirement (along with the legislative intent language) emphasizes the importance of early planning on the part of parents, teachers, and students. As soon as feasible, the student's curriculum should reflect courses that support desired postschool outcomes. For example, a student who is interested in a career in computers may have a statement connected to technology course work, and a student who plans to go on to college may have a statement regarding participation in advanced placement courses. For all students, a statement regarding increased skills of self-advocacy and self-determination should be included (Cashman, 1998).

## Other Laws Related to Transition

IDEA mandates the provision of supports and services for eligible students with disabilities

pre-K through 12th grade. Once a young adult graduates, permanently drops out, or "ages out," that student is no longer eligible under IDEA. The student may, however, come under the auspices of other related laws that support persons with disabilities. Some of these laws provide legal protection through the transition process for students while they are enrolled in school and other laws provide legal protection for the individual's lifetime. Table 12.1 describes some of the major laws related to transition.

Two of these laws, the Rehabilitation Act of 1973 and the Carl D. Perkins Vocational Education Act of 1984, were passed several years ago but were amended in the 1990s. The table reflects just the amendments of these older laws. Section 504 of the Rehabilitation Act of 1973 is not listed because its substance is covered under the Americans with Disabilities Act (ADA).

## The Transition Individualized Education Program (TIEP)

There are many similarities and a few important differences between Transition IEPs and the IEPs completed for students before they need transition services. Table 12.2 summarizes the components of the IEP process that are different for students in need of transition services under IDEA. The components that are required for all IEPs before transition planning remain in effect.

The TIEP is different from a student's previous IEP in that participants now include the student and agency representatives, as appropriate, and the content must address postschool desires and needs. The TIEP is similar to the previous IEP in that it must be reviewed annually and the present level of performance, the goals, and the objectives should drive the services and supports provided to students.

Many local school districts develop Individualized Transition Programs (ITPs) separate from

**Table 12.1** Legislation Since 1990 Affecting Transition for Students with Special Needs

| Name | Year | Major Purpose (relating to transition) |
|---|---|---|
| Americans With Disabilities Act (ADA), PL 101-336 | 1990 | ADA protects people with disabilities from discrimination in employment, public accommodations (including schools), state and local government services (including transportation), and telecommunications relay services. It also requires employers to make "reasonable accommodations" for employees with a disability. |
| Rehabilitation Act Amendments, PL 102-69 | 1992 | New language in the Rehabilitation Act emphasizes that a person with a disability, regardless of the severity of that disability, can attain employment and other life goals if appropriate supports and services are made available. |
| Carl D. Perkins Vocational Education and Applied Technology Education Amendments, PL 101-392 | 1990 | The new amendments replace set-asides mandated by the previous legislation with strong assurances and guarantees for equal access to services and support supplementary services for "special populations" (including students with disabilities). Controversy exists as to the elimination of the set-asides for special populations. |
| School-to-Work Opportunities Act (STW), PL 103-239 | 1994 | The purpose of STW is to establish a national framework to expand educational and career opportunities for all youth (including young people with special needs). States may be funded to plan and develop a system that helps ensure a seamless transition from secondary education to meaningful, high-quality employment and continuing education. |
| Goals 2000: Educate America Act, PL103-227 | 1994 | Goals 2000: Educate America Act presents voluntary national standards describing what all students should know and be able to do at certain grade levels and establishes a national Skills Standards Board to promote development of occupational skills standards. |

the IEPs. Some choose to incorporate transition planning into the student's IEP, but with more emphasis on preparing students to attain their desired postschool outcomes. Regardless of the way your school district elects to accomplish transition planning, you will be responsible for writing goals and objectives that address the postschool needs of your students. Depending on the individual student, these objectives may include skills to prepare them for postsecondary

**Table 12.2** Transition-Related Elments of the IEP Process

### Content of IEP

- A statement of transition service needs that focus on student's existing program or courses (beginning at age 14).
- A statement of needed transition services (beginning at age 16 or younger if appropriate).
- A statement of each agency's responsibilities and/or linkages.
- Goals and objectives addressing instruction, related services, community experiences, employment, postschool adult living (and, if appropriate, daily living skills and functional vocational evaluation).
- Because of the outcome orientation of the process, some statement of the student's desired postschool outcomes is implied. It should address, as appropriate, postsecondary education, vocational training, integrated employment (including supported employment), continuing and adult education, linkage with adult services, independent living, community participation. If services are not needed in these areas, the IEP team must indicate this and state the basis for making this determination.

### Participants of IEP Meeting

- The student must be invited.
- Representatives from agencies responsible for providing or paying for transition services.

### Notice of Meetings

- An indication that a purpose of the meeting is to consider transition services for the student.
- Beginning at least 1 year before the student reaches the age of majority, the student is informed of his or her rights as an adult (including signing the IEP).

education, competitive employment, and/or community participation.

We encourage you to contact your local school district for copies of local transition guidelines and secondary IEP/Transition Planning formats. Examples of selected sections of TIEPs for two students appear in Figure 12.1. In our two examples, Bobbie G. is in 11th grade and working toward an alternate diploma. Her exceptionality is Specific Learning Disabilities. George B. is in 10th grade and working toward a standard diploma. His exceptionality is Behavior Disorders.

As a teacher of adolescents with special needs, you will be involved in helping your students and their parents make informed choices as they plan for transition. Part of this involves helping students understand the different diploma choices available to them and the consequences of leaving school with a document other than a standard diploma. For example, without a standard high school diploma, it is more difficult to access

many postsecondary education options such as a community college or university. The armed services usually will not accept anything except a standard diploma (or its equivalent), and some employers are reluctant to hire people who do not have one. Although you may not be responsible for the entire transition planning process, you will be a key player. Below are some of the steps that must be taken before, during, and after the TIEP meeting (State of Florida, 1993):

1. Become familiar with local adult services and supports.
2. Obtain appropriate releases of information for the student.
3. Plan the TIEP meeting, which should include the student's input.
4. Schedule the TIEP meeting to include teachers, administrators, counselors, family members, adult agency representatives, and the student.

**Figure 12.1**   Sample Transition IEP for Two Students

*Desired Postschool Outcome* is an expression of the student's dreams/visions 1 to 3 years after high school in the areas of employment, postsecondary education, community participation, residential preferences, etc. (i.e., live, work, and play).

**Bobbie** desires to enroll in a postsecondary program to become a child-care worker, continue to live at home, learn to drive a car, and participate in a bowling league.

**George** wants to live at home while he attends community college, continue his involvement with the local barbershop quartet group, and get a part-time job at the Big-Blue Video store.

The *Present Level of Performance* describes how the student is currently functioning. It should be stated so that the relationship between the student's current level of functioning and future level of functioning required to achieve the desired postschool outcome is apparent. It should include what the student *can do* and what the student *needs.* Test scores are acceptable if they are accompanied by an explanation of why they are important.

Based on student and parent interviews, past IEP summaries, other school records, and observation, **Bobbie** is on track to meet the requirements for an alternate diploma. She has mastered the performance objectives in the areas of functional academics at the independent level. Bobbie has volunteered at the on-campus day-care center and is near successful completion of the special needs vocational program in this area. She needs to investigate postschool training options available to her and have some paid work experiences. Bobbie is independent in all daily living and most postschool adult living skills, but still has problems with budgeting money. She has taken Driver's Education, but has not applied for her restricted license. Bobbie goes bowling with her siblings, but has not found a league. Her **priority transition needs are to (1) participate in a work experience program (preferably one that is paid), (2) apply for her restricted driver's license, (3) learn money management skills, and (4) locate and sign up for a bowling league.**

Based on prior IEPs and school records, **George** is successful with the academic work in his inclusion classes. He continues to participate in strategies instruction in the resource room. He has difficulty with time management. He has investigated some of the community colleges in the area, but has not selected his career. George is involved with a barbershop quartet and enjoys his once-a-week rehearsals. His parents report that he usually completes his chores at home with few reminders and is independent in community activities. Curriculum-based vocational evaluations indicate that George has strengths in the areas of listening and following directions. He has good personal hygiene and follows through on assigned tasks. George works well alone and has improved in his ability to control his temper in the classroom setting when he feels that classmates are making fun of him. According to his counselor, George can state the appropriate social skills for group participation in all settings. Although he has some informal job experience, usually working for relatives, he has not had any formal employment experience. George needs to *improve his group social skills, time management skills, and select a career.*

*Annual Goals* address discrepancies between the desired postschool outcomes and the present level of performance. All activity areas must be addressed either as a goal or a statement of why the IEP team feels a goal is not needed.

**Figure 12.1** Continued

We present **sample annual goals for each** student.

> **Bobbie** will find paid work experience.

> **George** will demonstrate appropriate social skills while working in groups in a variety of settings.

*Short-Term Objectives* must relate directly to the annual goal and must be measurable. We also include the criteria, schedule, and responsible person or persons.

To achieve the goal of paid work experience:

*Objective 1:* Using classified ads, **Bobbie** will find five employment opportunities by November 15. The OT instructor will assist Bobbie.

*Objective 2:* Given five possible employment opportunities, Bobbie will fill out and submit five applications without spelling and grammer errors by December 2. The OT instructor will assist Bobbie.

*Objective 3:* When invited to interview, Bobbie will meet with the interviewers and secure a position by January 15. The OT instructor will assist Bobbie.

*Objective 4:* When requested, Bobby will provide evidence of her ongoing employment on a monthly basis from February through May. The OT instructor will assist Bobbie.

To achieve the goal of displaying appropriate social skills in various settings:

*Objective 1:* In a pull-out group setting supervised by the school counselor, **George** will successfully role-play appropriate social skills 80% of the time by September 2.

*Objective 2:* In the pull-out group setting supervised by the special education teacher, George will demonstrate appropriate social skills 80% of the time by November 2.

*Objective 3:* In one inclusive class setting supervised by the special education teacher, George will demonstrate appropriate social skills 80% of the time by February 2.

*Objective 4:* In both pull-out and inclusive class settings, George will demonstrate appropriate social skills 80% of the time as monitored by the special education teacher by April 2.

5. Send notice of the TIEP meeting to all participating members.
6. Prepare for the actual TIEP meeting, which may include preparing a packet of information and a survey of the student's job interests and adult living goals.
7. Initiate the TIEP meeting, which includes setting the tone for planning the student's future centered around living, employment, community access, and friendship goals in the adult world.
8. Develop an outcome statement that projects future goals for the student 1 to 5 years after your student graduates.
9. Review the student's present level of performance, needs, preferences, and interests.
10. Develop annual goals and short-term objectives in the transition activity areas of instruction, community experiences, employment, postschool adult living, daily living skills, and functional vocational assessment.

11. Assign follow-up responsibilities for tracking the progress of transition services for the student after he/she graduates from high school.

 ### Activity 12.2

Make a list of the graduation requirements for a standard diploma in your school district (call the school district office, a local high school, or go to the school's Web site). Additionally, ask them about other diploma options such as GED, IEP-driven, modified diploma, and so on for students with disabilities.

 **IMPORTANT POINTS**

1. Transition is not just a postschool experience as it includes everything we do during school to prepare students for adult living.
2. Critical practices for successful transition found in the literature are vocational training, parent involvement, paid work, and social skills training (Kohler, 1993).
3. Other practices for successful transition include interagency collaboration, individualized plans/planning, community-based instruction, community-referenced curriculum, follow-up employment services, integration, and vocational assessment (Kohler, 1993).
4. Planning and preparation for adult roles do not begin in high school, but much earlier through experiences in the home, school, and community.
5. Career education is based on the infusion of critical skills for living and working throughout the school day from the earliest years and throughout a student's school life.
6. Leaving high school with any exit document other than a standard diploma can have serious consequences for a student's future.

7. The Life Centered Career Education (LCCE) curriculum model is a unique scope and sequence to teach career education.
8. Transition is ". . . an outcome-oriented process . . . which includes a coordinated set of activities . . . which promotes movement from school to postschool activities . . . must take into account the student's preferences and interests . . . and must include instruction, community experiences, the development of employment and other postschool adult living objectives, daily living skills, and functional vocational evaluation" (IDEA, PL 101-476).
9. The 1997 amendments to IDEA lower the mandatory age to start the transition planning process to 14.
10. The Transition IEP is different from a student's previous IEP in that participants now include the student and agency representatives, as appropriate, and the content must address postschool desires and needs.
11. The Transition IEP is similar to a student's previous IEP in that it must be reviewed annually and the present level of performance, the goals, and the objectives should drive the services and supports provided to the student.

## LINKING FOR TRANSITION

Planning and implementing transition supports and services is not something that can or should be done only by schools and teachers. Schools must join with *families, intraagency* personnel (people inside the school system such as general and vocational educators and guidance counselors), and *interagency* personnel (people from the wider community, such as representatives from adult service agencies and employers). In this section, we provide you with some ideas about how to connect or link with these key stakeholders.

## Family Linkages

Many families are very involved with their children during the early years. Young children require care and attention, and those with special needs may evoke more nurturing and protective impulses in families than typical children. By the time students reach high school, however, family involvement in the IEP process has usually declined (Thorin, Yovanoff, & Irvin, 1996). The 1990 amendments to IDEA attempted to reemphasize the importance of family involvement by including a requirement of special notification to families when the purpose of the IEP meeting was to discuss transition services. Salembrier and Furney (1997) list three reasons as to the importance of family involvement in the transition planning and implementation process:

1. Families know more about their adolescents' needs, interests, and preferences.
2. The transition process prepares family members to think about the new roles and responsibilities they will have when their adolescent leaves the protective atmosphere of high school and the entitlement of IDEA.

3. If done correctly, involvement can empower the family to advocate for the adolescent during and after high school.

Families can be involved in many ways during transition. They may be involved in creating a vision, in the transition planning process, and in facilitating self-determination (Morningstar, Turnbull, & Turnbull, 1996). Training parents to become active partners may result in improved services and opportunities, both during school and after graduation. Family members should be taught the process of adult agency referral, mechanics of developing a TIEP, strategies for supporting a working child, strategies for accessing adult community services, and other information specific to their adolescent's transition needs. Table 12.3 lists some potential barriers along with solutions to family involvement in transition suggested in the literature (Salembier & Fumey, 1998).

## Intraagency Linkages

It is important for you and the students to develop linkages with people in the school environment because transition is not just a

**Table 12.3** Some Barriers and Solutions for Family Involvement In Transition

| *Barrier* | *Solution* |
| --- | --- |
| **If the family lacks knowledge or awareness:** | **Then schools and techers should:** |
| of rights and responsibilities during transition | share information in family-friendly formats (brochures, tapes, etc.) |
| about the continuum of programs offered in high school | discuss array of services; provide written or taped information |
| about graduation requirements | provide written information; discuss early and often; readdress during each TIEP meeting |
| about eligibility requirements for and services provided by adult agencies | hold Agency Fair; provide written information; invite agency personnel to TIEP meetings |
| about postsecondary options | share information about people with similar disabilities who have been successful; provide job shadowing |
| about community resources | provide written or taped information |

postschool experience. These individuals are the ones who help students acquire the knowledge and skills that will allow them to be successful after school. These intraagency linkages include general education, vocational education, and guidance and counseling.

### General Education

Students who wish to pursue postsecondary education must first obtain a standard high school diploma or its equivalent. This makes linking with general education teachers important. Ways to support students academically in inclusive settings are discussed elsewhere in this text. Please see Section II for a discussion of academic techniques.

### Vocational Education

About 99% of high school students with disabilities who stayed in school for four grade levels enrolled in some type of vocational education during that time (Wagner & Blackorby, 1996). Students with learning or speech problems, who took a concentration of vocational education during high school, were employed after high school at near or above the levels of the general population (Wagner & Blackorby, 1996). Vocational education may include school-to-work programs or work experiences.

*School-to-Work Programs.* One of the most exciting initiatives related to vocational education and transition is the School-to-Work Opportunities Act. The purpose of the School-to-Work (STW) Opportunities Act is to establish a national framework to broaden educational, career, and economic opportunities for all youth through partnerships among business, schools, community-based organizations, and state and local governments. "All youth" includes young people with special needs (e.g., students with disabilities, disadvantaged youth, and youth with limited English proficiency). STW was designed to help states develop an integrated system that would provide students with a seamless transition from secondary education to meaningful, high-quality employ-

ment and continuing education. Successful school-to-work programs have three core components:

1. School-based learning (e.g., programs in which students learn math, science, language arts, technology, and other skills and standards in the context of the work world)
2. Work-based learning (e.g., programs in which students gain practical experience and training)
3. Connecting activities (e.g., links between employers, schools, teachers, students, and others)

These three components should be incorporated in kindergarten through postsecondary educational programs. The best-known types of school-to-work programs are Tech Prep, Career Academies ("Schools Within Schools"), Youth Apprenticeships, Cooperative Education, Vocational Technical Schools, Vocational Student Organizations (VSOs), and School-based Enterprises.

*Work Experiences.* Despite the common perception that work experience is effective in promoting future employment success, the National Longitudinal Transition Study (Wagner & Blackorby, 1996) found only a slight difference in the percentage of students (10.4%) competitively employed after high school between students with mild disabilities who did and did not have work experience. However, paid work experiences while in high school do make a difference in postschool outcomes (Rabren, Dunn, & Chambers, 2002; Benz, Lindstrom, & Yovanoff, 2000; Sitlington, Frank, & Carson, 1993). Students with disabilities who engage in paid employment before high school completion are more likely to stay in school, remain employed after school completion, seek postsecondary education opportunities, and become self-supporting adults (Edgar, 1987).

Paid work experiences should be closely integrated with school-based instruction in job search and job maintenance skills training. Ideally, each student enrolled in job search and job maintenance skills training is simultaneously placed in a part-time job in the community. Skills learned in the classroom can then be practiced and generalized in the real world for permanency. A system for ongoing support and monitoring is critical for successful paid work experiences. Additionally, all members of the transition team should fully understand and implement the monitoring and evaluation process.

### *Guidance and Counseling*

School counselors often take an active role in career planning for students with disabilities and initiate early career planning with parents and students. Students need to become aware of the many programs that can help them beyond high school, including community college programs, counseling and testing, student disability services, occupational preparation programs, vocational training programs, and adult agency services.

School counselors should become an integral part of the transition team so they are informed and knowledgeable about the multitude of postschool program options for this group of students. High school special education teachers, job coaches, and other special education support personnel can play a vital role in collaborating with school counselors and soliciting their support on behalf of students with special needs in their quest for successful employment and adult living.

 ## ACTIVITY 12.3

Interview a school counselor to determine the counselor's responsibilities as far as providing transition services to adolescents with mild disabilities. Design the interview form with a peer.

## Interagency Linkages

Under IDEA, schools must provide a description of "interagency responsibilities and/or linkages" needed before a student leaves school. This implies that schools need to have a working knowledge of and relationship with the public or private agencies that might provide or pay for services needed during transition. Unfortunately, students with disabilities often have little contact with representatives from postsecondary education, social, or rehabilitation agencies during their high school years (Roessler, Brolin, & Johnson, 1990).

The referral process to adult agencies must begin early so school personnel can assist with the application process and ensure active service status with the appropriate adult agency before graduation. Once a student with special needs graduates, there are a multitude of adult agencies to access. However, most of the agencies are burdened with high caseloads, bureaucratic complexities, discrepant eligibility criteria, and voluminous paperwork. Most adult agencies (such as state vocational rehabilitation agencies) require a formal application, medical exam, psychological exam, permission to access existing assessment information, interviews with the agency representative, eligibility determination, vocational evaluation, and/or extended vocational evaluation. This process can take anywhere from 12 to 24 months. A planned and systematic process of adult agency referral should be included in the student's TIEP during the tenth grade. The ultimate goal must be active client status with the adult agency, including postsecondary institutions, before the student's graduation date.

Once students with disabilities have completed the period of eligibility under IDEA (usually through age 21 or high school graduation, whichever comes first), they are no longer guaranteed services. The young adult will have to undergo the eligibility determination process for whatever adult services are desired. If determined eligible, the person may receive services from that agency as long as adequate state or federal funding is available or until the eligibility is reversed. There are many challenges in finding and getting the services necessary for young adults to make a successful transition. IDEA makes it clear that meeting these challenges is the shared responsibility of schools, parents, students, and agency personnel.

There are two main reasons for you to get to know local representatives of the adult agencies. First, the linkage gives you access to information that will be important to your students and their families, and second, it will give you a point of contact if one of your students has problems with an agency.

The most often accessed adult service agencies are listed and described in Table 12.4. This is not intended to be an exhaustive list but instead a beginning place for teachers, transition specialists, parents, and students.

Welfare reform is rapidly changing the types of programs available to people with limited means, including those with disabilities. As the federal government gives more and more discretion to state and local governments, fewer and fewer general statements can be made about national programs. You will need to become familiar with state requirements, especially for the programs described in Table 12.4. Because regulations change, including eligibility requirements, you should stay in close contact with local representatives of these agencies. For the most current and detailed information related to Social Security programs, contact your local Social Security Administration (SSA) office. You may locate the SSA office closest to you by calling 1-800-772-1213.

▼ **ACTIVITY 12.4**

Working with a small group, plan an agency fair, an event that provides an opportunity for many different adult service agencies to share information with family members and students in a school or nonschool setting (e.g., a mall). Determine the agencies to invite, incentives for student and parent participation, prior preparations, and follow-up activities.

 **IMPORTANT POINTS** ◀

1. For effective transition to occur, families, intraagency personnel such as people inside the school system, and interagency personnel such as representatives from adult service agencies must work together.

2. The 1990 amendments to IDEA attempted to reemphasize the importance of family involvement by including a requirement of special notification to families when the purpose of the IEP meeting was to discuss transition services.

3. Family members need to be taught the process of adult agency referral, the mechanics of developing a TIEP, effective strategies for supporting the efforts of a working student, strategies for accessing adult community services, and other information specific to their adolescent's transition from school to the adult community.

4. Intraagency linkages include general education, vocational education, and guidance and counseling.

5. Successful school-to-work programs have the three core components of school-based learning, work-based learning, and connecting activities.

6. Students with disabilities who engage in paid employment before high school completion are more likely to stay in school, remain employed after school completion, seek postsecondary education opportunities, and become self-supporting adults (Edgar, 1987).

7. Under IDEA, schools must provide a description of "interagency responsibilities and/or linkages" needed before a student leaves school.

8. Once students with disabilities complete the period of eligibility under IDEA (usually through age 21 or high school graduation, whichever comes first), they are no longer guaranteed services.

**Table 12.4**   Adult Agencies That Serve Students With Disabilities in Transition

| Agency | Description |
| --- | --- |
| Vocational Rehabilitation (VR) | VR's primary purpose is to assist eligible recipients to attain vocational goals and thereby become more economically self-sufficient. To be eligible for VR, a person must<br>(1) have a physical and/or mental impairment that constitutes or results in a substantial impediment to employment, and<br>(2) be able to benefit from an employment outcome from VR services.<br>VR is a federally funded program (80%) with state match. |
| Job/Employment Services Job Training Partnership Act (JTPA) | Job or Employment Services are often administered by the same state agency that administers VR. The Job Training Partnership Act (JTPA) may also be in this agency (JTPA may be referred to by different names in different localities). This act provides job-training services for economically disadvantaged adults and others who face significant employment barriers. |
| Developmental Disabilities (DD) Services | Developmental disabilities services may include services in the areas of employment, residential, advocacy, and day activity programs.<br>The most common developmental disabilities are mental retardation, autism, cerebral palsy, and epilepsy. |
| Community Colleges and Vocational Technical Schools | Community Colleges and Vocational Technical Schools typically have open enrollment and serve high school graduates from a certain catchment area. They can provide information about financial aid, academic counseling and guidance, special supports for students with disabilities, and, of course, an array of programs that usually includes both terminal degrees with certifications or 2-year programs that will allow students to go on to upper-division colleges and universities. |
| Social Security Administration (SSA) | The SSA is responsible for administering many federal and state funds for eligible elderly persons and persons with disabilities. The ones that may affect students in transition are: *Income Programs* [e.g., Supplemental Security Income Benefits (SSI)], *Medical Programs* [e.g., Medicare and Medicaid], *Work Incentive Programs* [e.g., Plans for Achieving Self-Support (PASS), Impairment-Related Work Expenses (IRWE), Student Earned Income Exclusion, etc.]. |

## TEACHING FOR TRANSITION

The specific skills needed by a student with special needs to prepare for life after school will, of course, depend on the desired postschool outcomes of that individual. In this section, we address these skills in the context of the following transition domains of IDEA: Instruction, Related Services, Community Experiences, Postschool Adult Living, Social and Interpersonal Skills, Employment, and as appropriate, Functional Vocational Assessment and Daily Living Skills. When required, we further divide the skills in these domains into those that are more likely to be priorities for students who will be going (a) into postsecondary education or (b) directly into the workforce. These two outcomes are not mutually exclusive. Many students work while they attend school. Moreover, many of the same types of skills are necessary for young adults regardless of whether they go on to postsecondary education or directly into employment. It is impossible to teach students *all* the skills needed for the remainder of their lives. Therefore, you and the rest of the TIEP team must set priorities.

In this section we describe general skill areas for students in transition and list some specific skills for transition to postsecondary educational settings and employment. Additionally, we describe commercially available programs for teaching these and other important skills.

### Instruction

The teaching of academic skills is necessary for transitioning to either postsecondary education or employment. We have discussed strategies for teaching academic content throughout previous chapters so we just highlight information here.

### Academic and Study Skills for Postsecondary Education

The importance of having an integrated transition planning process is especially relevant for students who are going on to postsecondary education. If the academic component of the TIEP is not developed in the context of the student's desired postschool outcomes, the student may not be adequately prepared for postsecondary education. Although most high school curricula are set up to be "college prep," teachers and parents must make sure not only that students enroll in the appropriate courses, but also that they are provided with supports and services to pass those courses. Necessary accommodations and modifications should be documented on each student's TIEP. This helps ensure that the student will have a sufficient grade point average for college admission and be prepared academically for college-level work. Additionally, teachers, parents, and the students should make formal preparation to take college entrance exams, including investigating possible testing accommodations that are available to students with documented disabilities (Hicks-Cooley & Kurtz, 1997).

Part of academic preparation is preparing for the increased study and organizational demands of postsecondary education. Students need to be taught study and work habits that will allow them to balance the demands of school with the need for some personal freedom and relationship building as a young adult (Hicks-Cooley & Kurtz, 1997; Hildreth, Dixon, Frerichs, & Heflin, 1994). See Chapter 9 for a thorough discussion of study skills that will enhance student success in postsecondary education and in the workplace.

 **ACTIVITY 12.5**

Call a nearby community college and inquire about any supports and services available for students with disabilities. List and report to class.

### Academic Skills for Employment

The SCANS (Secretary's Commission on Achieving Necessary Skills) Report (1991) identifies academic skill areas critical to functioning in the world of work. They include reading and writing on the job, figuring computations, estimating, making change, and using time wisely. Yet many students with special needs are not being exposed to functional curricula that prepare them for employment (California Education Transition Center, 1990). Students with special needs often have difficulty generalizing traditional academics to the real world of employment and adult living (Polloway, Patton, Epstein, & Smith, 1989; Steere, Pancsofar, Powell, & Butterworth, 1989; Taylor & O'Reilly, 2000). Job-related functional academics such as counting change, operating cash registers, and calculating net and gross pay are easily infused into existing mathematics courses.

## Related Services

The term *related services* is defined as "transportation and such developmental, corrective, and other supportive services as are required to assist a child with a disability to benefit from special education . . . " (Sec. 300.22). Related services have been a required part of every student's IEP since the original PL 94-142 legislation. The 1997 amendments to IDEA highlight related services as part of transition planning by adding it to the areas that must be addressed on IEPs for students in need of transition services. Examples of related services that may be especially important for students in transition include transportation to a community-based instruction site, accommodations to a workplace environment, and parent counseling regarding the impact of a student's job on the income of the family. Related services are usually listed on the IEP separate from goals and objectives. However, if the need for the services is expressed or implied in the present levels of performance, there may also be annual goals to support them.

## Community Experiences

Community experiences are mentioned specifically in IDEA for two major reasons:

(1) some students with special needs do not have opportunities for a wide range of community experiences, and (2) many students with special needs require assistance to generalize knowledge and skills acquired in the classroom to real-life settings. Issues surrounding community-based instruction (CBI) or community-referenced instruction (CRI) include: (a) who should receive the instruction, (b) how much is appropriate, (c) which skills to teach in the community, and (d) what is the impact on inclusion efforts.

The amount of time spent in CRI should vary inversely with the student's ability to generalize. The more a student generalizes academic and social skills from school to nonschool settings, the less community-referenced instruction is needed. Conversely, the less a student demonstrates skills in real-life application situations, the more the student needs CRI.

Many school systems, community colleges, and colleges are promoting community service for *all* students. Community service projects are a positive step toward giving all students opportunities to feel connected to their communities. For example, the author is involved with a community service project for high school students with special needs. The students visit a retirement home weekly and read to the residents.

## Postschool Adult Living

Postschool adult living is a broad area that encompasses the skills and knowledge required in the adult world outside of work and school. As adults, we shop for groceries, balance our checkbooks, make dental appointments, vote, and participate in community volunteer activities. We form and maintain relationships with others and make lifestyle decisions that affect our lives for years to come. Some students learn the skills to perform these activities through family modeling or incidental learning without direct instruction. Other students will need guidance and support in applying skills learned in and out of school to their own situations in the community. It may be difficult to find the instructional time to address postschool adult living skills in a period of time when the emphasis is almost exclusively on rigorous academics and higher graduation requirements. However, in the larger scheme of life, they may be more critical to students' survival for life after high school (Cronin & Patton, 1993). This section suggests possible ways to teach critical postschool adult living skills. It also addresses self-determination and interpersonal skills, which are critical for successful postschool adult living.

### Life Skills

There are two basic ways to approach the teaching of life skills in the school setting. One way is to embed life skills into academic instruction. The other is to embed academics in life skills instruction. The approach you choose depends on several factors. If students who have mild disabilities have opportunities to practice adult living skills at home and in the community, and are in a school setting that stresses academic instruction, then you will probably want to teach academics and application opportunities in simulated or actual community settings. If students are able to give you specific examples of how they might use this knowledge and skills in various settings in the community (use language to mediate the generalization), you can be fairly certain they will most likely use the skills in places outside the classroom.

If, on the other hand, the students are enrolled in a life skills curriculum and have great difficulty applying the skills in real-life settings, then you will probably want to teach life skills explicitly and embed the necessary functional academics into this instruction. Below are examples of these two different approaches.

EXAMPLE 1:   EMBEDDING LIFE SKILLS
INTO ACADEMICS
    Teach a lesson on fractions using direct instruction. As part of connecting the fractions

lesson to prior learning, ask students why they think knowing about fractions might be useful in everyday life.

Follow the lesson on fractions with a discussion about how fractions could be used in everyday activities (measurements for cooking, measurements for building, fractions of an hour). Or, give a homework assignment to identify three ways fractions are used in their home.

EXAMPLE 2:   EMBEDDING ACADEMICS
INTO LIFE SKILLS LESSONS
    Teach a cooking lesson focusing on measuring parts (fractions) of a cup. Use direct instruction and modeling/demonstration. For guided practice, you might read a line from the recipe and then have students measure out the amount as a group. For independent practice, assign each student to read a line from a recipe and then require the student to actually measure out that amount.

Even if they demonstrate mastery of the concept of fractions in the cooking context, there is no assurance that students, especially students with moderate cognitive disabilities, will be able to apply the concepts in real-life settings. This will require an additional step.

### Self-Advocacy and Self-Determination

In the past, teachers, agency personnel, and parents completed transition planning without much student input. There are many curricula available that use a variety of approaches to help students develop self-determination skills. Table 12.5 lists and describes several of these curricula. Research indicates a relationship between positive postschool outcomes and self-determination for individuals with mild disabilities (Wehmeyer & Schwartz, 1997).

Students should be encouraged to participate in the planning for transition. Many students do not see themselves as an integral part of the transition planning process, and some professionals do not see students as active participants in TIEP development. Suggestions for ensuring student involvement in TIEP development include (a) have students write a rough draft of their own TIEP as a written class assignment, (b) encourage students to make a list of their strengths and weaknesses, (c) ask students to prepare a tentative list of their own transition goals to bring to the TIEP meeting, (d) allow students to be the prime decision makers relative to the time and place scheduled for their TIEP meeting, and (e) ensure that no TIEP meeting is held unless the students can be in attendance. See Figure 12.2 for an example of a way of involving students in the TIEP process.

 **ACTIVITY 12.6**

> Interview a student in a secondary program. Ask the student about his or her job interests, strengths and weaknesses, living plans for the future, and postsecondary education interests, if any. Fill out the Goals for My Future form (see Figure 12.2).

*Self-Advocacy and Self-Determination in Postsecondary Education.* The biggest difference between high school and postsecondary education is that the burden of advocacy shifts away from teachers and parents and toward the student. Under IDEA, schools and parents form a partnership to provide a free and appropriate education for the student. As discussed previously, students in postsecondary educational institutions have rights under ADA and Section 504, but they must be able to advocate for themselves. Self-determination and participation in one's own IEP has been discussed previously.

The first step in preparing for postsecondary education for young people with disabilities is to open them up to the possibility and desirability of continuing education. Going on to college may not seem like a very good idea to high school students who struggle daily with academic work. Teachers and parents can promote continuing education by (a) helping the young person set

**Table 12.5**  Sample Self-Determination Curricula

| Title/Date | Author | Target Population | Comments |
|---|---|---|---|
| *Become Your Own Expert* (1995) | Carpenter | High school students with learning disabilities | One-semester course designed to teach self-advocacy skills |
| *The Education Planning Strategy* (1987) | VanReusen, Bos, Schumaker, & Deshler | High school students with learning disabilities | This strategy from the Learning Strategies curriculum teaches students to advocate for themselves during IEP and other conferences |
| *Learning With PURPOSE* (1995) | Serna & Lau-Smith | Youth 12–25 with mild to moderate disabilities | Comprehensive curriculum |
| *It's My Life* (1995) | Curtis | Middle and high school students | Materials are designed to be fun for students (i.e., a card deck) |
| *Whose Future Is It Anyway?* (1995) | Wehmeyer | Students with mental disabilities | A student-directed transition planning process that is age and developmentally appropriate |
| *Choicemaker Self-Determination Transition Curriculum* (1996) | Martin, Huber, Marshall, Maxson, & Jerman | One part targets high school students with disabilities; other parts target all students | Comprehensive (and field tested); includes *Self-directed IEP, Choosing Employment Goals,* and *Take Action* |

**Figure 12.2**  Goals for My Future

*Directions:* Read each question and fill in the blanks.

One to three years after high school, I want to be living
_____ in an apartment.
_____ with my family
_____ Other _____

In order to do this, I will need to do the following:

1. _____ by _____
                    (action)                                              (date)
2. _____ by _____
                    (action)                                              (date)

I want to be employed as a _____
                                                                        (job title)

In order to get this job, I will need to do the following:

1. _____ by _____
                    (action)                                              (date)
2. _____ by _____
                    (action)                                              (date)

I want to continue my education at a
_____ community college
_____ college
_____ university
_____ vocational technical school

In order to do this, I will need to do the following:

1. _____ by _____
                    (action)                                              (date)
2. _____ by _____
                    (action)                                              (date)

and work toward goals, (b) pointing out people with similar disabilities who have entered and completed college and done well, and (c) helping the student develop a more positive self-concept. This does not mean that you should encourage unrealistic goals, but you can help students develop realistic self-images in order to capitalize on strengths and accommodate deficits (Adelma & Vogel, 1990; Aune, 1991; McGuire, Hall, & Litt, 1991). Students need to know how they learn best. They not only need to be taught compensatory learning strategies, but also need to understand why the strategies are necessary for them and the importance of their continued use. Learning disabilities do not disappear when a student leaves high school.

Good self-esteem and a realistic self-image are not enough, however. Students must also be

effective at advocating for themselves for success in postsecondary education (Dowdy & Evers, 1996; Koller, 1994). Several authors (Aune, 1991; Brinkerhoff, Shaw, & McGuire, 1992; McGuire, Hall, & Litt, 1991; McWhirter, 1990; VanReusen, Bos, Schumaker, & Deshler, 1987) suggest that students need to:

1. Be aware of their strengths, weaknesses, and learning preferences.
2. Understand their legal rights (federal laws and regulations such as ADA and applicable state laws).
3. Understand the circumstances under which they can and should request accommodations.
4. Maintain records that document their disability (e.g., IEP, medical records, descrip-

tions of accommodations provided in high school).

5. Identify the types of supports and services that will help them most in their chosen postsecondary setting (e.g., note takers, readers, transportation, etc.).

6. Identify specific services and resources available in the postsecondary institution they wish to attend.

7. Identify the specific people or offices they should contact before, during, and after admission to their school of choice.

Most colleges and universities, including community colleges and vocational technical schools, have written policies regarding students with disabilities. As part of the transition planning process, teachers and guidance counselors should make students and their parents aware that these policies are usually found in the college catalog and/or on the college Web site. Examples of typical supports and services for students with documented disabilities include note takers, special testing conditions (extended time, quiet setting, etc.), sign language interpreters, readers.

*Self-Advocacy and Self-Determination Skills in Employment.* Self-advocacy and self-determination skills are important to the worker with a disability. Some of these skills are more critical during the job-seeking process and others are needed to help workers maintain employment and feel good about their jobs. In the area of employment, the following self-advocacy skills are suggested:

1. Listing strengths and accomplishments (in writing a job application or in person during an interview).

2. Discussing the disability and requesting appropriate accommodations.

3. Responding to criticism in an appropriate manner.

4. Self-evaluating performance, monitoring task completion, and providing self-feedback.

5. Goal setting, including developing short- and long-term goals, and monitoring progress.

6. Developing a vocational plan that includes goals for career advancement and job upgrading.

7. Standing up for one's rights on the job (not being taken advantage of) (Hanley-Maxwell & Collet-Klingenburg, 1997).

## Social and Interpersonal Skills

Interacting with other people is something we do every day in almost every aspect of our lives. Some of us are more socially adept than others. We seldom think of our social skills consciously. Research and anecdotal reports have clearly shown that for many students with disabilities, socialization is not a naturally occurring process (Chandler & Pankaskie, 1997). Lack of appropriate social skills may result in social isolation in the community and, worse, involvement with the criminal justice system. If we do not provide systematic instruction in social skills for students with disabilities, we may be preparing students to fail in school and in the broader world of work and community.

There are many commercially available curricula that address many aspects of social-interpersonal skills. Some of them are listed and described in Table 12.6.

### Social and Interpersonal Skills for Postsecondary Education

In addition to self-advocacy and academic skills, students in postsecondary educational settings need appropriate interpersonal skills (Aune, 1991; Hildreth et al., 1994; Koller, 1994). Social skills essential for postsecondary educational settings may include the ability to (a) use strategies to manage frustration and anger, (b) speak in a way that conveys a positive yet realistic self-image, (c) show awareness and concerns for the feelings of others, and (d) interact positively with college instructors, administrators, staff, and peers.

**ACTIVITY 12.7**

In a small group or individually, review some of the social skills curricula listed in Table 12.6 and discuss their importance for students who plan to attend a community college, college, university, or vocational technical school.

### Social and Interpersonal Skills for Employment

Lack of social and interpersonal skills is often cited as the primary reason for unemployment and underemployment of individuals with special needs (Sitlington, Clark, & Kolstoe, 2000; Black, & Rojewski, 1998). The specific skills related to successful employment are (a) independently managing one's activities, (b) meeting minimal cleanliness and dress requirements, (c) getting along with supervisors, (d) getting along with coworkers, (e) following directions, (f) being punctual, (g) managing time effectively and efficiently, (h) keeping an orderly work environment, (i) being friendly on the job, and (j) maintaining a moral work ethic (Archer & Gleason, 1994; Minskoff & DeMoss, 1994; Warger, 1990). *Job-Related Social Skills: A Curriculum for Adolescents With Special Needs* (Montague, 1988) and *Working II* (Foss & Vilhauer, 1986) are two programs that promote prosocial skills and address special considerations for social skills in employment settings.

The purpose of *Job-Related Social Skills: A Curriculum for Adolescents With Special Needs* (Montague, 1988) is to teach adolescents 18 job-related social skills that will increase their opportunity for job success. The skill sequence is hierarchical, with the skills ordered from simple to complex and easy to difficult. The social skills curriculum is developed around a task analysis of social behaviors to be learned, systematic instruction with repeated practice, and feedback to the learner regarding the appropriateness of responses. Because social skills are generally learned through observing the actions of others, students are taught to refine their

**Table 12.6**  Sample Social Skills Curricula for Transition

| Title/Author/Date | Description |
|---|---|
| *ASSET* Hazel, Schumaker, Sherman, & Sheldon-Widgen (1981) | A social skills program for adolescents age 13–18. It has a Leader's Guide, group activities, videotapes, and audiotapes. |
| *Social Skills in the School and Community* Sargent (ed.) (1991) | A CEC publication for mainstreamed primary, intermediate, junior, and senior high school levels. |
| *Teaching Social Skills* Rutherford, Chipman, DiGangi, & Anderson (1992) | A CEC publication that teaches socialization skills using a practical instructional approach. |
| *Skillstreaming the Adolescent. A Structured Learning Approach to Teaching Prosocial Skills* Goldstein, Sprafkin, Gershaw, & Klein (2002) | One of the most widely used, this curriculum provides a five-phase sequence to teach students critical social skills: (1) introduce the steps of the skill, (2) teach the steps, (3) demonstrate the skill, (4) have student rehearse and practice the skill, and (5) teach maintenance and generalization of the skill. |
| *Social Skills Strategies Books A & B* Gajewski & Mayo (1989) | This is a two-year program with daily activities that target students with skill, performance, and self-control deficits. |

observation skills. They are also taught to improve their interaction and problem-solving skills, in other words, to think before acting. Job-related social skills include (a) ordering job responsibilities, (b) understanding instructions, (c) making introductions, (d) asking questions, (e) asking permission, (f) asking for help, (g) accepting help, (h) offering help, (i) requesting information, (j) taking messages, (k) having a conversation, (l) giving directions, (m) receiving compliments, and (n) giving compliments. *Job-Related Social Skills* comprises six sections: (1) an instructional guide, (2) job skills training format, (3) self-management strategies, (4) job-related social skills evaluation, (5) monitoring students on the job, and (6) appendices.

*Working II* (Foss & Vilhauer, 1986) is a job-related social skills program designed to develop social competence in a range of employment settings for adolescents and adults with mild mental disabilities. The program includes an assessment component, the Test of Interpersonal Competence for Employment (TICE), and an instructional component, the Interpersonal Skills Training for Employment (ISTE). The ISTE incorporates a nine-step teaching procedure designed to develop knowledge based on behavioral mastery of key job-related social competencies. Homework assignments are included to facilitate both application of learned skills in naturalistic settings and the transfer of training effects. The content areas of *Working II* include most of the critical areas listed in the literature, such as interactions with supervisors, following instructions, requesting assistance, handling criticism and correction, conflicts with coworkers, verbal teasing and provocation, interactions with coworkers, cooperative work behavior, and making requests.

With the *Working II* program, you use videotaped vignettes of job-related social skill situations to begin the problem-solving process. As the instructional sequence progresses, you model appropriate social skills for your students, then guide your students into their own behavioral

rehearsal of the appropriate skills. The final step is for the students to demonstrate the appropriate skill in an actual job situation. You can adapt the instructional sequence to fit work-related social behaviors unique to your own students.

## Employment

Knowing how to seek, find, and acquire employment are critical elements in transition programs for high school students with special needs (Gerber & Brown, 1991; Polloway, Patton, Epstein, & Smith, 1989). Former special education students who used to rely primarily on a network of family and friends to find jobs now are more self-sufficient and use agency and school resources (Frank, Sitlington, & Carson, 1991). Adolescents with disabilities need instruction in such skills as conducting a personal job search, filling out job applications correctly, and preparing a résumé, as well as alternatives such as school-based vocational development and placement (Roessler, Brolin, & Johnson, 1990). Some guidelines for infusing these components into the high school curriculum are listed below.

1. Include at least 2 to 3 weeks of skill building in how to search for job opportunities. Examine the classified ads, network with family and friends, and create an awareness of where job openings are posted in the local area.

2. Include instruction in developing a résumé. Although young people may not have prior work experience, they do have life experiences that are transferable to the workplace. Critical content such as the mechanics of résumé development may be included in an English course. Teachers may require the completion of a neat and accurate résumé that can be mailed or taken to a prospective employer.

3. Include instruction in filling out job applications neatly, accurately, and completely. An English course may include the steps for filling out a job application using effective teaching methods so that the learned skill generalizes to

the real world over time. Teachers should require students to complete a minimum of at least six real job applications to apply for jobs with local businesses (e.g., supermarkets, fast-food chains).

4.  Include instruction in how to interview for a job. Instruction includes the skills of demonstrating appropriate personal appearance, personal hygiene, and the critical communication skills required for a successful job interview. Direct instruction and role playing using video technology may effectively teach these skills. Minimum proficiency should be the competent demonstration of interviewing skills for at least six jobs using video role-play techniques.

5.  Include instruction on what essential documents are needed for getting a job. Cover what documents are necessary (e.g., birth certificate, state ID card, work permit, Social Security card), and how to obtain these documents.

Job success depends more on effective job maintenance skills (such as communication and interpersonal skills and good work habits) than on the actual job skills (Montague, 1988; Black & Rojewski, 1998). Employers consider worker behaviors and attitudes to be important or essential to job performance (Campbell, Hensel, Hudson, Schwartz, & Sealander, 1987; Sitlington, Clark, & Kolstoe, 2000). When employers were asked to rank factors judged critical to job success for workers with disabilities, the five highest-ranking factors were (1) getting along well with others, (2) interest in the job, (3) efficiency, (4) dependability, and (5) being able to adapt to new work situations (Chamberlain, 1988).

Students with disabilities require systematic instruction to learn and practice the critical skills of keeping a job. They also need on-the-job support to ensure that appropriate job maintenance skills have been generalized in the workplace over time. Some implications for the high school curriculum and transition programs are:

1.  Include at least a semester-long course in job maintenance skills. Emphasize job-keeping behaviors (e.g., how to dress appropriately on the job, how to fill out time cards, how to practice punctuality on the job) and job-related social behaviors (e.g., how to get along with supervisors and coworkers, how to interact with the public, how to ask for assistance, and how to give and accept praise and constructive criticism).

2.  Include opportunities for part-time jobs while enrolled in a job maintenance skills course. The practice of learned skills in the natural environment is critical for generalization and also provides the opportunity for immediate feedback.

3.  Provide ongoing and frequent support to working students. Support strategies may include teaching skills on the job, maintaining close employer communication, and implementing spontaneous crisis intervention. This process may require that systems change to allow support personnel to have time for supervision in the workplace.

As a teacher, it is important for you to communicate with your administrator and solicit the support necessary for a successful vocational training program.

 **ACTIVITY 12.8**

Make a list of the top 10 jobs in your county or city by using the Internet or calling the local Chamber of Commerce. Find out the educational requirements for three of these jobs.

## Functional Vocational Assessment

Appropriate, functional vocational assessment is required but not defined in IDEA. There has been much discussion about what is considered *appropriate* and what is meant by *functional*. There are many types of vocational assessments and each type can potentially add to what is known about a student and provide information useful in the transition planning process. IDEA requires that the interests and preferences of each student be considered in planning for transition. Vocational aptitude and interest inventories can provide much of this information. The traditional vocational assessments of the past were used to determine eligibility. Some of the newer assessments may be more appropriate to assess training needs. In the following sections, we describe curriculum-based vocational assessment and situational assessment, two specific types of vocational assessment that have this orientation. We also discuss portfolio assessment. Any of these assessments meet the original IDEA requirements for a "functional vocational assessment" and provide a way of assessing student progress in ways more useful (functional) than more formal, standardized testing. Note how the results of each type of assessment are incorporated in the present level of performance in the sample Transition IEPs found in Figure 12.1.

### Curriculum-Based Vocational Assessment (CBVA)

CBVA is similar to curriculum-based measurement discussed in Chapter 3, but it has some unique characteristics. The main purpose of CBVA is to determine the career development and vocational instruction needs of students based on their ongoing performance within existing course content and curriculum. CBVA provides an alternative to the more traditional vocational assessment process. It has been found especially useful with students for whom written and simulated manipulation assessments are not appropriate. Table 12.7 provides a comparison of CBVA and traditional vocational evaluation.

CBVA includes three general assessment areas: work-related behaviors, generalized skill outcomes, and specific skill outcomes. *Work-related behaviors* are the attitudinal, problem-solving, and interpersonal behaviors that are critical for student success both in classroom and community job settings. *Generalized skill outcomes* are the prerequisite concepts and knowledge necessary for students to perform successfully skills required in many occupational areas. These skills include oral and written communication, math computation, and social-personal and problem solving. *Specific skill outcomes* are those skills needed for a particular occupational area. For example, in the woodworking trade, students may be observed for mastery of their use of hand tools and varnishes.

**Table 12.7** Comparison of Two Vocational Assessment Approaches

| *Traditional Vocational Work Evaluation* | *Curriculum-Based Vocational Assessment* |
| --- | --- |
| Requires a trained work evaluator experienced with special populations | Uses existing personnel such as vocational and special education teachers |
| Has high start-up costs and ongoing maintenance expenses | Has minimal start-up and maintenance costs |
| Includes a "snapshot" of a student's abilities at the time of the evaluation | Includes ongoing assessments from middle school through high school |
| Tends to result in very technical reports that require interpretation by a work evaluator | Tends to result in reports easily understood by parents and teachers |
| Has little or no relevance to what goes on in the classroom | Focuses on performance of course objectives and work-related outcomes |
| Provides information at the time of the work evaluation report | Provides at current base of information useful for transition planning |

For students with special needs, the results of CBVA can assist in developing transition outcome statements, developing meaningful TIEP goals and objectives, and determining mastery of exit competencies for each outcome area. The results of CBVA may assist teachers in implementing and evaluating instructional plans and in making more suitable job placements.

### Situational Assessment

Situational assessment is a system for evaluating work-related behaviors by observing a student in a controlled or somewhat controlled work environment. It is different from CBVA in that the assessed variables may be controlled during the assessment process. Situational assessment may be performed in contrived or simulated settings, such as a mock work station in a classroom, or in a real work setting. Wherever it occurs, the underlying purposes of situational assessment are to observe and assess the individual in the work situation and provide feedback to the person and other interested parties about demonstrated work-related behaviors. The steps in a well-done situational assessment are:

1. Planning (considerations such as a work site that is of interest to the student, appropriate supervision, and a means for gathering information that can be used in vocational planning and feedback)
2. Scheduling (consideration of the dates and times of the observations, number of observations, and total time period of the observation—not longer than one month)
3. Recording (describing behaviors in observable, measurable terms; providing information about the work environment; recording the frequency, rate, or duration of behaviors when they occur)
4. Reporting (summarizing the observations and making recommendations, including job placement, work adjustment training, or another situational assessment in the same or different environment)

### Portfolio Assessment

Although portfolio assessment has been discussed already in Chapter 3, a few words are in order here about the use of portfolio assessment in the area of employment. Students in secondary programs may use portfolios in a number of ways, but a common use is to document the student's employability skills (Stemmer, Brown, & Smith, 1992). Many of the basic academic, personal management and teamwork skills that are important to employers may be taught, assessed, and documented in classroom settings. Examples of this include the ability to read and understand written materials, to attend class on time, and to work with people from diverse cultural and ethnic backgrounds. Both general and special education classroom teachers may provide this kind of documentation as part of their ongoing assessment of students. Either they or a transition specialist can help young adults decide what should go in the portfolio. The portfolio may be used to demonstrate to employers that young adults have the work-ready skills even if they have no actual work experience. If the student does have job training or experience, this may certainly be documented in the portfolio.

 **ACTIVITY 12.9**

Divide into small groups and discuss how you might use vocational portfolio assessment.

## Daily Living Skills

Daily living skills include the many things that we need to know to help us meet the demands and expectations of each day. Daily living skills help us maintain our bodies, our personal possessions, and our homes. To some, they also include managing resources (money, time, and people), but these are more often included under postschool adult living skills.

Most students with mild disabilities do not need direct instruction in daily living skills. They learn them, as most children do, through observation and guidance from parents. Some children (e.g., students with physical disabilities or with moderate to severe mental disabilities) may need direct instruction in the how, where, and when of daily living skills.

The most effective and efficient way to teach daily living skills is to break these real-life activities/tasks into their component skills (task analyze) and teach them sequentially in natural time and location using appropriate levels of prompts and reinforcement.

Several curricula offer guidance in teaching daily living skills. The Life Centered Career Education (LCCE) Curriculum (Brolin, 1993) includes 9 competencies and 41 subcompetencies in the daily living skills area. It also provides teachers with suggested assessment and teaching strategies. The Adaptive Living Skills Curriculum (ALSC) (Bruinicks, Moreau, Gilman, & Anderson, 1991) covers personal living skills as well as skills for home living, community living, and employment. It is cross referenced with the Checklist on Adaptive Living Skills (CALS) and contains specific and detailed instructional suggestions.

It is often not enough to teach daily living skills in a classroom setting. Teachers must also attempt to ensure that these skills are transferred to the home and community settings where they are actually needed. One way to do this is to build in application activities in the student's home or in simulated homelike settings at school. Another way to do this is to assign "homework" that requires students to practice skills in "real" times and places.

## ▶ IMPORTANT POINTS ◀

1. Transition domains under IDEA include Instruction, Related Services, Community Experience, Postschool Adult Living, Social and Interpersonal Skills, Employment, and as appropriate, Functional Vocational Assessment and Daily Living Skills.

2. Although most high school curricula are set up to be "college prep," teachers and parents must make sure not only that students with disabilities enroll in the appropriate courses, but also that they are provided with supports and services to pass those courses.

3. The SCANS (Secretary's Commission on Achieving Necessary Skills) Report (1991) identifies academic skills such as reading and writing on the job, figuring computations, estimating, making change, and using time wisely as critical to functioning in the world of work.

4. Examples of related services that may be especially important for students in transition include transportation to a community-based instruction site, accommodations to a workplace environment, and parent counseling regarding the impact of a student's job on the income of the family.

5. Generally speaking, students with moderate to severe disabilities will need more actual instruction in the community, but all students should have some community experience for practice and validation of skills.

6. Self-determination and self-advocacy skills will be needed by all young adults, whether they are going on to postsecondary education or directly into employment. The specific skills, however, may be somewhat different.

7. Lack of adequate social and interpersonal skills is often cited as the primary reason for unemployment and underemployment of individuals with special needs.

8. Guidelines for teaching students with disabilities to find employment include (a) searching for a job, (b) developing a résumé, (c) filling out job applications, (d) interviewing for a job, and (e) completing and obtaining essential documents.

9. Employers rank getting along well with others, interest in the job, efficiency, dependability, and being able to adapt to new work situations as critical to job success for workers with disabilities.

10. Guidelines for teaching students with disabilities to maintain employment include (a) emphasizing job-keeping behaviors and job-related social behaviors, (b) enrolling students in part-time jobs, and (c) providing ongoing and frequent support to working students.

11. Alternative functional vocational assessments include curriculum-based vocational assessment, situational assessment, and portfolio assessment.

12. Many students with mild disabilities do not require specific instruction in basic daily living skills, but may require prompts, encouragement, and reinforcement to use them.

 **DISCUSSION QUESTIONS**

1. Compare and contrast three functional vocational assessments.

2. Why do you think that students with disabilities still lag substantially behind their peers without disabilities in all areas of employment? What do you suggest to overcome this trend?

3. Your principal has asked you to create linkages for successful transition. What resources would you include and how do you plan to use them?

# REFERENCES

Adelma, P. B., & Vogel, S. A. (1990). College graduates with learning disabilities: Employment attainment and career patterns. *Learning Disabilities Quarterly, 13,* 154–166.

Adelman, H. S., & Taylor, L. (1983). Enhancing motivation for overcoming learning and behavior problems. *Journal of Learning Disabilities, 16,* 384–392.

Ager, C. L., & Cole, C. L. (1991). A review of cognitive-behavioral interventions for children and adolescents with behavioral disorders. *Behavioral Disorders, 16,* 276–287.

Alberto, P. A., & Troutman, A. C. (1995). *Applied behavior analysis for teachers* (4th ed.). Upper Saddle River, NJ: Merrill.

Alberto, P. A., & Troutman, A. C. (1999). *Applied behavior analysis for teachers* (5th ed.). Upper Saddle River, NJ: Merrill/Prentice Hall.

Albion, F. M. (1980, April). *Development and implementation of self-monitoring/self-instruction procedures in the classroom.* Paper presented at CEC's 58th Annual International Convention, Philadelphia, PA.

Allen, V. L. (1976). The helping relationship and socialization of children: Some perspectives on tutoring. In V. L. Allen (Ed.), *Children as teachers: Theory and research on tutoring* (pp. 9–25). New York: Academic Press.

Alley, G. R., & Deshler, D. D. (1979). *Teaching students with learning problems* (3rd ed.). New York: Merrill/Macmillan.

Alley, G. R., Deshler, D. D., Clark, F. L., Schumaker, J. B., & Warner, M. M. (1983). Learning disabilities in adolescent and young adult populations: Research implications (part II). *Focus on Exceptional Children, 15*(9), 1–14.

Allinder, R. M. (1996). When some is not better than none: Effects of differential implementation of curriculum-based measurement. *Exceptional Children, 62*(6), 525–536.

Allsopp, D. H. (1997). Using classwide peer tutoring to teach beginning algebra problem-solving skills in heterogeneous classrooms. *Remedial and Special Education, 18*(6), 367–379.

Alvermann, D. E. (1983). Putting the textbook in its place—Your students' hands. *Academic Therapy, 18*(3), 345–351.

Anderson, J., & Reilly, M. (1995). Establishing performance standards. In T. Azwell & E. Schmar (Eds.), *Report card on report cards: Alternatives to consider* (pp. 49–58). Portsmouth, NH: Heinemann.

Anderson, L., Evertson, C., & Brophy, J. (1979). An experimental study of effective teaching in first grade reading groups. *Elementary School Journal, 79,* 193–223.

Anderson, T. H., & Armbruster, B. B. (1980). *Studying.* (Report No. CS 005 205). Arlington, VA. (ERIC Document Reproduction Service No. ED 181 427).

Anderson, T. H., & Armbruster, B. B. (1984). *Studying.* In P. D. Pearson (Ed.), *Handbook of reading research* (pp. 657–679). New York: Longman.

Anderson-Inman, L. (1986). Bridging the gap: Student-centered strategies for promoting the transfer of learning. *Exceptional Children, 52*(6), 562–572.

Archbald, D. A. (1992). Authentic assessment: Principles, practices, and issues. *School Psychology Quarterly, 6*(4), 279–293.

Archer, A. L., & Gleason, M. (1989). *Skills for school success.* North Billerica, MA: Curriculum Associates.

Archer, A. L., & Gleason, M. M. (1994). *Skills for school success* (2nd ed.). North Billerica, MA: Curriculum Associates.

Archer, A. L., & Isaacson, S. L. (1990). Teaching others how to teach strategies. *Teacher Education and Special Education, 13*(2), 63–72.

Argyle, M. (1975). The syntaxes of bodily communication. In J. Benthall & T. Polhemus (Eds.), *The body as a medium of expression* (pp. 143–161). New York: E. P. Dutton.

Armbruster, B. B., & Anderson, T. H. (1981). *Content area textbooks* (Reading Education Report No. 23). Urbana, IL: University of Illinois, Center for the Study of Reading.

Aronson, E. (1978). *The jigsaw classroom.* Beverly Hills, CA: Sage.

Ascher, C. (1987). *Trends and issues in urban and minority education.* New York: ERIC Clearinghouse on Urban Education.

Ashbaker, M. H., & Swanson, H. L. (1996). Short term memory operations and their contribution to reading in adolescents with and without learning disabilities. *Learning Disabilities Research and Practice, 11*, 206–213.

Aune, E. (1991). A transitional model for postsecondary-bound students with learning disabilities. *Learning Disabilities Research and Practice, 6*, 177–187.

Aurbach, E. (1993). *Grady Profile* (Computer Software). St. Louis, MO: Aurbach & Associates.

Ausubel, D. P., & Robinson, F. G. (1969). *School learning: An introduction to educational psychology.* New York: Holt, Rinehart, & Winston.

Baca, L., & Almanza, E. (1991). Language minority students with disabilities. *Council for Exceptional Children.* Reston, VA.

Baca, L. M., & Cervantes, H. (1998). *The bilingual special education interface* (3rd ed.). Upper Saddle River, NJ: Prentice Hall.

Bailin, A., & Grafstein, A. (2001). The linguistic assumptions underlying readability formulae: A critique. *Language and Communication, 21*, 285–301.

Baker, J., & Zigmond, N. (1990). Are regular education classes equipped to accommodate students with learning disabilities? *Exceptional Children, 56*(6), 515–526.

Baker, L., & Brown, A. L. (1980). *Metacognitive skills and reading* (Technical Report No. 188). Urbana, IL: University of Illinois, Center for the Study of Reading.

Bakken, J. P., & Aloia, G. F. (1998). Evaluating the World Wide Web. *TEACHING Exceptional Children, 30*(5), 48–53.

Bakken, T., & Kortering, L. (1999). The constitutional and statutory obligations of schools to prevent students with disabilities from dropping out. *Remedial and Special Education, 20*(6), 360–366.

Banjera, M., & Daily, R. (1995). A study of the effects of an inclusion model on students with specific learning disabilities. *Journal of Learning Disabilities, 28*, 511–522.

Banks, J. A. (1987). *Teaching strategies for ethnic students* (4th ed.). Needham Heights, MA: Allyn & Bacon.

Banks, J. A., Cookson, P., Gay, G., Hawley, W. D., Irvine, J. J., Nieto, S., Schofield, J. W., et al. (2001). Diversity within unity: Essential principles for teaching and learning in a multicultural society. *Phi Delta Kappan, 83*(3), 196–203.

Barnes, D. (1993). Supporting exploratory talk for learning. In K. M. Pierce & C. J. Giles (Eds.), *Cycles of meaning: Exploring the potential of talk in learning communities* (pp. 17–34). Portsmouth, NH: Heinemann.

Baskwill, J., & Whitman, P. (1988). *New direction-evaluation: Whole language, whole child.* New York: Scholastic.

Bauwens, J., & Hourcade, J. (1994). *Cooperative teaching.* Austin, TX: PRO-ED.

Bauwens, J., & Hourcade, J. J. (1997). Cooperative teaching: Pictures of possibilities. *Intervention in School and Clinic, 33*(2), 81–89.

Bauwens, J., & Hourcade, J. (2002). *Cooperative teaching: Rebuilding the schoolhouse for all students.* Austin, TX: Pro-Ed.

Bauwens, J., Hourcade, J. J., & Friend, M. (1989). Cooperative teaching: A model for general and special education integration. *Remedial and Special Education, 10*(2), 17–22.

Baxter, J. (1970). Interpersonal spacing in natural settings. *Sociometry, 33*, 44.

Beals, D. E. (1989). A practical guide for estimating readability. *TEACHING Exceptional Children, 21*(3), 24–27.

Beech, M. (1997). *Using the Sunshine State Standards in the classroom. Assisting Florida teachers: A series of handbooks. Vol. 1.* Tallahassee, FL: Florida Department of Education.

Behrmann, M. M. (1995). *Assistive technology for students with mild disabilities* (ERIC Digest No E529). Syracuse, NY: ERIC Clearinghouse on Information and Technology.

Beirne-Smith, M. (1989). A systematic approach for teaching notetaking skills to students with mild handicaps. *Academic Therapy, 24*, 425–437.

Belpre, P. (1973). *Once in Puerto Rico.* New York: Wame.

Benz, M. R., Lindstrom, L., & Yovanoff, P. (2000). Improving graduation and employment outcomes of students with disabilities: Predictive factors and student perspectives. *Exceptional Children, 66*(4), 509–522.

Berdine, W. H., & Cegelka, P. T. (1995). Collaborative consultation: A key to effective educational delivery. In P. T. Cegelka & W. H. Berdine (Eds.), *Effective instruction for students with learning difficulties* (pp. 19–43). Needham Heights, MA: Allyn & Bacon.

Berliner, D. C. (1984). The half-full glass: A review of research on teaching. In P. L. Hosford (Ed.), *Using what we know about teaching* (pp. 51–77). Alexandria, VA: Association for Supervision and Curriculum Development.

Berninger, V., Abbott, R., Rogan, L., Reed, E., Abbott, S., Brooks, A., Vaughan, K. & Graham, S. (1998). Teaching spelling to children with specific learning disabilities: The mind's ear and eye beat the computer or pencil. *Learning Disability Quarterly, 21*, 106–122.

Bernstein, V. (1997). *Decisions for health, Book one.* Austin, TX: Steck-Vaughn Company.

Bietau, L. (1995). Students, parent, teacher collaboration. In T. Azwell & E. Schmar (Eds.), *Report card on report cards: Alternatives to consider* (pp. 131–153). Portsmouth, NH: Heinemann.

Billingsley, B. S., & Wildman, T. W. (1990). Facilitating reading comprehension in learning disabled students: Metacognitive goals and instructional strategies. *Remedial and Special Education, 11*(2), 18–31.

Binder, C., Haughton, E., & Eyk, D. V. (1990). Increasing endurance by building fluency: Precision teaching attention span. *TEACHING Exceptional Children, 22*(3), 24–27.

Birdseye, T. (1990). *A song of stars.* New York: Holiday House.

Black, R. S., & Rojewski, J. W. (1998). The role of social awareness in the employment success of adolescents with mild mental retardation. *Education and Training in Mental Retardation and Developmental Disabilities, 33*(2), 144–161.

Blackhurst, A. E., & Berdine, W. H. (1993). *An introduction to special education* (3rd ed.). New York: HarperCollins.

Blackorby, J., & Wagner, M. (1996). Longitudinal postschool outcomes of youth with disabilities: Findings from the National Longitudinal Transition Study. *Exceptional Children, 62,* 399–413.

Blalock, G. (1991). Paraprofessionals: Critical team members in our special education programs. *Intervention in School and Clinic, 26*(4), 200–214.

Blalock, G. (1993). Strategies for school collaboration. In E.S. Polloway & J. R. Patton (Eds.), *Strategies for teaching learners with special needs* (5th ed., pp. 123–143). New York: Merrill.

Blalock, G. (1997). Strategies for school consultation and collaboration. In E.A. Polloway & J. R. Patton (Eds.), *Strategies for teaching learners with special needs* (pp. 520–550). Upper Saddle River, NJ: Merrill/Prentice Hall.

Blalock, G. (2001). Strategies for collaboration. In E. A. Polloway & J. R. Patton (Eds.), *Strategies for teaching learners with special needs* (pp. 125–160). Upper Saddle River, NJ: Merrill/Prentice Hall.

Blalock, G., & Patton, J. R. (1996). Transition and students with learning disabilities: Creating sound futures. *Journal of Learning Disabilities, 29,* 7–16.

Blanchard, J. S. (1985). What to tell students about underlining . . . and why. *Journal of Reading,* 199–203.

Bloom, B. M. (1956). *Taxonomy of educational objectives, handbook I: Cognitive domain.* New York: David McKay Co., Inc.

Bondy, E., & Brownell, M. T. (1997). Overcoming barriers to collaboration. *Intervention in School and Clinic, 33*(2), 112–115.

Bondy, E., Ross, D. D., Sindelar, P. T., & Griffin, C. (1995). Elementary and special educators learning to work together: Team building processes. *Teacher Education and Special Education, 18*(2), 91–102.

Borg, W., & Ascione, F. (1982). Classroom management in elementary mainstreaming classrooms. *Journal of Educational Psychology, 71*(6), 733–750.

Bos, C. S., & Anders, P. L. (1990). Interactive practices for teaching content and strategic knowledge. In T. E. Scruggs & B. Y. L. Wong (Eds.), *Intervention research in learning disabilities* (pp. 116–185). New York: Springer-Verlag.

Bos, C. S., & Vaughn, S. (1994). *Strategies for teaching students with learning and behavior problems* (3rd ed.). Needham Heights, MA: Allyn & Bacon.

Bos, C. S., & Vaughn, S. (1998). *Strategies for teaching students with learning and behavior problems* (4th ed.). Needham Heights, MA: Allyn & Bacon.

Bos, C. S., & Vaughn, S. (2002). *Strategies for teaching students with learning and behavior problems* (5th ed.). Needham Heights, MA: Allyn & Bacon.

Bott, D. A. (1990). Managing CBA in the classroom. In J. Salvia & C. Hughes (Eds.), *Curriculum-based assessment: Testing what is taught* (pp. 270–294). New York: Macmillan.

Bragstad, B. J., & Stumpf, S. M. (1987). *A guidebook for teaching study skills and motivation.* Needham Heights, MA: Allyn & Bacon.

Brandt, F. J., & Ellsworth, J. J. (1996). Effects of cooperative learning on the academic achievement and self-esteem of urban adolescents with learning disabilities. *Learning Disabilities, 7*(1), 9–13.

Bransford, J. D., Sherwood, R. S., Hasselbring, T. S., Kinzer, C. K., & Williams, S. M. (1990). Anchored instruction: Why we need it and how technology can help. In D. Nix & R. Spiro (Eds.), *Cognitive, education, and multimedia exploration in high technology* (pp. 115–142). Hillsdale, NJ: Erlbaum.

Brigance, A. (1981). *BRIGANCE Diagnostic Inventory of Essential Skills.* North Billerica, MA: Curriculum Associates.

Brigance, A. (1983). *BRIGANCE Diagnostic Comprehensive Inventory of Basic Skills Student.* North Billerica, MA: Curriculum Associates.

Brigance, A. (1999). *BRIGANCE Diagnostic Comprehensive Inventory of Basic Skills (CIBS)—Revised*. North Billerica, MA: Curriculum Associates.

Briganti, M. (1989). *An ESE teacher's guide for working with the limited English proficient student*. Orlando, FL: Orange County Public Schools.

Brigham, F. J., Scruggs, T. E., & Mastropieri, M. A. (1992). Teacher enthusiasm in learning disabilities classrooms: Effects on learning and behavior. *Learning Disabilities Research and Practice, 7*, 68–73.

Brinkerhoff, L. C. (1996). Making the transition to higher education: Opportunities for student empowerment. *Journal of Learning Disabilities, 29*(2), 118–136.

Brinkerhoff, L. C., Shaw, S. F., & McGuire, J. M. (1992). Promoting access, accommodations and independence for college students with learning disabilities. *Journal of Learning Disabilities, 25*(7), 417–429.

Brolin, D. E. (1993). *Life Centered Career Education: A competency-based approach* (4th ed.). Reston, VA: Council for Exceptional Children.

Brolin, D. E. (1995). *Career education*. Upper Saddle River, NJ: Prentice Hall.

Brooks, J. G., & Brooks, M. G. (2001). *In search of understanding: The case for constructivist classrooms*. Upper Saddle River, NJ: Prentice Hall.

Broome, S. A., & White, R. B. (1995). The many uses of videotape in classrooms serving youth with behavioral disorders. *TEACHING Exceptional Children, 27*(3), 10–13.

Brophy, J. E. (1979). Teacher behavior and its effects. *Journal of Educational Psychology, 71*(6), 733–750.

Brophy, J. E. (1980). *Recent research on teaching*. East Lansing, MI: Institute for Research on Teaching, Michigan State University.

Brophy, J. E., & Evertson, C. (1977). Teacher behaviors and student learning in second and third grades. In G. D. Borich (Ed.), *The appraisal of teaching: Concepts and process* (pp. 117–139). Reading, MA: Addison-Wesley.

Brophy, J. E., & Good, T. L. (1986). Teacher behavior and student achievement. In M. L. Wittrock (Ed.), *Handbook of research on teaching* (3rd ed., pp. 328–375). New York: Macmillan.

Brown, A. L., & Palincsar, A. S. (1982). Inducing strategic learning from texts by means of informed, self-control training. *Topics in Learning and Learning Disabilities, 2*(1), 1–17.

Brown, A. L., & Palincsar, A. S. (1989). Guided, cooperative learning, and individual knowledge acquisition. In L. B. Resnick (Ed.), *Knowing, learning, and instruction: Essays in honor of Robert Glaser* (pp. 393–451). Mahwah, NJ: Erlbaum.

Brown, G. L. (1991). *Reading and language arts curricula in elementary and secondary education for American Indians and Alaska Natives* (Report No. RC 018 625). Washington, DC: Department of Education, Indian Nations at Risk Task Force. (ERIC Document Reproduction Service No. ED 343 766)

Bruinicks, R. H., Moreau, L., Gilman, C. J., & Anderson, J. L. (1991). *Adaptive Living Skills Curriculum*. Itasca, IL: Riverside Publications.

Bryan, T., Donahue, M., & Pearl, R. (1981). Learning disabled children's peer interactions during a small-group problem-solving task. *Learning Disability Quarterly, 4*(1), 13–22.

Bulgren, J., & Lenz, B. K. (1996). Strategic instruction in the content areas. In D. D. Deshler, E. S. Ellis, & B. K. Lenz (Eds.), *Adolescents with learning disabilities: Strategies and methods* (2nd ed.). Denver: Love.

Bulgren, J., Deshler, D. D., & Schumaker, J. B. (1993). *The content enhancement series: The concept mastery routine*. Lawrence, KS: Edge Enterprises.

Bulgren, J., Schumaker, J. B., & Deshler, D. D. (1988). Effectiveness of a concept teaching routine in enhancing the performance of LD students in secondary-level mainstream classes. *Learning Disability Quarterly, 11*, 3–17.

Burke, C. M. (1993). Talk within the kindergarten: Language supporting a learning community. In K. M. Pierce & C. J. Giles (Eds.), *Cycles of meaning: Exploring the potential of talk in learning communities* (pp. 79–98). Portsmouth, NH: Heinemann.

Burnette, J. (1987). *Adapting instructional materials for mainstreamed students*. Washington, DC: Office of Special Education Programs, United States Department of Education.

Burnette, J. (1996). Including students with disabilities in general education classrooms: From policy to practice. In Educational Resources Information Center, U.S. Department of Education (Ed.), *Inclusion, 4*(3), 2–11.

Burns, P. C. (1980). *Assessment and correction of language arts difficulties*. Upper Saddle River, NJ: Merrill/Prentice Hall.

Burns, P. C., & Roe, B. (1985). *Informal reading inventory* (2nd ed.). Boston: Houghton Mifflin.

Bursuck, W., Polloway, E. A., Plante, L., Epstein, M. H., Jayanthi, M., & McConeghy, J. (1996). Report card grading and adaptations: A national survey of classroom practices. *Exceptional Children, 62*(4), 301–318.

Byars, B. (1974). *Summer of the swans.* New York: Avon.

California Education Transition Center. (1990). *Synthesis of individual transition plans: Format and process.* Sacramento, CA: Author.

Calkins, L. M. (1986). *The art of teaching writing.* Portsmouth, NH: Heinemann.

Callahan, J. F., Clark, L. H., & Kellough, R. D. (1998). *Teaching in the middle and secondary schools* (6th ed.). Upper Saddle River, NJ: Merrill/Prentice Hall.

Campbell, P., Hensel, J. W., Hudson, P., Schwartz, S. E., & Sealander, K. (1987). The successfully employed worker with a handicap: Employee/employer perceptions of job performance. *Career Development for Exceptional Individuals, 10,* 85–93.

Canter, L. (1979). Competency-based to discipline—It's assertive. *Thrust for Educational Leadership, 8,* 11–13.

Canter, L., & Associates. (1986). *Assertive discipline videotape No. 2: Implementing assertive discipline in the classroom.* Santa Monica, CA: Author.

Carlisle, J. F., & Felbinger, L. (1991). Profiles of listening and reading comprehension. *Journal of Educational Research, 84,* 345–354.

Carman, R. A., & Adams, W. R. (1972). *Study skills: A student's guide for survival.* New York: Wiley.

Carnine, D., Silbert, J., & Kame'enui, E. J. (1990). *Direct instruction reading* (2nd ed.). Upper Saddle River, NJ: Merrill/Prentice Hall.

Carnine, D., Silbert, J., & Kame'enui, E. J. (1997). *Direct instruction reading* (3rd ed.). Upper Saddle River, NJ: Merrill/Prentice Hall.

Carpenter, C. D., Ray, M. S., & Bloom, L. A. (1995). Portfolio assessment: Opportunities and challenges. *Intervention in School and Clinic, 31*(1), 34–41.

Cartledge, G., & Cochran, L. L. (1993). Developing cooperative learning behaviors in students with behavior disorders. *Preventing School Failure, 37,* 5–10.

Cartledge, G., & Kiarie, M. W. (2001). Learning social skills through literature for children and adolescents. *TEACHING Exceptional Children, 34*(2), 40–47.

Caruso, C. (1997). Before you cite a site. *Educational Leadership, 55*(3), 24–25.

Case, E. J. (1986). *Evaluation report: C-level aide program.* Albuquerque, NM: Albuquerque Public Schools.

Cashman, J. (1998, Winter). DCDT offers preliminary on IDEA regulations. *DCDT Network, 22*(2), 8.

Cegelka, P. T. (1995). Structuring the classroom for effective instruction. In P. T. Cegelka & W. H. Berdine (Eds.), *Effective instruction for students with learning difficulties* (pp. 135–159). Needham Heights, MA: Allyn & Bacon.

Chadsey-Rusch, J. (1986). Identifying and teaching valued social behaviors. In F. R. Rusch (Ed.), *Competitive employment issues and strategies* (pp. 273–287). Baltimore: Paul H. Brookes.

Chalfant, J. C., & Pysh, M. V. (1981, November). Teacher assistance teams: A model for within-building problem solving. *Counterpoint,* pp. 1–4.

Chalfant, J. C., & Pysh, M. V. (1989). Teacher assistance teams: Five descriptive studies on 96 teams. *Remedial and Special Education, 10*(6), 49–58.

Chalfant, J. C., Pysh, M. V., & Moultrie, R. (1979). Teacher assistance teams: A model for within-building based problem solving. *Learning Disabilities Quarterly, 2,* 85–96.

Chamberlain, M. (1988). Employers' rankings of factors judged to be critical to job success for individuals with severe disabilities. *Career Development for Exceptional Individuals, 11*(3), 141–147.

Chan, D. M. (1987). Curriculum development for limited-English-proficient exceptional Chinese children. In M. K. Kitano & P. C. Chinn (Eds.), *Exceptional Asian children and youth* (pp. 61–69). Reston, VA: Council for Exceptional Children.

Chan, S. (1987). Parents of exceptional Asian children. In M. K. Kitano & P. C. Chinn (Eds.), *Exceptional Asian children and youth* (pp. 36–53). Reston, VA: Council for Exceptional Children.

Chandler, L., Dahlquist, C., Repp, A., & Feltz, C. (1999). The effects of team-based functional assessment on the behavior of students in classroom settings. *Exceptional Children, 66*(1), 101–122.

Chandler, S. K., & Pankaskie, S. C. (1997). Socialization, peer relationships, and self-esteem. In P. Wehman & J. Kregel (Eds.), *Functional curriculum for elementary, middle, and secondary age students with special needs* (pp. 123–153). Austin: PRO-ED.

Checkley, K. (1997). The first seven . . . *Educational Leadership 55*(1), 8–13.

Chinn, P. C., & Plata, M. (1987). Perspectives and educational implications of southeast Asian students. In M. K. Kitano & P. C. Chinn (Eds.), *Exceptional Asian children and youth* (pp. 12–28). Reston, VA: The Council for Exceptional Children.

Christensen, M. (1992). *Motivational English for at-risk students.* Bloomington, IA: National Educational Service.

Christenson, S. L., Thurlow, M. L., & Ysseldyke, J. E. (1987). *Instructional effectiveness: Implications for effective instruction of handicapped students* (Monograph No. 4). Minneapolis, MN: University of Minnesota, Instructional Alternatives Project.

Christenson, S. L., Ysseldyke, J. E., & Thurlow, M. L. (1989). Critical instructional factors for students with mild handicaps: An integrative review. *Remedial and Special Education, 10*(5), 21–29.

Ciardello, A. V. (1998). Did you ask a good question today? Alternative cognitive and metacognitive strategies. *Journal of Adolescent & Adult Literacy, 42,* 210–219.

Cohen, E. G. (1994). Restructuring the classroom: Conditions for productive small groups. *Review of Educational Research, 64,* 1–35.

Cohen, L. G., & Spencimer, L. J. (1998). *Assessment of children and youth.* New York: Longman.

Cohen, S. A. (1987). Instructional alignment: Searching for the magic bullet. *Exceptional Researcher, 16*(8), 16–20.

Cohen, S. B. (1986). Teaching new material. *TEACHING Exceptional Children, 19*(1), 50–51.

Coker, H., Medley, D., & Soar, R. (1980). How valid are expert opinions about effective teaching? *Phi Delta Kappan, 62,* 131–134.

Collins, M., Carnine, D., & Gersten, R. (1987). Elaborated corrective feedback and the acquisition of reasoning skills: A study of computer-assisted instruction. *Exceptional Children, 54*(3), 254–262.

Colvin, G., Ainge, D., & Nelson, R. (1997). How to defuse confrontations. *TEACHING Exceptional Children, 29*(6), 47–51.

*Conference Checklist.* (1979). NM: New Mexico/Albuquerque Public Schools Center for Parent Involvement.

*Content Enhancement Series* published by Edge Enterprises Inc; 708 W. 9th St.; Lawrence, Kansas 66044; phone number: 708-749-1473.

Cooney, J. B., & Swanson, H. L. (1990). Individual differences in memory for mathematical story problems: Memory span and problem perception. *Journal of Educational Psychology, 82.* 570–577.

Cooper, A. (1981). Learning centers: What they are and aren't. *Academic Therapy, 16*(5), 527–531.

Cosgrove, M. S. (1992). *Inside learning centers.* (ERIC Document Reproduction Service No. ED 358 875).

Costa, A. L., & Garmston, R. J. (1994). *Cognitive coaching: A foundation for renaissance schools.* Norwood, MA: Christopher-Gordon Publishers.

Cowley, J., & Melser, J. (1981). *Mrs. Wishy-Washy.* Bothell, WA: Wright Group.

Craig, D. V. (1997). Telecurricular teaching and learning: The impact of World Wide Web access on the instructional process. *Telecommunications in Education News, 8*(3), 1.

Crisis Prevention Institute. (1983). *CPI workshop materials.* Milwaukee, WI: Author.

Cronin, M. E., & Patton, J. R. (1993). Life skills instruction for all students with special needs; A practical guide for integrating real-life content into the curriculum. Austin, TX: Pro-Ed.

Cummings, C. (1985). *Peering in on peers: Coaching teachers.* Edmonds, WA: TEACHING, Inc.

Czarnecki, E., Rosko, D., & Fine, E. (1998). How to call up notetaking skills. *Teaching Exceptional Children, 30*(6), 14–19.

Daniels, V. I., & Vaughn, S. (1999). A tool to encourage "best practice" in full inclusion. *TEACHING Exceptional Children, 31*(5), 48–55.

Darch, C., & Gersten, R. (1986). Direction-setting activities in reading comprehension: A comparison of two approaches. *Learning Disabilities Quarterly, 9*(3), 235–243.

Davis, A., & Clark, E. (1981, October). *High-yield study skills instruction.* (Report No. CS 006 323). Paper presented at the annual meeting of the Plains Regional Conference of the International Reading Association, Des Moines. (ERIC Document Reproduction Service No. ED 208 372)

Day, V. P., & Elkins, L. K. (1994). Promoting strategic learning. *Intervention in School and Clinic, 29*(5), 262–270.

De La Paz, S. (1999). Self-regulated strategy instruction in regular education settings: Improving outcomes for students with and without learning disabilities. *Learning Disabilities Research and Practice, 14,* 92–106.

Delquadri, J., Greenwood, C. R., Stretton, K., & Hall, R. V. (1983). The peer tutoring game: A classroom procedure for increasing opportunity to respond and spelling performance. *Education and Treatment of Children, 6,* 225–239.

Delquadri, J., Greenwood, C. R., Whorton, D., Carta, J. J., & Hall, R. V. (1986). Classwide peer tutoring. *Exceptional Children, 52*(6), 535–542.

Demchak, M., & Morgan, C. R. (1998). Effective collaboration between professionals and paraprofessionals. *Rural Special Education Quarterly, 17*(2), 10–15.

Demi, (1990). *The empty pot.* New York: Henry Holt.

Deno, S. L. (1985). Curriculum-based measurement: The emerging alternative. *Exceptional Children, 52*(3), 219–232.

Deno, S. L., & Fuchs, L. S. (1987). Developing curriculum-based measurement systems for data-based special education problem solving. *Focus on Exceptional Children, 19*(8), 1–16.

Deno, S. L., Marston, D., & Mirkin, P. (1982). Valid measurement procedures for continuous evaluation of written expression. *Exceptional Children, 48,* 368–371.

Deno, S. L., Mirkin, P., & Wesson, C. (1984). How to write effective data based IEPs. *TEACHING Exceptional Children, 16*(2), 99–104.

Deno, S., Fuchs, L., & Marston, D. (2001). Using curriculum-based measurement to establish growth standards for students with learning disabilities. *The School Psychology Review, 30*(4), 507–524.

dePaola, T. (1974). *Charlie needs a cloak.* New York: Simon & Schuster.

dePaola, T. (1975). *Strega nona.* New York: Simon & Schuster.

dePaola, T. (1983). *The legend of the bluebonnet: An old tale of Texas.* New York: G. P. Putnam's Sons.

Desberg, P., & Taylor, J. H. (1986). *Essentials of task analysis.* Lanham, MD: University Press of America.

Deshler, D. D., Ellis, E. S., & Lenz, B. K. (1996). *Teaching adolescents with learning disabilities.* (2nd ed.). Denver: Love Publishing.

Deshler, D. D., & Schumaker, J. (1986). Learning strategies: An instructional alternative for low-achieving adolescents. *Exceptional Children, 52*(6), 483–490.

Deshler, D. D., & Schumaker, J. B. (1988). An instructional model for teaching students how to learn. In J. L. Graden, J. E. Zins, & M. L. Curtis (Eds.), *Alternative educational delivery systems: Enhancing instructional options for all students* (pp. 391–411). Washington, DC: National Association of School Psychologists.

Deshler, D. D., Schumaker, J. B., Alley, G. R., Warner, M. M., & Clark, F. L. (1982). Learning disabilities in adolescents and young adult populations: Research implications (part I). *Focus on Exceptional Children, 15*(1), 1–12.

Deshler, D. D., Schumaker, J. B., Lenz, B. K., Bulgren, J. A., Hock, M. F., Knight, J., & Ehren, B. J. (2001). Ensuring content-area learning by secondary students with learning disabilities. *Learning Disabilities Research & Practice, 16*(2), 96–108.

Dettmer, P., Thurston, L. P., & Dyck, N. (2002). *Consultation, collaboration, and teamwork for students with special needs.* (4th ed.). Boston, MA: Allyn & Bacon.

Devine, T. G. (1981). *Teaching study skills* (2nd ed.). Needham Heights, MA: Allyn & Bacon.

Dodge, B. J. (1995). *Some thoughts about WebQuests.* Retrieved July 22, 2002, from the World Wide Web: http://edWeb.sdsu.edu/courses/edtec596/about_Webquests.html

Dowdy, C. A., & Evers, R. B. (1996). Preparing students for transitions: A teacher primer on vocational education and rehabilitation. *Intervention in School and Clinic 31,* 197–208.

Drasgow, E., & Yell, M. (2001). Functional behavior assessments: Legal requirements and challenges. *The School Psychology Review 30*(2), 239–251.

Drasgow, E., Yell, M., Bradley, R., & Shriner, J. (1999). The IDEA amendments of 1997: A school-wide model for conducting functional behavioral assessments and developing behavior intervention plans. *Education and Treatment of Children, 22,* 244–266.

Duffy, G. G., Roehler, L. R., Meloth, M. S., Putnam, J., & Wesselman, R. (1986). The relationship between explicit verbal explanations during reading-skill instruction and student awareness and achievement: A study of reading teacher effects. *Reading Research Quarterly, 21*(3), 237–252.

Duffy, G., Roehler, L., & Rackliff, G. (1986). How teachers' instructional talk influences students' understanding of lesson content. *Elementary School Journal, 87*(1), 3–16.

Duke, D., Showers, B., & Imber, M. (1980). Teachers and shared decision making: The costs and benefits of involvement. *Educational Administration Quarterly, 16,* 93–106.

Dunn, R., Griggs, S. A., Olson, J., Beasley, M., & Gorman, B. S. (1995). A meta-analytic validation of the Dunn and Dunn model of learning style preferences. *The Journal of Educational Research, 88,* 353–362.

Durrer, B., & McLaughlin, T. F. (1995). The use of peer tutoring interventions involving students with behaviour disorders. *B.C. Journal of Special Education, 19*(1), 20–27.

Dyck, N., Sundbye, N., & Pemberton, J. (1997). A recipe for efficient co-teaching. *TEACHING Exceptional Children, 30*(2), 42–45.

Dye, G. A. (2000). Graphic organizers to the rescue: Helping students link and remember information. *TEACHING Exceptional Children, 32*(3), 72–76.

Dynak, J., Whitten, E., & Dynak, D. (1997). Refining the general education student teaching experience through the use of special education collaborative teaching models. *Action in Teacher Education, 19*(1), 64–74.

Eaton, M. D. (1978). Data decisions and evaluation. In N. G. Haring, T. C. Lovitt, M. D. Eaton, & C. L. Hansen (Eds.), *The fourth R: Research in the classroom* (pp. 167–190). Upper Saddle River, NJ: Merrill/Prentice Hall.

Echevarria, J., & Graves, A. (1998). *Sheltered content instruction: Teaching English-language learners with diverse abilities.* Boston: Allyn & Bacon.

Echevarria-Ratleff, J., & Graf, V. R. (1988). California bilingual special education model sites (1984–1986): Programs and research. In A. A. Ortiz & B. A. Ramirez (Eds.), *Schools and the culturally diverse exceptional student: Promising practices and future directions* (pp. 104–112). Reston, VA: Council for Exceptional Children.

Edgar, E. (1987). Secondary programs in special education: Are many of them justifiable? *Exceptional Children, 53*(5), 555–561.

Edgar, E. (1988). Employment as an outcome for mildly handicapped students: Current status and future directions. *Focus on Exceptional Children, 2*(1), 1–8.

Elbaum, B., Vaughn, S., Hughes, M., & Moody, S. W. (1999). Grouping practices and reading outcomes for students with disabilities. *Exceptional Children, 25*(3), 399–415.

Elias, M. J., & Taylor, M. E. (1995). Building social and academic skills via problem solving videos. *TEACHING Exceptional Children, 27*(3), 14–17.

Elias, M. J., & Tobias, S. E. (1996). *Social problem solving: Interventions in the schools.* New York: The Guilford Press.

Elliott, S. (1998). Performance assessment of students' achievement: Research and Practice. *Learning Disabilities Research & Practice, 13*(4), 233–241.

Elliot, S. N., & Fuchs, L. S. (1997). The utility of curriculum-based measurement and performance assessment as alternatives to traditional intelligence and achievement tests. *School Psychology Review, 26,* 224–233.

Elliott, S. N., & Sheridan, S. M. (1992). Consultation and teaming: Problem solving among educators, parents, and support personnel. *The Elementary School Journal, 92*(3), 315–338.

Ellis, E. S. (1983). *The effects of teaching learning disabled adolescents an executive strategy to facilitate self-generation of task-specific strategies.* Unpublished doctoral dissertation, University of Kansas, Lawrence.

Ellis, E. S. (1989). A metacognitive intervention for increasing class participation. *Learning Disabilities Focus, 5*(1), 36–46.

Ellis, E. S., & Lenz, B. K. (1987). A component analysis of effective learning strategies for LD students. *Learning Disabilities Focus, 2,* 94–107.

Emmer, E. T., Evertson, C. M., Clement, B. S., & Worsham, M. E. (1994). *Classroom management for secondary teachers* (3rd ed). Needham Heights, MA: Allyn & Bacon.

Engelmann, S., & Bruner, E. C. (1988). *Reading mastery: Fast cycle.* Chicago, IL: Science Research Associates.

Engelmann, S., Hanner, S., & Johnson, G. (1989). *Corrective reading.* Columbus, OH: Macmillan/McGraw-Hill.

Engelmann, S., & Carnine, D. (1982). *Theory of instruction: Principles and applications.* New York: Irvington Publishers.

Engelmann, S., & Carnine, D. W. (1972). *Distar arithmetic level III.* Chicago, IL: Science Research Associates.

Engelmann, S., & Carnine, D. W. (1975). *Distar arithmetic level I* (2nd. ed.). Chicago, IL: Science Research Associates.

Engelmann, S., & Carnine, D. W. (1976). *Distar arithmetic level II* (2nd. ed.). Chicago, IL: Science Research Associates.

Englert, C. S. (1984). Effective direct instruction practices in special education settings. *Remedial and Special Education, 5*(2), 38–47.

Englert, C. S., & Mariage, T. V. (1996). A sociocultural perspective: Teaching ways-of-thinking and ways-of-talking in a literacy community. *Learning Disabilities Research & Practice, 11*(3), 157–167.

Englert, C. S., & Palincsar, A. S. (1991). Reconsidering instructional research in literacy from a sociocultural perspective. *Learning Disabilities Research and Practice, 6,* 225–229.

Englert, C. S., & Thomas, C. C. (1982). Management of task involvement in special education classrooms: Implications for teacher preparation. *Teacher Education and Special Education, 5*(1), 3–10.

Englert, C. S., Raphael, T. E., & Mariage, T. V. (1994). Developing a school-based discourse for literacy learning: A principled search for understanding. *Learning Disability Quarterly, 17,* 2–32.

Englert, C. S., Tarrant, K. L., & Mariage, T. V. (1992). Defining and redefining instructional practice in special education: Perspectives on good teaching. *Teacher Education and Special Education, 15*(2), 62–87.

Enright, B. E. (1983). *Enright Diagnostic Inventory of Basic Arithmetic Skills.* North Billerica, MA: Curriculum Associates.

Ensminger, E. E., & Dangel, H. L. (1992). The Foxfire pedagogy: A confluence of best practices for special education. *Focus on Exceptional Children, 24*(7), 2–15.

Erchul, W. P., & Conoley, C. W. (1991). Helpful theories to guide counselors' practice of school-based consultation. *Elementary School Guidance and Counseling, 25*(3), 204–211.

Erikson, H. L. (1995). *Stirring the head, heart, and soul.* Thousand Oaks, CA: Corwin Press.

Etscheidt, S. K., & Bartlett, L. (1999). The IDEA amendments: A four step approach for determining supplementary aids and services. *Exceptional Children, 65*, 163–174.

Evans, S. S. (1980). The consultant role of the resource teacher. *Exceptional Children, 46*, 402–404.

Evans, S. S., & Evans, W. H. (1986). Training needs of special education paraprofessionals: Results of a survey conducted by a community college. *New Directions, 1*, 4–6.

Evans, S. S., Evans, W. H., & Mercer, C. E. (1986). *Assessment for instruction.* Needham Heights, MA: Allyn & Bacon.

Evertson, C. M., Emmer, E. T., Clements, B. S., & Worsham, M. E. (1994). *Classroom management for elementary teachers.* Needham Heights, MA: Allyn & Bacon.

Evertson, C., & Emmer, E. (1982). Effective management at the beginning of the school year in junior high classes. *Journal of Educational Psychology, 75*, 485–498.

Faber, J. E., Morris, J. D., & Lieberman, M. G. (2000). The effect of note taking on ninth grade students' comprehension. *Reading Psychology, 21*(3), 257–270.

Fantuzzo, J. W., Davis, G. Y., & Ginsburg, M. D. (1995). Effects of parent involvement in isolation or in combination with peer tutoring on student self-concept and mathematics achievement. *Journal of Educational Psychology, 87*(2), 272–281.

Fantuzzo, J. W., King, J. A., & Heller, L. R. (1992). Effects of reciprocal peer tutoring on mathematics and school adjustment: A component analysis. *Journal of Educational Psychology, 84*(3), 331–339.

Farr, R. F. (1989). A response from Robert Farr. In K. S. Jongsma (Ed.), Questions & answers: Portfolio assessment. *The Reading Teacher, 43*(3), 264–265.

FDLRS (Florida Diagnostic and Learning Resource System). (1982). *Communication skills materials.* Daytona Beach, FL: Author.

Fewster, S., & MacMillan, P. (2002). School-based evidence for the validity of curriculum-based measurement of reading and writing. *Remedial and Special Education, 23*(3), 149–156.

Fisher, C., Berliner, D., Filby, N., Marliave, R., Cahen, L., & Dishaw, M. (1980). Teaching behaviors, academic learning time, and student achievement: An overview. In C. Denham & A. Lieberman (Eds.), *Time to learn* (pp. 7–32). Washington, DC: National Institute of Education.

Fister, S. L., & Kemp, K. A. (1995). *TGIF: But what will I do on Monday?* Longmont, CO: Sopris West.

Flake-Hobson, C., & Swick, K. J. (1984). Communication strategies for parents and teachers, or how to say what you mean. In M. L. & E. M. Nesselroad (Eds.), *Working with parents of handicapped children: A book of readings for school personnel* (pp. 141–149). Lanham, MD: University Press of America.

Flavell, J. (1976). Metacognitive aspects of problem solving. In L. B. Resnick (Ed.), *The nature of intelligence.* Hillsdale, NJ: Erlbaum.

Flood, J., & Lapp, D. (1989). Reporting reading progress: A comparison portfolio for parents. *The Reading Teacher, 42*(7), 508–514.

Florida Performance Measurement System (FPMS). (1984). *Domains: Knowledge base of the Florida Performance Measurement System.* Tallahassee, FL: Florida Coalition for the Development of a Performance Measurement System, Office of Teacher Education, Certification and Inservice Staff Development.

Foorman, B., & Torgesen, J. (2001). Critical elements of classroom and small-group instruction promote reading success in all children. *Learning Disabilities Research & Practice, 16*(4), 203–212.

Forness, S. R., Kavale, K. A., Blum, I. M., & Lloyd, J. W. (1997). Mega-analysis of meta-analyses: What works in special education and related services. *TEACHING Exceptional Children, 29*(6), 4–9.

Foss G., & Vilhauer, D. (1986). *Working I & II: Interpersonal skills assessment and training for employment.* Santa Monica, CA: James Standfield.

Fradd, S., & Hallman, C. L. (1983). Implications of psychological and educational research for assessment and instruction of culturally and linguistically different students. *Learning Disability Quarterly, 6*(4), 468–478.

Frank, A. R., Keith, T. Z., & Steil, D. A. (1988). Training needs of special education professionals. *Exceptional Children, 55*(3), 253–258.

Frank, A. R., Sitlington, P. L., & Carson, R. (1991). Transition of adolescents with behavioral disorders—is it successful? *Behavioral Disorders, 16*(3), 180–191.

Fraser, C., Belzner, R., & Conte, R. (1992). Attention deficit hyperactivity disorder and self-control. *School Psychology International, 13,* 339–345.

Frederick, W. C., & Walberg, H. J. (1980). Learning as a function of time. *The Journal of Educational Research, 73,* 183–194.

French, N. K. (2001). Supervising paraprofessionals: A survey of teacher practices. *The Journal of Special Education, 30*(1), 41–53.

Friend, M., & Bursuck, W. (1996). *Including students with special needs: A practical guide for classroom teachers.* Needham Heights, MA: Allyn & Bacon.

Friend, M., & Cook, L. (1992). *Interactions: Collaboration skills for professionals.* New York: Longman.

Friend, M., & Cook, L. (2000). *Interactions: Collaboration skills for professionals* (3rd ed.). New York: Longman.

Frisby, C. (1987). Alternative assessment committee report: Curriculum-based assessment. *CASP Today, 36,* 15–26.

Frith, G. H., & Armstrong, S. W. (1986). Self-monitoring for behavior-disordered students. *Behavioral Disorders, 18*(2), 144–148.

Frith, G. H., & Lindsey, J. D. (1980). Paraprofessional roles in mainstreaming multihandicapped students. *Education Unlimited, 2,* 17–21.

Frith, G. H., Lindsey, J. D., & Edwards, R. (1981). A noncategorical approach for serving exceptional children of low-incidence exceptionalities in rural areas. *Education, 101,* 276–278.

Frith, G. H., & Mims, A. (1985). Burnout among special education paraprofessionals. *TEACHING Exceptional Children, 17*(3), 225–227.

Fry, E. (1968). A readability formula that saves time. *Journal of Reading, 11*(7), 513–516, 575–578.

Fuchs, D., & Fuchs, L. (1994). Inclusive schools movement and the radicalization of special education reform. *Exceptional Children, 60*(4), 294–309.

Fuchs, D., Fuchs, L. S., Mathes, P. G., & Simmons, D. C. (1996). *Peer-assisted learning strategies: Making classrooms more responsive to diversity.* (Report No. NCRTL-EC-304-716). East Lansing, MI: National Center for Research on Teacher Learning. (ERIC Document Reproduction Service No. ED 393 269)

Fuchs, D., Fuchs, L., Thompson, A., Svenson, E., Yan, L., Otaiba, S., Yang, N., McMaster, K., Prentice, K., Kazdan, S., & Saenz, L. (2001). Peer-assisted learning strategies in reading: Extensions for kindergarten, first grade, and high school. *Remedial and Special Education, 22*(1), 15–21.

Fuchs, L. S., & Deno, S. L. (1991). Paradigmatic distinctions between instructionally relevant measurement models. *Exceptional Children, 57*(6), 488–500.

Fuchs, L. S., & Fuchs, D. (2001). Helping teachers formulate sound test accommodation decisions for students with learning disabilities. *Learning Disabilities Research and Practice, 16*(4), 174–181.

Fuchs, L. S., Fuchs, D., & Hamlett, C. L. (1989). Effects of alternative goal structures within curriculum-based measurement. *Exceptional Children, 55*(5), 429–438.

Fuchs, L. S., Fuchs, D., Hamlett, C. L., & Stecker, P. M. (1991). Effects of curriculum-based measurement and consultation on teacher planning and student achievement in mathematics operations. *American Educational Research Journal, 28*(3), 617–641.

Fuchs, L. S., Fuchs, D., Hamlett, C. L., & Whinnery, K. (1991). Effects of goal line feedback on level, slope, and stability of performance within curriculum-based measurement. *Learning Disabilities Research & Practice, 6*(2), 66–74.

Fuchs, L. S., Hamlett, C. L., & Fuchs, D. (1990). *Monitoring basic skills growth.* Austin, TX: PRO-ED.

Fuchs, L. S., & Shinn, M. R. (1989). Writing CBM IEP objectives. In M. R. Shinn (Ed.), *Curriculum-based measurement: Assessing special children* (pp. 130–152). New York: The Guilford Press.

Fulk, B. M., & King, K. (2001). Classwide peer tutoring at work. *TEACHING Exceptional Children, 34*(2), 49–53.

Fullan, M., & Pomfret, A. (1977). Research on curriculum and instruction implementation. *Review of Educational Research, 47,* 335–397.

Gable, R. A., Young, C. C., & Hendrickson, M. J. (1987). Content of special education teacher preparation: Are we headed in the right direction? *Teacher Education and Special Education, 10*(3), 135–139.

Gajewski, N., & Mayo, P. (1989). *Social skills strategies, Books A & B.* Verona, WI: Thinking Publications.

Gardner, H. (1983). *Frames of mind: The theory of multiple intelligences.* New York: Basic Books.

Gardner, H. (1995). Reflections on multiple intelligences: Myths and messages. *Phi Delta Kappan, 77*(3), 200–209.

Gardner, R. III, Cartledge, G., Seidl, B., Woodsey, L., Schley, S., & Utley, C. (2001). Mt. Olivet After-

School Program: Peer-mediated intervention for at risk students. *Remedial and Special Education, 22*(1), 34–47.

Gardner, R., Heward, W. L., & Grossi, T. A. (1994). Effects of response cards on student participation and academic achievement: A systematic replication with inner-city students during whole-class science instruction. *Journal of Applied Behavior Analysis, 27*, 63–71.

Gartin, B., & Murdick, N. (2001). A new IDEA mandate: The use of functional assessment of behavior and positive behavior supports. *Remedial and Special Education 22*(6), 344–349.

Gartner, A., & Riessman, F. (1993). *Peer-tutoring: Toward a new model* (Report No. NCTRL-SP-034-776). East Lansing, MI. National Center for Research on Teacher Learning. (ERIC Document Reproduction Service No. ED 362 506)

Gearheart, B. R., Weishahn, M. W., & Gearheart, D. (1995). *The exceptional student in the regular classroom* (4th ed.). Upper Saddle River, NJ: Merrill/-Prentice Hall.

Gearheart, B. R., Weishahn, M. W., & Schloss, C. N. (2001). *The exceptional student in the regular classroom.* Upper Saddle River, NJ: Prentice Hall.

Geisel, T. (Dr. Seuss). (1938). *The five hundred hats of Bartholemew Cubbins.* New York: Vanguard.

George, J. C. (1987). *Water sky.* New York: Harper & Row.

Gerber, P. J., & Brown, D. (1991). Report of the pathways to employment consensus conference on employability of persons with learning disabilities. *Learning Disabilities Research and Practice, 6*(2), 99–103.

Gersten, R. (1985). Direct instruction with special education students: A review of evaluation research. *Journal of Special Education, 19*(1), 41–58.

Gersten, R., & Baker, S. (2000). What we know about effective instructional practices for English-language learners. *Exceptional Children, 66*(4), 454–470.

Gersten, R., & Carnine, D. (1984). Direct instruction mathematics: A longitudinal evaluation of low-income elementary school students. *Elementary School Journal, 84*(4), 395–407.

Gersten, R., & Maggs, A. (1982). Teaching the general case to moderately retarded children: Evaluation of a five-year project. *Analysis and Intervention in Developmental Disabilities, 2*, 329–343.

Gersten, R., & Woodward, J. (1994). The language-minority student and special education: Issues, trends, and paradoxes. *Exceptional Children, 60*(4), 310–322.

Gersten, R., Carnine, D., & Woodward, J. (1987). Direct instruction research: The third decade. *Remedial and Special Education, 8*(6), 48–56.

Gersten, R., Darch, C., David, G., & George, N. (1991). Apprenticeship and intensive training of consulting teachers: A naturalistic study. *Exceptional Children, 57*(3), 226–236.

Gersten, R., Vaughn, S., & Brengelman, S. (1996.) Grading and academic feedback for special education students and students with learning disabilities. In T. R. Guskey (Ed.), *ASCD Yearbook 1996 Communicating student learning* (pp. 47–57). Alexandria, VA: ASCD.

Gersten, R., Woodward, J., & Darch, C. (1986). Direct instruction: A research-based approach to curriculum design and teaching. *Exceptional Children, 53*(1), 17–31.

Gettinger, M., & Fayne, H. (1982). Classroom behaviors during small group instruction and learning performance in learning-disabled and nondisabled children. *Journal of Educational Research, 75*(3), 182–187.

Giacobbe, A. C., Livers, A. F., Thayer-Smith, R., & Walther-Thomas, C. (2001). Raising the academic standards bar: What states are doing to measure the performance of students with disabilities. *Journal of Disabilitiy Policy Studies, 12*, 10–17.

Gilliam, H. V., & Van Den Berg, S. (1980). Different levels of eye contact: Effects on black and white college students. *Urban Education, 15*(1), 83–92.

Givens-Ogle, L. (1989). Data-based consultation case study: adaptations of researched best practices. *Teacher Education and Special Education, 12*(1-2), 46–51.

Givens-Ogle, L., Christ, B. A., Coleman, M., King-Streit, S. & Wilson, L. (1989). Data-based consultation case study adaptations of researched best practices. *Teacher Education and Special Education, 12*, 46–51.

Glatthorn, A. A. (1990). Cooperative professional development: Facilitating the growth of the special education teacher and the classroom teacher. *Remedial and Special Education, 11*(3), 29–50.

Goldstein, A. P., McGinnis, E., Sprafklin, R. P., Gershaw, N. J., & Klein, P. (2002). Skillstreaming the adolescent: A structured learning approach to teaching prosocial skills. Chicago, IL: Research Park. www. skillstreaming.com

Goldstein, C. (1998). Learning at CyberCamp. *TEACHING Exceptional Children, 30*(5), 16–21.

Gollnick, D. M., & Chinn, P. C. (2002). *Multicultural education in a pluralistic society* (6th ed.). Upper Saddle River, NJ: Merrill/Prentice Hall.

Good, R. H., III, & Jefferson, G. (1998). Contemporary perspectives on curriculum-based measurement validity. In M. R. Shinn (Ed.), *Advanced applications of curriculum-based measurement* (pp. 61–88). New York: Guilford Press.

Good, T. L., & Brophy, J. E. (1984). *Looking in classrooms* (3rd ed.). New York: Harper & Row.

Good, T. L., & Brophy, J. E. (1987). *Looking in classrooms* (4th ed.). New York: Harper & Row.

Good, T. L., & Grouws, D. A. (1979). The Missouri mathematics effectiveness project. *Journal of Educational Psychology, 71,* 355–362.

Goodman, G. (1998). *Inclusive classrooms from A to Z: A handbook for educators.* Columbus, OH: Teachers' Publishing Group.

Goodman, L. (1985). The effective schools movement and special education. *TEACHING Exceptional Children, 17*(2), 102–105.

Goodrich, H. (Dec, 1996–Jan, 1997). Understanding rubrics. *Educational Leadership, 54*(4), 14–17.

Goor, M., Schwenn, J., Elridge, A., Mallein, D., & Stauffer, J. (1996). Using strategy cards to enhance cooperative learning for students with disabilities. *TEACHING Exceptional Children, 29*(1), 66–70.

Graden, J. L. (1989). Redefining "prereferral" intervention as instructional assistance: Collaboration between general and special education. *Exceptional Children, 56*(3), 227–231.

Graden, J. L., Casey, A., & Bornstrom, O. (1985). Implementing a prereferral intervention system: Part II: The data. *Exceptional Children, 51,* (6), 487–496.

Graden, J. L., Casey, A., & Christenson, S. L. (1985). Implementing a prereferral intervention system. Part I: The model. *Exceptional Children, 51,* 377–384.

Graham, S. (1985). Teaching basic academic skills to learning-disabled students: A model of the teaching-learning process. *Journal of Learning Disabilities, 18*(9), 528–534.

Graham, S., & Harris, K. R. (1993). Self-regulated strategy development: Helping students with learning problems develop as writers. *Elementary School Journal, 94,* 169–181.

Graham, S., & Harris, K. R. (1994). The effects of whole language on children's writing: A review of literature. *Educational Psychologist, 29,* 187–192.

Graham, S., & Harris, K. R. (2000). The role of self-regulation and transcription skills in writing and writing development. *Educational Psychologist, 35,* 3–12.

Graham, S., Harris, K. R., MacArthur, C., & Schwartz, S. (1991). Writing and writing instruction with students with learning disabilities: A review of a program of research. *Learning Disability Quarterly, 14,* 89–114.

Graham, S., Harris, K. R., & Troia, G. A. (2000). Self-regulated strategy development revisited: Teaching writing strategies to struggling writers. *Topics In Language Disorders, 29*(4), 1–14.

Graham, S., MacArthur, C., & Schwartz, S. (1995). The effects of goal setting and procedural facilitation on the revising behavior and writing performance of students with writing and learning problems. *Journal of Educational Psychology, 87*(2), 230–240.

Grant, C. A., & Sleeter, C. E. (1989). *Turning on learning: Five approaches for multicultural plans for race, class, gender, and disability.* Upper Saddle River, NJ: Merrill/Prentice Hall.

Graves, D. K., & Stuart, V. (1985). *Write from the start.* New York: New American Library.

Great Falls Public Schools. (1981). *Great Falls precision teaching training manual* (5th ed). Great Falls, MT: Author.

Greene, G., & Albright, L. (1995). "Best practices" in transition services: Do they exist? *Career Development for Exceptional Individuals, 18,* 1–2.

Greenwood, C. R. (1991). Longitudinal analysis of time, engagement, and achievement in at-risk versus non-risk students. *Exceptional Children, 57*(6), 521–535.

Greenwood, C. R. (1996). Research on the practices and behavior of effective teachers at the Juniper Gardens Children's Project: Implications for the education of diverse learners. In D. Speece & B. Keogh (Eds.), *Research on classroom ecologies: Implications for inclusion of children with learning disabilities* (pp. 36–67). Hillsdale, NJ: Lawrence Erlbaum.

Greenwood, C. R. (1999). Reflections on a research career: Perspective on 35 years of research at the Juniper Gardens Children's Project. *Exceptional Children, 66*(1), 7–21.

Greenwood, C. R., Arreaga-Mayer, C., Utley, C. A., Gavin, K. M., & Terry, B. J. (2001). Classwide peer-tutoring learning management system: Applications with elementary-level English language learners. *Remedial & Special Education, 22*(1), 34–47.

Greenwood, C. R., & Delquadri, J. (1995). ClassWide peer tutoring and the prevention of school failure. *Preventing School Failure, 39*(4), 21–25.

Greenwood, C. R., Delquadri, J., & Hall, R. V. (1984). Opportunity to respond and student academic performance. In W. L. Heward, T. E. Heron, J. Trap-Porter, & D. S. Hill (Eds.), *Focus on behavior analysis in education* (pp. 58–88). Upper Saddle River, NJ: Merrill/Prentice Hall.

Greenwood, C. R., Finney, R., Terry, B., Arreaga-Mayer, C., Carta, J. J., Delquadri, J., Walker, D., Innocenti, M., Lignugaris-Kraft, J., Harper, G. F., & Clifton, R. (1993). Monitoring, improving, and maintaining quality implementation of the classwide peer tutoring program using behavioral and computer technology. *Education and Treatment of Children, 16,* 19–47.

Gregory, R. P., Hackney, C., & Gregory, N. M. (1982). Corrective reading programs: An evaluation. *British Journal of Educational Psychology, 52,* 33–50.

Griffin, C. C., Malone, L. D., Kame'enui, E. J. (1995). Effects of graphic organizer instruction on fifth-grade students. *Journal of Educational Research, 89*(2), 98–107.

Grisham, F. M., Sugai, G. H., & Horner, R. H. (2001). Interpreting outcomes of social skills training for students with high-incidence disabilities. *Exceptional Children, 67*(3), 331–344.

Grossman, H. (1990). *Trouble-free teaching: Solutions to behavior problems in the classroom.* Mountain View, CA: Mayfield.

Grossman, H. (1994). *Special education in a diverse society.* Needham Heights, MA: Allyn & Bacon.

Gutkin, T. B. Henning-Stout, M., & Piersal, W. C. (1988). Impact of a districtwide behavioral consultation prereferral intervention service on patterns of school psychological services delivery. *Professional School Psychology. 3,* 301–308

Guy, B., Shin, H., Lee, S., & Thurlow, M. L. (1999, April). *State graduation requirements for students with and without disabilities* (Tech. Rep. 24). Minneapolis MN: University of Minnesota, National Center on Educational Outcomes. Retrieved March 20, 2000, from World Wide Web: http://www.coled.umn.edu/nceo/onlinepubs/technicalreport24. html

Haight, S. H. (1984). Special education teacher consultant: Idealism versus realism. *Exceptional Children, 50,* 507–515.

Hall, G. E., & Hord, S. M. (1984). *Change in schools: Facilitating the process.* Albany: State University of New York Press.

Hammeken, P. A. (2001). *Inclusion: 450 strategies for success.* Minnetonka, MN: Peytral Publications.

Hammill, D. D., & Bartel, N. R. (1995). *Teaching students with learning and behavior problems.* Austin, TX: PRO-ED.

Hanley-Maxwell, C., & Collet-Klingenburg, L. (1997). Curricular choices related to work. In P. Wehman & J. Kregel (Eds.), *Functional curriculum for elementary, middle, and secondary age students with special needs* (pp. 155–183). Austin, TX: PRO-ED.

Hannah, G. G. (1982). *Classroom spaces and places.* Belmont, CA: Pitman Learning.

Haring, K. A., Lovett, D. L., & Saren, D. (1991). Parent perceptions of their adult offspring with disabilities. *TEACHING Exceptional Children, 23*(2), 6–10.

Haring, N. G., & Eaton, M. (1978). Systematic instructional procedures: An instructional hierarchy. In N. Haring, T. Lovitt, M. Eaton, & C. Hansen (Eds.), *The fourth R: Research in the classroom* (pp. 23–40). Upper Saddle River, NJ: Merrill/Prentice Hall.

Haring, N. G., & Gentry, N. D. (1976). Direct and individualized instructional procedures. In N. G. Haring & R. L. Schiefelbusch (Eds.), *TEACHING special children* (pp. 77–111). New York: McGraw-Hill.

Harper, G. F., Mallette, B., Maheady, L., & Brennan, G. (1993). Classwide student tutoring teams and direct instruction as a combined instructional program to teach generalizable strategies for mathematics word problems. *Education & Treatment of Children, 16,* 115–134.

Harris, K. R., & Graham, S. (1994). Constructivism: Principles, paradigms, and integration. *The Journal of Special Education, 28*(3), 233–247.

Harris, K. R., & Graham, S. (1996). *Making the writing process work: Strategies for composition and self-regulation.* Cambridge, MA: Brookline.

Harris, K. R., Graham, S., Reid, R., McElroy, K., & Hamby, R. (1994). Self-monitoring of attention versus self-monitoring of performance: Replication and cross-task comparison studies. *Learning Disability Quarterly, 17,* 121–139.

Harris, K. R., Schmidt, T., & Graham, S. (1997). *Every child can write: Strategies for composition and self-regulation in the classroom. Every child every day: Learning in diverse schools and classrooms.* Cambridge, MA: Brookline Books.

Harry, B. (1992). *Cultural diversity, families, and the special education system: Communication and empowerment.* New York: Teachers College Press.

Harry, B., Allen, N., & McLaughlin, M. (1995). Communication versus compliance: African American parents' involvement in special education. *Exceptional Children, 61*(4), 364–377.

Hasbrouck, J. E., & Tindal, G. (1992). Curriculum-based oral reading fluency norms for students in grades 2 through 5. *TEACHING Exceptional Children, 24*(3), 41–44.

Hasselbring, T. S. (1998). *The future of special education and the role of technology.* Peabody College of Vanderbilt University. Retrieved July 15, 1998, from the World Wide Web:http://peabody.vanderbilt.edu/ltc/hasselbringt/futute.html

Hasselbring, T. S., Goin, L., Taylor, R., Bottge, B., & Daley, P. (1997). The computer doesn't embarrass me. *Educational Leadership, 55*(3), 30–33.

Hauser, J., & Malouf, D. B. (1996). A federal perspective on special education technology. *Journal of Learning Disabilities, 29*(5), 504–511.

Hayek, R. A. (1987). The teacher assistance team: A prereferral support system. *Focus on Exceptional Children, 20*(1), 1–7.

Hayes, M. L. (1985). Materials for the resource room. *Academic Therapy, 20*(3), 289–297.

Hazel, J. S., Schumaker, J. B., Sherman, J. A., & Sheldon-Wigden, J. (1981). *ASSET.* Champaign, IL: Research Press.

HEATH Resource Center. (1990). *Transitions for young adults with learning disabilities and other special needs.* Washington, DC: National Clearinghouse on Postsecondary Education for Individuals with Handicaps.

Hefferan, M., & Diviaio, L. (1989). *A resource manual for the development and evaluation of special programs for exceptional students, Volume V-D: Techniques of precision teaching, Part 1: Training manual.* Tallahassee, FL: Bureau of Education for Exceptional Students.

Hefferan, M., & O'Rear, S. (1991). *B.A.L.A.N.C.E. training manual.* Orlando, FL: FDLRS/Action.

Heflich, D. A. (1998). Getting ready to connect to the World Wide Web. *TEACHING Exceptional Children, 30*(5), 6.

Heit, S. B. (1980). *Gameboards for everyone.* Carthage, IL: Good Apple.

Heller, L., & Fantuzzo, J. (1993). Reciprocal peer tutoring and parent partnerships: Does parent involvement make a difference. *School Psychology Review, 22*(3), 517–535.

Henk, W. A., Helfeldt, J. P., & Platt, J. M. (1986). Alternative approaches to reading instruction for learning disabled students. *TEACHING Exceptional Children, 18*(3), 202–206.

Hepworth, D. H., & Larsen, J. A. (1990). *Direct social work practice: Theory and skills* (3rd ed.). Homewood, IL: The Dorsey Press.

Herald-Taylor, G. (1987). How to use predictable books for K–2 language arts instruction. *The Reading Teacher, 40*(7), 656–663.

Hernandez, H. (2001). *Multicultural education: A teacher's guide to linking context, process, and content* (2nd ed.). Upper Saddle River, NJ: Prentice Hall.

Heron, T. E., & Harris, K. C. (1987). *The educational consultant* (2nd ed.). Austin, TX: PRO-ED.

Herr, C. M. (1988). Strategies for gaining information. *TEACHING Exceptional Children, 20*(3), 53–55.

Herrmann, B. A. (1988). Two approaches for helping poor readers. *Reading Teacher, 42*(1), 25–28.

Heshusius, L. (1989). The Newtonian mechanistic paradigm, special education, and contours of alternatives: An overview. *Journal of Learning Disabilities, 22*(7), 403–415.

Heward, W. L. (1994). Three "low-tech" strategies for increasing the frequency of active student response during group instruction. In R. Gardner III, D. M. Sainato, J. O. Cooper, T. E. Heron, W. L. Heward, J. Eshleman, & T. A. Grossi (Eds.), *Behavior analysis in education: Focus on measurably superior instruction* (pp. 283–320). Monterey, CA: Brooks/Cole.

Heward, W. L. (2000). *Exceptional children: An introduction to special education* (6th ed.). Upper Saddle River, NJ: Prentice Hall.

Heward, W. L., Courson, F. H., & Narayan, J. S. (1989). Using choral responding to increase active student response during group instruction. *TEACHING Exceptional Children, 21*(3), 72–75.

Heward, W. L., Gardner, R., Cavanaugh, R. A., Courson, F. H., Grossi, T. A., & Barbetta, P. M. (1996). Everyone participates in this class. *Teaching Exceptional Children, 28*(2), 4–10.

Hicks-Cooley, A., & Kurtz, P. D. (1997). Preparing students with learning disabilities for success in postsecondary education: Needs and services. *Social Work in Education, 19*(1), 13–45.

Hildreth, B. L., Dixon, M. E., Frerichs, D. K., & Heflin, L. J. (1994). College readiness for students with learning disabilities: The role of the school counselor. *The School Counselor, 41,* 343–346.

Hilton, A., & Gerlach, K. (1997). Employment, preparation and management of paraeducators: Challenges to appropriate service for students with developmental disabilities. *Education and Training in Mental Retardation and Developmental Disabilities, 32*(6), 71–76.

Hines, R. A., & Hall, K. S.(2000). Assistive technology. *Journal of Special Education Technology, 15*(4), 37–39.

Hoffer, K. H. (1983). Assessment and instruction of reading skills: Results with Mexican-American students. *Learning Disabilities Quarterly, 6*(4), 458–467.

Hogan, K., & Pressley, M. (1997). Scaffolding scientific competencies within classroom communities of inquiry. In K. Hogan & M. Pressley (Eds.), *Scaffolding student learning: Instructional approaches & issues* (pp. 74–107). Cambridge, MA: Brookline Books.

Hoover, J. J. (1997). Study skills. In E. A. Polloway & J. R. Patton (Eds.), *Strategies for teaching learners with special needs.* Upper Saddle River, NJ: Merrill/Prentice Hall.

Hoover, J. J. (2001). Study skills. In E. A. Polloway & J. R. Patton (Eds.), *Strategies for teaching learners with special needs.* Upper Saddle River, NJ: Merrill/Prentice Hall.

Hoover, J. J., & Patton, J. R. (1995). *Teaching students with learning problems to use study skills.* Austin, TX: PRO-ED.

Hoover, J. J., & Rabideau, D. K. (1995). Semantic webs and study skills. *Intervention in School and Clinic, 30*(5), 292–296.

Hoover-Dempsey, K., & Sandler, H. (1997). Why do parents become involved in their children's education. *Review of Educational Research, 67*(1), 3–42.

Howell, K. W., & Morehead, M. K. (1987). *Curriculum-based evaluation for special and remedial education.* Upper Saddle River, NJ: Merrill/Prentice Hall.

Howell, K. W., Fox, S. L., & Morehead, M. K. (1993). *Curriculum-based evaluation: Teaching decision making* (2nd ed.). Pacific Grove, CA: Brooks/Cole.

Http://www.cec.sped.org/ps/code.html, CEC Standards for Professional Practice Professionals in Relation to Persons with Exceptionalities and Their Families, 1997, retrieved 3/24/03.

Huefner, D. S. (1988). The consulting teacher model: Risks and opportunities. *Exceptional Children, 54*(5), 403–414.

Hughes, C. A. (1996). Memory and test-taking strategies. In D. D. Deshler, E. S. Ellis, & B. K. Lenz (Eds.), *Adolescents with learning disabilities: Strategies and methods* (2nd ed., pp. 209–266). Denver: Love.

Hughes, C. A., Ruhl, K. L., & Misra, A. (1989). Self-management with behaviorally disordered students in school settings: A promise unfulfilled. *Behavioral Disorders, 14*(4), 250–262.

Hughes, C. A., Ruhl, K. L., & Peterson, S. K. (1988). Promising practices: Teaching self-management skills. *TEACHING Exceptional Children, 20*(2), 70–72.

Hundt, T. A. (2002). Videotaping young children in the classroom: Parents as partners. *TEACHING Exceptional Children, 34*(3), 38–43.

Hunt, P. (1995). *Collaboration: What does it take? What's working: Transition in Minnesota,* p. 1. Minneapolis: University of Minnesota Institute on Community Integration.

Hunter, M. (1981). *Increasing your teaching effectiveness.* Palo Alto, CA: Learning Institute.

Hyun, J. K., & Fowler, S. A. (1995). Respect, cultural sensitivity, and communication: Promoting participation by Asian families in the Individualized Family Service Plan. *TEACHING Exceptional Children, 28*(1), 25–28.

Iano, R. P. (1989). Comments related to Professor Heshusius' application of paradigm change to special education. *Journal of Learning Disabilities, 22*(7), 416–417.

Idol, L. (1986). *Collaborative school consultation* (Report of the National Task Force on School Consultation). Reston, VA: Teacher Education Division, The Council for Exceptional Children.

Idol, L. (1988). A rationale and guidelines for establishing a special education consultation program. *Remedial and Special Education Program, 9*(6), 48–62.

Idol, L., Paolucci-Whitcomb, P., & Nevin, A. (1994). *Collaboration consultation* (2nd ed.). Austin, TX: PRO-ED.

Idol-Maestas, L., & Ritter, S. (1985). A follow-up study of resource/consulting teachers: Factors that facilitate and inhibit teacher consultation. *Teacher Education and Special Education, 8,* 121–131.

Individuals with Disabilities Education Act of 1997, 20 U.S.C. (Section ) 1401-1485.

Irmsher, K. (1996). Inclusive education in practice. In Educational Resources Information Center,

U.S. Department of Education (Ed.), *Inclusion, 4*(3), 18–19.

Jayanthi, M., Epstein, M. H., Polloway, E. A., Bursuck, W. D. (1996). A national survey of general education teachers' perceptions of testing adaptations. *Journal of Special Education, 30*(1), 99–115.

Jensen, W. R., Sloan, H. N., & Young, K. R. (1988). *Applied behavior analysis in education: A structured teaching approach* (2nd ed.). Upper Saddle River, NJ: Prentice Hall.

Johnson, D. R., Stodden, R. A., Emanual, E. J., Luecking, R., & Mack, M. (2002). Current challenges facing secondary education and transition services: What research tells us. *Exceptional Children, 68*(4), 519–531.

Johnson, D. W., & Johnson, R. T. (1980). Integrating handicapped children into the mainstream. *Exceptional Children, 47,* 90–98.

Johnson, D. W., & Johnson, R. T. (1986). Mainstreaming and cooperative learning strategies. *Exceptional Children, 52*(6), 553–561.

Johnson, D. W., & Johnson, R. T. (1991). *Learning together and alone: Cooperative, competitive, and individualistic learning* (3rd ed.). Englewood Cliffs, NJ: Prentice Hall.

Johnson, D. W., & Johnson, R. T. (1996). The role of cooperative learning in assessing and communicating student learning. In T. R. Guskey (Ed.), *ASCD Yearbook 1996* (pp. 25–46). Alexandria, VA: ASCD.

Johnson, D. W., & Wen, S. (1976). Effects of correct and extraneous markings under time limits on reading comprehension. *Psychology in the Schools, 13,* 454–456.

Johnson, J. R., & Rusch, F. R. (1993). Secondary special education and transition services: Identifications and recommendations for future research and demonstration. *Career Development for Exceptional Individuals, 16,* 1–18.

Johnson, M. J. (1987). American Indian parents of handicapped children. In M. J. Johnson & B. A. Ramirez (Eds.), *American Indian exceptional children and youth* (pp. 6–7). Reston, VA: Council for Exceptional Children.

Johnson, M. J. (1991). *American Indians and Alaska Natives with disabilities* (Report No. RC 018 629). Washington, DC: Department of Education. (ERIC Document Reproduction Service No. ED 343 770)

Jones, B. F., Palincsar, A. S., Ogle, D. S., & Carr, E. G. (1987). *Strategic teaching and learning: Cognitive instruction in the content areas.* Alexandria, VA: Association for Supervision and Curriculum Development.

Jones, C. J. (2001). CBAs that work: Assessing student's math content-reading levels. *TEACHING Exceptional Children, 34*(1), 24–28.

Jones, C. J. (2001). Teacher-friendly curriculum-based assessment in spelling. *TEACHING Exceptional Children, 34*(2), 32–38.

Jongsma, K. S. (1989). Questions and answers: Portfolio assessment. *Reading Teacher, 43*(3), 264–265.

Joyce, B. R., & Showers, B. (1983). *Power in staff development through research on training.* Alexandria, VA: Association for Supervision and Curriculum Development.

Kagan, S. (1992). *Cooperative learning.* San Juan Capistrano, CA: Kagan Cooperative Learning.

Kahn, E. H. (1981). Aides in special education—A boon for students and teachers. *TEACHING Exceptional Children, 55*(3), 101–105.

Kalkowski, P. (2001). Research series: Research you can use, snapshot #18. Retrieved from the World Wide Web: http://www.nwrel.org/scpd/sirs/9/c018.html

Kame'enui, E. J., & Simmons, D. C. (1990). *Designing instructional strategies: The prevention of academic learning problems.* Upper Saddle River, NJ: Merrill/Prentice Hall.

Kamens, M. W. (1997). A model for introducing student teachers to collaboration. *The Teacher Educator, 33*(2), 90–102.

Katsiyannis, A., Ellenburg, J. S., & Acton, O. M. (2000). Address individual needs, the role of general educators. *Intervention in School and Clinic, 36*(2), 116–121.

Kavale, K. A., & Forness, S. R. (1995). Social skills deficits and training: A meta-analysis of the research in learning disabilities. In T. Scruggs & M. Mastropieri (Eds.), *Advances in learning and behavioral disabilities* (Vol. 9, pp. 119–160). Greenwich, CT: JAI Press.

Kavale, K. A., Hirshoren, A., & Forness, S. R. (1998). Meta-analytic validation of the Dunn and Dunn model of learning-style preferences: A critique of what was done. *Learning Disabilities Research & Practice, 13*(2), 75–80.

Kavale, K. A., Mathur, S. R., Forness, S. R., Rutherford, R. B., & Quinn, M. M. (1997). Effectiveness of social skills training for students with behavior disorders:

A meta-analysis. In T. Scruggs & M. Mastropieri (Eds.), *Advances in learning and behavioral disabilities* (Vol. 11, pp. 293–312). Greenwich, CT: JAI Press.

Kea, C. D. (1987). *An analysis of critical teaching behaviors employed by teachers of students with mild handicaps.* Unpublished doctoral dissertation. The University of Kansas, Lawrence.

Kea, C. D. (1995, July). Critical teaching behaviors. *Strategram, 7*(6), 1–8.

Keel, M., Dangel, H., & Owens, S. (1999). Selecting instructional interventions for students with mild disabilities in inclusive classrooms. *Focus on Exceptional Children, 31*(8), 1–16.

Kellogg, S. (1984). *Paul Bunyan: A tall tale.* New York: William Morrow.

Kerka, S. (1995). *Techniques for authentic assessment practice application brief.* Columbus, OH: ERIC Clearinghouse on Adult, Career, and Vocational Education Center on Education and Training for Employment.

Killoran, J., Templeman, T. P., Peters, J., & Udell, T. (2001). Identifying paraprofessional competencies for early intervention and early childhood special education. *TEACHING Exceptional Children, 34*(1), 68–73.

Kimball, W. H., & Heron, T. E. (1988). A behavioral commentary on Poplin's discussion of reductionistic fallacy and holistic/constructivist principles. *Journal of Learning Disabilities, 21*(7), 425–428.

King-Sears, M. E., & Bradley, D. F. (1995). ClassWide peer tutoring: Heterogeneous instruction in general education classrooms. *Preventing School Failure, 40*(1), 29–35.

Kitano, M. K. (1987). Gifted and talented Asian children. In M. K. Kitano & P. C. Chinn (Eds.), *Exceptional Asian children and youth* (pp. 1–11). Reston, VA: Council for Exceptional Children.

Kleinert, H., Haig, J., Kerns, J., & Kennedy, S. (2000). Alternate assessments: Lessons learned and roads to be taken. *Exceptional Children, 7*(1), 51–66.

Kline, C. S. (1986). *Effects of guided notes on academic achievement of learning disabled high school students.* Unpublished master's thesis: The Ohio State University, Columbus.

Klinger, J. K., & Vaughn, S. (1996). Reciprocal teaching of reading comprehension strategies for students with learning disabilities who use English as a second language. *Elementary School Journal, 96*, 275–293.

Klinger, J. K., & Vaughn, S. (1998). Using collaborative strategic reading. *TEACHING Exceptional Children, 30*(6), 32–37.

Knackendoffel, E. A. (1996). Collaborative teaming in the secondary school. In D. D. Deshler, E. S. Ellis, & B. K. Lenz (Eds.), *Adolescents with learning disabilities* (2nd ed., pp. 579–616). Denver, CO: Love.

Knackendoffel, E. A., Robinson, S. M., Schumaker, J. B., & Deshler, D. D. (1992). *Developing collaborative relationships: Teaming techniques for communication, problem-solving, and decision making.* Lawrence, KS: Edge Enterprises.

Knapczyk, D. R., & Rodes, P. G. (1996). *Teaching social competence: A practical approach for improving social skills in students at-risk.* Pacific Grove, CA: Brooks/Cole.

Kohler, P. (1993). Best practices in transition: Substantiated or implied? *Career Development for Exceptional Individuals, 16*, 107–121.

Koller, J. R. (1994). Improving transition outcomes for persons with specific learning disabilities. *American Rehabilitation, 20*(2), 37–42.

Komoski, K. (1995). *Seven steps to responsible software selection.* Syracuse, NY: ERIC Clearinghouse on Information and Technology. (ERIC Digest No EDO-IR-95-6)

Koorland, M. A., Keel, M. C., & Ueberhorst, P. (1990). Setting aims for precision learning. *Teaching Exceptional Children, 22*(3), 64–68.

Kounin, J. S. (1970). *Discipline and group management in classrooms.* New York: Holt, Rinehart, & Winston.

Kounin, J. S., & Gump, P. (1974). Signal systems of lesson settings and the task related behavior of preschool children. *Journal of Education Psychology, 66*, 554–562.

Kounin, J. S., & Obradovic, S. (1968). Managing emotionally disturbed children in regular classrooms: A replication and extension. *Journal of Special Education, 2*, 129–135.

Kovalik, S., with K. Olsen. (1994). *ITI: THE MODEL: Integrated thematic instruction* (3rd ed.). Kent, WA: Books for Educators.

Krivacska, J. J. (1986). Selection of the IEP management systems. *Computers in the Schools, 3*(3), 91–95.

Kroth, R. L., & Edge, D. (1997). *Strategies for communicating with parents and families of exceptional children* (3rd ed.). Denver, CO: Love.

Kruelle v. New Castle County School District, 642 F.2d 687 (3rd Cir. 1981).

Kuykendall, C. (1992). *From rage to hope: Strategies for reclaiming Black & Hispanic students.* Bloomington, IN: National Educational Service.

Lago-Delello. (1998). Classroom dynamics and the development of serious emotional disturbance. *Exceptional Children, 64*(4), 479–492.

Lahm, E., & Morrisette, S. (1994, April). *Assistive technology.* Paper presented at the annual meeting of the Council for Exceptional Children.

Lambie, R. A. (1980). A systematic approach for changing materials, instruction, and assignments to meet individual needs. *Focus on Exceptional Children, 12*(1), 1–12.

Langer, J. (1984). Examining background knowledge and text comprehension. *Reading Research Quarterly, 19,* 468–481.

Larkin, M. (2001). Providing support for student independence through scaffolded instruction. *TEACHING Exceptional Children, 34*(1), 30–34.

Lazarus, B. D. (1991). Guided notes, review, and achievement of learning disabled adolescents in secondary mainstream settings. *Education and Treatment of Children, 14,* 112–127.

Lazarus, B. D. (1996). Flexible skeletons: Guided notes for adolescents with mild disabilities. *TEACHING Exceptional Children, 28*(3), 36–40.

Lazear, D. (1991). *Seven ways of knowing: Teaching from multiple intelligences.* Palatine, IL: Skylight Publishing.

Lazerson, D. B., Foster, H. L., Brow, S. I., & Hummel, J. W. (1988). The effectiveness of cross-age tutoring with truant, junior high students with learning disabilities. *Journal of Learning Disabilities, 21*(4), 253–255.

Lee, P., & Alley, G. R. (1981). *Training junior high LD students to use a test-taking strategy* (Research Report No. 38). Lawrence, KS: University of Kansas, Institute for Research in Learning Disabilities.

Leffert, J. S., Siperstein, G. N., & Millikan, E. (2000). Understanding social adaptation in children with mental retardation: A social-cognitive perspective. *Exceptional Children, 66*(4), 530–545.

Leinhardt, G., Zigmond, N., & Cooley, W. (1981). Reading instruction and its effects. *American Education Research Journal, 18*(3), 343–361.

Lenz, B. K., Alley, G., & Schumaker, J. (1987). Activating the inactive learner: Advance organizers in the secondary content classroom. *Learning Disabilities Quarterly, 10*(1), 53–67.

Lenz, B. K., Ellis, E. S., & Scanlon, D. (1996). *Teaching learning strategies to adolescents and adults with learning disabilities.* Austin, TX: PRO-ED.

Lenz, B. K., with Bulgren, J. A., Schumaker, J. B., Deshler, D. D., & Boudah, D. A. (1994). *The unit organizer routine* (Instructor's Manual). Lawrence, KS: Edge Enterprises.

Lenz, K., & Schumaker, J. (1999). *Adapting language arts, social studies, and science materials for the inclusive classroom.* Arlington, VA: Council for Exceptional Children.

Lerner, J. (1985). *Learning disabilities: Theories, diagnosis, and teaching strategies.* Boston: Houghton Mifflin.

Leslie, L., & Caldwell, J. (1990). *Qualitative reading inventory.* Glenview, IL: Scott Foresman.

Leung, E. K. (1989). Cultural and acculturational commonalities and diversities among Asian Americans: Identification and programming considerations. In A. A. Ortiz & B. A. Ramirez (Eds.), *Schools and the culturally diverse exceptional student: Promising practices and future directions* (pp. 86–95). Reston, VA: Council for Exceptional Children.

Lewis, J. D. (1998). How the Internet expands educational options. *TEACHING Exceptional Children, 30*(5), 34–41.

Lewis, M. B. (1993). *Thematic methods and strategies in learning disabilities: Textbook for practitioners.* San Diego, CA: Singular Publishing Group.

Lewis, R. (2000). Musings on technology and learning disabilities on the occasion of the new millennium. *Journal of Special Education Technology, 15*(2), 5–12.

Lewis, R. B. (1993). *Special education technology: Classroom applications.* Pacific Grove, CA: Brooks/Cole.

Lewis, R. B., & Doorlag, D. H. (1991). *Teaching special students in the mainstream* (3rd ed.). New York: Merrill/Macmillan.

Lewis, R. B., & Doorlag, D. H. (1999). *TEACHING special students in general education classrooms* (5th ed.). Upper Saddle River, NJ: Prentice Hall.

Lieberman, A. (1995). Practices that support teacher development: Transforming conceptions of professional learning. *Phi Delta Kappan, 76*(8), 591–596.

Lilly, M. S., & Givens-Ogle, L. B. (1981). Teacher consultation: Present, past, & future. *Behavioral Disorders, 6*(2), 73–77.

Lindsey, J. D. (1983). Paraprofessionals in learning disabilities. *Journal of Learning Disabilities, 16,* 467–472.

Lindsley, O. R. (1990). Precision teaching: By teachers for children. *TEACHING Exceptional Children, 22*(3), 10–15.

Little, J. W. (1982). Norms of collegiality and experimentation: Workplace conditions of school success. *American Educational Research Journal, 19,* 325–340.

Lloyd, J., Cullinan, D., Heins, E. D., & Epstein, M. H. (1980). Direct instruction: Effects on oral and written language comprehension. *Learning Disabilities Quarterly, 3*(4), 70–76.

Longwill, A., & Kleinert, H. (1998). The unexpected benefits of high school peer tutoring. *TEACHING Exceptional Children, 30*(4), 60–65.

Lovitt, D. L., & Harris, M. B. (1987). Important skills for adults with mental retardation: The client's point of view. *Mental Retardation, 25,* 351–356.

Lovitt, T., Rudsit, J., Jenkins, J., Pious, C., & Benedetti, D. (1985). Two methods of adapting science materials for learning disabled and regular seventh graders. *Learning Disabilities Quarterly, 8,* 275–285.

MacArthur, C. A., Schwartz, S. S., & Graham, S. (1991). Effects of a reciprocal peer revision strategy in special education classrooms. *Learning Disabilities Research & Practice, 6*(4), 201–218.

Maddux, C. D. (1986). Issues and concerns in special education microcomputing. *Computers in the Schools, 3*(3), 1–19.

Madelaine, A., & Wheldall, K. (1999). Curriculum-based measurement of reading: A critical review. *International Journal of Disability, Development, and Education. 46*(1), 71–85.

Maheady, L, & Harper, G. (1991). Training and implementing requirements associated with the use of a classwide peer tutoring system. *Education & Treatment of Children, 41*(3), 177–199.

Maheady, L., Harper, G. F., & Mallette, B. (1991). Peer-mediated instruction: A review of potential applications for special education. *Reading, Writing, and Learning Disabilities, 7,* 75–103.

Maheady, L., Harper, G., & Mallette, B. (2001). Peer-mediated instruction and interventions and students with mild disabilities. *Remedial and Special Education, 22*(1), 4–14.

Maheady, L., Sacca, M. K., & Harper, G. F. (1988). Classwide peer tutoring with mildly handicapped high school students. *Exceptional Children, 55*(1), 52–59.

Maher, C. A. (1984). Handicapped adolescents as cross-age tutors: Program description and evaluation. *Exceptional Children, 51*(1), 56–63.

Mahoney, M. (1974). *Cognition and behavior modification.* Cambridge, MA: Bollinger Publishing Co.

Maker, C. J., Nielson, A. B., & Rogers, J. A. (1994). Multiple intelligences: Giftedness, diversity, and problem-solving. *TEACHING Exceptional Children, 27*(1), 4–19.

Male, M. (1988). *Special magic: Computers, classroom strategies, and exceptional students.* Mountain View, CA: Mayfield.

Male, M. (1997). *Technology for inclusion: Meeting the special needs of all students* (3rd ed.). Needham Heights, MA: Allyn & Bacon.

*MARC: A resource manual for the development and evaluation of special programs for the students, V-C: Affective curriculum for secondary emotionally handicapped students.* (1983). Tallahassee, FL: Florida Department of Education.

Marion, R. L. (1981). *Educators, parents, and exceptional children.* Rockville, MD: Aspen.

Markwardt, F. C. (1989). *Peabody Individual Achievement Test—Revised.* Circle Pines, MN: American Guidance Service.

Marston, D. (1996). A comparison of inclusion only, pull-out only, and combined service models for students with mild disabilities. *The Journal of Special Education, 30*(2), 121–132.

Marston, D., Dement, K., Allen, D., & Allen, L. (1992). Monitoring pupil progress in reading. *Preventing School Failure, 36*(2), 21–25.

Marston, D., & Magnusson, D. (1985). Implementing curriculum-based measurement in special and regular education settings. *Exceptional Children, 52*(3), 266–276.

Martin, B. (1970). *Brown bear, brown bear, what do you see?* New York: Holt, Rinehart, & Winston.

Marzano, R., Pickering, D., & McTighe, J. (1993). *Assessing outcomes: Performance assessment using dimensions of learning model.* Alexandria, VA: Association for Supervision and Curriculum Development.

Masters, L. F., & Mori, A. A. (1993). *Teaching secondary students with mild learning and behavior problems: Methods, materials, and strategies.* Rockville, MD: Aspen.

Mastropieri, M. A. (1988). Using the keyword method. *TEACHING Exceptional Children, 20*(2), 4–8.

Mastropieri, M. A., & Scruggs, T. E. (1998). Constructing more meaningful relationships in the classroom: Mnemonic research into practice. *Learning Disabilities Research and Practice, 13,* 138–145.

Mastropieri, M. A., Scruggs, T. E., & Levin, J. R. (1986a). Direct vs. mnemonic instruction: Relative benefits for exceptional learners. *Journal of Special Education, 20*(3), 299–308.

Mastropieri, M. A., Scruggs, T. E., & Levin, J. R. (1986b). Maximizing what exceptional students can learn: A review of keyword and other mnemonic strategy research. *Remedial and Special Education, 6*(2), 39–45.

Mastropieri, M. A., Scruggs, T. E., Levin, J. R., Gaffney, J., & McLoone, B. (1985). Mnemonic vocabulary instruction for learning-disabled students. *Learning Disability Quarterly, 8,* 57–63.

Mastropieri, M. A., Scruggs, T., Mohler, L., Beranek, M., Spencer, V., Boon, R. T., & Talbott, E. (2001). Can middle school students with serious reading difficulties help each other and learn anything? *Learning Disabilities Research & Practice, 16*(1), 18–27.

Mather, S. R., & Rutherford, R. B., Jr. (1996). Is social skills training effective with students for emotional or behavioral disorders? Research issues and needs. *Behavioral Disorders, 22*(1), 21–28.

Mathes, P. G., Fuchs, D., Fuchs, L. S., Henley, A. M., & Sanders, A. (1994). Increasing strategic reading practice with Peabody Classwide Peer Tutoring. *Learning Disabilities Research and Practice, 9*(1), 44–48.

Mathes, P., Grek, M., Howard, J., Babyak, A., & Allen, S. (1999). Peer-assisted learning strategies for first-grade readers: A tool for preventing early reading failure. *Learning Disabilities Research & Practice, 14*(1), 50–60.

Mayer, R.E. (2001). What good is educational psychology? The case of cognition and instruction. *Educational Psychologist, 36*(2), 83–88.

McCarney, S. B., & Tucci, J. K. (1991). *Study skills for students in our schools: Study, skills and intervention strategies for elementary and secondary students.* Columbia, MO: Hawthorne.

McCarthy, B. (1987). *The 4MAT system.* Barrington, IL: Excel.

McDonnell, L., McLaughlin, M., & Morrison, P. (1997). *Educating one and all: Students with disabilities and standards-based reform.* Washington, DC: National Research Council.

McDougal, D., & Brady, M. P. (1998). Initiating and fading self-management interventions to increase math fluency in general education classes. *Exceptional Children, 64*(2), 151–166.

McFall, R. M. (1982). A review and reformulation of the concept of social skills. *Behavioral Assessment, 4,* 1–33.

McGuire, J. M., Hall, D., & Litt, A. V. (1991). A field-based study of the direct service needs of college students with learning disabilities. *Journal of College Student Development, 32,* 101–108.

McIntosh, R., Vaughn, S., & Bennerson, D. (1995). FAST social skills with a SLAM and a RAP. *TEACHING Exceptional Children, 28*(1), 37–41.

McIntosh, R., Vaughn, S., Schumm, J., Haager, D., & Lee, O. (1993). Observations of students with learning disabilities in general education classrooms. *Exceptional Children, 60*(3), 249–261.

McKenzie, R. G., & Houk, C. S. (1986). Use of paraprofessionals in the resource room. *Exceptional Children, 53*(1), 41–45.

McLaughlin, M. J., Nolet, V., Rhim, L., & Henderson, K. (1999). Integrating standards including all students. *TEACHING Exceptional Children, 31*(3), 66–71.

McLoone, B. B., Scruggs, T. E., Mastropieri, M. A., & Zcker, S. F. (1986). Memory strategy instruction and training with LD adolescents. *Learning Disabilities Research, 2,* 45–63.

McRobbie, J. (1992). *Using portfolios to assess student performance, knowledge brief, # 9.* San Francisco, CA: Far West Laboratory for Educational Research and Development.

McWhirter, A. M. (1990). Whole language in the middle school. *The Reading Teacher, 43*(8), 562–567.

Means, B. (1997). *Critical issue: Using technology to enhance engaged learning for at-risk students* (On-line). Retrieved July 15, 1998, from the World Wide Web: http://www.ncrel.org/sdrs/areas/issues/students/atrisk/at400.html

Means, B., Blando, J., Olson, K., Middleton, T., Moroacco, C., Remz, A. R., & Zorfass, J. (1993). *Using technology to support education reform.* Washington DC: U.S. Government Printing Office, 1993.

Medley, D. M. (1979). The effectiveness of teachers: In P. L. Peterson & H. J. Walberg (Eds.), *Research on teaching: Concepts, findings, and implications* (pp. 11–27). Berkeley, CA: McCutchan.

Meese, R. (1994). *Teaching learners with mild disabilities: Integrating research and practice.* Pacific Grove, CA: Brooks/Cole.

Mehrabian, A. (1969). Significance of posture and position in the communication of attitude and status relationships. *Psychological Bulletin, 71,* 359–372.

Mehring, T. (1995). Report card options for students with disabilities in general education. In T. Azwell & E. Schmar (Eds.), *Report card on report cards: Alternatives to consider* (pp. 11–21). Portsmouth, NH: Heinemann.

Meichenbaum, D. (1977). *Cognitive behavior modification: An integrative approach.* New York: Plenum Press.

Meichenbaum, D., & Goodman, J. (1971). Training impulsive children to talk to themselves: A means of developing self-control. *Journal of Abnormal Psychology, 77,* 115–126.

Meier, F. E. (1992). *Competency-based instruction for teachers of students with special learning needs.* Needham Heights, MA: Allyn & Bacon.

Mendez, P. (1989). *The black snowman.* New York: Scholastic.

Mercer, C. D. (1992). *Students with learning disabilities* (4th ed.). Upper Saddle River, NJ: Merrill/Prentice Hall.

Mercer, C. D., & Mercer, A. R. (1993). *Teaching students with learning problems* (4th ed.). Upper Saddle River, NJ: Merrill/Prentice Hall.

Mercer, C. D., & Mercer, A. R. (1998). *Teaching students with learning problems* (5th ed.). Upper Saddle River, NJ: Merrill/Prentice Hall.

Mercer, C. D., & Mercer, A. R. (2001). *Teaching students with learning problems* (6th ed.). Upper Saddle River, NJ: Prentice Hall.

Mercer, C. D., Mercer, A. R., & Bott, D. A. (1984). *Self-correcting learning materials for the classroom.* Upper Saddle River, NJ: Merrill/Prentice Hall.

Merkley, D. M., & Jefferies, D. (2001). Guidelines for implementing a graphic organizer. *The Reading Teacher, 54*(4), 350–357.

Meyer, L. A. (1986). Strategies for correcting students' wrong responses. *Elementary School Journal, 87*(2), 227–241.

Middleton, J. A., Flores, A., & Knaupp, J. (1997). Shopping for technology. *Educational Leadership, 55*(3), 20–23.

Miller, A. D., Barbetta, P. M., & Heron, T. E. (1994). START tutoring: Designing, training, implementing, adapting, and evaluating tutoring programs for school and home settings. In D. M. Gardner III, J. O. Sainato, T. E. Cooper, W. L. Heron, J. W. Heward, & T. A. Eshelman (Eds.), *Behavior analysis in education: Focus on measurably superior instruction* (pp. 265–282). Pacific Grove, CA: Brooks/Cole.

Miller, J. H., & Milam, C. P. (1987). Multiplication and division errors committed by learning disabled students. *Learning Disabilities Research, 2*(2), 119–122.

Miller, S. P. (2002). *Validated practices for teaching students with diverse needs and abilities.* Boston, MA: Allyn & Bacon.

Miller, S., Butler, F., & Lee, K. (1998). Validated practices for teaching mathematics to students with learning disabilities: A review of literature. *Focus on Exceptional Children, 31*(1), 1–24.

Miller, W. H. (1995). *Alternative assessment techniques for reading and writing.* New York: The Center for Applied Research in Education.

Minner, S., Beane, A., & Prater, G. (1986). Try telephone answering machines. *TEACHING Exceptional Children, 19*(1), 62–63.

Minskoff, E. H., & DeMoss, S. (1994). Workplace social skills and individuals with learning disabilities. *Journal of Vocational Rehabilitation, 4*(2), 113–121.

Miramontes, O. B. (1990). Organizing for effective paraprofessional services in special education: A multilingual multiethnic instructional service team model. *Remedial and Special Education, 12*(1), 29–36.

Mitchell, A. (1997). Teacher identity: A key to increased collaboration. *Action in Teacher Education, 19*(3), 1–14.

Montague, M. (1988). Job-related social skills training for adolescents with handicaps. *Career Development for Exceptional Individuals, 11*(1), 26–41.

Montague, M. (1997). Cognitive strategy instruction in mathematics for students with learning disabilities. *Journal of Learning Disabilities, 30*(2), 164–177.

Montague, M., & Leavell, A. G. (1994). Improving the narrative writing of students with learning disabilities. *RASE, 15*(1), 21–33.

Morgan, D. P., & Jenson, W. R. (1988). *Teaching behaviorally disordered students: Preferred practices.* Upper Saddle River, NJ: Merrill/Prentice Hall.

Morgan, L. (Ed.). (1988). *Langston Hughes: He believed humor would help defeat bigotry and fear.* Seattle: Turman.

Morgan, N. A. (1997). *An introduction to Internet resources for K–12 educators: Part II: Question answering, listservs, discussion groups, update 1997.* Syracuse, NY: ERIC Clearinghouse on Information and Technology. (ERIC Digest No. EDO-IR-97-04)

Morgan, N. A., & Saxton, J. (1994). *Asking better questions.* Markham, Ontario: Pembroke Publishers.

Morningstar, M. E., Turnbull, A. P., & Turnbull, N. R., III. (1996). What do students with disabilities tell us about the importance of family involvement in the transition from school to adult life? *Exceptional Children, 62*(3), 249–260.

Morris, S. (2002). Promoting social skills among students with nonverbal learning disabilities. *TEACHING Exceptional Children, 34*(3), 66–70.

Mortsweet, S., Utley, C., Walker, D., Dawson, H., Delquadri, J., Reddy, S., Greenwood, C., Hamilton, S., & Ledford, D.(1999). Classwide peer tutoring: Teaching students with mild mental retardation in inclusive classrooms. *Exceptional Children, 65*(6), 534–536.

Mosca, F. J., & Perkins, T. (1997). Help from hundreds of people you've never met: Cruising the Internet's world. *Beyond the Classroom, 8*(1), 16–17.

Munk, D. D., & Bursuck, W. D. (1997). Can grades be helpful and fair? *Educational Leadership, 55*(4), 44–47.

Munk, D. D., Bruckert, J., Call, D. T., Stoehrman, T. & Randandt, E. (1998). Strategies for enhancing the performance of students with LD in inclusive science classes. *Intervention in School and Clinic, 34*(2), 73–78.

Murphy, D. A., Meyers, C. C., Olesen, S., McKean, K., & Custer, S. H. (1996). *Exceptions: A handbook of inclusion activities for teachers of students at grades 6–12 with mild disabilities.* Longmont, CO: Sopris Press.

Myles, B. S., & Kasselman, C. J. (1990). *Collaborative consultation: The regular educator's view.* Manuscript submitted for publication.

Narayan, J. S., Heward, W. L., Gardner, R., III, Courson, F. H., & Omness, C. (1990). Using response cards to increase student participation in an elementary classroom. *Journal of Applied Behavior Analysis, 23,* 483–490.

NASBE. (1997). Students with disabilities and high school graduation policies. NASBE Policy Update, 5(6), 1–2. National Transition Longitudinal Study (1994). *Postschool outcomes of students with disabilities* (Contract No. 300-87-0054). Washington, DC: U. Department of Education.

National Center for Education Statistics. (2001). Inclusion of students with disabilities in regular education classrooms. (2002). *Condition of Education Report—Section 4.*

National Clearinghouse for English Language Acquisition. *Glossary of terms.* Retrieved October 17, 2002, from the World Wide Web: http://www.ncela.gwu.edu/askncela/glossary.htm

National Information Center for Children and Youth with Disabilities. The IDEA amendments of 1997. *NICHCY News Digest, 26,* 1–38.

National Joint Committee on Learning Disabilities (NJCLD). (1999). Learning disabilities: Use of paraprofessionals. *Learning Disability Quarterly, 22,* 23–30.

NCED. (1997). *Special education teacher responses to the 1997 basic standard testing.* Minneapolis, MN: NCED.

Nelson, C. M. (1988). Social skills training for handicapped students. *TEACHING Exceptional Children, 20*(4), 19–23.

Nelson, C. M., & Stevens, K. B. (1981). An accountable model for mainstreaming behaviorally disordered children. *Behavioral Disorders, 6*(2), 82–91.

Nelson, C. M., Smith, D. J., Young, R. K., & Dodd, J. M. (1991). A review of self-management outcome research conducted with students who exhibit behavioral disorders. *Behavioral Disorders, 16,* 169–179.

Nelson, Jayanthi, M., Epstein, M. H., & Bursuck, W. D. (2000). Student preferences for adaptations in classroom testing. *Remedial and Special Education, 21*(1), 41–52.

Noddings, N. (1989). Theoretical and practical concerns about small groups in mathematics. *The Elementary School Journal, 89,* 607–623.

Nowacek, J. E. (1992). Professional talk about teaching together: Interviews with five collaborating teachers. *Intervention in School & Clinic, 27,* 262–276.

O'Connor, R. E., & Jenkins, J. R. (1996). Cooperative learning as an inclusion strategy: A closer look. *Exceptionality, 6*(1), 29–51.

O'Melia, M. C., & Rosenberg, M. S. (1994). Effects of Cooperative Homework Teams on the acquisition of mathematics skills by secondary students with mild disabilities. *Exceptional Children, 60*(6), 538–548.

O'Shea, L. J., & O'Shea, D. (1988). Using repeated readings. *TEACHING Exceptional Children, 20*(2), 26–29.

O'Shea, L. J., Sindelar, P. T., & O'Shea, D. J. (1985). The effects of repeated readings and attentional cues on reading fluency and comprehension. *Journal of Reading Behavior, 17,* 129–141.

Ogle, D. M. (1986). K-W-L: A teaching model that develops active reading of expository text. *The Reading Teacher, 39,* 564–570.

Olion, L. (1989). Enhancing the involvement of Black parents of adolescents with handicaps. In A. A. Ortiz & B. A. Ramirez (Eds.), *Schools and the culturally diverse exceptional students: Promising practices and future directions* (pp. 96–103). Reston, VA: Council for Exceptional Children.

Olson, J. (1989). Managing life in the classroom: Dealing with the nitty gritty. *Academic Therapy, 24*(5), 545–554.

Olson, J., & Platt, J. (1996). *Teaching children and adolescents with special needs* (2nd ed.). Upper Saddle River, NJ: Merrill/Prentice Hall.

Olson, J., & Platt, J. (2000). *Teaching children and adolescents with special needs* (3rd ed.). Upper Saddle River, NJ: Merrill/Prentice Hall.

Ortiz, A. A. (1989). *Factors to consider when adapting materials for ESE/LEP students.* Handicapped Minority Research Institute, Department of Special Education, University of Texas, Austin, TX.

Ortiz, A. A. (1997). Learning disabilities occurring concomitantly with linguistic differences. *Journal of Learning Disabilities 30,* 321–332.

Ortiz, A. A., & Garcia, S. B. (1989). A preferral process for preventing inappropriate referrals of Hispanic students to special education. In A. A. Ortiz & B. A. Ramirez (Eds.), *Schools and the culturally diverse exceptional student: Promising practices and future directions* (pp. 6–18). Reston, VA: Council for Exceptional Children.

Ortiz, A. A., & Polyzoi, E. (1989). Language assessment of Hispanic learning disabled and speech and language handicapped students: Research in progress. In A. A. Ortiz & B. A. Ramirez (Eds.), *Schools and the culturally diverse exceptional student: Promising practices and future directions* (pp. 32–44). Reston, VA: Council for Exceptional Children.

Osborne, S. S., Kosiewicz, M. M., Crumley, E. B., & Lee, C. (1987). It worked in my classroom. *TEACHING Exceptional Children, 19*(2), 66–69.

OSEP Doc: IDEA'97 Final Regulations Major Issues. Retrieved September 18, 2002, from the World Wide Web: http://www.ideapractices.org/law/addl_material/majorissues.php

Paige, R. (2002). Secretary's Statement. *Strategic Plan 2002–2007.* U.S. Department of Education.

Palincsar, A. S. (1982). *Improving the reading comprehension of junior high students through reciprocal teaching of comprehension-monitoring strategies.* Unpublished doctoral dissertation, University of Illinois, Urbana.

Palincsar, A. S. (1986a). Metacognitive strategy instruction. *Exceptional Children, 53*(2), 118–124.

Palincsar, A. S. (1986b). The role of dialogue in scaffolded instruction. *Educational Psychologist, 21,* 73–98.

Palincsar, A. S., & Brown, A. L. (1984). The reciprocal teaching of comprehension fostering and comprehension monitoring activities. *Cognition and Instruction, 1,* 117–175.

Palincsar, A. S., & Brown, A. L. (1986). Interactive teaching to promote independent learning from text. *The Reading Teacher, 39*(8), 771–777.

Palincsar, A. S., & Brown, A. L. (1987). Enhancing instructional time through attention to metacognition. *Journal of Learning Disabilities, 20*(2), 66–75.

Palincsar, A. S., & Brown, A. L. (1988). Teaching and practicing thinking skills to promote comprehension in the context of group problem solving. *Remedial and Special Education, 9*(1), 53–59.

Palincsar, A. S., & Brown, A. L. (1989). Instruction for self-regulated reading. In L. B. Resnick & L. E. Klopfer (Eds.), *Toward the thinking curriculum: Current cognitive research: 1989 ASCD yearbook* (pp. 19–39). Alexandria, VA: Association for Supervision and Curriculum Development.

Pappas, C., Kiefer, B., & Levstik, L. (1990). *An integrated language perspective in the elementary school: Theory into action.* New York: Longman.

Paris, S. G. (1988). Models and metaphors of learning strategies. In C. E. Weinstein, E. T. Goetz, & P. A. Alexander (Eds.), *Learning and study strategies: Issues in assessment, instruction, and evaluation* (pp. 299–321). San Diego: Academic Press.

Paris, S. G., Lipson, M. Y., Jacobs, J., Oka, E., Debritto, A. M., & Cross, D. (1982, April). *Metacognition and reading comprehension.* Symposium conducted at the annual meeting of the International Reading Association, Chicago, IL.

Paris, S. G., Newman, R., & McVey, K. (1982). Learning the functional significance of mnemonic actions: A microgenetic study of strategy acquisition. *Journal of Experimental Child Psychology, 34,* 490–509.

Paris, S. G., & Oka, E. R. (1986). Self-regulated learning among exceptional children. *Exceptional Children, 53*(2), 103–108.

Patton, J. R., Polloway, E. A., & Smith, T. E. C. (1996). Individuals with mild mental retardation: Post-secondary outcomes and implications for educational policy. *Education and Training in Mental Retardation and Developmental Disabilities, 31,* 75–85.

Pauk, W. (1989). *How to study in college* (4th ed.). Boston: Houghton Mifflin.

Paulson, F. L., Paulson, P. R., & Meyer, C. A. (1991). What makes a portfolio a portfolio? *Educational Leadership, 48*(5), 60–63.

Pearson, P. D., & Johnson, D. (1978). *Teaching reading comprehension.* New York: Holt, Rinehart, & Winston.

Perl, J. (1995). Improving relationship skills for parent conferences. *TEACHING Exceptional Children, 28*(1), 29–31.

Peterson, N. L. (1987). *Early intervention for handicapped and at-risk children: An introduction to early childhood—special education.* Denver, CO: Love Publishing.

Phillips, V., & McCullough, L. (1990). Consultation-based programming: Instituting the collaborative ethic in schools. *Exceptional Children, 56*(4), 291–304.

Pickett, A. L. (1986). *Paraprofessionals in special education: The state of the art.* New York: City University of New York, New Careers.

Pickett, A. L. (1988). *A training program for paraprofessionals working in special education and related services.* New York: National Resource Center for Paraprofessionals in Special Education, New Careers Training Laboratory, City University of New York.

Pickett, A. L. (1996). *A state of the art report on paraeducators in education and related services.* New York: National Resource Center for Paraprofessionals, Center for Advanced Study in Education, City University of New York.

Pickett, A. L., & Gerlach, K. (1997). *Supervising paraeducators in school settings.* Austin, TX, PRO-ED.

Platt, J. M. (1987). Increasing the independence of learning-disabled adolescents through self-detection of errors. *Ideas in Education, 4*(1), 17–23.

Platt, J. M., & Olson, J. (1997). *Teaching adolescents with mild disabilities.* Pacific Grove, CA: Brooks/ Cole.

Platt, J. M., & Williams, K. (1988). Preservice and inservice teachers' reading comprehension skills and their metacognitive awareness of processing of text. *Eighth Yearbook of the American Reading Forum.* Sarasota, FL: American Reading Forum.

Polloway, E. A., Epstein, M. H., Bursuck, W. D., Roderique, T. W., McConeghy, J., & Jayanthi, M. (1994). Classroom grading: A national survey of policies. *Remedial and Special Education, 15,* 162–170.

Polloway, E. A., Epstein, M. H., Polloway, C. H., Patton, I. R., & Ball, D. W. (1986). Corrective reading program: An analysis of effectiveness with learning disabled and mentally retarded students. *Remedial and Special Education, 7*(4), 41–47.

Polloway, E. A., & Patton, J. R. (1997). *Strategies for teaching learners with special needs* (5th ed.). Upper Saddle River, NJ: Merrill/Prentice Hall.

Polloway, E. A., Patton, J. R., Epstein, M. H., & Smith, T. E. (1989). Comprehensive curriculum for students with mild disabilities. *Focus on Exceptional Children, 21,* 1–12.

Polloway, E. A., Patton, J. R., Payne, J. S., & Payne, R. A. (1989). *Strategies for teaching learners with special needs* (4th ed.). Upper Saddle River, NJ: Merrill/Prentice Hall.

Polloway, E. A., Patton, J. R., & Serna, L. (2001). *Strategies for teaching learners with special needs* (7th ed.). Upper Saddle River, NJ: Merrill/Prentice Hall.

Pomplun, M. (1996). Cooperative groups: Alternative assessment for students with disabilities? *The Journal of Special Education, 30*(1), 1–17.

Pomplun, M. (1997). When students with disabilities participate in cooperative groups. *Exceptional Children, 64*(10), 49–58.

Popham, W. J. (1997). What's wrong—and what's right—with rubrics. *Educational Leadership, 55*(2), 72–75.

Poplin, M. S. (1988). Holistic/constructivist principles of the teaching/learning process: Implications for the field of learning disabilities. *Journal of Learning Disabilities, 21*(7), 389–400.

Powers, D. A. (1986). Evaluating software for use by mentally handicapped learners. *Computers in the Schools, 3*(3–4), 41–49.

Prater, M. A., Serna, L., & Nakamura, K. K. (1999). Impact of peer teaching on the acquisition of social skills by adolescents with learning disabilities. *Education & Treatment of Children, 22*(1), 19–35.

Pressley, M., Borkowski, J. G., & O'Sullivan, J. T. (1984). Memory strategy instruction is made of this: Metamemory and durable strategy use. *Educational Psychologist, 1,* 94–107.

Pressley, M., Brown, R., Van Meter, P., & Schuder, T. (1995). Transactional strategies. *Educational Leadership, 52*(5), 81–87.

Pressley, M., Harris, K. R., & Marks, M. B. (1992). But good strategy instructors are constructivists! *Educational Psychology Review, 4,* 3–31.

Pressley, M., Hogan, K., Wharton-McDonald, R., Mistretta, J., & Ettenberger, S. (1996). The challenges of instructional scaffolding: The challenges of instruction that supports student thinking. *Learning Disabilities Research & Practice, 11*(3), 138–146.

Public Law 94–142. (1975). *The Equal Education for All Handicapped Children Act.* Washington, DC: The U.S. Congress.

Public Law 98–199. (1983). *Amendments to PL 94–142: The School to Work Transition Initiative.* Washington, DC: The U.S. Congress.

Public Law 101–476. (1990). *Amendments to PL 94–142: The Individuals with Disabilities Education Act.* Washington, DC: The U.S. Congress.

Pugach, M. C., & Johnson, L. J. (1989). The challenge of implementing collaboration between general and special education. *Exceptional Children, 56*(3), 232–235.

Pugach, M. C., & Johnson, L. J. (1995). *Collaborative practitioners, collaborative schools.* Denver, CO: Love.

Pugach, M. C., & Warger, C. L. (2001). Curriculum matters. *Remedial and Special Education, 22*(4), 194–196.

Putnam, J. W. (1998). *Cooperative learning and strategies for inclusion: Celebrating diversity in the classroom.* Baltimore, MD: Paul H. Brookes Publishing.

Putnam, J. W., Rynders, J. E., Johnson, R. T., & Johnson, D. W. (1989). Collaborative skill instruction for promoting positive interactions between mentally handicapped and nonhandicapped children. *Exceptional Children, 55*(6), 550–558.

Putnam, M. L., & Wesson, C. L. (1990). The teacher's role in teaching content-area information. *LD Forum, 16*(1), 55–60.

Putnam, M. L., Deshler, D. D., & Schumaker, J. B. (1993). The investigation of setting demands: A missing link in learning strategy instruction. In L. S. Meltzer (Ed.), *Strategy assessment and instruction for students with learning disabilities* (pp. 325–354). Austin, TX: PRO-ED.

Rabren, K., Dunn, C., & Chambers, D. (2002). Predictors of post-high school employment among young adults with disabilities. *Career Development for Exceptional Individuals, 25*(1), 25–40.

Ray, J., & Warden, M. K. (1995). *Technology, computers, and the special needs learner.* Albany, NY: Delmar.

Raygor, A. L. (1970). *Study skills test: Form A.* New York: McGraw-Hill.

Raygor, A. L., Wark, D. M., & Raygor, R. D. (1980). *Systems for study.* McGraw-Hill.

Rea, P. J., McLaughlin, V. L., & Walther-Thomas, C. (2002). Outcomes for students with learning disabilities in inclusive and pullout programs. *Exceptional Children, 68*(2), 203–223.

Reeve, P. T., & Hallahan, D. P. (1994). Practical questions about collaboration between general and special educators. *Focus on Exceptional Children, 26*(7), 1–12.

Reid, D. K., Kurkjian, C., & Carruthers, S. S. (1994). Special education teachers interpret constructivist teaching. *Remedial and Special Education, 15*(5), 267–280.

Reid, E. (1986). Practicing effective instruction: The exemplary center for reading instruction approach. *Exceptional Children, 52*(6), 510–517.

Reid, R., & Nelson, J. (2002). The utility, acceptability, and practicality of functional behavior assessment for students with high-incidence problem behaviors. *Remedial and Special Education, 23*(1), 15–23.

Rhodes, L. K. (1981). I can read: Predictable books as resources for reading and writing instruction. *The Reading Teacher, 34*(5), 511–518.

Rhodes, L. K., & Dudley-Marling, C. (1988). *Readers and writers make a difference: A holistic approach to teaching learning disabled and remedial students.* Portsmouth, NH: Heinemann Educational Books.

Rhodes, L. K., & Dudley-Marling, C. (1996). *Readers and writers make a difference: A holistic approach to teaching learning disabled and remedial students* (2nd ed.). Portsmouth, NH: Heinemann.

Rich, H. L., & Ross, S. M. (1989). Student's time on learning tasks in special education. *Exceptional Child, 55*(6), 508–515.

Rickards, J. P., & August, G. J. (1975). Generative underlining strategies in prose recall. *Journal of Educational Psychology, 67,* 860–865.

Riegel, R. H., Mayle, J. A., & McCarthy-Henkel, J. (1988). *Beyond maladies and remedies.* Novi, MI: RHR Consultation Services.

Rieth, H. J., Polsgrove, L., Okolo, C., Bahr, C., & Eckert, R. (1987). An analysis of the secondary special education classroom ecology with implications for teacher training. *Teacher Education and Special Education, 10*(3), 113–119.

Ritter, S., & Idol-Maestas, L. (1986). Teaching middle school students to use a test-taking strategy. *Journal of Educational Research, 79*(6), 350–357.

Rivera, B. D., & Rogers-Adkinson, D. (1997). Culturally sensitive interventions: Social skills training with children and parents from culturally and linguistically diverse backgrounds. *Intervention in School and Clinic, 33*(2), 75–80.

Rivera, D. P. (1995). Portfolio assessment. *Diagnostique, 20*(1–4), 207–210.

Rivera, D. P., & Smith, D. D. (1988). Using a demonstration strategy to teach midschool students with learning disabilities how to compute long division. *Journal of Learning Disabilities, 21*(2), 77–81.

Rivera, D. P., & Smith, D. D. (1997). *Teaching students with learning and behavior problems.* Needham Heights, MA: Allyn & Bacon.

Roberds-Baxter, S. (1984). The parent connection: Enhancing the affective component of parent conferences. *TEACHING Exceptional Children, 17*(1), 55–58.

Roberts, G. H. (1968). The failure strategies of third grade arithmetic pupils. *The Arithmetic Teacher, 15,* 442–446.

Robinson, D. H., & Keiwra, K. A. (1995). Visual argument: Graphic organizers are superior outlines in improving learning from text. *Journal of Educational Psychology, 78*(3), 455–467.

Robinson, H. A. (1975). *Teaching reading and study strategies: The content areas.* Needham Heights, MA: Allyn & Bacon.

Roblyer, M. D. (1989). *Making the most of computers in the classroom: Effective models for integrating computer courseware into school instructional programs.* Tallahassee, FL: Florida Department of Education.

Roblyer, M., & Edwards, J. (2000). *Integrating educational technology into teaching.* Upper Saddle River, NJ: Prentice-Hall.

Roessler, R. R., Brolin, D. E., & Johnson, J. M. (1990). Factors affecting employment success and quality of life: A one year follow-up of students in special education. *Career Development for Exceptional Individuals, 13*(2), 95–107.

Rooney, K., Polloway, E. A., & Hallahan, D. P. (1985). The use of self-monitoring procedures with low IQ LD students. *Journal of Learning Disabilities, 18,* 384–394.

Rosenberg, M. S. (1986). Maximizing the effectiveness of structured classroom management programs: Implementing rule-review procedures with disruptive and distractible students. *Behavioral Disorders, 11*(4), 239–248.

Rosenfield, P., Lambert, N., & Black, A. (1985). Desk arrangement effects on pupil classroom behavior. *Journal of Educational Psychology, 77,* 101–108.

Rosenshine, B. (1983). Teaching functions in instructional programs. *Elementary School Journal, 83,* 335–351.

Rosenshine, B. (1990). How time is spent in elementary classrooms. In C. Denharm & A. Lieberman (Eds.), *Time to learn.* Washington, DC: National Institute of Education.

Rosenshine, B. (1995). Advances in research on instruction. *Journal of Educational Research, 88,* 262–268.

Rosenshine, B., & Meister, C. (1994). Reciprocal teaching: A review of the research. *Review of Educational Research, 64,* 479–530.

Rosenshine, B., & Stevens, R. (1986). Teaching functions. In M. Wittrock (Ed.), *Third handbook of research on teaching* (pp. 376–391). New York: Macmillan.

Rosenthal-Malek, A. L. (1997). STOP and THINK: Using metacognitive strategies to teach students social skills. *TEACHING Exceptional Children, 29*(3), 29–31.

Roser, N. L., Hoffman, J. V., & Farest, C. (1990). Language, literature, and at-risk children. *Reading Teacher, 43*(8), 554–561.

Rounds, K. A., Weil, M., & Bishop, K. K. (1994), Practice with culturally diverse families of young children with disabilities. *Families and Society: The Journal of Contemporary Human Services, 75*(1), 3–14.

Rowe, M. B. (1974). Wait time and rewards as instructional variables, their influence on language, logic, and rate control: Part 1: Wait time. *Journal of Research in Science Teaching, 11,* 81–94.

Rowe, M. B. (1987). Wait-time: Slowing down may be a way of speeding up. *American Educator, 11*(1), 38–47.

Rozenholtz, S., Basler, O., & Hoover-Dempsey. (1985). *Organizational conditions of teacher learning* (NIE-G-83-0041). Urbana, IL: University of Illinois.

Rueda, R., & Garcia, E. (1997). Do portfolios make a difference for diverse students? The influence of type of data on making instructional decisions. *Learning Disabilities Research & Practice, 12*(2), 114–122.

Ruiz, N. T. (1989). An optimal learning environment for Rosemary. *Exceptional Child, 56*(2), 130–144.

Rutherford, R., Chipman, J., DiGangi, S., & Anderson, K. (1992). *Teaching social skill: A practical instructional approach.* Reston, VA: Council for Exceptional Children.

Ryan, E. B., Weed, K. A., & Short, E. J. (1986). Cognitive behavior modification: Promoting active, self-regulatory learning styles. In J. K. Torgesen & B. Y. L. Wong (Eds.), *Psychological and educational perspectives on learning disabilities* (pp. 367–397). New York: Academic Press.

Safran, S. P., & Safran, J. S. (1996). Intervention Assistance Programs and Prereferral Teams: Directions for the Twenty-first Century. *Remedial and Special Education, 17,* 363–369.

Sailor, W. (1991). Special education in the restructured school. *Remedial and Special Education, 12*(6), 8–22.

Sainato, D. M., Strain, P. S., & Lyon, S. L. (1987). Increasing academic responding of handicapped preschool children during group instruction. *Journal of the Division of Early Childhood Special Education, 12,* 23–30.

Salembier, G., & Furney, K. S. (1997). Facilitating participation: Parents' perceptions of their involvement in the IEP/transition planning process. *Career Development for Exceptional Individuals, 20,* 29–42.

Salend, S. J. (1995a). Modifying tests for diverse learners. *Intervention in School and Clinic, 31*(2), 84–90.

Salend, S. J. (1995b). Using videocassette recorder technology in special education classrooms. *TEACHING Exceptional Children, 27*(3), 4–9.

Salend, S. (2000). Strategies and resources to evaluate the impact of inclusion programs on students. *Intervention in School and Clinic, 35*(5), 264–270.

Salend, S. J. (2001). *Creating inclusive classrooms: Effective and reflective practices* (4th ed.). Upper Saddle River, NJ: Prentice Hall.

Salend, S. J., & Allen, E. M. (1985). A comparison of self-managed and externally managed response cost systems on learning disabled children. *Journal of School Psychology, 23,* 59–67.

Salend, S., & Duhaney, L. (2002). Grading students in inclusive settings. *TEACHING Exceptional Children, 34*(8), 8–15.

Salend, S. J., Jantzen, N. R., & Giek, K. (1992). Using a peer confrontation system in a group setting. *Behavioral Disorders, 17*(3), 211–218.

Salvia, J., & Hughes, C. (1990). *Curriculum-based assessment: Testing what is taught.* New York: Macmillan.

Sapon-Shevin, M. (1986). Teaching cooperation. In G. Cartledge & J. F. Milburn (Eds.), *Teaching social skills to children: Innovative approaches* (3rd ed.). Elmsford, NY: Pergamon.

Sargent, L. R. (1981). Resource teacher time utilization: An observational study. *Exceptional Children, 47*(6), 420–426.

Sargent, L. R. (1991). *Social skills in the school and community.* Reston, VA: Council for Exceptional Children.

Saver, K., & Downes, B. (1991). PIT Crew: A Model for Teacher Collaboration in an Elementary School. *Intervention in School and Clinic. 27*(2) 116–120.

Saville-Troike, M. (1976). *Foundations for teaching English as a second language: Theory and method for multicultural education.* Upper Saddle River, NJ: Prentice Hall.

Sawyer, R., Graham, S., & Harris, K. R. (1992). Direct teaching, strategy instruction, and strategy instruction with explicit self-regulation: Effects on learning disabled students' compositions and self-efficacy. *Journal of Educational Psychology, 84,* 340–352.

Schloss, P. J., & Schloss, C. N. (1987). A critical review of social skills research in mental retardation. In R. P. Barrett & J. L. Matson (Eds.), *Advances in developmental disorders* (pp. 107–151). Greenwich, CT: JAI Press.

Schloss, P. J., Schloss, C. N., & Harris, L. (1984). A multiple baseline analysis of an interpersonal skills training program for depressed youth. *Behavior Disorders, 9,* 182–188.

Schloss, P. J., & Sedlak, R. A. (1986). *Instructional methods for students with learning and behavior problems.* Needham Heights, MA: Allyn & Bacon.

Schloss, P. J., Smith, M. A., & Schloss, C. N. (2001). *Instructional methods for secondary students with learning and behavior problems* (3rd ed.). Needham Heights, MA: Allyn & Bacon.

Schmidt, J. L. (1983). *The effects of four generalization conditions on learning disabled adolescents' written language performance in the regular classroom.* Unpublished doctoral dissertation, University of Kansas, Lawrence.

Schneider, W. (1985). Developmental trends in metamemory-memory relationships: An integrative review. In D. Forrest-Pressley, G. E. McKinnon, & T. G. Waller (Eds.), *Metacognition, cognition, and human performance* (pp. 57–109). New York: Academic Press.

Schniedewind, N., & Salend, S. J. (1987). Cooperative learning works. *TEACHING Exceptional Children, 19*(2), 22–25.

Schuler, L., Ogulthorpe, R. T., & Eiserman, W. D. (1987). The effects of reverse-role tutoring on the social acceptance of students with behavioral disorders. *Behavioral Disorders, 13*(1), 35–44.

Schumaker, J. B. (1989). The heart of strategy instruction. *Strategram: Strategies intervention model, 1*(4). Kansas City, KS: The University of Kansas Institute for Research in Learning Disabilities, pp. 1–5.

Schumaker, J. B., & Deshler, D. D. (1988). Implementing the regular education initiative in secondary schools: A different ball game. *Journal of Learning Disabilities, 21*(1), 36–42.

Schumaker, J. B., Deshler, D. D., & McKnight, P. (1989). *Teaching routines to enhance the mainstream performance of adolescents with learning disabilities.* Final report submitted to U.S. Department of Education, Special Education Services.

Schumaker, J. B., Nolan, S. M., & Deshler, D. D. (1985). *The error monitoring strategy.* Lawrence, KA: The University of Kansas.

Schumaker, J. B., & Sheldon, J. (1985). *Learning strategies curriculum: The sentence writing strategy, instructor's manual.* Lawrence, KS: The University of Kansas.

Schutt, P. W., & McCabe, V. M. (1994). Portfolio assessment for students with learning disabilities. *Learning Disabilities, 5*(2), 81–85.

Scruggs, T. E., & Mastropieri, M. A. (1984). Improving memory for facts: The "keyword" method. *Academic Therapy, 20*(2), 159–166.

Scruggs, T. E., Mastropieri, M. A., Levin, J. R., & Gaffney, J. S. (1985). Facilitating the acquisition of science facts in learning-disabled students. *American Educational Research Journal, 22,* 575–586.

Secretary's Commission on Achieving Necessary Skills (SCANS). (1991). *What work requires of schools.* Washington, DC: U.S. Department of Labor.

Shanahan, T., Robinson, B., & Schneider, M. (1995). Integrating curriculum: Avoiding some of the pitfalls of thematic units. *The Reading Teacher, 48*(8), 718–719.

Shields, J. M., & Heron, T. E. (1989). Teaching organizational skills to students with learning disabilities. *TEACHING Exceptional Children, 21*(2), 8–13.

Shin, J., Deno, S., & Espin, C. (2000). Technical adequacy of the maze task for curriculum-based measurement of reading growth. *The Journal of Special Education, 34*(3), 164–172.

Shinn, M. (Ed.). (1989). *Curriculum-based measurement: Assessing special children.* New York: The Guilford Press.

Showers, B. (1985). Teachers coaching teachers. *Educational Leadership, 42*(7), 43–48.

Showers, B. (1990). Aiming for superior classroom instruction for all children: A comprehensive staff development model. *Remedial and Special Education, 11*(3), 50–53.

Shumm, J. S. (1999). *Adapting reading and math materials for the inclusive classroom.* Arlington, VA: Council for Exceptional Children.

Silbert, J., Carnine, D., & Stein, M. (1990). *Direct instruction mathematics* (2nd ed.). Upper Saddle River, NJ: Merrill/Prentice Hall.

Simmons, D., & Kame'enui, E. J. (1999). *Toward successful inclusion of students with disabilities: The architecture of instruction.* Arlington, VA: Council for Exceptional Children.

Simpson, R. L. (1982). *Conferencing parents of exceptional children.* Rockville, MD: Aspen.

Sindelar, P. T., Bursuck, W. D., & Halle, J. W. (1986). The effects of two variations of teacher questioning on student performance. *Education and Treatment of Children, 9*(1), 56–66.

Sindelar, P. T., Griffin, C. C., Smith, S. W., & Watanabe, A. K. (1992). Prereferral intervention: Encouraging notes on preliminary findings. *The Elementary School Journal, 92*(3), 245–259.

Sindelar, P. T., Smith, M., Harriman, N., Hale, R., & Wilson, R. (1986). Teacher effectiveness in special education programs. *Journal of Special Education, 20*(2), 195–207.

Sitlington, P. L., Frank, A. R., & Carson, R. (1993). Adult adjustment among high school graduates with mild disabilities. *Exceptional Children, 59*(3), 221–233.

Skelton, K. J. (1997). *Paraprofessionals in education.* Delmar Publishers.

Slavin, R. E. (1984). Team-assisted individualization: Cooperative learning and individualized instruction in the mainstreamed classroom. *Remedial and Special Education, 5*(6), 33–42.

Slavin, R. E. (1985). Cooperative learning: Applying contact theory in desegregated schools. *Journal of Social Issues, 41*(3), 45–62.

Slavin, R. E. (1988a). Cooperative learning and student achievement. *Educational Leadership, 46*(2), 31–33.

Slavin, R. E. (1988b). *Student team learning: An overview and practical guide* (2nd ed.). Washington, DC: National Education Association.

Slavin, R. E., Stevens, R. J., & Madden, N. A. (1988). Accommodating student diversity in reading and writing instruction: A cooperative learning approach. *Remedial and Special Education, 9*(1), 60–66.

Smith, D. D. (1998). *Introduction to special education: Teaching in an age of challenge* (3rd ed.). Needham Heights, MA: Allyn & Bacon.

Smith, J. O. (1995). Getting to the bottom of social skills deficits. *LD Forum, 21*(1), 23–26.

Smith, S. W. (2000). *Creating useful individualized education programs (IEPs).* (Report No. EDO-EC-00–9),

ERIC Digest # E600. ERIC Clearinghouse on Disabilities and Gifted Education, Arlington, VA. (ERIC Document Reproduction Service No. ED 449636)

Smith, S., Boone, R., & Higgins, K. (1998). Expanding the writing process to the web. *TEACHING Exceptional Children, 30*(5), 22–26.

Snell, M. E. & Janney, R. (2000). *Collaborative Teaming,* Baltimore, Maryland: Paul H. Brooks Publishing Co.

Snider, V. E. (1992). Learning styles and learning to read: A critique. *Remedial and Special Education, 13*(1), 6–18.

Soldier, L. L. (1989). Language learning of Native American students. *Educational Leadership, 46*(5), 74–75.

Sonnenschein, P. (1981). Parents and professionals: An uneasy relationship. *TEACHING Exceptional Children, 14*(2), 62–65.

Spache, E. B. (1982). *Reading activities for child involvement.* Boston, MA: Allyn & Bacon.

Sparks, S. (2000). Classroom and curriculum accommodations for Native American students. *Intervention in School and Clinic, 35*(5), 259–263.

Speece, D. L., MacDonald, V., Kilsheimer, L., & Krist, J. (1997). Research to practice: Preservice teachers reflect on reciprocal teaching. *Learning Disabilities Practice, 12*(3), 177–187.

Sprick, R. S. (1981). *The solution book: A guide to classroom discipline.* Chicago: Science Research Associates.

Sprick, R. S. (1985). *Discipline in the secondary classroom: A problem-by-problem survival guide.* West Nyack, NY: Center for Applied Research in Education.

Squires, D. A., Huitt, W. G., & Segars, J. K. (1983). *Effective schools and classrooms: A research-based perspective.* Alexandria, VA: Association for Supervision and Curriculum Development.

Stahl, B. J., & Lorenz, G. (1995). Views on Paraprofessionals. Saint Paul: Minnesota Department of Education.

Stahl, S., McKenna, M., & Pagnucco, J. (1994). The effects of whole-language instruction: An update and a reappraisal. *Educational Psychologist, 29*(4), 175–185.

Stainback, S., & Stainback, W. (1996). *Curriculum considerations in inclusive classrooms: Facilitating learning for all students.* Baltimore, MD: Paul H. Brookes Publishing.

Stainback, W., Stainback, S., & Stefanich, G. (1996). Learning together in inclusive classrooms. *TEACHING Exceptional Children, 28*(3), 14–19.

Stallings, J. (1980). Allocated academic learning time revisited, or beyond time on-task. *Educational Researcher, 9,* 11–16.

Stamm, J. M. (1980). Teacher competencies: Recommendations for personnel preparation. *Teacher Education and Special Education, 3*(1), 52–57.

Stanciak, L. A. (1997). Curriculum integration and brain-based learning. *Connections, 2*(1), 2.

Standal, T. (1978). Readability formulas: What's out, what's in? *The Reading Teacher, 21,* 642–646.

Stanley, S. O., & Greenwood, C. R. (1983). How much "opportunity to respond" does the minority disadvantaged student receive in school? *Exceptional Children, 49,* 370–373.

Stanovich, K. (1986). Cognitive processes and the reading problems of learning disabled children: Evaluating the assumptions of specificity. In J. K. Torgesen & B. Y. L. Wong (Eds.), *Psychological and educational perspectives on learning disabilities* (pp. 85–131). Orlando, FL: Academic Press.

Stanovich, K. (1994). Constructivism in reading education. *The Journal of Special Education, 28*(3), 259–274.

Stanovich, P. J. (1996). Collaboration—the key to successful instruction in today's inclusive schools. *Intervention in School and Clinic, 32*(1), 39–42.

State of Florida. (1993). *Transition the IDEA way.* Tallahassee, FL: Florida Department of Education, Bureau of Education for Exceptional Students.

Steere, D. E., Pancsofar, E. L., Powell, T. H., & Butterworth, J. (1989). Enhancing instruction through general case programming. *TEACHING Exceptional Children, 22*(1), 22–24.

Stein, C. L. E., & Goldman, J. (1980). Beginning reading instruction for children with minimal brain dysfunction. *Journal of Learning Disability, 13*(4), 52–55.

Stein, M., Carnine, D., & Dixon, R. (1998). Direct instruction: Integrating curriculum design and effective teaching practice. *Intervention in School and Clinic, 33*(4), 227–234.

Stein, M., Carnine, D., & Dixon, R. (1998). Direct instruction: Integrating curriculum design and effective teaching practice. *Intervention in School and Clinic, 33*(4), 227–234.

Stemmer, P., Brown, B., & Smith, C. (1992). The employability skills portfolio. *Educational Leadership, 49*(6), 32–35.

Stephens, T. M., Blackhurst, A. E., & Magliocca, L. A. (1988). *Teaching mainstreamed students* (2nd ed.). New York: Pergamon.

Steptoe, J. (1987). *Mufaro's beautiful daughters.* New York: Lothrop, Lee, & Shepard.

Stevens, R. J., & Slavin, R. E. (1991). When cooperative learning improves the achievement of students with mild disabilities: A response to Tateyama-Sniezek. *Exceptional Children, 57*(3), 276–280.

Stilington, P. L., Clark, G. M., & Kolstoe, O. P. (2000). *Transition education and services for adolescents with disabilities* (3rd ed). Boston: Allyn & Bacon.

Stilington, P. L., Frank, A. R., & Carson, R. (1992). Adult adjustment among graduates with mild disabilities. *Exceptional Children, 59* (3), 221–233.

Stump, C., Lovitt, T., Fister, S., Kemp, K., Moore, R., & Schroeder, B. (1992). Vocabulary intervention for secondary-level youth. *Learning Disability Quarterly, 15,* 207–222.

Sugai, G., Maheady, L., & Skouge, J. (1989). Best assessment practices for students with behavioral disorders: Accommodation to cultural diversity and individual differences. *Behavioral Disorders, 14*(4), 263–278.

Suritsky, S. K., and Hughes, C.A. (1996). Notetaking strategy instruction. In D. D. Deshler, E. S. Ellis, & B. K. Lenz (Eds.), *Adolescents with learning disabilities: Strategies and methods* (2nd ed.) Denver, CO: Love.

Swaggert, B. L. (1998). Implementing a cognitive behavior management program. *Intervention School and Clinic, 33*(4), 235–238.

Swanson, H. L. (1991). Learning disabilities and memory. In D. K. Reed, W. P. Hresko, & H. L. Swanson (Eds.), *A cognitive approach to learning disabilities* (2nd ed., pp.159–182). Austin, TX: PRO-ED.

Swicegood, P. R., & Parsons, J. L. (1991). The thematic unit approach: Content and process instruction for secondary learning disabled students. *Learning Disabilities Research & Practice, 6*(2), 112–116.

Tarver, S. G. (1986). Cognitive behavior modification, direct instruction and holistic approaches to the education of students with learning disabilities. *Journal of Learning Disabilities, 19*(6), 368–375.

Tateyama-Sniezek, K. M. (1990). Cooperative learning: Does it improve the academic achievement of students with handicaps? *Exceptional Children, 56*(5), 426–437.

Taylor, B. M., & Beach, R. W. (1984). The effects of text structure instruction on middle-grade students' comprehension and production of expository text. *Reading Research Quarterly, 19,* 134–146.

Taylor, I., & O'Reilly, M. F. (2000). Generalization of supermarket shopping skills for individuals with mild intellectual disabilities using stimulus equivalence training. *The Psychological Record, 50*(1), 49–62.

Tharp, R. G. (1975). The triadic model of consultation. In C. Parker (Ed.), *Psychological consultation in the schools: Helping teachers meet special needs* (pp. 133–151). Reston, VA: Council for Exceptional Children.

Tharp, R. G., & Wetzel, R. J. (1969). *Behavior modification in the natural environment.* New York: Academic Press.

*The Grady Profile*™ (Computer Software). (1995). St. Louis, MO: Aurbach and Associates.

*The Portfolio Assessment Kit* (Computer Software). (1996). New York: Super School.

Thomas, C. C., Correa, V. I., & Morsink, C. V. (1995). *Interactive teaming: Consultation and collaboration in special programs* (2nd ed.). Upper Saddle River, NJ: Merrill/Prentice Hall.

Thorin, E., Yovanoff, P., & Irvin, L. (1996). Dilemmas faced by families during their young adults' transitions to adulthood: A brief report. *Mental Retardation, 34*(2), 117–120.

Thurlow, M., Christenson, S., & Ysseldyke, J. (1987). *School effectiveness: Implications of effective construction for handicapped students* (Monograph B. 3). Minneapolis, MN: Instructional Alternative Project, University of Minnesota.

Thurlow, M. L., & Johnson, D. R. (2000). High-stakes testing of students with disabilities. *Journal of Teacher Education 51*(4), 305–314. Minneapolis, MN: University of Minnesota, National Center on Educational Outcomes.

Thurlow, M., Ysseldyke, J. E., & Anderson, C. (1995). *High school graduation requirements: What's happening for students with disabilities?* (Tech Rep. No. 20).

Thurston, L. P. (1987). *Survival skills for women: Facilitator manual.* Manhattan, KS: Survival Skills and Development.

Tiedt, P. L., & Tiedt, I. M. (1986). *Multicultural teaching.* Needham Heights, MA: Allyn & Bacon.

Tindal, G. A., & Marston, D. B. (1990). *Classroom-based assessment: Evaluating instructional outcomes.* Upper Saddle River, NJ: Merrill/Prentice Hall.

Tindal, G. A., Shinn, M. R., & Rodden-Nord, K. (1990). Contextually based school consultation: Influential variables. *Exceptional Children, 56*(4), 324–336.

Tobin, K. (1987). The role of wait time in higher cognitive level learning. *Review of Educational Research, 57*(1), 69–95.

Tolan, S. S. (1978). *Grandpa and me.* New York: Charles Scribner's Sons.

Torgesen, J. K. (1977). Memorization processes in reading disabled children. *Journal of Educational Psychology, 69,* 571–578.

Torgesen, J. K. (1982). The learning disabled child as an inactive learner: Educational implications. *Topics in Learning and Learning Disabilities, 2*(1), 45–52.

Trammel, D. L., Schloss, P. T., & Alper, S. (1994). Using self-recording, evaluation, and graphing to increase completion of homework assignments. *Journal of Learning Disabilities, 27*(2), 75–81.

Turnbull, A. P., Strickland, B. B., & Brantley, J. C. (1982). *Developing and implementing individualized education programs.* Upper Saddle River, NJ: Merrill/Prentice Hall.

Turnbull, A. P., & Turnbull, H. R. (1986). *Families, professionals, and exceptionality: A special partnership.* Upper Saddle River, NJ: Merrill/Prentice Hall.

Turnbull, A. P., Turnbull, H. R., Shank, M., & Leal, D. (2001). *Exceptional lives: Special education in today's schools.* Upper Saddle River, NJ: Prentice Hall.

U.S. Department of Education. (2000). To assure the free appropriate public education of all children with disabilities. *Twenty-second Annual Report to Congress on the Individuals with Disabilities Education Act.* Washington, DC: U.S. Government Printing Office.

Udvari-Solner, A. (1997). Effective accommodations for students with exceptionalities. *CEC Today, 4*(3), 1, 9–15.

United States Internet Council. (2000). *State of the Internet 2000.* Retrieved September 18, 2002, the World Wide Web: from http://usic.wslogic.com/intro.html

Utley, C. A., Mortsweet, S. L., & Greenwood, C. R. (1997). Peer-mediated instruction and interventions. *Focus on Exceptional Children, 29*(5), 1–23.

Utley, C., Reddy, S., Delquadri, J., Greenwood, C., Mortsweet, S., & Bowman, V. (2001). Class Wide peer tutoring: An effective teaching procedure for facilitating the acquisition of health education and safety facts with students with developmental disabilities. *Education & Treatment of Children, 24*(1), 1–28.

Valencia, S. (1990). A portfolio approach to classroom reading assessment: The whys, whats, and hows. *The Reading Teacher, 43*(4), 338–340.

Van Luit, J. E. H., & Naglieri, J. A. (1999). Effectiveness of the MASTER program for teaching special children multiplication and division. *Journal of Learning Disabilities, 32*(2), 98–107.

VanReusen, A. K., & Bos, C. S. (1994). Facilitating student participation in individualized education programs through motivation strategy instruction. *Exceptional Children, 60*(5), 466–475.

VanReusen, A. K., Bos, C. S., Schumaker, J. B., & Deshler, D. (1987). *The education planning strategy: A motivation strategy.* Lawrence, KS: Edge Enterprises.

VanReusen, A. K., Bos, C. S., Schumaker, J. B., & Deshler, D. D. (1994). *The self-advocacy strategy for education and transition planning.* Lawrence, KS: Edge Enterprises.

Vaughn, S., Gersten, R., & Chard, D. (2000). The underlying message in LD intervention research: Findings from research syntheses. *Exceptional Children 67*(1), 99–114.

Vaughn, S., Hughes, M. T., & Moody, S. W. (2001). Instructional grouping for students with LD: Implications for practice. *Intervention in School and Clinic, 36*(3), 131–137.

Vaughn, S., Klinger, J., & Bryant, D. (2001). Collaborative strategic reading as a means to enhance peer-mediated instruction for reading comprehension and content-area learning. *Remedial and Special Education, 22*(2), 66–74.

Vaughn, S., & Schumm, J. S. (1995). Responsible inclusion for students with learning disabilities. *Journal of Learning Disabilities, 28*(5), 264–270, 290.

Veit, D. T., Scruggs, T. E., & Mastropieri, M. A. (1986). Extended mnemonic instruction with learning disabled students. *Journal of Educational Psychology, 78,* 300–308.

Viorst, J. (1972). *Alexander and the terrible, horrible, no-good, very bad day.* New York: Atheneum.

Voltz, D. L., & Elliot, R. N. (1997). Collaborative teacher roles in facilitating inclusion: Preservice preparation for general and special educators. *The Teacher Educator, 33*(1), 44–60.

Voltz, D. L., Elliot, R. N., & Cobb, H. (1994). Collaborative teacher roles: Special and general educators. *Journal of Learning Disabilities, 27*(8), 527–535.

Vygotsky, L. S. (1962). *Thought and language.* New York: Wiley.

Wadsworth, D. E., & Knight, D. (1996). Paraprofessionals: The bridge to successful full inclusion. *Intervention in School and Clinic, 30*(3), 166–171.

Wagner, M. M., & Blackorby, J. (1996). Transition from high school to work or college: How special education students fare. *The Future of Children,* 103–120.

Wagner, M. M., Blackorby, J., & Hebbler, K. (1993). *Beyond the report card: The multiple dimensions of secondary school performance for students with disabilities.* Menlo Park, CA: SRI International.

Walker, D. M., Schwarz, I. E., Nippold, M. S., Irvin, L. K., & Noell, J. W. (1994). Social skills in school-age children and youth: Issues and best practices in assessment and intervention. *Topics in Language Disorders, 14*(3), 70–82.

Walker, J. L. (1987). Language and curriculum development for American Indian handicapped children. In M. J. Johnson & B. A. Ramirez (Eds.), *American Indian exceptional children and youth* (pp. 17–23). Reston, VA: Council for Exceptional Children.

Walker, J. L. (1988). Young American Indian children. *TEACHING Exceptional Children, 20*(4), 50–51.

Wallace, G., & Kauffman, J. M. (1986). *Teaching students with learning and behavior problems* (3rd ed.). Upper Saddle River, NJ: Merrill/Prentice Hall.

Wallace, T., Shin, J., Bartholomay, T., & Stahl, B. (2001). Knowledge and skills for teachers supervising the work of paraprofessionals. *Exceptional Children, 67(4),* 520–533.

Walther-Thomas, C. S., Korinek, L., McLaughlin, V. L., & Williams, B. (2000). *Collaboration for inclusive education.* Boston, MA: Allyn & Bacon.

Warger, C. L. (1990). *Can social skills for employment be taught using cognitive-behavioral procedures with adolescents with mild disabilities?* (Research and Resources on Special Education, No. 28). Reston, VA: Council for Exceptional Children.

Washington, V. M., & Miller-Jones, D. (1989). Teacher interactions with nonstandard English speakers during reading instruction. *Contemporary Educational Psychology, 14,* 280–312.

Watson, D. L., Northcutt, L., & Rydele, L. (1989). Teaching bilingual students successfully. *Educational Leadership, 46*(5), 59–61.

Watson, O. M. (1970). *Proxemic behavior: A cross-cultural study.* The Hague: Mouton.

Weaver, C., Chaston, J., & Peterson, S. (1993). *Theme exploration: A voyage of discovery.* Portsmouth, NH: Heinemann.

Wehman, P. (1993). *Life beyond the classroom: Transition services for youth with disabilities.* Baltimore, MD: Paul H. Brookes.

Wehmeyer, M. L., Morningstart, M., & Husted, D. (1999). *Family involvement in transition planning and implementation.* Austin, TX: PRO-ED.

Wehmeyer, M. L., & Schwartz, M. (1997). Self-determination and positive post-school outcomes: A follow-up study of youth with mental retardation or learning disabilities. *Exceptional Children, 63,* 245–256.

Weinstein, C. S. (1981). Classroom design as an external condition for learning. *Educational Technology,21*(8), 12–19.

Welch, M., Judge, T., Anderson, J., Bray, J., Child, B., & Franke, L. (1990). COOP: A tool for implementing prereferral consultation. *Teaching Exceptional Children, 22*(2), 30–31.

Wesson, C. L. (1987). Increasing efficiency. *TEACHING Exceptional Children, 20*(1), 46.

Wesson, C. L., & King, R. P. (1996). Portfolio assessment and special education students. *TEACHING Exceptional Children, 28*(2), 44–48.

West, J. F., & Cannon, G. S. (1988). Essential collaborative consultation competencies for regular and special educators. *Journal of Learning Disabilities, 21*(1), 56–63.

West, J. F., Idol, L., & Cannon, G. (1989). *Collaboration in the schools: An inservice and preservice curriculum for teacher, support staff, and administrators.* Austin, TX: PRO-ED.

West, J. F. & Idol, L. (1990). Collaborative consultation in the education of mildly handicapped and at-risk students. *Remedial & Special Education, 11,* 22–31.

West, R. P., Young, K. R., & Spooner, F. (1990). Precision teaching: An introduction. *TEACHING Exceptional Children, 22*(3), 4–9.

White, A. E., & White, L. L. (1992). A collaborative model for students with mild disabilities in middle schools. *Focus on Exceptional Children, 24*(9), 1–10.

White, O. R. (1980). *Precision teaching workshop.* Orlando, FL.

White, O. R., & Haring, N. G. (1976). *Exceptional teaching.* Upper Saddle River, NJ: Merrill/Prentice Hall.

White, O. R., & Haring, N. G. (1980). *Exceptional teaching* (2nd ed.), Upper Saddle River, NJ: Merrill/Prentice Hall.

Whitten, E., & Dieker, L. (1995). Intervention Assistance Teams: A Broader Vision. *Preventing School Failure.* 40(1) 41–45.

Wiig, E., & Semel, E. (1984). *Language assessment and intervention for the learning disabled.* (2nd ed.). Upper Saddle River, NJ: Merrill/Prentice Hall.

Williams, R. M., & Rooney, K. J. (1986). *A handbook of cognitive behavior modification procedures for teachers.* Charlottesville: University of Virginia Learning Disabilities Research Institute.

Wilson, A. B. (1989). Theory into practice: An effective program for urban youth. *Educational Horizons, 67,* 136–144.

Wilson, R. (1987). Direct observation of academic learning time. *TEACHING Exceptional Children, 19*(2), 13–17.

Winograd, P., & Hare, V. C. (1988). Direct instruction of reading comprehension strategies: The nature of teacher explanation. In E. T. Goetz, P. Alexander, & C. Weinstein (Eds.), *Learning and study strategies: Assessment, instruction, and evaluation* (pp. 25–56). New York: Academic Press.

Winzer, M. A., & Mazurek, K. (1998). *Special education in multicultural contexts.* Upper Saddle River, NJ: Merrill/Prentice Hall.

Wissick, C. A., & Gardner, J. E. (1998). A learner's permit to the World Wide Web. *TEACHING Exceptional Children, 30*(5), 8–15.

Wohlge, N. (1983). Keeping communication clear. In O. Miramontes (Ed.), Application of research and theory in the classroom (p. 538). *Learning Disability Quarterly, 6*(4), 535–542.

Wolf, D. P. (1989). Portfolio assessment: Sampling student work. *Educational Leadership, 46*(7), 35–39.

Wolford, P. L., Heward, W. L., & Alber, S. R. (2001). Teaching middle school students with learning disabilities to recruit peer assistance during cooperative learning group activities. *Learning Disabilities Research & Practice, 16*(3), 161–173.

Wong, B. Y. L. (1986). Metacognition and special education: A review of a view. *The Journal of Special Education, 20*(1), 9–29.

Wong, B. Y. L. (1991). The relevance of metacognition to learning disabilities. In B. Y. L. Wong (Ed.), *Learning about learning disabilities* (pp. 232–261). San Diego: Academic Press.

Wong, B. Y. L., & Jones, W. (1982). Increasing metacomprehension in learning-disabled and normally-achieving students through self-questioning training. *Learning Disability Quarterly, 5,* 228–240.

Wong, B. Y. L., Wong, R., & LaMare, L. (1982). The effects of knowledge of criterion-task on comprehension and recall in normally achieving and learning-disabled children. *Journal of Educational Research, 76,* 119–126.

Wood, J. W. (2002). *Adapting instruction to accommodate students in inclusive settings.* Upper Saddle River, NJ: Merrill/Prentice Hall.

Wood, J. W., & Wooley, J. A. (1986). Adapting textbooks. *Clearing House, 59*(7), 332–335.

Woodward, J., & Gersten, R. (1993). Innovative technology for secondary students with learning disabilities. In E. L. Meyen, G. A. Vergason, & R. J. Whelan (Eds.), *Challenges facing special education* (pp. 141–161). Denver: Love.

Working Forum on Inclusive Schools. (1994). *Creating schools for all our students: What 12 schools have to say.* Reston, VA: Council for Exceptional Children. (ERIC Document Reproduction Service No. ED 377 633)

Yasutake, D., Bryan, T., & Dohrn, E. (1996). The effects of combining peer tutoring and attribution training on students' perceived self-competence. *Remedial and Special Education, 17*(2), 83–91.

Yell, M. L., & Shriner, J. G. (1997). The IDEA amendments of 1997: Implications for special and general education teachers, administrators, and teacher trainers. *Focus on Exceptional Children, 30*(1), 1–19.

Zaragoza, N. (1987). Process writing for high-risk and learning-disabled students. *Reading Research and Instruction, 26*(4), 290–301.

Zigmond, N., Jenkins, J., Fuchs, L., Deno, S., Fuchs, D., Baker, J. N., Jenkins, L., & Coutinho, M. (1995). Special education in restructured schools. *Phi Delta Kappan, 76*(7), 531–540.

Zigmond, N., Levin, E., & Laurie, T. (1985). Managing the mainstream: An analysis of teacher attitudes and student performance in mainstream high school programs. *Journal of Learning Disabilities, 18,* 535–541.

Zigmond, N., Sansone, J., Miller, S. E., Donahoe, K. R., & Kohnke, R. (1986). *Teaching learning disabled students at the secondary school level.* Reston, VA: Council for Exceptional Children.

Zirpoli, T. J., & Melloy, K. J. (1993). *Behavior management: Applications for teachers and parents.* New York: Macmillan.

# Name Index

# Subject Index

426